Lost and Found
Coin Hoards and Treasures
Illustrated Stories of the Greatest American Troves and Their Discoveries

One of thousands of double eagles found
in the wreck of the SS *Central America*.

Lost and Found

Coin Hoards and Treasures

Illustrated Stories of the Greatest American Troves and Their Discoveries

by Q. David Bowers

Forewords by Kenneth Bressett and Bob Evans

Whitman Publishing, LLC
PUBLISHING SINCE 1934

Whitman.com

Lost and Found
Coin Hoards and Treasures
Illustrated Stories of the Greatest American Troves and Their Discoveries

ISBN: 0794842933
Printed in the United States of America
© 2015 Whitman Publishing, LLC

Correspondence regarding this book may be mailed to Whitman Publishing, Attn: Lost and Found, 3101 Clairmont Road, Suite C, Atlanta, GA 30329; or emailed to info@Whitman.com (subject line: Lost and Found).

Disclaimer: No warranty or representation of any kind is made concerning the accuracy or completeness of the information presented, its use in purchases or sales, or any other use. Much information in this book has never been published in a single volume before, and in the future corrections, amplifications, and additions may be made.

If you enjoy *Lost and Found Coin Hoards and Treasures*, you will also enjoy *America's Money, America's Story* (Doty), *History of the United States Mint and Its Coinage* (Lange), *Numismatic Art in America* (Vermeule), *100 Greatest American Medals and Tokens* (Bowers and Sundman), *Pictures From a Distant Country: Seeing America Through Old Paper Money* (Doty), *Abraham Lincoln: The Image of His Greatness* (Reed), *Milestone Coins: A Pageant of the World's Most Significant and Popular Money* (Bressett), and other books by Whitman Publishing. Whitman is a leading publisher in the antiques and collectibles and American history fields. For a catalog of related books, hobby supplies, and storage and display products, please visit Whitman Publishing online at Whitman.com.

Foreword

by Kenneth Bressett

Do not think of this as simply another book with stories about coins to be added to your shelf for future reference. It is far more than that. This, you will learn, is more like a gateway to the study and appreciation of the legacy of numismatic history. The stories herein will transport you to places and times that are the genesis of the treasures we now hold in our collections and will serve to enhance our appreciation of them. That is what a proper book should do for the reader. That is why books are of such critical importance to the understanding and enjoyment of our hobby.

President Thomas Jefferson, in a letter to John Adams in 1815, said "I cannot live without books; but fewer will suffice where amusement, and not use, is the only future object." He was right on target then, and his words still resonate with truth. Books on any subject are meant to be used as well as enjoyed. His library at one time contained more than 6,500 volumes that were acquired over a 50-year period of careful selection. They included works on such diverse subjects as history, mathematics, sciences, ethics, law, politics, religion, literature, and fine arts. Jefferson drew his ideas, inspiration, knowledge, and pleasure from the information found in his books, and he commented on how he turned to reading as a welcome escape from the daily tedium of business affairs.

Not everyone can hope to build a library such as Jefferson's, but fortunately for us today we have public lending libraries and a number of new resources like the Internet where almost unlimited information can be had at the touch of a button. Those of us who have targeted interests, such as numismatics, have been blessed with a plethora of fine literature on nearly every phase of the hobby. Yet if those books are not used, we are missing out on the very essence of why so many people enjoy the beauty and lure of coins.

When I contemplated writing this at David Bowers's request, I first took a book from my shelf for inspiration. It was no special book; just the first one that caught my eye. It wasn't until much later, and with four other books by my side, that I went back to my mission. I had been drawn away by jumping from one book to another while exploring one coin after another in a quest to learn more about a subject that I had not taken time to fully investigate in the past. For more than an hour, I was once again totally absorbed in my favorite pastime. All cares of the world or other distractions were completely overlooked. It was book time; a time to regenerate enthusiasm and slake my thirst for appreciating the beauty and lore of numismatics.

Yes, I am a bibliophile. That is to say, someone who loves books. A bibliophile may be, but is not necessarily, a book *collector*. The classic bibliophile is one who loves to read, admire, and collect books, quite often to the point of amassing a large and specialized collection. And I am not alone. According to Arthur Minters, "the private collecting of books was a fashion indulged in even by many ancient Romans, including Cicero and Attticus."

Over the years, several people have asked me to name my favorite numismatic book. When I glance about my shelves with thousands of volumes, I find it nearly impossible to single out just one, but when pressed on the issue I usually name *Coins of the World* by R.A.G. Carson. It is probably the book I most often refer to for guidance and inspiration. It is not some weighty tome full of dry statistics; not a colorful picture book; not a list of prices. This, like the present volume, is another "gateway" book that leads me down numerous pathways to savor and explore the fascinating history of coins and money from the most ancient to the present.

Now, you may find it odd that I did not mention a more ubiquitous book or something closer to my heart, like *A Guide Book of United States Coins*. Many have used the *Guide Book* (or the "Red Book" as it is nicknamed) as their introduction to the world of coins and have found it to be a bountiful source of useful information on their nation's money from beginning to the present. Yes, I too use it often, but I never forget the lesson projected in the frontispiece coin that has always been shown at the beginning of the book. In case you have never thought about it, check the motto on those Spanish pillars. It says PLUS ULTRA, which means "more beyond." The words apply to more than just the Spanish Empire at that time, or even our own country's coinage that grew from those beginnings. It is also an inspiration to go beyond the world of information in that book—and all others.

No collector can fully appreciate his coins without learning all there is to know about them. While my personal library is large, I haven't read all of the books I own—at least not cover-to-cover. That is because many are references that are used only when I need to look something up for verification or additional information. I do, however, have a pretty good working knowledge of what is in each of them, and where to find them.

There are also a few that I read and reread for pure entertainment. This book, *Lost and Found Coin Hoards and Treasures*, by Q. David Bowers, is one of those kinds of books that will never grow old. One that you will use over and over again and still find it a passageway to extended or forgotten adventures.

As Sara Nelson says in *So Many Books, So Little Time*, "Reading's ability to beam you up to a different world is a good part of the reason why people like me do it in the first place—because dollar for dollar, hour per hour, it's the most expedient way to get from our proscribed little 'here' to an imagined, intriguing 'there.'"

The value of numismatic reference books cannot be overstated if one desires to fully enjoy the hobby or engage in any activity related to understanding, buying, selling, or simply knowing the history of these tiny objects of art, beauty, and commercial necessity. Choose your topic, field

of interest, or coins that you like best. There are numerous books on just about every subject from the most ancient beginnings of commerce to the most recent developments in special designs and finishes on the coins from nations around the globe.

Helen E. Haines is quoted as saying: "From every book invisible threads reach out to other books; and as the mind comes to use and control those threads the whole panorama of the world's life, past and present, becomes constantly more varied and interesting, while at the same time the mind's own powers of reflection and judgment are exercised and strengthened."

Author Q. David Bowers and I have occasionally discussed and contemplated the growing trend toward e-book publications and their merits. The advancement of available information presented this way should be admired and appreciated by all, especially for in-depth searches for material that is not easy to obtain in printed book form. We can understand that for a novel—read it today and toss it tomorrow—an e-book saves using shelf space for something that is only read once. There is always the question of whether electronic publications will ever replace a printed book that is filled with compelling, interesting information that is consulted again and again. Neither of us can imagine that ever happening. How can anything surpass the look, feel, or smell of a freshly printed book; or the anticipation of opening it and seeing for the first time a new adventure nearby? Who would give up the pleasure of nodding off while reading, only to awake with book in hand and reread those last couple of paragraphs? Will there ever be a society without books? Of course not. I imagine that three thousand years ago, when writing was first invented and inscribed on clay tablets, some wag must have wondered if speaking would someday go out of style.

There has never been a time when so many numismatic references have been available to collectors and students. They seem to appear almost weekly, and cover topics never before explored in depth. The quality and quantity of new publications is astounding. To quote Toni Morrison, "If there's a book you really want to read but it hasn't been written yet, then you must write it," and this seems to have been taken to heart by many now that it is quite possible through the advent of self-publishing.

Thomas Jefferson spent his life surrounded by books. For him, books were "a necessary of life." We should all take inspiration from him to respect, use, and enjoy the vast world of books that are available to all through libraries like that of the American Numismatic Society and the free lending library of the American Numismatic Association, and for books you want to own and enjoy, from many sellers, online sources to corner bookstores.

As the noted author Heinrich Mann wrote, "A house without books is like a room without windows." Let this book now be a window to your world of numismatics and an inspiration to explore all the avenues it will open for you.

Kenneth Bressett
Author, historian, numismatic leader
Colorado Springs, Colorado

Foreword
by Bob Evans

Treasure and the desire for treasure permeate the world's cultures. We are taught about treasure in our fables; in *Treasure Island*, in the tale of *Ali Baba and the Forty Thieves*, when Tom Sawyer and Huck Finn go searching for treasure in a haunted house, when the Hardy boys sleuth out the location of the stolen *Tower Treasure*, and more recently by the created treasure conceived and concealed with clues in the book *Masquerade* by Kit Williams. More recently yet the gender barrier was broken when a Nancy Drew computer game, *Treasure in the Royal Tower*, entered the lists in the mid-1990s. There are countless other examples of treasure tales, from the ancient to the modern.

As a boy in the 1960s, spurred on by fantasies of treasure, I began digging a hole in the backyard woodlot of the suburban home where I grew up— in Whitehall, an east-side suburb of Columbus, Ohio. I credit my parents for allowing me to play in the dirt. I don't remember what exactly I hoped to find, probably a chest of gold or something. However, this was playing at adventure, and each shovel-full held the possibility of something wonderful.

I dug down a couple of feet, through the leaves, through the black topsoil, and into the yellow clay. As I dug down I thought about this becom-ing my "hole to China," like in the Bugs Bunny cartoon. As it deepened it began to expand laterally as well. I recall that I worked on it for a couple days at least, whenever I was bored. Digging was hard work. Before I lost interest, while working the edge of my excavation, a few inches down, I heard a "clink." Soon I pulled a horseshoe from the loam. My young mind swam with the possibilities, and I ran inside with my "treasure" to show Mom. This artifact was the topic of some discussion around the dinner table that evening. Soon afterward, a trip to the library and a check of references revealed that our backyard was once part of the "Doney Woods," a forested tract that obviously used to be traversed by people on horseback.

Although this was not a fabulously valuable artifact, I was hooked on the idea of finding things, and my lifelong love of exploration and discovery was kindled. This soon morphed into an interest in fossils, then geology. I ultimately followed that path academically through college and into professional life.

Many readers of this book will know something of my connection with coin treasures, or at least one amazing treasure. As a young scientist (geologist) back in 1983, I was recruited by a neighbor of mine, marine engineer Tommy Thompson, to take over the scientific and historical research of his project to locate and recover the treasure of the SS *Central America*, the greatest lost treasure in U.S. history. Since this was at the inception of the project, I became in fact the "Chief Scientist and Historian," although the official title came somewhat later. The subject of this treasure has been an important part of my professional life ever since, providing me with decades of fascinating historical, scientific, and numismatic activities.

At first the historical research drew me into the lives of the people that survived to tell the tale of the sinking of the steamship in 1857. Reading their accounts in the sometimes difficult-to-discern microfilm copies of the period newspapers, I feel like I got to know them pretty well. Their compelling stories of loss and rescue served as the raw data, the basis of the search for the fabled shipwreck and its treasure. When Thompson turned the research over to me, he had a primitive manuscript spreadsheet that he called the "data correlation matrix." The different accounts were arrayed in columns, with blocks of passages from the accounts arranged horizontally to represent three-hour time slots, covering the period two days before the sinking until a day after, by which time all the nearby survivors had been rescued.

I cleared out a wall in my den at home, and posted the spreadsheet so the whole array could be viewed and compared. The goal in arranging the historical accounts in this way was that the data could be compared and contrasted, and a composite story emerged that was collectively more accurate than any one account.

It was clear that the SS *Central America* had foundered in a hurricane, known only as "The Great Storm of 1857." It sank well out of sight of land, so there were no shoreline points of reference. There was a smattering of latitude and longitude positions determined using celestial observations at various times during the sinking scenario. These had to be considered based on the relative skill of the mariners using sextants and related nautical instruments under the trying conditions of a strong hurricane.

There were also accounts or hints about the strength of the wind and the progress of the hurricane as it overwhelmed the steamship. I used these to construct an hourly chart of the estimated wind speed and direction during the storm. Several accounts mentioned the condition of the vessel at different times as its machinery struggled and then failed. The focus was on such "critical path information," that which represented something of the physics of the final hours and the immediate aftermath. Modern National Oceanic and Atmospheric Administration records provided some statistical information about the variable ocean currents in this part of the world, 100 to 200 miles off the Carolina coast. But that was essentially all we had to work with to find the mathematics in a very human story.

Thus, the historical information was key. Fortunately there were 153 survivors of the disaster and a few other reliable witnesses on the vessel that rescued them. As I found more little nuggets of information hiding in the small print of 1857 newspapers, I plugged these pieces into the puzzle, finding both corroborative and conflicting data. Not everyone had the same skills for accurate observation. There were mariners with years of experience at sea. There were well-seasoned travelers, and there were first-timers on the steamship. The vessel was a very large ship, almost the length of a football field, with multiple decks. Not everyone had the perspective, and they all had lived through a harrowing, stressful, life-altering event.

In the end, there were 33 accounts of survivors, eyewitnesses (on the rescue ships), or contemporary experts that yielded useful information for our mathematical analysis. Ultimately the manuscript version of the spreadsheet was rendered as a digital file, and submitted to Dr. Larry Stone, one of the world's top authorities on search theory mathematics. A "probability map" resulted, showing areas of higher and lower probability for the seabed location of the shipwreck site of the SS *Central America*. From this, combined with engineering design and financial projections, a business emerged.

But what exactly was this fabled treasure, the economic incentive for the business? Historic accounts related that $1,219,189.43 in specie had been aboard as a commercial shipment. This notion was my adult introduction to numismatics. As a boy I had briefly delved into the world of coins, probably prompted by ads in comic books and the also brief interest of an older foster brother. However, after plugging a few dozen cents into the blue Whitman Lincoln cent folders, my interest waned as I switched focus to fossil collecting and bird watching. Now as an adult I found myself coming back into the subject from the top down, so to speak. It was fairly obvious that the treasure would consist of thousands of double eagles, probably mostly the products of the San Francisco Mint, and likely in pretty nice condition. I really had no idea, but I was a quick study.

After a few struggles, our enterprise was successful, and we verified the shipwreck site and the presence a large pile of gold in 1988. As first revealed by our remotely operated submarine's cameras, the treasure was a childhood storybook dream. We dubbed it "The Garden of Gold," a glittering tumble of coins and ingots strewn among lumps of coal amidst the degraded timbers of the once-great steamship.

There is a special wonder around coins from hoards and treasures. They each tell a story that enriches the totality of the history, whether it is the confirmation of the standard tale or a colorful quirk. It did not surprise us at all (nor should it surprise anyone) that there were thousands of Mint State 1857-S double eagles in the SS *Central America* treasure. The presence of a couple 1857 *Philadelphia* Mint double eagles was a surprise and a delightful revelation, as were the hundreds of assayers' ingots previously unknown in modern times. And the privately minted California gold coins, the half eagles from the Charlotte and Dahlonega branch mints, and other unanticipated treats imbued the treasure with even more character. This money, part of a regular commercial shipment, brought to the history of the ship and its era information not found in the surviving documentary record, and it served as hard evidence of a richer reality.

From the discovery, I wrote articles about the treasure. I gave talks and seminars at numismatic and non-numismatic events. The treasure became a character of sorts in my life. Then, after 23 years, I was able to return in 2014 to the SS *Central America* shipwreck site.

Representing the interests of the original company, along with Craig Mullen—a legend in undersea operations—and working with the world-class mariners and personnel of Odyssey Marine Exploration, we set out in April of 2014 to find and recover what we had missed with the technology of the time of our first trip (1988 through 1991). The operators were highly skilled and experienced, and the new equipment was an impressive improvement. We not only salvaged the remaining commercial shipment, but we also found some new wonders.

One amazing find was a safe holding some parcels that appear to be passenger consignments, as well as what preliminary examination suggests may have been the operating funds of the ship itself, used to pay the crew and the operating expenses of the steamship as it traveled back and forth from New York to Panama. A separate compartment inside the safe contained one bag with more than $290 in U.S. silver half dollars and quarters, along with a few colonial Spanish 2 reales (the classic "two-bits"). Another heavy bag held an incredible abundance of dimes—more than 8,800 pieces—along with a smaller bag that had exactly $400 in small U.S. gold coins within: 41 half eagles, 56 quarter eagles, and 55 gold dollars.

Other parts of the shipwreck and its debris field yielded a number of "coin piles," fairly coherent and separate deposits of varying size, but some of them substantial in the number of coins. The presence of treasure outside the area of the commercial shipment deposit led me to conclude that the SS *Central America* treasure was no longer monolithic, but in fact comprised many treasures. Any one of these pluralities of coins would constitute a separate treasure in its own right (and maybe its own place in this book) if found by itself in an abandoned building or buried in a garden.

Speaking of other potential locations for finds, remember that a treasure or hoard can be born in a number of ways. While it might be the result of accidental loss (such as the sinking of a ship with significant wealth on board as I have related here), it could also be deliberately hidden or buried. Sometimes it is the result of a life's work, the accumulation of decades of gradual effort, occasionally obsessive. In another instance, it could be the actions of a government, withholding coins from circulation, and then releasing them much later when policy changes. Sometimes the reasons are unknown, leaving the finder and others puzzled.

What's more, treasures and hoards are found in a number of ways as well. Sometimes it is merely by accident, in the furrow of a farmer's plow, by children playing along a creek bed, or by workers tearing down an old house. Other times it can be a matter of awareness, by following the tales of concealed or buried treasure somewhere on a piece of property or within a particular area. Still others are found by highly complex and technical projects using sophisticated mathematical modeling and high-tech equipment, such as the treasure of the SS *Central America*.

For each of these scenarios and many more, there is at least one story, and it's those stories that give life to pieces from treasures or hoards. Gazing at a coin or ingot from a treasure can transport the examiner back to the time of its genesis or discovery. This is transformative, when a coin can become more than just a coin, not only an object of art and beauty, but also an artifact of history and experience.

This book is full of such stories, giving context to thousands upon thousands of coins. You will find a wealth of information within these pages. There is much to learn, and much to delight.

Bob Evans
Salvor, historian, and conservator of the
SS *Central America* treasure
Hopewell, Ohio

Introduction

Buried treasure! Gold! Pirates! This is the stuff of which dreams are made. When in the early 1950s I discovered the world's greatest hobby and started building a numismatic library, I was off to a good start in reading about the lore and lure of treasures. Back issues of the *American Journal of Numismatics* and *The Numismatist* had many stories and news accounts of coins found hidden in the walls of buildings, buried in chests, or recovered from the sea. But usually such narratives were tantalizingly incomplete.

As time went on, I learned more from other magazines, newspapers, books, and elsewhere. I built a "treasure file." In the 1990s, I organized these, corresponded with dozens of collectors, dealers, and researchers, and endeavored to make my information as accurate as possible. Along the way, I learned of many other hoards.

Since then, many things have happened. In 1999, I wrote *The Treasure Ship S.S. Brother Jonathan*, which details the recovery of double eagles and other coins—based upon my personal and my firm's involvement in marketing the treasure. And soon after, in 2002, the SS *Central America* was

the focus of a 1,055-page book of mine, *A History of the California Gold Rush Featuring the Treasure from the S.S. Central America*, created with help from Bob Evans and Tommy Thompson (discoverers of the lost ship) and the sponsorship of the California Gold Marketing Group (Dwight Manley and associates). I also wrote *The Treasure Ship S.S. New York: Her Story 1837–1846* regarding another find in which I was involved.

And beyond my books, Odyssey Marine Exploration—founded by Gregory Stemm and based in Tampa, Florida—has become a factor in shipwreck treasure recovery, in 2003 and 2004 salvaging more than 51,000 coins from 1,700 feet below the surface of the Atlantic Ocean at the site of the wreck of the SS *Republic*, lost in a hurricane in October 1865. Then, in 2014, Odyssey was commissioned to revisit the SS *Central America* site, with more good results. Meanwhile, other finds large and small, on land and at sea, have added to the narrative.

Now, some notes on treasures. In numismatics, there are many stories of coin treasures that have come to light, most often under circumstances a

bit less exciting than written in buccaneer lore, but often quite intriguing. Typically, notices of such finds have been reported first in newspapers or other popular periodicals, often with incomplete or inaccurate information. Then, if a numismatist was consulted, the facts might have been recorded.

Otherwise, coins were usually spent, sold, or otherwise scattered without any inventory being made of them. The latter is the usual scenario, especially for finds made a generation or longer ago. I have reviewed thousands of news accounts of robberies, finds of buried coins, losses of ships laden with coins, and the like, but only a tiny percentage of such narratives have any interesting or important numismatic information. The exceptions form many of the stories given here.

How did hoards come to be? This is a natural question, and one that has many answers. Some groups of coins were buried in yards or hidden in house partitions by wealthy people in an era when there were no banks or safe deposit boxes to offer secure storage. Many coins, including some fabulous cargoes of gold, went down with ships. Still others were concealed in cornerstones, secret compartments, or basement walls.

Uncle Sam also did his share of putting coins away. Bags of sparkling silver dollars were held in Mint and Treasury vaults for many years, only to come forth to delight a new generation of numismatists. Then there is the marvelous story of crates of patterns hidden in the Philadelphia Mint for many years, only to be revealed and to figure in an exchange of hitherto unknown $50 gold pieces in 1909.

Some hoards known today were concealed years ago to avoid capture by Indians, or by robbers, or by Yankee troops about to overrun a Louisiana plantation. Certain gold and silver coins found in the Midwest and West were taken in holdups or by some other illegal method and con-

cealed in order to permit fast escape. The idea was that the site of the hidden loot would be visited later and under more leisurely circumstances, and the coins or paper money would be retrieved to be spent and enjoyed. Meanwhile, the crooks might have been killed by members of posses, jailed by the local sheriff, or met some other end. After reading accounts of railroad robbers, ship pirates, bank holdups, and marauding soldiers, one can easily conclude that transporting or even owning a large holding of silver and gold coins in the 1700s and early 1800s was fraught with danger.

And reminiscent of the famous "Purloined Letter" story by Nathaniel Hawthorne, still other caches of coins and currency have been hidden in an obvious place—where else?—in a bank vault or in the Treasury Building in Washington.

As you read this book, many reasons why coins were concealed or lost will be revealed. Then again, in numerous instances no one will ever know who secreted these precious coins or why they did, as those involved died years or generations before their treasures were brought to light. For example, we do not know now, and may never know, who hid the thousands of large copper cents of the 1816 to 1820 years in the famous Randall Hoard (named after a later owner of the pieces). Coins keep their secrets well; they tell no tales as to where they have been, what they have seen, and the roles they played.

To qualify for inclusion in this book, a hoard or find had to include American coins, paper money, or other numismatic items relating to the United States or its antecedent colonies. Such hoards were mostly found within the borders of our country, but some were not (the SS *Central America*, SS *Republic*, and the "Bank of France" treasures are but three examples of exceptions).

Hoards consisting entirely of foreign coins are not within the scope of his book, but much information can be found elsewhere, including on the website of Odyssey Marine Exploration, which has found multiple wrecks with coins not related to the United States.

No listing of hoards can ever be comprehensive, as there are countless thousands of instances in which members of the public have brought long-forgotten rolls, money purses, and other holdings to coin dealers or have otherwise disposed of finds without giving details to the press. Indeed, more than just a few treasure finders have found that publicizing their good luck was just about the worst thing they could have done, as the news attracted many who sought to claim part of the coins as their own—based on former ownership of a property, a long-ago insurance settlement, or a modern desire to claim tax liability.

Case in point: while doing research for this book, I contacted several manufacturers and distributors of electronic treasure-detecting devices, and the typical reply to my inquiries was that "most of the people who find coins with our detectors keep the details secret." And in other instances—including in contemporary accounts—misinformation has been given out to throw other treasure seekers off the track, as in an 1850s newspaper account of early salvage attempts for the treasure of the SS *Yankee Blade*.

Adding even more intrigue are accounts of the "hoarders among us," detailing the activities of numismatists such as Virgil M. Brand, George W. Rice, John A. Beck, Colonel E.H.R. Green, and

others who were collectors, but who enjoyed squirreling away quantities of favorite items. For example, Brand cornered six of the ten known 1884 silver trade dollars, and Colonel Green had each and every specimen of the five known 1913 Liberty Head nickels.

Finally, chapter 26—"Hoaxes, Fantasies, and Questioned Finds"—discusses holdings of coins and fantasy pieces that have been questioned and are believed to have been made later than the dates they bear or the eras from which they appear to be. Some such "hoards" are not hoards at all, but represent contrived stories: capers and taradiddles, many of which make fascinating reading today.

All in all, it is hoped that the accounts will provide interesting reading, perhaps your own "treasure" of numismatic information and entertainment. Certainly, this book has been a lot of fun to research and write.

chapter 1

Finds of Colonial and Early Coins

VISITOR'S GUIDE TO THE U. S. MINT.
COLONIAL AND CONTINENTAL COINS.

"Sommer Islands" Brass.

New England Sixpence.

"Granby" or "Higley" Coppers.

"Chalmer's" Shilling.

"I. Chalmer's" Three-Pence.

Pine Tree Shilling.

J. Chalmer's Six Pence.

Lord Baltimore Groat.

Virginia Half Penny.

The Pitt Token.

A selection of coins relating to early America.

Many numismatists know that the Philadelphia Mint began operations in 1792. In that year, the staff of that facility prepared several varieties of pattern coins, including some copper cents, the dies for which were cut by someone surnamed Birch, but whose first name has proven elusive to historians. In the same year, apparently in the nearby cellar of a saw maker named John Harper, some little silver half dismes (an early word for dimes) were struck from official dies, the nearby federal mint not being quite ready to produce such pieces.

Unfortunately, 1792 pattern Birch cents are too rare to figure in any accounts of hoards. Indeed, some are known only to the extent of one, two, or three pieces (however, chapter 20, "Secrets of the Philadelphia Mint," reveals that some traces of 1792 patterns remained at the Mint site for many years thereafter; see page 335). The 1792 silver half dismes are not known from hoards either, although Frank H. Stewart, in his *History of the First United States Mint* published in 1924, quoted a letter received from a descendant of the Mint's first director, David Ritten-

A 1792 Birch pattern cent in copper.

house, in which he said that Rittenhouse's grandson had once owned eight or nine uncirculated half dismes. Apparently, the 1,500 or so pieces made were widely distributed at the time they were made.

The first coins struck at the Philadelphia Mint in quantity for circulation were the copper half cents and cents of 1793, followed by the first silver coinage in 1794 (half dollars and dollars), the first half dimes in 1795 (from 1794-dated dies), and the first gold coinage in 1795 ($5 half eagles and $10 eagles). It was not until 1796 that silver dimes, quarter dollars, and gold $2.50 quarter eagles were made for the first time.

At what point were U.S. coins—that is, those struck at the Philadelphia Mint—first hoarded?

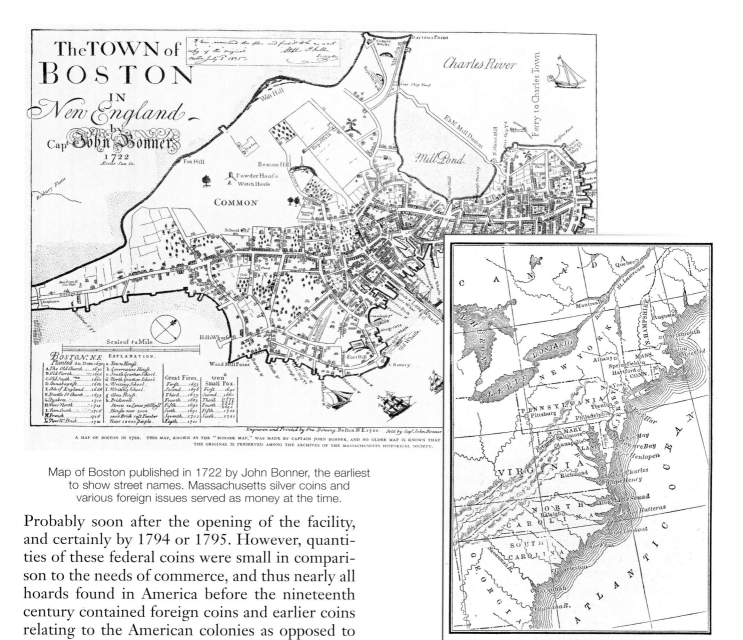

Map of Boston published in 1722 by John Bonner, the earliest to show street names. Massachusetts silver coins and various foreign issues served as money at the time.

Probably soon after the opening of the facility, and certainly by 1794 or 1795. However, quantities of these federal coins were small in comparison to the needs of commerce, and thus nearly all hoards found in America before the nineteenth century contained foreign coins and earlier coins relating to the American colonies as opposed to those federal issues.

The 13 American colonies. The Republic of Vermont (not depicted) was not included because of claims by New York against the land.

In the Absence of Federal Coinage

At the time early settlements were established in Massachusetts, Virginia, and other Atlantic seaboard colonies, circulating coinage consisted primarily of foreign issues—particularly the divisions of the silver 8 reales ("dollars") of Mexico and other Spanish-American areas, though coins of England, Holland, France, and other lands were in wide circulation in America as well. Many such pieces remained legal tender all the way up

to the implementation of the Act of February 21, 1857. By that time, the Philadelphia Mint and its branches—Charlotte (opened in 1838), Dahlonega (1838), New Orleans (1838), and San Francisco (1854)—had produced enough pieces to make the United States self-sufficient in coinage.

In addition, several state and private mints in America produced coins prior to the opening of

Mexican silver dollar or 8 reales of 1758. These and related coins were legal tender in the colonies and circulated widely.

the Philadelphia Mint in 1792, and some facilities abroad made coins with America-related inscriptions intended for circulation here. Silver coins of Massachusetts (mostly dated 1652, see "Introduction to Massachusetts Silver Coinage" in this chapter); 1722–1724 Rosa Americana coins made in England to be distributed in the American colonies; Nova Constellatio coppers of 1783–1786; copper coins made by or for the states of Connecticut, Massachusetts, New Jersey, New York, and Vermont in 1785–1788; and various tokens with portraits of General George Washington are examples.[1] Some of these coins subsequently found their way into hoards, this being particularly true of Massachusetts Bay Colony silver issues, which seem to have been ubiquitous in the Northeast at one time.

The gold and silver coins of the Spanish Main and most pieces captured and buried by pirates were not American coins and thus are not a significant part of this chapter, although scattered mentions concerning pirates and their treasure will be found in some later chapters relating to the sea. Captain Kidd, Blackbeard, and other knaves of the sea plundered gold doubloons (Spanish-American eight-escudo coins worth about $16 at the time), the aforementioned silver 8-real coins (worth about $1), and their fractions. Without doubt, these buccaneers saw their share of Pine Tree shillings as well.

Thus, although the present chapter describes many fascinating caches of coins buried, stolen, or otherwise put away in the years before 1800, it could be expanded to the length of several books if it were to include non-American issues. How-ever, unlike hoards of American coins, much has been published elsewhere on pirate and other early treasures, and a veritable bookshelf of already-written volumes can be acquired. Unfortunately, only a very few such texts are accurate from a numismatic viewpoint—to the average "popular" writer, all pirate coins are "doubloons" or "pieces of eight" whether they actually were or not. One particularly uninformed delineator of pirate tales decided that "double eagle" was the correct modern translation of "doubloon," never mind that double eagles, or $20 gold pieces, were not made until 1850, long after the pirate era had ended.

Introduction to Massachusetts Silver Coinage

As Massachusetts silver coins figure prominently several other treasure accounts in the present chapter (as well as the remainder of the work), it is appropriate to include a few remarks concerning them.

This numismatically fascinating coinage was effected under authority of the General Court of Massachusetts, and mintage took place under contract with John Hull and Robert Sanderson, who operated a mint in the Boston area. While Pine Tree shillings are the best remembered today, they are only a part of the silver coinage that consisted of the following main styles, here given with the approximate dates they are believed to have been struck:

NE (New England) coinage, undated, struck 1652. On one side is the stamped impression NE and on the other is the denomination expressed in pence as III, VI, or XII. Twelve pence (XII) equaled one shilling[2]

Willow Tree coinage, dated 1652, struck 1653–1660. Threepence, sixpence, and shillings (shilling shown on next page)

Oak Tree coinage, dated 1652 (except for the twopence dated 1662), struck 1660–1667. Twopence, threepence, sixpence, and shillings

Pine Tree coinage, dated 1652, struck 1667–1682 (with the large planchet Pine Tree shillings struck in the earlier part of the range, 1667–1674). Threepence, sixpence, and shillings (large planchet shilling shown on this page)[3]

NE silver coins are rare, Willow Tree pieces of all denominations are exceedingly rare, and Oak Tree coins are somewhat scarce. The most readily available issues are of the Pine Tree style, especially the shillings. The last-named coins have been the subject of several romantic accounts including a dramatization by Nathaniel Hawthorne.

In summary, denominations include three-pence, sixpence, and shillings, undated (in the case of the NE coins) or dated 1652. In addition,

1662-dated Oak Tree twopence pieces were made. Today, several thousand specimens of all kinds combined exist in private and museum collections, and each is highly prized and of significant value.

And now, our stories begin—logically enough, with some of these first silver coins to be minted in this country.

New England shilling.

A Fabulous Find!

Hidden: 1600s or early 1700s • **Found:** 1737 • **Treasure:** Massachusetts silver

One of the earliest known notices of a hoard of American coins was carried in the *Boston Weekly News-Letter*, July 21, 1737:

> We hear from Salem [Massachusetts] that on Friday last William Brown, Esq., the youngest surviving son of the Hon. Col. Brown, deceased, having had information that some money had been concealed in a place which he owned, caused search to be made for the same, where were found five or six jars full of silver, containing about one thousand and ninety-three ounces of silver of several species, among which were about six thousand New England shillings scarcely discolored.[4]

Unfortunately for generations of numismatists not yet born, it may be assumed that these pieces were simply spent in commerce, there being no collectors' premium for them at the time in America. By that time the New England shillings

(a general term for Massachusetts silver coins) were only a few decades old.

Interestingly, numismatics as a hobby and historical discipline was slow in developing in America, and by a century after the aforementioned 1737 find, serious coin collectors in the United States probably numbered fewer than two dozen and the Mint Cabinet (formed in June 1838) was still a year away.

One of the most famous and popular colonial coins is the 1652 Massachusetts Pine Tree shilling variety known as Noe-1 (Whitman-690).

The Castine Hoard of Silver

Hidden: Late 1600s • **Found:** 1840 • **Treasure:** Massachusetts silver

Over a period of time between November 1840 and April 1841, many silver coins (one account says about 500, another says nearly 2,000) were dug up by Captain Stephen Grindle and his son Samuel on their family farm in the town of Penobscot, near Johnson's Narrows on the Bagaduce River about six miles upstream from the harbor of Castine, Maine.[5] But before continuing with the tale of the hoard, a bit to set the scene:

Castine was established as a post to trade with Indians in the winter of 1613, pre-dating Plymouth by seven years. At various times, the town has been under French, Dutch, Massachusetts Bay Colony, British, and U.S. flags. During the War of 1812, the British invaded and then occupied Castine from the summer of 1814 until April 1815.

Of numismatic interest, the Castine Bank was established there in 1815 with an authorized capital of $100,000. At the time the town was in the Maine District of Massachusetts. On March 15, 1820, Maine achieved statehood. Thus, the bank was located in two states but did not move. Currency of the bank is very collectible today.

At the location above Castine that the coins were found, the inlet from the Atlantic Ocean becomes narrow, and the water is of great depth. A small indentation on the shoreline furnished a landing suitable for mooring in the early days. The location was on a path that had been used for

Pine Tree shilling, Noe-2, Whitman-700, "Straight Tree" variety, examples of which were found in the Castine Hoard.

Castine, Maine, as shown on an 1835 map.

many years by Abenaki Indians and others and may have been an overland route to Blue Hill (and Bay) and Mount Desert Island on the way to Frenchman's Bay. At the time of the earliest discovery in 1840, the landscape was covered with second growth forest, the original stands of tall pines having been cut about 75 years prior.

A Fortuitous Find

In the waning days of November 1840 Captain Grindle and his son were hauling wood down to the shore. Near a mostly buried large rock on the side of a hill about 75 feet from the water, young Samuel spotted a coin—a French silver crown. He and his father started digging and clearing away the top of the rock. In short order they unearthed about 18 to 20 other silver coins. Excitement prevailed! Dusk came all too quickly, and the pair abandoned their search, resolving to come back the next day to recover more. Fate intervened and nighttime brought a severe snowstorm, rendering further exploration impossible.

Accounts were carried in various papers, this from the *Worcester (MA) Palladium*, June 30, 1841, being typical:

> *Money Digging*—A farmer in the vicinity of Castine, in Maine, the present season, preparing his land for tillage, had occasion to excavate the top of a ledge, and on removing the earth, found lying loose, on the top of a rock, a quantity of ancient coin, of pure silver. Many of these coins are a curiosity, being of all possible shapes and forms. It would seem they were cut down to an exact weight. They all have upon them a coinage, but most of them very uncouth and without date, and clearly show the great improvements made since the days of our fathers, in the coinage of money.[6]

Treasure Found, Treasure Spent

After the spring thaw in April, the Grindles came back to the site. By removing some alder trees and rooting around the large rock they came across 400 to 500 coins, according to a February 17,

1859, letter from Joseph Williamson to Dr. Joseph Stevens. Additional pieces were found downhill some 10 to 12 feet closer to the water, having probably washed away from the original group at some former time. According to Joseph Williamson, in his 1859 booklet, *Castine; and the Old Coins Found There*, "Mr. Grindle's wife held her apron, which her husband and son soon loaded with, as she afterwards remarked, 'The best lapful she had ever carried.'"

Apart from several dozen Massachusetts silver coins, the Castine Hoard comprised silver issues from England, France, Spain (and Spanish America), Holland, and Portugal, of the types once prevalent in America in the absence of any sizable indigenous coinage. The latest-dated piece was a 1690 French demi-écu from the Bordeaux Mint. Thus, the hoard was secreted on or after that date, but probably within a few years of that time; otherwise, later-dated pieces would have been included. Opinions have varied, however. For example, Sydney P. Noe, of the American Numismatic Society, New York, commented that "the date deduced for the burial of the deposit was about 1704."[7]

There was scarcely any information available concerning the historical or numismatic significance of Massachusetts silver coins at the time of the discovery, and most of the coins were paid to a creditor of Captain Grindle and were subsequently melted into bullion by a silversmith who may have used the metal to make tableware, etc. The first book with an American imprint to treat in detail a numismatic subject was Joseph Barlow Felt's opus, *An Historical Account of Massachusetts Currency*, published in 1839 at an impressive 248 pages in length. Legislation and information about the well-known silver coins minted beginning in 1652 and of various paper money were presented in a time-line sequence. A later edition of the book was 259 pages long and included an index and three plates, one of which illustrated the curious 1652-dated Good Samaritan shilling. Nearly all of the information presented by Felt in 1839 is relevant and highly useful today.

By 1840 when the Castine Hoard was found, likely no one involved had learned of the Felt book, and it is sad to contemplate that some Massachusetts silver coins may have been among those melted by the silversmith.

Although no other coins were ever found at the site, the discovery became known in the area, and during the next 20 years a number of fortune seekers made excavations. Today, the Castine Hoard is one of the better remembered of early American finds, and accounts of it appear in several books and on the Internet.

Massachusetts Silver in the Hoard

In the Castine Hoard were 1652-dated Massachusetts silver coins described in various accounts as totaling from 30 to 75 pieces. Examples said to have been from this remarkable find passed to Dr. Joseph L. Stevens of Castine (mentioned above), and from this holding 17 coins went to the Maine Historical Society. An examination of the Society's pieces by Sydney P. Noe revealed four different varieties including Pine Tree shillings attributed to his own Noe numbers 2, 25, and 29, and a sixpence. In two W. Elliot Woodward auction sales coins were described as being from this hoard, indicating that pieces apart from the Maine Historical Society specimens may have reached numismatic channels with stories or labels attributing them to Castine. Woodward's offerings include his sale of April 28, 1863, lots 1870–1873 and October 20, 1863, lots 2460 and 2467.

One coin from the hoard, later known by the attribution Crosby 6-K (Noe-12), was featured in *Historical Magazine*, October 1863. It remains unique today and is almost certainly a product of the Boston mint. Eric P. Newman, the current owner, exhibited it at the 1991 Coinage of the Americas Conference at the American Numismatic Society at its headquarters in New York City.

The Roxbury Hoard

Hidden or lost: Late 1600s • **Found:** 1863 • **Treasure:** Massachusetts silver

In late summer 1863, George Wilber Reed, the young son of George P. Reed of Roxbury, Massachusetts, was playing outdoors. Climbing up an embankment made during the recent cutting through of a new street, he put his hand in the crevice of a rock to aid his ascent. He felt something within, and it proved to be a silver 1652-dated Pine Tree shilling of Massachusetts, to which two other coins adhered. His interest aroused, young George continued prospecting in the crevice and was eventually rewarded by finding 28 Massachusetts silver coins of various 1652-dated denominations plus several 1662-dated twopence.

It was later reported that the 28 coins consisted of one 1652 Oak Tree shilling, seven sixpence of the same design and date, two 1652 Oak Tree threepence, and six 1662-dated twopence. Among Pine Tree coins, all dated 1652, there were six shillings, two sixpence, and four threepence. The latest-produced coin was a small-planchet Pine Tree shilling of the type made circa 1675–1682, but bearing the standard 1652 date.

Presumably, the hoard was buried no earlier than 1675 or possibly not too much later than that, as evidenced by the coins showing relatively little wear.[8]

Oak Tree shilling, Noe-1, Whitman-430. A coin of this type, specific die variety unknown today, was found in the Roxbury Hoard.

The Exeter Hoard

Hidden: 1600s • **Found:** 1876 • **Treasure:** Massachusetts silver

In 1876, an underground hoard was found in Exeter, New Hampshire, and is said to have included 30 to 40 Massachusetts silver shillings among which may have been an example of the exceedingly rare and quite valuable Willow Tree shilling type.

This remarkable discovery was made when a cellar was being excavated under the extension of a store located close to the town railroad station. The store owner had given the sandy fill to an Irish laborer with the condition that he haul it away.[9] Quite probably, some former owner of the property had hidden the pieces for safekeeping purposes, there being no public security facilities such as banks in the area at the time.

In the process of dumping the sand into a cart, the Irishman saw a Massachusetts silver shilling, then another, then some more. At this point he decided to sift through the earth. In short order he located further specimens, as did several bystanders. Also found were the remains of what seemed to be a decomposed wooden box, which probably was used to bury the coins at some earlier date when the area was used as a garden for a private residence.

Upon examination, all of the pieces were reported to be of the Oak Tree and Pine Tree denominations dated 1652. In W. Elliot Woodward's sale of the Ferguson Haines (of Biddeford, Maine) Collection in October 1880, however, there was a notation that Lot 1084, a rare *Willow Tree* shilling, was pedigreed to "Treasure trove, Exeter, N.H., 1876."[10]

A Willow Tree shilling, Noe-1-A, Whitman-10. This is far and away the rarest of the three "tree" types of 1652-dated Massachusetts silver coins. All are irregularly struck with the inscriptions and devices incomplete in areas.

The Boothbay Harbor Find

Hidden or lost: 1600s • **Found:** 1880 • **Treasure:** Pine and Oak Tree shillings

In a note captioned "Treasure Trove," W. Elliot Woodward in his sale of the William J. Jenks Collection, September 1880, lots 429–432, related that "the four following pieces were found, quite recently, in a small cove in Boothbay Harbor, Maine. The entire find consisted of five pieces, and the finder, hoping to secure more, very judiciously keeps secret the exact place of discovery."[11]

Giving more details is this commentary, signed "W." and probably submitted by Woodward, printed in the *American Journal of Numismatics*, October 1880:

Milton Ambrose of Boothbay, Maine, several months since, found in Wall's Cove, East Boothbay Harbor, five Pine Tree and Oak Tree shillings. Description of four of these will be found in the catalog of coins sold by Bangs & Co.,[12] New York, September 1–3, nos. 429, 430, 431, 432; the fifth is now in possession of a gentleman at Boothbay. They have evidently been long in salt water, having lost about half of their original weight and thickness, and are destitute of ring, but are of unquestionable genuineness, being of well-known varieties. W.

In a subsequent offering of his own collection in an 1884 auction, Woodward described Lot 354 as: "1652 Oak Tree shilling. Found in a little cove with a number of others at Boothbay, Me., where it had lain long under salt water, the action of which reduced its weight nearly one-half. Piece broken from edge."[13] This might indicate that Woodward found the provenance to be sufficiently interesting that he kept one from his September 1880 sale for his own cabinet, or that Milton Ambrose was rewarded by not disclosing the precise location of his discovery, and found some other pieces later, one of which was acquired by the well-known Roxbury dealer.

Oak Tree shilling, Noe-4, Whitman 460.

Boothbay Harbor was famous for its shipbuilding industry, depicted here.

Talbot, Allum & Lee Coppers

Accumulated: 1795–1796 • **Sold:** 1795–1796 • **Treasure:** Copper one-cent tokens

At 241 Water Street in lower New York City, the firm of Talbot, Allum & Lee engaged in the India trade, importing goods by ship. Formed in 1794, the partnership operated only until 1796. Principals included William Talbot, William Allum, and James Lee. This particular district of the city was a beehive of activity with vessels continually arriving and departing. Numerous ships' chandlers, grog houses, cheap lodging places, and other establishments for the convenience of sailors did a lively business.

Obverse and reverse of a 1795 Talbot, Allum & Lee copper cent. These were made in Birmingham, England, to the order of a New York City merchant. (Whitman-8620).

To facilitate this trade, copper tokens dated 1794 and 1795 bearing the image of the standing goddess of Commerce on the obverse and a fully rigged sailing ship on the reverse were struck to the order of Talbot, Allum & Lee by Peter Kempson & Co., Birmingham, England, and imported into America by the partners. The quantity has been estimated at more than 200,000 coins, but no original records have been located.

At the time, copper coins in circulation in New York and nearby areas were a curious assortment of issues made by or for various states (Connecticut, Massachusetts, New Jersey, New York, and Vermont), British halfpence, counterfeits, and other pieces. The Liberty Head copper cents made at the Philadelphia Mint beginning in March 1793 were not particularly numerous. Generally, just about any copper coin the size of a British halfpenny (about the same size as an American cent) would trade in commerce at the value of one cent. Thus, it was a popular speculation and at the same time a worthwhile advertising scheme to have copper tokens privately struck for a cost of less than a cent apiece, and pay them out at one cent.[14]

In accordance with this practice, Talbot, Allum & Lee tokens dated 1794 were put into circulation, where they served at the value of one cent in local and regional commerce. However, pieces dated 1795 seem to have been less popular. Apparently, undistributed tokens piled up at the waterfront store. What should be done with the hoard?

To the Philadelphia Mint

The answer came quickly. On April 23, 1795, the firm sold 1,076 pounds of the tokens to the Philadelphia Mint for 18¢ per pound, or $193.68. On December 10, 1796, the remainder of the token stock amounting to 1,914 pounds of copper was purchased by the Mint from William Talbot for $319, or 16.6¢ per pound. These tokens weighed in at about 46 to 50 to the pound, equivalent to around 140,000 to 150,000 pieces acquired in the Mint's two purchases.

The coins were a godsend to the Mint, which had been experiencing severe difficulties obtaining copper stock from which to strike half cents and cents. Supplies of this metal were erratic and of uncertain quality and included such varied sources as copper sheet for roofing and the protection of ships' hulls as well as old pots and kettles.

Planchets for U.S. half cents were cut by punching discs from the Talbot, Allum & Lee tokens, most of which were probably in mint condition. Today it is not unusual to find a 1795 or 1797 U.S. half cent (but not one dated 1796) with faint traces remaining of the token undertype— usually some of the ship's rigging and/or some of the letters around the border of the token. Such half cents are highly prized by numismatists as they are literally two coins in one.

The Secret of an Old Desk

Hidden: 1780s • **Found:** Circa 1844 • **Treasure:** 1783 federal pattern coins

This story begins more than two centuries ago, in 1783. In that year a remarkable group of pattern coins was struck: the 5-unit piece, the "bit" of 100 units, the "quint" of 500 units, and the "mark" of 1,000 units. Sylvester S. Crosby, in his landmark *Early Coins of America* book, commented "These are undoubtedly the first patterns for coinage of the United States and command an interest exceeding that of any others in this class."

The unique 1783 pattern silver 1,000 units or mark from the desk of Charles Thomson. (Whitman-1835)

This being said, for a long span of decades the one-time existence of these coins had been forgotten by most numismatists and historians, until circa 1844 when the marvelous discovery was made of two specimens in an old desk. The dating of this find is implied from a commentary by Dr. Montroville W. Dickeson, *American Numismatical Manual*, 1859, p. 91:

> [The two pieces we have described as Figures 2 and 3 on Plate 9] formerly belonged to Charles Thomson—a contemporary and particular friend of Benjamin Franklin—who was a very decided advocate of the just rights of the colonies, and distinguished himself greatly by his uniform patriotism.
>
> They were discovered after the death of his son, which occurred, we are informed, some 15 years ago, near Newark, Delaware, in the secret drawer of an old desk that formerly belonged to the father. They are now in

the possession of a gentleman of this city, who values them very highly, not only as memorials of the past, but for their direct association with one of those noble men, whose visions were never obscured by anything that was, or could be, interposed between them and their country.[15]

These two rarities were acquired from the "gentleman of this city," Rathmell Wilson, by Philadelphia dealer John W. Haseltine and years later were sold into the Garrett Collection. In a statement to John W. Haseltine, May 28, 1872, Wilson gave further information concerning the pieces:

> The history of the two coins which you obtained from me, viz. Nova Constellatio 1783 U.S. 1,000, Nova Constellatio, 1783 U.S. 500 is as follows:
>
> They were the property of Hon. Charles Thomson, secretary of the first Congress. At his death the property was left by will to his nephew, John Thomson, of Newark, state of Delaware. These two coins were found in the desk of the said deceased Charles Thomson, and preserved by his nephew during his life; at his death they came into the possession of his son Samuel E. Thomson of Newark, Delaware, from whom I received them. So you will perceive that their genuineness cannot be questioned; as they were never out of the possession of the Thomson family, until I received them.

A bit of background on the original owner of these pieces before returning to the coins themselves. Charles Thomson, born in County Derry, Ireland, in 1729, came to America at the age of 11. He became a teacher and merchant in Philadelphia. Interested in politics, Thomson espoused the feeling for independence and was described as "the life of the cause of liberty" in Philadelphia.

From 1774 to 1789 he served as secretary of the Continental Congress, recording with enthusiasm the details of the birth of the United States. It was Thomson who was tapped to inform General George Washington of his nomination as president. Washington later sought to have Thomson appointed to service of the new government, but Thomson replied that he wished to retire. In his later years he lived on his estate and engaged in biblical scholarship. He died near Philadelphia in 1824.

When They Were Made

The 1783 pattern silver 500 units from the desk of Charles Thomson. (Whitman-1835)

As these are the first U.S. pattern coins, it is appropriate to tell more about them. Among the accounts of the United States, under the category of "Expenditure for Contingencies," between January and July 1783, the following entries appear in relation to coinage and bear upon the Nova Constellatio patterns:

February 8. Jacob Eckfeldt, for dies for the Mint of North America, $5 and 18/90ths.[16]

March 21. Benjamin Dudley employed in preparing a mint. $75 and 24/90ths.[17]

April 17. John Swanwick, for dies for the public mint $22 and 42/90ths.

May 5. A. Dubois, for sinking, casehardening, etc., for pair of dies for the public mint $72.[18]

June 30. Benjamin Dudley employed in preparing a mint $77 and 60/90ths.

Further circumstances surrounding the issue of 1783 pattern coins were recorded by Robert R. Morris, the financier. His diary noted that on April 2, 1783, "I sent for Mr. Dudley who delivered me a piece of silver coin, being the first that has been struck as an American coin."

On April 16, it was noted that he "sent for Mr. Dudley and urged him to produce the coin to lay before the Congress to establish a mint." On the following day, he "sent for Mr. Dudley to urge the preparing of coins, etc., for establishing a mint."

Morris reported on April 22 that "Mr. Dudley sent in several pieces of money as patterns of the intended American coins."

On July 5 he noted that "Mr. Benjamin Dudley . . . also informs of a minting press being in New York for sale,[19] and urges me to purchase for the use of the American Mint."

On August 19 he reported as follows:

> I sent for Mr. Benjamin Dudley, informed him of my doubts about the establishment of a mint, and desired him to think of some employment in private service, in which I am willing to assist him in all my power. I told him to make out an account for the services he had performed for the public and submit at the Treasury office for inspection and settlement.

On August 30 it was reported that "Mr. Dudley brought the dies for coining in the American Mint."

The dies were cut by hand and show numerous irregularities, with the same letters appearing in different configurations on the same coins. The largest denomination, the mark, was punctuated as "1.000" on the coin.

Rarities Today

Of the 1783 mark just one specimen is known today, the example which traces its pedigree to the Honorable Charles Thomson and was found in his desk. The obverse displays an all-seeing eye surrounded by rays and stars, with the legend NOVA CONSTELLATIO around. The reverse bears the legend LIBERTAS JUSTITIA 1783, a wreath, and within the wreath U.S 1.000.

Of the quint there are but two specimens known to exist, each of which is a slightly different design. The obverse of one is similar to that of the mark, but of reduced size, and with the legend NOVA CONSTELLATIO surrounding an all-seeing eye with rays and stars. The second variety has the all-seeing eye with rays and stars, but lacks the NOVA CONSTELLATIO inscription. Both reverses are from the same die and similar in concept to the mark, but with the denomination 500.

Of the bit there are three examples known, each with the same obverse and reverse designs: similar to those of the mark but of reduced size and bearing the denomination 100. There are two treatments of the edge, the Garrett Collection piece having an edge with an olive leaf design, and the Eric P. Newman Collection piece having a plain edge. A third example was discovered in England in the 1980s and was auctioned by Stack's.

Related to the preceding is a 1783 Nova Constellatio 5-unit copper coin of a similar design, but with the denomination expressed as ". . . 5" on the reverse. This is said to have been in various private collections in England, then the property of an English coin dealer in Paris in 1977, then American dealer Fred S. Werner in the same year, then into the collection of John J. Ford Jr.[20]

The Bank of New York Hoard

Put away: Circa 1788 • **Found:** Circa 1860 • **Treasure:** Fugio copper coins

The Bank of New York, founded in 1784, came into possession of a keg of original 1787 Fugio copper cents sometime around the time they were manufactured. Over a period of many years, beginning at least by 1859, bank officials passed these out to favored clients and employees and made some available to numismatists. Included were some of the scarce type with UNITED above and STATES below on the label at the center of the reverse (in contrast, most other varieties have these words to the left and right sides).

The variety known as Newman 13-X and Whitman-6855 was represented in quantity in the Bank of New York hoard.

Walter H. Breen's account of this keg includes a few more specific details: he claims that it contained fewer than 5,000 coins, was deposited in 1788 at the Bank of New York (44 Wall Street), and remained unopened until 1856. Whether the last date is a fact or a guess is not known, but many Breen's "facts" were invented. It is confirmed that after this time the hoard became widely known and, among other citations, was mentioned as follows by W.C. Prime in his book, *Coins, Medals and Seals* (copyright 1860, published in 1861):

> Within the past year a keg of these [Fugio] coppers was found in the vault of a New York City bank, in fresh proof condition.[21] This statement has been doubted; but we are indebted to the cashier for fine specimens of the contents of the keg, which abundantly prove the truth of the story. A recent discovery of the old dies, and possibly a manufacture of new dies, or repairing and retouching the old, has made these coins very common in various metals.[22]

Numismatic Commentary

By about 1948 some 1,641 pieces remained in the possession of the Bank of New York and were numismatically analyzed by Damon G. Douglas. By 1998, when Tony Terranova examined the group, there were 712 still on hand. It was learned that the pieces were made from two batches of planchets weighing on average 143 grains and 155 grains, respectively.

Today, numerous Bank of New York Fugio coppers are in private collections, and a selection is in the cabinet of the American Numismatic Society, New York.[23] The typical piece (such as the plentiful Newman variety 12-X) is somewhat casually struck, lightly defined in certain areas (especially at the bottom of the obverse), and is apt to have carbon streaks or planchet rifts. Coloration is likely to be a blend of original mint red with brown toning.

The Bank of New York as depicted on a $1 note of the bank.

Hoard Remnants? Restrikes?

First minted: 1795 • **Found:** 1850s • **Treasure:** Washington "Grate Cents"

Is the following an account of a hoard, or were restrikes being made? One way or another, by 1860 there was as supply of these tokens readily available per a popular author of the time. These words appeared in W.C. Prime's 1860-copyrighted work, *Coins, Medals and Seals*, p. 94:

> Another English token was issued with a head of Washington, and on the reverse a [fireplace] grate. This is called the Washington Grate cent or token, and was issued by Clark and Harris, a firm whose name it bears.
>
> The die is doubtless still preserved in England, as fine proof specimens are furnished to order in any quantity. It is a coin of little interest or value, and only to be noted as a compliment paid to the American patriot by an English house of tradesmen. The legend around the bust is "G. WASHINGTON, THE FIRM FRIEND TO PEACE & HUMANITY."

Apart from the foregoing, no information concerning this source of supply has been confirmed. However, Walter H. Breen attributed the dies for this piece to Thomas Wyon and suggests that they were struck by Peter Kempson & Co. in Birmingham.[24] At least two die varieties exist, one with small coat buttons and the other with large buttons, the former considerably the rarer. There are several variations of the edge treatment, the most often seen being with diagonal reeding.

1795 Grate halfpenny, Whitman-10955.

The Colonel M.I. Cohen Hoard

Put away: Circa 1775 • **Found:** By the 1870s • **Treasure:** 1773 Virginia halfpennies

In 1773, the colony of Virginia ordered a supply of copper halfpence from the British Crown. Examples were struck at the Tower Mint in London, and in due course exported to America.[25] In February 1774, the ship *Virginia*, under Captain Howard Esten, arrived at the York River (which empties into the Chesapeake Bay) with five long tons of new halfpence aboard, equivalent to about 672,000 coins. The coins bore the portrait of George III on the obverse and a heraldic shield on the reverse, the latter side inscribed VIRGINIA.

1773 Virginia halfpenny from the Colonel M.I. Cohen hoard. Many die varieties were found in that group.

Distribution of the pieces in commerce was quite slow. In late winter 1775, Robert C. Nicholas, treasurer of the Virginia colony, published notices that the halfpence were on hand and ready for exchange "either for gold, silver, or any Treasury notes."

As it turned out, the American colonies and Britain commenced war with each other less than two months after the availability of Virginia halfpence was announced. Widespread hoarding by the citizenry commenced, as it usually does during times of extreme political and economic uncertainty. Thus, many of the Virginia coins that were distributed were immediately saved, rather than used in everyday commerce. Enough reached circulation that numerous examples later became lost or misplaced as pocket change, though, and many others have been found by metal detectorists in recent decades.

Colonel Cohen

Colonel Mendes I. Cohen (1796–1879) of Baltimore, Maryland, served at Fort McHenry in 1814 during the bombardment by the British. After the war he joined his brothers in the banking business in Baltimore, and for a time conducted a branch of J.I. Cohen, Jr. and Brothers in New York City. He was also involved in Cohen's Lottery & Exchange in Baltimore. By then a wealthy man, from 1829 to 1835 he toured Great Britain, Europe, Asia Minor, and the Middle East. In Egypt he traveled up the Nile River to the Second Cataract. Years later he served with distinction in the Mexican War.

An inveterate collector in many fields, Cohen acquired art, coins, and other objects. His extensive collection of Egyptian antiquities was given to The Johns Hopkins University in Baltimore. He was also an early member of the Baltimore Numismatic Society and must have known such notable numismatists as Robert Gilmor Jr., Dr. George Massamore, and T. Harrison Garrett. It is interesting to note that of all American cities, Baltimore has had more than its share of very special numismatic connections over the years, and several of the most memorable cabinets ever formed were assembled within its city limits.[26]

Cohen, a bachelor, died on May 7, 1879. Sometime in the nineteenth century, he had acquired more than 2,200 bright Uncirculated specimens of the 1773 Virginia halfpenny under circumstances not recorded, but perhaps from his father, Israel I. Cohen. In 1952, Walter H. Breen speculated that they may have been found in a Maryland state government building in Annapolis and may have been in an original wooden keg. By 1988, Breen had modified his theory and forthrightly stated that they were "from a keg found in Richmond before the Civil War and long owned by Col. Mendes I. Cohen."[27]

Much of Cohen's collection was sold at auction October 25–29, 1875, by Edward D. Cogan. The

The J.I. Cohen, Jr. and Brothers bank in Baltimore.

Engraving for Cohen's Lottery Office in Baltimore.

offering was remarkable for its quality and included many rare early pieces, an extensive run of U.S. gold Proof sets, and other treasures, but Virginia halfpence did not play a notable part. Apparently, most of these sparkling copper pieces were subsequently bequeathed to Cohen's nieces and nephews, who also received many art objects.

In his January 21, 1880 auction catalog of properties from various sources, John W. Haseltine gave brief notice of a find of 1773 Virginia halfpennies without mentioning either their quantity or how they were located, but he did tie them to Cohen.

Haseltine wrote under lot 713:

> Many persons think that these Virginia 1/2d are restrikes, but that is not so; they were the property of the late Mr. Cohen, of Baltimore, and descended to him from his father; I purchased quite a number from him and found 12 different varieties among them, all from different dies.

Raymond Acquires Many

The Colonel Cohen cache remained nearly intact until 1929 when antiques and other items belonging to Bertha Cohen were auctioned in Baltimore. About 2,200 1773 Virginia halfpennies were sold loosely and in bulk and fetched a few cents each. From that time forward, these pieces have been relatively plentiful in numismatic circles.

Apparently, many of these were later resold by Wayte Raymond. At least a few hundred of these coins passed to a Mr. Gottschalk of Syracuse, New York, who had groups of these for sale in the 1950s and would bring several dozen pieces at a time to conventions of the Empire State Numismatic Association.[28]

About 20 different die pairings were represented in the Cohen hoard. Modern scholars have identified these Newman number die varieties as having been included in the Cohen Hoard: 2-E, 3-F, 4-G, 4-O, 4-P, 5-B, 5-Z, 6-X, 7-D, 8-O, 9-B, 20-N, 20-X, 21-N, 22-S, 23-Q, 23-R, 24-K, 25-M, 26-Y, and 27-J.[29]

The Knoxville and Easton Finds

Dr. Montroville W. Dickeson, in his 1859 work, *American Numismatical Manual*, commented (p. 84) concerning two other hoards of 1773 Virginia halfpence:

> Some few years since, a quantity of these copper coins was dug up from the summit of the hill on which the college now stands at Knoxville, Tennessee, and quite a number were exhumed from a locality near Easton, Pennsylvania, showing that they must have been extensively circulated, and have amply rewarded the projectors.

Little if any other information is known about the Knoxville and Easton finds, the condition of the pieces, where they went, and their relationship (if any) to the Colonel Cohen hoard. Apparently, Dickeson did not know of the Cohen holding if, indeed, it was owned by Cohen as early as 1859.

Today, the 1773 Virginia halfpennies are the only colonial (pre-1776) American coins that are readily available in Mint State. In fact, Mint State examples are, by a large margin, more often encountered than are pieces with extensive evidence of circulation.

These coins are commonly collected by two major variations in obverse punctuation, with or without a period after GEORGIVS. Relatively few have pursued the series by minute die varieties as described in Eric P. Newman's 1956 study, quite possibly because this monograph has been out of print for a long time. Thus, exceedingly rare die varieties, if found, are apt to cost no more than common ones.

A Handful of Copper Coins

Lost: 1780s • **Found:** 1924 • **Treasure:** Nova Constellatio coppers and other coins

It is not often that a find of copper coins makes news in the general press. This notice told of finding a 1783 Nova Constellatio copper and a few other pieces:

> "Sand hogs" working 80 feet underground on the foundations of the New York Telephone Company building recently, in New York, unearthed several American coins dating back to the latter part of the eighteenth century. An official in charge of the work said 50 feet underground the men found the hulk of an old vessel about the size of a modern canal boat.
>
> While digging out the hulk the men found the coins, which were bronze or copper. One bears the word "Libertas" and is dated 1783. On the reverse side is the inscription "Constel-latio Nova." Another coin found is dated 1780. Of the nine coins found no two are alike.[30]

It would be interesting to know more.

A 1783 Nova Constellatio copper, variety Crosby 2-b, Whitman-1865.

The "Solitude" Hoard

Hidden or lost: 1780 • **Found:** By 1925 • **Treasure:** New Jersey copper coins

In 1734, on a site well watered and fertile, a lovely house was built which later was named "Solitude" due to its secluded location.[31] Within a space of a few years, the home became the family seat for Justice John Cleves Symmes, a member of the New Jersey Supreme Court and a very important politician in state affairs.

In 1787, Justice Symmes, along with other influential members of Northern New Jersey's political elite, invited one Walter Mould to reside near Solitude and commence coining New Jersey coppers. Less than one year earlier, Mould, in conjunction with two other Englishmen, had successfully bid for and won a contract to supply the state of New Jersey with a copper coinage. But after a falling-out among the partners, Mould removed himself to Morristown and placed his operations under the tutelage and political protection of Justice Symmes.

For the next year and a half, Mould struck coins in Morristown, but the venture was not a commercial success, and both he and his backers reaped only substantial losses where they had expected equally large profits. By the summer of 1788, Walter Mould had died on a journey to Ohio, leaving behind a destitute wife and young son. Meanwhile, Justice Symmes—in whose entourage Mould had traveled to Ohio—began a successful legal career in the western territories.

1787 New Jersey copper with PLURIBS misspelling on reverse, Maris 61-p, Whitman-5340.

Meanwhile, back home at Solitude, Justice Symmes's house was sold and turned into a tavern named the Wheat Sheaf, run by Captain Benjamin Holloway. Holloway's establishment soon became a favorite stopping place along the Morristown to Elizabethtown turnpike. A copper mine on the site of Solitude (from whence it is believed that Mould obtained the copper for his coins) flooded due to the absence of pumping, and the pond then served as the inn's chief water supply.

A View of the Mint
In the way of further background, see this related commentary concerning the Symmes house from a letter dated August 8, 1855, from W.C. Baker of Morristown, New Jersey, to numismatist Charles I. Bushnell:

There were two mint-houses in this state, one located in Morristown, and the other in Elizabethtown. The mint-house in the former place, which is still standing, was the residence of John Cleve [sic] Symmes, chief justice of the state of New Jersey, uncle to John Cleve Symmes, author of *The Hole at the North Pole*, and father-in-law of Gen. Wm. H. Harrison, president of the United States.

The residence was called "Solitude." It was at one time occupied by a Mr. Holloway, and is known by some as the "Holloway House." The mint here was carried on by Walter Mould, an Englishman, who previous to his coming to America, had been employed in a similar way, in Birmingham. In the coinage of the New Jersey coppers, a screw with a long lever was employed. This information is vouched for by Mr. Lewis Condict, of Morristown, who saw the mint in operation.[32]

Wheat Sheaf Farm
In 1897 a German immigrant, Gustave Kissel, bought the old place and renamed it "Wheat Sheaf Farm." At some later time Kissel or his heirs sold the farm to Edwin S.S. Sunderland, who commenced renovations to the property. During one of these efforts, Sunderland discovered behind an old mantelpiece a series of New Jersey coppers of the large planchet type, which had been sealed behind the wall for more than a century. In addition, at least one other coin was discovered in the garden during the course of landscaping. These coppers, numbering 30 or more pieces, were placed into the pages of a National Coin Album and proudly shown to visitors.[33]

In 1955 Sunderland published *A History of Old Wheat Sheaf Farm, formerly "Solitude."* In the book, on page 13, he mentioned the 30 coppers that he had found while doing restoration work on the house and its grounds. This was the first notice that came to the attention of specialists in New Jersey coppers that any pieces had been found on the old site of Walter Mould's New Jersey mint. By 1964 several collectors had traveled to Sunderland's home to see the coins.

In October 1964, Everett T. Sipsey published his narrative account of the examination of the coins he had made in Sunderland's house. By the time Sipsey had seen them there were only 17 pieces left, and they had clearly been mixed up out of their places in the National Coin Album page, as no longer corresponded to the coins contained in those apertures. It is clear that at some point someone had attributed these coins to their particular Maris varieties, but that, over time, the coins had been taken out and put back so many times by inexperienced collectors that attributions underneath each slot no longer corresponded to the coins contained therein.

Sipsey did note that eight of the coins included were large planchet pieces, and that one variety, the popular PLURIBS reverse—which was noted as having been found in 1925—was missing from the group. Sipsey further noted that it was no longer possible to be sure exactly which large planchet coins had been plowed up in the garden, discovered behind the fireplace or, perhaps, added later to augment the collection. However, Sipsey suggested that all Maris numbers, 59-o through 67-v, could confidently be attributed to the Morristown Mint based upon their large planchet size.

While the "Solitude Hoard" was not an important find in terms of either individual coin values or overall numismatic content, for New Jersey specialists it marked a turning point. As the site was known to have been where Mould's mint was located in Morristown, and as the coins were discovered on site, confidently datable to the late 1780s, and large planchet varieties, it could safely be assumed that the large planchet pieces were Mould's products and not those of the Rahway Mint.

The Stepney Depot Hoard

Hidden: 1788 • **Found:** 1950 • **Treasure:** Copper coins of the 1700s

1787 Vermont copper made at Machin's Mills. The obverse utilizes a Vermont die and the reverse is the inadvertent use of a false die for a counterfeit British halfpenny deliberately made with light details to give the appearance of a coin that had been accepted in circulation for a long time. Two of these were in the Stepney Depot hoard.

A detailed report of this find was given by Walter H. Breen in 1952, based upon his examination of it in 1951:

Some excavations during 1950 on a pre-Revolutionary War estate in Stepney [Depot], Fairfield County, Connecticut, brought to light an old iron kettle apparently filled with earth. The kettle was of eighteenth century vintage, was undamaged, and probably had lain undisturbed since its burial next to one of the posts in the old barn (built 1760) whence it was unearthed. It proved to contain some 200 coins, encrusted, which the owners subsequently sold to Stack's in New York. The encrustations were cleaned off without damage to the coins, and some pieces were sold (reportedly including eight Uncirculated Vermont cents of the portrait types and 20-odd Connecticut cents in the same condition). I later had the opportunity to study the remainder of the hoard.

What I saw included 181 coins, as follows:

One was a 1787 Nova Eborac, three were Vermont cents (two having the BRITANNIA. reverse, the third being Ryder 27), 72 were counterfeit halfpence, all with correct legends (*i.e., no bungtowns*), the remainder were Connecticut cents 1785–1788, mostly in Mint State or almost as fine, though many were poorly struck.

The Connecticuts were just as noteworthy for variety as for condition. Fully 74 different die varieties, including some extreme rarities, were represented. Among these I might mention 1786 Miller 4.2-G (unlisted muling), 5.2-H.1, 5.2-L, 5.8-F, 5.11-R, 5.14-S, 33.13-Z.1, and 33.40-Z.2—all Rarity 5 or 6, all represented by one to three specimens.[34]

Probably of equal importance are the quantity and character of the counterfeit halfpence. Sixteen of the 72 were dated 1778–1787, *all* being in Mint State, all on planchets of the same fabric, all having identical letter and figure punches and die workmanship. Three of the 1787s have the identical die for reverse that was later used with Vermont obverse to make Ryder-13, the BRITANNIA variety; this die is attributed to James F. Atlee and the coins to Machin's Mill near Newburgh, New York. One of the three 1787 counterfeits has both obverse and reverse the same as that illustrated by Howard Kurth as "Machin's Halfpenny" in his introduction to Richardson on Vermont cents (May 1947 *Numismatist*). These Machin-made halfpence will be discussed below.

Some of the conclusions that can be drawn from this hoard follow, the complete catalog of the contents being omitted for lack of space:

1. The hoard was buried in 1788, unless most of the Connecticuts of that date were pre-dated. I would suspect it was fairly early in the year, too, inasm uch as the 1788-dated coins are extremely few in proportion to the 1787s, and all of the 1788s are choice Mint State. There are only four 1788 Connecti-cuts, but 75 1787s, thirteen 1786s and eight 1785s. Purely negative evidence seems to confirm this; there are no late Machin issues such as the GEORGIVS III REX / INDE ET LIB pieces, Immune Columbias, or "emergency" issues overstruck on earlier pieces such as Nova Constellatios or half pence.

2. Since coppers passed current then at six to eight for a penny, the whole current value of the hoard at time of burial cannot have exceeded two Spanish dollars (even allow-ing the maximum number of specimens to have been sold from the hoard before I saw it), and probably did not even equal one dollar. The answer to the natural question, "To whom would this junk have seemed treasure worth burying?" immediately sug-gests itself: this was a small boy's hoard, made up of his acquisitions of a few coppers at a time, gathered over a period of a couple of years (hence the great diversity of variet-ies). This hypothesis incidentally provides one of two possible explanations for the great number of counterfeit halfpence: either it was a child's ignorance of base coin, or else false halfpence really circulated in those times as if genuine—or both.

3. In any event, this hoard provides an extraor-dinary illumination of the kinds of currency of low value that passed in Connecticut and the surrounding area in that period. Com-pare the account in S.S. Crosby's *Early Coins of America* (pp. 291–292) which applied to New York, but is largely confirmed by this hoard buried only a few miles east of the New York-Connecticut border. There is one anomaly for which no explanation seems satisfactory, however: the complete absence of Massachusetts, Fugio, or New Jersey coppers.

4. The base halfpence mentioned above, dated 1778 and attributed by implication to Atlee and Machin, were certainly *predated*, judg-ing both by condition and by the fact that stylistically they are connected with 1788 Connecticuts and halfpence—not to men-tion the identity of letters and figure punches. This confirms a conjecture of C. Wyllys Betts (*Counterfeit Half Pence*, p. 16) that they were so made. I suspect that the "1778" was an error for 1787.

5. The "base coins in similitude of British half-pence" repeatedly mentioned by Crosby (pp. 291, 172–174) were these counterfeits, both Birmingham-made (circa 1736–1776, as in this hoard) and Newburgh-made (1778–1787–1788). They were mostly cer-tainly NOT the so-called "Pennsylvania coppers" or bungtowns. Strictly speaking, a *bungtown* is a bogus British copper of half-penny or farthing size, with legends (such as GLORIOVS IER VIS, CORNWALLIS IND., GEORGE RULES, GREGORIVS III. PON., etc.) designed to evade drastic British anti-counterfeiting acts—and, at worst, to deceive the illiterate. These are better termed "evasions" and left com-pletely out of the American colonial series, as most of the legends have been shown to refer to [British] historical events of the period 1789–1805, making it absurd to say that they circulated in Pennsylvania in 1781–1788. (See J.D.A. Thompson's article "Evasions," No. 373, *Seaby's Bulletin*, June 1949, for evidence.) There is plenty of evi-dence both inside and outside of the Fair-field County hoard that counterfeit British halfpence with correct legends circulated in the colonies. There is, however, NO evi-dence (other than Dr. Maris's conjecture quoted by Crosby, pp. 172–173) that these evasions ever did; and there is some evi-

dence, namely the present hoard, that they did not circulate in quantity, if at all—for there is not a single specimen in evidence. I suggest therefore that the coins suppressed in Pennsylvania were simply British counterfeits of the kind which form a good part of the present hoard, and that the Maris conclusions otherwise were based on too little evidence.

Another conclusion (perhaps weakened by my lack of metallurgical experience) that might be drawn from this hoard is that the same source apparently supplied copper for both the Machin halfpence and many of the Connecticut coppers of 1787–1788, as the fabric and finish are identical. If the conclusion that these latter were made in Machin's Mill be correct, then the statement on Crosby's p. 202 (concerning the insignificantly small output of the Newburgh manufactory of hardware before 1789) will need revision—especially as the false halfpence are fairly common. There was also, apparently, a good bit of shipping of dies from one mint to another.

I may also briefly mention here that there were several hubs or head-punches used concurrently among obverse dies of Connecticuts, Vermonts, and halfpence. One was the Mailed Bust seen on Connecticut 1785 obverses 7 and 8; 1786 types 4 and 5.1, 5.3, 5.6; and Vermont obverses of Ryder 10, 11, and 15. Another was the Draped Bust used for Connecticut obverses of 1787, numbers 16 to 56 and all of the 1788 Draped Busts. Still another was the hub found on Vermont coppers attributed as Ryder 1, 14, 20, 21, etc., and some others, and also on a GEORGIVS III REX obverse listed as Ryder 31. A fourth was that seen on 1787 Connecticut obverses 9 and 15; 1788 obverses 7, 8, 10, 11, 12, and 13.[35]

Note that Breen went on to write much more in numismatics, with the capstone of his career being the publication by Doubleday in 1988 of *Walter Breen's Complete Encyclopedia of U.S. and Colonial Coins*.

Fate and Findings

It is believed that many of the Stepney Depot Hoard state copper coins went into the collection of Edward Hessberg.[36]

A key piece in the Stepney find was a 1776 Machin's Mills imitation halfpenny, the variety today known as Vlack 76 B-9, which Eric P. Newman used as the center point to his 1958 article, "A Recently Discovered Coin Solves a Vermont Numismatic Enigma," in the *Centennial Publication of the American Numismatic Society*.

Newman recalled the purchase of this piece and made a few other comments:

> I bought this coin from Stack's, with Walter Breen handling the matter for them. There were about 10 to 12 Machins I bought from the group sent me and only one offered me was in Mint State. This was in May 1951 according to a recent article by John Kleeberg in *The Colonial Newsletter*, January 1996, page 1608. Walter knew I was working on the matter.
>
> While Walter may not have known the full significance of the 1776 coin he sold me he did note in his 1952 *Numismatist* article that the head punch matched some Connecticut and Vermont pieces, as stated in your adaptation of his article.
>
> I believe you should correct some of his erroneous guesswork. He makes it appear that Bungtown was an English name for evasive legend halfpence. When I wrote this up in 1976 to show it was strictly an American word for counterfeit halfpence he helped and was later delighted with the Shakespearean association. When I wrote more in 1991 on Shakespeare's bunghole usage Walter was responsible for the filthy Rabelais tie in.
>
> Walter's comment about "six to eight for a penny" is an error or mix up. There were six to eight shillings to a Spanish dollar in money of account, but before rejection of halfpence there were 14 to 18 coppers to a shilling and after rejection never more than 60.[37]

The Umpqua River Hoard

Buried: 1800s • **Found:** 1950s • **Treasure:** 1820 North West Co. tokens

The North West Company was one of Canada's premier trading outfits, running a profitable business buying beaver and other furs from Indians across the length of Canada. The company had a near monopoly on trade with the natives in the northwest regions of Canada and the United States, the areas that later became the provinces of British Columbia and the states of Washington and Oregon.

By the first decade of the 1800s, however, the North West Company had lost its control of the western fur trade to the bigger and more aggressive Hudson's Bay Company. By 1820, North West was no longer capable of directing its own business affairs, and one year later, it was forced to merge with its rival.

North West Company token of 1820, holed at the top for suspension, as usual. Whitman-9250.

Before that, though, the North West Company decided to issue brass tokens which would entitle the bearer to one prime beaver pelt's worth of trade goods at one of the company's forts. These tokens bore a male head on one side, possibly that of George IV, and the inscription TOKEN 1820. The other side showed a beaver, indicating the token's value in trade, and the inscription NORTH WEST COMPANY. These tokens may have been made by John Walker & Company, or by Cotterhill, Hill & Company, both of which firms were located in England. The tokens appear to have been holed at the time they were made, so they could be stored strung on leather cords at

the company's stores and carried easily by Indians. A couple of tokens are known not holed.

Presumably, these brass tokens were used in the district at least circa 1820–1821 by the North West Company, and possibly even later by the Hudson's Bay Company after its assumption of the former firm.

Demise of the North West Company

To shine some extra light on the end of the North West Company, see this account, printed in 1840:

The mercantile rivalry of the two great British corporations, the Northwest [*sic*; spelled North West in many other accounts and on the tokens] and the Hudson's Bay Company, which had been long strengthening, now began to rage in the wilderness, and in 1814 had broken out into actual war. A colony of Scotch highlanders had been established upon the Red River (now in Manitoba) by Lord Selkirk, in virtue of a grant of the country from the Hudson's Bay Company. On the other hand, the Northwest Company denied the validity of that grant, and it was of great injury to the last-named body, as their posts had been almost entirely supplied from the Red River lands. In consequence, numerous acts of violence ensued, and in 1814 the Scotchmen were driven away, their houses demolished, and the colony subverted.

It was re-established, however, during the following year when the hostilities were renewed, the posts retaken and burned. On the 19th of June, 1816, a more formidable battle was fought between the rival traders; the Scotchmen were routed, and their governor, Mr. Temple, and five others, were killed.

These facts having been brought before the British Parliament, an act was passed on the 2d of July, 1821, uniting the two companies by the name of The Hudson's Bay

Company, under a charter giving to them the privilege of trading in the Indian territory claimed or belonging to Great Britain for the period of 21 years. . . .

The system of the Hudson's Bay Company is one calculated to further the exercise of its despotic power. . . . The trade of this company at the west is prosecuted by a resident governor, agents, factors, and clerks, some of whom have a share in the profits of the trade; also by a more active class of agents, the hunters, voyageurs[38], and trappers, consisting of French Canadians, half-breeds, and Indians, who are paid a small salary with the promises of future advancement according as they shall render themselves of value to the trade. They are allowed only a small share o f miserable food, and are kept by promises in a state of entire subjection to the will of the company.

The furs which are collected are procured mainly from the Indians, in exchange for manufactured goods, which are imported into the country free of duty. . . .[39]

Expanding on the above, modern historian Scott M. Hopkins stated that North West Company was founded in 1779 informally as a reaction of Montreal traders—notably McTavish—to the Quebec governor's ruling against trading with Americans.[40] Initially it was a nine-member partnership. It continually brought in new firms and independent partners, expanding its reaches and separating itself from the style of the Hudson's Bay Company. All of the founding members—Nor'Westers—had experience in fur trading personally in remote regions.

By 1783, the company was a permanent entity after a stable and more business-friendly agreement was settled. This is the date that the current North West Company grocery chain traces their roots to and most academics agree.

On March 26, 1821, the North West Company and the Hudson's Bay Company signed an agreement to combine, although the NWC senior management lost much of their roles, and in order to maintain the royal charter the HBC name had to be maintained.

Caches

By the late 1800s, the North West Company tokens were considered to be rare and were of special interest to those collecting numismatic specimens of Canada. In 1894, P.N. Breton, in his landmark book, *Illustrated History of Coins and Tokens Relating to Canada*, illustrated the piece as his No. 925.

In time, collectors south of the Canadian border took a fancy to this token as well. Today it is listed in *A Guide Book of United States Coins* and is firmly on the "want lists" of many stateside numismatists.

Then, in the 1900s, several caches of North West Company tokens came to light in the Columbia River and Umpqua River valleys of Oregon, including 26 highly oxidized tokens unearthed with a copper kettle (which had contained the pieces) and a skull in a burial mound along the Umpqua River near the coast in central Oregon. Twenty-two of these were consigned to my company and were sold to collectors.[41] Concerning the other four pieces in the find, one was donated to a museum, and three were so extensively corroded that their edges were crumbling.

Other hoards of North West Company tokens have been variously reported. One consisting of 14 pieces is currently in a Western museum. Others have been excavated from the ruins of western forts, including two pieces shown by Steve Bibler at the October 28, 1954, meeting of the Seattle Coin Club, which were excavated from the ruins of Fort Vancouver.[42]

The Long Island Potato Field Find

Lost: 1700s • **Found:** 1990 • **Treasure:** New England silver sixpence

Among early American colonial coins the silver NE (New England) coinage combines rarity and history to an exceptional degree. Three denominations were made: the threepence denominated III, the sixpence (as here) with VI, and the XII shilling or 12 pence.

The NE (New England) silver sixpence found in a potato field. Much excitement followed!

Of the threepence, just two have been confirmed to exist. One is on exhibit at the Massachusetts Historical Society. The other was stolen from Yale University in the early 1960s and, hopefully, exists somewhere—eventually to be repatriated. Of the NE shilling, dozens are known, but they are so much in demand and so important that auction sales run into five figures when even a low-grade piece crosses the block.

Of the sixpence there are eight known pieces, including one belonging to the American Numismatic Society, one at the British Museum, the Eric P. Newman example, the Bushnell-Garrett coin, the Loye Lauder piece (in a Long Island collection), and the specimen that is the focus of this commentary.

That silver sixpence was found by Lillian Rade of East Hampton, Long Island, New York, in February 1990, in frozen ground in a potato field by use of a metal detector. The find caused no end of excitement, was published in nearly every major American newspaper, and was featured in "Ripley's Believe It or Not." It was auctioned by Sotheby's in 1991 and purchased by Stack's for $35,200 and sold to a client. It was the most

valuable coin ever found in American soil with a metal detector at that point, later surpassed by the $41,400 realization for a Maryland denarium sold by Stack's in August 2007.

In November 2012 Stack's Bowers Galleries auctioned the Jack Royse Collection of early American coins, of which the sixpence in question was now a part. The venue was the Whitman Coin & Collectibles Expo in Baltimore, an event held three times a year. The cataloger, John Kraljevich, combined numismatic and historical information in the coin's description, including this:

> Eastern Long Island had more in common with New England than New York in the 17th century. The Connecticut River, just across the narrowest part of Long Island Sound, was the main north-south thoroughfare into the interior of New England. It is no accident that today an Interstate parallels its path from Hartford to northern Vermont. The town at the mouth of the Connecticut River, Old Saybrook, was founded in the 1630s by a group led by John Winthrop, and Massachusetts held a firm grip on its commerce and governance for the better part of a century. It is no coincidence that, perhaps 20 miles away as the crow flies, this coin would turn up in that place.
>
> It survived its time in the ground well, attracting a pleasing deep gray-brown patina over most of the obverse and reverse. A lighter area of silver is present near 8 o'clock on the obverse and directly beneath the NE punch, similar texture at central reverse. The punches are both good and strong, matching the other known specimens of Noe 1-A—the only genuine variety of NE sixpence—in both shape and depth. A long old scratch runs from 10 o'clock on the obverse rim past center to near 3 o'clock opposite on the obverse; two lighter scrapes parallel it at top. A thinner, newer scratch is present from center of obverse to 6:30 or so. The light reverse scrapes have

now been laid subtle by the earthen patina on that side. The shape of the planchet is nearly round, about the same as other NE coinages, hand-cut to size and weight at the time. The weight is essentially full for the issue, 31.8 grains; the Garrett coin weighed 33.7 grains.

What happened at the sale? Would you believe that it sold for $431,250? It is true!

Hoard of Kentucky Tokens

Put away: 1790s • **Found:** 1996 • **Treasure:** "Kentucky" tokens

In June 1996, a small hoard of about 25 gem Mint State Kentucky tokens with lustrous red surfaces was found in England and sold to an American dealer.[43] Doubtless, these had remained in the British Isles since the time of their coinage, circa 1792, in Birmingham.

These tokens feature an obverse inscription that includes UNANIMITY IS THE STRENGTH OF SOCIETY and OUR CAUSE IS JUST. On the reverse are the legend E PLURIBUS UNUM and a pyramid made of 15 letters abbreviating states' names, with a K, for Kentucky, at the top. Hence the popular name of Kentucky token. Kentucky, the 15th state, was admitted to the Union on June 1, 1792. The 16th state, Tennessee, was admitted on June 1, 1796. Thus, it is presumed that the Kentucky tokens were minted sometime between the summer of 1792 and the summer of 1796.

It is my view that few, if any, of these tokens ever circulated in America. Such pieces are part of more than a dozen different America-related Conder tokens, a vast panorama of copper halfpenny-size token designs struck in the 1780s and 1790s to create varieties for collectors in England (there being no significantly developed numismatic activity in the United States at the time). Other Conder tokens with American themes include Talbot, Allum & Lee cents of 1794–1795, the 1794 Franklin Press token, and several pieces relating to George Washington.

Walter H. Breen stated that Kentucky tokens, struck as part of the Conder token series, "circulated widely along the Eastern Seaboard, while the floundering Philadelphia Mint's cents remained unfamiliar curiosities," certainly a different opinion of the history of this piece.[44] He further suggested that they were ordered from England by "New York or Philadelphia merchants."

Kentucky token, circa 1792–1795. On the token (Whitman-8800), Kentucky is represented by the K at the top of the pyramid.

Lord Baltimore Surprise

Put away: 1600s • **Distributed:** 1902 • **Treasure:** Lord Baltimore silver sixpence

On June 20, 1632, Cecil Calvert, the second Lord Baltimore, received from King Charles I of England a grant for a new province named for the queen, Mary, and designated as "Terra Maria," or Maryland. The land was settled, and the colonists prospered. During the Commonwealth period in England, Calvert lost control, but he regained it in November 1657 and soon afterward appointed Josias Fendall as governor and Philip Calvert (Lord Baltimore's brother) as provincial secretary.

Not long after that, Lord Baltimore worked to initiate a coinage with his brother, who was the "point man" for having a coinage prepared in England for use in Maryland. Dies were prepared accordingly and specimens were struck, probably at the Royal Mint. On October 16, 1659, Cecil

Calvert sent letters to the governor and council and also to his brother. To the Council went the following communication:

> After my hardy commendations, having of great pains and charges procured necessaries for a particular coin to be current in Maryland, a sample whereof, a piece of a shilling, a sixpence, and a groat [a silver coin of the value of four pence], I herewith send you, I recommend it to you to promote, all you can, to dispersing it, and by proclamation to make current within Maryland, for all payments upon contracts or causes happening or arising after a day to be by you limited in the said proclamation; and to procure an act of Assembly for the punishing of such as shall counterfeit the said coin or otherwise offend in that behalf, according to the form of an act recommended by me last year to my governor and secretary; or as near it as you can procure from the assembly, and to give me your advice next year touching upon what you think best to be further done in that matter touching coin; for its encouragement be given by the good success of it this year, there will be abundance of adventurers in it the next year.

Lord Baltimore actively tried to get the Maryland Assembly to consent to accepting his coinage in 1659 or 1660, but the legislation was put on hold. There was serious Protestant opposition to Baltimore's stand on several issues that almost resulted in an overthrow of the government in 1660. This attempted coup resulted in Baltimore having Governor Fendall sent to trial for treason and, following the trial, promoting his brother Philip Calvert as governor. In 1661 Maryland passed an act to establish its own mint, but this never saw fruition.

In 1671, John Ogilby, referring to Maryland in his *America: Being the Latest and Most Accurate Description of the New World*, noted that:

> The general way of traffic in commerce there is chiefly by barter, or exchange of one commodity for another; yet there wants not, besides English and other foreign coins, some of his lordship's own coin, as groats, sixpences, and shillings, which his Lordship at his own charge caused to be coined and dispersed throughout that province; 'tis equal in fineness of silver to English sterling, being of the same standard, but of somewhat less weight, and hath on one side his Lordship's coat of arms stamped, with this motto circumscribed Crescite & Multiplicamini, and on the other side his Lordship's effigies, circumscribed thus, Caecilius Dominus Terrae-Mariae, &c.[45]

Fast forward to 2002. A member of the Fales family of Lincolnshire, England, consigned a group of coins, medals, tins, and other collectibles to Morton & Eden Ltd., London auctioneers. Included was a silver box of the 1600s intended to store tokens or game counters. Surprise! James Morton of the firm opened the tube and found one game counter and 19 Lord Baltimore silver sixpence!

"I would have been happy finding one," Morton said. "It's pretty good finding 19."

Of these, 18 were of the most often encountered variety with Small Bust obverse and with MVLTIPLICAMINI in the reverse inscription. The 19th coin was a rarity lacking the P in that word. Grades ranged from Fine to Very Extremely fine, indicating that some of them had seen many years of circulation.

At the auction held in November 2002 the rare variety crossed the block at the equivalent of $50,432. The buyer was Stack's of New York City, a firm that also landed other pieces. Tony Terranova was also an important buyer at the sale. All of the Maryland coins went to American bidders. Prices for the 18 Small Bust variety coins ranged from $3,961 to $17,104.

How these coins came into possession of the Fales family was not recorded. It is presumed that someone visited America in the late 1600s and for some reason brought Maryland coins only of this denomination back to England. This is the most important hoard of Maryland silver ever found.[46]

chapter 2

Coins Hidden Here and There

Rare-coin treasures are where you find them, and that can be just about anywhere! Over the years valuable coins have been located in many unusual places, often as much by chance as by intention. However, as some of the accounts about metal detectorists and "coinshooting" relate, checking old maps and other planning can increase the chance of success.

The finds in this chapter cover a wide range of coins and circumstances—setting the scene for later stories and accounts. Descriptions of hundreds more were encountered during research for the present book, but only those with a degree of numismatic information were among those selected for inclusion. It is truly amazing how many popular accounts of hoards appear in newspapers and go on and on for paragraph after paragraph, telling about the weather, the age, and a brief biography of the person making the find—

as well as just about everything else—yet give no facts at all concerning the actual coins discovered! Is an "old coin" a common 1910 Lincoln cent or a rare cent of 1799? Many such questions are left unanswered.

Mint Reports issued over a long period of years tell of half cents, large cents, early half dollars, gold coins, and other items that have been turned into the Treasury Department for redemption. It is amazing to note that these records indicate only a few half cents (minted from 1793 to 1857) have ever been redeemed, and that tens of millions of 1793–1857 large cents are still missing, as are untold millions of nickel three-cent pieces, Liberty Seated coins, and other issues. Thus, the potential for discovery is immense.

The finds are listed here in the approximate order in which they were found or publicized.

Treasure Stolen from a Bank

Hidden: 1818 • **Found:** 1846 • **Treasure:** Gold and silver coins

On July 8, 1848, the *Worcester* (MA) *Palladium* printed this exchange item from a New Haven paper:

Stolen Money Found
Attending Circumstances

A gentleman of this city has put into our hands, a letter from a friend residing in Portland, Me., containing the following interesting intelligence, which is believed to be entitled to credit.

Considerable excitement, says the writer, has been caused in this city for a few days past, by a report of money having

been found buried on a hill back of the city. The story is, and I suppose it to be correct, that two boys were playing on the hill last Sabbath, and discovered a stake driven in the ground some distance. They attempted to pull it up, but as there appeared to be something at

A $5 note of the Cumberland Bank signed, dated, and issued in 1813.

the bottom of it, their curiosity was excited, and they dug down till a chest, keg, or box, was discovered, which, on opening, was found to contain about $11,000 in gold and silver. It is supposed to be a part of the money stolen from the Cumberland Bank, in this place, some 18 or 20 years ago—or money which had been buried there by pirates or other villains.

The story of the bank robbery is this. A man who was about the bank considerably, named Manly, formed the determination to relieve the vault of its *weighty* responsibility, and as he could not well do it alone, he entrusted his plan to another man named Roth. The night was fixed upon and every preparation made to carry their plans into effect—but Roth, when the night came, backed out, or attempted to, saying that he had rather do nothing about it. Manly thereupon threatened to kill him if he refused, and held a pistol to his breast till he consented to go. The bank was opened by means of false keys, and many thousands of dollars removed—all there was in it, at any rate—and the country was scoured in every direction in search of the lost *rhino*.

Much of it was found, and still no one suspected. Manly came down to the bank the succeeding morning, as bold as any one, and made the observation—"Upon my word, that was a *manly* trick." At length, through the fear manifested, and strange conduct of Roth, he was suspected, charged with the robbery, and confessed it at once; but would not tell who was his accomplice. He also informed where most of the money was buried; but Manly had the precaution to remove the largest deposit, and of course it was not found. As Roth came down the hill with the officers, under arrest, he asked permission to step into a hollow by the side of the road for a specific purpose, which was granted. While there, he placed a pistol to his own head and *blew his brains out*!

From something said by him, Manly was apprehended, convicted, and sent to prison for a term of years. A year or two after his imprisonment expired he died with the smallpox, he being the only man who had it at the time. It is supposed that the money was buried near the hospital, on the hill, and in digging for it, he must have caught the infection from some of the bodies which are there buried, of which he died.

This, however, may be only surmise, but so the belief tends, and such is the story prevalent in that vicinity.—*New Haven Courier.*[47]

From a paper, "Portland Banks," read by William E. Gould before the Maine Historical Society, December 31, 1883, a slightly different and more detailed version of the story was gleaned. In 1818 the Cumberland Bank of Portland, Maine, had relocated to new premises. The locks to the vault were old, and they were sent over to a blacksmith named Edis to be inspected and adjusted. While the locks were in the shop, Daniel Manley—who kept a junk shop near Clay Wharf—happened by, saw the keys, and had an idea. He went to the foundry of Joseph Noble and borrowed some molding sand. Returning to the blacksmith shop he made impressions of the keys and later had duplicates cast. The locks were replaced on the bank vault doors.

On a Monday morning not long afterward cashier Joseph Swift opened the vault and found "all the valuables gone, absolutely nothing left in the way of money except small change."

After a bag of the type to contain specie was found in Manley's yard, suspicion focused on him and an associate named Rolf. Manley suspected that something was amiss and dug up the coins from the spot where he and Rolf had buried them. A bank officer told Rolf that he was suspected of the burglary, but if he would turn state's evidence no prosecution would be made. More directly from Gould's account:

Rolf went with his party down to a spot between the present location of the Portland Company's works and Fish point, and told them to dig up the buried treasure; when lo! the hole was empty and the game was gone. Rolf had not been without distrust of his confederate. He doubtless had feared that Manley would beat him, and thus his story would have no proof.

Seeing his position, and finding that he was in a very sorry plight he took a small pistol from his pocket, put it to his head and shot himself, falling lifeless over the empty spot where in a dark night they had put all the valuables of the Cumberland bank.

The case now looked more dark for the recovery of the money. However, the quick-witted old men who managed the case for the bank, went at once to Manley, before he could in any way hear of Rolf's death, and told him that Rolf had confessed all, and that to save himself he might as well own up, which he did.

The bank had offered a considerable reward for the stolen treasure, and Manley was bargained with that if he would deliver the goods he should receive the reward. Accordingly he informed the directors that if they would accompany him to a place in Scarboro they might possibly find something valuable. They went along the road until they came to a spot where Manley remarked that it looked to him as if this would be a good place to bury money. There were some men named Libby, who living near, were attracted by the strangers, and they, hearing the remark, remembered some recently upturned earth which they had been unable to account for, hastened to the spot and unearthed the buried treasure before Manley could reach the place; one screamed out to his father, "Dad, I've found it." Of course the Libbys claimed the reward. But it was afterward divided, so that Manley received one-half as a reward for his own wickedness. The bank recovered all but one small bag of gold and a bag of pistareens. Manley was afterward tried and sentenced to the prison at Charlestown, Massachusetts, for twelve years. His latter days were spent in this city where he lived several years apparently quite unmoved by his former career.

Still more to the story, including information that diverges from the preceding, can be found in contemporary newspapers. The amount of gold and silver coins Manley stole on Saturday night, August 1, 1818, was upward of $200,000. In addition, there was a large amount of the bank's paper money. He must have been surprised by someone upon leaving the scene, as "part of the specie was left behind in the yard of the bank. His aide was named Captain Benjamin Rolfe. A quantity of bank notes was found "concealed under a hedge fence in Scarborough and the rest in Manley's garden."[48]

On September 5 Manley's brother-in-law, Fobes Dela, visited Manley in jail and attempted to smuggle some tools and a loaded pistol to him to allow escape. Dela was caught and jailed as well.[49] In October, Manley was sentenced to 30 days solitary confinement and 12 years of hard labor in the State Prison. His brother in law was fined $100.[50]

Ms. Rea's Birthday Present

Hidden: 1795 • **Found:** By the 1860s • **Treasure:** 1795 half dimes

In 1795, a Roxbury, Massachusetts, lady named Rea is said to have received a "little hoard" of glittering new half dimes dated that same year as a birthday present. She kept these for many years—possibly until the early 1860s—at which time the hoard was sold to a numismatist, the identity of whom is not known today. One of the Rea coins was offered in W. Elliot Woodward's John F. McCoy Collection sale, May 1864, Lot 609.

A Mint State half dime of 1795.

The quantity in the hoard has been estimated at from a dozen or so up to 100 pieces. Specimens attributed to this lightly documented cache are of Valentine die varieties 4, 5, and 6, with most being V-4 or V-6.[51]

The circumstances surrounding Ms. Rea's hoard are a mystery, as is the answer to the question of what happened to all the coins.

A Sag Harbor Physician

Hidden: 1836 • **Found:** 1880 • **Treasure:** 1836 half dollars

The story of this hoard is told by this item in the Long Island *Evening Transcript*, August 20, 1880:

> A gentleman of Southampton, Long Island, writes that a great deal of curiosity has been excited by the sudden appearance in circulation of a large number of silver half dollars, all bearing the date of 1836, and as bright as when they came from the Mint.
>
> The mystery is thus explained:
>
> An old resident of Sag Harbor, formerly well known as a practicing physician, but who for several years has led a comparatively secluded life, at the time of the panic of 1836 [*sic*] hoarded 1,500 half dollars of that date. He kept them in total disregard of interest or premium until the present time. He has now put this hoarded treasure into circulation.[52]

It was the Panic of 1837—not the Panic of 1836—but this report seems otherwise plausible considering that in early 1837 anyone seeking a large quantity of silver coins might likely have found them to be dated 1836. Indeed, by May 10, 1837 financial problems had increased to the point at which most leading eastern banks stopped paying out coins, and at the time, the half dollar was the largest currently minted silver coin of the country, silver dollars having been last struck in large numbers in calendar year 1804 (and bearing dates of 1803 and earlier). Note that about 1,600

1836-dated Gobrecht silver dollars were made, but these were primarily placed into circulation in Pennsylvania and would not have been available in quantity to anyone seeking a bag or any other notable quantity of them at a bank in distant Long Island.

But back to the release of these coins: it must have been a free-for-all among collectors on Long Island, as by 1880 Capped Bust half dollars (minted 1807–1836) had long since disappeared from circulation. In fact, such pieces had not been generally seen since the early 1850s, when many if not most of the remaining pieces were melted down for bullion as the price of silver rose in international markets.

Today no 1836-dated half dollars are known with specific pedigrees to the Sag Harbor physician, but some of them probably did reach numismatic channels at the time of their release.

A Mint State 1836 Lettered Edge half dollar of the type made from 1807 to 1836.

An Obscure "Celebrated" Find

Hidden or lost: Circa 179 • **Found:** Before 1884 • **Treasure:** 1794 half dimes

In his catalog of the Heman Ely Collection, January 8–10, 1884, W. Elliot Woodward offered Lot 356, a silver half dime dated 1794 described as a "splendid Proof, from the celebrated Wadsworth find in Hartford." What seems to be the same coin was subsequently offered as Lot 897 of Woodward's December 16–19, 1885, sale of the A.W. Matthews Collection.

A 1794 half dime, the first year of issue of the Flowing Hair design.

But however "celebrated" this Wadsworth find may have been to Woodward and his knowing readers in 1884, little else has been heard of it in numismatic circles. Certainly, the find could not have been acclaimed solely for this solitary 1794 half dime. Thus, it must have contained other notable pieces.

Adding to the confusion, in 1988 Walter H. Breen suggested that about 15 Mint State 1794 half dimes were saved "as first of their kind," but there is no mention of the Wadsworth hoard in reference to this date. Instead, the Wadsworth name is used for a group of *1795* half dimes (see "Ms. Rea's Birthday Present," page 35).[53]

Wadsworth is a well-known Hartford surname, and the Wadsworth Athenaeum is one of the city's leading institutions. Jeremiah Wadsworth (1743–1804) was a major supplier for the Continental Army during the Revolution and was a banker after the war. If a Wadsworth was involved, it was probably he, not his son Daniel, who founded the Wadsworth Athenaeum.

It is worth noting that any cache of 1794-dated half dimes could not have been secreted earlier than 1795, for that is the year that this denomination was first struck at the Mint (those made early in the year were from dies dated 1794).

The Wadsworth Athenaeum in Hartford, Connecticut.

Judge Putnam's Souvenirs

Put away: 1864 • **Disclosed:** 1885 • **Treasure:** Half cents of 1855

In 1864 (and again in 1868, 1871, and 1877), Judge John P. Putnam of Boston journeyed to Philadelphia to participate in the annual Assay Commission procedure. Putnam, born in Hartford, Connecticut on March 21, 1817, was a numismatist and a personal friend of Roxbury (Massachusetts) dealer W. Elliot Woodward.[54] To participate in Woodward's November 1862 sale of "Selected Specimens from the American Portion of the Finotti Collection," the first major auction held by Woodward in New York City, Putnam made the trip from Boston to attend in person.[55] He was in good company in the saleroom and must have visited with such numismatic luminaries as Charles I. Bushnell, Edward Cogan, Charles Betts, William Harvey Strobridge, and John F. McCoy, each of whom purchased lots in the same section of the auction.

A brilliant 1855 half cent, possibly from the Judge Putnam hoard.

But back to the Assay Commission: for this event, the various mints (at the time these being Philadelphia, Carson City,[56] and San Francisco) set aside samples from quantities of silver and gold (but not copper) coins struck. These were sent to the Philadelphia Mint and reserved for the Commission, which met early in the year to review the preceding year's precious-metal coinage. Thus, on Monday, February 8, 1864, the commission members gathered to review coins bearing the date 1863.[57]

Also on hand in 1864, by virtue of their offices, were the Honorable Judge John Cadwalader (judge of the U.S. District Court for the Eastern District of Pennsylvania), George A. Coffey (United States attorney for the same district), and William B. Thomas (collector of the Port of Pennsylvania). These men had served in meetings of earlier years as well. In addition, a group of officers from the Mint itself were in attendance: James C. Booth (melter and refiner), John G. Butler (chief coiner), Jacob R. Eckfeldt (assayer and numismatist), Henry R. Linderman (secretary of the Assay Commission and a numismatist), James B. Longacre (chief engraver), and Archibald McIntyre (treasurer).

From the quantities of sample coins on hand, random pieces were selected by the commissioners. These were weighed to determine their compliance with coinage statutes. Some pieces were also assayed to determine their percentage of silver and gold (authorized at 90% with 10% copper alloy).

Undoubtedly, Judge Putnam enjoyed being a part of the 1864 ceremony, for it was considered an honor to be named to the select group. Apparently, while he was there he sought to acquire some souvenirs of his visit, obtaining a supply of bright Uncirculated copper half cents bearing the date 1855. Coins of this denomination had not been made at the Mint since early 1857, and most if not all supplies on hand had been melted shortly afterward.[58] However, the Mint acted as a depot for citizens, banks, and others seeking to redeem the obsolete copper cents and half cents of years before, and, quite probably, someone had recently brought these sparkling little copper 1855 half cents to the facility. From there, one of the numismatically interested people on the staff—Jacob R. Eckfeldt is a good candidate—must have set them aside, rather than consigning them to the melting pot.

Exactly what Putnam intended to do with these inexpensive pieces is uncertain—perhaps he thought they would make nice mementos for friends back home in New England—but it seems he held on to most, if not all, for some time. He passed on January 4, 1882, survived by his wife and two daughters. The fate of the coins is revealed in this account of W. Elliot Woodward's sale of the A.W. Matthews Collection and other properties (December 16–18, 1885), to which certain coins sold by Putnam to an unknown party had been consigned.[59] Described among the offerings were these items:

> Lot 1761: 1855 [half cents] Bright red Uncirculated. In 1855 [*sic*] Judge J.P. Putnam, of Boston, was a member of the Mint Assay Commission; he bought these half cents from the Mint, and parted with them only just before his death. All are perfect, and nearly all are selected for fineness of impression, as well as other qualities. Another lot so fine probably does not exist. 10 pieces.
>
> Lot 1762: 1855 Another lot of the same perfect quality.[60] 10 pieces.
>
> Lot 1763: 1855 Another lot from the same source and equally fine. 8 pieces.
>
> Lot 1764: 1855 Red Uncirculated. 6 pieces.
>
> Lot 1765: 1855 Perfectly Uncirculated, a handsome lot; one I think is a Proof impression. 10 pieces.
>
> Lot 1766: 1855 Very fine to red Uncirculated. 13 pieces.[61]
>
> Lot 1767: 1855 Very fine lot. 18 pieces.

The same sale continued with quantities of 1856 and 1857 half cents, including 19 Uncirculated examples of the last date of the denomination.

The number of gem Mint State 1855 half cents in the Putnam hoard was most certainly the sum of Lots 1761 through 1763, these being specifically cited as having been acquired by Putnam at the Mint. Using this total, the Putnam hoard would have amounted to 28 coins. If Lots 1764 through 1767 are added (although it is unclear if these were from Putnam's acquisition at the Mint), the total swells to 75.

The Ill-Fated Donner Party

Hidden: 1846–1847 • **Found:** 1891 • **Treasure:** Silver coins

One of the most chilling (literally) and gruesome accounts of western migration is that of the Donner Party, stranded in the high Sierras near the California-Nevada border.[62] In spring 1846, a group of 29 adventurous people gathered at Springfield, Illinois, to plan a trip by wagon westward to the Pacific Coast. This group, the Reed-Donner Party, organized by James F. Reed and George Donner, would later be joined by others to form the Donner Party.

At the time, that most precious yellow metal had not yet been discovered on the American River, and thus the Gold Rush was a couple of years away. Still, California represented a land of opportunity for many hundreds of Easterners who sought to better their lives, including perhaps as many as 500 who came to California in 1846 by land through Nevada and the high Sierra Nevada Mountains, the "Truckee route."[63] Many

more went north to the Oregon Territory and other points in the Pacific Northwest.

Typically, adventurers would form in wagon trains at a jumping-off spot on the Missouri River. The Reed-Donner Party set off from Springfield on April 15 for the most popular point of assembly—Independence, Missouri—and reached there on May 11. From May to July

An 1845 half dollar of the Liberty Seated design that, with several changes, was in use from 1839 to 1891.

of that year about 2,000 emigrants left Independence to take various routes west. For mutual protection and convenience, the travelers assembled into large groups, chose a leader, and made other communal arrangements. The name of the leader was assigned to each group, such as the Boggs, Cooper, Donner, Jacob, and Ritchie parties, among numerous others. In such wagon caravans family groups usually remained together, but sometimes loners would switch from one party to another.

At the time the routes to the West—especially to California—were uncertain, poorly marked, and fraught with hazards. Many discussions were held as to which way was the fastest and, to a lesser extent, which route offered the most safety. There was no single best way to go.

Composition of the Donner Party

On July 20, 1846, the Donner Party—now 87 people, including new faces—assembled at Little Sandy River in Wyoming Territory. In the train of ox-drawn covered wagons were 36 men, 21 women, and 30 children, including five infants. The travelers were members of four families surnamed Green, Donner, Graves, and Murphy. Their geographic origins were various, as the group included members of the original Reed-Donner Party from Springfield, Illinois; 10 from Keokuk, Iowa; and others.

The backgrounds of the Donner Party members were varied, too, and included those of American, Irish, and German extraction and of such religious inclinations as Catholic, Mormon, and Protestant. Their economic status ranged from rich—in the case of George Donner, who took with him a stock of merchandise to sell when he reached California and, apparently, quite a bit of money—to poor, which characterized the majority of the travelers. All shared the hope that California would be the Promised Land.

At Little Sandy River they found an "Open letter" posted by Lansford Hastings, an explorer and guide, who stated that a new route had been found from Fort Bridger though the south end of the Great Salt Lake that would save 200 miles as compared to the traditional path. Although this,

the so-called Hastings Cutoff, had been partially explored by John Frémont years earlier, its characteristics were not completely known. In his open letter Hastings said that he would be at Fort Bridger and could personally describe the characteristics of the new route.

Historian Hubert Howe Bancroft wrote that "Hastings, in his partisan zeal, supported by the proprietors of [Fort Bridger in Wyoming] for their own interests, exaggerated the advantages and underrated the difficulties of the new route; but though not a very wise counselor in such matters, he doubtless acted according to his judgment honestly."

The sandy and alkali plain areas in Utah and Nevada, known as the Great American Desert, were particularly barren, desolate, and hostile, but this was usually learned of only when passing through them. In 1846 there were no reliable guides for emigrants across those trackless wastelands. Even if there had been, not many eager travelers would have paid attention. It was recorded that all among the travelers except the cautious Mrs. Donner embraced the idea.

Important to the present account, the Donner Party caravan included Franklin W. Graves, his wife Elizabeth, sons William C., Jonathan B. (age 7) and Franklin Jr. (age 5), daughters Mary A., Eleanor, Lovina, Nancy (age 9), and Elizabeth (infant), his son-in-law Jay Fosdick and his wife Sarah (née Graves). Together with a fellow named John Snyder, the 12 members of the Graves clan had come from Marshall County, Illinois.

Difficulties Along the Route

On July 28, 1846, the Donner Party set out for the West, only a few days behind the Harlan and Young parties guided by Lansford Hastings. Soon after their departure, they received a letter from Hastings, who advised that great difficulties had been encountered in the Weber Cañon, and that another route should be taken. It later developed that the advance group encountered many problems, lost much livestock in the Great Salt Lake desert country, but succeeded in crossing the Sierra Nevadas in late 1846.

Seeking to learn more, the party dispatched James Reed and two others to catch up with Hastings. This took a week or more, after which the Donner group continued on another trail. The new way proved to be very difficult, and it was not until the beginning of September that they reached Great Salt Lake. The season was becoming late. On September 3, the first casualty occurred when Luke Halloran, who had come from Missouri, died of consumption at the southern reaches of the lake. This was the year before Brigham Young and the Mormons established Great Salt Lake City, which later became an important stop for emigrants.

An artist's conception of the Donner camp in late 1846.
Not long afterward, the settlement was covered with many feet of snow.

Sutter's Fort.

From September 9 through 15, the Donner Party traveled through the alkali flats and desert areas, headed in a northwest direction. With virtually no grass and no untainted water, many of the cattle perished. One family lost all of its oxen. Wagons had to be abandoned for the lack of power.[64]

Finally, a clear stream was reached when the party arrived at the headwaters of the Humboldt River. However, food and other provisions were seriously short, and two of the group members, William McCutchen and Charles T. Stanton, volunteered to ride ahead on horses to obtain relief. With cold weather approaching and the trail difficult, this was a long shot, but in the absence of any other ideas it was deemed best. Increasingly, those remaining in the Donner Party realized they were in great danger.

Around the end of September, the group found the old emigrant trail along the Humboldt and began following it westward, down the river and toward the Sierra Nevada range.[65] On October 5, James F. Reed became involved in a violent argument with fellow traveler John Snyder and killed him, which led to Reed's expulsion from the group. Reed went ahead, taking with him Walter Herron, also from Springfield, in the hope of finding some provisions to bring back to his wife and children, who stayed with the party.

On October 12, Indians stole 21 head of cattle. By this time, several families had neither oxen nor cattle and were plodding westward on foot. Hardcoop, a Belgian immigrant in the party, became sick and was left behind to die. Wolfinger, one of several Germans in the group, also was abandoned, under circumstances suggesting foul play on the part of his fellow countrymen.

On October 19, advance man Stanton returned to the Donner Party, having gone ahead to Sutter's Fort near Sacramento, California, an outpost established in 1839 by John Sutter, a Swiss. His fort included shops for provisions and repairs, and serviced the surrounding agricultural industry. Stanton, accompanied by two California Indians, Luis and Salvador, brought seven mules, five of which, laden with flour and other provisions, were a great help. McCutchen, who had gone

with Stanton, became ill and remained in California. Stanton's return to the distressed Donner Party was all the more remarkable and altruistic in that he had no family members in the group.

In the region of what is now Reno, Nevada, the travelers stopped for several days to rest. On October 23, the journey westward was resumed. Within the week they arrived at a lake in the Truckee region. Snow was falling, and at higher elevations the accumulation reached several feet. Obviously, travel across the Sierras was now impossible.

Winter Takes Its Toll

For the next several weeks, the party members were in chaos. Some tried to set out on their own through the snowy mountains, only to meet with failure and return to camp. Most of the remaining cattle and oxen strayed. Meanwhile, a week-long storm brought an estimated 10 feet of snow to the areas of higher elevation, rendering any escape from the area impossible. Soon, deep snow covered the Donner camp as well. With little food and only primitive shelter, the situation went from bad to worse. By the time a small relief party reached the camp on February 19, 1847, many had died, and the remains of some had been eaten by the survivors. The leather shoelaces from a pair of boots had furnished New Year's dinner for some.

In the spring, several other relief parties set out from California to seek the survivors. One group of nine men left on April 13 under the charge of William Fallon. As an inducement, the group had been promised half of the value of anything that could be saved. Fallon eagerly looked forward to divvying the large amount of money that George Donner was reported to have with him. Upon arrival at the Donner Party site on the April 17, Fallon found that Donner had died from privation, and that Mrs. Donner had been killed, apparently by Louis Keseberg, who was said to have stolen her money. Keseberg, when threatened with being hanged, surrendered some coins that he claimed Mrs. Donner had given him to care for on behalf of her children.[66]

By the spring of 1847, of the 87 people originally in the Donner Party, 22 men, 5 women, and 12 children—or a total of 39—had died. Later, the remains of those who could be located were given burials. Their campsite came to be known as Donner Lake and the nearby gap in the mountains as Donner Pass.

Many Years Later

In 1891, Edward Reynolds, a prospector from Sierra Valley, was poking around the Donner Lake area when he found a handful of dollar-sized foreign silver coins. Digging in the earth, he found many more pieces, including U.S. half dollars. Seeking to return at a later date, he reburied the treasure, rejoined several other miners with whom he was exploring, and went back to Truckee. Later, he and a friend returned and dug up the cache of silver coins, which amounted to about $146 in face value.

It was subsequently determined that the pieces had been carefully hidden in holes bored into the undersides of cleats mounted on the floor of the wagon of Elizabeth (Mrs. Franklin W.) Graves, who, realizing that she might never cross the Sierras, took the coins from the wagon and buried them. By this time the remains of her husband had been consumed as food by the survivors. Mrs. Graves, too, would die.

An inventory of the coins revealed these pieces (per published listing; numbers in parentheses represent multiples of a date):

Argentina 8 reales

1835

Bolivian 8 reales

1836

French "dollar" with Louis Phillippe portrait

French 5-franc pieces of the Republic

Year 8
Year 11 (2)
Year 13

French 5-franc pieces

1806	1820	1832 (2)
1808 (3)	1822 (2)	1833 (3)
1809	1823	1834 (2)
1811	1824	1837
1812 (10)	1825	1838 (2)
1814 (2)	1827 (2)	1839
1816	1828	1840
1818	1829 (2)	1841 (2)
1819	1831 (3)	1844

Mexico City silver 8 reales

1805	1831 (2)	1839 (3)
1810 (2)	1832 (3)	1840 (3)
1812	1833	1841 (5)
1821	1834 (4)	1842 (4)
1826	1835 (3)	1843 (2)
1827	1836 (4)	1844
1828 (2)	1837 (3)	1845 (2)
1830	1838 (3)	

Plus an additional coin, date not completely readable, but from the 1830s

Saxony 5 marks

1835

Spanish silver 4 reales

1800
1805[67]

U.S. half dollars

1810	1826 (3)	1835 (3)
1813	1827 (2)	1836 (4)
1815	1828	1837 (4)
1817	1829 (6)	1838 (2)
1818 (3)	1830 (6)	1839 (3)
1822 (2)	1831	1840
1823 (2)	1832 (6)	1841 (3)
1824 (2)	1833 (3)	1842 (3)
1825 (2)	1834 (2)	1843 (4)

From a numismatic viewpoint today, the coins may represent a cross-section of large-denomination silver pieces in circulation in the United States circa 1845 (the latest date on a coin). For some reason, no silver dollars were included, although they actively circulated in the early 1840s. Perhaps the source(s) for the coins had none on hand. French 5-franc and Mexican 8-real coins were legal tender at the time.

Others in the Donner Party had coins, including the group's unfortunate leader, but no description of them has been located.

The Collins Find

Hidden or lost: 1828 • **Found:** By 1894 • **Treasure:** 1828 half cents

In his catalog of the Allison W. Jackman Collection, June 28–29, 1918, Philadelphia dealer Henry Chapman inserted this commentary after Lot 879, a rare *1811* half cent, to shed light on the ready availability in Uncirculated grade of 1828-dated half cents, the variety with 13 obverse stars:

> This [1811] coin was discovered in 1884, being brought by an old colored woman of Alexandria, Va., to Mr. Benjamin H. Collins of Washington, to whom she stated she had a bag of them! He, thinking there was not any mistake about the hoard, sold it [*i.e.*, the 1811] to S.H. & H. Chapman for $3! with the remark, "How many more will you take?"
>
> We said the lot.
>
> The woman subsequently brought him the bag, but to his astonishment they were all 1828 13 stars! It has always been a mystery to me that an 1811 equally fine as the 1828s should have been in with the later date, and that her pick at random should have alighted on the only 1811 in the bag! It was subsequently sold in the Warner Sale, $67, and there bought by Mr. Jackman.

How Many Coins Were There?

The preceding account has a number of inaccuracies and requires some amplification and modification including the following:

B.H. Collins of Washington, D.C.—a specialist in early copper coins, especially cents, and known for the fine specimens he handled, including several notable pieces imported from Europe—was an employee of the Treasury Department in 1884. It was not until the 1890s that he became a

rare-coin dealer; thus, the date of the hoard is moved up a decade to 1894. Also, the 1811 half cent was sold by Collins to Chapman for $18, not $3, and the Warner and Jackman specimens were two different coins.

On the subject of the 1828 13-stars half cents, the number in the hoard was stated to be 50 by Collins in a conversation with John F. Jones in December 1899. However, this has not been confirmed, and while the figure of 50 may be correct, it probably is not. Many more than that are known today. In 1988, Walter H. Breen commented that the hoard "apparently originally numbered 1,000; as late as 1955 a remnant containing several hundred pieces was in the holdings of F.C.C. Boyd."[68]

In confirmation of the preceding, in 1996 John J. Ford Jr. stated that many of these pieces were owned by David U. Proskey, who sold them to Boyd along with other material. In the early 1950s, about 200 to 300 bright red coins were sold by Boyd to New Netherlands Coin Co.[69]

Fact-finding concerning hoards is never an easy task, and absolute definition is often impossible.

The typical Collins Find specimen seen today is bright orange-red with spotting.[70]

An 1828 half cent, possibly from the Collins Find.

Fooling an English Dealer

Exported to England: 1700s and 1800s • **Found:** Early 1900s • **Treasure:** Rare early copper coins

In the late 1700s and early 1800s, quite a few U.S. coins emigrated to England as souvenirs in the pockets of returning travelers and as specimens desired by British numismatists who collected coins of the present and former British colonies.

A 1905 newspaper account told of a New York City coin dealer, name not disclosed, who visited a well-known London dealer, name also not given, who "thoroughly versed as he is in every phase of the old coin business, still he is not well up on American rare coin values." Quite possibly, the London dealer had acquired some old "American souvenirs" that in the meantime had acquired significant numismatic value:

> The English dealer brought out about 25 specimens of early American copper coins, the greater part of them dating from 1793 to 1800. They were all in superb condition, and every one of them was a rare variety.[71]

The story went on to relate that the Englishman asked $75 for the lot, which figure was eagerly accepted. Upon returning to the United States, the other dealer "in less than a month disposed of the whole lot, realizing a total profit of nearly $1,500." Upon learning of this, his British counterpart advised the U.S. dealer never to darken his doorway again.

A high-grade copper cent of 1794, Sheldon-38 variety.

The Chapman Hoard of Half Cents

Hidden or lost: 1806 • **Found:** Circa 1906 • **Treasure:** 1806 half cents

Sometime around 1906, Philadelphia dealer Henry Chapman found a hoard of 1806 half cents (the variety today known as Breen-4, Cohen-4) variously estimated to contain from about 200 pieces up to "many hundreds."

Most of these seen today have generous areas of original mint red, but are spotted. Examples are always weakly struck at the upper part of the wreath.[72]

A Mint State 1806 half cent, Cohen-4 variety.

The "Bank Holiday" and Related Hoards

Hidden: 1800s • **Found:** 1930s • **Treasure:** 1833 and 1835 half cents

In the 1930s, New York dealer Julius Guttag found a large hoard of 1833 half cents. During the same era, dealer Elmer Sears found a hoard of 1835 half cents, "probably a bag of 1,000 pieces, possibly more than that. They were in spotty mint red Uncirculated state."[73] The total for both half cent dates was in the thousands of coins. Most were bright red, usually with some tiny black flecks. Some of the 1833 half cents were prooflike and were offered as Proofs.

This was a period in which times were hard, the Depression was pervasive, and long-held cash assets were often liquidated, including some possibly from bank reserves (more on that momentarily). Many of the aforementioned half cents were sold during this time, during which the going price was approximately 25¢ each on the market. In the mid-1950s, the remainder of the coins were distributed in New York and sold for several dollars apiece, and for several years thereafter, half cents of these two dates were fairly plentiful in dealers' stocks. Then, with the great boom in numismatics that took place in the 1960s, most became widely scattered.[74]

On a different but related topic, Walter H. Breen commented that certain large cents of the 1850s are common in numismatic circles because of caches which came to light in this era: "Some of these hoards appear to have come from banks' cash reserves during the 1933 Bank Holiday, when examinations of bank vault assets yielded quantities of obsolete coins. There may have been a full keg or more of 1853 cents, which would mean at least a ballpark figure of about 14,000 coins."[75]

Cent varieties mentioned as coming from these hoards include 1850 Newcomb-7, 1851 N-2, 1852 N-3, 1853 N-25, 1855 N-5, and 1856 N-14.

A Mint State 1833 half cent.

An 1853 large cent.

The Boston Hoard of Half Cents _____

Hidden or lost: 1800s • **Found:** Circa 1935–1937 • **Treasure:** 1800 half cents

In the 1930s, a hoard of several dozen or more 1800 half cents (the variety known today as Breen-1b, Cohen-1) turned up in Boston. Specimens from this holding display mint red, but are usually spotted. Estimates of 30 to 100 pieces have reached print. Where had they been hidden? Who found them? No one knows.

Other 1800-dated half cents of the same variety, typically with lustrous brown surfaces, are said to have come from another hoard discovered in New England. This other cache is believed to have been found before 1910 and to have contained "hundreds of pieces."[76]

A Mint State 1800 half cent.

Treasure on the Beach _____

Hidden: 1834 or later • **Found:** 1942 • **Treasure:** Various coins

A find made on a Massachusetts beach was reported by United Press on August 15, 1942, and published in many periodicals:

Century-Old Treasure Box Found at Plymouth Beach

Discovery of a century-old treasure trove buried in the historic sands of Pilgrim's Beach at Plymouth, Mass., was revealed by a Colebrook, N.H. man, Ben Lay.

Lay said that he and his son, Fred, were skipping stones on the ocean surface at the beach a few weeks ago when the son picked up an object which proved to be an old silver dollar. Looking around, they soon found several more coins scattered about the beach, and they noticed the corner of an old box protruding from the same.

Without attracting the attention of the hundreds of bathers in the vicinity, they covered the spot with sand and went away. Several times during the ensuing fortnight they returned and salvaged all the coins that the box contained.

An inventory showed that the booty included 400 silver half dollars, 38 silver dollars, $50 in gold coins, and 45 foreign pieces. The oldest gold coin was dated 1834, and the oldest silver piece, 1795.

Wrapped in an old Boston newspaper, the treasure was believed to have been buried at about the time of the Mexican War 1846–47. How the newspaper survived the years was not stated.

Lay reportedly has been offered $2,000 for the collection.

A Little Bag in an Old Safe

Hidden: 1855 • **Found:** 1940s • **Treasure:** 1855 half cents

Charlie and Arline French are still remembered today by old timers in numismatics. Charlie, who had changed his surname from Lehrenkraus (in the 1930s a few coin leaflets were issued under this name by him), did business from a basement-level hobby shop in Troy, New York, typically trading as "A. French" or "French's." Probably his sales of model airplanes, stamp kits, and other hobby supplies paid the rent and heating bills, while his first love, coins, occupied most of his attention.

A Mint State 1855 half cent.

Speaking of, Charlie and Arline conducted 113 coin auctions from 1939 to 1976. I recall attending several of their sales and, having looked at the lots beforehand, selecting some nice pieces in competition with a small roomful of bidders. These events were staged in the glory days of the Empire State Numismatic Association, which each year held small conventions, more like informal gatherings. Such coin-collecting greats as Fiore Pipito, John Jay Pittman, Charles W. Foster,[77] Jonah Shapiro, Jake Cheris, Jasper Robertson,[78] Dave Nethaway, and Ken Sartoris, to give just a short list, were on hand, and all had a good time. Among the "youngsters" often attending were Jim Ruddy, Bill Vanco, Les Zeller, and myself.

But on to the story of the hoard: in the 1940s, French purchased a small cloth bag containing 500 bright red half cents, each bearing the date 1855, the same year as the Putnam pieces (see "Judge Putnam's Souvenirs," page 38). The coins had been found in a small metal safe of the type painted black with a scene on the front, as were commonly used in the late 1800s and early 1900s.

Half cents were seemingly an ideal denomination for hoarding purposes. No doubt the low face value of such pieces was a factor in their having been put away; and once put away, not readily spent. At the time of this find, French feared a reduction in the numismatic market value of the denomination and thus said little while parceling them out to clients and in small groups to dealers. By about 1960, most or all were gone.[79]

A Few Asides

It is worth noting that Troy—a town with many traditions, where numerous old commercial buildings remain—was home to many manufacturers and tradesmen that advertised via copper tokens. These were made from amateurishly cut dies and were crudely struck but are still highly collectible today. For example, Bucklin's Interest Tables, a creation of Troy schoolteacher Isaac B. Bucklin, were advertised via copper tokens. The N. Starbuck & Son machine shop also put out tokens, as did the dry goods firm of Carpenter & Mosher. It requires but little imagination for the traveler to envision what the city must have been like in the 1800s, when Troy was one of the leading manufacturing centers of the state, horses were clip-clopping with their carts down the streets, and Hudson River steamers were discharging passengers and cargo from New York City.

By the 1940s and 1950s, most Troy tokens had for the most part long since disappeared, but now and then a local resident would bring a handful of old tokens, large cents, and other coins into

Charlie French's shop. It is not difficult to imagine that the safe containing the sparkling little 1855 half cents that he bought had rested comfortably in some dusty old attic or room in Troy for the best part of a century.

Also worth noting is that French's best retail customer was Ellis H. Robison, who lived locally and conducted a drug wholesaling firm. Robison had all of his purchases checked by French, who had to put his stamp of approval on each. His goal

was to acquire one each of the various coins listed in the *Guide Book*, and he certainly gave it a good try. Later, the Robison collection was auctioned by Stack's.

And one final fact: each month for *Hobbies* magazine, Charlie French conducted a question and answer column. In 1967, some of this material was incorporated into the *American Guide to U.S. Coins*, a paperback distributed in bookstores.

Half Dollars in the Sand

Lost: 1840s • **Found:** 1950s • **Treasure:** 1841-O and 1843-O half dollars

In the 1950s, when Grover C. Criswell and his brother Clarence were partners in the rare coin and Confederate currency business, the author met with them in their hotel suite one evening at a coin show. These were the days when theft was not a problem at such events, and guarded "security rooms" were not provided for the safekeeping of collectors' and dealers' coins. The Criswells set up in elegant style with fresh flowers around the room and a cart of beverages.

Displayed before me were several 1843-O Liberty Seated half dollars—not a rare date (2,268,000 were minted), but one not often seen, then or now, in high grades such as Mint State. I bought one or two and also purchased some Proof Barber dimes of the 1892–1915 years that the Criswells had as part of their stock.

Upon inquiring about the 1843-O coins, I was told that a few months earlier a beachcomber in the St. Petersburg, Florida, area had stumbled upon a small metal can or container in the sand, and in it were between a dozen and 20 of these 1843-O halves, all Mint State and all of the same general appearance—indicating that they had been kept together for a long period of time.

As I recall, the coins were fairly brilliant and lustrous and had no evidence of saltwater etching. If indeed they had been on the beach for more than a century, one would think they would have shown evidence of that. Was this a cover story for coins found somewhere else?[80]

1841-O Halves at an Old Fort

Somewhat related may be a group of 1841-O half dollars mentioned in *Walter Breen's Complete Encyclopedia of U.S. and Colonial Coins*, p. 395, here paraphrased: "1841-O A hoard of this (possibly 40 Uncs.) turned up in Clearwater, Florida, before 1957."[81]

More information is found under lot 2166 of Coin Galleries' mail bid sale of November 9, 1988, where an example of an 1841-O is described as being Mint State, of a better strike than usual, "a handsome specimen from the 'Clearwater Hoard' of 40 pieces found in Florida on the site of the former Fort Harrison and presumably buried by a soldier on duty there at about the time of issue."

An 1843-O half dollar in Mint State.

Hidden in an Old Woodstove ———

Lost: Early 1900s • **Found:** 1954 • **Treasure:** Gold and silver coins

Bob Ross tells of an interesting treasure that started him in the hobby of numismatics:

The year was 1954. The location was in my pool room, which I had just opened in Glasgow, Kentucky.

A man walked in and wanted to sell some gold and silver coins to me. They all looked like they were just minted, and some were over a hundred years old. I settled on a half dollar minted in 1850 and paid him four dollars. I was afraid word would get out I had paid someone four dollars for a half dollar and they would put me in the loony house.

The man I bought these from had been on a construction site when a bulldozer pushed an old shack and the contents into a 20-foot dug water well. He spotted some coins on the path to the well and picked them up. The owner of the property arrived shortly afterward and found enough one-dollar gold coins to make his wife a necklace. He picked up several other gold and silver coins as well. Apparently, the coins were dropping out of an old wood stove that years earlier had been used to heat the now long-abandoned building. It was later learned that any time the old black man, Stephen Landrum ("Uncle Steve"), who lived there, received money he would exchange most of the bills for coins. The story was that most of the coins are still down at the bottom of the well. Maybe yes, or maybe no.

In a book of our county's history, Landrum's attorney, E.H. Smith, commented:

"One time I helped him in his negotiations to purchase a building in Glasgow for which he was to pay $4,500. The deed was drawn and ready for delivery, and it was time for 'Uncle Steve' to pay. 'Just wait a little while and I'll be back,' he said.

"He was gone some 15 or 20 minutes, and when he returned he had exactly $4,500 in a little split-bark basket with a napkin over the money. There was nothing larger than a $10 bill in the basket, and there were many ones and several hands full of silver."

Landrum was further described as a generous man who carefully managed rental properties, bought houses for his relatives, provided for needy blacks, and was a benefactor of the Ratliff Industrial Institute and Teachers Normal College.

I still have the 1850-O half dollar and it's not for sale.

That started me on the road to collecting coins for the next 10 years. Then I gave up interest, but I started again about a year ago. The hobby surely is different now.

There have been two other "finds" here that I have heard about. Back in the 1940s a man was plowing a garden in his backyard and unearthed a jar of gold coins. The other "find" was from a fireplace in another section of town. I have not been able to learn anything specific about either of these hoards.[82]

An 1850-O half dollar similar to one in this Kentucky treasure.

An Elderly Druggist

Saved: Early 1900s • **Revealed:** 1954 • **Treasure:** Two-cent pieces

During the early 1900s, a druggist whose store was on the west side of Market Street, Kingston, Pennsylvania, thought that bronze two-cent pieces (minted 1864–1873) were curious. Whenever he received one in change, he set it aside in a cigar box.

In 1954 he saw an advertisement placed by myself, as I had recently begun my numismatic career. I was invited to come and inspect the several hundred pieces he had accumulated. I did this and bought them on the spot. Most of the two-cent pieces were dated 1864 and 1865, but there were some of all other dates through 1872. The typical grades were Good to Very Fine, although a few were far finer.

An 1864 two-cent piece, the first year of issue.

Treasure on a Virginia Farm

Saved: 1849 • **Revealed:** 1959 • **Treasure:** Mostly silver coins

In late February 1959, Tom Reid was operating a bulldozer on the Alpine Hills farm of Dr. A.A. Houser in Rockbridge County, Virginia, when he dug up a coin-filled earthenware crock. He did not notice his find until he started dumping his load of dirt. The find included 1 large cent, 1 copper-nickel cent, 43 trimes, 195 half dimes, 285 dimes, 534 quarters, 112 half dollars, a 1798 silver dollar, and 3 gold coins among the U.S. coins, the latest of which was dated 1849. In addition, there were 129 Spanish-American silver coins which were legal tender at the time of that latest-dated U.S. coin. The earliest U.S. coin was dated 1797. The foreign coins were dated before the 1840s.

Word of the find spread, and before long more than 200 people came to comb the area for more treasure. Emmet W. Tardy, a numismatist from Lexington, Virginia, examined the coins and reported that about 90% of the coins were "very fine or second in quality only to mint condition." Tardy said the hoard was worth "between $1,000 to $1,050." He valued the 1798 dollar at $9. Apparently, he bought most or all of them, as he was quoted as saying, "Having this much money around worries me. I am going to get this into the bank right away."

Some local historians suggested that they had been hidden in the foundation of a home by a Mr. Berger, perhaps hidden away to avoid capture during the Civil War. As that conflict did not begin until April 1861, this seems unlikely.[83]

Maine Half Dollar Hoard _____

Hidden or lost: 1830s • **Found:** By 1963 • **Treasure:** Early half dollars

John J. Ford Jr. told of a group of about 2,000 Capped Bust half dollars of various dates, but mostly dated in the 1820s and 1830s. The hoard was brought to him at New Netherlands Coin Co., 1 West 47th Street, New York City. The seller was Canadian dealer Fred Samuels, who said that the hoard had come from Maine, where it had been hidden for more than a century, but specific details were not provided. Ford speculated that the coins might have been hidden by someone fearful of banks circa 1837–1838, during the financial panic.

Some of these halves—but not the best ones—were cataloged and appeared as part of "a splendid run of half dollars" in New Netherlands' Sale 57, December 10–11, 1963, there mixed with material from other consignments. The catalog made no mention of any hoard, however.

Meanwhile—circa 1963—about 1,000 coins averaging between Extremely Fine and About Uncirculated were wholesaled by New Netherlands to Philadelphia dealers Harry J. Forman and Ruth Bauer, who paid $15 apiece and later sold many of them to New York dealer Edwin Shapiro. In turn, Shapiro consigned them to New Netherlands' 66th Sale, July 21–22, 1976, by which time the firm was operated solely by

Charles M. Wormser, Ford having retired. Beginning with Lot 28 and ending at Lot 747, the pieces appeared in single- and multiple-coin lots under the title of "Extraordinary Collection of Bust Half Dollars—Possibly the Largest Ever Offered at Public Auction," again with no specific mention of the Maine hoard.[84]

About 150 to 200 of the Maine hoard half dollars were "absolute gems" and were reserved for the New Netherlands Coin Co. inventory. Many if not most of these selected pieces remained with Wormser, and in the 1980s were sold by Wormser's widow, acting on the advice of dealer Lester Merkin, to dealer Kevin Lipton. The best of these coins were dated 1831 and were sold into the market in various transactions.[85]

A beautiful 1831 half dollar, possibly from a hoard.

An Array of Sparkling Half Dimes _____

Hidden or lost: 1835 • **Found:** 1960s • **Treasure:** 1835 half dimes

In the 1960s, I purchased a quantity of lustrous gem Mint State 1835 half dimes from a California numismatist who had obtained them from some source not revealed to me. Perhaps the explanation was provided years later (1988) by Walter H. Breen: "The 1835 Small Date with Small 5 C. has become [the commonest variety of the year in Mint State] owing to a hoard of at least 100 specimens found in a Boston bank in 1969 and dispersed by Q. David Bowers."[86]

A splendid Mint State 1835 half dime, Small Date, Small 5 variety.

If the pieces were indeed found in a Boston bank, it seems likely that they were in someone's safe deposit box, not a part of a bank's cash assets.

I never thought to ask Breen the source of his information before his passing.

An Englishman Visits America

Acquired: 1795 • **Disclosed:** 1964 • **Treasure:** High-grade early U.S. coins

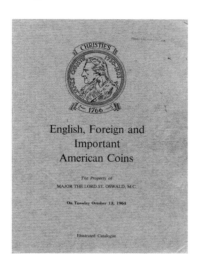

This is not the story of a secret of the Philadelphia Mint or a "find" there, but of a long-ago visit to that institution, then in the early years of its existence:

In October 1795, Sir Rowland Winn, an English traveler from a distinguished family, visited the United States and was an honored guest at the Philadelphia Mint. While there he was given selected specially struck presentation coins on hand from the previous year, 1794, and new high-quality examples of the current 1795 coinage were made especially for him.

Although a number of very choice U.S. coins survive from the 1790s, the visit of Sir Rowland Winn is the only instance of a specifically identified numismatist from anywhere being given the red carpet treatment at the United States' minting institution. Equally significant, the coins descended in a single family and remained together until 1964, each accompanied by this remarkable direct-from-the-Mint pedigree.

Or so the story went.

Years Later

On October 13, 1964, the venerable London firm of Christie, Manson & Woods had an auction of coins from the Lord St. Oswald Collection. Emphasis was on ancient and other classic issues, but in addition to this cabinet of fine numismatic material, the consignor furnished a small pasteboard box containing miscellaneous and seem-ingly unimportant "loose change." Presumably, an ancestor or someone else had probably brought this from the United States in 1795, and it had long since been more or less forgotten.

A.H. Baldwin & Sons, Ltd., of London cataloged the pieces. It was soon recognized that such "loose change" items as Uncirculated 1794 large cents, two Uncirculated 1794 silver dollars, and other U.S. coins primarily dated 1794 and 1795 were quite special, and some were among the finest known of their varieties.

A Mint State 1795 dollar from the Lord St. Oswald sale in London, lot 139, sold to Norman Stack for £460.

The sale was not widely publicized in the United States, and some dealers on this side of the Atlantic thought perhaps some really good buys would be made. Professionals from the United States, including Lester Merkin, Norman Stack, and James F. Ruddy were present on sale day, as were some collectors, including silver dollar specialist Jacque C. Ostheimer. It was evident at the outset that there would be some strong competition. When all was said and done, this group of U.S. coins far overshadowed the ancient and other coins in the Lord St. Oswald consignment, and created a sensation. This handful of "loose change" with a face value of less than $10 brought a whopping $72,000! Today the decimal point of that total sale price could probably be moved over two places to the right.

Each of the 1794 dollars fetched $11,200 from U.S. buyers, again eligible today for decimal point shifting. The first was knocked down to Ostheimer. The second was awarded to A.H. Baldwin & Sons, Ltd., on behalf of Ambassador and Mrs. R. Henry Norweb. Which was the better coin has been a toss-up in discussions since,[87] but the Norweb coin—later in the D. Brent Pogue Collection—seems to have the edge.

Theories

After a time, theories of the pieces' origins began to develop, and before long Walter H. Breen firmly stated that the coins were "obtained by Sir Rowland Winn, about October 1795 on his visit to the Philadelphia Mint," as described above. Subsequently, numismatists were informed by Breen and others that Winn not only visited the Mint, but that he was rewarded by receiving "presentation pieces," certainly a rare honor.[88] Breen even described how a certain 1795-dated dollar had been made as a presentation piece—on a burnished planchet, struck from polished dies (possibly struck twice to assure extra sharpness), etc. This made a nice story, but one not supported by even the slightest shred of fact.[89]

Obviously, this story of an accomplished numismatist being an honored guest at the Mint in 1795 furnished the possibility for further information to be gained, especially as it was the only known instance of such a visit by a knowledgeable collector during the 1790s.

Detail of one of the plates in the Lord St. Oswald Collection, this showing two Mint State 1794 dollars and a Mint State 1795 dollar.

Who Was Lord St. Oswald?

Enter Michael Hodder, who in 1993 and 1994 enlisted the assistance of Jack Collins and wrote an essay, "Who Was Major the Lord St. Oswald?" which in due course appeared in *The Asylum*, Fall 1994, and thus he did not visit America in the 1790s.[90]

First, by reviewing the 1964 catalog issued by Christie's, Hodder noted that nothing was said there about anyone visiting the Mint or even going to the United States, nor were there any claims about presentation or other special coins. All that was stated was that the coins were included in a catalog that featured a consignment from the St. Oswald family, living in Wakefield, Yorkshire, and nothing more.

From that point, Michael Hodder learned that Major the Lord St. Oswald (Major Sir Rowland Denys Guy Winn, M.C., the Fourth Baron St. Oswald), *born in 1916* and died in 1984, was not a coin collector. The nice story of Sir Rowland Winn visiting the Mint in *1795* began to unravel.

In 1993, Jack Collins wrote to the Winn family in England seeking to learn more.[91] Derek Edward Anthony Winn, Fifth Baron St. Oswald, replied that he had no knowledge of which of his ancestors might have gone to the United States. The Sixth *Baronet* St. Oswald (1775–1805) was living in 1795, but "was never in good health and consequently would not have traveled much," Collins' correspondent advised. After his death, unmarried, at age 30, the direct male line died out, and the title seems to have lapsed, to be revived years later in 1885 and elevated at that time to a full barony.

As for the name of Sir Rowland Winn, multiple individuals bore that moniker over the years, but none was linked to any transatlantic trip in 1795. There were, however, members of the Winn family who did collect coins. Andrew W. Pollock III found information published by the National Trust in England that a Sir Rowland Winn in 1767 ordered a mahogany coin and medal cabinet to be custom made by Thomas Chippendale. Today this is National Trust inventory no. 959798 and is preserved in its original location hidden behind a door in the library of Nostell Priority in

West Yorkshire. But this Winn died suddenly in 1785, while on a trip to London.

The Final Word

The matter remained a mystery until 2015, when at long last David E. Tripp solved it. Delving into archival and genealogical documents, he found that the man who actually collected these coins was named William Strickland. He visited America from September 20, 1794, to July 29, 1795, married into the Winn family, and later deposited the pieces in Nostell Priory, the family seat.

Strickland was a collector of many things, including coins, and he appears to have gathered a sensible and organized grouping of American coins during his 10-month visit, although there is no record that he crossed the portal of the Philadelphia Mint. The coins from the Lord St. Oswald / Strickland collection span the breadth of the Philadelphia Mint's production until the time of Strickland's departure from Philadelphia at the end of July 1795, ranging from half cents to dollars (curiously omitting half dimes) and including a lightly worn Chain cent and perfect gem coins struck in the weeks before his return home. Notably, coins struck after that date—including 1795-dated gold coins (first delivered on July 31, 1795), Draped Bust issues, and more—are not present here, verifying that his American collection was formed entirely during his visit and never augmented later.

Interestingly, Strickland rubbed elbows with John Adams in Boston, raised glasses with George Washington at Mount Vernon, and talked farming with Thomas Jefferson at Monticello. Each of those men being collectors, perhaps coins and medals came up in conversation as well.

Since 1964 many of the pieces have been resold in the marketplace. Today each of the Lord St. Oswald coins has the possibly unique distinction of being pedigreed back to the very time of issue!

Church Cornerstone Yields Rarities

Hidden: 1877 • **Found:** 1972 • **Treasure:** Coins dated 1877

In 1877, the First Methodist Church was built in Lynn, Massachusetts. At the start of construction a metal box was placed in the cornerstone. Among the contents were current coins.

As events would prove, 1877 was indeed a fortunate numismatic year, for Proofs of this year included key issues in the Indian Head cent, nickel three-cent, Shield nickel, and other series.

Nearly a century later in 1968, the First Methodist Church merged with St. Paul's Methodist Church to form the present-day Christ Church. In 1972, the old First Methodist Church structure burned. The cornerstone box with its many books, documents, papers—and 1877 Proof and other coins—was recovered unharmed.

The numismatic contents were:

1877 Indian Head cent (prooflike Uncirculated)
1877 nickel three-cent piece (Proof)

1877 Shield nickel (Proof)
1877-S Liberty Seated dime (Uncirculated)
1877-S Liberty Seated quarter dollar (Uncirculated)
1877-CC Liberty Seated half dollar (Uncirculated)
1877 trade dollar (Uncirculated)[92]

1877 Philadelphia Mint trade dollar.

The Cogswell Time Capsule

Sealed: 1879 • **Opened:** April 1979 • **Treasure:** Silver coins

Once each month members of the Cogswell Society gather at one saloon or another in Washington, D.C., to lift their glasses to the memory of Dr. Henry Daniel Cogswell (March 3, 1820–July 8, 1900) and his *failure*.[93]

Cogswell, a San Francisco dentist active in the 1870s, made a small fortune as a securities and real estate trader. Similarly, Cogswell College, a trade school he founded in San Francisco, went on to success and, in fact, is still highly esteemed. These were his successes—significant, but perhaps not quite worthy of camaraderie and celebration among beer drinkers of a century later.

But about his seemingly important failure. You see, Cogswell did not like alcohol. In fact, he detested it. He came up with a novel idea to combat demon rum: for every 100 saloons in a town, he would donate a drinking fountain to dispense water.

Not every city wanted such a reminder of temperance, but enough did that some 20 fountains were erected at his expense, including about half this number scattered around San Francisco, a place with more than its share of rum sellers and grog shops. One such fountain was erected in San Francisco's Washington Square and was topped with a statue not of the Father of our Country, but of Benjamin Franklin, who, presumably, was seen as epitomizing the virtues of abstinence or, possibly, thrift. This particular dispensary of *aqua pura* was also outfitted with a time capsule, which was placed there in 1879 to be opened a century later.

Other fountains, often surmounted by the effigy of Cogswell himself, were installed in San Jose, California; Dubuque, Iowa; Buffalo, New York; Rockville and Willimantic, both in Connecticut; Pawtucket, Rhode Island; and Washington, D.C. Several efforts to remove the Washington, D.C., statue have been resisted over the years by the aforementioned Cogswell Society.

What a Time Capsule Revealed

Years passed, and in 1979 the long-sealed capsule in San Francisco's Washington Square was opened and revealed many souvenirs, messages, and other memorabilia placed by quite a few donors. Cogswell himself inserted a number of items, including a letter warning future readers of "Irish Catholic hoodlums."

Relevant to the present text, a handful of U.S. coins came to light along with several medals and foreign coins. Nearly all showed wear, indicating they were probably taken from pocket change at the time. Exceptions were the half dimes, dimes, and silver dollars, each of which was lightly toned Uncirculated. Federal issues included these:

> 1851 silver three-cent piece
> 1873-S half dimes (9, all Uncirculated)
> 1877-S dimes (9, all Uncirculated)
> 1876-S quarter dollar
> 1877-S quarter dollars (2)
> 1878-S quarter dollars (2)
> 1875-S half dollar
> 1879-S Morgan silver dollars (2, both Uncirculated)
> 1873 Open 3 gold $1

1873 gold dollar, variety with Open 3 in the date.

The Single Failure

Cogswell was an easterner who departed Philadelphia on May 9, 1849, aboard the *Susan G.*

Owens, and after a long journey arrived in San Francisco in October. There, while he was drinking water, just about everyone else, so it seemed, was drinking whiskey, wine, and other alcoholic beverages, often to excess. Cogswell went from one dental, real estate, and stock market success to another, because his mind was never clouded.

Thus was born his temperance crusade, apparently his only *failure*, as there was no measurable decrease in alcohol consumption following the erection of his statues.

Back to the meetings of the Cogswell Society:

Lift your glasses high! Here's a toast to the memory of Henry Cogswell!

Silver Coins Aplenty

Hidden: 1951 or later • **Found:** 1979 • **Treasure:** Thousands of silver coins

An old whisky still![94] Sealed jugs of liquor! Such were the surprises discovered in an old grocery store building in Pontiac, Michigan, in 1979.

The business had been owned for a long time by Joseph Polasek, who had died eight years earlier. Apparently, during Prohibition in the 1920s the facility was used for certain less-than-legal activities. Now in 1979, the premises at 534 Franklin Street were being dug out to make a cellar for the Gethsemane Bethel Apostolic Church.

As demolition and excavation work continued, crane operator Brad Bronkhorst of the Jonkisch Excavating Company cracked open a large crockery pickle jar, one of many leftover store items that were of no use to anyone and were destined to be hauled to the dump. You can imagine his surprise when out poured a silvery cascade of coins in the form of quarters, half dollars, and silver dollars dated from 1879 to 1951! Silver, silver everywhere! The staggering total eventually reached $9,000 face value! Workers had wondered if more whiskey would turn up, but no one suspected a treasure of coins was in the offing.

The coins were loaded into two large garbage cans that became so heavy that it took four men to carry each one.[95] The cache was taken to the police department to be stored and inventoried.

1927-S half dollar struck during the Prohibition era.

Meanwhile, word of the find spread around town; the prospect of finding free coins drew fortune seekers from far and wide, and caused several traffic jams. Equipped with metal detectors, rakes, and shovels, latecomers poked further around the site and found about $200 more in coins.

At the time a report was filed on the matter, the coins had been transferred to the Pontiac State Bank, and a protracted court session was expected as the present as well as previous property owners each filed claims. No numismatic inventory was published, but likely some of the coins stashed away during the Prohibition era 1920 to 1933 were Mint State and had significant value.

The New Orleans Excitement

Hidden: Early 1840s • **Found:** October 28, 1982 • **Treasure:** New Orleans Mint silver coins

On Thursday, October 28, 1982, a few minutes past noon, excitement prevailed in the French Quarter in downtown New Orleans as earthmoving equipment brought to light a vast treasure of silver coins.[96] The site, scheduled to be used for a new Meridien Hotel, may have secreted a long-forgotten bank reserve.

Passersby grabbed what they could in a frantic free-for-all. In the melee no accounting was ever made of what was found. However, it is estimated that more than 1,000 (perhaps *well* more than) silver pieces were found, including large numbers of Spanish-American silver coins. Apparently, these had been buried in two, perhaps three cedar boxes.

An 1840-O Liberty Seated quarter dollar.

On October 29, the *State Times*, published in Baton Rouge, carried an account that included this:

Coin Find Starts Gold Rush

New Orleans (AP): Construction workers digging the foundation for a hotel pulled up two boxes of pre-Civil War coins from the mud, setting off a gold rush by well-dressed prospectors from nearby office buildings.

Businessmen in suits and women in heels began sloshing in the muck to grab some of the gold and silver coins that scattered after one of the boxes broke open Thursday. . . . "They were down in the ground in coats and suits and ties like groundhogs," said Guy Montana, a construction worker. . . .

Most of the coins, gathered after a backhoe digging 13 feet below ground hit pay dirt, were silver. A few were gold. The coins included a 1726 Mexican coin, a large 1838 coin bearing the words "Est Nor Peruano," and French coins from the early 1700s.

Roy Mouledous, job superintendent for Gervais F. Favrot Co., the contractor at the site, said there were two wooden boxes, each measuring 10 by 12 by 8 inches. They held about 1,000 coins, he estimated. When the first one fell, "It broke open and 200 hands got in it," Mouledous said. . . .

The site used to be a bank, said Jack Serio, who owns the building next door.

How Many Coins Were Found?

Among large-denomination U.S. silver coins, various half dollars from about 1811 to 1837 were registered, as was a solitary 1798 dollar. Local dealer James H. Cohen evaluated many and furnished comments for the press. However, most attention by numismatists was centered on a remarkable cache of Liberty Seated quarter dollars struck at the nearby New Orleans Mint in 1840 and 1841, many if not most of which were Mint State!

A few were of the 1840-O No Drapery variety, but most were 1841-O With Drapery,[97] and the exact quantity of 1840-O and 1841-O quarters found has been a matter of conjecture ever since. In 1988, Walter H. Breen suggested that there were about 40 of the most plentiful variety, 1841-O, but I believe that several multiples of that number were found. Indeed, Larry Briggs in his book, *The Comprehensive Encyclopedia of United States Liberty Seated Quarters*, noted that of one die variety of 1841-O alone, more than 200 coins are known from this hoard.[98]

The latest-dated coin in the New Orleans hoard was an 1842 quarter dollar, which dealer Cohen graded as "About Uncirculated, which indicates that the hoard was buried shortly thereafter."

The typical coin was blackened from 150 years of immersion in damp soil. Many were cleaned soon thereafter, judiciously and otherwise, by numismatists. Fortunately, some were carefully conserved using archival methods. Today, survivors from this hoard can be identified by having a somewhat matte-like surface (not lustrous mint frost), usually with some traces of gray or black in areas.

Reflective of today's world and its thinking is this commentary:

> While quite understandable from an insurance viewpoint, but most unfortunate for the numismatic fraternity, the hotel owners promptly put a police guard around the site. This prevented people from coming in after hours with metal detectors and possibly being injured in the process. Additionally, the construction company accelerated its schedule and has poured concrete into the treasure hole, thus making the balance of the coins forever inaccessible.

The Ash Interviews

Additional information on this fascinating find is revealed in these personal interview notes by James D. Ash, taken with New Orleans coin dealers and collectors and an investment broker who was on the scene, as well as a later (September 16, 1986) interview with James H. Cohen:

> The coins were found in three cypress [*sic*] wood boxes. The first was broken open, and the coins were mingled with mud and dirt. Many passersby entered the excavation area to gather the coins, stuff them in their pockets, etc.; this was the account that was widely publicized. Some of these coins were later purchased by collectors and dealers.
>
> The second box was picked up at the scene by two individuals and loaded into a pickup truck. They left the scene quickly without opening the box at the time. So far as is known, the contents of this box never came on the local coin market.
>
> The third box was more systematically distributed at the scene, and numerous specimens from it were traded and sold on the local market. For several years thereafter these could be purchased without difficulty. I recall buying about a dozen quarters from James Cohen in the late 1980s. I also recall seeing an interesting pair of matched gem brilliant Uncirculated 1841-O quarters in a frame. One had a gem obverse, but a severely corroded reverse, while on the other the reverse was gem and the obverse was corroded. Together, with their best sides up, they made a nice display. This pair was offered to me for $650, but I passed. These had come from the third box.
>
> I was able to learn from witnesses that boxes one and three each contained two cloth bags filled with silver coins, possibly weighing about 50 pounds per bag, and estimated to contain about $1,000 face value per bag. Considering that a $1,000 bag of silver dollars weighs about 56 pounds, this estimate may have been close to the mark. Later, there were some rumors that box number two had gold in it, but this is probably not true.
>
> I understand that all verified coins were dated 1841 or earlier, although there were rumors of an 1842 quarter. The coins were 80% foreign and 20% United States. Most of the foreign pieces were Spanish-American silver 2-real and 8-real pieces. The United States coins were all quarters plus a few higher denominations. I heard of no half dimes or dimes. If each of the three boxes contained about $2,000 worth of coins, or a total of $6,000, it might be reasonable to assume that perhaps $800 of this was in quarters, or 3,200 pieces. Most I have observed were of the 1841-O, and more than half of these were from a slightly doubled obverse die.[99]

Here is a treasure for the future. The Meridien Hotel will not stand forever, and perhaps in the distant future when it, too, succumbs to "progress," someone will dig out a dusty old copy of this book and learn that beneath the broken-up concrete foundation are more silver coins!

Kept in the Family

Set aside: Circa 1824 • **Brought to market:** 1992 • **Treasure:** Capped Bust half dollars

On Tuesday, June 23, 1992, at Sotheby's sale rooms in New York City, coins described as "The Property of a Gentleman" crossed the block.[100] Offered were 37 examples of Uncirculated (mostly) half dollars bearing dates from 1820 to 1824. The catalog noted:

> This collection of half dollars was assembled in the years in which they were struck, by an ancestor of the present consignor. Not only is it unusual to find a group of coins assembled over a century and a half ago, but the quality and freshness of all of the coins is extraordinary.

The following half dollars were included, all Mint State except as noted:

1820, 20 Over 19, Overton-101
1821 O-103 (nearly Mint State)
1821 O-105a
1822 O-104
1822 O-106 (2)
1822 O-106a late die state (4)
1823 O-103 (3, two nearly Mint State and one full Mint State)
1823 O-105 (3)
1823 O-106a
1823 O-108
1823 O-108a (2)
1823 O-112 (5)
1824, 4 Over 1, O-101 (9 including 3 later die states)
1824 O-104
1824 O-108[101]

An 1821 half dollar, Overton 105a variety.

Surprise in a Dog Pen

Hidden: Circa 1916 • **Found:** 1996 • **Treasure:** Gold and silver coins

In July 1996, Betty Brauer struck it rich! Until that time her greatest stroke of luck was finding a $5 bill while shoveling snow.[102] The Valmy, Wisconsin, woman had been pulling weeds around a pen she was preparing for her beagles near the home she and her husband had owned for 33 years. There, exposed in the earth, was a gleaming treasure, hidden years earlier in a fruit jar, which upon inspection was found to consist of 21 gold and 29 silver coins! Dealer Mike Worchek, of Card & Coin Corner in Green Bay, examined the coins and pronounced them to be worth more than $7,000.

George Evenson, president of the Door County Historical Society, conjectured that the coins had been buried there by frugal former owners who

A $20 double eagle of 1901.

did not trust banks. A thrifty couple who had a couple of cows and sold milk locally had lived there. From the dates on the coins, it was determined that the pieces had been put away at least 80 years before, which would place the date at 1916 or earlier. Betty Brauer remembered that there had been a hint of such a find years ago when her sons dug for night crawlers for fish bait and found some old silver dollars.

Perhaps displaying more sense than the earlier owners of the house, Mr. and Mrs. Brauer quickly took the coins to a safe deposit box for security.

More than $7,000 worth of rare coins was found buried in a beagle pen.

The Newcastle Bank Hoard

Hidden: Circa 1864 • **Found:** 1996 • **Treasure:** Cents and two-cent pieces

Publicized in July 1996, the Newcastle Bank hoard contained six rolls of uncirculated 1864 two-cent pieces at 20 coins per roll, with an additional roll of 16 coins (pictured here).[103] There were 10 rolls of Uncirculated 1863 Indian Head cents and one and a half rolls of Uncirculated 1864 Indian Head cents (copper-nickel variety) at 25 coins per roll. The coins were rolled in paper.

The story is that the coins were originally bought with a $20 gold piece in 1864. The coins were purchased in the Hudson River Valley and comprised $10 in cents and $10 in two-cent pieces. That's 1,000 cents and 500 two-cent pieces. Over the years, the hoard was divided up between family members with all the other known coins being previously sold. All that remained was the present group.

This makes a nice story, a family legend. The problem is that in the summer of 1864, it took $258 in cents or two-cent pieces or in Legal Tender notes to buy $100 in gold. Accordingly, a $20 double eagle would have bought $51.60 in cents or two-cent pieces, not $20 worth. Thus it is more likely that $20 in Legal Tender notes, not a $20 gold piece, was used to make the purchase.

Mint-fresh 1864 two-cent pieces wrapped in a roll made of paper.

Finds at Colonial Williamsburg

Hidden: In colonial times • **Found:** 1900s • **Treasure:** Coins that circulated in colonial times

In 1956, in his monograph *Coinage for Colonial Virginia*, Eric P. Newman gave an accounting of examples found during the restoration of Colonial Williamsburg in Virginia:

> 1773-dated Virginia halfpennies (40 pieces; this is evidence that many of these circulated in Virginia, although many others were hoarded by the citizenry)
>
> Circa 1695–1701 William III British halfpenny, date apparently not readable
>
> 1722 Rosa Americana pennies (2)
>
> 1722 British regal copper halfpennies (2)
>
> George II British copper halfpence, various, only two with dates readable, these being 1738 and 1740 (5 total)
>
> George II Irish copper halfpence, circa 1737–1760, date not readable (2)
>
> George III copper halfpence, all counterfeits, one dated 1774, another 1775, with the balance being unreadable

> (5 total; such British issues were widely imitated, including by counterfeiters in the United States perhaps concentrated at Machin's Mills, Newburgh, New York, where coppers bearing inscriptions of Connecticut, Vermont, and other entities were also struck)
>
> Charles II Scottish sixpence, circa 1677–1679, date not readable
>
> 1785 Danish 2 skilling of Christian VII
>
> 1763 Hungarian 1 poltura, Maria Theresa
>
> Mexico City Mint silver coins of the 1700s, various (7 total)[104]

The preceding coins were found scattered over a wide area at Williamsburg and thus do not represent hoards, but, instead, finds. The distribution indicates that Spanish-American silver coins—in this case, all from the Mexico City Mint—dominated the larger coins in the monetary system in Virginia during this period.

The Massachusetts State House Time Capsule

Hidden: 1795 • **Opened:** 1855, again in 2015 • **Treasure:** Various coins

"This capsule was embedded in a cornerstone of the Massachusetts State House when construction began in 1795. It was placed there by Revolutionary luminaries including Paul Revere and Samuel Adams, governor of Massachusetts at the time."[105]

So began an account published in January 2015 of a long-forgotten time capsule containing several newspapers of 1795 and a group of coins that are now rare. But before explaining the reason for that account—the most recent unearthing—it is worth exploring happened in 1855, when the same capsule surprised everyone upon being discovered during the building of an addition to the State House. In 1795, the items had been in some

sort of leather portfolio or case sealed between two sheets of lead and set in the masonry between the stones.

The story of its original placement in 1795 and its rediscovery in 1855 was told in "Corner-Stone of the State House, Boston," in the *Freemason's Monthly Magazine* published in Boston on October 1, 1855 (here excerpted):

> On the seventh day of August last (1855), while the workmen employed by the commissioners in making repairs to the foundation of the State House were removing a portion of the earth at the south-east corner of the build-

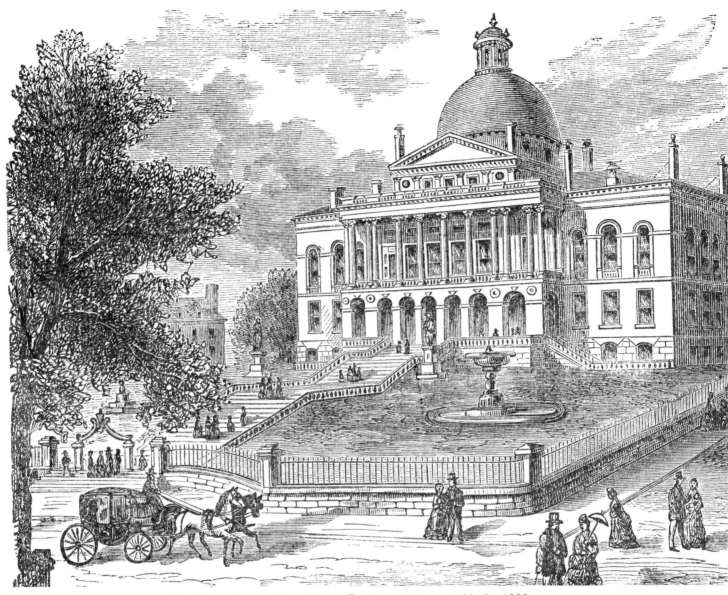

The Massachusetts State House, Boston, as it appeared in the 1800s.

ing, they were surprised by the appearance of a few copper coins and a small leaden box (if such it may be called) which consisted of two pieces of sheet lead loosely put together without the usual solder generally used by workers in that metal. This accident disclosed the fact that the rough granite stone still in its place was the corner-stone of the Capitol, and that the deposit made in 1795 was placed upon the soil with no other protection than a small quantity of the cement employed by the operatives in the construction of the foundation of the building.

With praiseworthy alacrity Messrs. Joseph R. Richards and Samuel K. Hutchinson, two of the commissioners on the alterations of the State House, secured all of the deposits, together with the material that formerly enclosed them, and after consulting with his Excellency the Governor of the Commonwealth and an antiquarian gentleman of Boston, resolved upon having the same plate and coins replaced, without any special display, under a new stone in a securely prepared metal box hermetically sealed.

As it may not be known to all that the corner stone was originally laid on the 4th of July, 1795, with considerable pomp and ceremony by the Hon. Samuel Adams, then governor of the Commonwealth, assisted by the Most Worthy Paul Revere, Grand Master, and other officers and Brethren of the Grand Lodge of Massachusetts, the following account is furnished for the information of the Masonic Brethren and for the future reference of those who are curious in such matters. . . .

On the morning of the 4th of July, 1795, it being Saturday, the papers of the day stated that the day would be celebrated in more than usual magnificence, and that the festivities of the occasion would be heightened by the laying of the corner-stone of the new State House with Masonic ceremonies. . . .

The day was ushered in by the ringing of bells and a federal salute by the company of artillery under the command of Capt. Samuel Bradlee. The infantry honors of the day were performed by the Independent Fusiliers of Boston under the command of Captain Joseph Laughton. . . .

[After an oration] the civic and Masonic procession—in which was the stone intended for the foundation corner of the new edifice, drawn by fifteen white horses (the number of states in the Union) decorated with federal emblems, colored ribbons and other insignia— moved from the meeting house and proceeded through Milk Street, Liberty Square, State Street, Main, (now Washington Street), Winter Street, and across the Common, arriving on the ground at one o'clock. . . .

The procession moved to the spot intended for the edifice; and being opened, the Agents, His Excellency the Governor, the Lt. Governor, the Grand Lodge, &c., passed through, and the operative Masons having prepared the stone, his Excellency laid it, with the assistance of the Grand Master and Deputy Grand Master, after having made the deposit thereunder. . . .

After the ceremony the whole company moved to the Council Chamber where the

precession was dismissed. The papers of the day state that it would be impossible to do justice to the scene which this grand occasion presented. . . .

[The contents of cornerstone included a silver plate upon the back of which] were placed the following coins: a Massachusetts cent, (commonly known as bearing an Indian on one side and an eagle on the other) of the year 1787; another of the year 1788, two half cents of the same currency and bearing the same dates; cents of the United States, coined in 1793 and 1794; New Jersey cent (Nova Caesarea,) of the year 1787; an old half penny of the time of George the Second; a half dollar of the United States currency, 1795; half dime of the same currency and year; a pine tree shilling of the currency established in Massachusetts in 1652; and a copy of the small medal struck in England in 1794 in honor of Washington, bearing the following on the obverse, head and bust of Washington in regimentals, with the legend, "George Washington, born in Virginia, Feb. 11, 1732," the parallel lines, "General of the American Armies 1776. Resigned 1783. President of the United States 1789." . . .

On Saturday, August 11, 1855, just sixty years and thirty eight days from the date of the original laying of the corner-stone, the ancient deposits were placed in a new metallic box made for the purpose, and re placed without any special ceremony, by the regular successors of those who officiated in 1795, in the same corner, but under a newly hammered granite ashlar, resting upon another block of granite, firmly laid upon a new foundation. . . .

The box was held in place on the underside of the stone by a layer of plaster that filled the remainder of the recess. Apparently when they plastered the box into the recess someone added five more coins by pressing them into the plaster before it hardened.

The 2014 Rediscovery

After 1855, the capsule was all but forgotten until December 11, 2014, when it was removed as problems of water infiltration were being checked at the State House. Pam Hatchfield, head of objects conservation at the Museum of Fine Arts, Boston, removed the brass box containing the artifacts from the cornerstone that day. Then, on January 6, 2015, with Governor Deval Patrick and other dignitaries and museum officials in attendance and a contingent of the media, she opened the box at the museum and removed its contents on live television. After being displayed, the contents were scheduled to be resealed once again.

The 2015 media account included an illustration of a Pine Tree shilling in perhaps Very Fine condition. An interviewee was quoted as saying that it might be worth as much as $75,000, "although given the context of this particular coin and the association with Paul Revere and Samuel Adams the valued would likely be much higher." Never mind that the current value as listed in *A Guide Book of United States Coins* is about $5,000.

These items are from an inventory made in 1855, a numismatic expansion of the earlier-quoted account published at that time:

> 1652 Pine Tree shilling (large planchet)
> 1787 Massachusetts copper half cent
> 1787 Massachusetts copper cent
> 1788 Massachusetts half cent
> 1788 Massachusetts half cent
> 1787 New Jersey copper
> Washington "Born Virginia" copper
> 1793 large cent, Chain AMERICA reverse
> 1794 cent
> 1795 half dime
> 1795 half dollar
> Very worn British copper halfpenny of George II, date not visible

These coins were added to the capsule in 1855:

1851 half cent	1852 cent
1853 half cent	1853 cent
1854 half cent	1854 cent

The time capsule as rediscovered in 2014.

1855 cent	1855 dime
1855 trime	1855 quarter
1855 half dime	1855 half dollar

Found in the plaster that was used to seal the box in 1855 were an 1855 trime, 1854 half dime, 1843 dime, 1854 dime, and an 1855 (?) dime with the date partially obscured.[106]

Now the question: Once re-interred, will the time capsule be forgotten again, to be discovered a century or two hence to the delight of everyone involved?

Museum of Fine Arts conservator Pam Hatchfield at the media presentation of the discovery.

chapter 3

Hoarders and Misers

Hoarding coins has been a popular thing to do since ancient times. *Silas Marner: The Weaver of Raveloe*, a novel by George Eliot published in 1861, epitomizes a recluse who finds comfort in hoarding gold guineas in an iron pot. In the United States there have been some famous real-life hoarders—Aaron White is an example—as well as obscure personalities such as the unrelated Charles White. Hoards assembled by numismatists who primarily bought their coins from dealers (rather than finding them in the hands of the general public) are discussed separately in chapter 4, "Dealer and Collector Hoards."

"Never Keep a Paper Dollar in Your Pocket Till Tomorrow"

Hidden: 1860s • **Found:** By 1888 • **Treasure:** Thousands of U.S. coins

Early in 1857 the country was riding a wave of feverish speculation in real estate and in railroad stocks, the latter comprising the vast bulk of the most actively traded issues on the New York Stock Exchange. Railroads were America's growth industry, lines were expanding rapidly including to the West, and profits in some instances were immense. However, not all was well with banks, insurance companies, and financial markets.

Aaron White's satirical token, brass, 35 mm.

On August 24, 1857, the New York City division of the Ohio Life Insurance & Trust Company failed, followed by its parent company shortly afterward.[107] Following that August announcement, "conditions in the money market rapidly approached a state of panic."[108] This triggered a wave of financial crises. Banks in some larger eastern cities stopped paying out silver and gold coins, and by year's end several thousand companies were bankrupt. A later government report, *Condition of Banks in 1857*, revealed that throughout the year most banks in America issued paper money equal to many multiples of the amount of coins on hand to redeem such notes if they were offered. What's more, railroad shares fell precipitously as the year went on, examples being the January-to-October crashes of Michigan Southern stock from $88 to $15 and Illinois Central stock from $123 to $79.

Concerning New York City banks, the report noted that on January 1, 1857, banks had liabilities of $43,974,000 and held $6,557,000 in specie (gold and silver coins). By June 6, specie had increased sharply to $14,370,000, but liabilities had increased far more dramatically to $127,703,000. Thus, although there were more coins in banks' hands, wild speculation in railroads, lands, and other areas put many bank assets in non-liquid form.

Banks began to weaken noticeably on September 4, when a broker protested a non-payment of just $250. Two more small protests occurred with other banks on September 12 and 15. This precipitated a call for redemption of paper notes in coins, further accelerating a trend that had been increasing each month since June. Indeed, toward the end of September, three leading banks failed

"The Panic in Wall Street."

The Merchants' Exchange in New York City was an important financial center in the 1837 era and was depicted on a Hard Times token and a popular print.

in Philadelphia, and the other leading banks there suspended specie payments. And by October 1, more than 30 banks had failed in New York state.

On October 13, 1857, all banks in New York City (with the single exception of the Chemical Bank) stopped paying out silver and gold coins.[109] Most banks remained solvent, but not liquid. Paper currency issued by insolvent private banks became worthless or, for a time, sold for pennies on the dollar, later to become valueless as well.[110] Meanwhile, notes of solvent banks sold at various small discounts in terms of cash, although some clothing merchants and others took the opportunity to advertise that they would accept paper currency at par in exchange for merchandise.

Following the suspension of specie payments, banks in New York (mainly) and New Orleans accumulated unprecedented amounts of coin, of course to the detriment of the value of their circulating paper. On November 7 the first steps were taken for solvent banks to resume paying out coins, and this was accomplished on December 11. In New York state, certain obligations—particularly of inland banks—were allowed to be paid out via a time schedule, these and other arrangements to be administered by the state banking superintendent, James M. Cook. New England banks were generally more solvent than those in New York state, and in the southern United States there was little problem at all.

Back to the Past: 1837

By 1857, the Panic of 1837 was a distant memory for most American citizens, but it is worth mentioning here due to its similarity to the Panic of 1857 and its pertinence to the hoard to be described. Following widespread land speculation combined with reckless issuance of paper money by banks with questionable assets, New York City and many other eastern banks suspended specie payments on May 10, 1837. Coins were hoarded, and few federal issues were to be seen in general circulation.

To fill the need for a commercial medium, a wide variety of what today are called Hard Times tokens were minted. Depreciated currency of the era, known then as wildcat notes and shinplasters and today as broken bank notes, are also of great interest to numismatists.

Didn't Like Paper Money

Aaron White, a New Boston, Connecticut, lawyer, may have been left holding the currency of a failed bank or otherwise suffered depreciation of his assets during the uncertain times of 1837, 1857, or both periods. Whatever the reason, he had a deep and abiding dislike of banks, financial institutions, and paper money.

In fact, he is known for having issued a satirical medal depicting on one side a sow hanging from a hook, and the inscription 1837–1857 SUS PENDENS[111] (probably a reference to banks' suspension of specie payments in 1837 and again in 1857) and NEVER KEEP A PAPER DOLLAR . . . (continuing on reverse) IN YOUR POCKET TILL TOMORROW. Depicted on the reverse was another sow, this one rooting in a jar inscribed 10, and the inscriptions DI OBOLI, DEUX SOUS, and SUS TOLL ENS.[112] "These tokens were suppressed by the government and are now very rare," Dealer W. Elliot Woodward stated at a later date.[113] Unsurprisingly, White was also known for being a hoarder of coins. But while most hoarders who disliked paper money preferred gold, he had a penchant for copper and nickel coins. Copper-nickel 1862 and 1863 Indian Head cents were bought by him directly from the Mint and stashed, and old half cents, large cents, colonials, and other copper coins were squirreled away as well. Gold and silver coins were very few by comparison. All told, the American pieces in the hoard seem to have amounted to around $2,000 or so in face value, but as most coins were of smaller denominations the *quantity* was vast.

After White's death his hoard was taken to the attic of a warehouse, where it remained for years. Later it was examined by dealer Édouard Frossard, who disposed of the majority of pieces privately and offered the rest in an auction on July 20, 1888, billed as "18,000 American and foreign copper coins and tokens selected from the Aaron White hoard."

Just What Did White Have?

Benjamin P. Wright, an early student of tokens and medals, summarized certain of White's holdings as follows:

250 colonial and state copper coins

60,000 copper large cents (which were mainly "rusted" and spotted; 5,000 of the nicest ones were picked out and sold for 2¢ each)

60,000 copper-nickel Flying Eagle and Indian Head cents (apparently most were dated 1862 and 1863)

5,000 bronze two-cent pieces

200 half dollars

100 silver dollars

350 gold dollars

20,000 to 30,000 foreign copper coins

The Frossard auction catalog omitted the bulk coins and concentrated upon those of numismatic value. That listing included the following federal coins:

Half cents dated 1800–1855 (945)

1795 plain edge copper cents (19)

1795 lettered edge cents (2)

1796 Liberty Cap cents (2)

1797 cents (26)

1800 cents (14)

1802 cents (34)

1803 cents (42)

1804 cent (altered date)

1805 cents (23)

1806 cents (16)

1807 cents (34, including some 1807/6)

1808 cents (24)

1809 cent

1810 cents (29)

1811, 1 Over 0, cent

1811 cents (6)

1812 cents (65)

1813 cents (18)

Miscellaneous cents 1795–1813, "worn, holed, stamped" (471)

Miscellaneous cents 1816–1856, Poor to Very Good (3,902)

Copper-nickel cents (338)

These miscellaneous items are adapted from the original catalog descriptions; modern commentary in brackets:

Wood's halfpence, 1723, low grades (47)

Rosa Americana coin

Nova Constellatio coppers (7)

Fugio cents (41)

Connecticut coppers (56)

New Jersey coppers (29)

Massachusetts coppers (42)

1787 Nova Eborac copper

Vermont coppers, 1788 (5)

North American tokens, 1781 (7)

Hard Times tokens (174)

Civil War tokens (534)

Brass tokens with inscription including CONTRAHENDO ET SOL-VENDO, etc. (559) [This legend translates approximately to: "I drag (or pull) together and loosen up," apparently a reference to pants suspenders, a punning allusion to the suspension of specie payments. Today these are known as Rulau Y-3, Y-3C, Y3E, and Y3G.[114] Y-3 is described as brass, 27 mm. diameter, with obverse legend: CONTRAHENDO ET SOL-VENDO / PUN. GO. / SEM. PAR. Russell Rulau theorizes that SEM. PAR may refer to Semper Paratus ("always prepared")]

White's own NEVER KEEP A PAPER DOLLAR, etc., token (105 copper, 147 brass, 1white metal)

Brass calendar medals of the type sold in 1863 by White (16) [The obverse displays a calendar of seven columns and six lines headed CALENDAR / FIG. DAY / CHANGE YEARLY. On the same side of the medal are far-ranging inscriptions including EMANCIPATION / JAN. 1, 1863, INDEPENDENCE / JULY 4, 1776, and CONSTITUTION / MARCH 4, 1789. In reference to the year at hand is the notation EQUINOXES / MAR. 20 SEP. 23. The reverse gives life dates of men from history: Franklin, Jefferson, Washington, and Lafayette. The medal is signed at the bottom: AARON WHITE, / NEW BOSTON CONN. / JAN. 1, 1863. PRICE 25 CTS.][115]

Proof strikings of a token, COLONEL PERCIE CLARK, etc. (191) [Russell Rulau advises that Frossard, a careless cataloger, should have referred to Percie Kirk, a figure from British history.

Kirk, a major-general by 1688 and remembered by historians as being a very cruel man, led the relief of Derry in 1689; Aaron White's tokens depict a bust facing left, presumably that of Kirk, with the inscription COLONEL PERCIE KIRK around]

An examination of the foregoing Frossard listing shows it is not particularly valuable for present-day research inasmuch as certain coins (*e.g.*, cents of 1798, 1801, and 1814) must have been grouped or sold separately, no dates are given for the copper-nickel cents, and so on.[116] However, Frossard's descriptions of White's token productions open the door to a veritable fun house of modern numismatic research possibilities!

A Fortune Found on a Farm

Hidden: Before 1910 • **Disclosed:** 1910 • **Treasure:** Banknotes and coins

On February 28, 1910, Elizabeth Hays died suddenly in her farmhouse in Burlington, New Jersey. The next day her heirs and her executor visited and found that over the course of 50 years she had been secreting money in various places on the premises. A report titled "Over $100,000 Found in Woman Miser's House" stated:

Bed and table linen yielded $10 and $20 bank notes by the scores. Bed springs, old coffee pots, several old purses, and other receptacles were found to contain hundreds of dollars. An old family Bible was almost completely interleaved with $20 notes, some of them bearing dates of issue shortly after the Civil War. The book stood on a parlor table.

In a cupboard among odds and ends of every description was a little pasteboard box. The investigators were about to toss it aside

when a jingle of coin drew their attention and they raised the lid to discover the box filled with gold coins, mostly eagles and double eagles, amounting to nearly $800. Old salt bags and leather wallets filled with gold were picked from an odd assortment of trash. . . .

Rolls of bank notes, all of big denominations, were stuffed between the mattresses, and mixed in with them were quantities of Civil War "shinplasters." It is said the searchers could not pick up a book without finding money between the leaves. Linen dropped to the floor, disclosing $10 notes between the folds.

Most of the old bank notes bearing early dates almost crumpled to dust when found, and it will take an expert to decipher their value.[117]

It Was Just Pocket Change

Buried: 1900s onward • **Disclosed:** 1975 • **Treasure:** Various coins

In 1975, Wayne Miller was a fledgling in the coin business in Helena, Montana.[118] He would become well-known in the field, particularly so with his landmark *Analysis of Morgan and Peace Dollars*, released in 1976, followed by *The Morgan and Peace Dollar Textbook*, published in 1982. Along the way he would handle quite a few silver dollar bags from the famous Treasury dispersal of 1962–1964 and the Redfield Hoard of 1976. However, that is not the thrust of this account.

A Mint State 1916 Denver Mint
Liberty Walking half dollar, first year of the design.

As Wayne relates the story:

I received a telephone call from a couple who had some coins for sale. They invited me to their home in the Helena Valley. As I parked my car I noticed a most unusual dog house—it consisted of three bales of hay! The husband was an ex-Marine in Army fatigues, over six feet tall. His wife was Chinese and at least a foot shorter.

The interior of their home consisted of narrow pathways to the kitchen, bathroom, and bedroom, and a very constricted view of a television set in the living room. The rest of the house was crammed from floor to ceiling with an assortment of newspapers, magazines, old appliances, car parts, etc. Glancing at what must have been many tons of worthless junk, my expectations for their coin collection

plummeted. However, when the first coin I saw was a nice Uncirculated 1916-D half dollar, my heart raced!

As I examined the somewhat dusty group (they had been buried loose in their dirt floor basement and had been removed when there was a threat of flooding). I noticed that the latest dated coin was from 1948. The wife explained that she was the eldest daughter of a Chinese family that had moved to Helena in the early 1900s. (Helena had a sizable Chinese population because of its beginnings as a mining town in 1864.) It was the family's custom to set aside extra money and pass it on to the oldest daughter in each generation.

After I sorted the pieces I was amazed at their high quality. There were virtually no worn or circulated coins! This was no ordinary coin collection!

The wife said that for many years her family would put extra money into a jar. What I was looking at was pocket change from 1916 to 1948. No one in the family was numismatically knowledgeable; no effort was made to find or save anything rare, or unusual.

After looking through about 135 marginal to gem brilliant Uncirculated 1916-S Mercury dimes, I realized why I had never bought a single 1916-D dime from the local public. If there had been any released in Helena, surely some would have been in this hoard. Obviously, when Mercury dimes were sent to Helena around 1916 and 1917 they came from the San Francisco Mint, not from the closer mint in Denver.

There were several dozen high grade 1916-D half dollars, several hundred Denver Mint Washington quarters from 1932 to 1939 (including 30 or more of the rare 1932-D), and many other Denver and San Francisco coins. However, there were only a few silver dollars, and there were no Indian Head cents or Buffalo nickels. These had been sold earlier to another "coin dealer" at double face value!

My generous offer for their 1,500 coins delighted them. They thought that the most they would be able to get would be twice their face value!

About six months later the couple brought in their gold coins. Included were about 20 $20 double eagles, 50 $10 pieces, 90 $5 coins, and 200 $2.50 pieces. Most of these were quite nice. There were also about 100 gold dollars, but most had been damaged or used as jewelry, including about 30 that had been holed and put on a chain. The gold coins realized another $15,000 for the owners. Of course, the coins were worth a lot less in 1975 than they would be today.

About a year later the couple called again: Would I know anyone who would buy sapphires? We met at the bank. They handed me a quart fruit jar full of raw sapphires (one of

the largest sapphire deposits in the world is about 20 miles east of Helena, on the banks of the Missouri River.) The jar contained over 20,000 carats of sapphires!

After disposing of the silver coins, the gold, and the sapphires, I waited for the next call. But I never saw either of them again. Too bad—I had come to expect the unexpected from this unusual couple.

Many 1916-S Mercury dimes were released into circulation in and around Helena, Montana. Some were added to the hoard discussed here.

A "Ton" of Coins—Really!

Put away: 1950s onward • **Found:** Circa 1983 • **Treasure:** Various coins

Wayne Miller, the aforementioned Montana professional numismatist, has had his share of unusual properties, but few matched a hoard that came to light in the early 1980s.[119] He seems to have a knack for stumbling onto treasures! Here is another story adapted from his own account:

Sometime in 1983 I received a call from a fellow tenor in the Helena Symphony Chorale. He told me that his father had recently passed away and left him a coin collection. He was a bit vague describing its contents, but he was sure that it weighed over a ton. I was skeptical, but intrigued.

About a month later I traveled to Los Angeles to meet my friend at a storage facility. He ushered me into a room measuring about 16 feet square. I was stunned by the sight of a gigantic pile of coins measuring about two feet high in the center and spreading out to the walls!

My friend explained that he and his late father had been estranged for 20 years. His dad had been a Greek merchant who ran a neighborhood grocery store. For over 30 years he saved every unusual coin that came his way. At the end of each week he would package these in penny-candy bags and take them home. The son had not seen his father for a long time and had never visited his home. Upon opening the front door to his father's house he found a well-worn trail leading to the kitchen, bedroom, and bathroom. The entire rest of the house was piled to the ceiling with newspapers, magazines, broken appliances, and other things.

It took my friend 45 days to clear all the debris away. As he did this, he came across the little bags of coins and set them aside. There were about 1,600 sacks, each with varying amounts of pieces therein. After he had sorted the loose and bagged coins from the tons of newspapers and other worthless junk he called me.

It took four people four 12-hour days just to empty the little bags and divide the coins by denominations. There were about 200,000 wheat-back Lincoln cents, 35,000 silver dimes, 15,000 silver quarters, 12,000 silver half dollars, 2,000 or so silver dollars, 22,000 Eisenhower dollars, and about 5,000 assorted world coins. The accumulation had been started about 1950 and continued until the father's death in 1983. Imagine an accumulation of nearly 300,000 coins weighing over 4,800 pounds, assembled from 1950 to 1983. One would assume such a hoard would contain hundreds, even thousands of scarce coins. But there was virtually nothing exciting at all. So much for the numismatic desirability of Los Angeles pocket change!

My friend's father also had a hoard of countless filled liquor bottles upstairs over his business, in a stifling hot, unventilated, upper room. The wine had of course deteriorated, but the whiskey was okay. The retail value was easily $100,000. These bottles were sold for $15,000 as a lot. Imagine how many hangovers were generated by this "rotgut" liquor!

Under the Schoolhouse Floor

Put away: 1946 onward • **Found:** 1996 • **Treasure:** Various coins and tokens

Alexander K. Miller was a peculiar sort of fellow.[120] Miller and his wife Imogene moved to the isolated village of East Orange, Vermont from New Jersey in 1946 to retire and, as it turned out, remained for the rest of their lives. The town, reachable only after traveling several miles on unpaved roads, is sufficiently remote that it has no zip code and was not included in the 1990 U.S. census. It was the ideal place for privacy, it seems. With only a few exceptions, people in the outside world did not know of the Millers, nor would they during their lifetime. This would change dramatically in 1996—but first, a bit of background.

Born on July 14, 1906, the only child of Edward S. and Jane Kennedy Miller, Alexander spent much of his early life in Montclair, New Jersey. He became a collector of license plates by age 16. In the 1930s, he engaged in "expert automobile repairing" and offered Miller's Flying Service for "aeroplanes rebuilt and overhauled," according to one of his old business cards. In World War II, he served in the Royal Canadian Air Force.

After the war, Alexander maintained his interest in aviation, as evidenced by his acquisition of an old World War I biplane which for a time he stored in a barn on his Vermont farm; this he eventually sold or traded away. He also kept active with automobile repairing after the move, though no longer on a commercial basis; rather, he collected and restored cars that interested him, and that included just about everything from classics to rusted modern junk. Miller would often trade cars or other items with other collectors, and along the way he accumulated many parts, seemingly far more than he could ever use.

Throughout their years in East Orange, Alexander and his wife did very little socializing. They kept to themselves and rarely discussed their interests or affairs. However, Alexander must have reached out now and then, as his next-door neighbor remembered him as treasurer of the local church for two decades. He was a student of the Bible and often quoted verses from it.

More peculiarities: When Miller's father died in 1957 and left his son a substantial amount of money, the latter apparently converted some or much of this into "hard assets" such as coins. Alexander was also known to give the impression that he had no telephone (though he did) and would engage in protracted negotiations via letters and postcards, often demanding gold, silver, or cash in payment. Other times he would have a check made out to one of his favorite religious organizations. Obviously, he was a generous man, if odd.

W. Murray Clark, owner with his family of Clark's Trading Post, Lincoln, New Hampshire,

A small part of the Miller Hoard.

recalled communicating with Miller over the years and visiting him upon occasion in East Orange.[121] At one time Miller had some Indian Head cents, and Clark had some brass lamps and other auto parts. A trade was to be arranged. The two met on the first floor of the Miller home, but after some give-and-take discussions, Clark came to the conclusion that the Vermonter wanted high retail prices for his coins, but wanted to acquire the auto parts below wholesale, and thus the transaction ended.

Clark noted that he had the impression that Miller had brought many of his various coins with him from New Jersey, and had acquired relatively few after his move.

A Great Surprise!

Alexander Miller relished his surroundings and remained there until the autumn of 1993, when a fall from a ladder while installing storm windows resulted in his death. He was 87. His wife Imo-gene, age 78, died in Montclair, New Jersey, in February 1996.

Upon her passing, the couple's assets were intended nearly entirely to go to religious groups. When administrators visited the property, they were amazed at what they found on the rundown farm. Cars, antiques, gold and silver ingots, coins, and other items were estimated to be worth about $3 million!

Underneath an old schoolhouse and other out-buildings on the property was found $82,000 in silver coins, including a small but interesting cache of 1878-S Morgan dollars. Some $100,000 worth of gold coins is said to have been located as well. However, most of Alexander's gold was in bullion form—about $900,000 in large ingots. Silver was in 70-pound ingots that a representa-tive of Christie's later said "resemble loaves of bread." About $200,000 worth of stocks and $700,000 in promissory notes were also located.

A pack rat deluxe to outsiders, and perhaps a clever buyer in the view of his fellow collectors, over a period of time Alexander Miller accumulated about 40 old automobiles, some of which had great collectors' value. Meanwhile, the tin-roofed house in which the Millers lived had not seen serious repair or renovation for a long time. Mrs. Miller scrimped—instead of buying raincoats she made them from plastic bags. Apparently, both husband and wife scraped by with just the barest of essentials in their personal life. They were good people, even if a bit eccentric.

Dispersal of the Treasures

From May 24–26, 1996, Archie and Joshua Steenburgh sold at auction the first group of accumulations from the Miller buildings.[122] By this time the state of Vermont had filed claims totaling nearly $900,000 against the Miller estate, Uncle Sam was in there with a demand for $7,300,000 (noting that the Millers neither had Social Security numbers nor had ever filed tax returns), and 50 other claims had been recorded!

At that first sale, about 600 to 700 people were on hand, a combination of serious bidders and curiosity seekers. Among the items crossing the block were typewriters, furniture, mechanical gadgets, and music boxes. Murray Clark recalled that prices were quite high the first day, but after the novelty wore off, there were some excellent values to be had, including for a half dozen or more antique sewing machines that Murray acquired for his collection.

Later, at a sale held by Christie's auction house at the Vermont farm in September 1996, such marques as a 1935 Stutz Bearcat and (from more recent times) a 1962 Rolls Royce Silver Ghost Piccadilly Roadster crossed the block. Stutz had apparently been Miller's favorite brand, as he had quite a few stored in old, but well-maintained buildings around his property. If one has to have a favorite marque of old car to buy in quantity, fewer names are better than Stutz, the Indiana manufacturer that went out of business before World War II.

About 3,000 people crowded into East Orange For the first day of Christie's sale (September 7). Most had come to look around, but quite a few registered as bidders. The highlight of the car auction was a 1916 Stutz 4C Bearcat which fetched $173,000. The Rolls Royce went to a new home for $129,000. On the other hand, "Volkswagens sold for pocket change; one brought $23 (the buyer was an eight- or nine-year old boy bidding with his allowance money and his dad's approval), and another brought $12.08."[123]

Littleton Coin Company, which seems to always be on the lookout for quantities of interesting things to sell, latched on to the 1878-S Morgan silver dollars found under the schoolhouse floor, and in that same September began to offer them for sale. Thus, before long quite a few

Indianapolis-based Stutz was Alexander Miller's preferred make of automobile.

collectors around the country had a bit of Vermont folklore to go with the coins they bought.

Miss Millie J. Drury

Sometimes when a business or person is long gone and largely forgotten, a numismatic memento will serve as a souvenir to excite the curiosity of a later generation of collectors. Such is the case with one final story relating to Alexander Miller's hoards.

Among the treasures found on that Vermont farm was a cache of 48 aluminum cent-sized tokens was found. Each one bore on the obverse the inscription MISS M.J. DRURY / WILLIAMSTOWN / VT., with the reverse reading GOOD FOR ONE 5¢ CIGAR.[124] Used in the early 1900s, such pieces were probably stored in the payout slot of a trade stimulator and given as prizes in an era when cash rewards were prohibited.

Such mechanical devices were made by the Mills Novelty Co., Exhibit Supply Co., Watling, Caille Brothers, and others. These were usually placed on top of a store counter, often near the cash register. Upon the deposit of a cent, wheels would turn, or dice would be shaken, or another game of chance would be activated. If a lucky combination was hit, a token would be dispensed. This token could be exchanged for merchandise—in the case of these tokens, a cigar.

Somewhere along the line Miller preserved this little group of 48 tokens, most showing signs of

use, to be purchased in 1996 by Littleton Coin Co. These pieces have relatively nominal numismatic value in the overall scheme of market prices, but like many tokens, they certainly have an interesting history! When Russell Rulau heard about these he became very interested—he had never heard of a "Good For" token issued by a "Miss." He bent the rules and listed this slightly later piece in the 4th edition of his *Standard Catalog of U.S. Tokens 1700–1900*.

It turns out that in the early years of the last century, continuing into the 1920s, Miss Millie J. Drury operated a retail business and, later, a lunch room in the lower level of the Grange Hall in Williamstown, Vermont.[125] The building later burned, and today no trace of it remains, although the local historical society has an old-time photograph showing part of her sign there.

In 1909 her business consisted of selling "fancy goods," toys, and novelties. At the time, fancy goods were generally defined as including small items that added to the enjoyment of life, such as clocks, vanity mirrors, binoculars, china plates, etc. Her business was not particularly well-financed, and in 1909 it was said that her assets were less than $500.[126] Of course, in that era, such an amount went much further than it would today.[127]

One of the 48 tokens issued by Miss M.J. Drury, found in the hoard.

chapter 4

Dealer and Collector Hoards

Hoards traceable to dealers and collectors—in other words, those with numismatic knowledge—form a special segment of the present narrative. Such hoards have the common thread that the pieces were set aside for numismatic purposes. Most coins in such hoards or accumulations were bought from other dealers and collectors and were already known to the numismatic community. Thus, these holdings differ from the "find" type of hoard.

These hoards, many of which are well-known and others of which are delineated here for the first time, are caches made by numismatists who were not content with owning just one example of a given item. In other instances, the hoards were the result of dealers accumulating inventory in a special area of interest. The greatest of all numismatic hoarders was Virgil M. Brand, but he had quite a bit of company.

Before 1950

Investment in coins has been a part of the hobby for many years—in fact, as far back as the 1870s and 1880s one dealer attempted to "corner" Proof sets of the year 1858, as an example. Various appealing coins, including leftover, unsold current minor Proofs from the Mint, were often squirreled away as store stock. The market was generally rising, and in this time period, as also in the years to come, dealers often found that it was more profitable to hold a coin in inventory than to sell it.

In the early 1900s, various dealers set aside "new" coins as they were produced, usually of minor denominations, especially cents and nickels. To have saved quarter dollars or half dollars in quantity would have tied up too much precious capital, a commodity never in long supply among the majority of professional numismatists. In time such dealers as John Boss, F.C.C. Boyd, B. Max Mehl, David U. Proskey, William Pukall, and John Zug had in their safes and vaults many bank-wrapped rolls of minor denomination coins.

The 1930s represented a watershed era for numismatics. Despite the Great Depression and its nationwide impact, coin collectors were marching to the beat of a different drummer. Among the catalysts for this uptick in activity were the appeal of the low-mintage 1931-S Lincoln cent (the first cent in a generation to have a mintage below the million mark); the introduction by Wayte Raymond of the *Standard Catalogue of United States Coins*; the 1935–1936 commemorative boom; the debut of easy-to-use and fun-to-fill coin albums by M.L. Beistle and Wayte Raymond; the related mass production of "penny boards" by J.K. Post of Neenah, Wisconsin (which activity was continued by Whitman Publishing Company); and the list goes on. These were happy, exciting times. Coin values rose tremendously. The cat was out of the bag: coins were one of the best investments ever, it was said.

Beginning about 1934, many people started putting away current rolls of Uncirculated coins from cents to half dollars (silver dollars were virtually ignored and might as well have been struck on a different planet; there was hardly any collecting interest in them). The pace would continue, despite a crash in mid-1936 of the overblown market for commemorative half dollars. In the same year, Proof sets were sold to collectors for the first time since 1916. The *Numismatic Scrapbook*, launched by Lee F. Hewitt in 1935, became popular and served as a forum for buying and selling coins.

During World War II, cash was plentiful, but consumer goods were rare. Thus, a lot of money was put into coins, perhaps starting in a big way with Abe Kosoff's September 1943 sale of the Michael F. Higgy Collection, which saw coins sell for two, three, five, or more multiples of the latest catalog prices.

Common-date gold coins also became exceptionally popular, and for the first time a widespread interest developed in the large and heavy $20 double eagles, each of which contained nearly an ounce of gold. The original passion for such pieces started in the 1930s when Louis E. Eliasberg, Floyd Starr, and other established collectors realized that the calling-in of gold coins by Franklin D. Roosevelt would catalyze inflation, and now momentum picked up as more individuals realized that gold coins, which were allowed to be held by numismatists, were a good hedge.

After all, displaced citizens of European countries had long sought financial comfort in gold—now the sentiment extended to our own shores. Common-date double eagles, previously with a market value of less than $40, jumped to $50, $60, or even more. Richard S. Yeoman's *Guide Book of United States Coins* made its debut in 1946, adding fuel to the market fire.

All the while, hoards small and large were being assembled by collectors, dealers, and investors who continued to put away bank-wrapped rolls of current coinage.

The 1950s

In the decade or so prior to 1960, coin collecting was mostly a leisurely pursuit, notwithstanding lots of exciting market news and a dazzling run-up in prices. Information was obtained monthly through *The Numismatic Scrapbook Magazine* and *The Numismatist* magazines; and out in Iola, Wisconsin, Chet Krause published his newspaper-format *Numismatic News* beginning in 1952. Pricing information was primarily gathered from Yeoman's *Guide Book*, which was published annually.

Bank-wrapped rolls made up from coins taken from mint-issued cloth bags continued to be popular items to buy and put away in quantities. Proof sets, which were made again in 1950 following suspension after 1942 due to the pressing needs of World War II, also attracted a wide following and had a remarkable way of escalating in price. Furthermore, the 1950-D nickel (of which more will be said subsequently) was a brilliant beacon to anyone interested in buying coins that, as certain as sunset follows sunrise, would go up in price.

However, investment was still secondary to most numismatists in the 1950s; the formation of a collection by date and mintmark sequence was primary.

The 1960s Onward

In 1960 there were several changes. The 1960 Small Date Lincoln cent was produced at Philadelphia and immediately became valuable. Several bags containing $50 face value (5,000 pieces) of this variety were obtained by various people from banks and sold immediately at sharp advances, some for $10,000 to $12,000. This was exciting news, and stories were carried in newspapers nationwide, in *Time* magazine, and on television. In Syracuse, New York, dealer Jonah Shapiro made a market in these, and his telephone kept ringing off the hook. In Philadelphia, Harry J. Forman and his associate Ruth Bauer also had their hands full with 1960 Small Date cents.

Meanwhile, in Sidney, Ohio, newspaper publisher J. Oliver Amos decided to issue a weekly newspaper about a hobby or sport, and after some consultation with his staff narrowed the field down to potential categories beginning with the letters A, B, and C; specifically, antiques, bowling, or coins. The last was picked, and *Coin World* was launched under the editorship of D. Wayne Johnson. Englewood, Ohio, dealer James Kelly was tapped to write a new feature, "Trends," which on a weekly basis gave coin values, a hitherto untried concept. Within a short time the publication had tens of thousands on its subscription list, and within a year or so it would cross the 100,000 mark, an all-time high which to this day has not been re-attained.

Perhaps in part because of these developments, *investment* was the key word from 1960 through 1964. The market rose rapidly, and in a cause-and-effect relationship, thousands of people entered the hobby to satisfy their intent to make a profit. Teletype networks (with several systems in place, including one operated by the Professional Numismatists Guild) linked dealers all over the United States; *The Coin Dealer Newsletter* was launched in 1963; and jet airplane travel made it possible to transact over breakfast in New York City and lunch in Los Angeles.

The darling of the investors was the aforementioned low-mintage 1950-D nickel, which rose from $10 to $15 per roll (of 40 coins) in the mid-

1950s to more than $1,200 at one point in 1964. However, in the next year the market softened, and in 1965 it foundered. The 1950-D nickel did the impossible: It fell from grace, and the situation was the same for quite a few other "winners." Recovery of the coin market (but not the 1950-D nickel price) took place a few years later, and there were other investment peaks in 1979–1980 and again in 1989.

The advent of third-party grading services, pioneered by the American Numismatic Association and its ANA Certification Service (ANACS) started a trend that in time launched more than 100 such businesses, the most successful of which were the Professional Coin Grading Service (PCGS) in 1988 and the Numismatic Guaranty Corporation of America (NGC) in 1989. Nearly all others have disappeared.

Walter Breen's Complete Encyclopedia of U.S. and Colonial Coins was published by Doubleday in 1988 and became popular in a short time. Within a year my company sold more than 10,000 copies. This study, which since then has been found to have had quite a few errors, was extremely influential and important in its time. In one handy volume a reader could learn much information about die varieties and rarity ranges, for example, with much less effort than could their predecessors a generation or two earlier.

In Later Years

Today the market is very cosmopolitan. On one side there are more dedicated scholars than ever before, and more interest in numismatic specialties. Publications such as the *Colonial Newsletter*; *Colonial Coin Collectors Club Newsletter*; *The Asylum* (published by the Numismatic Bibliomania Society, a group of collectors of printed material), along with its electronic newsletter counterpart, *The E-Sylum*; *Penny-Wise* (about copper cents and other issues); *Longacre's Journal* (Flying Eagle and Indian Head cents); *John Reich Journal* (early silver coins); *Gobrecht Journal* (Liberty Seated silver

coins); *Token and Medal Society Journal*; and *Paper Money* provide technical information and historical notes for specialists in various series.

At the same time, general interest periodicals including *Coin World*, *COINage*, *Coins* magazine, *Numismatic News*, and *The Numismatist*—as well as *The Coin Dealer Newsletter* and a few other pricing sources—cater to the wider popular market for coins. What's more, in the early 2000s Anderson Press (whose principals have been involved in numismatics for many years and who own several book and retailing businesses) acquired Whitman Publishing and launched an expanded, dynamic company that continued to print standard references such as *A Guide Book of United States Coins* plus countless new titles by leading authors.

Meanwhile, the modern market constituting sales to coin buyers ranges from numismatically oriented and very knowledgeable dealers with clienteles of serious collectors to investment-oriented sellers who offer coins to the public by telephone, television, and mass mailings.

All of the preceding elements give a rich diversity to the coin market as it is today.

With these comments as a preface, it is appropriate to comment on various hoards, groups, accumulations, and other holdings of coins that have been set aside by numismatically knowledgeable people over a long span of years. No such enumeration will ever be complete, as virtually every dealer who ever sold a coin also set aside a few "extras" now and then, and collectors often acquired duplicates for investment or trading purposes. Moreover, the estates of many dealers included coins in quantity, few of which have been recorded in published inventories.

Some of the dealer and collector hoards worthy of mention—ranging from well known to obscure—are given below in approximate chronological order. By including all in the same section, they can be compared to each other, as many dealer hoards are related.

Quite a Few Proof Sets

Acquired: Late 1870s and early 1880s • **Dispersed:** 1886 • **Numismatic hoard:** Proof coins

In his October 1886 sale of the J. Colvin Randall Collection, W. Elliot Woodward offered quantities of Proof sets of the 1878–1882 era. Undoubtedly, these had been bought at the Mint by Randall, a Philadelphia dealer; it was the custom of the Mint to sell for face value any undistributed remainders, while those not placed with dealers were simply spent. The Woodward-Randall offering is simply representative of multiple such groups held by dealers in this era and included the following:

   1878 three-piece Proof sets (10; included Indian Head cent, nickel three-cent piece, Shield nickel)
   1879 three-piece Proof sets (82)
   1880 three-piece Proof sets (76)
   1880 Proof sets (35; content not specified, but probably complete from the cent to the trade dollar)

   1880 Proof trade dollars (64; these were favorite coins for speculation in 1880)
   1882 Proof sets (32; content not specified)[128]

A Proof 1880 trade dollar.

Charles White:
Banker, Numismatist, Hoarder

Gathered: Early 1800s • **Dispersed:** 1886–1887 • **Treasure:** Early quarter dollars, etc.

Charles White, cashier of the Northampton Bank in Massachusetts beginning in June 1850 and continuing until August 1861, is little remembered today.[129] Collectors of notes issued by the bank will sometimes find a bill signed in ink by him, but such are rare. When that institution

evolved to become the Northampton National Bank in April 1865 (charter 1018), most of the earlier notes were redeemed and burned. By that time he had moved on, apparently relocating to New York City at one point.

Besides a cashier, White was also a coin collector, and like many numismatists, he could not resist some hoarding, too. Little survives about his hoard(s) in print, but what does—courtesy Harlan P. Smith, fruit wholesaler and part-time coin dealer of 269 West 52nd Street, New York City—is fascinating.

Smith, who was himself a first-rank collector, cataloged the White cabinet in 1886 and offered it for sale. The auction took place in a well-known gallery rented for the purpose. His introduction to the offering noted:

A Mint State 1818 quarter.

The cabinet of Mr. Chas. White of New York City, comprising a remarkably fine and full series of U.S. silver and copper coins, with few medals, to be sold at public auction, without reserve, on Tuesday, March 9th, 1886, at two o'clock, p.m., by Messrs. Bangs & Co., Auctioneers, 739 and 741 Broadway, N.Y.

A $2 note of the Northampton Bank signed at the lower left by cashier Charles White.

What Was In the Hoard?

The flavor of this long-ago event is gained by reprinting some of the catalog descriptions beginning with Lot 121, the prices in brackets being those realized. Note in particular Lot 128, which gives a hint of a hoard of a particular date, but which, unfortunately for present-day aficionados in the early quarter dollar field, leaves much unsaid. How many were there? Where were they found? What happened to the others?

A sampling of the quarter dollar listings follows:

Lot 121: 1796 Very Fine, bold impression; slightly touched by circulation; a handsome piece [Price realized at the sale: $9.25]

Lot 122: 1804 Very Good [$2.00]

Lot 123: 1805 Uncirculated, except for two minute nicks in field: beautiful sharp impression generally: few stars flat: surpasses my own specimen and all others I've seen. [$2.87]

Lot 124: 1806 over '5; Good. [$0.60]

Lot 125: 1806 Fine; perpendicular crack across obverse die [$0.90]

Lot 126: 1807 Uncirculated: splendid impression: excels the 1805 in some points: a very desirable specimen: in the Randall sale Lot 558 brought $90: that piece claimed to be the only Uncirculated specimen existing; this proves the contrary. [$26]

Lot 127: 1815 Uncirculated: sharp impression. [$2.90]

Lot 128: 1818 Uncirculated: sharp: rev. die cracked across; this is the last specimen of the hoard discovered by Mr. White, while cashier of the Northampton Bank; he naturally reserved the best specimen for his collection. [$1.40]

Lot 129: 1818 Uncirculated: sharp: plain edge; only specimen known. [$1.20]

Lot 130: 1819 Very Fine, sharp impression: barely touched by circulation: Reverse with colon after the "25 C," the "5" engraved twice; desirable in this condition. [$1.40]

Lot 131: 1820 Uncirculated; sharp impression [$2.40]

Lot 132: 1821 Uncirculated; sharp impression [$2.30]

Lot 133: 1822 Uncirculated; stars flat; seldom equaled [$3.10]

Lot 134: 1823 over '22; Good for date; the most difficult date to obtain, except '27. [$30.00]

Lot 135: 1824 Very Fine, but little circulated. [$5.00]

Lot 136: 1825 Uncirculated; sharp impression. [$2.80]

Lot 137: 1828 Very Fine; rubbed only on highest points. [$0.65]

Lot 138: 1831 Uncirculated. [$0.45]

Lot 139: 1832 Uncirculated; desirable so perfect. [$0.95]

Lot 140: 1833 Uncirculated. [$0.70]

Lot 141: 1834 Uncirculated; sharp [$0.90]

Lot 142: 1834 Uncirculated; sharp; lacks the period after "25 C." [$0.40]

Lot 143: 1835 Uncirculated; cracked die. [$0.50]

Lot 144: 1836 Very Fine; cracked die. [$0.40]

Lot 145: 1837 Uncirculated. [$0.50]

Lot 146: 1838 Uncirculated. [$0.55]

Lot 147: 1838 Liberty Seated; Uncirculated. [$0.45]

Lot 148: 1839 Very Fine. [$0.40]

Lot 149: 1840 Uncirculated; draped elbow; "O" mint; splendid specimen. [$0.75]

Later in the catalog a half dollar was described as follows, an overdate not known to numismatists today:

Lot 218: [Capped Bust half dollar] 1820 over '18 Fine, and now first described; only specimen I've seen. [$2.00][130]

Also of interest is an 1840 Liberty Seated half dollar:

Lot 246: [1840 Liberty Seated half dollar struck at New Orleans, but lacking an O mintmark] Fine: large lettered reverse; this appears to be the same die used in the New Orleans Mint in 1839, and re-engraved; this variety seldom found.[131]

It is evident from the listings that these were the cradle days of American numismatic information. For example: as part of the description of Lot 182, an 1879 Uncirculated Liberty Seated quarter (which brought $0.45), cataloger Smith noted concerning issues from that year through 1885: "None issued for circulation."

A rare Mint State 1879 Liberty Seated quarter dollar.

It is known that circulation strikes were indeed made, and contemporary *Mint Report* issues mention them. Curiously, such pieces were made to prevent the dates becoming rare (as they would have been had only Proofs been struck). Inasmuch as the Mint and certain of its officials were exploiting the numismatic community for all it was worth, this in retrospect seems to have been a curious motive.

With regard to aforementioned the remark in the listing, it could have been the case that by the time these were auctioned in 1886, the relatively restricted circulation strike mintages of these dates were still in storage and were not generally available. That being said, the offering of "Uncirculated" examples indicates that at least a few got out.

Also note a gratuitous comment concerning trade dollars appeared before Lot 353, the first coin in a set of Proofs by date from 1873 through 1883 inclusive. The introduction read as follows: "It will be noticed that Mr. White wasn't an advocate of the lightweight dollars, which must eventually be recoined; as they are actually tokens." Harlan P. Smith, apparently no fan of trade dollars, was incorrect in his information as, in fact, trade dollars were heavier than regular silver dollars.

Finally: a mini-hoard of sorts followed Lot 474, a collection of 1864–1873 Mint State two-cent pieces except for the 1872 and 1873 which were Proofs. Next were presented four separate offerings of Proof 1873 two-cent pieces—the rarest date in the series.

More White Coins for Sale

On April 15, 1887, part II of the Charles White Collection was offered by Smith, who by this time had exited the fruit business and was devoting much if not all of his time to coins. The 1887 catalog bore these introductory comments:

Having concluded to dispose of the balance of the White Collection, the reader will find described in the following pages many very choice specimens of the U.S. coinage. The exceptionally fine condition of so large a number of pieces will be found worthy of attention of the most prominent collectors.

In this second sale, in remarks preceding Lot 134, the cataloger noted this in connection with an offering of silver Proof sets: "Prices of Proof sets are now as low as they possibly can get, and now would be the opportunity for parties desiring an investment to obtain a series which will undoubtedly greatly increase in value in a few years."

An 1884 Liberty Seated half dollar
from a Proof set of that year.

Interestingly, Lot 162 was described as a set of "1884 brilliant Proofs, no trade," while Lot 163 was described as "1885 brilliant Proofs," with no mention of a trade dollar being either absent or present. This would seem to indicate that in 1887 Smith was aware of the existence of an 1884 trade dollar, but realized that there was not one in this particular 1884 Proof set; otherwise, there would have been no reason to have noted its absence. The numismatic community at large, however, did not know of silver strikings of the trade dollar until 1906 when John W. Haseltine and Stephen K. Nagy made known the existence of 10 pieces (although the rumor of silver 1884 trade dollars had surfaced earlier, and some copper impressions had appeared on the market).

Beginning with Lot 315 in the second sale, quarter dollar listings included the following. Note that Lot 320 alludes to White's hoard of quarters, implying via "of this period" that dates other than 1818 may have been included:

Lot 315: 1796 Strong, sharp, brilliant impression; entire surface Proof: 6 in date almost touches bust; I believe this

to be the finest known specimen; a gem for any collection. [$57.00]

Lot 316: 1796 6 more distant from bust: Fine, strong impression; everything sharp except centers of stars on left; hair clear and well defined; eagle's head perfectly struck up (more so than in preceding); it has seen but the slightest, if any, circulation. [$44.00]

Lot 317: 1796 Broken die; Very Fair. [$1.20]

Lot 318: 1807 Uncirculated; all sharply struck except for a few stars; mint lustre still retained; one of the finest specimens known; that in Randall's sale sold for $90. [$42.00]

Lot 319: 1815 Barely circulated; clear, bold impression. [$2.10]

Lot 320: 1818 Uncirculated, brilliant and sharp; nearly all the extra fine quarter dollars of this period came from Mr. White's hoard, as he seems to have paid more attention to this series than any other. [$2.10]

Lot 321: 1819 Very slight trace of circulation; strongly struck; very desirable in this condition. [$2.10]

Lot 322: 1820 Large O; Uncirculated. [$3.20]

Lot 323: 1821 Uncirculated. [$2.10]

Lot 324: 1822 Very Fine specimen; barely circulated; desirable in this condition. [$3.10]

Lot 325: 1824 Very Fine for this date, in fact, I think it the best I have seen; very desirable. [$14.00]

Lot 326: 1825 over '22; Uncirculated; sharp. [$1.80]

Lot 327: 1828 Uncirculated; sharp. [$1.65]

Lot 328: 1833 Very faint traces of circulation; sharp, bold impression, and equal to any I ever saw. [$1.60]

Lot 329: 1834 Handsome impression. [$0.40]

Lot 330: 1837 Uncirculated. [$0.60]

Lot 331: 1840 Draped Elbow; Uncirculated. [$0.75]

Lot 332: 1842-O mint; fine. [$0.60]

Lot 333: 1852 Uncirculated; sharp. [$1.20]

Lot 334: 1853 Without arrows; Uncirculated; very desirable specimen. [$12.25]

Lot 335: 1863, '4 Brilliant Proofs, 2 pcs. [$0.55 each]

Lot 336: 1865 Brilliant Proof. [$0.60]

Lot 337: 1867, '8 Brilliant Proofs. 2 pcs. [$0.65 each]

Lot 338: 1873 Without arrows, '72, '75; brilliant Proofs, 3 pcs. [$0.37-1/2 each]

Lot 339: 1880, '3, '5, '6 Brilliant Proofs, 4 pcs. [$0.40 each]

Lot 340: 1881, '2, '4, '6 Uncirculated, 4 pcs. [$0.50 each]

The commentaries after lots 339 and 340 no longer mention that 1880 and 1881 quarters were not released; possibly by 1887 they had been. Also of interest was Lot 421, described under patterns as:

1877 Copper Fifty Dollars: large head of Liberty left, by Barber, 13 stars surrounding. Reverse similar to double eagle but enlarged: FIFTY DOLLARS below: fine broad planchet (size 32); fine Proof. A prominent Philadelphia dealer recently had one of these and held it at $300, which alone will give an idea of the great rarity of this remarkable piece: this fact, however, has not influenced the owner to place any limit whatever on the piece, which will be sold on its merits solely; *first and only one ever offered*. [$20]

Several later lots are representative of the eclectic nature of Charles White's holdings:

Lot 436: Original steel hub die for California octagonal $50 gold piece (1850): eagle on a rock, with upraised wings, long ribbon in beak: shield, arrows, olive branch in talons; perfect.[132] [$2.20]

Lot 437: Hub die for pattern $10 (or a Half Do.), head in circle of stars; unfinished.[133] [$1.00]

Lot 438: Hub die for small bust of Franklin, perfect.[134] [$0.25]

Harlan P. Smith's Later Career

As it turned out, the second part of the Charles White Collection was the last of Harlan P. Smith's catalogs under his own imprint. Later in the same year, 1887, he joined forces with David U. Proskey in the New York Coin & Stamp Company. In due course, the pair handled many fine collections at auction, among which were the cabinets of R. Coulton Davis, Lorin G. Parmelee, Francis Worcester Doughty, and George D. Woodside.

To quickly touch on each of these sales, as they were all numismatically significant: Davis, a Philadelphia druggist, had close ties to the inner circle of coiners at the Mint and thereby acquired many interesting rarities, especially in the pattern series, for which he wrote the first numismatic check list. The holding of Boston bean baker Parmelee crossed the block—or at least some of it did, as the owner bought quite a bit back—in June 1890 and at the time was considered to be the most complete cabinet of U.S. coins ever formed (however, the collection of the late T. Harrison Garrett of Baltimore was more important, but its contents were not generally known). Doughty was a writer of children's fiction, student of large cents (in particular), and a couple of decades later would become a screenplay author. Woodside, whatever his vocation may have been, was a hobbyist of refined numismatic tastes who acquired many gems.

As for Smith, he departed this earthly sphere on March 2, 1902. His private collection was auctioned a few years later in May 1906 by the Chapman brothers and, among other things, included an 1822 half eagle, one of just three known to exist. The next month, the same catalogers offered the balance of Smith's coins, after which Samuel Hudson Chapman and Henry Chapman dissolved their partnership which had been formed in June 1878. Later, both brothers conducted many illustrious auctions separately.

George W. Rice's Passion

Acquired: 1890s to 1906 • **Dispersed:** After 1906, especially 1911 •
Numismatic hoard: 1856 Flying Eagle cents

Of all American rarities of the 1800s, the 1856 Flying Eagle cent is one of the most famous. The Mint struck somewhat less than 1,000 of these as patterns for wide distribution to newspaper editors, congressmen, and others to acquaint them with the lighter-weight, smaller replacement for the time-honored "large" copper cent. Made of a new copper-nickel alloy, the new cents weighed 72 grains.

The obverse was designed by James B. Longacre, who copied Christian Gobrecht's flying eagle motif used on the illustrious silver dollars of 1836. The reverse was Longacre's own "agricultural" wreath, which consisted of corn, cotton, and tobacco leaves and was used earlier on the gold $1 and $3 pieces of 1854. These pattern cents captured the fancy of collectors, and a great demand arose for them.

The 1856 Flying Eagle cent,
one of the United States' most famous rarities.

Luckily, the supply would not remain quite so limited. Within the next few years, Mint Director James Ross Snowden (who served 1853–1861) sought to acquire Washington tokens and medals for the Mint Cabinet in preparation for a special ceremony dedicating the Washington display to take place on February 22 (Washington's birthday), 1860. Snowden announced that restrikes of certain pattern cents—including the Flying

Eagle—would be available to interested collectors, these in trade for desired Washington pieces.

This was just the beginning of restriking, of course; soon, it became a big business that had nothing to do with trading. A criticism of the practice arose among dealers (in particular) and collectors, and the activity went "underground." Still, restrikes of 1856 Flying Eagle cents continued to be made through at least the early 1860s and perhaps later, and all told, an estimated 2,500 or so 1856 Flying Eagle cents were made, considering originals and restrikes combined.

All through the late 1800s, the 1856 Flying Eagle cent continued to be an object of desire for just about every amateur collector. While the other two (regular) issues of Flying Eagle cents of 1857 and 1858 were inexpensive and easily obtained—and while all Indian Head cents from 1859 onward presented no problem either—the centerpiece of the small cent collection was the 1856. By the 1890s, examples were selling for several dollars apiece.

Among the many who clamored for examples of this piece was George W. Rice of Detroit, who in the 1890s and early 1900s took a fancy to the rare 1856 Flying Eagle cent and ultimately amassed a hoard of 756 pieces. Many of these were sold in 1911 and went into another hoard, that of John Beck, Pittsburgh industrialist (see "John Andrew Beck," page 98).

Note that while the Rice and Beck hoards were the most famous holdings of this coin, there were several smaller accumulations formed over the years. Just about everyone *enjoyed* owning an 1856 Flying Eagle cent. Perhaps reflective of this sentiment, dealer Abe Kosoff stated in the 1960s that it was good luck to have an 1856 Flying Eagle cent as Lot No. 1 in an auction sale, and from time to time his catalogs had such a feature.

Virgil M. Brand

Acquired: 1880s to 1926 • **Dispersed:** After 1926 • **Numismatic hoard:** Just about everything

A wealthy Chicago brewer, Brand began collecting coins in the 1880s and continued until his death in 1926.[135] Along the way he acquired more than 300,000 coins of all descriptions. He was a hoarder *par excellence*, and his holdings included six 1884 trade dollars (only 10 were minted), one or more wooden barrels filled with Uncirculated Civil War tokens, gold coins by the thousands, and more.

His coins were dispersed for decades after his death by his heirs—his brothers Armin and Horace—and their descendants. These provided a nice "working stock" for many coin dealers in the 1930s, 1940s, and 1950s, New Netherlands Coin Co. among them.

Major auction sales featuring some of Brand's U.S. rarities were held in 1983 and 1984 by Bowers and Merena Galleries via the Jane Brand Allen family and the Morgan Guaranty Trust Co., New York, for which David E. Tripp acted as numismatic advisor.

Virgil M. Brand.

David U. Proskey

Acquired: 1880s to 1928 • **Dispersed:** After 1928 • **Numismatic hoard:** U.S. minor coins

Entering the coin business in 1873, David Ulysses Proskey worked with several partners and firms over a long period of time and remained active until his death in 1928. One account stated that "he had a habit of going to the Mint early each January and buying up the stock of unsold Proof coins."[136] He seems to have concentrated upon minor Proof coins—those of the cent, nickel three-cent, and nickel five-cent denominations. Most likely, he ignored Proof gold.

Probably most of his purchases were in the 1880s, an era in which minor Proofs were made in record quantities. In addition, Proskey acquired various coins in quantity from other sources, included bank-wrapped rolls. By the 1920s he had a vast holding of rolls and early Proof coins, many of which are said to have passed to F.C.C. Boyd, who in turn sold many to Howard E. MacIntosh of the Tatham Stamp & Coin Co., Springfield, Massachusetts.[137]

The biography of Proskey makes interesting reading. An active dealer from the 1870s onward, he had what might be called situational ethics. A competitor, Édouard Frossard, stated Proskey had a "level head and an India rubber conscience."

David U. Proskey had large quantities of minor coins of the late 1800s and early 1900s. Shown is a 1908-S Indian Head cent.

A.M. Smith

Acquired: 1870s–1890s • **Dispersed:** 1935 • **Numismatic hoard:** Proof sets, etc.

Anders Madsen Schmidt, who was born in Denmark on February 4, 1841, came to America at an early age and changed his name to Andrew Mason Smith.[138] Today, he is best remembered as A.M. Smith, rare-coin dealer.

Before becoming a professional numismatist, he did many other things including sailing aboard merchant ships, selling chickens in New Orleans, and serving in the Civil War with the 13th Indiana Regiment. (If anything, the backgrounds of many professional numismatists have been diverse!) In 1872 he married Botilla Elberg, a fellow Dane he met when he was working on the transcontinental railroad. The couple had six children.

A.M. Smith (from an 1886 catalog).

Also in 1872, Smith became a wine dealer in Salt Lake City. The business must have yielded sparse trade due to the Mormons' abstinence from alcohol, and by the middle of the decade he pulled up stakes and relocated to Philadelphia. There, he must have learned numismatics rapidly and well, for by 1879 he is said to have issued his first price list, and in 1880 he published a quarterly numismatic newsletter.

By the mid-1880s a guide he had written about the Philadelphia Mint had gone through several editions. Interestingly, he also published *Luck of a Wandering Dane* under the pseudonym of Hans

Lykkejaeger in 1885. This work—price 25 cents, "For sale by all news dealers"—seems to be a combination of his biography and fantasy.

Once a wine dealer, always a wine dealer, it may be. In any event, in 1886 he moved to Minneapolis, where he became a dealer in spirits and a saloonkeeper until about 1905. Still, he kept his hand in the coin trade, at least casually, and ordered Proof coins from the Mint for several years thereafter. He died in 1915.

About 20 years later, his widow Botilla had a Minneapolis bank consign her late husband's coin stock to dealer M.H. Bolender. In June 1935 Bolender published an announcement for his sale of June 29:

> The [A.M. Smith] collection contains over 3,000 large cents worth up to $100 each; over 2,000 half-cents worth up to $50 each, over 1,500 U.S. Proof sets. It is a well-balanced collection, with something in every series.
>
> It was shipped to me by express in five boxes weighing nearly 500 pounds. Over 15,000 coins in the collection. It required two weeks for Mr. Bolender and a capable assistant, and two stenographers, to appraise them.

Smith's 1,500 Proof sets from the 1800s (which certainly ranks him as among the most prominent of dealer hoarders) and other properties were offered in Bolender's sales numbered 98, 99, and 100, all three of which included Proof sets dated 1878 through 1889 and 1893. Included in one sale was the unique 1884 Proof set, which was struck in copper and included the 1884 trade dollar in that metal. This would suggest that Smith had close ties to the Mint at one time, as would also be suggested by his having published multiple editions of his visitors' guide to that institution.

Ella Wright Sells Some Delicacies

Acquired: Late 1800s and early 1900s • **Dispersed:** After 1935 • **Numismatic hoard:** Dealer stock

After the death of Philadelphia dealer Henry Chapman (1859–1935), his inventory was liquidated over a long period of time by his secretary, Ella Wright. At the 1937 American Numismatic Association convention held in Philadelphia, dealers converged upon the erstwhile Chapman office and bought many standard dates and mintmarks of U.S. coins, generally ignoring a vast stock of important tokens and medals.

In 1942, John J. Ford Jr. was in the earlier years of his numismatic career (born in 1924, he had begun by collecting Lincoln cents as a pre-teenager in 1935). Every few weeks in the early 1940s, Ford took the train from New York City, where he was working with Stack's at the time, to Philadelphia to visit various dealers and buy coins. During this time and in the course of several visits, Ella Wright reached into some long-hidden reserve stock and sold him a large group of prooflike gem 1857 Liberty Seated quarter dollars, perhaps 50 to 100 in all; many prooflike gem 1858 Large Letters Flying Eagle cents; and several or more Proof 1921 Morgan dollars, the last from a stock of a dozen or so that Ella Wright said Chief Engraver George T. Mor-

gan "made especially for Mr. Chapman." Proof Morgan dollars were not in demand by collectors at the time, thus Ford bought only a few.[139]

It seems that Wright on her own account bought many Proof 1942-P Jefferson nickels, as Ford also bought thousands of those from her, each wrapped in a cellophane sleeve.

Wright had thousands of Proof 1942-P nickels.

Leftover Chapman inventory coins and other properties went to many diverse locations in the 1940s and 1950s, including to Edmund A. Rice (of Cranbury, New Jersey) and David M. Bullowa (Philadelphia professional numismatist).

Colonel Edward H.R. Green

Acquired: 1920s to 1936 • **Dispersed:** Late 1930s and early 1940s •
Numismatic hoard: U.S. gold, rarities, currency, etc.

In the annals of American coin hoarders, Green's name is in the first chapter, right along with Virgil M. Brand. However, while Brand was a consummate numismatist and devoted much if not most of his life to the hobby, Green had many other interests to divide his attention.

Born to eccentric millionairess Hetty Green (nicknamed "The Witch of Wall Street"), Green became heir to her fortune and enjoyed life as a roué and hoarder. On July 10, 1917, he married one of his favorite "ladies of the night," Mabel E. Harlow. Green collected and hoarded with a pas-

sion and acquired boats, real estate, a railroad, stamps (he once owned all 100 of the 1918 24¢ "Jenny" airmail inverts), and especially coins.

At the time of his death in 1936, it took eight armored cars to move his collectibles, the numismatic part of which was estimated to be worth $5 million.[140] Among his coins were all five known 1913 Liberty Head nickels (these were later sold through B.G. Johnson of the St. Louis Stamp & Coin Co. to Eric P. Newman, and by the end of the 1940s were dispersed in the market). In 1996 I was auctioneer at the podium when one of those coins—a beautiful Proof—sold for more than a million dollars, being the first coin in the world to achieve such a level. The record was soon broken.

Green also owned a reported seven specimens of the famous 1838-O half dollar; hundreds of $5 gold coins (his favorite gold denomination; some of these were sold through Stack's in the early 1940s); "many" 1796 dimes including numerous choice examples;[141] 200 or more Uncirculated 1796 quarter dollars;[142] and a vast holding of early large-size American currency notes including great rarities. Unfortunately, Green stored his paper money in cellulose nitrate album pages which caused the notes to break apart into bits and crumbs. Moreover, some of the albums purchased by Newman caught fire due to spontaneous combustion of the unstable nitrate.

Today the Green name is not as remembered as it should be, perhaps because his collection was not memorialized by catalogs. Much of it, however, passed through Burdette G. Johnson and into the hands of another great collector, Eric P. Newman.

COLOR PLATE XIII

Lot 807
The Fabulous 1913
Liberty Head Nickel
Finest Known

Green once owned all five of the known 1913 Liberty Head nickels. Shown is a page from the 1996 sale of the Louis E. Eliasberg Collection.

A.C. Gies, Numismatist and Hoarder

Put away: Early 1900s • **Dispersed:** In the 1930s • **Treasure:** Rolls of coins of the early 1900s

A Civil War token issued by Buffum's Mineral Water in Pittsburgh, die variety known as Fuld PA-765-C-1a. In the 1800s, the final "h" in the city name was sometimes omitted, as on this token.

August Charles Gies was born on January 29, 1855. He grew up and spent the whole of his life in the Pittsburgh area. He began collecting in 1864, at age nine, when he sought to obtain one each of the various Civil War store cards issued by merchants in and near Pittsburgh. These were generally called "copperheads" and circulated at the value of one cent.

By the mid-1870s he had increased his interest in Civil War tokens to the extent of visiting many of the firms and individuals that had issued them, Buffum's Mineral Water being an example. His cabinet contained nearly 100 different store cards, including numismatic strikes in brass, German silver, and white metal. This implies that he was probably a customer of the shop of Murdock & Spencer of Cincinnati and its successors, which provided pieces for collectors after the war ended.

In 1879, Gies moved to East Liberty and gained employment with a jeweler. On January 31 of that year, he joined the Western Pennsylvania Numismatic Society; he remained active with that group for the rest of his life. He also participated in the activities of the American Numismatic Society and, later, the American Numismatic Association, attending a number of the latter group's conventions.

In 1883, Gies opened his own jewelry business, and he remained active in the trade until 1941. He was mentioned frequently in accounts of this business, sponsored trophies, and prepared exhibits. His coin collecting interests were varied, and to maintain a level of enthusiasm he added new series now and again. His collection of large copper cents was probably impressive, and his collection of pioneer and territorial gold coins included rarities. However, it was half dollars by die varieties that were his main forte, and he pursued these for many years.

An account published in October 1924 of the August American Numismatic Association convention held in Cleveland reveals that for half dollars Gies had some competition: "Messrs. Gies, Kraft and Locker, of the Pittsburgh, Pennsylvania, district, were inseparable conventionites. They are a long-time friendly trio of rivals for die varieties of the early United States half dollars. What they did not have on public display they had to show in private. Based on their combined collection of varieties, a new 'type table' is in order."

The reference is to John W. Haseltine's 1881 *Type Table*, that being the standard reference for the series. Stack's auctioned the Gies collection of half dollars on Saturday, October 19, 1940. Included were the two obverse varieties of 1796 half dollars and two half dollars of 1797, each described as Very Fine.

Gies felt that new coins as they were issued were an excellent store of value. It has been said that he had at least one bank-wrapped roll of every issue from cents to half dollars from 1900 onward, and that may be true. And apart from the foregoing, circa 1935 Gies happened upon a marvelous group of 1,000 half cents dated 1854, each coin being a bright orange-red, typically with some minor spotting. These 1854 half cents were distributed in numismatic channels in due course and provide the source for most such pieces seen today.

Gies died in 1944.

A 1901-S quarter.

The Ford Commentary

As to his bank-wrapped rolls, stories of Gies's holdings grew in the retelling. Did he have *multiple* rolls of rarities?[143] Enter John J. Ford Jr., who as a precocious teenager was hired by Stack's and worked there for a time in 1941 and 1942.

As noted, Stack's—the partnership formed in New York City in 1933 by Joseph and Morton Stack—sold Gies's remarkable collection of half dollar varieties in 1940. Gies also sold quantities of other coins through the firm in the 1930s. I spent much time over the years interviewing Ford on various numismatic matters, including in 1996 concerning his recollections of certain coin hoards. He informed me that accounts of Gies putting away rare rolls of higher coin denominations were "pure hogwash."[144]

Of course, the Stack brothers were not likely to have given the details of past dealings to the ever inquisitive teenaged Ford. As you know by now—having read the preceding chapters—facts can be elusive.

This much is known for certain: in 1941, as his first job when working for Joe and Morton Stack, young John J. Ford Jr. had to catalog cents and other coins from the Gies holdings. Thomas L. Elder may have been involved in the transaction as well. At the time, Ford was given the opportunity to buy some bright red 1854 half cents for $1 each, which he did. These several coins were consigned to my company by 1980 and realized between $2,000 and $3,200 apiece—not a bad investment return![145]

John Zug

Acquired: 1910s–1940s • **Dispersed:** 1940s • **Numismatic hoard:** U.S. minor coins

John Zug, born in Washington, D.C., on May 1, 1869, became interested in coins by the turn of the century. Like many collectors, he was fond of putting away quantities of lower-denomination pieces. Circa 1918 he is said to have disposed of 25,000 1909-S V.D.B. cents for one and three-quarters cents each. He had purchased these at face value from the Mint in August 1909, according to an account.[146]

By 1920, then living in Bowie, Maryland, Zug was in the mail-order rare-coin business. He continued to buy quantities of coins as they were issued, and at the same time would parcel some of them out to his customers. Thus, his "numismatic hoard" was more of a large working inventory, a movable hoard, so to speak. Interestingly, when Treasury Secretary Henry Morgenthau Jr. (successor to numismatist William H. Woodin in that post) formed a collection of commemoratives, he bought them through John Zug.[147]

In time, Zug became well liked and well known. For more than 25 years, he ran full-page advertisements on the inside back cover of *The Numismatist*. He did not leave behind a corpus of coin books, auction catalogs, or philosophical articles (as did Thomas L. Elder, for one), thus he is little remembered today, but he was very highly esteemed in his lifetime, and any comprehensive account of the rare-coin business of the first half of the 1900s must necessarily include him.

John Zug is said to have sold
25,000 Mint State 1909-S V.D.B. cents.

Zug died on October 23, 1949. Among the last letters he wrote was one to Louis E. Eliasberg Sr. of Baltimore, congratulating him on completing his collection of U.S. gold coins by date and mintmark.

William Pukall

Acquired: Circa 1914–1950 • **Dispersed:** 1950s • **Numismatic hoard:** U.S. minor coins

A New Jersey dealer, William Pukall began buying Uncirculated coins directly from the Philadelphia, Denver, and San Francisco mints about 1914, and continued to do so for many years (by which time the Treasury Department in Washington handled sales from the three mints). He seems to have concentrated on Lincoln cents and Buffalo nickels, but he acquired other coins as well, among which were commemorative half dollars from various issuing commissions. He related to me that his orders were often for small amounts and were placed multiple times each year.

At one unknown point he acquired many Proof Indian and early Lincoln cents, nickel three-cent pieces, and Shield, Liberty, and early Buffalo nickels, all wrapped in thin paper tissue as put up by the Mint at the time of issue. Possibly, these came through David U. Proskey, Henry Chapman, John Zug, or John Boss, all of whom had quantities in the 1920s. In any event, Pukall still had many of these coins in the 1950s, by which time there was a ready sale and most remainders were sold to me at the time my coin business was getting underway and was in a rapid growth stage.

Nearly all of the coins approached perfection. The bronze mirror Proof Indian Head cents and Matte Proof Lincoln cents all had hints of iridescent blue toning over their natural color. Also set aside were large quantities of small-denomination foreign coins, although I never bought any of those.[148]

A receipt William Pukall received for an order of 1928 Denver Mint coins in the year of issue.

Frederick C.C. Boyd

Acquired: 1910s–1930 • **Dispersed:** 1950s • **Numismatic hoard:** U.S. minor coins, rarities

New Jersey businessman F.C.C. Boyd, who headed a company that operated newsstands and kiosks in railroad stations, is remembered as one of the all-time great figures in American numismatics of the 1900s. From his office in New York, Boyd purchased quantities of Proof coins from David U. Proskey (and later, the latter's estate). He acquired many bank-wrapped rolls of coins, especially small denominations, at the same time.

Boyd was a major advertiser in *The Numismatist* during this era, although he is best remembered as the owner of what was billed as "The World's Greatest Collection" when it was sold at auction by the Numismatic Gallery in 1945 and 1946. Other sections of U.S. coins in Boyd's collection were purchased *en bloc* by Numismatic Gallery, and were sold to King Farouk in Cairo, Egypt. In addition, certain ex-Proskey hoard coins were sold by Boyd to Howard E. MacIntosh of Tatham Stamp & Coin Co.

In the later years of his life, Boyd sold many of his non-federal coins such as tokens and medals to his close friend, John J. Ford Jr. I purchased many of these pieces from Ford. All were of uniformly high quality. Also involved were quantities of fractional currency notes.

Wayte Raymond

Acquired: 1920s to 1940s • **Dispersed:** 1950s •
Numismatic hoard: Rolls of minor coins, commemoratives, etc.

Born in 1886 in Connecticut, Wayte Raymond became interested in coins as a teenager. By 1908, he was issuing lists of coins for sale. Meanwhile, he put food on the table from his salary as a bank teller.

For a time, a partnership was envisioned with Texas dealer B. Max Mehl, but this did not materialize. Had this come about, the history of the rare-coin trade in America may have been quite different from what is known today. Raymond's coin knowledge and Mehl's marketing acumen would have made for either a sensational partnership, a bitter lawsuit—or possibly both!

Wayte Raymond had quantities of many coins of the late 1800s and early 1900s, including 1914-D Lincoln cents, one of the scarcer varieties.

As it turned out, Raymond formed an arrangement with Elmer Sears and conducted 43 auction sales from 1912 to 1918. Later, in the 1920s, Raymond had his own business and, among other things, handled the $100,000 purchase through art dealer Knoedler & Co. of the James W. Ellsworth Collection; financing was provided by John Work Garrett, who was given first choice of the rarities. In the meantime, Raymond acquired large quantities of bank-wrapped rolls and Proof coins of the 1800s and early 1900s, some of which were apparently acquired from old-time dealer David Proskey.

During the 1930s and 1940s, Raymond ran the numismatic department of the Scott Stamp & Coin Company. In 1934, he launched the expanded version of the *Standard Catalogue of United States Coins and Currency*, the first regularly issued price guide to the American series. This work was the standard text until it was supplanted in 1946 by the *Guide Book*. The last edition of the *Standard Catalogue* appeared in 1957, a year after Raymond's death, and was edited by his protégé, John J. Ford Jr.

And on the topic of pioneering numismatic products, Raymond's line of "National" cardboard album pages, made by M.L. Beistle in Shippensburg, Pennsylvania, made its debut in the 1930s and revolutionized the coin hobby. Now for the first time collecting coins was like filling in a crossword puzzle: empty spaces beckoned and made it instantly obvious which coins were still needed. John J. Ford Jr. related that this enabled Raymond to find an eager market for the untold thousands of dates and mintmarks he had accumulated earlier.[149] Earlier, collectors usually stored coins in two-by-two-inch paper envelopes or in cabinet drawers.

In the early 1950s, Raymond underwrote the expenses of young Walter H. Breen in his research in the National Archives, which led to the finding of much information not previously known to the numismatic community.

Upon his death in 1956, Raymond was mourned as one of the best-liked and most influential persons the hobby had ever called its own. After that time, large quantities of Raymond's coins were purchased by John J. Ford Jr., who sold many to me. I also purchased coins from Raymond's widow, Olga, who took a liking to me. One time in the 1960s, she had F.A.O. Schwarz deliver some stuffed toy animals to my young sons Wynn and Lee, who were staying with me in the Plaza Hotel. She lived in a condo overlooking the East River.

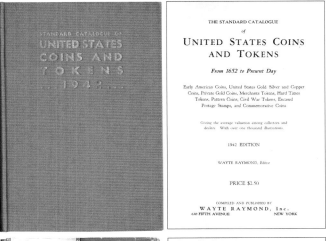
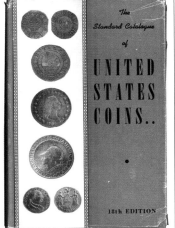
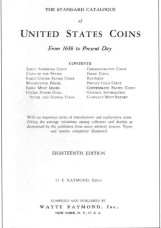

Wayte Raymond's *Standard Catalogue* was the main reference book in numismatics until the advent of the Red Book.

Charles and Ruth Green

Acquired: 1940s and 1950s • **Dispersed:** Late 1950s • **Numismatic hoard:** Proof 1886 quarters

The Chicago husband-and-wife team of Charles and Ruth Green—whose trade style was R. Green—liked the 1886 Proof quarter dollar, of which only 886 were minted. They were determined to buy as many as possible, and by the late 1950s they had acquired several hundred.

I later purchased many of these from Ruth. The quality was very "miscellaneous," as she purchased every Proof she was offered, or so it seemed. No matter, the 1886 quarter is scarce in any and all grades, and they all sold quickly.

As is the case with all of the brief biographical notes of dealers given in this chapter, much more could be written about the Greens—perhaps a project for another time.

Ruth Green loved Proof quarters of 1886 and hoarded them.

Don Corrado Romano's Favorites

Acquired: 1950s and 1960s • **Dispersed:** Unknown • **Numismatic hoard:** 1795 halves, 1878 trade dollars

In Boston, Don Corrado Romano operated the Worthy Coin Company, an issuer of yellow-covered premium catalogs giving prices paid to the public for selected rare coins. As an amusement, Romano took a liking to half dollars dated 1795 and Proof trade dollars of 1878, these being his two favorite issues. Over a period of time he hoarded many.

I visited him in Boston in the 1950s and saw a few dozen of each, but these did not represent his entire holdings. The half dollars were mostly in grades from Very Good to Very Fine.

Don Corrado Romano had hundreds of 1795 half dollars.

MacIntosh Had Much, Lost All

Acquired: 1930s to 1958 • **Dispersed:** After 1958 • **Numismatic hoard:** Quantities of coins

In Springfield, Massachusetts, Howard E. MacIntosh operated the Tatham Stamp & Coin Co. The firm dealt mainly with the general public and sold starter kits, packets, and groups of coins which were sent on approval to those requesting them. In the course of business, he was an eager buyer whenever quantities of U.S. coins became available, as these could be advertised in his newspaper-style catalogs and other listings, and he would have the ability to fill multiple orders.

At one time in the 1950s, I purchased about 300 scarce 1879 Liberty Seated dimes from him, each coin being a prooflike gem. Later, in August 1958, I received a telephone call from MacIntosh, who asked me if for about $200,000 I would like to buy his entire rare-coin inventory, which he assured me was worth more than a million dollars. He needed cash for a real estate development deal, he said, and would sacrifice his coin stock. I was skeptical that a coin dealer would offer such a discount for worthwhile material and did not investigate the matter further. On September 5, 1958, he became despondent and took his own life with a handgun, a tragedy.

It turned out that his coin inventory included many bank-wrapped rolls of Indian Head cents; early mintmark issues of Lincoln cents (including 1909-S V.D.B.); Proof coins of the 1800s; large quantities of 1936 P-D-S Rhode Island commemorative half dollars; certain Boone commemoratives of the 1930s by the hundreds (perhaps he had made a deal with the distributor, Frank Dunn, in that era); and much more, many pieces

having come from F.C.C. Boyd. The MacIntosh coins were later mainly sold through New Netherlands Coin Company.

Yes, the total amounted to well more than a million dollars. This is one opportunity that given the chance to take again, I would approach much differently.

Among the MacIntosh holdings were large quantities of low-mintage commemorative half dollars, such as this 1939 Arkansas issue.

Michael Kolman Jr.

Acquired: 1950s • **Dispersed:** 1960s • **Numismatic hoard:** 20-cent pieces

In the 1950s, Cleveland dealer Michael Kolman Jr. took a fancy to worn 20-cent pieces, which were selling for about $5 to $15 each, depending upon the grade. He amassed many hundreds of them, perhaps even more, while his colleagues looked on with amusement.

Kolman had the last laugh, however, for in the 1960s there arose a great interest in collecting coins of the 1800s by design types—when new albums were marketed by the Coin and Currency Institute and by Whitman Publishing Co.—and the value of his worn 20-cent pieces multiplied several times over!

This account may be related to one told by David Sundman, who heard from a West Coast dealer that in the 1960s another dealer had accumulated "nearly a bag" of worn 20-cent pieces. The "grapevine" is very active in numismatics!

A lightly worn 1875-CC 20-cent piece. This denomination was minted for circulation only in 1875 and 1876.

Cornering the 1881 Gold $1 Market

Acquired: 1950s–1972 • **Dispersed:** 1973 • **Numismatic hoard:** 1881 gold $1

A Proof 1881 gold dollar.

David W. Akers reported this cache:

> In 1973 Paramount International Coin Corporation handled an interesting group, the Leon Lindheim hoard of 1881 'Proof' gold dollars. Lindheim, a well-known Cleveland collector and numismatic writer (with a regular column in the Cleveland *Plain Dealer*), set out to acquire as many specimens as he could from the reported 87-piece Proof mintage for

this date, and over a period of many years he purchased many "Proofs." As it turned out, only eight coins were actually Proofs, the rest being circulation strikes. Some were fully prooflike circulation strikes, but many others were only partially prooflike or were frosty![150]

Apart from the Lindheim holdings, there have been other hoards, often larger, of 1881 gold dollars. In the 1950s, John J. Ford Jr. dispersed of a quantity of 300 pieces. Over the years I have handled hundreds each of 1879, 1880, and 1881 gold dollars, all Mint State and prooflike, and many of 1889, these being frosty and lustrous.

Years ago many prooflike pieces were sold at auction and elsewhere as Proofs, as distinguishing characteristics of Proofs were not widely known. Later, David W. Akers and Walter H. Breen were among those who published identification information for Proofs.

John Andrew Beck

Acquired: 1880s to 1924 • **Dispersed:** 1970s •
Numismatic hoard: 1856 Flying Eagle cents, $50 gold, etc.

John Andrew Beck, a collector of many items and owner of one of world-class displays of rare and unusual smoking pipes and Indian relics, hoarded 1856 Flying Eagle cents and ultimately amassed a hoard of 531 pieces, some of them from the Rice Collection. Beck, a Pittsburgh industrialist, also liked $50 gold "slugs" and bought dozens. Ditto for certain other types of coins.

Beck was born in Chestnut Ridge, Pennsylvania, on January 5, 1859. He spent part of his youth with his parents in Texas, but the family was forced to return to the Keystone State because of Indian depredations. In Pennsylvania, Beck's father engaged in drilling for brine (a source of salt) near Pittsburgh.

At the age of 10, John collected his first coins, and after that time the passion grew. Following

California $50 gold slugs were a Beck specialty.

his father's death, John and his brothers maintained the brine business. John eventually acquired a 100% interest in the enterprise, and for a number of years traveled around western Pennsylvania selling salt, groceries, and other goods. Later, he went into the oil business and was probably acquainted with numismatist John M. Clapp, who in the late 1800s and early 1900s was an oil producer in the same state.

By that time, Beck decided that if owning one coin was nice, having two or three was better yet, and owning 100—and often many more—was a great accomplishment. The most famous "popular rarity" of the time was the 1856 Flying Eagle cent, and he set about tracking down as many as possible, including with a massive postcard-mailing campaign to collectors and dealers. At one time he had a standing order to pay $10 each for any and all offered. Another passion of his was $3 gold coins, as were $50 gold "slugs" from the Gold Rush era.

His activity attracted wide notice. In March 1906, *The Numismatist* reported that Beck was about to corner the market in $50 gold pieces of various types, and that his collection had some 56 of these "slugs," including nine Wass, Molitor pieces and one Kellogg & Co. coin.

Beck passed away on January 27, 1924. His estate was handled by the Pittsburgh National Bank & Trust Company (Beck had been a director of several banks which were merged into this institution).

In ensuing decades, many dealers and others knocked on the bank's door seeking to see or buy the Beck Collection, but to no avail. Finally, in the early 1970s, the administrators consigned the Beck estate to Abner Kreisberg and Jerry Cohen, who had a coin store on North

Beverly Drive in Beverly Hills and also conducted auctions under the name of Quality Sales. The arrangement was that the partners could decide how the coins would be sold. Most were presented at auction, but the 1856 cents were sold privately—nearly all to dealers and in groups.

Being a friend of both Abner and Jerry, I was called in when the dispersal began. I found that nearly all were somewhat dull, some with gray "vault grime," mostly ranging from about PF-58 to PF-62 or so (per today's grading; no such refinement of numbers existed in the 1970s). There was not even one sparkling, brilliant piece in the lot.

The coins were carefully conserved by removing grime and grease with solvents that did not disturb the metal. The result was that the entire hoard was sold quickly without disturbing the market price at all.

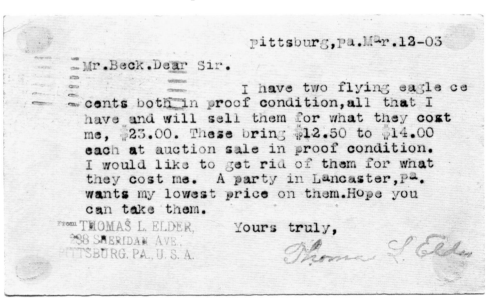

Beck made mass mailings of postcards to dealers and collectors in his search for 1856 Flying Eagle cents and other favorite hoard items. Here dealer Thomas L. Elder offers two coins to him.

The Missing Numismatist

Acquired: Before 1961 • **Dispersed:** 1977 • **Numismatic hoard:** Quantities of coins and notes

In 1966, under court order, a safe deposit box belonging to Charles Coble of Wichita, Kansas, was opened. Coble, who lived in a shack and who was remembered by neighbors for his picking up

old bottles, had disappeared in 1961. Later, the "shantytown" where he had lived was bulldozed by the Urban Renewal Agency in an effort to "eliminate blighted areas."

Not much could be learned about Coble, and no local coin collectors or dealers could recall him when asked at a later date. Seemingly, he disappeared without a trace, leaving valuables behind. His safe deposit box . . .

> . . . was brim full of coins and bank notes. On the table before the group was spread a pirate's delight hoard: gold coins that glowed under the overhead light, bank notes crisp and notes greatly worn, a pile of silver dollars. The more than 90 notes looked to viewers like a small fortune. More than a third of them were obsolete bank notes including three Republic of Texas notes, a $500 and two $50 bills. . . . The hoard contained a set of the $1 Legal Tender bills of 1869–1917 missing only the scarce 1874. . . . In the box were 59 silver dollars from 1797 down to 1928.

Many of the pieces were numismatically identified and were in two-by-two-inch paper coin envelopes marked with sale prices. Years later an announcement was made that the coins were to be auctioned on January 14, 1977.[151]

After Charles Coble disappeared, his safe deposit box yielded numismatic treasures.

Hoarding Panama-Pacific $50 Gold Coins ———

Acquired: 1970s–1980s • **Dispersed:** Unknown •
Numismatic hoard: 1915-S Pan-Pacific $50 gold pieces

Coin World, July 16, 1980, reported that seven years earlier a small group of investors led by Chicago insurance executive Arthur L. Weiner sought to invest $250,000 in rare coins. "The intent going in to this was to buy the coin we felt had the greatest upside appreciation with minimal downside risks, and we came to the conclusion that the U.S. $50 gold piece was *the* coin. And, we haven't changed our minds," read a quote from the story.[152]

Based upon current market prices, a *Coin World* writer estimated that the investors held between 19 and 26 of the coins, although the owners weren't talking numbers. Mr. Weiner made this further comment: "We went into it for materialistic reasons and not aesthetic reasons, and that's what upsets some of your friends like Dave Bow-

ers, who believes the coin is probably one of the most aesthetic things man has ever created. I don't think so."

An octagonal 1915-S Panama-Pacific gold $50.

Long Forgotten Coins

Set aside: 1800s • **Brought to market:** 1991 • **Treasure:** Liberty Seated silver coins

Friday the 13th can be a lucky day for coin collectors.

On Friday, September 13, 1991, at Christie's auction rooms in New York City a consignment of coins from the estate of Mrs. Sumner A. Parker crossed the auction block. Assets from the Parker family home—known as The Cloisters—in Brooklandville, near Baltimore, Maryland, had been given to found the Cloisters Children's Museum of Baltimore.

There was no information concerning how Mrs. Parker, not a numismatist, came into the possession of the coins. From an ancestor? The offering was eclectic—multiples of many coins—suggesting either a dealer's long-forgotten stock

or the holdings of a hoarder. The term "Baltimore Hoard" was used in the catalog. Collectors were delighted to be able to compete for many high-quality specimens from the 1800s and 1900s, among which were these quantity groups:

1879 nickel three-cent pieces (6, Mint State)
1880 nickel three-cent pieces (12, Mint State)
1881 nickel three-cent pieces (10, Mint State)
1862 half dimes (7, Mint State)
1888 Liberty Head nickels (5, Mint State)
1919 Buffalo nickels (20, Mint State)
1882 Liberty Seated dimes (4, Mint State)
1875-S twenty-cent pieces (12, Mint State)
1918-S Standing Liberty quarters (12, Mint State)
1860-O Liberty Seated half dollars (15, Mint State)
Sheets of $5 Federal Reserve Bank Notes from Atlanta, variety known as Friedberg-789, each sheet containing four notes (5 sheets)

A Mint State 1860-O half dollar similar to those in the hoard offered by Christie's.

A Wise Museum Curator

Acquired: 1920s • **Dispersed:** 1995 • **Numismatic hoard:** Scarce coins of the 1920s

Born on May 22, 1856 in Tariffville, Connecticut, Joseph C. Mitchelson entered the family tobacco business after completing his education. At the time, the Connecticut River Valley was a leading producer of tobacco, and Mitchelson was a wholesaler of that then-popular substance. Seeking markets and visiting clients, he traveled widely, including frequent trips to the Midwest and West. For a time he was located in Kansas and had branch outlets in Kansas City and San Francisco. In 1900, he returned permanently to Tariffville and conducted his business from that location,

The Connecticut Museum Hoard contained quantities of coins of the 1900s, including rolls of scarce issues such as 1925-D nickels.

which included the family farm comprising more than 1,000 acres in nearby Simsbury.[153]

In the 1890s and early part of the 1900s, Joseph C. Mitchelson of Tariffville, Connecticut, was also a coin collector and dealer.[154] Actually, he seems to have been a collector first, and if while he was buying coins he needed he saw some interesting duplicates or pieces that his friends wanted, he would buy these as well. Thus, he acquired many coins as duplicates or selling stock. Among his clients was John M. Clapp, oil man and banker from Pennsylvania, whose collection was sold via Stack's to Louis E. Eliasberg Sr. in 1942 for $100,000—a very impressive sum and one rivaled at the time only by the J.W. Ellsworth Collection (which sold for the same amount in 1921 through art dealers Knoedler & Co. to Wayte Raymond and John Work Garrett).

Mitchelson passed to his reward on September 25, 1911, and his collection was bequeathed to the State of Connecticut. Before long, his accumulations—valued at $70,000—were on display in specially constructed vaults in the Connecticut State Library in Hartford. Visitors were dazzled at the display which included sets of Proof gold coins from the second half of the 1800s; colonial rarities; early silver dollars; Fractional Currency; and other treasures.

Provision was made for the collection to be supervised by the state librarian, who was, by legislative authorization, "to continue the Joseph C. Mitchelson Collection of coins, tokens, and medals by adding each year a Proof specimen, or if not so coined, an Uncirculated specimen of each variety of coin minted in the several mints of the United States." As it turned out, in the 1910s and 1920s curator George Godard not only bought one each of certain coins, but acquired numerous duplicates as well. Prominent among these purchases were two examples of the later-to-be-rare 1927-D double eagle; roll quantities of 1924-D and 1925-D Buffalo nickels and Mercury dimes; a roll of 1924-D Standing Liberty quarters; and many other delicacies.

Over a period of time, leading rare-coin dealers and auctioneers beat a path to the steps of the Connecticut State Library, seeking to handle the Mitchelson coins as well as later acquisitions. In 1994 and 1995, the Library decided to deaccession certain coins acquired after Mitchelson's gift. Included were many sparkling gems from the 1920s, among which were the aforementioned nickels, dimes, quarters, and one of the 1927-D double eagles. The nod was given to Heritage Numismatic Auctions, which featured them in a sale held June 1–3, 1996, with the Long Beach Coin & Stamp Exposition in California. Great collector and dealer interest was shown, and intense bidding activity resulted.

The Conneticut State Library.

New York Subway Hoard

Acquired: 1940s–1950s • **Dispersed:** 1991–1996 • **Numismatic hoard:** Various U.S. coins

In 1942, a working dime die at the Philadelphia Mint was begun with a 1941 master die and completed with a 1942 master die, thus creating a working die that had the previous figure 1 visible under the final 2. This resulted in a variety of dime that became known as the 1942, 2 Over 1 overdate.

In early 1943, it was found that many of these dimes had been released in the New York City area. Token sellers operating kiosks in the subway system began to scan their change, and over a period of time several thousand 1942, 2 Over 1 overdates were found and sold into the numis-

The 1942, 2 Over 1, overdate dime created a lot of excitement when the variety was first discovered.

matic market, where they eventually became worth several dollars or more apiece.

This spurred a certain token seller named Morris Moscow, a clerk on the D Train, to learn more about coins. Soon, he was seeking other scarce coins including 1916-D Mercury dimes and 1914-D Lincoln cents, a rewarding pursuit that continued for much of the next 20 years. Many of his finds were marketed through his brother-in-law, George Shaw, a Brooklyn rare-coin dealer who advertised in the *Numismatic Scrapbook Magazine*.[155]

Numerous pieces remained unsold after Shaw's death and from 1991 through 1996 were acquired in a series of transactions by the Littleton Coin Co. amounting to about $250,000. Morris Moscow himself lived until 1993.

Highlights of the hoard included:

1914-D Lincoln cents (44)
1912-S Liberty Head nickels (160)
1918-D, 8 Over 7, Buffalo nickels (29)
1916-D Mercury dimes (241)
1921 dimes (600)
1921-D dimes (450)
1942, 2 Over 1, dimes (166)
1896-S Barber quarters (29)
1901-S quarters (8)
1913-S quarters (20)
1916 Standing Liberty quarters (19)
1918-S, 8 Over 7, quarters (3)

Barber half dollars

1892-O (14)	1897-O (16)	1913 (29)
1892-S (8)	1897-S (10)	1914 (25)
1893-S (6)	1898-O (22)	1915 (36)[156]
1896-S (17)	1901-S (16)	

Other Littleton Finds

The Subway Hoard was the latest in a string of interesting "finds" acquired over the years by Littleton Coin Co.[157] For example, in the mid-1980s, the firm acquired from a dealer 90 unsearched bags of worn Liberty Head nickels (minted for circulation from 1883 to 1912), which amounted to exactly 360,000 coins! David Sundman, president of Littleton Coin, stated that his staff found about 25 specimens of the rare 1885 Liberty Head nickel when they sorted through the trove, and other scarce and rare issues were found as well. The intermediary in the transaction related that for many years the nickels had been stored in a barn under a pile of hay.

The same person who held those nickels is said to have another 100 bags of Liberty Head nickels and more than 100 bags of Indian Head cents!

The New York City D Train as it appears today.

Stack's 123 West 57th Street Hoard ————

Acquired: Circa 1960 onward • **Dispersed:** 2014
Numismatic hoard: More than 1 million U.S. coins

In March 2014 this news release created headlines all across the hobby:

> One of the greatest American coin hoards ever to be found has been acquired by Stack's Bowers Galleries. The hoard, which contains over a million coins, ranges from bags of large copper cents and Capped Bust half dollars, to Morgan and other silver dollars. Other coins include Washington quarters, Franklin half dollars, bags of Flying Eagle and Indian Head cents, nearly 10,000 1909 V.D.B. cents, and more. Most are in circulated grades, and will appeal to collectors seeking coins that are both historical and affordable. The market value is estimated to be well into eight figures, with initial estimates ranging from $15 to $20 million.

> Designated as The Stack's West 57th Street Collection, the coins were obtained in New York City and around the country, then stashed away and never reviewed for key dates or attributed by varieties. Armed guards kept watch as the 30-ton hoard was unloaded from two large transport trucks and transferred into secured vaults. The sorting process has now just begun, and announcements of collection highlights will be made in the upcoming months as the hoard is examined.

> "Going through samples from this collection has been amazing," said Lawrence R. Stack, a founder of Stack's Bowers Galler-

Staff members looking at some coins from the hundreds of bags, boxes, and other containers, more than a million coins in total. Left to right: Jenna Arsenian, Scott Reiter, John Pack, and Andrea Espindola.

ies. "Each of the thousands of groupings has remained sealed as originally closed by the owner. We expect to find many rare varieties and discoveries as the review process continues. I have never seen anything like it, and I am unaware of any comparable hoard of copper, nickel, and silver coins that has ever come to the numismatic market. This will have a profound effect on new collectors coming into the hobby, for the vast majority of the coins will be very affordable — quite a change from the usual business of handling rarities."

It is thought that most of the coins were put in bags starting in the early 1960s. The find generated a lot of excitement, and much of the hoard found buyers throughout the rest of 2014.

However, before sales took place, John Konop of Stack's Bowers Galleries contacted Allen R. Ross and Dennis Fuoss, members of Early American Coppers, Inc., who expressed interest in examining the large copper cents in the holding. Arrangements were made, and Allen paid a visit. John Konop started with an old canvas bag on a cart, labeled *Bag 11 of 14, 29,000 large cents.* Wow!

This initiated a series of visits on Wednesday mornings—which Dennis joined in—spent in a room examining the previously unsearched treasure. Early on, a rare 1796 Sheldon-96 Draped Bust was found.[158]

Allen and Dennis told of their experience in an article in *Penny-Wise.* This excerpt gives some of their general impressions:

> There is little doubt that the coins were "untouched" for a long time. The raw cents came out of the bags coated with a thick residue of dirt and grime which blackened our hands. We quickly resorted to wearing thin latex gloves. The coins were held in bags inside the Stack's Bowers vault, which was not only exhilarating, but a little intimidating at first.
>
> Neither of us had seen this many large cents in one place before. There was absolutely no arrangement to the large cent accumulation, with all types, all dates, and all grades thrown together at random. Our job was to make some sense of all this raw copper stock. Once we had a two-man team, Dennis spent more time with early-date and middle-date cents, while Allen looked at middle-date and late-date cents. . . .

The two "adventurers," if they can be called that, concluded that at an early time some scarce and rare coins that were obvious were plucked out and sold. Meanwhile, the vast remainder were bagged and put away, probably in the early 1960s.

> A large fraction of the large cents in the hoard (70–75%) are dated 1840–1857. Approximately 15–20% overall are dated 1816–1839. Only 5–10% of the coins in the hoard are early-date cents (1793–1814). . . .

Among early-date cents the following were found:

1793 Wreath	1802 (55)	1810 (70)
1794 (36)	1803 (75)	1811 (4)
1795 (32)	1804	1812 (63)
1796 (16)	1805 (14)	1813 (20)
1797 (11)	1806 (7)	1814 (17)
1798 (67)	1807 (77)	
1800 (32)	1808 (24)	
1801 (28)	1809 (12)	

chapter 5

Hoards of Old Copper Cents

Today, few series are more avidly collected than old copper "large" cents minted from 1793 to 1857. Some of these can be pedigreed to old-time hoards, including certain finds mentioned in passing earlier. Interestingly, although the famous Nichols Find and Randall Hoard have been known for a long time and mentioned extensively in literature concerning cents, little is known of the circumstances of their original concealment.

In the early 1800s, the copper cent was the most ubiquitous of all American coins. But since 1857, when these began to be redeemed in quantity by the Treasury Department, many millions of coins have gone missing and remain unlocated. Most probably disappeared one at a time during the era in which they were used. But who knows—perhaps a few hoards are yet to be discovered.

Domestic tranquility (presumably) in the era of large cents, as illustrated in an engraving of the 1800s.

Unwanted Bags of Large Copper Cents

In the news: 1846 • **Treasure:** Cents of the era

An article in the October 1846 issue of *Banker's Magazine*, "Cents as Legal Tender," told this:

> In a case pending before the Baltimore County Court, sitting as a court of appeals, Judge Purviance presiding, a question arose as to whether cents are a legal tender. From the evidence, it appeared that the appellant had tendered, in payment of a debt amounting to upwards of $20, in bags of cents, which were refused.

On the part of the appellee it was contended, upon the authority of a decision of the Supreme Court of South Carolina, that cents are not legal tender in payment of any debt amounting to more than four cents, as the smallest silver coin is a half dime or five-cent piece, and as the Constitution of the United States uses only the words gold and silver.

For the appellant it was maintained that the Act of Assembly of Maryland, 1812, makes the coins of the United States current money, which may be tendered in payment of debts in Maryland, and that cents are as much the coins of the United States as any coins issued from the Mint.[159]

In the course of the evidence it appeared that the tender was not made to a person authorized to receive it, and therefore the case passed off upon this point. The learned judge, however, in the course of his opinion, intimated that no difficulty could exist as the fact of cents being a legal tender, and in support of his opinion referred to a note to *Greenleaf on Evidence*, page 436, an able work, sanctioned by the approbation of the late Judge Story, in which it is declared "copper cents and half cents are established as part of the currency, and by implication made a legal tender, by statute in 1792, Chapter 39, Section 2."

What a treasure these bags of cents would be today!

The William Pickman Hoard

Hidden: Circa 1803 • **Found:** Circa 1856 • **Treasure:** Mint State cents

The *American Journal of Numismatics* published this in July 1875:

About 1856–7 Mr. A.F. Walcott of Salem, Mass., a young collector of coins, was presented with a bag of "bright cents" by a relative, Mr. William Pickman of that city. They had been laid away for very many years—quite forgotten—and when found were as bright as the day they were coined. Of the Mint series there were those of 1795, 1796, 1797, and 1798, and 1803, also a few Massachusetts *Indian Head cents.*

Mr. Walcott exchanged them with various collectors and at the Mint, where they were looked upon with suspicion and inquiries made as to where they came from, &c., &c. We remember that several collectors looked upon them doubtingly, thinking that some expert had been making them. The prices paid for some of these pieces at the present time would astonish our friend if he were in this part of the world.

A.F. Walcott, son of Samuel B. Walcott, later served in the 21st Regiment of the Massachusetts Volunteer Infantry in the Civil War. After the war he was active in gatherings of the Grand Army of the Republic veterans. Was this exchange with the Mint done when he was a "young collector," or was it made later?

The Massachusetts cents would have been of the coinage of that state in 1787 and 1788. The preceding indicates he may have traded some to the curators of the Mint Cabinet. William Pickman, a wealthy merchant, died in Salem on Friday, May 1, 1857, at the age of 82.

The Nichols Find

Hidden: 1797 • **Found:** By 1859 • **Treasure:** Cents of 1796 and 1797

Chances are excellent that if you encounter a Mint State 1796 or 1797 copper large cent, it will be linked by pedigree to the famous Nichols Find (also known as the Goodhue-Nichols Find).

According to numismatic tradition, these pieces came from an original bag of cents obtained in late 1797 or early 1798 by Benjamin Goodhue, who was born in Salem, Massachusetts in 1748 and died there in 1814. Goodhue, a Federalist, was a representative to Congress from 1789 to 1796 and a senator from 1796 to 1800.

If Goodhue obtained the pieces at the Mint, it would probably have been after November 21, 1797, since during 1797 coins were only delivered by the coiner to the treasurer from November 22 to December 18. Blank planchets had been imported recently from Matthew Boulton of Birmingham, England—such planchets being remarkable for their high quality (in sharp contrast to those made within the Mint, often from copper of uncertain purity and often irregular). As a result, coins in collections today, and attributed to this hoard, are apt to have particularly smooth and glossy surfaces.

It is believed that Goodhue gave the coins to his daughters, from whom they descended in the family. Eventually, they were distributed from the Salem area.

A Mint State S-119 1796 cent, probably from the Nichols Find.

One account (Breen, 1952) quotes a rumor that the coins came from Major C.P. Nichols of Springfield, Massachusetts. As is true of many hoards, facts are scarce.

David Nichols of Gallows Hill

In any event, by 1858 and 1859 the numismatic community was aware of the coins, at which time they traded for about $1 each. By 1863 all of the pieces had been dispersed—apparently by David Nichols—now having a market value of about $3 to $4 apiece. Reminiscing about the "good old days" John Robinson, who began collecting in 1857, commented on those coins:

> The older collectors helped us too. David Nichols, who lived near Gallows Hill, would occasionally open the bag of mint-red cents of 1796 and 1797 and give us one of each. The lot came, it was said, from the Hon. Benjamin Goodhue, who received them in part pay for his service in the U.S. Senate. As I remember them, at the time there were about 50 or 60 of each date in the bag.[160]

The assigning of the quantity of 1,000 pieces to the hoard is assumed from Mint records which show that in 1797 the Mint regularly issued cents in bags of 1,000 and boxes of 5,000 coins. As at least several hundred specimens are known to exist today, the 1,000 estimate may be reasonable. On the other hand, it seems unlikely that in 1797 senators would get bags of cents for their pay.

Varieties Included

Today, the typical Nichols Find cent is apt to be glossy brown with somewhat prooflike fields, toned a medium brown. Varieties attributable to this source include 1796 Sheldon-119, 1797 S-123 and 135, and, to a lesser extent, 1796 S-104 and 118 and 1797 S-122(?), 136, and 137.

Specimens of 1798 S-154, not in the Nichols Find, appear to have been struck on planchets from the same Boulton lot and were probably made very early in 1798, possibly as part of a shipment arriving from England on the HMS *Adriana* in spring 1797.[161]

The Randall Hoard

Hidden: Circa 1830s • **Found:** By 1869 • **Treasure:** Thousands of large cents

Of all American coin finds of the 1800s, the most famous is the so-called Randall Hoard, named after a later owner of the cache. Even today, mention of the Randall Hoard recurs with frequency in auction catalogs and sale lists. Probably just about any numismatist who has collected large copper cents for more than a few weeks has heard of it.

Among U.S. large cents of the early years of the Matron Head design, nearly all are very elusive in Mint State—except for the first five years, 1816 through 1820. Today, many of these exist, with

Railroad and station platform of the mid-1800s, of the general type mentioned in certain accounts of the Randall Hoard.

A selection of large cents attributed to the Randall Hoard: 1816 Newcomb-2, 1817 N-14, 1818 N-10, 1819 N-9, 1820 N-13, and a typical reverse.

1818 and 1820 being the most numerous. Such coins are commonly attributed to the Randall Hoard. Note, however, that cents dated 1816 are in the minority and are not even mentioned in some historical accounts of the hoard and may be from another source.[162]

While notices about the Randall Hoard differ in some details, it seems to be the consensus that a *small* wooden keg (or perhaps more than one keg) filled with Uncirculated copper cents was found beneath a railroad station platform in Georgia after the Civil War, but before autumn 1869. The cents may have been hidden during the war years to prevent discovery, or they may have been stored in such a railroad facility before that time, possibly as early as the late 1830s.[163] Alternatively, the hoard may have had nothing to do with any railroad platform (as usual, hard facts are scarce).

Walter H. Breen related that in the period between 1816 to 1820, the Philadelphia Mint reused wooden kegs that had been obtained from Matthew Boulton's establishment in Birmingham, England, from which the Mint bought blank planchets.[164] These kegs typically held about 14,000 cents or cent planchets, although Mint records exist of kegs containing 12,000 to 18,000. Since the Randall Hoard coins were described as being in a *small* keg, quite possibly the number it contained was less, perhaps on the order of 5,000 to 10,000 coins. Again, hard facts are lacking.

An early citation (given below) indicates that some 1825-dated cents were included as well, but for a long time specialists (*e.g.*, Walter H. Breen) considered this unlikely, as Mint State cents of that date were very rare and had been for a long time. Also, in his sale of August 16, 1887, under Lot 654, W. Elliot Woodward, stated the Randall

Hoard contained cents from 1817 to 1856, but the latter date was probably a slip of memory.

What the Hoard Contained

Details on this hoard in large part come from the publication in 1869 of an answer to a correspondent. Ebenezer Locke Mason Jr., Philadelphia coin and stamp dealer, published this in his magazine:

L.M. Troy. Beware of bright pennies of old dates. Buy them as restrikes, but not as originals. We can send 1816, 1817, 1818, 1819 (large and small dates) and 1820 U.S. cents for 25 cents each, or fair ones for 2 cents each.

This evoked a response from veteran dealer Edward D. Cogan, who thought Mason wrote more than he knew, and sent this to Dr. Charles E. Anthon for publication in the *American Journal of Numismatics*. The date was January 11, 1870:

My Dear Sir:—

When I presented to our Society, through my friend Mr. Betts, at the last meeting, the cents of 1817, '18, '19, and '20, I did so upon the full conviction that they were from the issues of the U.S. Mint, struck in the years of which they bear the date. Judge, then, of my surprise to find in Mason & Co.'s Magazine, of this month, a caution against buying these pieces as being re-strikes.

I believe all these pieces were purchased of Mr. J. Swan Randall, of Norwich, in the state of New York, and I immediately wrote to this gentleman, asking him whether he had any idea of their having been re-struck from the original die, and herewith I send his reply, which exculpates him from having reason to believe that he was offering anything but original pieces; and from his statement I must say I believe them—as I have from the time I purchased them—to have been struck at the Mint in the years of their respective dates.

Yours faithfully,

Edward Cogan.

Randall's letter, datelined Norwich, January 7, 1870, is given herewith:

Edward Cogan, Esq.
Dear Sir:—

I should not sell coin that I knew or believed to be re-strikes without letting it be known. The bright, Uncirculated cents I have sold of 1817, 1818, 1819, 1820, and 1825, I am very sure *are not re-strikes*. I bought them of Wm. H. Chapman & Co., dry goods merchants of this village, and the head of the firm, W.H.C., informed me that he got them of a wholesale merchant in New York, who informed him that he got them from a merchant in Georgia; that he took them as a payment on a debt, and that the Georgia merchant wrote him that they were found since the war in Georgia, buried in the earth.[165]

Mr. Chapman said to me that he was in New York about the time the cents were received there, and that the merchant who had (ditto) thought they were too large to use, and did not know what to do with them; and that he (Chapman) thinking that his customers here would be pleased with bright cents, offered ninety cents a hundred for them, which was immediately taken.[166]

Chapman & Co. commenced paying them out here, and their bright appearance and old dates made many think they were counterfeits, and they were called "Chapman's counterfeits," and the firm stopped paying them out.

I then went to the store and asked W.H. Chapman if he had disposed of many of his bright cents. He replied, "No. I made a bad bargain," and laughed about their being regarded as his counterfeits.

I then offered to take them at the price he paid—ninety cents a hundred—and he was very willing to let me have them. They were loose together in a small keg,[167] and the great mass of them were of 1818; and a great many, though apparently Uncirculated, were more or less corroded or discolored. I enclose herewith one of the 1817 and 1818, discolored on one side and bright on the other, From this statement, you will see that there can be very little doubt about their being the genuine issues of the United States Mint of their respective dates.

Very respectfully,

John Swan Randall

Randall passed to his final reward on January 1, 1878. Shortly thereafter, from May 6–9, 1878, Edward D. Cogan offered the remaining coins at auction, comprising 85 pieces dated 1817; 1,464 of 1818; 67 of 1819; and 500 "various dates," presumably including many dated 1820.

Becoming Elusive

The typical specimen seen today with a Randall Hoard pedigree is a mixture of bright original red with flecks and stains of deep brown or black. Few if any are pristine (uncleaned, undipped) full mint red.

According to Walter H. Breen's research sponsored by Wayte Raymond in the 1950s, the most readily available variety attributable to the Randall Hoard is 1818 Newcomb-10, followed by 1820 N-13.[168] Curiously, both of these varieties are usually seen with die breaks linking the stars and date. Then following in descending order of rarity, the 1817 N-14, 1816 N-2, and the 1819 N-9 and N-8 are encountered.

By 1988, Breen revised his thoughts and stated that 1816 N-2 and 1819 N-9, although traditionally ascribed to this hoard, were from other groups,

and that the Randall hoard included specimens of 1825 N-9.[169] Inasmuch as a few commentaries from the 1800s did not mention 1816, but did include 1825, perhaps this is nearer the truth.

As late as the 1950s it was not unusual to see groups of Randall Hoard coins in dealers' stocks. By the turn of the 21st century the supply had become widely dispersed, and when seen such coins were apt to be single specimens.

In Retrospect: Not Plentiful in 1859

In 1859 in his *American Numismatical Manual*, Dr. Montroville W. Dickeson wrote of the cents of various years, but at this time the hoard was not known, nor would it be, apparently, until after the Civil War. Thus, in 1859, the 1820 was viewed as being rare. Extracts from Dickeson:

> 1816 cent: They are quite plenty, and can be procured looking as fresh as when they first came from the Mint.
> 1817: The metal of which they were composed is well milled and very hard, which protects the face of the coin. They are hence in a good state of preservation.
> 1818: Plenty and well preserved.
> 1819: Equally plenty, and in good order with the preceding emission out.
> 1820: The slight milling of the edges of these coins render good specimens difficult to be obtained.[170]

The Mansion House Cornerstone

Hidden: 1809 • **Found:** By 1871 • **Treasure:** Cents dated 1809

Thomas Birch & Sons' June 21, 1871, sale of the M.W. Nickerson consignment offered as Lot 183 an 1809 large cent, "One of nine taken from the cornerstone of the Mansion House, Philadelphia; extremely rare."[171]

Years earlier the Mansion House, located at 122 South Third Street, was considered to be one of the leading stopping places in the city, with its well-known contemporaries including the U.S.

Hotel (opposite the Bank of the United States), City Hotel, National Hotel, Washington Hotel, and Congress Hall.[172]

Today, 1809 is considered to be the scarcest date among U.S. large cents of the 1808–1814 Classic Head design. It would be interesting to learn more concerning the opening of the old cornerstone and what else, if anything, was found there.

The Hidden Find

Secreted: Early 1800s • **Found:** Before 1889 • **Treasure:** Large cents

In his catalog of the Charles Stetson Collection, January 21, 1889, W. Elliot Woodward offered as Lot 26 an 1802 large cent, not otherwise attributed, described as: "One of the few known as the Hidden Find, discovered many years ago in Rhode Island."[173]

As A. Conan Doyle did in his Sherlock Holmes detective stories with mysterious otherwise unexplained references such as the "giant rat of Sumatra," Woodward and his contemporaries printed many asides in their catalogs, some of which were probably recognized at the time by the knowing ones, but most of which probably left readers with no clue as to the meaning of the references. A certain William E. Hidden was a well-known antiquarian and numismatist in the late 1800s and early 1900s (his collection was sold by Thomas Elder in 1916); could he have been associated with the "Hidden Find"?

Of course, if the coins had been concealed prior to their finding, this group could be referred to as the *hidden* Hidden Find.

A Mint State cent of 1809.

A Copper-Filled Stump

Hidden: 1800s • **Found:** Before 1914 • **Treasure:** Many large cents

An acquaintance of Walter B. Gould of Winterport, Maine, related in 1914 this account, which would have occurred some time before that date:

> [Gould] had copper cents ever since he was a small child, and before he knew what money was, or copper was, and thinks that copper is to him a magnet, or that he possesses a magnetism for coppers.
>
> At one time in the Maine woods several miles from any habitation he kicked several hundred of the U.S. copper cents out of an old rotten stump where they had been for a great many years. This find was advertised at the time, but no one ever claimed the coins. He never knew, then, who owned the land the stump was on that held the coins.
>
> The most of these cents from that stump were dated before 1849 [although a listing showed some dated as late as 1855], and a few

> were so much worn that the date cannot be seen. For years friends who had seen the cents he had in a showcase in his store would contribute now and then one or more as they happened to get them, and he received some from Eastport (Maine), Oregon, California, and many other places.
>
> Anyway, he has kept all that came to him and bought large lots, until he has now about two bushels altogether of this one kind of coin. For the past two weeks Mr. Gould and his family have worked spare time sorting dates and dies. . . .

In the Gould hoard of many thousands of large cents, somewhat more than 80 to 100 pieces were found with counterstamps of certain merchants (for example, USE / G.G.G. & G.G.G.G., a patent medicine) and were believed to be of special interest and value. In 1914, Gould offered to exchange such counterstamped cents to anyone "for most any relic or coin worth a few cents." The eventual disposition of this vast hoard of copper cents, most of which were not counterstamped, was not recorded.[174]

Note that in this same era, George C. Arnold, proprietor of the Arnold Numismatic Company in Providence, Rhode Island, made a specialty of buying old large copper cents in quantity and had thousands of them on hand.

A Mint State cent of 1802.

An 1853 copper cent counterstamped with USE / G.G.G. & G.G.G.G., patent medicines made in Exeter, New Hampshire.

A typical well-circulated large copper cent (1801 S-220).

This 1856 advertisement by Charles H. Goodwin deciphers certain initials used with his patent medicines and other products.

The South Shore Hoard

Hidden or lost: 1800s • **Found:** By 1910 • **Treasure:** Large cents

In the catalog for the Allison W. Jackman Collection, sold June 28–29, 1918, Philadelphia dealer Henry Chapman presented 42 "bright Uncirculated" United States large cents in the offering of various lots from No. 762 intermittently to 772. These were said to have been from the South Shore Hoard once in the possession of Boston dealer H.E. Morey.

Born in Malden, Massachusetts, on April 21, 1848, Morey became fascinated with coins at a young age—specifically, in 1857, when the old copper "large" cents were discontinued. Although he graduated from the Massachusetts Agricul-

tural College in 1872 and pursued other lines of work, his interest in coins was maintained, and at one time he was offered the curatorship of the Mint Cabinet.

In 1890, he became a professional numismatist and bought out the interests of Boston dealer Henry Ahlborn, who had published coin premium lists since at least 1875. Morey seems to have conducted a business based upon the widespread sale of his coin-buying catalog, a forerunner of what B. Max Mehl would produce in the next century. Along the way, Morey bought many things from the public.[175]

A Sleepy Tramp?

Lost: 1897 or later • **Found:** 1910 • **Treasure:** Miscellaneous coins

Sometime in 1897 or soon thereafter, a tramp or other itinerant may have fallen asleep on the Boston Common, the large park-like area in the downtown of that Massachusetts city.[176]

A few years later, in 1910, workmen "unearthed over 75 coins, not to mention various badges and a gold ring." Although it seems unlikely that such a large number of items would have been lost casually, Howland Wood, a prominent numismatist and a leading figure at the American Numismatic Society, seemed to think so and wrote this:

A "bright Uncirculated" cent of the 1850s.

> The recent excavations furnish an instance of hidden treasure unconsciously deposited by man, for these pieces rolled out one by one from the pocket of someone lying down to rest, and were lost for the time as surely as if they had been purposely buried.
>
> The coins found were of various dates from 1779 to 1897, many of them being old cents of our fathers, struck between 1800 and 1852. Quite a number of foreign coins as well were exhumed.

If such coins were in the pocket of a snoozing citizen, he or she must have been carrying the family coin collection, for by 1897—the latest date on any of the coins—copper large cents of the 1800–1852 era had long since passed from circulation, to say nothing of other coins dated as early as 1779. Likely, the "someone lying down to rest" idea can be dismissed.

The New Bedford Coin Blast

Hidden or lost: 1798 or later • **Found:** 1914 • **Treasure:** Various coins

New Bedford, Massachusetts, is a storied town and figures prominently in American maritime history, particularly in the annals of the whaling industry. In the early 1800s, square-rigged sailing ships departed from there and were often gone on voyages lasting up to a year or two seeking oil for lamps that illuminated homes across the nation.

Years later, for a short time in 1914, the community received attention of another sort. An account datelined New Bedford, January 9, tells the tale:

> Granite workers preparing for a blast near the road between this city and Fall River dug up a bag of coins, some of them dated before the Revolution and none of them dated later than 1798. All were of copper, and it took considerable cleaning before they could be deciphered.
>
> Of the 11 coins two were of the famous old Liberty pennies, dated 1797 and 1798 respectively, and there is one King George [English] penny dated 1774.
>
> As interesting and peculiar as any of them, however, are the old Fugio pennies. These pennies have on one side a design of the sun and below it a sundial. Under this design are the date, 1787, and the legend "Mind Your Own Business," while the Latin inscription, "Fugio," is printed on the edge.[177]

On the reverse are 13 links in a circular chain, emblematic of the 13 original states. These Fugio coins were manufactured in Connecticut by a citizen there, and under a special act of Congress in 1786 and 1787, and there was but a limited number to the issue. They are rare now and eagerly sought by collectors.[178]

No great treasure here, it seems. However, the unidentified newspaper writer at least had access to a numismatic book telling about Fugio cents.

A 1787 Fugio copper (Whitman-4900, Newman 19-M variety).

A Cache of Large Cents

Hidden: 1800s • **Found:** By the early 1940s • **Treasure:** Cents dated 1826

The late Oscar G. Schilke lived on the shore of Dodge Pond in Niantic, Connecticut, in the 1950s and 1960s. Prominent on the numismatic scene for many years beginning in the early 1930s, he would often set up exhibits in banks. These displays served to attract customers to the financial institutions, and for Oscar it meant getting leads which often resulted in his acquiring choice pieces for his collection.

On one particular day a gentleman told him that in the course of doing some work in the Boston harbor area, he came across what was left of an old building which was once the office of a customs agent or toll-taker of some kind—the informant wasn't sure. In any event, cemented into the floor of the structure was a little metal vault or strongbox which, through an opening, appeared to contain a bunch of old coins.

Oscar went to Boston with the gentleman in question and after some effort pried the top off the box to reveal an early-day version of a piggy bank. All in a heap were dozens of large cents dated 1826. Grades ranged from worn nearly smooth on up to lustrous Uncirculated, or close to it. Apparently, some long-forgotten person once took a fancy to this particular date, and each time an 1826 cent was found in the course of commerce it was dropped through a slot in the floor into this tiny chamber. As large cents did not circulate much after 1857 and not at all after the summer of 1862, presumably this cache was formed in the 1840s or 1850s, after which it was untouched for the best part of a century.

Perhaps the original depositor passed away and never told anyone about the cents, or perhaps he realized that their value was insufficient to warrant tearing up the floor. For several years afterward, Oscar Schilke had a good trading stock of cents of this date![179]

The Boston Cornerstone

Hidden: 1821 • **Found:** 1981 • **Treasure:** Cents dated 1821

In 1821, a building was constructed in Boston, and to memorialize the event at least seven new copper cents were placed in its cornerstone. In 1981 the structure was razed, and the long-forgotten pieces came to light.

These coins were attributed as two specimens of 1821 Newcomb-1 and five of 1821 N-2. Both N-1 coins were called MS-63 by the cataloger, while four of the five examples of N-2 were graded MS-63 and the fifth MS-60.

Adding to their appeal was the appreciation of the 1821 cent as the second-scarcest (after 1823) of the later-date large cents. Sold at auction by New England Rare Coin Galleries in 1981, six of

the pieces went to Garry Fitzgerald, and one went to Roy E. Naftzger Jr.[180]

A Mint State 1826 Newcomb-6 cent.

A Remarkable Find of Large Cents

Hidden or lost: 1800s • **Found:** 1996 • **Treasure:** Large cents

In 1996 a feature article by Burnett Anderson in *Numismatic News* told of "a remarkable hoard of 4,700 large cents" that came to light in New Jersey and was acquired by Stephen K. Ellsworth, a Clifton, Virginia dealer.[181] "It appears to have been untouched by two or three generations, and may go back to the 1880s," Ellsworth was quoted as having said.

Grades of the coins are said to range from Good to Very Fine. Among the pieces were a number of scarce issues, including two of the rare 1799 (but none of 1793). The hoard was acquired through New Jersey numismatist Robert W. Miller, who first learned of it from a friend.

It was related that 3,500 of the cents were dated from 1816 to 1839, about 600 in the range of 1794 through 1814, and the balance from 1840 through the end of the series in 1857. The hoard was assumed to have come from somewhere in "eastern Pennsylvania."

A later account in *Numismatic News* reiterated that the hoard had more than 4,000 coins, but 3,559 were from the period 1816 through 1839.[182] The name "Butternut Hoard" had been assigned to the group, from owner Ellsworth's business, Butternut Coins. Details were given in various later issues of *Penny-Wise*, the journal of Early American Coppers, Inc.

A Mint State 1821 cent, rare in this grade.

chapter 6

Hoards of Small Cents

Flying Eagle cents (1856–1858), Indian Head cents (1859–1909), and Lincoln cents (1909 to date) have come in for their share of hoard stories, too. In fact, many families in America have a "hoard" of Lincoln cents at this very moment, if all of the pieces in piggy banks, drawers, shelves, purses, and other places are put together in a pile!

The following are some interesting and quite varied accounts of hoards from the past.

The Collapsing Floor

Stored: 1862 • **Treasure:** Copper-nickel cents

An 1858 Flying Eagle cent. By 1862, millions of Flying Eagle and Indian Head cents were in general circulation.

By early 1862, the outcome of the Civil War was uncertain, and the public began to hoard "hard money." At first, gold coins were saved, and then silver. By early summer 1862, Liberty Seated half dimes, dimes, and other silver issues were nowhere to be seen in commerce. The only federal coins in general circulation were copper-nickel cents. These cents had been minted for circulation since 1857, when the Flying Eagle cents made their debut, to be followed in due course by Indian Head cents in 1859.

In order to make handling of cents easier, many people wrapped them in paper rolls or put them up in packets of 25, 50, or 100 coins, to later use them in trade. American financial historian Neil Carothers told what happened: "Bus companies, theatres, and restaurants accepted these rolls everywhere. A retail store in New York received so many that the floor of the room in which they were stored collapsed."[183]

By the second week of July 1862, no federal coins of any kind were to be seen in circulation in the larger eastern cities. Even the

A country store in the 1800s. The hoarding of coins in summer of 1862, continuing through 1863, caused many hardships for those in the retail and service trades.

once-plentiful copper-nickel cents had disappeared. The lack of cents caused great difficulty with ordinary transactions, such as paying for barber services, newspapers, and public transportation.

Several types of substitutes arose, including printed cards or "chits" valued from 1¢ upward, postage stamps glued to cardboard or put in paper envelopes, postage stamps in brass frames ("encased postage stamps"), federal postage currency notes, and, especially, private tokens.

Cents at a Premium

Copper-nickel Flying Eagle and Indian Head cents continued to be hoarded, probably as late as December 1863, if an advertisement in the December 1 number of *Thompson's Bank Note &*

Commercial Recorder is any indication. At that time, there must have been some demand for these at a premium, enough to warrant this notice:

> *New Pennies*: U.S. Pennies for sale in bags from Ten to One Hundred Dollars, at Ward's Shirt Manufactory, 387 Broadway, N.Y.[184]

Unfortunately for numismatists, such vast hoards of what must have been several tons of copper-nickel Flying Eagle and Indian Head cents are not known to have been preserved, and likely as not, most of the coins were back in general circulation by spring 1864, by which time the shortage of small change had eased.[185]

A Remarkable Hoard of Indian Head Cents

Hidden: 1862 • **Found:** Before 1918 • **Treasure:** 1862-dated cents

On January 25 and 26, 1918, Thomas L. Elder, New York City, conducted an auction featuring the Robert Hewitt and B.C. Bartlett collections. Included was a remarkable hoard of 1862-dated Indian Head cents.

Lot 318 was described: "1862 C. Nickel. Bright. Unc. 125 pcs." This was followed by lots 319 to 323, each described as "Bright Unc." and each containing 100 coins. Then came Lot 324, also of 100 coins, "Unc. Red"—apparently, these were toned. Lot 325 featured 50 specimens, "Unc. Bright."

To this point, 775 pieces of Mint State 1862 cents had been offered. Then followed three lots of 100 coins each, described as containing mixed cents dated from 1857 to 1862, each including "many" 1862 cents, but without the number specified.

Accordingly, it is probable that this hoard sold by Elder consisted of about 1,000 specimens of the 1862 date.[186] Perhaps the accumulation had remained intact from that pivotal era in U.S. history until this sale.

An Indian Head cent of 1862.

Lincoln Cents of 1922

Saved: 1920s and 1930s • **Treasure:** 1922-D Lincoln cents

The Numismatist, July 1937, included this letter from Maurice Scharlack of Corpus Christi, Texas:

> In the interest of throwing a little more light on the much discussed 1922 Lincoln cent, I am jotting down these notes. The United States Mint record shows a coinage of only 7,160,000 coined from the Denver Mint only. This is a comparatively small issue, and the writer feels confident that these pennies will increase in value as time goes on and collectors begin to take notice of their absence from circulation.
>
> I have 25,000 of them packed away in a little wooden chest, and in all due modesty I honestly believe this is the largest collection of this one cent. There is an interesting little fact I want to bring out. I said above that the 1922 Lincolns were minted only at the Denver Mint. Yet you will occasionally find a 1922 plain Lincoln cent (which ordinarily means they were minted at the Philadelphia Mint). In this particular instance I do not believe that is the case, but the only explanation I can give is that the die might have broken or worn off and thus coined a 1922 sans the D. I have in my lot some specimens showing no signs of wear, yet no D is visible, even under a lens. . . .

A later generation of numismatists solved the mystery. Several pairs of dies used to coin 1922-D cents became worn to the point at which the D is barely visible. On coins struck from these, the rest of the obverse is weakly detailed as well. The reverse can range from weak to sharp, as reverse dies were replaced as needed, not necessarily at the same time as obverse dies.

Others were struck from what is known as die pair "No. 2," the obverse die of which had the D mintmark deliberately effaced from the die, in the process of removing some damage that occurred in the coining press. Coins from this pair only are those that are sought as the 1922 "Plain" or "No D" variety. Others are simply "Weak D" coins that should be classified as such.

Today, as you read these words, a high-grade 1922 "No D" cent is extremely valuable. It was not always so. Years ago many veteran collectors dismissed the 1922 "No D" cent as nothing more than a defective coin. *The Numismatist* printed this in May 1945:

> In 1922 the U.S. government coined 7,160,000 Lincoln head cents at the Denver Mint. None were coined at Philadelphia or San Francisco. Some of these cents are poorly struck and show only a faint outline or no sign of the D mintmark. That's all there is to the story. Collectors who feel they "must" own a 1922 cent with an obliterated mintmark should use a tack-hammer on the mintmark of a well struck specimen. With a little practice they will become as expert as the next fellow.

A 1922-D cent without the D mintmark.

The Endicott Hoard of Cents

Put away: Early 1900s • **Disclosed:** 1950s • **Treasure:** Rolls of early Lincoln cents

In the late 1950s, a gentleman who lived in Endicott, New York, located a cache of bank-wrapped rolls of Uncirculated Lincoln cents, mainly of the dates 1910 through 1915. These were all from the Philadelphia Mint, with not a Denver or San Francisco coin in the lot. Each coin was sparkling and brilliant, virtually as nice as the day of mintage, save for a trace of natural light toning.

Many dozens of these rolls were eventually sold to the Empire Coin Company, which Jim Ruddy and I conducted beginning on April 15, 1958, and in due course were distributed into numismatic channels.[187]

A Mint State 1915 Lincoln cent.

"This Is Your Life," Dr. Kate

Gathered: 1954 • **Treasure:** Millions of cents

Stories about caches and accumulations of Lincoln cents have filled coin magazines, newspapers, and popular journals for many years. However, possibly the Lincoln cent hoard to end all Lincoln cent hoards was one described by television producer Ralph Edwards, a friend of mine, who in 1992 responded to a letter about an earlier campaign he started nationwide to gather these coins. In his words:

> I presented "THIS IS YOUR LIFE, DR. KATE PELHAM NEWCOMB" on March 17, 1954. Dr. Kate was a country practitioner serving patients in 300 miles of wilderness in the north woods of Woodruff, Wisconsin. She ministered to wounded hunters, trappers, injured lumberjacks, and Indians. She revived half-drowned vacationers and trudged miles on snowshoes through frozen woods to deliver babies by the light of a kerosene lantern. She was called "an angel on snowshoes."
>
> Dr. Kate Newcomb was born on July 26, 1885, in Wellington, Kansas, daughter of Thomas Pelham and Kate Callahan Pelham, country school teachers. After her mother's death when Kate was three years of age, she went to live with her grandparents in Leoti, Kansas. When her father remarried, she moved to Buffalo, New York, to live with him and his new wife.
>
> Dr. Kate opened her medical practice in Detroit, and in 1920 married a husky auto plant employee, Bill Newcomb. Bill became seriously ill, and Dr. Kate left a thriving medical practice to move to Crandon, Wisconsin (south of Lake Superior), where Bill recovered. An elderly Dr. Torpy pleaded with Dr. Kate to assist him on an emergency case. That was the last case Dr. Torpy was able to take, which left the backwoods without a doctor. Therefore, Dr. Newcomb met the challenge of becoming the country doctor in a remote wooded area with no hospital within a 300 mile radius.
>
> After the show, I told the television audience of the hospital Dr. Kate had dreamed of building which would be opened formally the next Monday morning. I said to the viewers: "It takes a lot of pennies to build and equip a hospital. There's still a construction debt to

pay off, and there's a lot of equipment to buy *before* it can truly fulfill its mission. And that'll take a lot of pennies, too. We thought maybe you folks in our audience would like to share in Dr. Kate's great work. . . . "

Over $250,000 worth of pennies was received in Woodruff, Wisconsin, for the new hospital."

This $250,000 in face value translates to 25,000,000 "pennies," far eclipsing any other hoard of these coins that has come to our attention.

Indian Head Cents in a Virginia Mansion

Hidden or lost: 1880s • **Found:** 1970 • **Treasure:** Indian Head cents

Around 1970, James F. Ruddy purchased a large group of common-date Indian Head cents that had been found in the attic of an old mansion in Virginia. Nearly all were dated in the 1880s— nothing rare here. Each coin was Mint State, indicating that the group had been put away decades earlier, quite possibly at the time of issue.

Upon careful examination, two of the 1888 Indian Head cents were determined by Jim to be overdates, 1888, 8 Over 7, a variety previously unknown to numismatists. Publicity was given to the issue, and every expectation was that additional pieces would turn up. However, years went by, and the variety remained rare. Today, these

two specimens remain among the finest known of their kind, as only a few other Mint State coins having come to light.

A Mint State 1888 Indian Head cent.

Several Other Lincoln Cent Hoards

Additional examples of Lincoln cent hoards include that of Edwin Rommel. In 1979, the Cold Brook, New York, resident deposited in his bank 1 million cents that he had gathered over a period of 20 years. The stash filled 200 cloth bags and weighed three and one-half tons.[188]

Another came to light with a front-page article in *Coin World* in the 1990s that was captioned: "Adage 'a penny saved is a penny earned' becomes lifestyle for 70-year old Ohioan. Eight million cents fill 40 large cans." Ray Amoroso,

collection manager for the Steel Valley Bank in Dillonvale, Ohio, age 70, had been collecting cents since he was five years old. Talk about a long-term interest!

Also of note here, and possibly even more prevalent in the press than accounts of deliberately acquired hoards of cents, are stories of accumulations made out of spite—instances in which someone who disliked paying a debt, such as taxes, fulfilled the obligation with a bucketful or wheelbarrow load of Lincoln cents.

chapter 7

The Incredible Economite Hoard

This is the story of a communal society in Pennsylvania, the storing of the society's wealth in the form of coins hidden away, and the remarkable find of many of the coins in 1878. The following history of the Economy settlement is paraphrased and edited from information received in the 1996 from Raymond Shepherd, curator of the museum complex there, and from related material: Along the way the reason for the dispersal of the Economite Treasure in 1878 will be revealed.[189]

The Economite Treasure

Hidden: Circa 1836 • **Found:** 1878 • **Treasure:** A vast trove of silver coins

The Economite treasure is one of the most remarkable in American numismatics. It was discovered in Old Economy Village, the third and final home of the Harmony Society, a Christian communal society in the 1800s on the Ohio River, not far from Pittsburgh. Best known for its piety and industrial prosperity, the Society believed in the economic use of time, material, and labor.

A half dollar of 1795, variety known as Overton-117.

The story of the community begins in 1804, when the Harmonists (later also called Economites) followed leader George Rapp (1757–1847) to the United States from Ipptingen in southwest Germany to seek religious and economic freedom. A group of nearly 800 farmers and craftsmen under the official title of Georg Rapp mit Gesellschaft, or "George Rapp and Company," settled first in Butler County, Pennsylvania, establishing a settlement named Harmony and staying for 10 years.

The Society then relocated to Posey County, Indiana, and created a new settlement, also named Harmony. During the group's time there, there was apparently some unrest about the sharing of property, and in 1818 George Rapp burned the book containing the list of original contributions to the Society in an effort to help quiet the problem. The Harmonists stayed in this location for another 10 years and then vacated in May 1824, after which the Indiana facilities were assumed by Robert Owen, a wealthy Scottish cotton manufacturer who paid $150,000 for the property and established the utopian community of New Harmony there to explore his "New Moral Order."

Finally, the Society moved to the aforementioned Ohio River location, which was referred to differently over the years: names included Economy, Harmony, OEkonomie, Harmonie, Harmony Village, and Economy Village. *Harmony* may have been the most used in the early years, while *Economy* was the most used in later times, including today.

Note that most (but not all) Harmonists adopted celibacy in 1807 in order to purify themselves for the Millennium or Christ's 1,000 year reign on earth.[190] They worked for the good of the Society and received what they needed to live simply and comfortably. Rapp himself claimed to have a special connection to God and His messengers, including the angel Gabriel (who, it was said, visited Rapp personally and left two footprints in a stone preserved at Harmony, Indiana).[191] Another tale of divine contact asserts that the design for one of the church buildings was revealed in a dream. In its final form, the building was 120 feet long and being supported by 28 pillars "of walnut, cherry, and sassafras, varying in circumference from five to six feet, and in height from 21 to 25 feet."[192]

From the beginning of the Society's time in the United States, all of the property was in the name of Frederick (1775–1834), adopted son of the founder and designer of all three towns. For this final settlement in Pennsylvania, the plan was primarily in the form of rectangular blocks separated by streets, with brick communal factory and other work buildings in the center and with houses on the periphery.

Prosperity in Pennsylvania

Rapp's followers worked quickly on the banks of the Ohio upon their arrival, and by winter 1825 the Harmony Society members had constructed cotton and wool factories powered and heated by steam as well as centralized steam laundries and a dairy. Among their number were blacksmiths, tanners, hatters, wagon makers, cabinet makers, wood turners, linen weavers, potters, and tinners. Agriculture was important as well and included the planting of flowers and ornamental shrubs.

The Harmonists developed new technologies for their daily needs and in due course also made quality industrial products, the latter being sold into American commerce. Their output of silk, cotton, and wool goods achieved an outstanding reception in the marketplace, and the silk specifically received gold medals during exhibition competitions in Boston, New York, and Philadelphia.

Meanwhile, the village had many fine facilities, including the Great Hall or Feast House, the second floor of which was given over to Love Feasts held several times a year in celebration of various holidays or simply as occasions for good cheer. The first floor was devoted to the Museum formed 1825–1827 and added to for many years later. Intended for the education and instruction of adults, it contained many interesting and valuable items.

For example, oil paintings signed by Rubens and Mengs and such American artists as Peale, Doughty, and Otis were on view. A collection of plants, mechanical devices (such as an air pump and a static-electricity generator), an exhibit of butterflies, and other man-made and natural curiosities added to the interest. Included in the Cabinet of Curiosities within the Museum were items crafted of precious metals and a fine collection of rare coins. Some of the coins, but not the main collection, were stolen in 1846.

Marquis de Lafayette visited the Museum in May 1825 during his tour of the United States. At the time, he was particularly interested in viewing some of the industries in the Pittsburgh area. Rudyard Kipling and Charles Dickens were among the many other distinguished guests who paid calls on the Harmony Society.

Silver and Gold Coins

Through the years, silver (especially) and gold coins poured into the coffers of the Society, and in due course some of this treasure was cached in various places, including, it is said, in the

Hired field hands cutting hay in Economy Village in the 1800s.

bedroom of the founder. Later, it was stored in three brick vaults. Most probably, a goodly amount of wealth was also on hand from the earlier and quite prosperous days in Indiana.

Records show that on June 5, 1826, a substantial deposit of coins was made, this being in addition to many funds that were constantly being received and paid out and a substantial extra reserve.[193] Those deposited coins may have been the foundation of the Economite Hoard; they were mostly silver issues, denominations not known, but probably mostly half dollars, and consisted of the following:

11 boxes of silver coins, each containing
  $1,000 for a total of $11,000
1 box containing $1,005
2 boxes each containing $1,020
2 boxes each containing $1,025
1 box containing $1,035
1 box containing $1,050
1 box containing $1,056
2 boxes each containing $1,065
1 box containing $1,075

The above separate boxes totaled $11,441 face value. This plus "1 bag of gold" worth $3,567 and the first group of 11 $1,000 boxes added up to a total deposit of $25,008. In the absence of any records to the contrary, I assume that the $3,567 in gold coins represented U.S. issues and probably totaled $3,567.50, for there were no $1 or $3 gold coins at the time, and the total would have included some $2.50 gold pieces.

The above items are the stuff of which numismatic dreams are made. One can imagine that the boxes containing $1,000 face value in silver were filled with newly minted half dollars (most likely), old silver dollars (none had been minted since 1804), or quarter dollars. And for the gold coins, wow! *Anything* in the group would be a numismatic prize today, and any pieces dated in the 1820s would be major rarities!

Further Financial Matters

In 1832, about one-third of the members of the Harmony Society left under the leadership of Bernhard Müller, a self-proclaimed prophet also known as the Lion of Judah, Count de Leon, Proli, and the Archduke Maximilian von Este, among other cognomens. The 1818 burning of the Harmony Society's records was cited as an excuse to escape, and those who decamped demanded cash settlements for what they thought they deserved or had put into the Society. The total sum of $105,000 was decided upon, to be paid in three installments.

Two payments were made, but as signed releases could not be obtained from some of the secessionists, the third payment was denied. An angry mob of former Harmonists subsequently returned to Economy to demand their due, but were repelled by militia. A mill was later destroyed in the village in what was believed by some to be a case of arson, quite possibly by the dissidents. Apparently, Müller later converted some of the $105,000 payment to his own use.

Meanwhile, the Society members did not have a bank, but employed their own system of credits, loans, deposits, bills of exchange, etc., that served the community well. As previously mentioned, a cash reserve of coins was built over a period of time. However, following the payments to Müller and his followers, some changes were in order.

First, George Rapp established a special fund to provide for any such future withdrawals. He told Romelius L. Baker to assemble $500,000 in specie, and the latter brought in large quantities of silver coins and a lesser amount of gold.[194] This goal was accomplished by 1845.

Also, in 1846, money was moved to the three secret vaults discussed earlier. These were located in the cellar of the Great House, which had been home to George's son Frederick until his passing in 1834. After the money was moved, the walls were plastered over to hide the location of the treasure. Once Rapp died in 1847, R.L. Baker and Jacob Henrici were the keepers of the secret cache.

Planning a Railroad

With nearly all Harmonists practicing celibacy and with few new members coming in from the outside, the average age of the members advanced over the years. Youthful vitality was gone by the mid-1850s, and production of silk, cotton, and woolen goods had diminished to just a fraction of what it had been two decades earlier. However, after George Rapp's death the Harmonists turned to new ventures, including railroads, oil, and building the town of Beaver Falls and its industrial complex.

The first of those pursuits came about after a group of promoters tried to develop a railroad along the Ohio River near Beaver Falls in 1874 with little success. That was when Harmonist Jacob Henrici became interested and felt that he could make such a line profitable. Of course, to do this, money was required.

As it turns out, what is known now as the Economite Treasure, publicized in 1878, was probably just a small part of a very large group of silver coins brought out of hiding in the late 1870s to provide financing for the railroad. Karl J.R. Arndt, later historian of the Society, related:

> It will be remembered that Henrici had been George Rapp's trusted agent and assistant at the time when he was determined to collect and bury the fund which he believed he should have on hand as part of the Appropriation of the Second Coming of Christ. Henrici would not have touched this religious fund without the inner conviction that the building of this railroad was a link in the chain of events that would bring on the glorious day when man would be restored to the original image in which God had created him.
>
> Accordingly, Henrici had the money which Father Rapp had buried for that special purpose brought up to the directors' meeting in the Monongahela House. The boxes containing the money were emptied of their contents in the center of the room, forming a large pile of silver, all of which had to be cleaned before it could be put back into circulation.[195]

Details of the Treasure

As to the total scope of the Harmonists' hoards, it seems probable that at one time there were three substantial caches of silver (primarily) and gold coins stored in as many vaults. The Economite Treasure of silver coins here discussed was taken from one of these hiding places. While the single vault in question seems not to have been added to after 1836, deposits of silver and gold coins in the other two chambers apparently continued well past that date, at least into the 1840s, and in 1838 included newly acquired gold English sovereigns.[196] However, it is not known today what happened to the contents of the other two vaults.

As noted earlier, the coins in the 1878 Economite Treasure discovery were mostly U.S. silver issues from 1794 onward—but some foreign pieces were present as well. All pieces were blackened from being stored in damp surroundings for more than 40 years. After their discovery, they were all cleaned to remove tarnish.[197] It seems that earlier issues dated from 1794 through the next two or three decades showed evidence of wear, but it is likely that many coins struck in the 1820s through 1836 were Uncirculated.

At the time of the discovery, the viewers of the coins did not know the details of how they were gathered and hidden. Word of the find spread, though some newspaper stories erroneously stated that the coins had been hidden a cellar in 1863 to avoid capture by Confederate raider General John Hunt Morgan.[198] Of course, the contents reveal that the coins were hidden in 1836 or shortly afterward. If, indeed, any coins were quickly hidden in advance of Morgan's anticipated depredations, they must have been other than those forming the Economite Treasure discussed here.

An account of this find published in the March 1881 issue of *The Coin Collector's Journal* is numismatically detailed:

The Economite Treasure

Our worthy correspondent, Mr. Jos. M. Lippincott, has furnished us with particulars concerning the long secreted treasures of the Harmony Society at Economy, Pa., of which we have written an odd line heretofore, but lacking positive information we could say but little. The aforesaid gentleman has kindly obtained for us all the points to be desired, in particularizing just what kind of coins and their number, which will be of great interest to all collectors. When we consider the many years during which the quantities were being amassed, especially during the earlier years of the Mint, we may safely judge the rarity of the respective dates by the quantity of each discovered in this vast amount.

Mr. Lippincott had the pleasure of examining the entire lot soon after its recovery from the underground vault, in the latter part of 1878. . . . When the silver was brought to light it was black or tarnished from oxidation, and our correspondent says, "sore fingers were plenty in Economy" from cleaning the coins, as all were scrubbed before sold or circulated. Before their great value was discovered, two half dollars of 1796 and one of 1797 and several other dates were paid out at face value.

Mr. Morrison, cashier of the Economy Savings Institution, furnished our correspondent with the information; consequently we regard it as authentic. The amounts[199] are as follows:

Quarter Dollars
    1818 to 1828: 400 pieces.

Half Dollars
1794: 150	1803: 300
1795: 650	1805 over '04: 25
1796: 2	1805: 600
1797: 1	1806: 1,500
1801: 300	1807: 2,000
1802: 200	1815: 100

Common half dollars 1808–1836:
    111,356 pieces

Silver Dollars
1794: 1	1798 Small
1795: 800	Eagle
1796: 125	reverse: 30
1797: 80	

1798 Large Eagle	1799: 1,250
reverse: 560	1800: 250
1799 5 stars facing: 12	1801, '02, and '03: 600

Foreign silver (French, Spanish, and Spanish-American), total face value: $12,600

Total face value of the hoard: $75,000.00

A well-known dealer purchased the scarce dates, $4,000.00 face value, for $6,500, and the 1794 silver dollar for $22.

Our readers here have all the facts; the coins are now scattered all over the country, and it may be safe to say that less remain in Economy than at any other point.

Postscript

After the unearthing of the Treasure, the economic vitality of Harmony continued to wane as its members aged. By 1880, the average age was 70. Many, if not most, had simply run out of energy. By 1890, the Society was experiencing severe financial difficulties.

Jacob Henrici died in 1892, after which John Duss (1860–1951) was in complete charge. During this time, most assets "disappeared."[200] The state of Pennsylvania endeavored to take over the remainder of the property in 1894, and after protracted litigation became heir in 1916.

Today, the village is a 16-acre site administered by the Pennsylvania Historical and Museum Commission. Structures built between 1824 and 1830 house more than 16,000 Harmonist objects which are exhibited and can be viewed on self-guided tours.

As of 1996, the Old Harmony Village Museum had the following half dollars, the gift of Ms. Christiana Knodeler in 1975: 1817, 1818, 1819, 1821, 1823, 1826 (2), 1827 (2), 1828, 1833, 1834, 1835, and 1836 (2).[201] Although there are no specific records, it is believed that these half dollars were kept locally over a long period of time and are survivors from the 1878 Economite Treasure.

chapter 8

Silver Coins from Various Places

Interesting finds here and there, beginning with a long-time numismatic enigma.

The Mysterious 1815 and 1825 Quarter Dollars

Hidden or lost: 1825 or later • **Found or distributed:** Sometime 1825–1881 • **Treasure:** 1815 and 1825 quarters

One of the greatest unsolved mysteries, at least for lovers of numismatic esoterica, pertains to a hoard of certain U.S. silver quarter dollars of the Capped Bust type.[202] The identity of the hoarder is not known today, although in the 1880s some information must have been available to the knowing ones. It is possible, although not particularly probable, that the aforementioned Harmony Society may have had something to do with it.

Or perhaps Latin and English school prizes are relevant to the enigma. Then, there is the matter of Lafayette and the Erie Canal . . . theories abound!

An 1815 quarter with the mysterious E counterstamp above the head and a close-up view of the same.

An 1825 quarter with the somewhat rarer L counterstamp.

Sound confusing?

Well, it is, and has been for a long time.

These curious quarter dollars bear the dates 1815 (one die variety, known to specialists as Browning-1)[203] and one of the three die varieties known of 1825 (B-2, the 1825, 5 Over 3, overdate).[204] During the 1815–1825 period many different die varieties of quarter dollars were coined, but only these two varieties bearing two different and widely separated dates concern us here.

Specifically, the coins that concern us are certain of these two varieties known today with one or the other of two letters, E or L, carefully counterstamped above and close to Miss Liberty's head. Most often seen are 1815 quarters with the E counterstamp. The letters are both from related punches—thin cross members and uprights and each with light serifs—and, in view of their relative consistency of impression and location were probably all done by the same person(s) at the same time.

Moreover, as only two die varieties bearing these marks are known, and as presumably hundreds or more pieces were originally counterstamped, the coins must have been taken from groups of Uncirculated coins from specific press runs that had been accumulated or stored somewhere, and counterstamped no earlier than 1825. If coins had been retrieved from circulation, other dates such as the large-mintage 1818 and issues through 1824 surely would have been involved. Further, among 1825 quarters there would have been some of the Browning-1 and 3 variety in addition to the counterstamped B-2 examples known to exist of that particular date. Thus, a hoard originally consisting of Uncirculated coins is indicated.

Debut at a Haseltine Sale

Karl Moulton, who has been studying these counterstamps carefully, reports that the first auction appearance he has been able to find in an extensive search of catalogs beginning with those published in 1859 was in a Captain John W. Haseltine sale of December 12, 1881, offering an 1815 quarter dollar with an E counterstamp, the coin described as Uncirculated. From that time onward, examples in sales were numerous, and nearly 20 pieces crossed the block in 1882 and 1883. This is rather curious, considering their absence earlier.

It should be noted that John W. Haseltine's *Type Table*, actually the miscredited work of J. Colvin Randall and essentially an auction sale conducted on November 28, 1881, did not include any E or L counterstamps.[205] On the other hand, I—being a collector of counterstamps of various sorts, but mostly large copper cents, since 1955— recall that in the 1950s and 1960s, quarter dollars with these letters were considered to be "mutilated." Thus, while a specialist with an academic bent might have taken an interest, the casual buyer was apt to ignore one of these in favor of acquiring an "undamaged" piece. Over the years, I have cataloged my share of quarter dollar collections, and only infrequently has a specialist been interested in counterstamped pieces.

Accordingly, it is *likely* that 1815 and 1825 quarter dollars with E or L counterstamps were known in numismatic circles prior to the 1880s but were not considered worthy of notice in auction catalogs. Of course, such words as *likely*, *possible*, *maybe*, and *perhaps* have been attached over the years to most discussions of these curious counterstamps.

Woodward Takes Notice

Indeed, the philosophy of viewing these counterstamped pieces as being mutilated or damaged was hardly new when I first learned of such pieces in the 1950s. In his auction of the Blanchard Collection, December 11–12, 1882, W. Elliot Woodward—coin dealer, druggist, and historian who lived in Roxbury, Massachusetts—suggested that such counterstamped quarter dollars were from a "recent, mutilated find."

Further, in his October 16–18, 1882, sale of the Prof. J. Grier Ralston Collection, Lot 323, Woodward mentioned the hoard tangentially: "1815 [quarter dollar]. Barely circulated; it will be noticed that this is not one of the inexhaustible lot, stamped with the letter 'E' or 'L' above the head; rare."

Thus, as an "inexhaustible lot" certainly implies a hoard, these interesting quarter dollars of 1815 and 1825 are included in the present book.

I'll mention here because the previous extract attests to the notion: Woodward, the most talented rare-coin cataloger of his era, was as good an iconoclast as the best of them. Then, and sometimes now, if a particular rare-coin dealer didn't think of something first, or felt he was upstaged, the result was "sour grapes," Aesop's early equivalent of today's "not invented here" syndrome.

Presumably, if the "recent, mutilated find" had come to Woodward first, the commentary would have been different. Recall (see chapter 1, "The Boothbay Harbor Find," page 22) that in 1880, Woodward expressed some degree of enthusiasm in handling Pine Tree shillings that were found in a cove on the seaside, and had been corroded to the extent that they had lost half their weight. Quite possibly, if Haseltine had handled them, rather than Woodward himself, these would have been candidates for the "mutilated" adjective.

As it was, the estimable cataloger from Roxbury continued his animus toward these counterstamps, even stretching the truth a bit and also denigrating the counterstamp *in absentia*, as in his sale of June 29, 1885, Lot 560, a quarter dollar: "1815 Unc.; the obnoxious letter E or L stamped above the bust on all other known quarters of this date is happily wanting on this." In actuality, there were many other 1815 quarters without either an E or an L. In his sale of June 28–29, 1886, the counterstamp received a similar knock:

"Lot 348: 1815 The obnoxious letter is absent over the head; very good, scarce."[206]

Note that in more recent times, counterstamped coins have come into their own due to enlightenment and interest on the part of many people, the expansion of the Token and Medal Society, and the publication of a reference book on U.S. and Canadian counterstamps by Dr. Gregory Brunk. Today, there are many instances in which a counterstamped coin is worth more than an unstamped one, sometimes *much more*.

However, with regard to the 1815 and 1825 quarter dollars with the stamped E and L letters, these in higher grades tend to sell for a bit less than their unmarked cousins.

Theories and More Theories

If the counterstamps on the quarter dollars of these two dates had been intended to advertise a person or business or to commemorate an occasion, certainly something more than a single initial or letter would have been used. A quarter dollar with an E or L would have no meaning to someone encountering it later. However, it could have been used as an admission check or identification of some type.

For many years it was suggested that these were notations to identify the weight of the coins, with L meaning the coin was *light*, E referring to *extra* or *excess* weight.[207] The only problem with this theory is that careful weighing of such counterstamped coins does not disclose any significant deviation from the standard, and E-stamped pieces are not heavier than L-marked coins.

Walter H. Breen in his 1988 *Encyclopedia*, p. 340, suggests that they may have been school prizes, "E = English, L = Latin, which would account for the high grade of survivors; they were kept rather than spent." However, what about school subjects such as arithmetic and reading? For my part, I will dismiss the prize idea, although I will be the first to stand corrected if any documentation should ever be found.

Other related E-L letter-word pairs could be devised and have been suggested by numismatists, as Early-Late (or Earlier-Later, such as seating times in a dining hall or aboard ship), Elephant-Lion (attractions at a circus), etc.

Another idea concerning the counterstamped quarter dollars: The E and L letters could have indicated ownership, possibly by two family members, if the coins were stored for a long time. In that way if some were stolen, they could be easily identified. This idea is not as foolish as it might seem at first consideration. Realize, for example, that businessman and collector James Vila Dexter (1836–1899) boldly counterstamped his surname initial D on the reverse of his most prized coin—an 1804 silver dollar—to give it permanent identification.[208]

Mark Hotz Commentaries

The *John Reich Journal* carried two articles relating to these quarters by Mark Hotz in 1987 and 1990, the first accompanied by a separate, related commentary by Bill Subjack.[209] In 1987, Hotz examined existing theories and proposed one of his own: that in order to improve the quality of strike, coin presses were adjusted "Left," "Right," or no adjustment ("Even"). The same writer observed that "the counterstamped issues are at least 15 times rarer than the same dates without counterstamps," which would seem to infer that in W. Elliot Woodward's era of the 1880s there had been a flood of counterstamped pieces on the market, thus making non-counterstamped pieces seem rare, but in the century or more since then, the true rarity ratio has become apparent.

In the same 1987 venue, Bill Subjack mused that the E and L could have referred to changes in the minting technique: "Could the E stand for 'Edge collar die reeding?' Could the L mean 'Lathe' application of the same reeding?"

In 1990, Mark Hotz re-explored the subject. R.W. Julian had advised him that in the 1890s, assistant treasurers of the United States "did stamp gold and silver coins with an L to indicate light weight." This may shed light on the origin of the old and now largely discounted theory that the E meant "Extra" or "Excess" weight and L referred to "Light." After discussing several other ideas, Hotz remarked that the weight and school prize theories did not seem logical with regard to the 1815 and 1825 counterstamped quarters, but he had no definite answer, and the mystery still remained.

Contemporary America

I suggest that the answer may lie in American history, and that the counterstamping was done either to identify these coins at a later date (for example, if they were stolen or fell into the hands of an enemy—much like the HAWAII overprints on World War II currency—thus they could be declared invalid), or to serve as a pass or admission check for use at a one-time event (25¢ being a popular price for certain amusement and transportation services at the time).

One historic occasion that called for several such one-time events was the return visit of Marquis de Lafayette, French hero of the American Revolution, from 1824 to 1825. Declared by Congress to be "The Nation's Guest," the marquis was honored with celebrations in many eastern cities. Could the L be related?

Of course, one would need to find an E connection as well. (E)conomy, the Harmonists' settlement in Pennsylvania (see chapter 7, "The Incredible Economite Hoard," page 125), springs to mind; and for the juxtaposition of L and E, consider that Lafayette visited that settlement

toward the end of May 1825. Besides, the Harmonists just might have had wooden boxes filled with Uncirculated quarter dollars dated 1815 and 1825, as vast quantities of coins were stored for long periods of time at Economy, and it is an easy supposition that coins the Harmonists had marked in 1825 could have been stored for decades in wooden boxes, and then brought to light for the first time in 1881.

Per contra, although E could have been used for Economy, the town was also called Harmony (or Harmonie) in the mid-1820s, although the Harmony name was usually reserved for the two other communities the Rappites established before moving to their final location in 1824.

Another occasion which could potentially be connected: In 1825, the 360-mile Erie Canal from Albany to Buffalo, New York, was opened amid much celebration and fanfare. Could the E be related? One would need to find an L connection as well. Donald Davis has noticed that E and L are the first and last letters of (E)rie Cana(L).[210]

In June 1825, Lafayette visited that waterway and traveled some distance on two vessels, the Rochester and the Governor Clinton. Special notice was paid by Lafayette to Lockport, which had recently been constructed and already boasted a large hotel and a newspaper. Thus

Erie Canal.

there is an Erie-Lafayette connection and also an Erie-Lockport pairing.

Seemingly, it is possible to go back and forth on the E-L situation all day long!

Before leaving Lafayette, it may be of interest to note that E and L counterstamp speculation aside, his 1824–1825 visit to America did have many provable numismatic connections. Hundreds of large copper cents were counterstamped with his image on one side and that of George Washington on the other, as were a lesser number of half dollars and some other denominations as well.

Also, on June 17, 1825, the marquis was the honoree of the Bunker Hill Monument Association at the Revolutionary War battle site near Boston, this being the 50th anniversary of the military engagement. Lafayette, with tens of thousands in attendance, participated in the laying of a cornerstone which contained, among other things, "Coins of the United States" (per an 1825 program); Comitia Americana medals of George Washington (two varieties), John Egar Howard, and John Paul Jones; medals of Benjamin Franklin, Thaddeus Kosciuszko, and Christopher Columbus; and "specimens of old Continental money."[211]

What is Known, What is Assumed

The observable realities seem to be as follows:

1. The counterstamping was done at a single time by one or more persons in 1825 or later.

2. A hoard of several hundred or more Uncirculated quarter dollars from 1815 and 1825 was on hand when the counterstamping was done. The estimate of several hundred is assumed as an extrapolation of the dozens of auction appearances of the counterstamps over the years. Karl Moulton reported that there have been about 100 auction offerings since World War II and, of course, many before that time.[212]

3. Nearly all known pieces described in the literature and known to several interested numismatists are in higher grades such as Extremely Fine, About Uncirculated, and Uncirculated.[213] The occasional Very Fine coin could have remained in circulation for years after the 1880s.

On the other hand, most known 1815 and 1825 quarters without E or L are in lower grades from Good to Very Fine (although higher-grade pieces exist, they are in the minority). This suggests that counterstamped coins may not have been released into general circulation in 1825 or in the immediately following years, but were kept in storage until circa 1881 and then distributed via numismatic channels or even released into circulation at that time.

Silver coins had been hoarded by the public beginning in the spring of 1862, and it was not until April 20, 1876, that such coins achieved parity with Legal Tender notes and were again seen in circulation. At that time, large quantities of silver coins dating back to the early 1800s appeared, much to the delight of numismatists.

4. Several hundred or more are estimated to be known today, indicating that at least this many were counterstamped. Such would have required a considerable amount of effort and time. Thus, there must have been a purpose for the counterstamping.

5. These pieces were not generally known to numismatists until late 1881 or were not published until that time, after which time offerings became numerous.

What is the answer? At present, no one knows. What are your ideas? Sherlock Holmes, where are you?

A Valuable Wedding Present ___

Hidden or lost: 1800 or earlier • **Found:** Late 1800s • **Treasure:** Early half dimes

The Numismatist, August 1892, included this:

Mr. Wm. E. Woodward related that at one time he bought a roll of 50 half dimes which was one of the wedding presents of an old lady 90 years of age. They were all dated before 1800 and were as bright and sharp as if just coined.

The old lady had laid them away and never disturbed them. The idea of contributing to an old ladies' home induced her to part with them. Mr. Woodward realized as high as $100 for some of them.

A Flowing Hair half dime, one of two designs that might have been present in this hoard.

A Draped Bust, Small Eagle Reverse half dime, the other design which might have been present in this hoard.

Secret of the Old Porter Mill ___

Hidden: 1800s • **Found:** 1906 • **Treasure:** American and Spanish silver coins

On November 9, 1906, the Portland, Maine *Evening Press* published this:

Two Maine townships and two prominent families are in a complicated tangle that is almost a feud over $1,250 in Spanish and American coins of ancient date which have been found buried in old tin cans in the ruins of an old mill on the land of Leonard Hackett of New Vineyard.

It is asserted by the heirs of Alexander Porter, who died a miser fifty years ago, that the money was buried by him. When the money was buried it was in the town of Strong. Later the town boundaries changed and the spot became New Vineyard.

Under the law the town where buried treasure is found may claim and hold one-half of the treasure found and the individual persons making the find the other half. That is to say, unless lawful heirs or the person who concealed the treasure arise and prove their rights to the property.

There are seven direct heirs of Alexander Porter, the children and grandchildren of these being numerous.

Now the Hacketts claim half on their land, the heirs of Porter claim half because he buried it, the town of Vineyard claims half because the Hacketts' land is in New Vineyard, and the town of Strong claims half because the money was originally buried there.

Nothing has been found about what happened to the coins. What little can be found about Porter is unrevealing: his address given as New Vineyard (then a district on the east side of Strong); he was granted a patent on January 23, 1835, for a "Threshing and cleaning machine for grain"; and his "saw mill and clover mill" was located at the outlet of Mill Pond there.[214]

"Souvenir of the Old Porter Treasure. Found on Sept 29, 1906, in the ruins of the Old Porter Mill, New Vineyard, Me., by L.J. Hackett's workmen. The Old Porter Mill burned on Sept. 25, 1906."

Half Dimes and Dimes Near the Mississippi River

Hidden or lost: 1857 or later • **Found:** 1961 • **Treasure:** Half dimes and dimes

The Baton Rouge, Louisiana *State Times Advocate* carried this Associated Press story on June 14, 1961 (this account was also widely printed elsewhere):

> Natchez, Miss. (AP) A group of boys playing near the Mississippi River bank retrieved a small chest floating on the water and threw it out. The impact split the box open, and a stream of silver coins spilled out—touching off a stream of treasure seekers armed with picks and shovels to the spot on the banks of Natchez under the hill.
>
> Police were placed on guard today to keep the hunters from starting a landslide with their picks and shovels. Officers said a man saw what happened when the boys threw out the chest and grabbed it.
>
> The youngsters sold most of the spilled coins—mostly silver dimes and half dimes dating from 1848 to 1860.

The New Orleans *Times-Picayune* printed this story on Thursday, June 15, 1961:

> Natchez, Miss.—Natchez policemen stood guard Wednesday on the Mississippi River

bank at the foot of Silver Street in Natchez-Under-the-Hill to prevent eager treasure hunters armed with picks and shovels from conducting excavations and undermining the street.

Tuesday afternoon a group of small boys playing at the old ferry landing at the foot of Silver Street noticed what appeared to be a small chest which had been washed out of the river bank by the current. The river has been at an extremely high stage during the spring rise.

Not realizing that the chest contained anything of value the boys started tossing it about, and when it struck the ground the impact caused it to break open and a stream of coins spilled out. The boys picked up a number of coins which were sold afterwards to local collectors. They said that a man who had been attracted to the scene grabbed the box with most of the contents and made off in a boat across the river to Vidalia, Louisiana.

The report that buried treasure had been found on the river bank, once the notorious resort of gamblers and river pirates, spread quickly, and treasure seekers rushed to the scene prepared to start digging operations. Wednesday, public works director Ed Spyles and Natchez policemen took measures to protect the bank and street from further digging.

No estimate could be made of the probable value of the old coins to collectors. The coins are all dimes and half dimes with dates ranging from 1848 to 1860.

Later accounts—including one by John M. Kleeberg, who interviewed Larry Bolyer by telephone years later on March 27, 2007—held that the 7-year-old Bolyer was poking around the ruins of an old brick house near the river. A friend, Don Hunter, who was in the area to watch the arrival of the Greene Line steamship *Delta Queen*, happened by and saw the coins. He told others, and soon there was a mad scramble.

The authorities took notice that the find had been made on land owned by the City of Natchez and seized as many of the coins as they could find. No report has been located as to what was done with those pieces seized.[215]

Half dimes and dimes in this hoard were of the Liberty Seated design.

The Mohawk River Hoard

Hidden or lost: 1842 • **Found or distributed:** 2001 • **Treasure:** Mostly American silver coins

One of the more remarkable finds of the early 2000s is what has been called the Mohawk River hoard. In 2001, detectorists using electronic equipment discovered 18 separate groups of coins, about 650 to 700 in total, the latest dated 1842. These comprised U.S. silver coins, mostly half dollars (one cache found below a rotted tree trunk yielded 30 or more half dollars), dated from 1794 (the first year of issue) to 1848; and more than 100 Spanish-American coins, mostly 2-real pieces, dated from 1775 to 1842.

Most of the coins had similar marks reflecting some unknown intent or purpose. "The marks appear as a notch or chisel mark along the obverse rim between the twelve and one o'clock positions, as a round punch in front of or in the obverse portrait of Liberty, or as an oblong gouge in the field in front of the portrait."[216] No similarly marked coins have been reported in numismatic or historical literature. As the coins were privately sold, no die variety attributions were made, and the finders were not identified. Records concerning the hoard are not complete, thus only approximations may be given.

Mike Capawan of Keshequa Coins of Nunda, New York, took an interest in the coins and bought or viewed nearly 350, including from private sources and coin shows. He copyrighted the "Mohawk Valley Hoard" for use in marketing and placed many of his pieces in Numismatic Conservation Service holders with that inscription. These later pieces were attributed as to variety.

The Draped Bust, Heraldic Eagle Reverse and Capped Bust, Reeded Edge half dollar designs might have been represented in this cache.

chapter 9

Silver Coins Go to Foreign Lands

Over the years, many silver coins minted of the United States have been shipped to and later found in foreign lands. Often such pieces return to America to the delight of numismatists. In other instances, no one is sure what happened to them.

The American Silver Nuisance

Exported: 1858–1870 • **Treasure:** U.S. silver coins

Today it is impossible for a numismatist to conceive of tons of Liberty Seated silver coins being a *nuisance*, but that is exactly what a great surplus of them was called in Canada in 1870.[217] There were simply too many of our half dimes, dimes, quarters, and half dollars (but only a few silver dollars) in circulation north of the border.

The story begins in British North America—specifically, in the area that would later become Canada—in the early 1800s. In the absence of a native mint in this region or the production in England of coins especially for the territory, commerce was largely conducted in foreign coins. Among silver issues, most were old Spanish-American coins and various U.S. denominations, with a lesser number being English pieces.

It was not until 1858 that the territory had its own coinage, which consisted of 5-, 10-, and 20-cent pieces in addition to an issue of bronze cents; however, these coins were far short of the amount needed to sustain commerce. Thus, U.S. silver coins continued to come into Canada.

However, there eventually came to be an overabundance of them north of the border. Historian Neil Carothers wrote:

> From 1858 to 1862 a steady stream of subsidiary silver [coins of less than the $1 denomination] went across the border. After the [newly issued U.S.] greenbacks fell to a discount in 1862, the profit on export to Canada became large, and in a short while Canada was overrun with United States silver. When the saturation point was reached in the fall of 1862, the Canadian market was wiped out. . . .
>
> Before the end of 1862, United States silver was at a discount of 3% in Canadian gold. The *Detroit Advertiser* said that the city treasurer of Toronto had half a ton of U.S. silver coins that he could not dispose of. In this country [the United States] a greenback dollar would buy about 80 cents in subsidiary coin. Across the line a Canadian paper dollar would buy $1.03 in the same coin.[218]

Some Canadian merchants would receive U.S. silver coins only at a discount. No one wanted to ship them back to their country of origin and exchange them for paper notes of uncertain value. For a period of years during the 1860s, it was estimated that in the city of Montreal alone there were 30 or more brokers who derived most of their income from trading in U.S. coins in bulk at the rate of more than $80,000 per day.[219]

As U.S. silver coins had no fixed values in Canadian commerce and traded at varying discounts, they were complained about by the public, as

Countless Liberty Seated silver coins piled up in Canada in the 1860s and were considered to be a nuisance! Certainly there would have been thousands of 1853 half dollars, shown here, as this was one of the most plentiful dates.

those holding such coins were always fearful of sustaining losses.

Ironically, such coins disappeared from circulation in the United States around this time, as citizens began hoarding hard money after New York banks stopped paying out gold coins on December 28, 1861, and Legal Tender notes ("greenbacks" not redeemable in coins) were launched in 1862.

What To Do With Them All

In 1869, William Weir, an agent of the Canadian government, made arrangements with merchants to export $2 million worth of U.S. silver coins to New York City to be sold to brokers there. Not long after (January 27, 1870), Sir Francis Hincks, government finance minister, circulated to various merchants and bankers a proposal to fix the rates of U.S. coins at a 20% discount.[220] This resulted in an . . .

> . . . official proclamation, February 12, which fixed April 15, 1870, as the last day of grace for 'the old lady with the broomstick' and other barbarisms of the United States Mint. After that date our half dollars must take forty cents for themselves or give up passports, and all the other coins, even to five cent pieces, in the same ratio.[221]

Throughout 1870, more than $3,500,000 in U.S. silver coins went from Canada to brokers in New York City, causing a glut there, after which additional pieces were said to have been shipped to England as bullion.[222]

Old Silver Coins Reappear

Despite these measures, quantities of U.S. silver remained in Canada, as well as a few Latin American countries to which coins had "fled" in the 1850s and early 1860s. Carothers takes up the story in 1877, by which time the U.S. government had been minting record quantities of silver coins and had recently exchanged about $36,000,000 face-value worth of them for paper money:

Further exchanges of newly-minted silver coins for paper notes were brought to a complete stop by an unexpected and dramatic development. In the winter of 1877 there suddenly reappeared in circulation literally hundreds of millions of the silver three-cent pieces, half dimes, dimes, quarters, and half dollars that had as suddenly departed in 1862. They streamed in from Canada, from Central America, from South America, and from the West Indies. A small quantity, probably, was brought out from domestic hoards. With the value of silver going down and the value of greenbacks rising toward parity with gold a point had been reached where these long absent coins were worth more at home than they were in foreign countries.

The most interesting feature of this unexpected homecoming was the information it afforded as to the fate of the coins in 1862. It showed that they had not been melted or exported to Europe as bullion, although there was a definite profit in melting the coins at that time. They had gone to Latin America, served as local currency for 15 years, and then returned. Sen. John Sherman in 1880 estimated the value of the coins returned in the preceding two years at $22,000,000, and a large amount came back after that time.[223]

Where Are They Now?

No numismatic connection with specific Canadian, Latin American, or related hoard pieces is known today, and, presumably, most of the coins were melted in the 1870s and later. However, the occurrence at one time of large numbers of U.S. silver coins in Canada—a situation that persisted well into the 1900s, but to a lesser degree than in the 1850s and 1860s—accounts for specimens still found there from time to time.

It is appropriate to mention that in the 1860s, when old copper "large" cents were no longer common in general circulation in the United States, there was a glut of these, too, in Canada, where countless thousands were in commercial

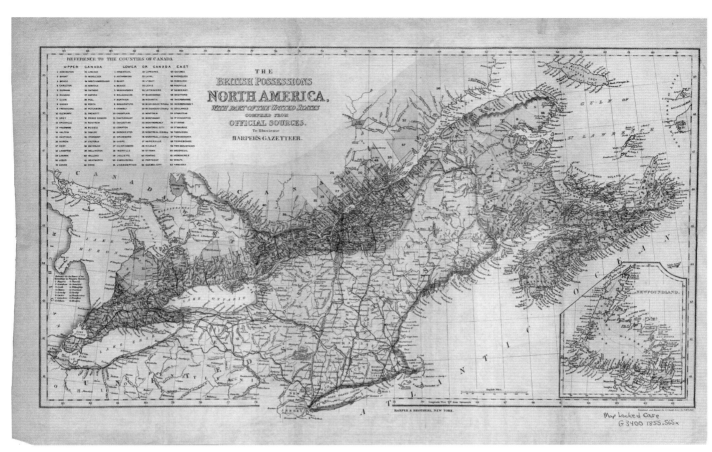

An 1855 map of British North America, part of the future nation of Canada.

channels along with various copper tokens issued by Canadian banks and merchants. Devins & Bolton, Montreal druggists, counterstamped thousands of these cents with their advertisement during the same decade.

U.S. large copper cents of 1810 and 1848 counterstamped by Devins & Bolton in Montreal.

Half Dollars in Guatemala

Exported: Circa 1853–1864 • **Found:** By 1942 • **Treasure:** Half dollars

An 1861-S half dollar similar to
those found in the hoard described here.

This hoard is described by John J. Ford Jr. as follows (also see "Half Dollars in Guatemala—Again, 1956," page 147):

> About 1942 the Stack's dealership [Joe and Morton Stack] in New York City bought a tremendous hoard of Liberty Seated half dollars. These were somewhat oxidized and were said to have been dug up in Guatemala. Perhaps they were buried during the Civil War. Dates ranged from 1853 to about 1864. I remember that there were a lot of San Francisco coins, especially 1861-S, but there was no 1855-S.
>
> I studied the lot carefully and was the first, I believe, to notice that the S mintmarks from this era came in three different sizes. These

coins were retailed to customers, including in price lists I wrote in 1942.[224]

After the spring of 1862, silver half dollars were no longer seen in commerce in the majority of the United States due to the hoarding of hard money during the Civil War. The New Orleans Mint had last struck half dollars in 1861, including when it was in the hands of the Confederacy, and was shut down after the Union retook the city until 1879. However, on the West Coast the story was different: the San Francisco Mint produced half dollars and other coins which, unlike the situation in the East, went readily into the channels of commerce. What's more, paper "greenback" notes were not used in California, and thus silver and gold coins continued to be employed, despite the suspension of specie payments in the East. Any Legal Tender notes brought to California could only be spent at a deep discount in relation to coins—the inverse or opposite of the situation in the East.

Thus, with the San Francisco Mint being the only source during the period, many San Francisco silver and gold coins were exported as payment in international transactions. Presumably, the half dollars that went to Central America as late as 1864 were as part of some type of foreign exchange.

Trade Dollars Come Back from China

Exported: 1873–1878 • **Found:** 1940s onward • **Treasure:** Trade dollars

An 1874-CC trade dollar with Chinese chopmarks.

From 1873 to 1878, many millions of silver trade dollars were shipped to China from the United States. Minted at Philadelphia, Carson City, and (mainly) San Francisco, the pieces weighed 420 grains each, slightly more than the 412.5 grains of a standard silver dollar. While going from hand to hand in China, these trade dollars were usually privately stamped with Chinese figures called "chopmarks" to indicate that they were made of good silver and were acceptable in commerce.

Merchants in China preferred silver coins to gold or any other form of payment, and the slightly heavier weight of the U.S. trade dollar made it a formidable competitor to several other varieties of silver "trade" coins issued by various countries, most notably the Mexican silver pesos. In fact, U.S. trade dollars were so extraordinarily popular in China in 1873 and 1874 that the West Coast mints (San Francisco and Carson City) could for a time not keep up with the demand. However, by 1876 the pieces were plentiful in China. Many of the trade dollars sent there were later sent to India in payment for opium, and in India were melted.[225]

Trade dollars remained legal tender in the United States until July 22, 1876, after which they were used only for export purposes. Domestically, trade dollars sold after that time at prices based upon their bullion or melt-down values, which in all instances was less than face value.

In 1887 and later years, trade dollars could be redeemed for face value under a new law, but those with chopmarks were not accepted. The trade dollars that were taken in by the Treasury Department were melted and mostly recoined into silver dollars (of the current Morgan design). As an example, many 1891-O (New Orleans Mint) Morgan dollars were made from melted-down trade dollars, although most numismatists today are not aware of this historical connection.

Numismatic Considerations

Large quantities of U.S. trade dollars remained for many years in Hong Kong and other Chinese cities. Meanwhile, there was very little numismatic interest in the denomination in the United States, and as a result few pieces were retained in cabinets. Even the Proofs of the 1873–1883 dates, which by Mint policy were included as a part of silver Proof sets of those years, were often spent by collectors who acquired them in those sets or otherwise.[226]

Decades later, the tables turned: in the 1940s, there developed a strong collector market for trade dollars among U.S. numismatists, and many thousands were brought back to this country. The reasons for the new interest include the listing of the denomination by date and mintmark in Wayte Raymond's *Standard Catalogue of United States*

How many silver U.S. trade dollars were sent by Chinese traders to India in exchange for opium?

Coins beginning in the 1930s and, starting in 1946, Richard S. Yeoman's *Guide Book of United States Coins*. With such coins illustrated and described, a desire to acquire them arose.

While most of the repatriated trade dollars had chopmarks, many did not. At the time, it was felt that those with chopmarks were more valuable, as they "told a story" and showed evidence of having been circulated in China—the intended purpose of such pieces. However, by the 1950s the situation had changed, and in the United States trade dollars without chopmarks were considered to be more valuable.

These pieces continued to be imported by the thousands through at least the 1960s, after which most supplies ran out. Later finds were mostly of a few hundred or so coins. Perhaps more are in hiding in China. The world of numismatic hoards and treasures is ever changing, and surprises are bound to occur.

The San Francisco Silver Mystery

Although the story of the trade dollar is well known, relatively unchronicled is the vast departure of other silver coins from San Francisco from the 1850s through 1872, the latter year being just before the advent of the trade dollar.

In 1859, the San Francisco Mint struck 20,000 Liberty Seated silver dollars for export to China.

Beginning in the early years of the Gold Rush, there developed an extensive sea trade with China. As noted, merchants and banks there preferred payment in silver. Gold coins were not popular, and no one would hear of payment in any kind of paper. It was an era of "hard money" deals, and the money wanted was to be in the form of silver coins.

During most of the decade of the 1850s, merchants in San Francisco bought Mexican silver 8-real "dollars" from bullion dealers and brokers, paying a premium for them, as these were readily accepted in China. The premium added to the cost of doing business, though, and so the shipping firms of the city in 1859 petitioned the San Francisco Mint—which had opened for business a few years earlier in 1854—to make silver dollars.

Accordingly, in 1859 some 20,000 Liberty Seated dollars were struck for export purposes, but what happened to all of these 1859-S dollars remains a mystery, as very few have ever been found in the Far East. Quite possibly, many were melted down or shipped to India, the same fate that befell many of the later 1873–1878 silver trade dollars. Even more of a mystery is what happened to what is believed to be the vast majority of other silver coins minted at San Francisco in the 1850s, denominations from the dime to the half dollar (half dimes were not made there until 1863). Most probably, much of the 1855-S half dollar coinage went to China, but what happened to most of them after that is not known. Some circulated in China and were affixed with merchants' and bankers' chopmarks.[227] Apparently, half dollars after 1855-S were not as actively used for hand-to-hand transactions, for examples are not seen today. The Irving Goodman holding of U.S. half dollars found in China (see "Half Dollars from Hong Kong" in this chapter) sheds some light on the matter, but did not include an 1855-S.

Note that most other Liberty Seated dollars made in the last years before the trade dollar's advent—from the 1860s through the early 1870s—were also used in the export trade. Most of these later dates were struck at the Philadelphia Mint continuously, though some others were made at Carson City, New Orleans, and San Francisco.

Half Dollars in Guatemala (Again)

Exported: 1850s–1860s • **Found:** 1956 • **Treasure:** Half dollars

This hoard is described by Walter H. Breen as follows:

> [Half dollar] dates from the San Francisco branch (and to a lesser extent 1863–1865 from Philadelphia) were formerly believed scarce or rare. However, about 1956 unidentified individuals discovered an immense hoard in Guatemala, reflecting massive wartime shipments of coins as bullion.
>
> The Guatemala hoard coins are readily recognizable: they are dated between 1859 and 1865 Philadelphia Mint, and between 1860 and 1865 San Francisco Mint, most often 1861–1862 from either mint, ranging from VF to nearly Mint State, all cleaned with baking soda or some other abrasive.
>
> There were many hundreds of each date, possibly a couple of thousand of 1861–1862. As there were no later date coins in the part of the hoard I saw (at New Netherlands Coin Co., 1956), most likely the hoard was buried about 1865 or early 1866. Either there were no 1866-S No Motto coins, or they were fished out beforehand; but I have seen none that match the hoard coins.[228]

From a numismatic-historical viewpoint, there seem to be some flaws in the above account. Indeed, in the latter decades of his career, many of Breen's supposed facts have been found to have been based on imagination more than research. The problem is that it is sometimes difficult to separate the two in his extensive writing.

The truth of the matter is this: beginning in 1862, the federal government stopped paying out silver coins at par, and Philadelphia Mint coins struck after early summer 1862 and continuing until after 1865 (the latest date seen in the hoard) never circulated. Thus, it is virtually impossible that such pieces, if buried in Guatemala in 1865 or 1866, could have been worn down to the "Very Fine" level.

However, San Francisco Mint silver coins, unlike the Philadelphia issues, *were* circulated at par in the 1860s. Probably, most were shipped to China, but some could have gone to other places such as Guatemala. Still, it seems unlikely that half dollars minted at San Francisco from 1860 to 1865 (the years of the S-Mint coins mentioned by Breen), even if they had circulated on the West Coast, would have been worn so much that they would be only Very Fine. Perhaps there is some other explanation.

For a somewhat similar story, refer back to "Half Dollars in Guatemala," page 144.

Half Dollars from Hong Kong

Exported: 1800s • **Found:** 1960 • **Treasure:** Half dollars

Half dollars were shipped in quantity to China in the 1800s, but unlike trade dollars shipped to the same place, numismatic accounts of such pieces are seldom encountered. A pleasant exception is provided by Superior Galleries' sale of May 1996, Lots 977, 985, and 1000, comprising the Irving Goodman holding of Liberty Seated half dollars brought back to the United States from Hong Kong in the early 1960s.

All coins were described as being "either cleaned or damaged." A few were chopmarked (one 1843, the 1846, one 1863-S, and one 1864-S), but most were not. The offering included the following:

1843 (2)	1865-S (8)
1843	1866-S, With Motto (9)
1846	1867
1848-O	1867-S (2)
1849	1868-S (5)
1854	1869-S (4)
1855-O (2)	1870
1856	1870-S (6)
1857-O	1871 (2)
1858-O (2)	1871-O
1858-S (2)	1871-S (20)
1859	1872-S (2)
1859-O	1873, Close 3
1859-S	1875 (2)
1860-S (4)	1875-S (2)
1861	1876 (6)
1861-O	1876-S
1861-S (19)	1877
1862-S (20)	1877-S (7)
1863-S (16)	1891
1864-S (5)	1895-O (3)

From a numismatic-historical viewpoint, this offering is quite significant. Among other things,

it reflects that many San Francisco Mint half dollars were shipped to the Far East; that Philadelphia Mint coins of the 1862–1873 era (when the Treasury Department was not paying them out, but was keeping them in vaults or selling them at a premium for export) were less frequently used in overseas; and that of the half dollars used there, only a few were chopmarked. As recited in our earlier account of trade dollars, the Chinese strongly preferred silver as a store of value and disdained gold.[229]

Quite possibly, the sample represents coins sent to the Far East over a long period of years. In general, prior to the advent of the U.S. trade dollar in 1873, larger quantities of U.S. half dollars and other silver coins were shipped to overseas than were sent in later years. Note that in addition to pieces sent across the Pacific for commercial purposes, large numbers of silver coins were brought back to China by natives who had worked for several years or more in the United States (such as on track-laying gangs for railroads) and who returned to China to visit or to remain home.

Traders in Hong Kong Harbor in the late 19th century.

In Mexico? On the West Coast?

Hidden, lost, or exported(?): 1874 • **Found:** By 1949 • **Treasure:** 1874-S quarter dollars

In the 1960s, Lester Merkin, a well-known New York City dealer, acquired several dozen choice Uncirculated 1874-S quarter dollars, many of which were sold to me. These examples were mostly brilliant with light silver-gray and iridescent toning and of a quality that in a later time (when grading by numbers became popular) would be an easy call at MS-65 or MS-66. Nearly all were dipped to sell in a market in which "brilliant is best"—a period when toned coins, even if beautiful, were rejected as "tarnished" by most buyers. The story was told that these pieces turned up in Mexico.[230]

In 1988, *Walter Breen's Complete Encyclopedia of U.S. and Colonial Coins* was published and contained this brief comment (p. 355) indicating another origin:

> A hoard of 80 to 100 Uncirculated 1874-S quarters turned up in a West Coast bank about 1949; they were dispersed one at a time, more frequently after 1974, to dealers and type collectors, so as not to depress prices.

Presumably, these are the same coins as those distributed by Lester Merkin, but one never knows when it comes to hoards, for factual information is often scarcer than the coins themselves.

Update

A draft of this article was sent to John J. Ford Jr., who shared many recollections. Thus, here is probably the most accurate account, per his commentary:

> I bought the hoard of 1874-S quarters from Henry Christensen for New Netherlands [Coin Co.]. You remember Henry; his office was in New Jersey. He had 300 or 400 of them in the early 1960s, which he had bought somewhere in Latin America. Mexican, Central American, and South American coins were his specialty, and somewhere along the line he stumbled on to these Liberty Seated quarters.
>
> After Lester Merkin sold the Helfenstein large cents in the summer of 1964,[231] he had some extra money and bought 15 or 20 of the quarters from New Netherlands. We kept selling them various places, including to you. Some later appeared in stocks and auctions of your company and Superior Galleries. By the time I left New Netherlands in 1971 there were still 30 or 40 in stock. I think some of these ended up in [my former business associate] Charles Wormser's estate.[232]

A Mint State 1874-S quarter.

chapter 10

Gold Is Where You Find It

"Gold Mining in California."

Gold! gold! gold! gold!
Bright and yellow, hard and cold,
Molten, graven, hammered, and rolled;
Heavy to get, and light to hold;
Hoarded, bartered, bought, and sold;
Stolen, borrowed, squandered, doled;
Price of many a crime untold
Gold! gold! gold! gold![233]

Hoards and treasures containing gold coins have always had a certain mystique. The story of Silas Marner—the weaver of Raveloe, who spent his evenings gloating over and enjoying his hoard of gold guineas—is just the most famous of the extensive lore that captures this feeling.[234]

Years ago, many who contemplated hoarding coins selected gold, as such pieces offered the possibility of storing a large amount of value in a small space. The following are several accounts of finds whose contents were of that precious yellow metal.

Gold Rush Twenties ___

Hidden: Early 1850s • **Found:** 1854 or 1855 • **Treasure:** Rare $20 gold pieces

Ballou's Pictorial Drawing-Room Companion, Volume VIII, 1855, page 286, recounts this:

> A rag picker in San Francisco, while tearing out the lining of an old trunk that had been thrown from the Crescent City Hotel, discovered twenty $20 gold pieces snugly stored upon their edges. Some former owner of the trunk had doubtless placed them there for concealment.

By the time of this account, the San Francisco Mint had been making double eagles—that is, federally issued $20 gold pieces—for only a short while. Presumably much more numerous in circulation were the private issues of Moffat & Co.,

the United States Assay Office of Gold, Kellogg & Co., and others. As this trunk was discarded in early 1855 or perhaps in 1854, it is possible that some or all of the 20 pieces bore those names. Today, how rare and desirable they would be!

A $20 gold coin minted in 1853 by the United States Assay Office of Gold, San Francisco.

The South Mountain Treasure ___

Hidden: Early 1700s • **Found:** 1857 • **Treasure:** Gold coins

Ballou's Pictorial Drawing-Room Companion, January 31, 1857, p. 79, printed this account:

> About one thousand dollars in old Spanish and American gold coins and French silver was found by a servant girl in the smokehouse of Peter Texter, South Mountain, Bucks County, Pennsylvania.
>
> The house has been used every day for many years, without any suspicion of the treasure. It is supposed to have been hidden away by some of Mr. Texter's ancestors, who died without revealing its existence.

In 1857, there was very little numismatic interest in gold coins—even very early ones—and it can be supposed that these pieces were spent or sold to a bullion exchange.

An 1841-O gold eagle.

Gold Dollars in an Anthill —————

Hidden: 1851 or later • **Found:** Circa 1874 • **Treasure:** Gold dollars

The October 1874 issue of the *American Journal of Numismatics* included this brief item:

A boy found a gold dollar on an ant hill in the old commissary building at Fort Fillmore, New Mexico, a short time since. The following day three dollars were found in the same place. They had evidently been brought up by the ants. Search was made, and a small wooden box, badly decayed, containing one hundred and eighty gold dollars was found about a foot below the surface.

Fort Fillmore was established by the U.S. Army in September 1851 in the territory later known as New Mexico. The fortification was intended to protect gold seekers taking the southern route to California.

A Mysterious Gold Coin Treasure ————

Hidden: 1860s • **Found:** 1880 • **Treasure:** Gold coins

Did this treasure exist? Apparently so. Was it discovered? That is the question. The following is adapted from an account in the September 14, 1890, issue of the *New York Times*:

During the days when the famous Confederate raider John Morgan was slashing into southern Ohio with his troop of irregular cavalry, attacking the fat farms of the Union's breadbasket, there lived in Summit County a wealthy farmer named William Huddleston. War prices made farming profitable, and Huddleston, wary of any sort of paper money in unsettled times, put his savings into gold, which was then at a high premium. He had accumulated $6,000 in gold when Morgan's Raiders began to pillage farms in his region.

Sensibly mistrusting banks or bonds or other ventures based on conventional commerce, Huddleston buried his treasure somewhere on his land.

The war ended, leaving the resourceful Huddleston still farming his property. Content that he had buried enough gold to fall back on in case of misfortune, he never bothered to dig up the hidden hoard. He shared the secret of the gold's location only with his wife. His children scattered as soon as they grew up, and one of them, Elizabeth, wound up in Cleveland, where she managed to earn a good living.

The elder Huddlestons died, and the farm passed into other hands. A Clevelander, Charles F. Brush, acquired the property, but he immediately rented it out to a series of tenant farmers.

One of these, a man named Wilkinson, unearthed the gold while plowing his rented acres in the 1880s. He spread the news of his windfall widely,[235] and it came to the attention of Elizabeth Huddleston, who was still living in Cleveland. She could not remember the location of the hoard, but she clearly remembered that her father had asked her to gather a number of empty oyster cans, in which he buried the coins. She immediately took steps to recover the treasure.

Discovering that Judge Timballs of Akron had been retained by Wilkinson to help him clear his title to his find, Elizabeth Huddleston consulted another judge named Marvin, and asked him to investigate the Wilkinson claim and her own rights in the treasure matter.

To Miss Huddleston's chagrin, Marvin returned from his conference with Timballs and informed his client that he could tell her nothing without violating the confidence which obtains between lawyers and those who retain them. Said Judge Marvin, "All lawyers have secrets which they must keep, and Timballs could not tell me what he knew. All that I know positively is that a large amount of money was found."

The canny Wilkinson, when questioned, would say nothing about the matter except that he had found "a few bogus dollars." Defeated by the legal fraternity, which almost certainly shared in the Wilkinson windfall, Miss Huddleston made a last effort, going the rounds of the banks to try and find out if Wilkinson had made any large deposit recently. In this attempt she ran square into the protocol of the banking community, which guards its secrets as carefully as do the lawyers. The bankers smugly told her nothing.

Presumably Wilkinson died rich. As for Miss Huddleston, deponent sayeth not.[236]

"Bring Down the Stocking"

Hidden: 1800s • **Found:** 1894 • **Treasure:** Gold coins

In 1894, an agent of the Mutual Life Insurance Co. of New York had been soliciting a prospective client for some time on the isolated Canadian island of Newfoundland, but to date had achieved no success.[237] Then this happened, as described in his report to the firm's home office:

Dear Sir:—

We are apt to receive a good many kinds of money in some of the remote places here in Newfoundland. Having canvassed one man until I had almost given up, on his plea that he had "no money," he said at last (turning to his wife), "You may as well bring down the stocking," and when that stocking came with its shining mass of stuff poured out on the table, I wondered if I could tell whether I had enough for the premium or not.

Attached please find memo of the different kinds of specie given me for the premium. I hardly knew whether I had $30 or $60. I invested in a small pocketbook to put the premium in, to show the friends how business is done here. Will keep it until I return.

The memorandum showed a variety of world coins, including a solitary U.S. gold coin, a $2.50 piece of 1851. Among Canadian coins, there was an 1870 Newfoundland $2 gold piece. Most of the others were Spanish-American gold, with the largest being a 1788 doubloon. The latest-dated coin was 1887.

A later numismatic writer, R.J. Graham, suggested that the pieces may have been acquired via trading with a foreign fishing fleet.

An 1851 gold quarter eagle.

Canyon City Gold Hoard

Hidden: Circa 1874 • **Found:** 1906 • **Treasure:** Gold coins

In October 1906, a group of gold miners trading as the Jin Que Company found a cigar box filled with gold coins at the ghost town site of Canyon City, California. More than 220 pieces were found, including 17 $50 octagonal gold slugs from the Gold Rush era. It was suggested that they had belonged to Jacob Kiplinger, who had been killed in a mine cave-in several decades earlier.[238]

An octagonal $50 from the Gold Rush era.

The Secrets of Old Buildings

Hidden or lost: 1800s • **Found:** By 1907 • **Treasure:** Gold coins

Contractors in the business of building demolition often find strange and valuable things. An unsigned account in the *Boston Herald*, September 17, 1907, featured an interview with a New York City contractor, who regaled the reporter with many interesting stories.[239]

"A short time ago," apparently in 1906 or 1907, "an old woman died of starvation in her home in the Bronx, and afterward it was discovered that she had hidden gold pieces in flower pots concealed under the stairs," the man related.

Unfortunately, the numismatic content of these flower pots was not revealed, but even if there were only two flower pots, and they were small ones—the logical minimum in this account—there must have been many hundreds of gold coins.

The Sugar House as illustrated A.B. Sage's Odds & Ends No. 2 token issued in 1858. Dies by George H. Lovett.

Prisoners of Long Ago

Another find was described as follows:

> The most interesting of the many finds made in tearing down old houses was unearthed in the old Sugar House, at Rose and Duane streets, New York, built in 1763, and transformed during the Revolution into a military prison. When the baseboards were torn away many old coins were found. They were discovered in little piles and were of different mints—Spanish, Swedish, English—as if each prisoner had put his money away for safekeeping and there had been a feeling that one prisoner should not interfere with another.
>
> Many of these prisoners were shot, many others died there, and so there was none to claim their little hoards of money and none to know about them. Year after year they stayed there until a blow of the hammer revealed them.[240]

Another account by the same contractor told of an old residence on Bleecker Street in which he found "a complete counterfeiter's outfit for making silver money. It is illegal to have anything of that kind in your possession, and we destroyed it as soon as possible."

The home had been occupied by a "man and woman of quiet ways, who never visited or received anyone." Finally, the couple moved away, after which the building was closed up, until it was demolished.

The Old Sugar House and the Middle Dutch Church.

But Somebody Did Find It

Hidden: 1800s • **Found:** February 1907 • **Treasure:** Double eagles

The first decade of the last century was a good time to find double eagles in the Midwest, it would seem. The *Granite State News*, March 2, 1907, told of this hoard:

> Norfolk, Nebraska. February 20, 1907:
> Over $4,000 in gold, all in double eagles, has been found in the barn of William Boche, the miser, who died several weeks ago. Boche did not believe in banks, and when he got any money he hid it, and told his wife he had hid his money where no one could find it.

What happened to miser Boche's 200 or more golden double eagles? No one knows. Perhaps some were saved to be examined by collectors, but likely they were cashed in at a local bank.

Note that in the same year, a few gold coins—not really a hoard—were found in Iowa. The *Granite State News*, July 20, 1907, printed this:

> Iowa City, Iowa:
> While John Curry, a farmer living near here, was plowing, he turned up three gold pieces, a $20 piece, and two of $5 each. All three had dates in the early '50s. The land on which the treasure was discovered was entered by Byron Dennis in the '40s.

The Abernathy-Bennett Hoard

Hidden: 1867 • **Found:** 1908 • **Treasure:** 1854–1855 Kellogg $20

A $20 gold coin minted by Kellogg & Co. in San Francisco in 1854.

This gold hoard—lost in 1867—was found in the early 1900s, but its present whereabouts remain a mystery. The following narrative by Thomas J. Hammond was contributed for use in the present book.[241]

Abernathy and Bennett

The rush for gold is usually associated with Western expansion. Many have visions of rugged pioneers, ambitious souls blazing trails west through a trackless wilderness. Rarely does one hear stories of those pioneers of the 1850s who returned eastward, having already found that idyllic dream of monetary wealth in the West, but this did indeed occur.

In just such a scenario, a man named William Abernathy converted his bright yellow dust into gold coin and headed east to Nebraska to homestead a ranch with a man named Joseph Bennett. This is the story of Abernathy's hoard of Kellogg $20 gold pieces, which is only briefly mentioned in a couple of numismatic books and periodicals. Unfortunately, as is often the case with tales of treasure, the story in incomplete, and some questions remain.

My research on the matter took me to Thayer County, Nebraska, a fertile valley which was described in the 1800s as "surrounded by as fine an agricultural and grazing country as is found in Southern Nebraska."[242] It remains so today. The Little Blue River meanders through thick stands

of cottonwood trees, and wild berries and underbrush abound. At the time of my visit, ripening August corn hugged the river road which led to the old Abernathy and Bennett homestead. The thickness of vegetation, combined with recent rains, stifled the air.

The Oregon Trail passed by this area, and many travelers settled this land instead of traveling farther westward through the "Great American Desert."

A Tragic Tale

Despite its charm, this land was the setting for a tragic event in 1867. I discovered that Joe Worrell, a printer and publisher who settled in Thayer County in 1871, collected the story from firsthand witnesses of the time. An expanded account was printed for a larger audience by Mr. Clarence S. Paine of the Nebraska Historical Society, who interviewed Mr. Worrell, and an identical account was also published by Erasmus M. Correll, editor of the *Hebron Journal*.

The tale begins with Abernathy, a rancher and miner who had been in California during the Gold Rush. Authentic ranchers recognize that money is only temporary wealth, but the wealth of the land is eternal;[243] perhaps it was this wisdom that brought William back to Nebraska with at least $1,160 face value in Kellogg & Co. gold $20 pieces, minted in San Francisco in 1854 and 1855, to become partner with Bennett on a ranch bordering the Little Blue River about four miles east of Hebron in Thayer County.

Unfortunately, Indian attacks in this valley during this time were numerous and destructive. Only the Otoe tribe lived in consistent peace with white settlers. Reports are graphic and perhaps even biased in their depiction of the slaughter:

All alike were made to feel [the Indians'] cruelty. . . . No mercy was shown. No captives were taken but women, and death was preferred to the captivity that awaited them. Could the Eastern philanthropists who speak so flatteringly of "the noble red man of the West" have witnessed the cruel butchery of unoffending children, the disgrace of women, who were first horribly mutilated and then slain, the cowardly assassination of husbands and fathers, they might, perhaps (if fools can learn), be impressed with their true character.[244]

This was the wrath which faced Bennett and Abernathy in August of 1867. A band of Pawnee attacked almost every homestead along the river valley and the bluffs which bordered it. Erasmus Correll, writing in *History of the State of Nebraska*, described the event with less prejudice than most:

> When the helpless and innocent fall into the hands of such monsters, their fates are too terrible for pen to relate. Of what fearful metal are their natures made, how basely turned, and what a multitude of sins their unfeeling bosoms hold! And yet we must admit that among the white men there are nature's kindred to these, whose crimes are more revolting when we consider their advantages of civilization—education and nurture in pious homes. . . . From what an altitude, by comparison, have they fallen, or to what loathsome depths.

This early account addresses the fate of Abernathy and Bennett:

> The Indians proceeded to the Abernathy and Bennett ranch. A cave in a limestone bluff bordering the Little Blue River was converted into a dwelling by the construction of an extended front of logs. The thick underbrush in front of the cave provided the Indians the advantage of surprise. After a short battle, the Indians eventually set fire to the front of the dwelling, and Bennett and Abernathy were killed. The Indians were later overcome about 20 miles east in Superior by a militia of soldiers including A.C. Ring of Hebron.

A group of soldiers commanded by Captain L.P. Luce found the bodies of Abernathy and Bennett "in so charred and mutilated a condition as to be scarcely recognizable."[245] The cave was quickly sealed. In 1869 or 1870, a portion of the bones was buried, while a skull and the bones of one of the victims were taken to Davenport, Iowa, as a museum donation.

Settlers knew of Abernathy's missing gold, and the cave was supposedly ransacked. Many suspected their neighbors of theft, but no solid reports were made in the remainder of the 1800s.

A Remarkable Find

Some decades later, in August of 1908, two boys named James McFarland and John May were swimming in the Little Blue River. While resting on a small sandbar near the limestone bluff, May kicked up a gold coin. It turned out to be a Kellogg and Co. $20 coin minted in San Francisco during the Gold Rush. John, an orphan who lived in Belvidere, was able to rake two more coins from the sand near the bluff.

May lived with a man named Spaulding, who confiscated the coins and demanded to know where they were found. According to the *Hebron Journal*, the boys refused to tell Spaulding and returned to the bluff the next day. It was then that McFarland found a small hole near the old mouth of the cave and retrieved a sack containing $1,100 in Kellogg $20 gold coins.

The *Journal*'s story gave some geographical details of the location: "The spot where the coins were said to be found was a little south and east of the old Leland Mill where the stream flows to the southeast and then to the north in a bend, two miles north and two and one half miles west of Gilead. . . ."

Evidently, the seemingly heartless Spaulding—who was not May's legal guardian—kept the boy's three Kellogg coins. The whereabouts of the coins are unknown today, and Spaulding has no known living relatives in the area at the present time.

Reports indicate that the remaining $1,100 in Kellogg $20 coins was deposited into a bank in Geneva, Nebraska. The coins were received into a general account identified as a cash deposit, so tracing the coins has become quite difficult.[246]

The Abernathy-Bennett Site Today

Today, the site of the find has been destroyed, pushed in years ago for safety reasons. The limestone bluff is fragile, and the residents feared a cave-in. The rocks surrounding the exact location show black stains, probably left from many smoking fires.

Much is left to be discovered. Is more gold buried in that limestone bluff? What happened to the 58 $20 coins? How were they disbursed, and who has them now? Or were they melted decades ago?

The beauty of research and the enjoyment of numismatics often come not from the actual acquisition of a coin or a bit of information, but from what occurs during the search for discovery. It is through the search that the community learns, grows, and shares. The contemplation today of an actual specimen of an 1854 or 1855 Kellogg & Co. $20 gold piece becomes all the more interesting when one considers the coin's history—how it was minted and what its later experiences may have been.

A Teakettle Filled With Gold

Hidden or lost: 1800s • **Found:** December 9, 1907 • **Treasure:** $20 gold coins

The *Granite State News*, December 28, 1907, included this:

> New Milford, Connecticut, December 10:
> $3,000 in $20 gold pieces were dug up late yesterday by T.T. Jones on his farm in the Merryall district while he was digging a trench. Mr. Jones was formerly a New York businessman and then about a year ago bought the farm of Edgar Peet. The gold was in a teakettle, and Mr. Jones states that it is evident the kettle had been buried for many years.

Treasure in the Treasury Building

Hidden: 1800s to 1907 • **Revealed:** 1911 • **Treasure:** $1, $3, $10, and $20 gold coins

The time is 1911 and the place is the Treasury Building in Washington.[247] There were rumors in Congress that some old gold dollars—a denomination that had not been minted for circulation since 1889—were in Treasury vaults and had been paid out as "souvenirs" on occasional requests.

Senator John D. Works heard of this and on August 8 asked for two of the coins in exchange for two bills. Secretary of the Treasury Franklin MacVeagh sent one gold dollar and expressed regret that no more could be supplied.

On December 11, Representative William D. Ashbrook of Ohio and Representative Arthur W. Kopp of Wisconsin, both numismatists and members of the ANA, sent a message that they sought "to examine the one and three dollar gold pieces now in the hands of the Treasurer with the idea of securing therefrom any such as may be of peculiarly rare date or mintage."[248] Assistant Secretary

A Mint State 1889 gold dollar.

of the Treasury A. Piatt Andrew inquired of Treasurer Lee McClung, who had jurisdiction over these coins and some others that had been set aside.

Andrew subsequently prepared a memorandum on the subject for MacVeagh that said in part:

I have talked with Mr. McClung about the question of the rare coins in the treasurer's office. It appears that there are 320 one dollar gold pieces, 337 three dollar gold pieces, 129 ten dollar Saint-Gaudens pieces of rare and early strike, and 58 twenty dollar Saint-Gaudens pieces of an early strike, all of which have a market value considerably above their face value.

The one dollar and three dollar pieces ceased to be coined in 1889, and the rare strikes of the Saint-Gaudens ten dollar and twenty dollar gold pieces were issued only in 1907. It is possible that some of the individual pieces bearing special dates or the marks of particular mints have a value considerable above the rest. All of these coins are held in the Treasurer's cash room and constitute part of his cash at their face value. They have been given to applicants from time to time at the discretion of yourself or of the treasurer. For about a year the distribution of the twenty dollar gold pieces has been confined entirely to your option. The unsatisfactory feature of this present method is the necessary discrimination between the applicants. If a school teacher from New Hampshire were to ask for one of these dollar pieces as a souvenir of her visit, she would undoubtedly be refused. On the other hand, an application by a congressman or a senator would probably never be denied. An application endorsed by a senator or congressman might or might not be granted according to circumstances.

The issue of these pieces involves the conferring of a favor which has a certain financial value and ought, therefore, to be carefully considered. A request from such as that recently presented, to be allowed to select from among those more or less valuable pieces those of peculiarly rare dates or mintage, involves the conferring of a favor of possibly very large financial value and is open to serious objection on the grounds of propriety and of precedent. Such permission might yield the beneficiary a very considerable profit which, if known, might subject the Treasury to disagreeable criticism, and the precedent established of allowing outsiders to examine coins in the cash room for the purpose of obtaining rare pieces might lead to undesirable results.

As regards the stock of rare coins now in the cash room, there are several possible alternatives:

1. To continue the present policy of leaving the distribution to the discretion of the secretary and the treasurer.
2. To limit the distribution to senators and congressmen at their personal request for their personal ownership and enjoyment, and
3. To transfer the present supply to the Mint with orders for their melting and recoinage.

Mr. McClung favors the first alternative, believing that no harm comes from the present practice and that if embarrassment should arise in the future then reconsideration may be given the question in the light of developments. I am inclined to the third alternative—the recoinage of these pieces—on the general ground that it is peculiar and not quite proper for the Treasury to be distributing through its cash room, to selected recipients, coins of exaggerated market value.[249]

The listed gold dollar count was later revised to 313, and the number of $3 gold coins was changed to 335. Some of the coins were very special pieces, such as the "early strike" Saint-Gaudens eagles, which would have been the rare type with periods on the reverse.

Apparently, no record was kept of the numbers passed out or to whom. This created a dilemma as to what to do. One proposal was to give them to the Mint at face value, to be used in exchange

A rare 1907 Saint-Gaudens eagle with periods in the legend on the reverse.

An MCMVII (1907) Saint-Gaudens double eagle.

for pieces needed for the Mint Collection. Treasurer McClung rejected the idea, seemingly as he wanted to maintain the control and distribution of pieces to special requests.

It was finally decided to send the coins to the Mint. The coins were tossed into a bag marked "Uncurrent Gold Coin" and shipped to Philadelphia. Upon receipt, T. Louis Comparette, curator of the Mint Collection, found that all of the gold dollars except one were dated 1889, the $3 coins were all in circulated grades, and the double eagles were all of the MCMVII (1907) type.

From that point, most of the coins were dispersed. On June 28 and 29, 1912, local dealer Henry Chapman purchased all of the gold dollars for $2 each and 36 of the $3 pieces for $4 each.[250] The remaining $3 coins, except for one mutilated piece, were sold to New York City dealer Thomas L. Elder for $1 to $1.50 above face value for each.

Beyond these transactions, many of the rare 1907 eagles with periods on the reverse were sold for $15 each and all of the MCMVII $20 coins for $23 each, with the buyers not disclosed. On July 18, there were 80 remaining eagles on hand (79 with periods and 1 regular circulation issue) at an asking price of $15 each. By October, another four eagles had been sold.

Then, tired of holding the remaining eagles, Comparette ordered the remaining ones to be melted! Today, if gems, they would be worth tens of thousands of dollars each!

Note that apart from the above scenario, Representative Ashbrook pursued his numismatic interests. On January 17, 1913, he entered this in his diary: "I spent three hours in the Treasury looking over a bag of 5,000 quarter eagles, but did not find one that I wanted. I expect it is foolish, but I enjoy my coin fad." He returned to the Treasury Building on January 18, 20, and 21 and spent the better part of each day looking through a total of 30,000 quarter eagles without finding anything to keep. Perhaps he hoped to find 1796–1834 issues, all of which are rare.

Gold Dollars Come Back to America

Hidden or lost: 1800s • **Found:** By 1923 • **Treasure:** Gold dollars

From the beginning of the 1900s into the 1930s, Thomas L. Elder was one of the United States' leading rare-coin dealers. He maintained a store and conducted many auctions in New York City. Elder wrote many articles on the lore and lure of numismatics. In January 1926, *The Numismatist* published this by Elder:

Four Thousand Gold Dollars Sold in Two Lots

A few details as to how over 4,000 United States gold dollars—those tiny coins of two sizes, coined between the years 1849 and 1889, covering a period of just 40 years—were disposed of to an American, and by him to Americans, may be of more than passing interest. It took the World War, or, rather, its aftermath, to uncover these two hoards and remove them from their hiding places in old and dusty bags in foreign vaults and bring them again into the land of their origin. The vicissitudes of foreign paper tender must have had a great deal to do with it, possibly the shrinkage of the mark, or even the franc, but most likely the former.

At any rate, one day about two and a half years ago a tall young man with a slightly foreign accent, evidently British, drew a few samples of the coins from his pocket and extended his hand with them in its palm across the counter of a well-known New York dealer. Said he: "What will you offer for each? There are more of them—quite a few more."

The price was quickly agreed on per coin and no limit was placed on the number. The next day, in a spacious, well-furnished office resembling that used by directors in their meetings, three men sat around a table as two small bags were opened and 1,700 of the tiny coins were rolled out into view. They were counted into three piles, viz., the fine, the simply good, and the damaged gold dollars. The deal being completed, the matter was thought to be ended, when, behold! some three months later the same tall Britisher telephoned the collector and asked if he would not come downtown, since another bag of gold dollars had arrived. Well, in that bag there were not only more than 2,000 gold dollars but perhaps 20 of our $3 gold pieces. Here a really remarkable find had been disposed of, and all to one individual in the city of New York.

Now, collectors, you will ask what did that immense lot of gold dollars contain and what did it prove as to the commonness or rarity of gold dollars? Surely this is a question of interest to at least those who try to keep close records on current prices of coins and priced catalogues of coin sales. One of the singular things about this big find was that the second

portion of the collection contained only gold dollars of the small size.

Another just as singular thing about this big find was that the second portion of gold dollars contained the rarest assemblage of dates and mintmarks, proving in a way, that in the long run the larger gold dollars—that is, the later dates—include more rarities than the smaller and older ones. The buyer paid no attention to what the lot might contain when he made the offer, because he had no way of finding that out in advance. The owner, or broker, or agent wanted a price per coin in a stated condition, and the buyer, in a business-like way, immediately made his offer and got the coins, taking a chance on what the lots might contain.

Well, in that lot of over 4,000 gold dollars there were almost all dates, not quite all, nor quite all the mintmarks. There were two 1863s, two 1864s, and all the other dates in the 1860s, except 1865. The dollar of 1865 therefore, must be rated as one of exceptional rarity—not one in over 4,000! Neither was there an 1875, but all other dates in the 1870s of the Philadelphia Mint were there, including an Uncirculated 1870 of the S mint. Just imagine coming across perhaps the finest 1870 of the San Francisco Mint in a pile of coins like this! However, there was only one. In the first lot also were a few of the C and D mints, but not nearly all. There was no 1855, 1859, 1860, nor 1861 of the D mint. There were a considerable number of the San Francisco Mint, such dates as 1856, 1857, 1858, 1859, and 1860. There was only one 1850 of the New Orleans Mint. Strange to say the larger lot of the two, the one of over 2,000, contained very few rarities.

Now, you may inquire, what became of all these gold dollars, and does the buyer still have them tucked in the little bags in his safe-deposit vault? Just here I will tell you how quickly those 4,000 gold dollars were absorbed—taken up so completely that not more than about 100 of them remain in the original buyer's hands. Were these gold dollars taken by dealers, to be scattered throughout the country, to keep down the value of gold dollars? Collecting Americans need not worry, for most of these coins rest today in collections which will not be sold, at least not for a good many years, for the dealers did not get them, and, except for a few scattering very small lots, they went into the hands of less than four collectors. In fact the biggest buyer of them has never been known to deal in coins or sell coins.

If the knowledge that a large lot or two of gold dollars has been 'around' during the past two or three years has tended to keep speculation in these coins slightly on the bear side, let not the numismatic gold dollar 'bulls' despair, because the day of the gold dollar—its best day—has not yet come, but is surely coming. Knowing that this large lot is now off the market, and knowing that these little yellow pieces have always enjoyed favor among collectors, and still continue in favor, it is certain we are going to see less gold dollars in the future than we have been seeing and hearing about recently.

Only the other day a big New York dealer said to me: "Gold dollars? Why, a gold dollar—we wouldn't sell one for less than $4!" I say the present craze for late-date quarter eagles is simply nothing compared with the craze that will one day seize the Americans in their search for gold dollars. The gold dollar

is just as scarce as ever. It sold for $4 four years ago, and will sell for $4 for common issues in the very near future, I predict. See if I am not right.

The popularity of the gold dollar has been very great, and is destined to become still greater as the supply diminishes. Mr. [Lyman H.] Low told of having gone to the Philadelphia Mint in 1889, the last year of their coinage, and how the mint master urged him to take a thousand brilliant new gold dollars, which had just been struck, for their face value, but the numismatist either did not have the means or the inclination to accept this suggestion and passed up the wonderful opportunity.

Since that day things have changed as regards the gold dollar, and as early as 1908 or 1910 the gold dollar of 1861 of the Dahlonega Mint made a record of $250 or more. The writer sold several for over $225 apiece. DeWitt Smith paid, I think, $280 for one specimen and valued its rarity extremely high. One of this mint and date came over the writer's counter back about 1910. Recent fluctuations in the prices of the common dates have shown very clearly how the law of supply and demand governs the price of coins.

To this day the identities of the principals in the 4,000-coin gold dollar hoard are not known.

Tobacco Farm Gold Cache

Hidden or lost: Civil War era or before • **Found:** 1926 • **Treasure:** Gold coins

For two brothers, a fortunate find paid for an automobile. The year is 1926 and the location is Kentucky:

$675 in Gold Found
on Tobacco Farm

Buried gold has interfered with tobacco planting on the edge of Stewart County, Tennessee, a few miles from the Kentucky town of Hopkinsville. Two youths told the story when they came to Hopkinsville to buy

an automobile with part of the treasure they had found buried.

Ernest Roberts, 20, and his brother Austin, 18, made the find. The boys were setting out tobacco on the farm of their uncle, William Thweatt, when one picked up a five dollar piece. When they made another row of tobacco, they found a twenty dollar coin. Thereafter the tobacco planting languished while the youths searched for treasure. Before long they had uncovered $675 in gold of a coinage antedating the Civil War. They took their treasure home, where they told their mother about the finds.

Coin collectors are offering premium prices for some of the gold pieces. Seven of the five dollar gold pieces, dated 1834, are worth $15 each, it is said.[251] The finders say the gold was scattered about with the remains of a glass jug which had been buried just under the surface and had been broken, letting the coins fall out. It is believed that the money was buried during the war to hide it from one side or the other of the fighting forces.

No steps have been taken by anyone else to claim the money, so the boys will get their auto.[252]

A half eagle of 1834, first year of the Classic Head design by William Kneass.

Some Really Rare $20 Gold Coins

Hidden or lost: 1800s • **Found:** May 22, 1926 • **Treasure:** $20 gold coins

In 1926, numismatists and others were startled when they read this Associated Press dispatch datelined Demopolis, Alabama:

Aided by old papers his father left him, Gayus Whitfield, of Middleboro, Ky., has unearthed buried gold valued at more than $200,000 on the Whitfield farm, near here. Discovery of the treasure came as the result of a search which began May 22. Directions for locating the gold were contained in papers left his son by C. Boaz Whitfield, member of one of the oldest and most aristocratic families of Alabama and descendant of the pioneer general, Nathan Bryan Whitfield.

When Gayus Whitfield began his search 35 Negroes were employed to uncover an old boundary stake on the Shady Grove farm, 18 miles from Demopolis, near Jefferson. For a week the large force worked without results, but today a large cache of gold coins was discovered. They consist of $20 gold pieces, minted in 1850 and before, buried by the wealthy Boaz Whitfield during Civil War days.

While news of the discovery was confirmed tonight, the exact amount involved was not divulged. There are eight heirs who may put in claims for the gold, all of them sons and daughters of the four Whitfield brothers, born in Civil War days, themselves sons of General Nathan Whitfield.

Other gold coins had been found on the old Whitfield place prior to today's discovery, but the matter of instituting an active search for buried treasure was never given much attention by the Whitfield family until the ancient key left by C. Boaz Whitfield was found in Kentucky. Citizens here expressed the belief that Boaz Whitfield buried the gold to prevent its seizure by Union forces during the Civil War. Similar instances were recalled by older inhabitants of the region, but in no case has so large an amount been involved.[253]

A double eagle of 1850, the first year of issue.

Later Associated Press dispatches from the same location stated that the value of the coins was much less than that originally stated. Numismatists were still left wondering, however, about all of those $20 pieces "minted in 1850 *and before*," as 1850 was the first year such coins were made for circulation.[254] Such are the "facts" about treasure troves in the daily press.

Readers who want to know more about mythical double eagles minted *before* 1850 will find the next account, "The Secret of the Dump," to be likewise amusing.

The Secret of the Dump

Hidden or lost: 1800s • **Found:** August 1927 • **Treasure:** Gold coins

In August 1927, there was quite a commotion in downtown Philadelphia at the dump at the eastern end of the Spring Garden Street Bridge. It seems that an old house was torn down at Fifth and Noble streets, and the debris was hauled to the disposal site.

Among the dirt, mortar, and other rubble, some gold coins, including an "1843 double eagle," were found. Word spread, and before long hundreds of citizens were scrambling among the litter.

"Gold coins only, of all denominations, are reported to have been found, nearly all of which are dated prior to 1850," one account related. Estimates of the amount of money recovered varied widely. In addition, as numismatists know, there is no such coin as an 1843 double eagle, as the first patterns were made in 1849, and the first coins for circulation in 1850.[255]

On September 7, 1937, F.D. Langenheim of Philadelphia summarized the find:

> Late reports are that some $3,000 in gold coins has been found. An old lady, 86 years old, living near Fifth and Noble streets, says that a French doctor lived in the house being torn down, who died some forty or fifty years ago. He attended many Quaker families living near the Fifth and Noble Street Meeting House and was probably the one who hid the gold.

Under an Old Gambling Hall

Lost: Late 1890s • **Found:** 1929 • **Treasure:** Gold coins

During the wild and woolly days of the late 1890s, Seattle was the jumping-off spot for treasure seekers going "north to Alaska" (as the popular song went). All of the United States eagerly read accounts of the excitement as laborers, city slickers, and even novelist Jack London went to Skagway and over the Chilkoot Pass (at one time littered with the bodies of 4,000 dead horses) to the land of the midnight sun.

Many of the fortune hunters on the way to the Klondike or on the way back stopped at the M&N Saloon at the corner of Washington and First Avenue South in Seattle to live it up, lift a bottle or mug, roll the dice, and perhaps make the acquaintance of a lady for the evening.

Chilkoot Pass on the overland route to the Klondike.

Apparently, the floor boards in the M&N had a few cracks between them, and every now and again a gold coin, nugget, necklace, or other item would fall through.

Fast forward to December 1928:

A gold rush stopped street repairing operations at Washington street and First Avenue South, Seattle, Washington, for several hours when a workman turned up a gold nugget with his shovel. Jobless onlookers saw him make the find, and the stampede was on.

Over the site of what once had been the M&N saloon and gambling house, a Mecca for returning prospectors during the Klondike gold rush, fighting crowds of men reenacted the scenes in the North of 30 years ago on a miniature scale. The muddy streets yielded gold nuggets, gold chains, gold coins, South American currency, rings, lockets, necklaces and brooches, and brought Christmas to that part of town where December 25 is just another day without work. Old-timers suggested that the treasure uncovered was lost by patrons of the M&N three decades ago and probably had slipped through floor cracks and become buried in the mud under the building.

As is often the case in such situations, no coin collectors were on hand, or if they were, no specifics were given.[256]

Crates of Klondike gold being loaded on a steamship for transport to the Canadian Bank of Commerce in Seattle.

A Double Handful of Gold

Hidden or lost: 1800s • **Found:** 1931 • **Treasure:** Gold coins

The following account appeared in a Wisconsin newspaper in 1931:

Near the foot of an old willow stump, Martin A. Born, town of Oconomowoc, Wis., unearthed a cache that netted him perhaps a thousand dollars more or less. He declines to state the exact amount. With the exception of one silver dollar it's all gold—$10 and $20 pieces. He and his uncle, Herman, live on an 80-acre farm that once was the property of the late Patrick Olwell and adjoining Henry Rose-now on the east.

Down at the edge of the pond, Martin Born was plowing for corn a few days ago.

Every inch that could be turned into possible productive land was upturned by the plowman. Close to the stump the plowshare brought up pieces of leather and an innumerable quantity of what appeared to be buttons. Partial cleaning revealed the "buttons" to be gold pieces, genuine American coined money, in all as much as could be held in his two hands.

The following morning he went back to the cache and put the gold and single silver dollar into a satchel, thoroughly sifting the earth through his fingers to make certain he had all the gold. He carried his find to the house, cleaned the coins, and then headed for

Milwaukee, where he made a deposit in the National Bank of Commerce.

How the money came to be in the stump Mr. Born has no means of knowing. His one guess is that it was hidden away in an old leather boot and placed in the base of the tree by someone who left that section during the Civil War days, and who never returned to reclaim his hidden treasure. He said one coin bore the date of 1847 and another that of 1863.[257]

In 1931, gold coins could be paid into or received from any bank. Presumably, they were not scanned by a numismatist prior to being cashed in.

The Illinois Gold Rush

Hidden: Circa 1880 • **Found:** July 14, 1931 • **Treasure:** Hundreds of gold coins

A half eagle of 1810; half eagles were the only gold denomination minted in that year.

On July 14, 1931, all work came to a standstill in downtown Buffalo, Illinois, in a latter-day version of the Gold Rush. A contemporary account noted:

Employers and employees dropped whatever tools they were using and made haste to be the first to peer into a narrow airway between two buildings when it was learned that workmen on the property of Alex M. Booth had unearthed two ancient jugs containing more than $6,000 in gold coins. The coins, believed to have been hidden nearly fifty years ago by a pioneer physician, Dr. Peter Leeds, dated back to 1810. Many children saw their first gold money and some grown-up residents saw their first gold dollar. Older residents stood in groups and reviewed stories heard during their childhood of the strange, almost mythical "Doctor Leeds."

Mr. Booth claims ownership of the money because it was found buried on his property.

He has another point in his favor—actual possession—for the money has been placed in his safety deposit vault.

On the other hand, Edward Jack and James M. Rogers, two workmen who unearthed the gold, feel that they should come in for a share. Jack and Rogers were digging a drainage ditch from a new building erected by Mr. Booth, when they uncovered the two old jugs.

Still other claimants appeared today in the person of relatives of Dr. Peter Leeds, recluse of the eighties, who is generally believed to have buried the money. Dr. Leeds' relatives live in Lincoln, Clinton, and California, and today two granddaughters, Miss Anna and Miss Jennie Leeds, of Lincoln, hired attorneys to protect their interests.

Threats of litigation over the find indicate that by the time the final disposition of the gold is made, much of it may be dissipated in attorney's fees and court costs.[258]

The money was counted only hastily the day it was found, and a recount was made the following day, some of which were badly weathered, in the belief that the total may run close to $7,000. Numismatic authorities also were to be called in to check the pieces in the belief that some of which date back to 1812 [sic; earlier, the date 1810 was given] may have a value for collectors far higher than their actual value.

The hoard was taken to the bank, where Ed McCann, cashier, and G.F. Lester, assistant, began the task of counting it. One of the coins dated as far back as 1812 and the most recent one was 1880, about the time the money is believed to have been buried. The coins ranged from $1 to $20 gold pieces.

Mr. Lester counted a total of $6,028.50. Included were 228 $1 gold pieces. There were 159 $20 gold pieces and $2.50, $3, and $5 gold pieces.

Although in 1931 most of the $20 pieces may have been worth just face value, all $1 and $3 coins sold for a premium, and $2.50 pieces commanded a slight premium regardless of date.[259]

Two Hundred Men Dig 'Em Up

Hidden or lost: 1880 or later • **Found:** July 25–26, 1926 • **Treasure:** Gold coins

In the vacation resort of Saratoga Springs, New York, on July 25 and 26, 1926, there was what was described as a "gold rush on state property."

In an area famous for its natural springs, a foundation was being excavated for a new "drink hall." Workers found scattered old coins, word spread, and by the afternoon of the second day, "200 men with shovels and picks were delving into the earth." No casual treasure hunt, this!

One man was said to have found $300 in gold coins in a milk bottle, and others found silver and gold coins in tin cans, preserve jars, and other containers. Denominations ranged from silver three-cent pieces to $20 gold double eagles. The latest date seen was 1880.

State Attorney General John J. Bennett Jr. was a spoil sport, for when he learned of the frenetic activity, he ordered New York state troopers to put an end to the free-for-all. What if any coins were found later (by the state troopers?) was not recorded.[260]

Gold Hidden in a Baltimore Cellar

Hidden: Circa 1856 • **Found:** August 31, 1934 and later • **Treasure:** Gold coins

On August 31, 1934, two young boys, described as poor and underprivileged, were playing in the cellar of a house at 132 South Eden Street, East Baltimore, owned by sisters Elizabeth H. French and Mary P.B. Findlay and rented by the mother of one of the boys.[261]

Henry Grob, age 15, and his companion, Theodore Sines, 14, came upon a cache of gold coins. After a brief discussion as to what should be done, the lads took the treasure to the local police station and turned the find over to the authorities. Later that evening, the boys said that they had "held out" some of the pieces, and these were subsequently added to the first group. One *Baltimore Evening Sun* article put the amount as 3,556 coins with $11,424.00 face value. All were dated before 1857. Meanwhile, at the police station some of the patrolmen "tried their hand at cleaning them with coal oil [kerosene] and vinegar," a procedure definitely not recommended by numismatists!

How had the coins been hidden and by whom? One story had it that they were secreted by a sea captain of a ship in the coffee trade between Brazil and the port of Baltimore, this captain having lived in the house with his two sisters. Another story suggested that "the coins may have been buried in April 1861 by a resident who was frightened by the passing of federal [sic] troops through the city; the house is located close to the depot at which the troops landed in Baltimore."[262]

Multiple claims were filed for ownership. For the rest of 1934 and into May 1935, the matter was in the courts. Meanwhile, although the gold coins were to have remained undisturbed pending the outcome, the family of one of the finders sold

$185 worth for face value. Judge Eugene O'Dunne of the Second Circuit Court of Baltimore eventually awarded proceeds from the entire find to the two teenagers, negating an offer by the two ladies who owned the house to give the boys 50%. During the litigation, all parties agreed that the coins could be sold at auction.[263]

The sale was held on May 2, 1935, at the Lord Baltimore Hotel downtown, with Perry W. Fuller serving as auctioneer. About 100 attended, including a few out-of-town dealers and many local curiosity seekers. Grouped into 438 lots and casually described in a printed catalog (most pieces were simply called "very fine"), the hoard realized $19,746.15.

The star of the sale was a "very fine" 1856-O double eagle, which went to a Virginia numismatist at $105. An 1849-O eagle, also "very fine," commanded $45, while an 1841 half eagle, "fine, scratch on date," found a buyer at $26 and an 1847-O of the same denomination, "fine," fetched $22. In an era in which there was very little numismatic interest in gold coins of higher denominations, most pieces sold for double face value.

Leonard Augsburger created the following inventory (note that both the 1834 quarter eagle and 1834 half eagle were of the "Classic Head" design):

A gold dollar of 1849, the first year of issue.

$1 gold (listings apparently omit mintmarks)

1849 (95)	1853 (976)
1850 (78)	1854, Type I and II (322)
1851 (452)	1855 (215)
1852 (322)	1856 (296)
Various damaged coins 1849–1856 (39)	

1834 Classic Head quarter eagle.

Quarter eagles

1834 (2)	1845 (2)	1853 (14)
1836 (5)	1847-O	1854 (7)
1839-D	1848-D	1855 (3)
1843	1850 (3)	1856 (4)
1843-O (4)	1851 (5)	
1843-C	1852 (11)	

1855-D half eagle.

Half eagles

1834 (15)	1844-C (2)	1852 (20)
1835 (2)	1845 (10)	1852-C (5)
1836 (12)	1845-O (3)	1852-D (2)
1837 (3)	1846 (4)	1853 (12)
1838 (6)	1846-C (4)	1853-C (3)
1838-C	1846-O	1853-D (3)
1839	1847 (20)	1854 (11)
1840 (8)	1847-O	1854-O
1841	1847-C	1854-D (6)
1842-D	1847-D	1855 (15)
1843 (12)	1848 (8)	1855-C (3)
1843-O (5)	1848-C (5)	1855-D
1843-C (2)	1848-D	1856 (3)
1843-D	1850 (5)	
1844 (6)	1850-D (2)	
1844-O (6)	1851 (13)	

1847 eagle.

Eagles

1839 (2)	1847 (13)	1851-O (3)
1840	1847-O (7)	1852
1841	1848 (5)	1853 (4)
1842 (2)	1848-O (2)	1853-O (3)
1842-O	1849 (10)	1854
1844-O	1849-O	1854-S
1845	1850 (6)	1855 (7)
1845-O	1850-O (2)	1856 (3)
1846-O	1851	

1852-O double eagle.

Double eagles

1850 (92)	1852-O (2)	1856
1850-O (5)	1853 (27)	1856-O
1851 (79)	1854 (12)	1856-S (23)
1851-O (10)	1855 (6)	
1852 (47)	1855-S (12)	

That same month that the auction took place, while other Eden Street residents dug up their own cellars with absolutely no success, the same two young boys revisited the site after one said he was "feeling lucky." They claimed that in due course more than $8,000 face value of additional gold coins was found! This find, too, went to court, and meanwhile an unauthorized sale of coins representing $2,500 face value (for $3,005, the buyer being Yale Merrill and his brother Eli) took place around September.[264]

The "second find" story was debunked in 2008, when Augsburger published a book on the find titled *Treasure in the Cellar*. The work was a masterful study and gained warm reviews. It turns out the second lot was actually a group of coins that the boys initially held back rather than turn over to the authorities.

Regardless, the young lads did not receive long-term benefit from their good fortune. The Grob boy died in 1937, by which time Sines had been sentenced to prison for reckless driving. Grob's share was given to his mother, while Sines's share was disbursed to him by the Baltimore City court in 1939. Their attorney, Harry O. Levin, who had taken the case on contingency, received one-third of the proceeds.

Few coins can today be attributed to the Baltimore Hoard. An 1856 (upright 5) gold dollar, ex Tom Elder and attributed to the find, appeared in the Stack's Bowers Galleries Americana Sale in October 2010 and sold for $4,600.

The Fearful Guest

Hidden: 1854 or later • **Found:** 1935 • **Treasure:** Gold coins

Workmen tearing down an old hotel in Tuskegee, Alabama, found $185 face value in gold coins dated from 1834 to 1854 when they pried a mantle from a wall. It was conjectured that a "fearful guest" hid the money there during the Civil War (1861–1865). No account of the coin denominations or specific varieties was given.[265]

A Strange 1861-S Double Eagle

Hidden or lost: 1800s(?) • **Found:** 1937 • **Treasure:** Gold coins

In 1937, numismatists were startled to learn of a very strange 1861-S double eagle that came to light with a few other U.S. gold pieces under an old barn in Hull, Texas. This particular 1861-S was unlike the regularly seen double eagle in that the letters in UNITED STATES OF AMERICA and TWENTY D. on the reverse were in letters taller and narrower than usual.

The editor of *The Numismatist* consulted a copy of the 1912 work on pattern coins by Edgar H. Adams and William H. Woodin and found a somewhat similar piece listed, but as a pattern made in Philadelphia. There was no mention of an 1861-S coin. He concluded that the 1861-S was a new variety of pattern made—possibly by inadvertently using a pattern die—in San Francisco, as evidenced by the tiny "S" mintmark.

As time went on, coin collectors searched their holdings, quantities of double eagles became available from Europe, and numismatic interest increased in the pieces. It was found that the 1861-S "Paquet Reverse" double eagle, as it became known, was rare, but hardly unique. Today several hundred are known, most of which grade in the Very Fine to Extremely Fine range.

What other varieties of gold coins were found in Hull, Texas, in 1937? The information remains unpublished to this day.[266]

1861-S Paquet double eagle with distinctive tall letters on the reverse.

Dozens of Double Eagles

Hidden: Before the 1930s • **Found:** 1938 • **Treasure:** Gold coins

In 1938, Robert K. Botsford of Nescopeck, Pennsylvania, reported that a hoard of gold coins was unearthed in nearby Bloomsburg when workmen were digging out the cellar of a house. The hoard, no numismatic details of which were given, was said to have consisted mainly of double eagles with a total face value of about $3,000. At the time of the report, ownership was being contested in court.[267]

An Eccentric Kentuckian

Hidden: 1911 or later • **Found:** 1942 • **Treasure:** Gold coins

William H. Cooper had lived in Hodgenville, Kentucky—birthplace of Abraham Lincoln—for nearly all of his life, including from 1898 until his death in October 1932 in a house he had purchased there.

"He was a splendid citizen, but eccentric: what we would term a peculiar man," the administrator of his estate wrote. "Mr. Cooper retired from active business in 1923 and spent practically all of his time at his home. He was a great lover of game chickens and spent much of his time with them. He did not confide in anybody and kept his business strictly to himself. He left a will in which he provided that no inventory should be made of his estate, leaving his property to his wife for her life, and at her death to be equally divided between her people and his people."

By the time of his death, Cooper had suffered memory loss and was in failing health. His wife and heir, who had not been told where the deceased kept his investments, sought to identify his assets. She found a small sum of money in a local bank. Believing there was more, she started a search and in due course located $3,500 in another bank in a nearby town and several thousand dollars in still another bank in Louisville. Meanwhile, she razed the chicken house that her husband had used for his game fowl.

In 1937, Mrs. Cooper, too, passed away. The real estate passed to a man named Hubbard, who lived there through the early 1940s, except for a four-month period when an Army officer stationed at Fort Knox rented the property. The property was then sold to a man who had not moved in by 1942.

In 1942, Otis Enlow—who had been employed by a neighbor, Mr. Routt, to cultivate land for a garden—ran his plow over the old chicken house site and struck gold! Enlow scooped up $600 in eagles and double eagles, and neighbor Routt found $360 worth. The coins, the dates of which ranged from 1850 to 1911, were taken to the Lincoln National Bank, at which point they were intercepted by Judge Handley, who had handled the estates of the Coopers.

The matter went to court in LaGrange, Kentucky, with claims presented by the finder and the administrator of the two Cooper estates. Judge Ballard Clark reviewed the evidence and concluded the coins must have been hidden by the late William H. Cooper sometime around 1911 or later and thus belonged to his heirs. What, if anything, went to the finder was not stated in the account seen.[268]

The Bain Farm Hoard

Hidden: 1866 • **Found:** 1947 • **Treasure:** Gold coins

In 1947, Jack Glasgow—a tenant farmer on acreage owned by A.L. Bain 12 miles south of Keran, Texas—and his employees Clifton Glasgow, Henry Crook, Fred Burton, Wilmer Ely, and Fred Rhynes plowed up a cache of 166 gold coins with a face value of $1,775. Included were these dates and mintmarks (note that it was not indicated whether the 1866-S double eagle was of the "With Motto" or "Without Motto" variety):

Quarter eagles

1861
1866

Half eagles

1834 (4)	1838 (2)	1842-D
1835	1840	1842-O
1836 (5)	1841	1843 (5)

1843-D	1850 (2)	1855-D
1844 (2)	1851 (3)	1855-S
1844-O (6)	1851-O	1856 (2)
1845	1852 (5)	1856-D
1846 (2)	1852-D	1856-S
1846-D (2)	1853 (5)	1858-C
1846-O (2)	1853-C (2)	1858-D
1847 (7)	1853-D	1861 (10)
1848 (2)	1854	
1849 (2)	1854-O	

Eagles

1842	1849 (2)	1853
1843 (2)	1850	1854-S
1847 (3)	1852	1856
1847-O (4)	1852-O	1857

Double eagles

1850 (2)	1856-S	1862-S
1851 (2)	1857 (2)	1863
1851-O	1857-S (2)	1863-S (3)
1852	1858 (3)	1864 (2)
1852-O	1858-S (2)	1864-S (2)
1853 (4)	1859-S	1865 (2)
1854 (3)	1860 (3)	1865-S (2)
1855-S (2)	1861 (8)	1866-S
1856	1861-S (4)	

Concern was expressed that holding gold coins might not be legal, and Bain determined to find out. The curator of history at the Smithsonian Institution stated that there was no problem, after which Bain said he wanted the find to benefit Glasgow and his employees.

William Philpot Jr., a well-known collector of the time, examined the coins. It was stated that coin dealers would be contacted for bids.[269] What happened after that is not known.

The Loxahatchee River Bayou Find

Put away: 1930s • **Found:** 1950s • **Treasure:** Gold and silver coins

In the early 1930s, a man lived aboard a houseboat in a bayou near the outlet of the Loxahatchee River near Jupiter, Florida.[270] Distrustful of banks, he kept gold and silver coins in an iron kettle which he dangled over the boat rail by a wire. A hurricane came up, the boat was tossed about, and the kettle was lost in deep water.

Octagonal $50 gold coin struck in California by Augustus Humbert in 1851.

Years later in the 1950s, Dr. Body, a graduate of the Heidelberg University in Germany, now retired and operating a general store, learned of the missing kettle and contacted F.L. Coffman, who operated a treasure salvage business in West Palm Beach. After one hour and 45 minutes of effort, Coffman located the kettle with an electronic device, brought it to the surface, and found to the delight of Dr. Body and himself that each would be sharing in $7,920 face value worth of rare coins!

The treasure, not numismatically described, was said to consist of the following:

$50 gold: 6
$20 gold: 111
$10 gold: 309
$5 gold: 388
Silver dollars: 217
Miscellaneous silver: 306

Upon reflection today, this was a rather remarkable cache, as $50 gold coins never circulated in Florida or anywhere near it. Such pieces were produced in California in the early 1850s and circulated in that state, and some commemorative $50 coins were produced for the 1915 Panama Pacific International Exposition in San Francisco that year, though these were never intended for circulation.

In any event, it would have been unusual for anyone to have had such pieces as non-numismatic holdings in the early 1930s. More-over, the number of $10 coins in this hoard is remarkably large. Typically, a hoard of gold coins saved for their bullion value is found to be oriented toward pieces of the $20 denomination.

Perhaps the houseboat owner had been a numismatist? This would explain the presence of $50 gold pieces. If so, storing $50 gold coins, silver dollars, and other specimens in salt water would have been a very curious way to keep them!

As is the case with many treasure stories, much is left unanswered.

The Merkers Kaiseroda Mine Treasure

Hidden: 1939–1945 • **Found:** 1945 • **Treasure:** Gold coins and other plunder

During World War II, under orders from Nazi leadership—primarily Hermann Goering and Heinrich Himmler—conquered people and nations were systematically stripped of art, gold, and other valuables.[271] The German Schutzstaffel (SS), or "Protective Squadron," swarmed over conquered Europe confiscating nearly everything of value from governments, many religious groups and individuals. Among the loot were numerous public and private coin collections. The national collections of the Netherlands and Belgium were stolen in their entirety, others were decimated in part;[272] private coin collections spanned the range of typical holdings, from a few dozen pieces kept as much as mementos and family heirlooms, to extensive assemblies of ancient, medieval and modern gold pieces.

The following excerpt sets up our numismatically relevant tale:

On April 4, 1945 the Third Army, 90th Infantry Division took the village of Merkers, a few miles inside the border in Thuringia. On the morning of the 6th, Pfc. Clyde Harmon and Pfc. Anthony Kline, U.S. military policemen, stopped two women on a road outside Merkers. Since both were French displaced persons and one was pregnant, the MPs decided rather than to arrest them to escort them back into the town. On the way, as they passed the entrance to the Kaiseroda salt mine in Merkers, the women talked about gold that the Germans had stored in the mine—so much gold, they said, that unloading it had taken local

One room, approximately 75-by-150-feet in area, of the Merkers mine containing thousands of bags of gold. Bags in the foreground are labeled Reichsbank. Other rooms contained paintings, sculpture, and other art works.

civilians and displaced persons who were used as labor seventy-two hours.[273]

When U.S. soldiers entered the mine, they discovered a room 75 feet wide and 150 feet deep. The floor was covered more than 7,000 numbered bags, each bag containing gold bars or gold coins. The gold amounted to nearly 250 tons. Additionally, paper money was in bales and amounted to 98 million French francs and 2.7 billion Reichsmarks; suitcases contained jewelry, dental fillings and other valuables stolen from individuals; and in other mine passages were 400 tons of fine art works stolen from museums and individuals throughout Europe.

Inventorying and examining the gold treasure was well outside the Army's expertise. For this the Army turned to the Treasury Department on April 20, and they, in turn, recommended using U.S. Mint personnel. The Mint was the only government department that had routine expertise in evaluating gold bullion and coins. The Bank of England also offered the services of two bullion experts. The Treasury provided any needed bags, tags, and seals, and the Army provided ten enlisted men to move and count gold and silver and two clerks to handle clerical work.

Analysis of the inventory committee records and reports by Roger W. Burdette revealed that U.S. gold coins were contained in 738 bags. This amounted to 1,022,919.67 troy ounces of fine gold, or 1,136,577.41 troy ounces of standard 0.900 fine coin gold, representing approximately $21,145,630 at face value. Further analysis broke down the U.S. gold coins by denomination and showed that most of the coins were double eagles. No determination of dates or mintmarks was possible since this information was not recorded during inventory.

The quantities of U.S. gold coins in the hoard:

$1 gold: 1,000
Quarter eagles: 12,714
Half eagles: 136,141
Eagles: 301,534
Double eagles: 870,840

After the inventory, in early 1946, the gold found at Merkers was turned over to the Inter-Allied Reparation Agency and eventually to the Tripartite Commission for the Restitution of Monetary Gold (TGC) for distribution to countries whose central bank gold had been stolen by the Nazis. The TGC began the process of getting the gold returned to most countries as quickly as possible. However, Cold War factors resulted in some of the gold not being returned to its owners until 1996.[274]

It is likely that most of the gold coins were retained in their original condition following restitution. All of the post-war governments were in need of cash, and selling a double eagle for $48 on the open market was a much better deal than melting it and getting only $33.86 for the same gold. There is no way to tell how much of the present stock of U.S. gold coins came from the Merkers treasure and how much came from bank vaults in neutral Switzerland or South and Central American countries.

Hidden in a Staircase

Put away: Early 1900s • **Revealed:** 1957 • **Treasure:** Gold coins

Raymond Shepherd, curator of Old Economy Village (see chapter 7, "The Incredible Economite Hoard," page 125), told of a cache of gold coins within his own family:

My grandmother, Katherine Matlack, called me to her bedside just days before she died late in November of 1957. I was home from college for the Thanksgiving holiday. She was very frail, and I was rather sad to see her in her condition. However, she was happy to see me and asked me to stay when the nurses left.

She motioned me to come closer to whisper in my ear, "Raymond, I want you to go into my sewing room and go to the closet. Under the sheets on the fourth step—pull it toward you—it will come out. In the cut out you will find something for you! Bring it to me!"

To my surprise I only found a cloth bound by a ribbon and something hard inside. However, upon opening it I saw a 1924 $20 gold coin of the Saint-Gaudens design, three Liberty Head $10 gold coins dated 1899, 1900, and 1907, and a gold dollar of 1853. She said they were for hard times and hoped I never had to use them. Happily, I still have them in my safe deposit box.

My grandfather, William Shepherd, had also had retained gold pieces in spite of their possibly being seized. He had given them to

my father, as he collected coins as a young boy in the 1920s. When I was 21 my father gave them to me including a $2.50 Indian head, a $5 Indian, and four Liberty Head $10.[275]

An 1853 gold dollar.

Gold Dollars in Baltimore

Put away: 1880s • **Found:** 1950s–1960s • **Treasure:** Rare gold dollars

Beginning in 1879, there was a popular speculation in certain U.S. coin series, especially the gold dollar, but to a lesser extent the silver trade dollar and the $3 gold denominations. By this time, gold dollars—first minted in 1849—had ceased being a meaningful part of the U.S. commercial coinage system, and examples mainly reposed in bank vaults. In contrast, years earlier in 1853, gold dollars were struck to the extent of 4,076,051 examples and were common sights in business transactions.

A glance at mintage figures reveals enticingly low production quantities for circulation strike gold dollars of 1879 and the two following years:

1879: 3,000
1880: 1,600
1881: 7,620

Large quantities of gold dollars bearing the three aforementioned dates were bought by a Baltimore investor whose identity is not known today. However, it has been suggested that T. Harrison Garrett—an heir to the Baltimore & Ohio Railroad fortune who resided in Evergreen House, a mansion on North Charles Street in Baltimore— is a likely candidate. If he was the buyer, those gold dollars were not transferred to The Johns Hopkins University in 1942 when Garrett's coins were gifted to the institution by one of T. Harrison Garrett's sons, John Work Garrett.

Years later, in the 1950s and 1960s, glittering prooflike gem gold dollars of 1879, 1880, and 1881 began appearing on the market in quantity,

An 1880 gold dollar.

especially through the offices of Abner Kreisberg in California and Thomas Warfield in Baltimore. It was generally acceded at the time that the source for these coins was a Baltimore bank vault, but no other details were given. Kreisberg recalled to me that he had purchased some of his coins from old-time dealer Joe Block (who also had large quantities of 1938-D Buffalo nickels).[276]

I was involved in the numismatic distribution of these pieces and acquired examples to the extent of many hundreds of each date. If memory serves, there were more of 1881-dated coins than of the other two. Today, high-grade gold dollars of all three dates are often encountered and are highly prized for their quality and their low mintage.[277]

A Cache of 1889 Gold Dollars

In addition, worthy of mention is a small hoard of a couple hundred or so 1889 gold dollars, each coin frosty and lustrous (not prooflike) and stored in a small rectangular brown envelope, that I bought from Maurice Storck in the 1950s. These had turned up in a safe deposit box in a bank in Maine.

A brilliant and lustrous 1889 gold dollar.

Evergreen House, the residence of T. Harrison Garrett, who by the late 1880s had the largest private coin collection in the United States. He also collected books, autographs, and prints.

He Liked Gold!

Accumulated: 1930s • **Found:** 1960 • **Treasure:** Gold coins

On Wednesday, March 30, 1960, the normally quiet Chicago suburb of Mount Prospect was thrown into a dither, according to a story which broke in the *Chicago Daily News* and immediately was sent out on the wires by the Associated Press.[278]

It seems that Stanley R. Pierce, a wealthy Chicago investment broker at the time recently deceased (December 25, 1959), liked gold. However, he kept his liking secret; when his estate had been appraised at $500,000, the valuers were not aware of any gold coins. But, indeed, there were quite a few!

The circumstances of the find were not revealed, nor was it said why appraisers of his estate did not know of the cache earlier. However, he left a map behind in a safe he owned, which was found by representatives of the executor, the Continental-Illinois Bank. Thus, on one memorable day in early spring, the coins—said to "total nearly $100,000"—were unearthed in his yard, where they had been buried beneath two fruit trees. This was no old-time hoard, but instead had been secreted by Pierce within the preceding 10 years (his home was built in 1950). Apparently, though, the coins had been accumulated by him in the early 1930s.

Pierce, a widower, left no children, and his entire estate went to his alma mater, the University of Chicago, where in 1913 he had been a star fullback on the football squad. Unfortunately, no numismatic details of the cache appeared in the popular press, and it is not known if the $100,000 represented the face value or an appraised numismatic worth.

Four Double Eagle Rarities

Put away: 1931 or later • **Disclosed:** 1960 • **Treasure:** Rare 1931-D double eagles

In 1960, a Sidney, New York, businessman took from his bank safety deposit box four "ordinary" double eagles and brought them to me, for he had heard there was a premium above face value for all gold coins.

I glanced at them, found they were all of the extremely rare 1931-D variety and in blazing gem Mint State, showed him the listing in *A Guide Book of United States Coins*, and expected that the finder would be delighted.

Just the opposite occurred. Uncertainty set in—what were they *really worth*? Could they be sold for more elsewhere? Maybe they shouldn't be sold after all.

Back into the safe deposit box the pieces went. Where they are now I do not know.[279]

A rare 1931-D double eagle.

Long-Hidden Gold Coins

Hidden or lost: Early 1900s or before • **Found:** 1965 • **Treasure:** Gold coins

In Amity, Arkansas, J.C. Bean was clearing a lot in preparation for building a new house. While his bulldozer was scraping out the foundation area, a hoard of $538 face value worth of gold coins was revealed.

After the coins were counted, onlookers pressed forward, and two observers "made off with several of the coins during the confusion," reducing the remaining hoard to $438. No list of dates and mintmarks was made available to the press.[280]

Soldiers' Gold at Pyramid Lake (?)

Hidden or lost: 1800s • **Found:** 1967 • **Treasure:** Gold coins

In 1967, members of the Nicon Tribal Council, Pyramid Lake Indian Reservation, near Reno, Nevada, found a cache of "gold coins dating back to 1814 with a face value of $3,500."[281]

The coins were taken to Nick Jackson, a shop owner in Reno, who inspected them and pro-nounced that "many are quite valuable." He conjectured that the coins might have been left from a military encampment in the area during the Second Pyramid Lake Indian War in 1860.

Gold in Beverly Hills

Stored: 1916 • **Found:** 1970s • **Treasure:** Gold coins dated 1911 and 1916

In the 1970s, I received a call from a trust officer at the Beverly Hills branch of the Bank of America on North Beverly Drive. The John Estate was being sold, and investigation had revealed a cache of gold coins had been hidden in a vault for decades.

Upon visiting the bank, I was greeted by the sight of three white cloth bags with mint inscriptions on the outside of each, one containing 500 1916-S eagles—considered to be a somewhat scarce date—and 500 each of 1911-S and 1916-S double eagles. Each coin was brilliant and lustrous. A deal was struck, and the coins were mine.

These were subsequently advertised and were completely sold out *within four hours* of the time our offering appeared![282]

A 1916-S eagle.

Gold in a New England Bank Vault _____

Hidden: 1873 or later • **Found:** By 1976 • **Treasure:** Gold dollars

There is a romantic link between numismatics and New England, the latter representing the source not only of many coins in our history (beginning with the 1652 Massachusetts silver coinage), but also collections, accumulations, and hoards.

Further, the undisclosed contents of safe deposit boxes are always fascinating to contemplate. Any old bank vault is likely lined with scores of such steel-faced boxes, imprinted with numbers, within which may lurk all sorts of treasures.

Thus, when an old safe deposit box in a New England bank yields a treasure, so much the better for romantic and historical purposes. Seem-ingly, finding a cache of coins in a bank vault in a modern shopping center in Delaware would have less appeal. Anyway . . .

It was circa 1976 when a box was opened in New England and dis closed 11 different speci-mens of 1873-dated U.S. gold dollars—not a rare date, but an issue usually found one at a time. Grades ranged from About Uncirculated to choice Uncirculated. Nine of the 11 were from an obverse die with a raised die line on Miss Liberty's neck. All coins were toned alike and showed evidence of having been kept together for a long time.[283]

A Long-Buried Snuff Pot _____

Hidden: Circa 1910 • **Found:** 1977 • **Treasure:** Gold coins

It is not often that museum curators, the custodi-ans of many valuable coins, find a numismatic treasure first-hand.[284] However, it has happened, and this account is of such an instance.

In late spring 1977, Donald R. Touhy, a curator at the Nevada State Museum, Carson City, had a singular stroke of good fortune. Excavation was to be done at Lovelock, Nevada, for the right-of-way for the Interstate 80 highway. Chinese labor-ers had lived in the area in the late 1800s and early 1900s, and it was felt that the site, which had yielded some artifacts, should be professionally explored before construction crews came in with heavy equipment.

At the site, Touhy was digging in the basement of what had once been a house when he came across a crockery pot of the type that had been commonly used as a snuff container. Upon inspec-tion, the container was found to contain gold coins dated from the late 1800s through 1910 with a total face value of $1,800. The coins, which became the property of the Nevada State Museum, were appraised as having a numismatic worth of about $26,000.

The Nevada State Museum is housed in the impressive stone building that was home to the Carson City Mint. Wonder if any of those buried gold coins had CC mintmarks? If so, they came back home.

Gold in the American River (Reprise) _____

Hidden: 1850s • **Found:** 1979 • **Treasure:** Gold coins

Historians know well that the American River was the site in January 1848 of the fabulous dis-covery of gold by James Marshall.[285] An employee of John Sutter, owner of a wood-sawing mill on the American River, Marshall saw some gleaming yellow gold flakes in the tail race. This set in motion the great California Gold Rush, the ensu-ing arrival of the forty-niners, and, eventually, the development of the West as it is today.

At some later date, an individual whose identity is not known today put part of his personal fortune in a little sack, dug a hole about two feet deep, and buried it nearby, on the North Fork of the American River where it joins with Indian Creek. This small stash consisted of San Francisco Mint gold coins dated in the 1850s, mostly double eagles but two half eagles as well. Also included were three Kellogg $20 gold pieces of the 1854–1855 style.

Fast-forward to 1979, when Joe Soule was looking for gold nuggets with a dredge on the North Fork of the American River. *Voilà*—a "second find" of gold on the American River! Under a couple feet of gravel and enclosed in what remained of the old sack were found a handful of the long-hidden double eagles, the two aforementioned half eagles, and some gold nuggets. As good fortune would have it, these were sold into numismatic channels and today quite probably rest in a number of different collections, the owners of which may not be aware of their romantic history.

The California Gold Rush district, as shown on an 1850 map.

A Society Lady's Security

Acquired: 1933 • **Dispersed:** Early 1980s • **Treasure:** Gold coins

In early 1933, the U.S. government placed stringent restrictions on the ownership of U.S. gold coins.[286] Hearing rumors to this effect, a prominent lady of the East Coast, possibly with the cooperation of her mother, decided to acquire and set aside some pieces for the comfort and

financial security they seemed to represent in that troubled economic time.

Years later, the woman's heirs enlisted numismatist David Enders Tripp to assist with their sale into the numismatic market. The group was found to contain the following pieces, a valuable informational find for scholars, as it shows typical gold coins that could be acquired at banks in early 1933. The earlier-dated coins were for the most part worn, while some of the later pieces were gem Mint State, the 1927 gold eagles being in the latter category.

In his 1988 *Encyclopedia*, Walter H. Breen erroneously attributed certain of these pieces to the Virgil M. Brand estate, as in this example: "1923-D $20. Manfra, Tordella & Brookes handled a hoard of over 1,000 Uncs. including many from the Brand estate 1981–1982." As is seen in the inventory below, the number of 1923-D double eagles from this source amounted to 154 coins, hardly a quantity to be sniffed at, but not a serious challenge to the 1,000 figure mentioned by Breen.[287]

Note that the 1834 half eagles were of the Classic Head design; the 1908 half eagle was of the Indian Head design; the 1907-D and 1907-S eagles were of the Liberty Head design, while of the 1907 (Philadelphia Mint) issue, 4 were of the Liberty Head design and 29 were of the Indian Head design; and the 1907-D double eagles were of the Liberty Head design.

$1 gold

1850
1852

Quarter eagles

1843-O (2)	1857-S	1893 (2)
1845	1859	1895
1845-O (2)	1859-S	1896 (2)
1846-O (2)	1861 (15)	1897 (2)
1847-O (2)	1862	1898 (3)
1850 (4)	1871-S (2)	1899 (6)
1851 (7)	1873 (12)	1900 (12)
1852 (14)	1878 (21)	1901 (22)
1852-O (2)	1878-S (8)	1902 (23)
1853 (19)	1879 (13)	1903 (48)
1854 (7)	1879-S (3)	1904 (43)
1854-O (2)	1879 (13)	1905 (56)
1855 (2)	1879-S (3)	1906 (56)
1856 (8)	1887 (2)	1907 (88)
1857	1890 (4)	1908 (51)

1909 (11)	1912 (3)	1914-D (11)
1910 (2)	1913 (6)	1915 (10)
1911 (17)	1914 (7)	

Half eagles

1834 (2)	1877-S	1900-S
1836 (3)	1879-S (3)	1901-S (12)
1838 (2)	1880 (5)	1902-S (4)
1839 (2)	1880-S (8)	1903-S (8)
1839-C	1881 (9)	1904
1840	1881-S (5)	1905-S (6)
1843	1882 (11)	1906-S
1844-O (2)	1882-S (2)	1906-D (5)
1845 (6)	1884-S	1907
1846 (4)	1885-S (2)	1907-D (5)
1847 (7)	1886	1908 (17)
1848 (3)	1886-S (11)	1908-S (22)
1849	1887-S (3)	1909 (6)
1851	1888-S (2)	1909-S (5)
1852	1893-S (4)	1910 (8)
1853	1895	1911 (9)
1854 (holed)	1897 (5)	1911-S
1855-S	1897-S (3)	1912 (8)
1856-S	1898 (2)	1913 (7)
1857	1898-S (8)	1913-S
1861 (8)	1899	1914
1863-S	1899-S (5)	1915 (6)
1874 (3)	1900 (10)	

Eagles

1840	1880-S (4)	1893-S
1842-O (2)	1881 (9)	1894 (2)
1844-O	1881-S (7)	1894-O
1845-O	1882 (11)	1894-S
1847 (3)	1882-S	1895-O
1847-O (3)	1883	1896-S
1849 (4)	1884-S	1897 (12)
1850 (3)	1885 (2)	1897-S (5)
1852 (2)	1885-S	1898 (3)
1853	1886-S (2)	1898-S
1854-S (2)	1887-S (6)	1899 (6)
1856-S	1889-S (2)	1899-S (5)
1857	1890	1900-S
1879-S (2)	1892 (3)	1901 (11)
1880 (7)	1893 (3)	1901-S (10)

1902	1907-D	1910-S (5)
1902-S (2)	1907-S (2)	1911 (5)
1903	1907 (29)	1912 (6)
1903-S (2)	1908 (7)	1912-S (2)
1905 (2)	1908-D (2)	1913 (4)
1905-S (5)	1909 (2)	1914
1906	1909-D	1914-D (2)
1906-D (15)	1909-S (2)	1915 (4)
1906-S (3)	1910 (2)	
1907 (4)	1910-D (3)	

Double eagles

1878-S	1904	1927 (14)
1879-S	1907-D (99)	
1890-S	1923-D	
1895	(154)	

A Mint State 1923-D double eagle.

Four Teenagers Strike Gold

Hidden: 1897 or later • **Found:** 1984 • **Treasure:** Gold coins

In 1984, four teenagers were remodeling the home of Robert Poehling in LaCrosse, Wisconsin.[288] The house had been built circa 1864. In the basement beneath the kitchen was found "a hidden hoard of late nineteenth century United States gold coins." The pieces were contained in an iron pot.

Upon inspection, the treasure was found to contain half eagles, eagles, and double eagles dated from 1870 to 1897. It was theorized that a former owner, local merchant Mons Anderson, had secreted the coins. Previously wealthy, Anderson was poor at the time of his death in 1905, deepening the mystery of why the gold coins remained there.

Help Me Find the Missing Half Eagle

Hidden: 1876 or later • **Found:** 1984 • **Treasure:** Double eagles and others

Bob Van Camp, owner of Comstock Metal Detectors, Chico, California, received a call for assistance.[289] A lady had lost a gold coin from her necklace while rototilling her garden. The necklace itself had been found, but the coin—a half eagle—had in all probability been plowed under somewhere in an acre of freshly turned earth. Help!

Van Camp switched his detector on and began searching in the area where the chain part of the necklace had been found. A few signals indicated "nails," but to be sure he was not missing the valuable half eagle, the detectorist turned over a few spades of dirt. Nothing particular turned up.

A few minutes later, eureka! There was a tremendous blast in Van Camp's headphones. The missing half eagle had been found, according to the "gold" setting on the meter. Bob dug to extract it, but, what was this? He found a *double* eagle! Bob showed it to the waiting landowners and was told that in recent years a few other gold coins had been turned up here and there during the rototilling season.

Excited about the possibilities of finding a cache, Van Camp asked questions and found that an old stage line had once passed nearby. A deal was made to split any find, and he went to work. Soon Bob found another double eagle, then another, and then still another! By day's end, a half eagle (but not the necklace specimen) and six double eagles had been found, the last including an 1875-CC with a scar from the rototiller blade.

The next day, Van Camp was on the site early, and in short order found two eagles stuck together, perhaps indicating that he was near the original spot where the coins had been buried. Some more looking disclosed the remains of an old iron pot and some more coins. The following day brought still more. Then, the finds stopped.

When all the coins were counted, the total stood at 44 gold pieces, of which 35 were of the $20 denomination. The oldest coin was a rare 1839 eagle, while the most recent was a double eagle with the date 1876. And, oh yes, the missing half eagle from the necklace was found, too.

Scrambling for Coins in Jackson, Tennessee

Hidden: 1859 • **Found:** 1985 • **Treasure:** Gold coins

On September 12, 1985, in Jackson, Tennessee, land was being graded in preparation for the building of a parking lot.[290] A bulldozer driven by "Buddy" Crick dug up a glass jar filled to the rim with glittering gold coins, many from the Charlotte and Dahlonega mints. A mad scramble ensued as crew members were joined by others. Within a short time, hundreds of coins were claimed by a dozen or more people.

Word spread to gold buyers and to coin dealers, who descended upon Jackson and bought whatever they could. One man traded eight gold coins for a 1983 Pontiac. Some workers, not aware of their value, sold coins for as little as $50 each. Dealer Jeff Garrett reported that "the workers all jumped in, and the coins were scattered among several individuals. I had the opportunity to examine many of the pieces and they were all of very high quality."

John Dannreuther advised, "There were several hundred 1853 quarter eagles. I know of a hundred piece lot that traded and I sold 50 to 60 at another time."[291] Dannreuther himself purchased many coins at the time, including five Mint State 1858-O eagles. A Mint State 1858-O double eagle was also among the treasure, and there was rumor of two $50 octagonal slugs from the California Gold Rush, though that was not later confirmed. The illustrated 1854 double eagle was among his acquisitions.

Taking stock of the situation slightly after the fact and responding to media, Jackson mayor Robert Conger was quoted as saying, "We've accounted for 177 [coins], and that's just by

A Mint State 1853 quarter eagle.

An 1854 double eagle from the Jackson find.

talking to people who said they possessed some." At Conger's request, a judge issued an order that people who had coins should not sell them until it was learned to whom the title belonged (perhaps the city). This caused a lot of pro-and-con discussion in the local papers, and it seems that few of the dispersed coins were surrendered.

One Evening in 1859

There is a tragic background to this story. The scenario swirled about the Jackson branch of the Union Bank of Tennessee. The institution had been chartered in 1832 with an authorized capital of $3 million and opened in 1833 with headquarters in Nashville and branches in Jackson, Knoxville, Columbia, Chattanooga, and Memphis, the last of which transacted more business and had far more capital than did the Memphis headquarters or any other branch.[292]

In August 1856, *Banker's Magazine* reported that the branch in Jackson—located in a two-story red brick building with a vacant top floor—had been reorganized, and Ebenezer F. McKnight was named as cashier.[293] As was normal for many banks, the cashier was provided with a room to reside in adjacent to the banking office. This was to provide security at times when the bank was closed. However, McKnight never slept there as he felt it was too dangerous.[294]

On February 2 of 1859, McKnight went by train to Augusta, Georgia, where he checked into the City Hotel. A clerk, George E. Miller, occupied the sleeping room at the bank in the meantime and stayed overnight. McKnight had left some sheets of signed cashier's checks with Miller.

At about nine o'clock in the evening of the next night, a visitor—probably a person well known to Miller—called and requested a cashier's check drawn on Memphis. While the clerk was at a desk filling out the check, the visitor grabbed a heavy hammer used to cancel redeemed bank notes and struck him on the head with great force, crushing his skull and killing him instantly. The assailant then took the bank and vault keys from under

Miller's pillow, entered the banking room and vault, stole a large amount of coins and paper money, and then put the keys back under the pillow. The gruesome situation was discovered the next morning when the bank remained closed.

A $4 note, an unusual denomination, of the Jackson branch of the Union Bank of Tennessee. Printed by Woodruff, Tucker & Co., bank-note engravers in Cincinnati.

Stories

Many sensational stories were then told in newspapers, often varying widely. According to early accounts, McKnight had taken *all* of the bank's paper money to Atlanta the day before the robbery (for reasons undisclosed), leaving only about $16,000 in coins in the vault. The losses, however, were later amended to $6,000 in gold coins and $11,000 in Union Bank notes, which does not square with the story that cashier McKnight took all of the bills to Atlanta.

Still another account stated that $20,000 in bills was stolen, and a few months later (June 1859) a large amount of the bank's currency was discovered in Cohocksink Creek near Philadelphia, Pennsylvania.[295] The truth seems to have been that about $23,000 was stolen, including $5,700 in gold.[296]

In the meantime reward notices for information were posted in many newspapers. A few weeks later a young man named James Rigdon, known at the time as Irwin or Irving, was arrested and found to have some suspected stolen coins on his person. For lack of evidence he was soon set free.[297] It has been said that the bank president was strongly suspected of the crime, but was not charged. I found no evidence of this charge.

Thus, no prime suspects were ever identified. As the coins were hidden not too far from the bank, it seems likely that the intruder was a local person who took the coins home or to another location, transferred them to a jar, and buried them sometime before the discovery of the crime the next morning. In that way, there was no chance they would be found in the possession of anyone or on any premises. And seeing as the coins were never claimed, it is likely that this robber died not long afterward.

Today, apart from the coins that have come on the market now and then and which have been said to have come from Jackson, little is known. No inventory of the hoard will ever be compiled, as most finders of the coins and the dealer buyers—some of whom I interviewed in the late 1900s—seem to think that the less said the better! Likely, the quantity was between 500 and 700 coins.

The Chicago Double Eagle Hoard

Hidden: Circa 1929–1933 • **Found:** July 1986 • **Treasure:** Double eagles

Thomas K. DeLorey tells the story of this remarkable group:

A rare 1932 double eagle.

In July of 1986 I received a call at the coin shop in Chicago where I was working at the time to ask if we would be interested in doing an appraisal on "some gold coins at a bank." Naturally, I said yes and made an appointment to meet the lady who had them.

At the bank I met the owner. While she went to get the coins for me to view, I waited in a conference room. After some time she returned with a vault attendant who was pushing a heavily laden cart. I noticed that the bank employee left the cart with the coins, as this was easier than having to lift the box off of it. After he departed, the owner opened the box and began pulling out some 10-inch by 10-inch sheets of purple felt sewn into squares, checkerboard fashion, five rows of five squares each. There were 43 of the sheets.

The owner produced a pair of scissors and handed them to me and said that the gold coins were inside the cloths. I carefully began cutting the felt along one side of a sheet, and removed five double eagles from the five pockets in the row thus exposed. Every pocket in each sheet contained a double eagle, for a total of 25 coins per sheet.

As I spent the next few hours carefully opening the sheets, I noticed a definite pattern in their contents. One sheet might have 25 ordinary mixed-date Very Fine to Extremely Fine Liberty Head or Saint-Gaudens double eagles, while the next one might have 25 absolutely gorgeous specimens all of the same date and mint. The Uncirculated coins all had a deep rich patina with a hint of green in it, which I assume was from prolonged contact with the felt, and were remarkably free of bag marks due to their protection by the felt and the fact that they had never been subjected to an ocean voyage to a Swiss bank and back. Most would grade MS-65 or *better* by today's standards.

In chatting with the owner, I learned that her grandmother, who had been born and raised in the "old country" and had married a successful businessman after emigrating to America, did not trust banks and was in the habit after the stock market crash of 1929 of taking $500 in cash to a bank every so often and converting it into double eagles. She then took the coins home where she sewed them into the squares that made up each cloth sheet. Whatever the bank happened to have a particular day—and there may have been more than one bank involved—was what she received.

Approximately 40% of the pads contained circulated Liberty Head $20s, and there were two or three pads of circulated Saint-Gaudens pieces from the 1907–1916 period. There were no pads of mixed circulated Liberty Heads and Saint-Gaudens coins, which might mean that banks routinely separated the two, though it could just as easily mean that she just happened to draw on one bag of each from two different banks.

Among the Uncirculated pads, there were two or three that were Liberty Head coins dated 1907 and five or six of the 1907-D, plus one to five each of the Saint-Gaudens varieties such as 1907, 1908 no motto, 1911-D, 1914-D, and 1923-D, and perhaps one or two common dates from the 1920s. The 1923-Ds were exceptionally nice.

All of these pads were of solid dates, except for one exceptional pad which yielded one each of the extremely rare 1927-S, 1929, 1930-S, 1931, 1931-D and 1932! I was astounded, to say the least, when I saw this pad filled with great rarities, and opened the last 10 or so pads hoping to find a legendary 1927-D or even a 1933, but the pattern reverted to normal. Once my pulse went back to its regular rate, I completed the appraisal and carefully repacked the coins in plastic tubes cushioned with a lot of tissue paper. Eventually we purchased the collection, and it was dispersed at the 1986 ANA convention in Milwaukee.

I have no idea how this hoard happened to have six rare dates in it. Perhaps one of her bankers, in the interest of keeping an important customer happy, arranged to get them for her. Perhaps she just got lucky. In the early 1930s little numismatic attention was paid to these almost-current dates, so it was probably simply the luck of the draw.

Several years later, as I was telling this story to another Chicago area coin dealer, he told me that he had purchased a smaller but similar lot from another heir, who had implied that there was yet another such group in existence. However, his purchase did not include any rare dates, and mostly consisted of 1923-Ds. I do not know if the other group referred to was the one we had bought, or if there is a third (or fourth) lot still out there.

I would have loved to have seen the entire group in its original hiding place—wherever that was—so that I could have recorded the dates of the strata as they were laid down in the 1930s, but the coins must have been moved several times during the process of distribution to the heirs. However, it is interesting to note that several different original bags of pre-World War I dates must have been in place in Chicago banks in the 1929–1933 period, and not just common Philadelphia Mint double eagles bearing such often-seen dates as 1924 through 1928.

Abe Kosoff once told me how he had assisted a few clients in having bags of U.S. $20s shipped to Swiss banks before the Gold Surrender Act of 1933 took effect, and I take it he was not alone in this endeavor. Perhaps this outflow of $20s caused a shortage of that denomination in this country, which in turn caused the Treasury in Washington and/or the Denver Mint to open its vaults of older dates long held in storage, similar to what was done with silver dollars in the 1962–1964 period. Of course, this is speculation on my part.[298]

Forgotten Gold Eagles

Hidden: 1932 • **Found:** 1989 • **Treasure:** Gold eagles

It is said that in 1932, a sea captain living on a rocky inlet on Penobscot Bay on the coast of Maine liked gold—as in gold coins.

In that year, he obtained from his bank 61 freshly minted $10 gold eagles of the same date and put them in a place for safekeeping. There they remained forgotten for many years, until a descendant came across them and showed them to a leading Eastern U.S. dealer in art and antiques, who contacted a rare-coin dealer. The coins proved not to be rarities, for 1932 is one of the more plentiful issues of the Saint-Gaudens Indian Head design.

However, nearly all were particularly nice choice or gem Mint State examples, and when they were auctioned in 1989, there was a wild bidding scramble as collectors competed to acquire them.[299]

A 1932 eagle.

A Leather Pouch

Hidden: 1856 or later • **Found:** Early 1990s • **Treasure:** Dahlonega Mint gold coins

Jeff Garrett recalled a significant find of gold coins located in the early 1990s:

> About five or six years ago a hoard of Southern gold was discovered somewhere in North Carolina. The coins were found in a leather pouch and included a quantity of Dahlonega gold coins. The hoard ended up with a dealer in Atlanta. Al Adams, who saw the coins, said the quality was fantastic. I have heard from other people that the group contained many examples of 1856-D half eagles.[300]

This is a short but numismatically sweet account, as 1856-D half eagles are highly prized no matter what the grade. And these were only *part* of the find!

A rare 1856-D half eagle.

The "Rolling Stone" Hoard

Hidden: 1914 • **Found:** 1996 • **Treasure:** Gold coins

In 1914, a person unknown today decided to wrap in paper rolls a group of gold coins and carefully place them in a glass jar on a site that was once a mining area in Sun Valley, Idaho. Years later, that land was purchased by Jann Wenner, New York publisher of *Rolling Stone* magazine, as part of a 117-acre tract.

In 1996, Greg Corliss, working for Anderson Asphalt, was using a skip loader to prepare a drive to an area of Wenner's tract on which a guest house was to be constructed. Eureka! The blade unearthed and broke the long-buried jar. Corliss called over his employer, Larry Anderson, and the two agreed to split the find half-and-half and also to keep the coins secret. They went to a trailer parked on Anderson's gravel pit and examined the coins—96 pieces dated 1914 and earlier with a total face value of $1,160.

Despite the aforementioned agreement, pride overwhelmed Corliss, and he could not resist telling friends in a local bar about the treasure. He suggested that the coins might be worth somewhere between $30,000 and a half-million dollars once they were appraised. Meanwhile, most of the coins were stored for safekeeping by Anderson.

Trouble arose, as Corliss kept talking while Anderson wanted to keep the matter quiet. Soon they were adversaries. Both told Wenner of the find and hoped to work out some arrangement. Corliss thought fame would be his, that he might even be featured in *Rolling Stone*—but Wenner took the position that the coins were his.

The dispute went to mediation, which was unsuccessful. The next step was court, where Judge James May ruled in Wenner's favor. Afterward, Corliss sued Anderson without effect. Wenner secured two appraisals, one for $23,400 and the other for $25,500.[301]

The Wells Fargo Hoard

Hidden: 1908 • **Found:** 1997 • **Treasure:** 1908 No Motto double eagles

A double eagle from the Wells Fargo Hoard.

Ron Gillio told of his role in the remarkable Wells Fargo Hoard:

> Of all the different hoards I have bought in Europe, Asia, America, and elsewhere, for which you have interviewed me over a period of years and for which I have sent you various correspondence, this group of 1908s in the most interesting and highest quality group I have ever purchased. Here is the basic story, although some details must remain confidential:
>
> In the 1990s I bought 19,900 pieces of 1908 No Motto twenties. The coins were stored in one place in bags of 500 coins, each with a seal. The seals on the bags of all 19,900 coins were all dated in the 1960s. When I first met with the owners there were several people involved, and I was on hand with a colleague. They had a special book in which we had to register before they opened the first bag. The book contained the seal number and the date of the seal. We had to sign this book for every bag they opened. The person opening the bags was the person who sealed them originally.

At first glance I could tell the coins were fantastic and of high quality—as the bags were never tossed around or recounted over the years, in contrast to most bank hoards. I took the coins and put them in rolls of 50 and then put the rolls back in the bags. By the way, the bags were normal canvas bags that had been used to replace the original bags, which had deteriorated, in which they were sealed in 1917. The coins had something to do with an international settlement/payment of some kind in the World War I era. Except for the rebagging, the coins had remained unmoved and untouched since 1917!

After I bought the coins they were subsequently moved and stored for a time at a Wells Fargo Bank in Nevada, whose name was later attached to the hoard. Most of the coins were graded by PCGS and NGC receiving the highest grades of any hoard of $20s. Here is an approximate breakdown of the grades: MS-69 (10 coins), MS-68 (200+), MS-67 (1,700+), and MS-66 (6,000+), with the balance being MS-65 or below. I have never seen a hoard of $20s of this quality, all one date, before this group or after. I have since examined large caches of $20s in various places but none match the quality of the 1908s.[302]

The Saddle Ridge Hoard

Hidden: 1894 • **Found:** 2013 • **Treasure:** Liberty Head double eagles, etc.

An 1890-S double eagle from the Saddle Ridge Hoard before and after conservation.

In 2013, a husband and wife who live in the Gold Country of California (loosely defined as being in or around the Sierra Nevada Mountains more or less east of San Francisco) were walking their dog on their property.[303] They spied a metal can partially sticking out of the ground. Upon inspection, it was found to be filled with gold coins—mostly double eagles!

Their interest was piqued, and with a good deal of excitement they used a metal detector to explore the area carefully. Seven more gold-filled cans came to light. The treasure trove included 4 half eagles (including a scarce 1849-D), 50 eagles, and an amazing 1,373 double eagles! The earliest coin was an 1847-O eagle, the latest a number of 1894-S double eagles, suggesting that the coins were hidden in 1894 or shortly afterward. The total face value was $27,980, which would have been a small fortune at the estimated time of burial.

As the winners of a lottery ticket might do, the couple carefully considered their options. First, to insure safety, they put the coins in a cooler and buried it beneath a woodpile. Their secret was not shared with anyone. Then, they contacted an attorney, who contacted two coin dealers. Kagin's, of Tiburon, California, was decided upon, and Don Kagin jumped into what turned out to be a lot of excitement.

One of the tin cans.

The name "Saddle Ridge Hoard" was given to the find, as the cans were found on a ridge on their property. Wisely, the finders elected to remain anonymous—no doubt sparing them from countless intruders, not to mention lawsuits from those claiming to have links to former owners of the property.

As is usually the case with found treasure, facts were and are scarce—the wish of the owners. Meanwhile, there was no lack of speculation, including suggestions that the mystery of $30,000 face value of double eagles stolen from the San Francisco Mint had been solved! Of course, the stolen coins were freshly minted, whereas the coins from the find had seen various degrees of circulation. To settle the matter, the U.S. Mint eventually issued a statement that the Saddle Ridge Hoard had no connection with that theft.

An inventory of the hoard showed it was dominated by 416 1889-S double eagles in various grades. Among the most valuable in the accumulation was a beautiful 1866-S No Motto double eagle certified by PCGS as MS-62, the finest known example. Most of the coins were from the San Francisco Mint, suggesting that they had been gathered in the area before they were buried, as opposed to having been brought from a distant place.

The coins were offered for sale by Kagin's—to the numismatic community and also on Amazon.com—starting at midnight on May 27, 2014. By May 29, nearly half had been sold at fixed prices totaling $4,100,000.[304]

chapter 11

Down with the Ship

Over the years, shipwrecks on American inland and coastal waters have numbered in the tens of thousands. Doubtless, just about any vessel that departed from a river, lake, or ocean port and later sank took with it at least some pocket change. Thus, a complete enumeration of shipwrecks with coins would, in effect, be a multivolume listing of our country's shipping history.

That said, there are several notable shipwrecks that are mentioned here (and others in later chapters). Certainly, the HMS *Feversham* is numismatically important by any standard. The wreck of the *Arabia* is representative of many inland steamer incidents and has yielded only assorted pocket change. The tragedy of the *Lexington* is one of many nautical disasters that may in some future day yield specimens of numismatic value, but for the present the coins remain either lost or, if discovered, unreported.

Possibly more than in any other area of numismatic treasure research, published references concerning lost and sunken ships are apt to differ widely in details, possibly because later writers often romanticized and embellished their accounts. Because of this, I have listed multiple sources in many instances and has pointed out some differences in details.

Certain California Gold Rush era ships are discussed in later chapters.

The Wreck of the HMS *Feversham*

Lost: October 7, 1711 • **Location:** Scatarie Island, Nova Scotia •
Found: 1984 • **Treasure:** Massachusetts silver and other coins

In 1710, during one of the seemingly endless series of colonial military conflicts between England and France—this one called Queen Anne's War—the British government in America decided to mount an attack against the fortress at Quebec. Accordingly, a large fleet was assembled in Boston and sailed for Quebec City in August 1711.

The operation did not last long, as on August 14 the fleet was wrecked in the St. Lawrence River, eight ships being lost along with 900 men.

Massachusetts 1652-dated Pine Tree shilling, small planchet, Noe-23 variety, from the wreck of the *Feversham*.

The admiral of the fleet, Sir Hovendon Walker, decided to abandon the venture and retire to Nova Scotia.

Earlier, the HMS *Feversham*—a 32-gun frigate measuring 107 feet in length and built by Thomas Ellis in Shoreham, England in 1696—had been sent to the southern colonies to pick up food and naval stores in support of the ill-fated expedition. As such, the *Feversham* had been on station in the south during the disaster that befell Walker's fleet in the St. Lawrence and luckily escaped the August 1711 tragedy.

When he realized that his efforts against the fortress Quebec had to be abandoned, Admiral Walker sent letters by fast dispatch to New York, advising the governor there to have HMS *Feversham* wait upon Walker's return and not venture north, as there was no longer any need for her to do so. At the time, the *Feversham* was docked in New York Harbor to replenish her stores of coinage, which had been exhausted by purchases of supplies in the southern colonies—records show that on September 4, the ship's purser applied for and received from the New York office of the British Treasury some 569 pounds, 12 shillings, and 5 pence sterling in coins.

Unfortunately, Admiral Walker's letters reached New York one day too late; the *Feversham* and three transport ships—together carrying more than a thousand barrels of pork, as well as coins, bread, flour, butter, peas, rum, and tobacco—had sailed on September 17 for Quebec City. Subsequently, the ship was blown onto the rocky shore of Scatarie Island, Nova Scotia, during a fierce storm on Sunday, October 7, 1711.

Of the 149 officers and seamen aboard, about 49 survived, the others having drowned. The three transports that accompanied the *Feversham* on her doomed voyage north also foundered and sank, resulting in additional loss of life.

Salvage operations commenced in the summer of the following year, when HMS *Saphyr* was dispatched to Scatarie Island to attempt to recover the *Feversham*'s cannons and stores. The *Saphyr*'s captain stated, however, that he had no opportunity to salvage anything from the bottom of the bay, as the weather and the rocks were too dangerous to allow for such operations. No further salvage attempts were made for more than 250 years.

The HMS *Feversham* Found

Finally, starting in 1984 and continuing for the following several years, salvage operations were undertaken by a private venture group. The operation successfully located and recovered the HMS *Feversham*'s cargo, including a number of the coins she had originally taken on in New York City in 1711.

With the approval of the Canadian government and after having obtained the appropriate legal licenses for export and sale, coins from the wreck of the *Feversham* were first offered to the public by Christie's in February 1989. A further parcel of coins from this wreck was sold by Jeffrey Hoare Auctions, Inc., in February 1993; this latter portion, however, was restricted to purchases by Canadian citizens only, as none of the lots were allowed for export out of the country.

Massachusetts Silver Aboard

The importance of the treasure recovered from the wreck of HMS *Feversham* cannot be overstated. As the ship put into New York in September 1711, and as published records at the time show that she took on coins in that city to replenish her stock, it can be assumed that whatever was found in her wreck represents exactly what was in common circulation in New York City at that time. When one considers the number and types of coins discovered in the wreck, one can see immediately a nearly perfect cross-section of the coins one might find in daily circulation in a major colonial metropolis on the Eastern Seaboard.

With this in mind, it is the number of *American* coins found marks this wreck as one of the most significant dating to colonial times. Found in the wreck of the *Feversham* were 131 Massachusetts silver coins of the following types:

> New England shillings: 1 (Noe 3-C)
> Willow Tree shillings: 4 (Noe 1-A, 3-D,
>   3-E, unidentifiable)
> Oak Tree shillings: 35
> Oak Tree sixpence: 1
> Pine Tree shillings: 75
> Pine Tree sixpence: 1
> Cut quarters and halves of Pine Tree
>   shillings, to make small change: 9 (4 half-
>   shilling segments and 5 quarter-shilling
>   segments)

These pieces prove that the British Treasury paid out silver Massachusetts shillings and accepted the same as a medium of exchange. Various numismatic-historical accounts have suggested that the coinage of Massachusetts was inimical to the interests of the British Crown, and that the date 1652 was maintained on coins minted into the 1680s so that the British authorities would not be aware that pieces were made after 1652, but the coins salvaged say otherwise. Thus, certain aspects of this "conventional wisdom" are gradually undergoing revision.

It is interesting to note, on the other hand, that while Massachusetts silver coins may have been in common circulation in New York City in 1711, exactly 31 years later they were curious enough to be offered at auction in London! The earliest recorded auction appearance of any Massachusetts silver coin can be traced back to Christopher Cox's sale in Covent Garden dated March 18, 1742, where Lot 55 included six Massachusetts shillings, two threepenny pieces, and one twopenny piece, all of which were sold for 11 shillings. When it is realized that the face value of the coins in this lot amounted to 6 shillings and 8 pence, it is clear that a considerable premium had been paid for these pieces, which by then must have been both curious and collectible.[305]

Note also that in addition to the Massachusetts coins, there were numerous Lion daalders of the Netherlands, primarily strikes of the 1600s; numerous Spanish colonial silver cobs (1/2- to 8-real pieces), mostly of the reigns of Philip IV through Charles II (1621–1700); and a small quantity of British silver coins. The number of British coins was so small as to pale into insignificance when compared to the number of Spanish colonial pieces, and even the number of Massachusetts silver coins, showing quite graphically exactly how coinage-poor the mother country intended to keep her American colonies!

Cut Coinage

Lastly, before leaving the topic of the wreck of the HMS *Feversham*, the Pine Tree shillings which were found deliberately cut into half- and quarter-shilling segments warrant discussion. Clearly, there was a considerable need in colonial New York City for small change (denominations smaller than a shilling).

While both the Pine and Oak Tree series were struck in large numbers and included many of the smaller sixpence and threepence denominations and some of the twopence denomination, the number of these lesser coins must not have been sufficient to meet the needs of the general populace. Accordingly, expediency was resorted to whereby shilling pieces were carefully cut into quarters or halves to supply the need for sixpenny and threepenny pieces for daily transactions.

The cutting of coins into segments was hardly a new idea and had been practiced with Spanish-American silver 8-real coins. Some of these were literally "pieces" of eight. In 1728, this commentary appeared, reflective of the practice:

> *Cutting Coin in America*: I have been told, that among some of our poorest American colonies upon the continent, the people enjoy the liberty of cutting the little money among them into halves and quarters, for the conveniences of small traffic.[306]

Before the recovery of the fractional pieces from the wreck of the HMS *Feversham*, some scattered examples of cut fractional Massachusetts silver pieces had been known in the numismatic trade, but these had always been looked upon with some concern, for it could not be determined with any degree of certainty exactly when the original coin had been cut into pieces. As it's known that the *Feversham* took on her coins in September 1711, it's clear that her cut fractions must have been nearly contemporary with the 1652–1682 striking period of the entire Massachusetts silver coin series.

The *Lexington* Tragedy

Lost: January 13, 1840 • **Location:** Off Eaton's Neck, Long Island •
Found: By 1983 • **Treasure:** Gold and silver coins

On the night of January 13, 1840, the 488-ton steamer *Lexington* was en route from New York City to Stonington, Connecticut, with about 160 people aboard and a cargo of about 150 bales of cotton. She caught fire at sea in sub-zero weather, and in the ensuing tragedy all but four people died.[307] Still at the bottom of Long Island Sound among the wreckage may be $18,000 worth of silver and gold coins.

Before beginning the tale of the tragedy, though, let us visit a couple of interesting asides. First, Henry Wadsworth Longfellow—whose poem "The Wreck of the Hesperus," would be published the day after the *Lexington* departed—desired to make the trip, but missed the boat. Thus, the world today can enjoy "Hiawatha," "Evangeline," and other epic poems that later flowed from his pen, and a generation of scholars at Bowdoin College in Maine could tap the benefits of his instruction there.[308]

Also: this particular ship disaster launched Nathaniel Currier into the pantheon of American iconography. The man who was later a partner with James Merritt Ives in Currier & Ives published a hand-colored print of the disaster titled *Awful Conflagration of the Steam Boat LEXINGTON In Long Island Sound on Monday Eve'g, Jan'y 13th 1840, by which melancholy occurrence, over 100 PERSONS PERISHED.* In an era in which most newspaper accounts were not yet illustrated with black-and-white engravings (let alone any sort of color images), the Currier print—with its dramatic perspective of raging flames and smoke reaching high into the sky—was a sellout, and it had to be reprinted several times.[309]

A Harrowing Account

The steamer *Lexington* left its pier on Manhattan's East River for Stonington after three o'clock (possibly as late as four o'clock) on Monday afternoon, January 13, 1840, with eager passengers who looked forward to arriving at their destination early the following morning.[310] Those aboard settled comfortably in their chairs

and on benches awaiting entertainment soon to be provided by Charles Everle and Henry J. Finn, two actors from Boston who were going to present a variety show.

About half past seven o'clock, when the ship was about 50 miles out of the port of New York City and four miles off Eaton's Neck on the north shore of Long Island, the woodwork and casings about her smokestack were discovered to be on fire.

Pilot Stephen Manchester, who was at the helm,[311] later related:

> My first movement was to step out of the wheel-house and look aft. I saw the upper deck on fire all around the smoke-pipe and blazing up two or three feet, perhaps, above the promenade deck. The flame seemed to be a thin sheet and, apparently, but just commenced. The blaze seemed to follow up the smoke-pipe and was all around it. . . . I thought from my first view that it was a doubtful case whether it could be extinguished. . . .

Captain George Childs (of Narragansett, Rhode Island), who had been below deck, then came into the wheel-house and placed his hand on the wheel, at which time the drive-rope connected to the rudder gave way. The smoke quickly became so intense that the post had to be abandoned anyhow. An alarm was immediately given, and a small hand-pumped fire engine was brought out, but only two or three buckets could be located, although there were supposed to be several dozen aboard.

It was soon found that fighting the fire was futile as the flames roared toward the sky, so with much effort, the *Lexington* was directed at full speed toward the Long Island shore in the hope of beaching her. Unfortunately, her engine stopped two or three miles away from land, and she was dead in the water. Meanwhile, the forward motion of the ship had served to fan the flames to great intensity.

Manchester's testimony continued:

> In my opinion, the fire originated from the heat of the smoke-pipe, which was communicated to the woodwork. I have frequently seen the smoke-pipe red hot, and saw it so on the last night. I do not know whether the red heat extended to the flange or not. The cotton was piled within perhaps a foot of the steam chimney.

Shortly after the fire was discovered, the single lifeboat and two smaller boats were readied, but the lifeboat was smashed when it came into contact with one of the two 23-foot-diameter paddlewheels. As if that was not enough, according to later testimony the dispatching of the two small boats was marred "by mismanagement in lowering them into the water crowded with passengers." One was filled with about 20 passengers and then lowered toward the sea when someone cut the forward tackle, making her go into the water bow-first and flooding the interior. Essentially the same thing happened to the second small boat, and with the sea temperature about at the freezing point and the air below zero, the chances of unprotected survival were slim to none.[312]

The flames increased in their intensity still more, and before long there was no place of safety remaining on the ship. At this point, Captain Childs rigged a small raft "from a spar and flagstaff with a portion of the bulwarks; also throwing overboard four baggage carts after being emptied of their contents, with a line attached." Some of the cotton cargo was pitched into the water as well. For the passengers who had jumped overboard, the only hope for being saved was to cling to floating cotton bales or other objects, "but none of them succeeded except passenger Captain Chester Hilliard, pilot Stephen Manchester, fireman Charles Smith, and a second mate David Crowley who seemed to be on the brink of death (but who survived)."[313]

Hilliard, who had been a captain on other boats, first went to the improvised raft, then moved to a bale of cotton, to which he clung until 11:00 a.m. the next morning. Then, having been in the water about 15 hours, he was taken off by the sloop *Merchant*, which had sailed out from Southport under a Captain Meeker. That ship had jettisoned some of its cargo to permit it to be in shallow water during the rescue, and thus saved two more passengers who were clinging to a wood fragment. The bodies of two others were likewise taken from the wreckage on which they had perished from cold; other bodies, luggage, and articles were also recovered.

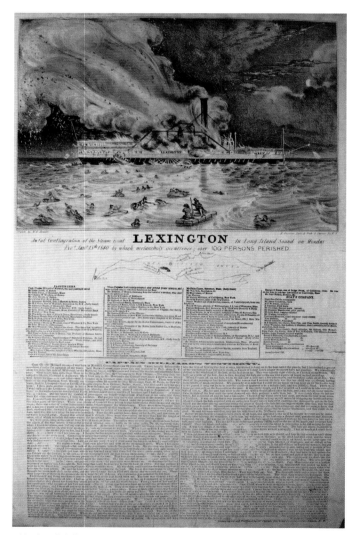

Nathaniel Currier's depiction of the *Lexington* tragedy, the first color print of a disaster to be made in the United States, plus lengthy narrative attached.

Sadly, it came to light later that much of this loss might have been avoided. The text appended to Currier's print included the unfortunate scenario:

On Friday night Captain Comstock dispatched a letter to the city, in which he says that:

"Captain William Terrill, master of the sloop *Improvement*, was, with his vessel, within four or five miles of the *Lexington* at the time she commenced burning, and thinks if he had immediately repaired to her assistance, he could have saved a great number of lives. The reason he gives for not doing so is, *that he would have lost his tide over the bar*, at the port to which he was bound, and accordingly he pursued his inhuman course, leaving upwards of 100 persons to die the worst of deaths.[314] The circumstances of this unparalleled cruelty will hereafter be more clearly exposed, and I trust he will receive his merited deserts."

This conduct of Captain Terrill has elicited a universal burst of indignation against him in this city, and for his safety's sake we advise him not to venture too much in public here.

The *Lexington* remained afire until about three o'clock in the morning, when the largely gutted hulk slipped beneath the waves, apparently carrying with it the bodies of passengers who had preferred death by fire to death by freezing—an awful choice to have to make.

As an aside, numismatist John J. Ford Jr. recalled many years later that as a young man living on Long Island, he would sometimes visit an old cemetery at the corner of Merrick Road and Ocean Avenue in Lynbrook (on the south shore and not close to the north shore wreck site). There he saw an overgrown patch of weeds and brush within which he discovered a modest size monument designating the burial sites of victims of the *Lexington*.[315]

An Inquiry into the Tragedy

Hearings were held to determine the circumstances of the ship's demise. Testimony related:

> The boat was built as a wood-fired steamer by Bishop & Simonson, New York, for Cornelius Vanderbilt [in the latter part of 1834 and beginning of 1835] of the best possible materials and bolted and fastened together and secured in the strongest possible manner without regard to cost or expenses. . . .
>
> She was 205 feet long on deck from stem to stern, 22 feet wide and 40 feet across the wheelhouses from side to side. She was launched in April 1835, and her first trip was in June of 1835. Her timbers were part oak and part chestnut, with planks of oak as far as the waist and then of pine. . . . About two months before the accident she was repaired in drydock and some new copper and other fittings were put in. Vanderbilt owned her until 1838 and then sold her to the Providence & Rhode Island Steamboat and Transportation Company. . . .
>
> The ship was the only boat that had navigated Long Island Sound for four or five years and never stopped because of weather or lost a trip. . . . Instructions to the captain were never to stop while they could see to go ahead, he had so much confidence in her strength.
>
> The *Lexington* was first built to burn wood and then converted to burn anthracite coal when the ownership changed. No reference as to whether the boat had ever caught fire from sparks, but such minor fires were common incidents.[316]

Coal burns with a much more intense heat, and certain precautions as to insulation and spacing from combustible materials need to be taken as a result. There had been trouble with the new fuel on the *Lexington* during a recent trip, and she had been laid up for repairs to the two 36-inch blowers, powered from a shaft on the main engine, that forced a draft in the fire box that became far too hot. The steam engine, built by the West Point Foundry, had a 48-inch cylinder that operated with an 11-foot stroke.

In the hearing, Captain William Comstock was examined. . . . He related that Robert Schuyler, then president of the company, purchased the *Lexington* from Vanderbilt for $60,000, and with additional expenses it cost $70,000 [or $72,000] before her first trip for our company. . . . Further: "I can't say whether or not that money was to induce Captain Vanderbilt to take his boat off that station, such a boat as the *Lexington* is worth $60,000.[317] She had not been running in opposition to us at the time she sunk, but when first she came on the line she ran in opposition to us. . . ."

Comstock testified that the ship burned about 10 to 13 tons of anthracite coal [on a typical trip] going from New York to Stonington and then from 2 to 3 cords of wood. She ran on about 8 to 13 inches of steam and could go 12 to 14 miles an hour. Goods were carefully stowed. "You never saw any goods stowed nearer than three or four feet of the casing of the steam chimney, although no danger would be found if it was stowed against the steam chimney."

Soon after the disaster, Colonel Harry A. Hunt, editor of the Sag Harbor *Corrector*, called the event a "willful, savage, horrid murder," further observing: "There was not an officer on the boat who did his duty—each acted for himself only. The Master [captain] was one of the first to desert his post."[318]

Some cotton bales washed ashore along Long Island Sound. From one or more of these, "Lexington shirts" were woven and hawked as mementos of the disaster. Thus, Nathaniel Currier with his prints was not the only person to profit from the tragedy.

Coins Aboard

One account included the information that among the passengers was "Adolphus S. Harnden of the Boston and New York Express Package Car Office, having with him about $18,000 in specie and $70,000 or $80,000 for brokers in eastern money." Stephen Manchester testified that Harnden was trapped on the forward deck by the flames and was one of the last to remain aboard the ship.

The $18,000 in specie would have consisted of silver and/or gold coins. "Eastern money" refers to paper money of Eastern state-chartered banks. While the coins would have held up to immersion in the water of Long Island Sound for years thereafter, the paper money would have deteriorated quickly.

Currier mentioned the coins in the text on his popular print, as well:

> Unfortunately, the painter [rope attached to the prow] gave way and the lifeboat was sucked under the wheel thus depriving those who looked for safety in this boat of all hope. Flames now advanced rapidly to the aft part, and to prevent its progress, the pilot and others broke open some specie boxes [filled with coins], and emptied them of the worthless dross, used the boxes [as fire buckets] to keep off the flames and prevent their progress. . . .

Another account—this written a year after the disaster—also commented on the coins, here called "dollars":

> Everything which could hold water was seized upon. The boxes containing specie were broken open, the dollars poured out and trodden under foot as worthless, whilst the boxes were used to throw water on the devouring flames.[319]

An attempt to recover the coins was made as early as 1842.[320] More than a century later in 1983, the *Lexington*—described as a "plush" passenger vessel—was said to have been found in about 80 feet of water off Port Jefferson, New York, by a the National Underwater and Marine Agency.[321] Susan Wynne, spokesperson for the Agency, commented that "the ship could be raised but is in about three pieces, sitting upright in the bottom, amazingly well preserved." It was not stated whether positive identification of the *Lexington* had been achieved, nor was there any mention of the hull being charred.

A leading dealer who wished to remain anonymous stated that he had purchased and privately sold two choice Mint State 1838 $10 gold eagles from the wreck. Each would have been worth into six figures.

A Collision in the Night

Lost: July 1840 • **Location:** Off the coast of South Carolina •
Found: 2000 • **Treasure:** Gold and silver coins

At one o'clock in the morning of July 26, 1840, with the sea calm and under starlight, two steamships—the SS *North Carolina* and the SS *Governor Dudley*—collided not three miles off the coast northeast of Georgetown, South Carolina. Each was going about 12 to 14 miles per hour. Both ships, as well as the *Vanderbilt* and *Wilmington*, were operated coastwise connecting Charleston and Wilmington under an entity of Commodore Cornelius Vanderbilt named Wilmington & Roanoke Railroad Co.

The *Governor Dudley*, while damaged, escaped without serious harm. Not so for the *North Carolina*, which broke apart into two pieces and sank in about 70 feet of water within 20 minutes. Aboard the ship were many prominent figures, including several congressmen and citizens of wealth. Fortunately, all aboard were rescued, although many were in their nightclothes, including Honorable Dixon H. Lewis, of Alabama, who weighed 500 pounds and whose appearance caused some mirth.[323]

The cargo, mail, and all of the passengers' personal effects were a complete loss as were many gold coins reported to have been placed with the purser for safekeeping. Congressman William Crosby Dawson of Georgia had taken $15,000 with him in a trunk.

Gold Found

By 2000, Marine Archaeological Recovery and Exploration (MAREX) had located the wreck site, filed appropriate court papers, and received title to the *North Carolina*.[324] The firm—founded in 1983 by James Herbert Humphreys Jr., a Memphis businessman who was an early and large investor in the Holiday Inn chain—had at this point found a number of wrecks, most notably the Spanish galleon *La Nuestra Senora de Las Maravillas*, which gave up thousands of artifacts including 7,600 silver pieces of eight, 116 gold coins, 29 gold bars, 25 silver bars, 193 silver ingots, and 21 gold ingots, as well as emeralds, diamonds, gold chains, rings, and broaches.

The *North Carolina* was about 40 miles offshore, 100 feet below the surface, and scattered over a wide expanse of sand. Exploration began. MAREX had at its disposal several vessels for the operation, including the 210-foot *Atlantic Explorer*, the 120-foot R/V *Beacon*, and the 65-foot R/V *Southland*, the last equipped for shallow water work.

In the absence of a rail line in the area Wilmington, North Carolina and Charleston, South Carolina were connected by steamship line conducted by Commodore Cornelius Vanderbilt.

Ben Marich, vice president of operations, reported later in 2000 that "a number of gold coins have been recovered with exceptional numismatic value because of their rarity" from among "scores of gold coins." CaymanCompass.com reported on March 22, 2012, that two rare coins from the wreck, not further identified, had sold for $420,000.

The SS *New York*

Lost: 1846 • **Location:** Off the coast of Texas • **Found:** 2005 • **Treasure:** Silver and gold coins

Constructed in 1837 at the yard of William H. Brown on the East River, New York City, the SS *New York* was a side-wheel steamship with auxiliary sails, a class of vessel generally known as a "steam packet." The machinery was made by the Allaire Iron Works, a leading manufacturer of marine engines and equipment.[325]

The *New York* was 160.5 feet long, had a 22.5-foot beam, and a 10.5-foot depth of hold. There was one main deck with a cabin section in the center, with decks fore and aft. The fore deck had a canvas cover. Above the aft (or promenade) deck was an open-air deck, essentially a platform, where passengers could relax if the passage was smooth, under the sun and in the open air, cooled by the breeze of forward motion.

Her hull was of wood, sheathed in copper. Once each year, in the summer, the vessel sailed to New York City, where its builder checked and cleaned the hull, replaced sheathing as needed, inspected the boiler, and performed repairs. An October 13, 1843, registration document notes

The SS *New York*.

there had been changes since an earlier registration; she was now listed as having two masts and displacing 365 tons, whereas an early depiction of her showed one mast. Perhaps a second mast was added during her summer 1843 visit to New York City.

Up to 200 passengers and several dozen crew members could be accommodated in addition to cargo, although it seems on most voyages only a few dozen passengers were aboard. The highest number noted in a contemporary account is slightly more than 100, and the accuracy of that particular observer is not known.

The first owners of the *New York* were Charles Morgan, James P. Allaire (of the aforementioned Iron Works), and John Haggerty, the three of whom formed the Southern Steam Packet Company. The new line acquired two other steam packets in addition to the *New York*: the *Home* and the *Columbia*. The *Columbia* was essentially a twin to the *New York*, but built a few years earlier. The *Home* was the flagship of the line, measured 220 feet in length, and displaced 537 tons. She was built for river voyages in 1836, and then refitted for ocean travel.

The *New York* made her first voyage on June 15, 1837, going into service carrying passengers, cargo, and mail on the coastwise route connecting New York City to Charleston, South Carolina. Prospects were bright for the two sister ships as well. The company landed contracts to transport troops and supplies to military outposts in Flor-

ida, commercial cargoes were profitable, and the vessels carried many passengers. All was well for a short time.

The wrecking later in the year of the *Home* in a hurricane at Cape Hatteras, with a loss of 90 lives, changed everything. Allaire left the company, and the remaining partners sent the other two ships to the Gulf of Mexico to engage in trade there. In late November 1837, the *New York* and the *Columbia* arrived in New Orleans. In ensuing years, the *New York* made many trips, including to Galveston, which served the Republic of Texas, formed in 1836.

In January 1846, the *New York* was sold to Captain John D. Phillips. By that time, the maritime business in the Gulf was very competitive. On April 29, 1846, early in the Mexican War, the venerable ship was chartered by the government to transport troops to the new U.S. Army depot at Brazos St. Jago. The lease payment totaled $2,196.

From then through the summer, she was chartered several more times, resulting in protests from travelers and shippers of merchandise who resented the interruption of regular service.[326]

Outward Bound

On Saturday, September 5, 1846, the SS *New York* departed Galveston at half past four o'clock in the afternoon carrying 30 passengers and a crew of 23. Fare was $15 for cabin passage, less for steerage. At the helm was the owner of the ship, Captain John D. Phillips, a seasoned commander. Among the passengers were Daniel J. Toler, who had been the postmaster general of the Republic of Texas; M.F. Bonzano, M.D., whose career was taking off; and the Follett family of five, the largest family aboard.

Money in the estimated amount of $30,000 to $40,000 was aboard, although no authoritative figures were ever published. This consisted of gold and silver coins and, it is likely, many bank notes. It is known that also among the cargo was a woodworking machine; probably there were barrels and crates of other goods as well, normal for the route, although one later account stated the hold was empty.

Additionally, animals such as cows, pigs, and chickens were taken aboard to provide fresh meat in an era in which spoilage was rapid and refrigeration was not available. These as well as pets, livestock, and work animals were tethered or caged on the foredeck. Still, the load was far short of capacity, indicating the voyage would be pleasant, with more than usual attention from the crew.

Pastimes on board the *New York* were typical for the day. Reading novels, magazines, and newspapers was popular. Likely, the ship had a small library on board. Parlor games were played, and cards were always good for gathering groups at a table or two. Wine and liquor were available from the steward or stewardess, as were small bottles of mineral water. These provisions, as well as utensils, bedclothes, lamps, and other items were provided by chandlers, or ship-outfitters, in the ports.

With its square steam engine fitted with a single low-pressure cylinder, the ship was reasonably quiet, the sound being limited to a non-stop series of regularly spaced puffing noises. Below deck, firemen worked shifts to continually stoke the boiler with coal. The captain or a mate in the wheelhouse manned the helm. Navigation was accomplished by sextant, compass, depth sounding, and an awareness of the elapsed time since leaving port.

All was set for a routine transit similar to those the ship had taken for many years. The voyage was expected to take two days, including overnight, with arrival on the evening of Sunday, September 6. That being said, the exact time of reaching New Orleans often varied, as the schedules of pilot ships to guide vessels to port were sometimes erratic, and the weather could be a factor; some trips took three days, including two overnights.

A "Perfect Gale"

Immediately before the trip, the weather had been foggy and rainy for nearly three weeks, and at departure time a light haze covered the harbor. Regardless, the ship steamed out of Galveston Bay and headed to the open sea, with no indication of anything unusual. However, once the bar—a ridge of sand about 12 feet below the surface—was crossed, a stiff breeze kicked up waves, and soon it began to rain heavily. The going was choppy, as sometimes happened, but the roughness was expected to soon pass.

A few hours later, in the dark, with the wind coming in even more strongly from the northeast and a heavy sea from the east, progress slowed. Captain Phillips dropped anchor several dozen miles offshore in about 50 to 60 feet of water and waited through the night for calm. There was a lull the next morning, and on Sunday at ten o'clock the anchor was weighed and the ship continued its course. Onward to New Orleans, never mind the slight delay.

As it turns out, the calm was temporary—perhaps the eye of the storm—though there had been no way to know for sure. The wind accelerated, and after traveling a short distance Captain Phillips decided to ride it out and dropped anchor again in 10 fathoms of water. Matters got worse, developing into what he described as a "perfect gale." A fierce hurricane, the scourge of the Gulf Coast, was in progress.

Throughout Sunday the storm worsened, and the ship was tossed about even more violently. The passengers huddled and tried to cheer each other. Surely the winds would subside and the sea would become quiet. Then on to New Orleans, as planned. But this did not happen; the worst was yet to come.

About midnight or within an hour afterward, a cable snapped, and part of the structure gave way on the starboard side. Water rushed into the hold, the boiler fires were extinguished, and for the first time, passengers seriously feared for their lives. Into the night men manned pumps, but to no avail. Early the next morning the ship sank, while some deck parts and the wheelhouse floated away.

Survivors included 19 passengers and 18 crew, including the captain. Lost were 11 passengers and 8 crew. One of the survivors, John Todd, published a detailed account of the tragedy. In time the ship was forgotten.

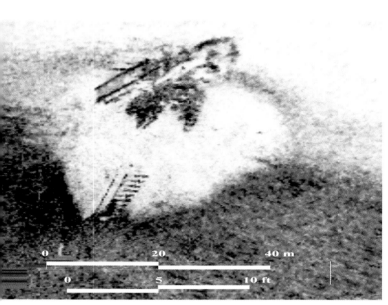

Side-scan sonar image of the wreck of the SS *New York*.

The bell from the SS *New York* shortly after it was found.

The Rest of the Story

Fast forward to modern times.

Avery Munson, of New Iberia, Louisiana, who loved scuba diving and exploring the sea, wondered whether there might be any historical accounts of lost ships with treasure aboard in the Gulf of Mexico within reach of his home port. For several years, he combed old newspapers and other records. Lightning struck! He found a telltale comment on the *New York* in the *Daily Picayune* of September 10, 1846. With this as a beginning, he enlisted friends Craig DeRouen and the husband-and-wife team of Gary and Renée Hebert, and they together formed a group of four and styled themselves as the "Gentlemen of Fortune."

The team studied newspaper articles, survivor accounts, charts, and underwater data. The Gulf of Mexico is a center for offshore oil rigs, and thus much mapping has been done. They took measurements and made estimates, and they also consulted shrimp fishermen and others familiar with the Gulf to seek clues and ideas. In time, success was theirs; they had their "eureka!" moment in early 2005, when the ship's bell was found. In due course, their ownership was successfully registered in a federal court, no other claims arose, and recovery commenced.

The Gentlemen (with one woman) of Fortune on board the *Barracuda*, with coins on the table. Left to right: Gary Hebert, Craig DeRouen, Renée Hebert, and Avery Munson.

I had the pleasure of spending some time at sea with the finders, while my son Andrew, a certified scuba diver, joined them in dives to the wreck. All of this was a memorable, indeed unique, experience.

Afterwards, I began work on my book on this wreck, *The Treasure Ship S.S. New York: Her Life and Loss, 1837–1847*. At the time, I did not know much about life in Galveston or New Orleans in 1846, so I spent some time at the American Antiquarian Society in Worcester, Massachusetts—of which I am a trustee—and looked through newspapers from both cities (the Society has the

A brilliant Mint State half eagle, reverse up, as seen on a dive, just before it was recovered.

Galveston and New Orleans as shown on an 1850 map.

Andrew Bowers about to dive.

largest archive in existence of American printed items from colonial days up to 1876). I learned that Galveston was a shipping port with relatively few amenities, whereas New Orleans had a lively social scene with glamour and many activities, perhaps more than any other city in the United States at that time.

I reviewed my historical notes, added information from the Gentlemen of Fortune, and described the numismatic characteristics of the coins found. In time, my book was published and drew nice reviews.

Inventory

The following inventory includes most of the federal gold coins found as of June 1, 2008. Most were graded by NGC, and the most important coins were auctioned by Stack's. Some holders had "Details" added to the grade; here that notation appears as "det." This is an exceedingly valuable insight into the money in common

circulation on the Gulf Coast in 1846. Many world silver and gold coins were legal tender and would remain so until 1859.

Quarter eagles

1835: AU det.
1836: AU det. (3); AU-55; AU-58; Unc. det.; MS-61 (2); MS-62 (2)
1839-O: AU-55; MS-62
1843, Large Date, Plain 4: MS-62
1843-C, Large Date, Plain 4: AU det.

1843-O: AU det. (3); AU-58; MS-60 (4); MS-61 (7); MS-62 (2); MS-63 (2); MS-64 (2)

1844-D: AU-53; AU-58

1845-D: MS-64

1846: MS-61

Half eagles

1834: EF det. (4); EF-45; AU det.; AU-53; AU-55 (5); Unc. det.; AU-58 (4); MS-61 (4); MS-62; MS-62

1835: EF det.; AU det. (3); AU-58; Unc. det.

1836: VF det.; AU det.; AU-55 (3); AU-58 (5); MS-60; MS-61

1837: AU det.; AU-58

1838: AU det. (4); AU-58; Unc. det.; MS-61 (4); MS-62

1839: MS-61

1839-D: AU det.; AU-58

1840: AU-58; Unc. det.; MS-60

1840-D: MS-62

1840-O: AU det.

1841-C: MS-60

1841-D: MS-61

1842-D, Small Date, Small Letters: MS-60

1842-D, Large Date, Large Letters: MS-61

1842-O, Small Date, Small Letters: AU det.

1843, Large Letters reverse: VF det.; EF-40; AU det.; AU-58 (2); Unc. det. (3); MS-60 (2); MS-61 (6); MS-63 (3)

1843-C, Small Letters reverse: AU-58; MS-61

1843-D, Large Letters reverse: AU det. (2); AU-55; Unc. det. (2); MS-61; MS-63

1843-O, Small Letters reverse: MS-61

1843-O, Large Letters reverse: AU-58 (3); MS-62 (2)

1843-O, unclassified: AU det. (4)

1844: (fragment), AU det.; AU-58; Unc. det. (3); MS-62 (3)

1844-C: AU det.

1844-D: AU det.; MS-61; MS-63

1844-O: AU det. (6); AU-58 (2); Unc. det. (3); MS-60 (2); MS-61 (2); MS-62 (8); MS-63 (3); MS-64 (2)

1845: Unc. det. (2); AU-58 (2); MS-61 (2); MS-62; MS-63; MS-64

1845-D: AU-58; MS-60; MS-61; MS-62

1845-O: AU det.; AU-58 (4); Unc. det.; MS-61; MS-62 (3); MS-63 prooflike

1846, Small Date and Medium Date varieties: Unc. det. (3); MS-61 (2); MS-63

Eagles

1842, Small Date: MS-61

1842, Large Date: AU-58; MS-60

1842-O, Large Date: AU-55; AU-58 (2)

1843: AU-58; MS-60

1843-O: AU det.; AU-58

1844-O: AU det.; MS-61 (3); MS-62; MS-63 (2)

1845-O: AU det.; AU-58 (3); Unc. det.; MS-61 (3); MS-62

Non-federal gold coins

Bechtler $5, 140 G., 20 CARATS., August 1, 1834: AU-58

In addition, nearly 2,000 silver coins were found. Most of these were of the half dollar denomination, including many of the Capped Bust design from 1807 to 1836 (including one of the rarest date, 1815), some others dating back to 1795, and many Liberty Seated issues. A single silver dollar was recovered, a 1795 of the Flowing Hair type. Generally, the Capped Bust and earlier coins are etched and thus certified with the notation "Shipwreck Effect," a term to denote treasure ship origin.

Certain later-date Liberty Seated issues are Extremely Fine to About Uncirculated, with very little etching. An 1842-O, Small Date, half dollar was well preserved and stands among the finer examples known and a highlight of the silver coins recovered. A large copper cent dated 1843, well-etched, was also found, as were many foreign gold coins. These are detailed in *The Treasure Ship S.S. New York: Her Life and Loss, 1837–1847*.

Today, coins from the SS *New York*, never plentiful to begin with, are scarce in the marketplace. A subculture has arisen of enthusiasts who enjoy collecting documented treasure ship finds. The result is that such coins attract a lot of attention when offered.

A Mysterious Treasure Ship

Lost: Late 1850s • **Location:** Off the East Coast • **Found:** Before 1974 • **Treasure:** Gold coins

The sea tells no tales, and, indeed, the majority of old wooden shipwrecks in American coastal waters are not identified as to name of the ship, owner, or time sunk. Such may be the case for an unknown wreck which yielded some highly important coins.

As for those coins: any specialist in U.S. gold coins will sooner or later encounter certain quarter eagles and half eagles, mostly dated in the 1850s, that are bright and sharp but also have a grainy, minutely etched surface instead of frosty luster. This effect was caused by particles of sand swirling over the coins in shallow water, perhaps near the ocean shore. These are often referred to as "seawater Uncirculated" or with "saltwater damage," the latter a pejorative term that deters bidders.

Writing about this find in 1988, Walter H. Breen stated:

> Many [$5 gold coins] surviving from Southern branch mints (notably 1853-O, 1853-C to 1855-C, and 1852-D to 1855-D) show full mint sharpness but dull matte surfaces; these are known as "seawater Uncs." They were retrieved from a wrecked ship, said to be a Confederate transport, sometime before 1974. Details have not yet become available, but the hoard also included double eagles and probably other denominations. . . .[327]

Of course, as is the case with many comments of Breen's, this assertion should be looked at with some scrutiny; considering that there was no such thing as a "Confederate transport" prior to April 1861 (when the Civil War started), it would be odd that the latest coins from such a vessel find would be dated 1855.

Some Possibilities

Most likely, the ship in question went down in 1855 or very early 1856 after having visited a Southern port such as New Orleans, Savannah, or Charleston. Such a scenario would at once account for the dating of the coins as 1855 or earlier and for the presence of significant numbers of Charlotte and Dahlonega issues.

Possibilities for shipwrecks that meet these criteria include the following. Note that the 1855 and January 20, 1856, entries seem to have greater possibilities for having all coins dated prior to 1856:

1855, November 5. *Inca*. Under Captain Dennison, this ship was en route from New Orleans to New York City, but the voyage was cut short when she was wrecked on Riding Rock, south of Cat Cay in the Bahamas.[328]

1856, January 20. *Valparabo*. With Captain Runnells in charge, this ship was on her way from New Orleans to Liverpool, England, when she went down close to where the *Inca* had sunk two months earlier.

1856, May 17. *Peterhoff*. On the way from Charleston to Havana with Captain Peabody at the helm, the *Peterhoff* was lost near Abaco Island in the Bahamas.[329]

1856, September 24. *Lizzie Lord*. This ship, en route from Savannah to New Orleans under Captain Kendall, went down in the Bahamas.[330]

Another possibility is that these Charlotte, Dahlonega, and New Orleans Mint gold coins could have been lost on a small coastwise sailing vessel or steamer out of one of many southern ports. There were so many small ships wrecked that standard sources on sailing ship or steamship history omit mention of nearly all of them. The only way to track down such wrecks is to peruse contemporary newspapers published at Charleston, Savannah, New Orleans, and other ports; however, the majority of these omit specific information about money aboard.

In yet another alternative scenario, the coins could have been buried or otherwise deliberately hidden on the shore of some bayou or inlet, or on a coastal strand where the groundwater was brine.

With regard to the quality of the coins recovered from this mysterious wreck, David W. Akers commented that the quarter and half eagles are generally more heavily etched than are "seawater" 1854-S, 1855-S, and 1856-S double eagles from another find from this era (see "Coins from the *William and Mary*" in this chapter).[331]

Coins from the *William and Mary*

Lost: May 1, 1857 • **Location:** Old Indian River outlet in Florida • **Found:** 1963 and 1964 • **Treasure:** Gold coins

In the early 1970s, hundreds of double eagles came on the market. Prominent among them were 1855-S and 1856-S coins with very lightly etched surfaces from the action of fine sand particles, otherwise appearing to be Mint State. The 1856-S pieces were the most numerous.

Many of these were sold through WorldWide Coin Investments of Atlanta and were said to have been from a "sunken treasure ship off the coast of Florida." However, the principals of WorldWide, John Hamrick and Bob Harwell, did not know where the pieces had been salvaged, as they had been acquired via an intermediary.

I myself handled dozens of pieces obtained from that source, advertised them in *Coin World* and offered them privately. They sold quickly. Their history remained a mystery, but there are many theories.

The Story Revealed

In 2009, John M. Kleeberg provided answers in an extensive narrative in *Numismatic Finds of the Americas*, which included the following information:

In the spring of 1857, $23,000 in coins was withdrawn from the sub-treasury in Charleston, South Carolina to pay government troops fighting in the Third Seminole War. The money was put aboard the *William and Mary*, in the custody of Army paymaster Major Jeremiah Yellot Dashiell. At the outlet of the Indian River between Vero Beach and Fort Pierce, Dashiell took the funds with him aboard a small boat that left the *William and Mary* and headed to Fort Capron. The boat capsized, and the bag containing the coins was lost in the swirling sand.

More than a century later, in the spring of 1963, James Robert Gordy, age 16, and Albert N.

Ashley were skin diving and fishing for crawfish on the coast at Fort Pierce. They were surprised to find a number of coins. James' father, Kenneth F. Gordy, applied to the Florida Internal Improvement Fund for the right to register the find and take possession of the coins. The State of Florida agreed and was to receive a 25% share.

The finders reported in September 1964 that they had retrieved 225 silver coins and 477 gold coins since July of that summer. They did not disclose that in 1963 they had salvaged 2,682 gold coins, for a total of 3,264 for the two years.

Treasure Exposed

The majority of the findings thus remained a secret until 1968, when the finders quarreled and sued each other in the Circuit Court of Saint Lucie County. Finally, on April 12, 1972, an agreement was reached whereby coins remaining at the Saint Lucie County Bank would be divided with 45% split between the James R. Gordy and Albert N. Ashley (nothing to Gordy's father) and 45% going to the State of Florida. Of these coins 114, were sold to WorldWide Coins for $101 each on or about June 23, 1972, per the scenario described above. Remaining by that time were 195 gold coins comprising:

$1 gold

1850-O
1855

Quarter eagles

1843-O	1852	1855
1851-O	1854 (2)	1856

Half eagles

1834	1846 (2)	1854-C (2)
1838 (2)	1846-D (2)	1855-D (2)
1841 (2)	1850-C (2)	1856-C
1843-C	1850-D	1856-D
1844-O	1853-D	

Eagles

1839	1847 (2)	1850
1845	1849 (2)	

Double eagles

1850 (7)	1852-O (3)	1855 (26)
1850-O (6)	1853 (23)	1855-S (7)
1851 (10)	1853-O (5)	1856 (11)
1851-O (4)	1854 (15)	1856-S (20)
1852 (17)	1854-S (3)	1857-S

Details concerning the full inventory of the 1963 and 1964 salvages are incomplete. John Kleeberg learned this:

> Half dimes: 28 reported to the State of Florida in 1964, later finds unknown
>
> Quarter dollars: 83 reported to the State of Florida in 1964, later finds unknown
>
> Half dollars: 26 reported to the State of Florida in 1964, later finds unknown
>
> Gold $1 (1849–1856): 159 reported to the State of Florida in 1964, 508 total found
>
> Quarter eagles (1834–1856): 137 reported to the State of Florida in 1964, 787 total found
>
> Half eagles (1834–1856): 125 reported to the State of Florida in 1964, 929 total found
>
> Eagles (1840–1852): 48 reported to the State of Florida in 1964, 490 total found
>
> Double eagles (1850–1857): 113 reported to the State of Florida in 1964, 550 total found

chapter 12

Gold Rush Treasure: SS *Winfield Scott*

As a prelude to this and other chapters about the California Gold Rush, it is appropriate to discuss both the history of the era as well as the methods of travel used. The story begins on January 24, 1848, when flakes of the yellow metal were discovered by James Marshall at Sutter's Mill on the American River in California. Thus was set in motion a great craze that not only attracted untold thousands of fortune seekers to the West over the next several years, but in the process also built an empire, completing the American map from the Atlantic to the Pacific.

Sutter's Mill, located on the American River east of Sacramento, was nearing completion when James Marshall saw a flake of gold in the tail race.

The news of Marshall's find spread slowly at first, and it was not until the following autumn that adventurers began to arrive in notable numbers in the formerly quiet port of San Francisco, which had recently changed its name from Yerba Buena. For the time being, this was one-way traffic, as the crews of the ships as well as their argonaut passengers did not want to return to sea.

With no one to man them on outbound voyages, abandoned ships accumulated in the harbor. One such vessel was brought close to shore and made into a hotel (called the Niantic).

Newspaper stories about gold and instant wealth became prevalent in the Atlantic states toward the end of 1848. Fact was often difficult to separate from fiction, as writers with little hard information on hand tried to outdo each other with wondrous tales of adventure and fortune. Eager readers became excited by the news of easy wealth to be obtained by a few days of digging in the West—gold was (seemingly) there for the taking. One story told of the Gold Bluffs, where nuggets littered the sandy beach just waiting to be picked up. A slightly more fanciful account told of a volcano spewing precious metal instead of the usual lava!

Among the first shipments of gold was received at the Philadelphia Mint in December 1848, and the precious ore was subsequently coined into quarter eagles ($2.50 gold coins), each with the distinguishing counterstamp "CAL." on the reverse to identify the origin of its metal. Sent by the U.S. representative in San Francisco, William L. Marcy, the small chest of treasure officially confirmed the new Age of Gold, the new Golconda, the new El Dorado, as it came to be known.

San Francisco in 1849.

Miners at work in the gold fields.

Forty-niners.

Thus, after late 1848 and early 1849, it was a free-for-all in the Eastern states as thousands dropped their saws, plows, fishing nets, and other implements of employment and commerce and headed west to make their fortunes.

By Land

There were a few ways to go to the Land of Gold. The overland trip by ox-drawn wagon took about five months in the early days of the Gold Rush, though the actual time varied depending upon the route taken (there were several) and the equipment possessed. Happy adventurers in high spirits formed wagon trains in Independence, Missouri, and a few other places, and singing *O Susanna* and other rollicking melodies, headed westward, with each night's stop being an occasion for festivities and celebration.

At least, this was typical at the start of the trip; in reality, there were many hazards along the way, including Indian attacks, outbreaks of cholera, lack of water, and extremes of temperature and weather. Many died, their bodies simply abandoned along the trail alongside dead and bloated cattle or buried in shallow graves only to be dug up by coyotes. Sometimes wagons broke down, and other times there were no oxen remaining

Wagon trains heading west.

alive to pull them. Much valuable equipment had to be abandoned.

Yet despite such travails—the trip was not easy for anyone—many thousands did arrive at their destination via land. Fewer and fewer chose this approach as time went on, though.

By Sea

Travel on the water was the main alternative to the overland journey. Both sailing ships and steamships made the trips, following one of two main routes.

One of these routes was around Cape Horn at the tip of South America. Going by sailing ship could take 150 days or even more, depending upon the vessel, the number of shore stops, and the weather. Few were interested in this arduous, largely unknown method of travel through unfamiliar seas. Note that beginning in the mid-1850s, clipper ships with billowed sails and sleek hulls cut the travel time to below 100 days, but these primarily carried bulky cargo, not passengers.

From 1849 into the 1860s, sidewheel steamships became the preferred vessels, and the route across the Isthmus of Panama won travelers' (and shippers') favor. By 1855, when the 48-mile-long Panama Railroad opened, travel from the East to San Francisco and vice-versa became routine, and it was not unusual for entire families to travel. The days of perilous adventure were over.

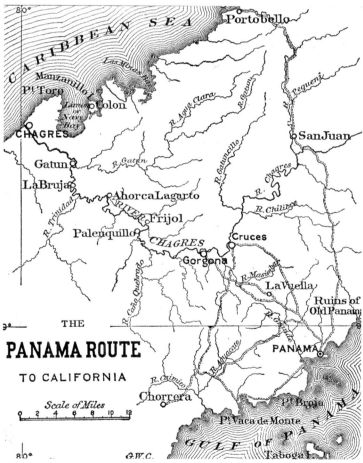

A map showing the Panama crossing on the route from the Atlantic to the Pacific. The Isthmus twists at this point, with the result that Chagres, the Atlantic port, is shown at the upper left and Panama (Panama City) is at the lower right. Passage was made up the Chagres River to Gorgona at which point travel was continued by using pack animals.

The port of Chagres in the early days of the Gold Rush.

Pack animals at Gorgona.

In 1849, Chagres had no deep-water dock,
and passengers had to be ferried in small boats.
The same was true at Panama City on the other side of the isthmus.

Sleeping accommodations in Panama City
for those waiting to board
a steamer connecting to California.

The dining room of French's Hotel in Panama.

In California

Upon arrival in California, many intrepid souls found a combination of wealth and excitement in the gold fields in the foothills of the Sierras inland from San Francisco. However, even more came to the realization that gold hunting was hard work and thus settled into other pursuits, including clerking, farming, lumbering, and other trades. For people in these positions, wages were higher than back home in Massachusetts, Illinois, or Pennsylvania, but living expenses were higher as well, and usually there was no net gain.

Eventually, gold mining became concentrated in the hands of large partnerships and corporations, which dug deep tunnels into the earth or used high-pressure streams of water to blast away hillsides in search of nuggets and ore. Though it was the dream of thousands, very few of the people that came to California from the East went to the gold fields, found enough to make themselves wealthy, and then returned home to live a life of luxury.

Beginning in the heady days of 1849, several assayers, bankers, and entrepreneurs in San Francisco and nearby towns produced gold coins and hallmarked ingots to serve as exchange in an economy in which gold was plentiful but coins were scarce. In 1850, additional privately produced coins were made. Then, in 1851, Augustus Humbert arrived by ship from New York City to become the government's agent under the title of United States Assayer of Gold, California, an arrangement which soon led to the establishment of the U.S. Assay Office of Gold.

The height of Gold Rush production was 1853, according to government statistics. In the early years, much of the precious metal was shipped to the East, particularly to the Philadelphia Mint, where it was converted into coins—including the gold dollar denomination (introduced in 1849) and the $20 double eagle (introduced in 1850). However, once the San Francisco Mint opened in March 1854, it became the main depository for such metal.

In time, large amounts of gold coins and ingots were concentrated in commercial channels, primarily in San Francisco, from which port the "treasure" (as it was openly referred to in newspaper accounts and shipping notices, seemingly with little thought for security) was sent by sea to Nicaragua, Panama, Liverpool, and other destinations. Large amounts of gold also continued to be received at the Philadelphia and New Orleans mints, though both experienced great difficulty in refining the metal so as to remove at least part of the large amount of unwanted silver that existed as an "impurity."

The SS *Winfield Scott*. The engraver has the flag blowing in one direction and the smoke in another.

Return Trips Become Treasure Troves

The next few chapters focus specifically on a few sidewheel steamers, particularly ones laden with gold coins and ingots (as well as a complement of passengers) that headed back from San Francisco and south on the Pacific Ocean to Panama, where the treasure would be carried to the far Caribbean Sea coast by pack animals or (after 1855) the railroad. Once on that side, the travelers and gold would be transferred to another steamship and carried to New York City or another port.

While many ships had difficulties or were lost on this journey, the several given individual chapters here were particularly important with regard to treasure of interest to numismatists.

The Story of a Steamship

Lost: December 2, 1853 • **Location:** Anacapa Island, California • **Found:** 1965 • **Treasure:** Miscellaneous gold coins

Among the vessels in service to and from San Francisco was the 1,291-ton SS *Winfield Scott*. The ship had been named for General Winfield Scott (born in 1786), who had distinguished himself in the Mexican War, during which he marched from Vera Cruz to Mexico City and served as the governor of the city from 1847 to 1848. Some have ranked him as the pre-eminent U.S. military figure of the first half of the 1800s. Scott was also the Whig party candidate for president in 1852, but he lost to Franklin Pierce.

The ship *Winfield Scott* was built by Westervelt and McKay in New York and launched on October 27, 1850. The sidewheel steamer measured 225 feet long, had a draft of 14 feet, and was powered by two 370-horsepower side-lever steam engines fed by coal stored in bunkers capable of holding 300 tons.[332] The specifications called for a capacity of 165 passengers in first and second cabins and 150 in steerage, but in practice, the passengers and crew usually totaled far more than that.

The dining salon, 96 feet in length, could seat more than 100 at a time. To each side of the dining area were staterooms. For the relaxation of passengers, an 80-by-14-foot parlor at the stern was lined with sofas on the sides, and part of one end could be closed off by folding doors to allow privacy for ladies or families. Another parlor was in the fore part of the ship.[333]

The *Winfield Scott* arrived in San Francisco for the first time on April 28, 1852, having made the transit from Panama with 700 passengers in just 14 days. She bore the flag of the Independent Line for the remainder of the year, after which she was in service for the New York & San Francisco Steamship Company.[334] She departed San Francisco for Panama on May 6, 1852, with 580 passengers, and was back in California on June 16 with 600 passengers, including 85 ladies.[335] Then, in May 1853, the ship was purchased by the Pacific Mail Steamship Company.[336]

On the Way to Panama

On December 1, 1853, the SS *Winfield Scott* weighed anchor in the harbor of San Francisco and headed toward Panama. Captain Simon F. Blunt—a graduate of the U.S. Naval Academy who later worked for the U.S. Geodetic Survey mapping the coasts of California and Oregon—was at the helm for what would be his first-ever command.[337]

On board were 450 (442 men and only 8 women) passengers, the crew, many sacks of mail, and $884,861 in gold treasure (per the manifest) plus coins and various personal effects carried by the travelers. By this time, travel along the Pacific Coast was routine, and the passengers enjoyed many amenities, including on-board games and entertainment; walking on the deck and observing the distant coast, provided there was no low fog (called "smoke" by sea travelers); and taking the opportunity to relax. Through a spyglass, sometimes glistening brown seals could be seen sunning or cavorting on rocks.

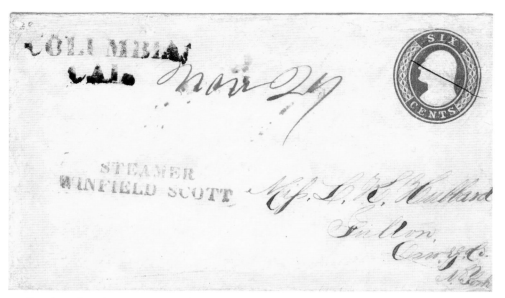

Envelope for a letter posted in Columbia, a gold-mining town, on November 29, 1853, and carried aboard the SS *Winfield Scott* on her last voyage.

Meals were of excellent quality, with the meat coming from poultry, sheep, cows, and pigs kept alive in pens on board.[338] Sumptuous tables were set for first cabin passengers, and while those in steerage often had to eat while standing at counters, the food was still good. Stocks of wine and other spirits were abundant and could be tapped at a reasonable cost.

First cabin accommodations provided travel at its finest—even better than the mail steamers on the Atlantic side of Panama. The later generation of Pacific steamers built after the first few years of the Gold Rush tended to be of larger size and with more commodious parlors and public rooms. However, on both coasts, steerage accommodations could be primitive, cramped, and noisy.

"Let Her Rip!"

On the same day as the *Winfield Scott*'s departure, the SS *Sierra Nevada* departed from San Francisco with a larger number of passengers, more cargo, and $1,635,000 in registered gold. This 1,300-ton sidewheel steamer—owned by the Vanderbilt-Nicaragua Line and under Captain C.H. Baldwin—was headed to Nicaragua. Both ships left at nine o'clock in the morning.

On the next day, December 2, Captain Blunt initiated a race in order to showcase the desirabil-ity of the *Winfield Scott* over the *Sierra Nevada*. Such competitions were not unusual, and the winner was guaranteed of favorable publicity. To make the best time, he decided to take a shortcut by cutting between the Channel Islands and the coast near Santa Barbara, rather than the usual route westward of the islands. This was a large area of open water except for a tiny island known as Anacapa about five miles distant from Santa Cruz Island and about 25 miles offshore of Santa Barbara. Nonetheless, it was a risky move, as a dense fog blanketed the ocean. Still, Blunt was confident, based on his earlier survey work of the coast.

The new course disturbed some of the officers of the ship, as it seems that the SS *Winfield Scott* came too close to a rocky point on Santa Cruz Island, and arguments arose. This was after dinner had been served, and most passengers had retired to their berths. The course could be changed to vast open ocean to the west; certainly, the more prudent heads asserted, the SS *Sierra Nevada* was proceeding slowly because of the fog, and the race could be "on hold" until the morning.

Captain Blunt was apparently not dissuaded. In fact, when the first officer questioned whether the ship should slow down around 9 o'clock so as to proceed carefully in dense fog, Blunt commanded, "Let her rip!"[339] As such, the *Winfield Scott* proceeded at full speed through the gloom.

Tragedy Strikes

This reckless decision proved costly, as shortly before midnight the ship struck the rocks on the north side of Anacapa Island, creating two large holes in her bow. The two large sidewheel paddles were thrown into reverse, but the damaged ship backed away only to hit other rocks and smash her rudder. Then "the boat drifted off a

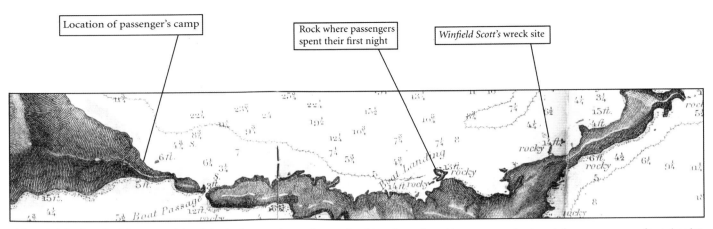

Location of passenger's camp

Rock where passengers spent their first night

Winfield Scott's wreck site

Map detail of part of Anacapa Island, including spots on the north side where the ship was wrecked and the passengers found safety.

distance of about 300 yards, and went ashore bow-on, striking upon a high bluff. She had already commenced filling, and soon after striking for the last time sunk up to her guards."[340]

In the wee hours of the morning of December 3, the passengers and crew took provisions and bedding to a tiny uninhabited island close to the shore about a mile west of the crash scene, where they spent the night in company with retrieved mail sacks and the gold treasure. The evacuation was supervised by Captain Blunt and were not over until the crack of dawn. Afterward, the hull drifted away, sank in deep water, and was a total loss.

Most of the passengers' baggage and personal effects, among which were at least a few gold coins, were left behind in the wreck. The next morning the passengers and saved cargo were transferred to a larger island nearby. This was comfortable for the time being, and a large cave afforded shelter.

Rescue Operations

At eight o'clock in the morning of December 4, someone on board the SS *California* (under Captain A.V.H. LeRoy) saw the smoke from a signal gun fired by the stranded voyagers, and within the next two to three hours that ship rescued the female passengers from the island and took the

gold treasure and mail on board.[341] However, the *California* could not hold all of the survivors—perhaps due to matters of capacity, as the ship had departed Panama with 500 of its own passengers—and had to leave some stranded while it continued to San Francisco. The *California* arrived there on December 6 at 8:00 a.m.; passengers disembarking (supposedly a mix of those originally on board and those rescued) numbered 309, of which 77 were women.

Thankfully, those not taken by the *California* were not doomed, though they did nearly run out of food. The SS *Southerner* arrived at the scene at daybreak on December 10 and brought ashore ample provisions for the remaining survivors while they waited for the SS *Republic*, which had been sent to take them aboard.[342] At five o'clock the same day, the *Republic* arrived. From that time until the morning of the December 12, rescue and additional salvage operations were conducted, after which the *Republic* headed back to San Francisco amid high winds and heavy seas. The ordeal was over.

By all accounts, throughout the entire incident Captain Blunt did a superb job of assisting with the landing of the passengers, the removal of what cargo and mail could be taken ashore, and other matters.[343] The matter of racing the ship seems to have been kept quiet.

Diving on an Unknown Wreck

Over the years, many divers visited the wreck site, including salvors Captain Maginn and Colonel George Baker. In 1894, that pair lifted a steam engine piston, an unopened chest (the contents of which were not disclosed by the finders), brass fittings, and other artifacts from the sea bottom. However, I have located no accounts of coins being found.

Apparently, additional pieces of copper and brass were salvaged as scrap for the defense effort during World War II. Years later, in 1965, scuba diver Glenn E. Miller operated the 62-foot charter boat *Emerald* out of Santa Barbara and often took divers on exploration trips to examine undersea life, including lobsters. On one such lobster-hunting sortie to Anacapa Island, one of the 28 undersea investigators reported seeing strewn pieces of iron, brass spikes, and other nautical items.

Here, possibly, was a wreck to be explored! Miller donned his suit to see for himself, and he was soon rewarded by the sight of the center part of an old paddlewheel sticking about 15 feet out of the bottom and remains of another about 40 feet away. In between were scraps of metal, perhaps from a long-forgotten sidewheel steamer, with the wooden parts long since rotted away.[344]

Afterwards, Miller returned home and headed for the local library to see what he could learn. Before long, the story of the ill-fated SS *Winfield Scott* emerged from the old clippings.

Treasure Found

Miller soon enlisted Jim Gurdy, who had come to Santa Barbara from Sacramento and done gold diving in rivers in the northern part of the state. Gurdy, who was to receive 10% of anything valuable found, had a portable dredge for underwater work. The two took the apparatus to the Anacapa Island wreck site and soon found pieces of lead and copper, spikes and nails, a well-preserved ceramic spittoon, and several gold nuggets.

Then, on Memorial Day 1969, Miller and other divers including Paul Tizimoulis, publisher of *Skin Diver* magazine, and Jack McKenney, editor, went to the site. Dick Anderson, who later

wrote several articles about the experience, including an account in the September 1969 issue of the *Skin Diver*, recalled:

As soon as I hit water I began fanning the sand away from bedrock crevices. In less than five minutes I spotted what had to be a gold coin. It is hard to describe the thrill associated with such an event, but monetarily speaking it would be much like finding a hundred dollar bill in the middle of a field and knowing that there had to be a lot more of them around.

I picked up the coin and looked at it. Even after 116 years of salty immersion the octagonal coin was in nearly perfect shape and the markings legible: "1 DOLLAR CALIFORNIA GOLD, 1853." Part of the coin still glistened with the original mint

Treasure historian and enthusiast Tom Sebring with the bell from the SS *Winfield Scott*.

lustre. I swallowed hard and continued fanning. In just moments I had uncovered two more gold coins: an octagonal half dollar and a round gold dollar.

Among those who read Anderson's article was Don Robinson, a former director of the Channel Islands National Monument, who gently advised Anderson and others that unauthorized salvage operations could not be conducted on any undersea wrecks within a mile of Anacapa Island, but divers were free to explore and look to their hearts' content.

From then on, Miller worked on the sea bottom, and he as well as Anderson, Pete Greenwood (charter operator of the *Scuba Queen* out of San Pedro, the port of Los Angeles), and Mark Williams found many gold coins. Separately, Cliff Croft obtained several small denomination gold coins.[345] Presumably, these pieces were from "passenger gold"—coins carried by travelers and left behind during the disaster. The "treasure gold" was carried off the ship soon after it was wrecked and, apparently, was saved intact.

The following gold coins are among those known to have been found by divers beginning in 1960s:

Small-denomination California gold coins

25¢ octagonal: 1853 Small Liberty Head by Frontier & Diviercy,[346] 9 stars. Breen Gillio-101 (5 pieces)

25¢ round: Undated. Small Liberty Head by Frontier & Diviercy, 12 stars. BG-205

25¢ round: Undated. Small Liberty Head by Frontier & Diviercy, 10 stars. BG-206

25¢ round: 1853 Small Liberty Head by Frontier & Diviercy, b 10 stars. BG-209 (2 pieces)

25¢ round: Undated. Small Liberty Head by A.L. Nouizillet,[347] 12 stars. BG-222 (die state I, an early impression)

25¢ round: Undated. Small Liberty Head, 12 stars. BG-222 (State II)

25¢ round: Undated. Small Liberty Head by A.L. Nouizillet, 12 stars. BG-223 (10 pieces)

50¢ octagonal: 1853 F.D. Liberty Head by Frontier & Diviercy, 13 Stars, eagle reverse (with rays behind the eagle, giving it at quick glance the appearance of a peacock, by which appellation it is sometimes known). BG-302 (3 pieces)

50¢ octagonal: 1853 BG number uncertain, 301 to 304. By Frontier & Diviercy

50¢ octagonal: Date and variety unknown

50¢ round: 1853 Variety unknown

50¢ round: 1853 Liberty Head by Frontier & Diviercy, 13 stars. BG-401

50¢ round: 1853 Liberty Head by Frontier & Diviercy on behalf of Gaime, Guillemot & Co.; with G.G. initials below portrait, 13 stars. BG-414

50¢ round: 1853 Liberty Head by M. Deriberpe and signed D,[348] 11 stars. BG-421

50¢ round: 1853 Liberty Head by M. Nouizillet, 13 stars. BG-428

50¢ round: 1853 Liberty Head by M. Nouizillet, 13 stars. BG-430 (3 pieces)

50¢ round: Date and variety unknown

$1 octagonal: 1853 Liberty Head, by M. Deriberpe and signed DERI. 8 stars. BG-514

$1 octagonal: 1853 Liberty Head by Deriberpe, 8 stars. BG-519 (2 pieces)

$1 octagonal: 1853 Liberty Head by Deriberpe, 8 stars. BG-525

$1 octagonal: 1853 Liberty Head by Deriberpe, 8 stars. BG-526 (2 pieces)

$1 octagonal: 1853 N. (A.L. Nouizellet). Liberty Head, 13 stars. BG-530 (15 or 16 pieces)

$1 octagonal: 1853 Liberty Head by A.L. Nouizillet, 13 stars. BG-531 (2 pieces)

Large-denomination California gold coins

$5 Moffat & Co. 1849

$5 Moffat & Co. 1850

$10 Augustus Humbert 1852 (found by Pete Greenwood, 1965)

Federal gold coins

$1 gold: 14 miscellaneous unattributed, some of which may have been California gold dollars, others federal

Quarter eagles: 5 pieces, varieties unknown

Half eagles: 3 pieces, varieties unknown[349]

Many if not most of these coins were sold to Southern California dealer Kenneth W. Lee, who did not realize the historical interest they might have to later researchers, but simply acquired them as stock in trade. "I guess at the time it did not occur to me to keep details!" he later commented to numismatic researcher Robert D. Leonard Jr.

Note that while collectors have long known that small gold quarters, half dollars, and dollars had been minted in San Francisco by various private interests and had served to facilitate small transactions, it was less clear when these first became popular. The situation is complicated by the practice employed after the 1850s of back-dating certain dies so as to give the coins the aura of age and, thus, acceptability. Such small-denomination gold coins were never officially sanctioned and, in fact, were made illegal by federal statute in 1864.

The presence of these small gold pieces in the littered remains of the *Winfield Scott* verified that the varieties in question actually circulated in California during the time indicated. Early documentation of these small gold coins is hard to find in newspaper accounts or travelers' reminiscences. Probably, they were too familiar at the time to be chronicled in print.[350]

chapter 13

Gold Rush Treasure: SS *Yankee Blade*

In the heady days of the Gold Rush, passenger travel advertising had two emphases: fastest total speed (combined time for the Atlantic leg, land crossing, and Pacific leg) from East to West, and the lowest fare. On these fronts, the Independent Steamship Company and Cornelius Vanderbilt's Nicaragua Line together competed with the longer-established Pacific Mail Steamship Company on the western run from San Francisco to Panama or the crossing at Nicaragua—although the latter route did not amount to much, despite the efforts made by Vanderbilt to establish it as a more solid presence in the mid-1850s.

Among the Independent Steamship Company's fleet was the 1,767-ton SS *Yankee Blade.* Built at Williamsburg, New York, in 1853 by Perrine, Patterson & Stack—the same firm that had launched the SS *Brother Jonathan* (see chapter 15, "The Fate of the SS *Brother Jonathan*," page 261) in 1850—she measured 274 feet long. Power was

provided by a single coal-fired steam engine, which sported a 6-foot, 4-inch cylinder and a stroke of 12 feet and was built by the Allaire Iron Works.

An "Opposition" Steamer

Lost: October 1, 1854 • **Location:** Near Port Arguello, California • **Found:** 1977 (or earlier?) • **Treasure:** Gold coins

The *Yankee Blade*'s first voyage, leaving in December 1853 and arriving the next month, was on the New York-to-Aspinwall run under the Independent Opposition Line flag. The incorporation of the word "Opposition" in a line's name had been common in the seafaring passenger trade for many years and was typically employed by entrepreneurs who sailed at lower rates (as extensively advertised) and with minimal amenities (not mentioned in publicity) compared to the longer-established and better-outfitted lines, which frequently held lucrative government or other contracts.

The ship's large capacity for passengers made her difficult to fill except at discounted rates—as in other areas of commercial endeavor and public service, high price and low quality were not compatible—and starting at the outset, the line sustained heavy losses. Additionally, amenities for passengers were often found wanting, and passage aboard the *Yankee Blade* was anything but an exercise in luxurious travel.

Reflective of the *Yankee Blade* and a related ship, a ballad of the day, *The Humbug Line*, noted in part:

The greatest imposition that the public ever saw,
Are the California steamships that run to Panama.
They have opposition on the route, with cabins very nice,
And advertise to take you for half the usual price;
They get thousands from the mountains, and then deny their bills,
So you have to pay their prices, or go back to the hills.
You are driven round the steerage like a drove of hungry swine,
And kicked ashore at Panama by the Independent Line;
Your baggage is thrown overboard, the like you never saw,
A trip or two will sicken you of going to Panama.
Chorus:
Then come along, come along, you that want to go,
The best accommodations and the passage very low;
Our boats they are large enough, don't be afraid,
The *Golden Gate* is going down to beat the *Yankee Blade*.[351]

Along the Pacific Coast

For her first voyage to the Pacific, the *Yankee Blade* left New York City on February 2, 1854, went around Cape Horn, and arrived in San Francisco on May 4, still in service for the Independent Opposition Line. Soon thereafter, however, she was under somewhat similarly named Independent Steamship Company.[352]

The first few months of the *Yankee Blade*'s Western service were rather uneventful. On September 1, 1854, she arrived in San Francisco from Panama, with six of her 500 passengers dead from cholera. This was not particularly unusual, though, as cholera—typically acquired in tropical Panama during the land crossing—ravaged many steamers of the era. Indeed, accounts of incoming ships published in the *Alta California* and *San Francisco*

Herald often gave death notices in the same accounts as cargo and passenger information.

Later in the same month—September 28, 1854—the *Yankee Blade* sailed for Panama with more than 900 aboard, advertising through rates (including the Atlantic connection by another steamer) to New York City of $175 first cabin, $150 second cabin, and $50 steerage.[353] The ship was packed to nearly overflowing, as revenue was the main concern of her owners. One estimate, later discredited, held that there were more than 1,200 aboard;[354] another later account placed the number at 812 passengers and 122 crew.

As was so often the case, an exact passenger count was not possible. While there was a list of those who had purchased their tickets by advance reservation, there were usually others who arrived at the docks at the last minute to buy passage and whose names were not recorded. This lack of passenger roster precision was true of virtually all vessels on both coasts.[355]

Trying for a Speed Record

On September 30, 1854, the *Yankee Blade*'s captain—Henry T. Randall—decided to try to establish a speed record from San Francisco to Panama, as such an accomplishment could have an excellent effect in advertising and focus favorable attention on the vessel.[356] After all, the ship was in need of some good publicity.

What's more, the presence of a competitor pushed the need for speed. Just outside of the harbor, the *Yankee Blade* "stopped her engine, and allowing the *Sonora* to pass her, raised her flag as a challenge of speed, and then getting again headway, passed the *Sonora* at the bar. It was understood at San Francisco that a bet of $5,000 was pending on the race to Panama."[357]

The two ships were rivals, not only flying flags of different lines, but also tied together by a previous encounter: recently, the captain of the *Sonora* had seen a distress signal from the *Yankee Blade*, but had not stopped to aid her when she was out of coal and instead only reported the stranded ship when he made port. Then, just as public sentiment against the crew of the *Sonora* was beginning to run high, the *Yankee Blade* had arrived under her own power after her crew and some volunteer passengers went ashore on Coiba Island and cut firewood.[358]

Supposed to be in Deep Water

The record-setting attempt came to an end at about 3:30 in the afternoon of October 1, when the *Yankee Blade* struck a submerged reef off Port Arguello while cutting close to the California coast in thick fog. Apparently, Captain Randall thought his ship was in deep water about 20 miles from shore; later, he suggested that a "powerful current" out of his control drew the boat onto the rocks. At the time, the ship's paddlewheels were turning at the rate of 13 revolutions per minute.

The vessel was stranded at a rakish angle with the first 60 feet of her bow raised on the reef and her stern submerged in about 50 feet of water. Confusion reigned among officers and crew as they sought safety, apparently with little concern for the passengers. Waves breaking over the stern caused extensive damage and broke away some wooden sections.

About $152,000 in specie[359] consigned by the San Francisco banking house of Page, Bacon & Co. was stored in a vault at the bottom of the quickly flooded hull. Upon first inspection after the crash, the treasure was found already covered by five feet of rapidly rising water, making recovery impossible. Note that Adams & Co. had also consigned a bag to New Orleans via Panama, but it contained only papers.

Interestingly, Fretz & Ralston—San Francisco agents for the *Yankee Blade*—advertised for shipments but apparently had no specie or bullion aboard for their own or anyone else's account booked through them. Page, Bacon & Co. must have made separate arrangements; it was common for agents to solicit shipments of treasure up to a few hours before a vessel's departure. Passengers had varying amounts of personal effects and money.

C.M. Welles, a member of the crew of the SS *Cortes*, gave a different account of the conditions of the crash and an even larger estimate of the passengers aboard, but did confirm that there was considerable wealth aboard:

> It was on board this ship I first knew the unfortunate steamship *Yankee Blade*. She lay upon the other side of the dock we occupied, and left the city at the same time with us. She was an immense vessel, crowded beyond all description. I gazed in perfect astonishment at the mass of human beings that crowded her every part as she glided away from the wharf into the bay.
>
> She could not have had less than fifteen hundred souls on board, more than a thousand of whom were lost this same trip, in the fearful wreck it experienced. Suspicions of foul play were in the minds of many, for she carried an immense treasure beside what was in the hands of the passengers, and ran upon the beach in a clear night, in calm weather, in a manner that has always remained a mystery.[360]

Captain Randall's Actions

Soon after the crash, Captain Randall took about 30 passengers on shore in a lifeboat, but elected to remain in safety there and not return to the wreck. His first officer did likewise, but as his lifeboat was nearing the shore it too wrecked, and 17 of the 22 aboard were drowned.

Meanwhile, Randall's young son, Henry Jr., was appointed to remain on board and supervise, but events quickly showed that he was incompetent to do so. By evening, about 200 of the passengers and crew had been transferred to the beach, where they stayed with the captain and first officer; the remaining occupants waited for the morrow.

The wind rose in the night, and the wooden hull began to break up on the rocks. Absent the commanding officer and his assistant, confusion and panic ran rampant aboard the ship. Steerage passengers broke into the liquor lockers, and many became drunk. A rampage of shooting, looting, and terrorizing the first-cabin passengers ensued.

Details appeared in the *Alta California*, October 10:

As soon as the ship struck, a gang of fiends armed themselves, broken open the bar, and then proceeded to cut and break open the trunks of passengers. The ship was entirely under their control, and passengers did not dare to go below for their baggage, which might in many instances have been saved. Knives and pistols were used, and passengers who dared to interfere to save their own property were summarily knocked down, and kicked, and threatened with being shot. Several pistols were fired, and it is said one or two passengers were killed. It is supposed by some that the compass had been tampered with, for the purpose of losing the ship, that these plunders might be committed.

The passengers have lost their baggage and nearly all of them their money. We think the loss of passengers, besides the treasure list, may be safely put down at half a million of dollars. . . .

When the steamer was threatening to go to pieces any minute, some of the gang of pirates on board got possession of the life preservers and demanded enormous prices of the passengers for them, in some cases taking gold watches for them. A Mr. Gaston informs us that he purchased one from the steward [J. Belknap] of the Yankee Blade, for which he paid him $40.[361] Such things as this speak little for human nature.

More of the same was printed in a subsequent account in the *New York Times*:

When the captain left the ship in the first boat, all on board was in confusion, and not five minutes had elapsed before the hell hounds were at their work. A band of robbers seemed organized at once, and began plundering the cabin. They were armed with revolvers and knives, and proceeded coolly to open carpet bags and trunks, which they ransacked with all possible dispatch, as it was necessary to hasten through their job in that portion of the boat where the water was rapidly coming in.

In the steerage they had full control all night, and no one dared to enter or to interfere. At one time cries of murder were heard below, and a young man called for help to protect his friend, but none were willing to go down. One passenger subsequently exhibited a severe gash in the back of his head which was inflicted while they were taking his watch.

Some passengers had to draw their pistols and present them in order to get the women and children on the boats the first day. The plunder party got possession of one of the boats, and money was exacted from several who got on board. A lot of men on shore of the same stripe would give up nothing that they had obtained without pay. They provided themselves with canvas and blankets, while the women were without covering or protection from the weather save a quantity of brush.[362]

Help Arrives

At eight o'clock the next morning, the small coastal steamer SS *Goliah*, under Captain Samuel Haley, came by and succeeded in getting about 600 of the stranded passengers on board via her lifeboats, even amid heavy seas.[363] Supplies including clothing, food, and canvas were landed on the beach for the use of the 200 or so still stranded.

At that point, the *Goliah* took the survivors to Santa Barbara and San Pedro (port of Los Angeles) on the way to its final port of San Diego, where the majority of the passengers disembarked. The *Goliah* then returned to pick up those who had remained on the shore near the wreck. Unfortunately, in the meantime the beach had become a scene of self-inflicted disaster, as the ship's firemen and a few others—brandishing firearms—took most of the provisions for themselves and also relieved helpless passengers of their money and other valuable goods that had been brought ashore. A rare exception to the behavior of the crew was J.H. Kennard, third officer, who expressed concern for the welfare of the passengers and did as much as he could to help them.

Various sources state that between 17 and 50 passengers, mostly women and children, lost their lives, all told.[364] Some accounts suggested an even greater mortality. J.P. Pittman of Downieville, California, a passenger who assisted with the rescue of many women and children, averred that "at least 200 perished."[365]

The survivors included Frank Jones (said by some to have been "the cleverest gambler in San Francisco," and by others to have been a prominent New York socialite); Jones's black servant Charley; and Charles Reed, all three of whom would later figure in the memorable voyage of the SS *Central America* in September 1857.[366]

Aftermath

By the morning of October 3, 1854, the *Yankee Blade* had broken apart. In the immediate area, nothing was to be seen afloat except the pilot house and part of the deck. The hull, ruptured by a break estimated to be a foot wide and 30 feet long, was on the ocean floor.

On October 15, survivors held a mass meeting in Portsmouth Square in San Francisco to address their concerns.[367] Resolutions passed included these:

> Resolved: That after a careful investigation and by an unbiased judgment, we have come to the firm conclusion that sheer negligence upon the part of the managers of the *Yankee Blade* in directing her course, and in running so near a coast well known to be dangerous, was the cause of the disastrous wreck.
>
> Resolved: That duty compels us to censure Capt. Randall, in so quickly deserting the wreck, and leaving the boat without a leading officer on board to quiet the passengers and prevent the plundering. Had the Captain remained on board, it is our candid opinion this could have been done.

Certain survivors were brought back to San Francisco by the *Brother Jonathan*, under Captain C.P. Seabury, and the crowd in Portsmouth Square proposed to present him with a gold watch "as a mark of esteem for the hospitable manner in which the destitute passengers were treated on board of his ship on the way from San Diego to this port."

On the darker side of events, the agents for the *Yankee Blade* "sent to the police office and requested the marshal to send down five or six police officers to prevent any outrage" at the mass meeting. A committee of five survivors was deputized to meet with the steamship agents, but an interview was denied.

All of the passengers had been on their way to Panama when the wreck occurred. General unhappiness was expressed at the line's policy of bringing them back to their port of embarkation, rather than giving them accommodations to their intended destination of Panama. In San Francisco, the line offered to refund *just 25%* of the ticket purchase price, "evidently taking refuge behind some clause that gave the purchasers passage on that particular steamer."[368]

Obviously, the entire *Yankee Blade* affair remains one of the sorriest chapters in the annals of the U.S. passenger steamship trade.

Divers on the Wreck

On October 22, 1854, the *Alta California* reported that the "body of a man, apparently 40 years of age, came ashore, badly cut about the head, and the pockets of his clothing rifled. . . . They thought that he had been murdered on board the steamer by some of the ruffian gang of whose horrible work much has been said." The same account noted that heavy waves were rolling over the shipwreck site, and that although a box of liquor and valise had been found by divers using underwater breathing apparatus, no trace of the treasure had been found.

Meanwhile, the empty wooden hull had separated from the heavy engine and had washed on shore, and back in San Francisco, the much-condemned Captain Randall offered his services to assist in salvage efforts. This offer and his subsequent actions would prove only to further reflect his cupidity.

On December 1, 1854, the *Weekly Alta California* (an adjunct of the usual daily edition) reported the return of Captain Fowler and his pilot boat,

Dancing Feather, which with its crew of divers had spent about five weeks seeking the lost treasure of the *Yankee Blade* under the watchful eye of Captain Randall. "It is reported that two boxes of specie have been recovered, the amount of which could not be ascertained," read the story. Among other artifacts seen but not brought to the surface was a brass cannon described as "a very valuable one, and it is said it was exhibited at the great exhibition [Crystal Palace, 1853] in New York, and cost originally $1,150."

Another account, this one datelined January 7, 1855, noted that the *Dancing Feather*—now under Captain Hutchins but with Randall still advising the recovery attempts—had recently returned from the wreck site, but that "the bad weather which prevailed most of the time prevented any successful operations, and no further amount of the sunken treasure had been recovered."

Other salvage efforts were going on at the same time, as evidenced by an account in the *Alta California*, January 5, 1855, which reported that Samuel Wheland, Thomas Matthews, and Robert Wilson had been charged for "stealing gold dust from the wreck of the *Yankee Blade*, the property of Page, Bacon & Co." They had recovered this dust clandestinely while ostensibly under the hire of official salvors and had brought it back to San Francisco aboard the *Pilgrim*.

Subsequent court reports concerning the alleged theft noted that Captain Randall "testified that at the wreck he saw some of the prisoners bring up two boxes, resembling treasure boxes. They might, however, have been decoy boxes, as the parties in search of the treasure were in the habit of deceiving and misleading each other."[369] Other discussions revealed not only that Page, Bacon & Co. had shipped about $152,000 (as mentioned before), but also that passenger Mrs. E. Bloomingdale lost $10,000, and another traveler lost $6,000. For whatever reason, though, the charges against the salvors aboard the *Pilgrim* were dismissed shortly afterward.

Separately, Captain Randall was charged by other parties with "having plundered a box of treasure of about $17,000 in gold dust." The rascal eventually settled claims against him by paying $6,000. All considered, the entire affair was beginning to sound farcical.

On January 14, the *Alta California* printed still more on the wreck salvage attempts, quoting a Mr. Haven, president of the Steam Tug Company, who had been hired by the insurance underwriters to help recover the treasure. He reported that a visit to the location by his ship, the *Caroline*, which had left San Francisco on October 16, was unproductive. However, Haven recalled, "The *Dancing Feather* on her first trip brought up four boxes of treasure, about $69,300, roughly." Under contracts given by the insurers, salvage ships and their operators were to receive 60% of what they found.

Even more efforts continued at the wreck into March 1855. In that month, the *Ada* was at the site but "did not procure anything." Also, Captain Hutchins was back on the scene—commanding the brig *Boston* "with a diving machine on board"— but he and this ship abandoned the *Yankee Blade* effort and sailed for Chile on March 11 "to search for copper lost in a vessel on that coast some time ago."

Later Salvage Efforts

For many decades after these last described attempts, the hull of the *Yankee Blade* remained in its watery grave off the coast of California. In 1948, the hull was located, but strong currents and unfavorable weather prevented any recovery.[370] Indeed, this area spelled doom for numerous other ships, often under circumstances of low-lying fog similar to those faced by the wreck currently in question.

Eventually, more artifacts from the *Yankee Blade* were salvaged by divers in 1977, and about 300 specimens of 1854-S gold $20 coins are said to have been found (although I have found no accounts of such coins in contemporary reports). As is often true of treasure salvage situations, little factual information found its way into print.

It is known, however, that a generous supply of Uncirculated 1854-S double eagles came on the rare-coin market about that time, and that these coins were uniform in appearance. All were sharply struck, had somewhat subdued luster from microscopic etching by seawater (which attacks the copper element of the 90% gold / 10% copper alloy of the pieces), and displayed a fine network of die cracks on the reverse.[371]

When these unusually fine 1854-S double eagles appeared in coin-collecting circles in the late 1970s, explanations as to their origin were not readily forthcoming. One person informed me that these coins were found between the studs of a wall in an old building in San Francisco when it was torn down. However, that did not account for the obvious indication that these pieces had been immersed in seawater with sand drifting over them.

The probable explanation is that the finders did not want to deal with any claims that others might make to the treasure, but that these pieces did indeed come from the *Yankee Blade*.

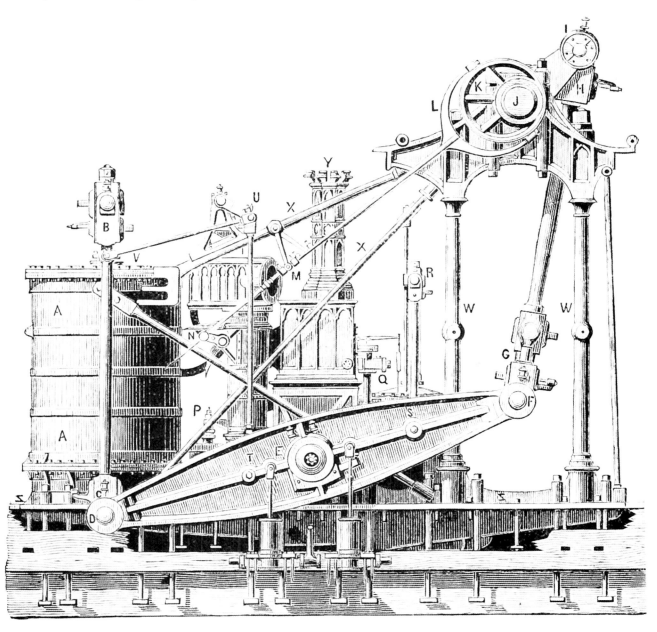

A side-lever engine powered the *Yankee Blade*.

chapter 14

Gold Rush Treasure: SS *Central America*

Lost: September 12, 1857 • **Location:** Off the coast of North Carolina •
Found: 1987 • **Treasure:** Vast quantity of gold coins and bars

To Panama on the SS *Sonora*

In the annals of undersea treasure hunting for United States coins the saga of the SS *Central America* is an adventure to end all adventures. Its final chapters are still being written in our own time.

In San Francisco on August 20, 1857, more than 400 people who had booked passage on the Pacific Mail Steamship Company's SS *Sonora* hastened aboard the vessel. The destination was Panama to be followed by a train trip across the Isthmus, then a connecting passage on another ship at Aspinwall (today known as Colón) for the Atlantic run. Accompanying the passengers were more than 100 bags of mail and a cargo of gold registered at over $1.2 million consigned by nine major shippers including Wells, Fargo & Co. The ultimate destination of the travelers and cargo was New York City.

In addition to more than $1.2 million in gold listed on the manifest, many passengers had their own treasures, variously estimated to average from about $1,000 to $5,000 per person, and when added to the commercial cargo, the total came to well over $2 million.

The gold was in various forms including rectangular ingots and bars from various assayers, recently struck $20 pieces from the San Francisco Mint, and an assortment of other coins ranging from British sovereigns to American issues struck in California by assayers and private minters. Some of the larger coins were $50 "slugs" of octagonal shape made by the U.S. Assay Office of Gold. The bulk of the coins and bullion

The SS *Central America*.

were destined for New York clearing houses and bankers, the New York Sub-Treasury, and the Philadelphia Mint, with a lesser amount to be transshipped to the London market.

As nearly always, the Pacific trip was an enjoyable experience, what with finely appointed salons and other public areas, fresh meat from livestock on board, and other amenities. The *Sonora* had a fine record and had experienced no major problems since it entered the Pacific service in 1854.

With a brief stop at Manzanillo on the Mexican coast, and an overnight respite at Acapulco to take on coal for the boilers, the *Sonora* arrived at the Gulf of Panama on the evening of September 2. The trip had been uneventful, and all aboard had seemingly savored the experience.

Across the Isthmus of Panama

Early the next morning the passengers were transferred to shore by small boats, after which they would ride the Panama Railroad across

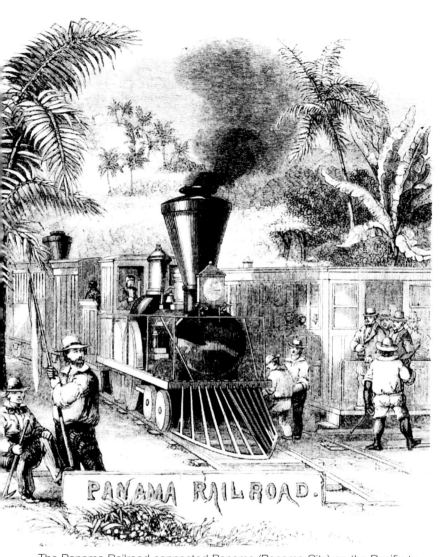

The Panama Railroad connected Panama (Panama City) on the Pacific to Aspinwall on the Atlantic, a 48-mile route. By 1857 travel on the line was routine, with occasional optional stops along the way.

nearly 48 miles of land. This took from three and a quarter hours for those who departed early, to nearly six hours for the last in line. Several transits were required to accommodate all of the travelers and cargo from the *Sonora*.

The Panama Railroad cars that traversed the track across the Isthmus to Aspinwall were hardly luxurious and were described as "toys" by one passenger. Along the way there were several concessions for food and drink set up by natives in tents, and those taking the ride could stop and be refreshed. Since its opening in 1855 the line had revolutionized travel from San Francisco to points on the East Coast and vice versa. What had been

an arduous trip combining pack animals on the Pacific side and small boats on the Chagres River on the Atlantic side was now very routine. The days of covered wagons trekking west on the alkali plains past Utah were but a memory now.

After arrival on the Atlantic side of the Isthmus at Aspinwall the travelers boarded at several hotels. Even though most large structures in the village, earlier called Chagres, were of relatively new construction, health and sanitation facilities were uncertain, and the passengers were advised to be careful of the quality of the food.

Ahead was the final leg of the trip to New York City, about 2,000 miles, taking less time than the Pacific part of the journey.

Captain Herndon and His Ship

On Thursday afternoon, September 3, 1857, passengers continuing from California plus others picked up at Panama were greeted at the dock at Aspinwall by Captain William Lewis Herndon as they boarded the SS *Central America* for the passage to New York.

Herndon, born in 1813, was a career Navy officer. Among his accomplishments was service under Commodore Matthew Calbraith Perry in the Mexican-American War and his 1847 command of a small steamer, the *Iris*.[372] In 1851 and 1852 he was the first American to traverse the Amazon River. He began on the Pacific side, climbed the Andes to the headwaters of the Amazon, built boats, and then navigated the river to its mouth on the Atlantic Ocean, a distance of about 4,100 miles. His published report on the exploration had been well received.

Once comfortably settled in their cabins and berths, the nearly 600 passengers and crew members aboard the *Central America* looked forward

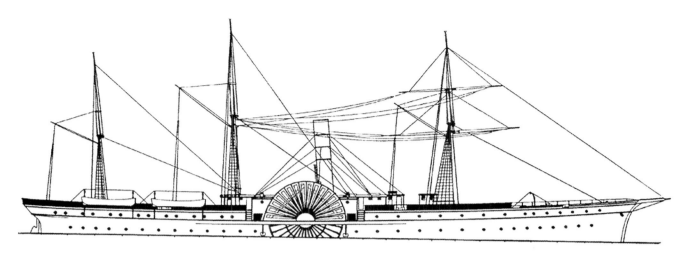

Sketch of the SS *Central America*. Images of the ship often vary in details.

to their voyage, traveling at slightly faster than 12 miles per hour, with a scheduled stop in Havana.

The 278-foot, 2,141-ton SS *Central America*, owned by the U.S. Mail Steamship Company and recently renamed from the SS *George Law*, was a veteran on the Atlantic coast-wise route, having traversed it 43 times since her first departure from New York City to Aspinwall on October 20, 1853, and having carried one-third or more of the total value of California gold shipped to Eastern banks and government agencies during that period.[373]

Captain William Lewis Herndon, here in his U.S. Navy uniform.

The *George Law* had been built in New York by William H. Webb and equipped with two oscillating steam engines made by the Morgan Iron Works. Launching took place on October 28, 1852, but it was nearly a year before she was fully outfitted and ready for her maiden voyage.

With many amenities for passenger comfort, entertainment, and food, and with a light breeze caused by the ship's forward motion, the trip in mild September weather was surely considered by many passengers to be the height of luxury in a tropical cruise. Many on board had taken this route before, as had their families. Indeed, travel from California to Panama and onward to New York City had become routine. The "adventurous" days were over. There seemed to be no real need for life preservers or safety drills.

Fall from Grace

However, there was another view, not so glamorous. Perhaps the glory days of the ship were past. Nearly a century later, historian Erik Heyl commented:

> In July 1857 the name of the *George Law* was changed to *Central America*.... The steamer continued on the same run as heretofore, but the new management was more interested in profits than in providing safe and satisfactory service. The newspapers published ever increasing complaints about skimpy and spoiled food, overcrowding, filthy accommodations, and insufficient and untrained crews.

It was rumored that the *Central America* was not seaworthy, having been allowed to deteriorate through neglect and stinginess.[374]

In checking contemporary as well as modern-day accounts concerning the accommodations on board any steamer of the 1850s, any historian can quickly learn that a dozen different passengers can describe the same vessel in a dozen different ways. This was caused in part by the type of accommodations purchased. Someone with comfortable first-cabin accommodations and fine meals with the other first-class passengers might well write a more favorable account than someone traveling in steerage with an economy ticket.

There is no doubt, however, that in the era of the *Central America*, ocean-going ships tended to deteriorate quickly, and after several years of service this particular vessel probably was in need of refurbishing. Indeed, later testimonies and an investigation would suggest this.

On to New York

The SS *Central America*, now on its 44th voyage, departed Aspinwall on September 3, 1857, in calm seas under bright blue skies interrupted by a few cumulus clouds. Every indication offered a good omen for another smooth, pleasant trip to New York. For those in the best class of accommodations, this was travel at its finest, a trip to be enjoyed and remembered. Others with lesser-priced tickets expected what they paid for, but in any event it was a fine season for an ocean voyage.

Previous passages of the *Central America* had been made without unfavorable incidents, save for a couple of groundings on reefs and a storm-tossed voyage of December 1853. Life preservers and lifeboats remained unused.

On Monday afternoon, September 7, 1857, the *Central America* arrived at the port of Havana. Coal was taken on and a few passengers ventured on shore, but not as many as usual, for yellow fever was rampant there. In Havana there were some slight changes in the passenger manifest, and on the continuing trip to New York City

there were an estimated 492 passengers and 105 officers and crew members including some newly boarded survivors from the recently wrecked bark *Vespasian*, which had met its fate on Old Providence Island in the Bahamas. Two intended passengers were disappointed, however. In Havana, J.C. Lenea had purchased passage on the *Central America*, but while he was arranging for his luggage to be brought from his rooms to the dock, the ship departed without him. Also left on shore was a Mr. Jacobs who had sought to buy a ticket, but was told that all the berths were filled.

At 9:25 a.m. on Tuesday, September 8, the fully loaded *Central America* hoisted anchor in Havana and headed toward New York City via the Straits of Florida. The weather was pleasant and as usual was made even more so by a light breeze from the ship's forward motion. Everything was set for the continuation of a really enjoyable voyage.

Strong Winds

At 5:30 a.m. on Wednesday, September 9, the ship's second officer noted that the ship had gone 286 nautical miles in the preceding 26 and one-half hours, and that there was a fresh breeze kicking up swells. Perhaps a storm was coming. In any event, there was no alarm. This was a large ship, well equipped, and with an experienced crew capable of handling any storm. Meanwhile, the ship plowed onward toward New York.

As the hours passed, the breeze intensified to a strong wind, finally reaching gale force. The *Central America* was tossed about in the waves, but continued on her course. Surely the discomfort would soon be over, as storms usually passed quickly, although this one seemed a bit rougher than usual. In the meantime, card games, reading, and other amusements in the finely appointed parlors were restricted. Many seasick passengers huddled in their cabins that afternoon, continuing into the night, waiting for the wind to subside and looking forward to a bright morning. Squalls and gales often sprang up along the Florida coast and were usually just a passing inconvenience. In this era there was no way to forecast them accurately or to predict their intensity or duration.

Passenger B.M. Lee later recalled:

> I again went to bed, thinking that it would be over in the morning. Down below at this time nothing was to be heard but the crying of children and the moans of those suffering seasickness, and rising above all the sounds that proceeded from the inside of the vessel was the continued dashing and splashing of the waves against the sides of the ship and the howling of the storm as the wind surged through the steamer's rigging. Amid all this I fell asleep.[375]

Thursday, September 10

The expected calm did not come. By daybreak on Thursday, conditions had worsened, wind was screaming through tattered sails and rigging, passengers remained below deck, and the *Central America* was in the middle of a raging hurricane. Throughout the day the fury of the storm and wind-whipped waves increased, but the ship remained watertight and the engines functioned properly. Certainly, the storm would end soon. There was no way to forecast its duration, and just about every year in the season of late summer and early autumn several such storms arose.

Passenger Alonzo C. Monson recalled:

> During Thursday evening the evening games of cards and other pastimes for diversion and amusement usual in the cabin were dispensed with. The storm was the leading topic of conference. Some expressed their apprehension, particularly the ladies, as to the safety of the steamer. Most of the gentlemen, I among others, did everything to prevent any alarm among the passengers.[376]

Friday: Fury of the Storm

Instead of subsiding as hoped, the fury of the storm continued to increase. High winds and waves wracked the ship, and it was all Captain Herndon could do to keep the bow headed into

Men on the bucket brigade attempted to lower the water level in the ship's hold.

the waves. This was important to do as otherwise control would be lost and the vessel would be at the mercy of the mountainous seas. Not to worry, even with the ship tossing and turning. Didn't the *Central America*, well-financed and with great experience on the route, have the best crew that money could hire?

On Friday morning, September 11, crew members were still in control, but matters grew worse. The steamer had begun to take on water through the drive shaft, some broken or open portholes, or elsewhere—the locations are not known. Alternatively, it could simply have been the working of the timbers that breached the caulking and allowed water into the hull. The ship was tossing violently, making it virtually impossible to feed coal into the boilers.

Meanwhile the rising water reached steam pipes and became hot. Conditions in the engine room worsened. The crew down below either did their best, or they were woefully unconcerned and neglectful (depending upon which later accounts are read). In any event, water was sloshing around and the boilers and engines could not be tended properly.

At 11 a.m. Captain Herndon told the passengers that the ship was in danger and enlisted the aid of all men to bail water with a bucket brigade. At one point the ship listed sharply to the starboard (right side), and the captain ordered all passengers to go to the port side for balance.

At 1:00 in the afternoon the main engines stopped, although an auxiliary steam engine operated a pump. From several accounts it seems that George E. Ashby, the chief engineer, made little serious attempt to keep the engines running. A cowardly man, he intimidated many others aboard and placed his personal safety above all else. Passenger Thomas W. Badger, himself a captain and certainly in a position to be a qualified observer, recalled that Captain Herndon had urged action: "For God's sake, Mr. Ashby, don't wait until the ship is full of water. Start the men to work bailing now."[377] Keeping the engines running so as to maintain control of the vessel was considered to be the first order of seamanship when running in high waves.

By mid-afternoon, the lower deck and many cabins were uninhabitable, food service had been suspended, and passengers scavenged to eat crackers and drink water or wine. A small spanker sail was rigged in an attempt to keep the ship headed into the wind, for if it was broadside to the waves it risked being swamped. However, it and all other canvas sails were soon ripped to shreds. Early in the evening the small auxiliary pump failed.

Saturday, September 12

After a tumultuous wind and wave-whipped night, the powerless *Central America* wallowed helplessly in a raging sea on Saturday morning. Decks were awash. This was disaster experienced first-hand, not an ordinary tropical storm, and passengers and crew alike feared for their lives.

Captain Herndon ordered the American flag to be flown upside-down as a distress signal. The Atlantic coastal route was well-traveled, and surely it would be a short time until other ships came along.

Despite the leadership of Herndon, problems developed on board as some male passengers refused to work on the bailing brigade and quarreled with each other and the crew. In contrast, others toiled ceaselessly, some of whom were men of leisure and knew little of physical labor. Women volunteered to help, but the men in a display of chivalry would not let them. Children frolicked one moment and cried the next. All were afraid.[378]

Before 8:00 a.m. the ship listed sharply on its side, and many broken portholes were now under water. Captain Herndon once again announced that if the ship could be kept afloat for a few more hours, surely help would come from other ships plying the same route. He reminded passengers that another steamship, the ill-fated SS *San Francisco*, had remained afloat for more than 11 days after being disabled in bitter-cold weather, beginning on December 23, 1853. Perhaps Herndon did not mention that the passengers aboard that vessel suffered great privation and many died.

Good news finally arrived. By 10:00 a.m. the hurricane showed signs of abating. The worst of the storm was over.

However, bad news took precedence. Seemingly, too much damage had already been done to save the ship.

Water continued to fill what air spaces remained in the cabins and compartments in the hull, and it seemed inevitable that the *Central America* had but a short time left. Still, the bucket brigade struggled, and by the use of hoists and barrels recently emptied of ice-packed pork, the men remaining on the line were able to purge the ship of about 400 gallons per minute. Unfortunately, this was not enough to make a difference. Distress flares and rockets were launched.

Free Gold Coins!

At about 1:00 p.m. on Saturday afternoon, the sail of the brig *Marine* was seen on the horizon. This storm-damaged vessel, under the command of Captain Hiram Burt and 10 crew members, drew closer. Aboard the sinking *Central America* Captain Herndon ordered women and children on deck, preparatory to boarding lifeboats. Women left behind unnecessary baggage. Some, "as if to illustrate how little value was the gold, brought out bags of coins and scattered them on the floor, asking all who wanted money to help themselves."[379] A few ladies picked up pieces, but none took more than two $20 coins.[380]

Meanwhile, a carpetbag filled with $16,500 in double eagles was too heavy to remove from a cabin, and Mrs. Jane Badger, who had packed it by emptying the coins from a trunk, left the golden array behind. Later, her husband, Captain Thomas W. Badger,[381] dumped the glittering coins from the bag onto the floor of the captain's stateroom. Several other men spread their coins about, amounting to an estimated several hun-

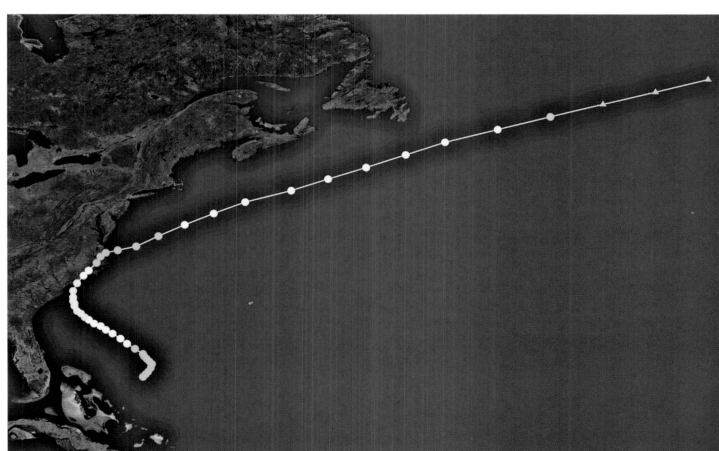

The path of the September 1857 hurricane (today recorded as a Category 2) that resulted in the loss of the SS Central America. Blue points indicate tropical storm strength; white points indicate Category 1 strength; yellow dots indicate Category 2 strength.

dred thousand dollars' worth.[382] Two women threw a further $10,000 in $20 gold pieces on the floor, but no one cared. Purses, containing in some instances thousands of dollars in gold coins, were left untouched on sofas.[383]

A later account summarized the golden scene:

> According to the statements made by many of the survivors, there was seldom so large an amount of money owned by the passengers as was the case with those who came by the *Central America*, and the quantity of treasure on board was, consequently, far greater than the one and a half to two millions named on the freight list. Many, indeed, were persons of large means, and there were but few whose immediate wealth did not amount to hundreds, while numbers reckoned their gold by the thousands of dollars.
>
> The greater portion of the passengers were returned miners, some on their way to invest the capital they had realized, in hopes to live a life of greater ease as a result of their industry,[384] and others to get their families and once more go to the land of gold.
>
> But, as the storm continued to rage, less and less was thought of gold, and when, on Saturday, it became evident that they were likely at any moment to be buried beneath the waves, wealthy men divested themselves of their treasure belts and scattered the gold upon the cabin floors, telling those to take it who would, lest its weight about their persons—a few extra ounces or pounds—should carry them to their death. Full purses, containing in some instances thousands of dollars, lay around untouched. Carpetbags were opened, and the shining metal was poured out on the floor with the prodigality of death's despair. One of the passengers opened a bag and dashed about the cabin twenty thousand dollars in gold and told him who wanted to satisfy his greed for gold to take it. However, it was passed by untouched, as the veriest dross.[385]

Rescue Attempts

The first lifeboat leaving the *Central America* was smashed, and other difficulties were experienced as women and children climbed into the small boats. Some were lowered sitting in hastily fashioned rope loops or nooses, but most jumped into the boats below. Some missed the target and landed in the sea, and were fished out by those already in the little vessels.

In the coming hours the storm-damaged brig *Marine* took dozens aboard. Finally, men were allowed into the lifeboats, and a few went over to the *Marine* including some of the crew of the *Central America*, an action that caused many unfavorable comments in later investigations, as passengers expected that crew members would remain in the rescue boats to shuttle regular passengers to safety. They were wrong.

Meanwhile, many incidents continued aboard the stricken steamer including threats and fights among the remaining passengers, drunkenness of several, and numerous injuries from falling or being hit with storm-tossed wreckage. In nine

A rescue effort.

shuttle trips 109 passengers were saved. The *Marine* eventually drifted several miles away and could no longer render aid.

The contemptible chief engineer, George E. Ashby, "turned out to be a thoroughgoing coward," according to historian Heyl. "He jumped into the last lifeboat as it was still loading, having only a half-dozen people in it, and by brandishing a huge knife prevented others from leaving the steamer and getting into the boat." The same writer laid the entire unfortunate incident at Ashby's feet.

Bob Evans, modern researcher of the ship, corrects the preceding:

> Historian Heyl has this wrong. Ashby was placed in charge of one of the lifeboats by Captain Herndon. It was actually passenger George Bassford who jumped into this lifeboat at the last moment, prompting Ashby to brandish his knife, etc., in order to discourage any such further attempts. It is interesting that Bassford gave some of the most damaging testimony as to Ashby's conduct.
>
> I think Ashby is far too convenient as a scapegoat in the overall analysis. Sure, he was the chief engineer, and the proper running and maintenance of the engines and equipment was his responsibility, but it appears that when the engines stopped it was not his shift. He appears, shirtless, moments later, having noticed the problems from somewhere else, probably his cabin. Herndon placed him in charge of a lifeboat, since reviving the engines at that point in the sequence of events was out of the question, and Ashby was a senior officer. There seems to be little doubt that he was not a terribly popular man, coarse in his language, and possibly with a combative personality. But this doesn't necessarily mean he was entirely to blame. Also at fault was the human tendency to believe that technology grants powers to humans that are greater than reality, and that nature can raise forces that can defeat any contrivance.[386]

Meanwhile, the Boston sailing ship *El Dorado* came close to the *Central America*, but it was too disabled by the storm to be able to help with rescue work, despite intentions of its captain to do so.

The *Central America* continued to fill with water. By now, all bailing efforts had ceased, and most of the ship was inundated. Pounding waves broke up cabin walls and floors and tore away sails, spars, and equipment. Some of the men ripped planks and railings off the ship to make crude rafts, while others found single boards. At about 7:50 in the evening, Captain Herndon ordered rockets to be fired downward to signal that the ship was sinking, meanwhile bravely trying to reassure the 438 men remaining on board that other rescue vessels were bound to come along.

The Last Moments of the *Central America*

A few minutes past 8:00 a tremendous wave hit the SS *Central America*. She shuddered, timbers broke, and with hundreds of men huddled at the front of the ship and Captain Herndon on the starboard paddle-box, she slipped at a sharp angle beneath the waves.

Many, including Herndon, went down with the ship, while others clung to wreckage or bobbed about in hollow tin or cork-filled life preservers. As passengers were drowning or clinging to flotsam, George Ashby and certain of his fellow crewmen were being comforted aboard the *Marine*.

James Birch, president of the California Stage Company, went down with the steamer, taking with him $70,000 in gold.[387] Two brothers from Missouri, John and Anson Horne, had $4,000 to $6,000 in gold in a valise, brought it on deck, took seats on either side of their treasure, clasped hands, and went down with the ship.[388] Luckier was Stephen C. Caldwell, a steerage passenger who had come to California from New York, who "had 20 pounds of gold dust and assorted coins in a belt about his waist; he kept himself afloat upon a cabin door which he secured shortly after the ship sank."[389]

The loss of the SS *Central America* in the evening
of September 12, 1857.

Soon thereafter the *Central America* came to rest in the darkness 7,200 feet below the surface, about 160 miles offshore of Charleston, South Carolina. Passenger gold was scattered here and there around the ship's hull and the surrounding sea bottom. In the hold, still stored in the wooden boxes that had been carried along the Pacific Coast by the *Sonora*, followed by a trip on the Panama Railroad, the registered treasure of gold coins and ingots remained intact.

Several dozen adrift passengers and crew members were rescued the next day by the Norwegian bark *Ellen* under Captain Anders Johnsen. Three more castaways from the *Central America* drifted at sea for many days and endured hardships, but were picked up on September 21 by the British brig *Mary*. Among the rescued was John Lorimer Graham Jr., a numismatist of some renown. Several years later in 1860, no doubt with mixed emotions, he purchased at auction a silver impression of a medal observing the loss of the SS *Central America*. By 1867 it was stated that Graham's

Adrift on the sea.

cabinet, "in intrinsic worth alone, is one of the most valuable in the country."[390]

At final reckoning of the *Central America* disaster, about 435 souls were lost. Only 162 were saved.[391] Many of the last were picked up adrift by passing ships in the ocean, often clinging to wreckage.

Uncertainty in Wall Street

On August 24, 1857, the Ohio Life Insurance & Trust Co., based in Cincinnati and with a large office in New York City, abruptly failed, sending a wave of shock throughout the financial community.[392] The company had been one of the leading lenders to stock traders and others and was viewed as sound. All of a sudden money became scarce. Bankers and others attempted to call in their loans, but debtors could not pay. Advances made on collateral such as bank stocks were found to be unsecured as the market took a sharp downturn.

Several brokerage houses and exchange offices collapsed, causing further distress. Newspapers played up the excitement by turning out extra editions to broadcast the latest failures. Depositors rushed to banks to exchange paper money for silver and gold coins and to withdraw funds from their accounts. Although New York City banks normally had sufficient reserves for ordinary redemptions, they could not withstand this flood. On October 13 all except the Chemical Bank stopped specie payments. This suspension was largely restored by the end of the year.

A later generation of historians blamed the non-arrival of the *Central America* as the precipitating cause of the panic, which it was not.

Scientists at Work

The scene changes to decades later in the 1980s:

Thomas ("Tommy") G. Thompson of the Battelle Memorial Institute, Columbus, Ohio, was a student of shipwrecks, and in 1980 he began directing his efforts toward trying to find the long-forgotten *Central America*. In 1985 a group of entrepreneurs and investors headed by Thompson and two associates, Robert Evans and Barry Schatz, formed Recovery Limited Partnership to finance the search for the *Central America*.

Evans and Thompson compiled the passenger and crew information from historical accounts including newspaper stories, reports by survivors, and other contemporary sources. The resulting matrix would provide clues leading to the location of the *Central America*. They entered the data on a 12- by 12-foot sheet of paper, arranging the historical accounts into three-hour time slots covering the period of the storm and shipwreck. The matrix also included information about the weather, the progress of the hurricane, and the physical deterioration of the steamship.

They took the matrix to Dr. Lawrence D. Stone, a leading expert on search theory, a method using probability and statistical analysis to find objects, particularly in the ocean. No one had ever applied search theory to a historical database such as this. Stone was able to create thousands of computerized models of possible sinking scenarios based on variables such as the *Central America*'s last known coordinates, the probable wind speed and direction of the hurricane, and the ocean currents likely at the time of the sinking.

With the data, Stone and the mathematicians working with him were able to construct a probability map with a 1,400-square-mile search area—still a vast expanse of open sea, but now reduced to a manageable field. Already, without leaving the confines of the Buckeye State, more useful ideas had been formulated than ever before!

The Search Begins

After listening to Tommy Thompson's projections, many leading citizens in and around Columbus, Ohio, stepped up to help with financing. Early fundraising was done in several stages. Eventually $12.7 million was raised even though investors were aware of the risks involved.

The sea operations started in 1986 when Thompson used the ship *Pine River* for the side-scan search. In 1987 he used the *Nicor Navigator* and recovered a lump of coal from an unidentified shipwreck to legally "arrest" the site in July 1987. The following winter of 1987–1988, Bob Evans again reviewed the side-scan images and turned up another target approximately 40 miles closer to shore. They decided to test new equipment on this target while on the way to the arrested site when operations resumed. Throughout the summer of 1988 a new ship, the R/V (Research Vessel) *Arctic Discoverer* was prepared and the first iteration of *Nemo*, a remotely controlled mini-submarine, was built. In late August they set out, finally diving on the new target on September 11, 1988. Suddenly Milt Butterworth, the team's

Gold at the bottom of the sea.

The brass bell found in the wreck of the SS *Central America*.

photographer-videographer, burst out, "Whoa. Whoa! WHOA!"

The empty screen was filling with dark shadows. An image was drifting up from the bottom of the video screen and taking shape.

Someone else cried out, "Oh, my God!"

"We could see now the ghostly image that *Nemo*'s undersea cameras were sending to the monitors: the half-circle shape of a rusting side-wheel. It was the one distinctive feature of the U.S. Mail Steamship *Central America*, and there it was, lying flat in the mud on the ocean floor," Bob Evans recalled.

"It was as if she was calling to us from a century ago, 'Here I am, the *Central America*! You found me!'"

Nemo had come so close with the cameras that the crew had to pull the robot up quickly to avoid striking the complex of engine works, which stood straight up.

Continuing Recoveries

The R/V *Arctic Discoverer* stayed in the area of the shipwreck through the end of October. On board, Evans served as mission coordinator in the control room, which served as the operations center for exploration and recovery, planning, and managing each dive. Meanwhile, the navigator monitored and controlled *Nemo's* position over the site, and the pilot directed recovery efforts. At the same time, Milt Butterworth recorded every moment of undersea activity to preserve whatever archaeological, historical, scientific, and numismatic data could be found.[393]

In time the *Central America's* identity was confirmed by the recovery of the ship's bell, which was marked MORGAN IRON WORKS NEW YORK 1853 by the ship's manufacturer. Much of the wood part of the steamer had rotted away and metal components had rusted. However, a video-camera image revealed that metal framework elements of one of the large side paddle-wheels were identifiable. A subsequent dive of the *Nemo* proved to be wondrous: visible through the cameras was a veritable sea-bottom carpet of glittering $20 and $50 gold pieces and other coins! Keeping the coins company were starfish and other deep-sea fauna.

In 1989 the recovery commenced on a grand scale by Columbus-America Discovery Group (CADG). The *Arctic Discoverer* was outfitted with additional gear including a vastly upgraded *Nemo*, now standing more than seven feet tall, fifteen feet long, and weighing over six tons. Of particular note was a mechanism which could dispense a chemical substance at the undersea wreck site. This liquid could surround coins and other objects, harden, and then be retrieved as a solid mass without harming the items encased. Later, after being brought to the surface, the hardened casing could be dissolved, and any encased treasures would be intact.

Discovery Announced

The September 1989 announcement of the discovery of the gold treasure created a sensation among professional numismatists. James Lamb, director of Christie's Coin Department and a consultant to CADG, described the recovered U.S. and pioneer gold coins as "magnificent."[394] The coins appeared to be in mint condition, he noted, and the bars included some heavier than any other previously known. Additional funds were needed, and in 1990 Columbus Exploration LLC was established and raised an additional $10 million, some of which was used to start funding other shipwreck projects. Given the golden prospect, investors were eager to participate. Recovery operations extended into 1991, and details of the find were kept secret.

The Treasure Revealed

In 1992 *Coin World* ran front-page stories and editorials about the effect of the news on collectors and dealers. "The numismatic community teemed with excitement," said editor Beth Deisher.[395] "The thought of being able to identify, recover, and preserve the SS *Central America's* coins and bars produced a wave of enthusiasm among numismatic researchers and collectors." *Numismatic News* was equally enthusiastic in its news coverage, and other periodicals followed suit.

The recovery of 427 gold coins struck at San Francisco and other federal mints, 11 pioneer gold coins, and more than 6,000 ounces of gold in the form of bars and ingots early in the recovery operation, proved to be just the beginning. Those involved in the find were eager to share details.

Early estimates of the 1989 *bullion value* of the treasure, insured for $1.25 million in 1857, ranged from $28 to $450 million, some of these figures being given by people who had little or no knowledge of what had actually been found. Similar to political contests, there were many opinions and many "experts." When asked about the value of the treasure, Tommy Thompson was realistic and said, "I get nervous about these estimates, because we don't want to disappoint any of our backers. Nobody really knows what this stuff would bring at auction."[396]

When pressed, he admitted that $1 billion "isn't out of the realm of possibility," no doubt as at that point conservation of the items had not begun and the detailed appraisal process was still in the future.

Soon thereafter, an intense publicity campaign was mounted, and glowing accounts of the find were carried in newspapers and magazines and on national television. Estimates of the worth of the treasure trove typically ranged up to $1 billion or even much more, obviously a rich reward for the stockholders and investors in the venture.

Walter H. Breen was tapped to write an article about the treasure for publication in *The Numismatist*, the promotional talents of Los Angeles sports tycoon Bruce McNall (who had launched his career by making a fortune in numismatics) were enlisted,[397] and James Lamb of the Coin Department of Christie's art-auction house greeted reporters and television crews. John J. Ford Jr. was signed as numismatic advisor based upon his knowledge of Western gold coins and bars. More money was needed. About $3 million from Bruce McNall and a secured line of credit of about $20 million from Christie's kept the venture on a solid footing. Nothing from the treasure had been sold yet.

Many other dives were made by *Nemo*, and more coins and ingots were recovered. A very large part of the program did not involve numismatics. Detailed records were made of undersea fauna, including many varieties not heretofore described in the literature. Great attention was given to passenger possessions and other items found. A number of scientific and historical studies were published as a result. These non-numismatic endeavors involved very large expenses with little in the way of having the costs monetized.

An Unexpected Turn of Events

Amid the hoopla, no specific distribution plans were announced. Numismatists, historians, romanticists, and others awaited news of how the

A small part of the coins and ingots from the recovered treasure.

coins, ingots, and other items would be sold or otherwise made available. Under the generally agreed-upon philosophy of "finders, keepers," this treasure far out in the ocean would soon yield a fortune to the scientists from Ohio and their financial backers. Numismatists would be blessed as well, with unprecedented opportunities.

Alas, that was not to happen, at least not for a while.

The excitement about hundreds of millions of dollars being found attracted a large swarm of claimants. Some were attorneys representing descendants of 37 long-gone old-time insurance companies. Others seeking to cash in claimed to have helped find the wreck or to have held ownership title. Still others said that their research facilities had been used in investigating the history, and therefore they now had a vested interest. Now the treasure finders and investors were confronted with seemingly endless lawsuits and controversies that would string out for seven years and gobble up millions of dollars.

Only a small part of the wreck had been explored—likely the safe room or purser's room—but much more remained untouched. Rumors swirled, including that there might have been an unregistered shipment of "Army-guarded gold" elsewhere in the hull. Tommy Thompson, who stood to take home 34% of the value of the recovery, hoped that another series of explorations would be made on the site. He had his own problems, including a contentious divorce in which he surrendered part of his intended share.

Inventing History

The entire matter deteriorated into a big mess. More money was needed. On December 14, 1998, *Coin World* ran a front-page article, "SS *Central America* investors seek $40 million to find gold," which began with this:

> Investors who financed the recovery of 3 tons of gold from the 1857 shipwreck of the S.S. *Central America* tentatively agreed November 24 to a plan to raise an additional $40 million to continue the search for another 18 tons of gold believed to have been aboard the ship. The Columbus, Ohio *Dispatch* reported in a November 25 news story that Thomas G. Thompson, who led the 1980s expedition to find the *Central America*, said about 3 tons of an estimated 21 tons in gold has been recovered. The remaining portions are reportedly part of a secret U.S. Army shipment from the San Francisco Mint to New York City banks, intended to strengthen banks during the Panic of 1857.[398]
>
> The ship sank during a hurricane off the South Carolina coast in 1857. Thomas has not revealed plans about marketing the gold recovered thus far, believed to be in the form of federal gold coinage struck by the San

Francisco Mint, pioneer gold coins and ingots from Gold Rush days and other ingots and forms of gold. Collectors, numismatists, and dealers are anticipating an eventual release of the gold coins and ingots, which include previously unknown ingots and could increase the surviving populations of S-Mint gold coins of the mid-1850s. None of the gold from the Army shipment has been found. The Army shipment may be buried deeper than the commercial gold coins and ingots found thus far, according to the *Dispatch*....

There is a fatal flaw in the preceding account. It was on August 24, 1857, that the New York City office of the Ohio Life Insurance & Trust Co, failed, the prelude to the Panic of 1857. In the meantime the SS *Sonora* had departed San Francisco on August 20 with its cargo of gold and passengers!

Continuing Complications

For years afterward, into 1999, the matter dragged through the U.S. District Court in Norfolk. Finally, in November 1999 Judge Calvin Clarke issued an order giving 92.4% to the Columbus-America Discovery Group, confirming a decision made in 1996. The remaining amount was to be distributed among the insurance companies. A large hassle erupted when everyone except CADG wanted the inventory of the treasure published. CADG wanted to maximize a marketing campaign being planned, anchored by a sale in New York City by Christie's, to determine market interest and prices. Robert W. Trafford, one of the attorneys representing CADG, stated, "There are people out there who would love to take information about this treasure and perhaps depress it for purposes of certain kinds of sales. I'll offer an example: coin dealers.... Neither of us [CADG and insurers] has any obligation to tell the world what we have."[399]

On March 2, 1999, Bill Gibbs, feature writer for *Coin World*, brought readers up to date:

> Gold coins and bars recovered from the wreck of the S.S. *Central America* were secretly

split up and distributed among their court-recognized owners in June 1998, but it's still unclear when any of treasure might reach the auction block. The owners of the smaller portion of the treasure—insurers whom the court recognized as paying off claimants after the 1857 shipwreck—want to sell their portion now, according to a Virginia newspaper account. However, they say they can't because officials of the Columbus-America Discovery Group, the finders of the shipwreck and the owners of the larger portion, are refusing to honor a court order to release the complete inventory of everything it recovered from the wreck site.

More was told by Paul Gilkes, *Coin World* feature writer, on April 12, 1999:

Sotheby's auction house in New York City is apparently in the running to auction off the insurers' 8 percent portion of the gold coins, assay bars, ingots, and bullion brought up from the sunken shipwreck S.S. Central America. A Sotheby's spokesman said because of confidentiality, the auction company could not comment on a proposed auction of the insurer's share until terms of an agreement were drafted and a full contract signed....

At the same time, another major New York auction house, Christie's, a division of Spink America, has reportedly sued the salvors and owners of 92 percent of the treasure, Columbus-America Discovery Group, for allegedly defaulting on an agreement in which Christie's loaned $35 million to CADG against the value of the treasure recovered from the wreck. However, a search of the records of the U.S. District Court for the Southern District of New York where the suit is supposed to be filed shows no public documentation. A source indicates not only is the suit filed under seal, there is no public documentation on the court docket being kept showing the suit even exists....

From August 11 to 15 at the American Numismatic Association's 108th Anniversary conven-

tion in Rosemont, Illinois, the insurers' 7.6% part of the treasure was displayed. It was announced that Sotheby's would be auctioning the items in New York City on December 8 and 9. In time a fine catalog was prepared by David E. Tripp. The remaining 92.4% was sealed in a warehouse awaiting the outcome of multiple lawsuits. No inventory was available. In September rumors swirled that the CADG treasure had been sold to one or more investors in California, settling the Christie's claim, but no specifics were forthcoming.

On December 7, the day before the Sotheby's sale was to begin, CADG obtained an order from the U.S. Fourth District Court of Appeals in Virginia (where its share of the treasure was stored) stopping the event. This caused all sorts of ill feelings, including on the part of those who had traveled to New York City to attend. In the meantime a transaction with CADG had taken place. Bob Evans, a consummate scientist, was enlisted to conserve the treasures from the ship and to take detailed numismatic notes concerning the characteristics of the coins and ingots, including many aspects of ingots in particular that were previously unknown to the numismatic community. This had the unintended consequence of proving certain other ingots from other sources, included a Justh & Hunter bar, to be modern forgeries. The state of the art was advanced considerably. Certain of his findings were published in *The Numismatist*.

The California Gold Marketing Group

On January 19, 2000, it was revealed that the California Gold Marketing Group (CGMG), headed by Dwight N. Manley, had purchased the entire 92.4% interest held by CADG and contested by others, and that all claims had been settled. The sum paid was not disclosed, but years later a figure of $52 million was suggested.

On January 20 representatives from the press were invited to visit the offices of the Professional Coin Grading Service (PCGS) to view certain of the coins put up in special holders with imprinted gold labels. This launched what was to be one of the most successful marketing campaigns in the history of American numismatics.

In February the first showing of the treasure was held at the Long Beach Coin & Collectibles Expo. In the meantime the Sotheby's sale was rescheduled for June 2000, at which time it was held. The same catalog was used.

As part of the agreement Christie's was to hold the first auction of coins and ingots received by CGMG, a small selection in terms of the overall find. I was asked by Christie's and CADG to write the catalog, which I did. The event was held on December 14, 2000, and was very successful.

The California Gold Marketing Group constructed a large "show front" display, "The Ship of Gold," measuring 50 feet from left to right. This was a representation of the side of the ship, with portholes through which gold coins and ingots could be observed. The "Kellogg & Humbert Assay Office" was set up nearby, and other exhibits were put in place. A small "movie house" consisting of a large screen and several rows of seats was assembled for continuous presentation of the History Channel's *Ship of Gold* film. This was the sensation of the 2000 American Numismatic Association convention in Philadelphia.

Bob Evans presented a program as part of the Numismatic Theatre (the ANA convention's educational programming), and I helped. The large room was filled with 400 people, more than ever attended such a program before or since. The "Ship of Gold" went on tour, including to the Tucson Gem and Mineral Show, where, for the first time in the history of that famous event, crowd control needed to be put in place in the form of stanchions and ropes. Previous attractions including the greatest collection of Fabergé eggs and the Hope Diamond required no such precautions.

The Ship of Gold display.

Treasure discoverer and curator Bob Evans with Christine and Melissa Karstedt.

Around the same time arrangements were made with me to document the historical setting of the SS *Central America* and its Gold Rush treasure, including information never before available

Myself, Tommy Thompson with an iron ingot mold, and California Gold Marketing Group president Dwight N. Manley.

Crowd control in Tucson.

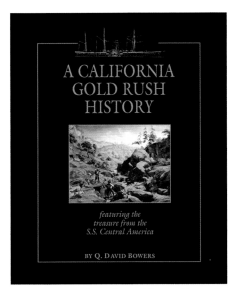

The *California Gold Rush History Featuring Treasure from the S.S. Central America* book.

in a single reference volume. *A California Gold Rush History Featuring Treasure from the S.S. Central America* was published in 2002 to the extent of about 4,000 deluxe hardbound copies and a special edition of 600 with an insert displaying gold dust from the treasure. The special edition was initially available only to those who bought coins or ingots from CGMG's distributors. These books have since commanded prices of several thousand dollars when sold on the secondary markets.

Christine Karstedt and I helped with the marketing and other publicity, a memorable and unique experience. In time everything was sold, and by a decade later almost all of the coins and ingots had increased in market value.

The Treasure

The following listings were prepared by Bob Evans from personal inspection, plus information from other sources including pieces taken by the insurers.[400] Certain coins in groups or unconserved "lumps" are listed at the end of each denomination, if attributable as such.

The gold coins recovered from the SS *Central America* in the late 20th century were dominated by the most popular of all gold denominations, the $20 double eagle. Most of the pieces are of the 1857-S variety and no doubt represented transfers of funds by the various banks, express companies, and merchants with "treasure" aboard. To facilitate packing and counting, it is likely that $20 coins were used in nearly all instances—as there would have been no advantage to make up a shipment with $2.50, $5, and $10 coins.

Most of the other gold coins, $1 to $10, were probably part of "passenger gold" or of private parcels placed with the purser. As gold dollars are very small in size, they would be more likely lost on the sea floor, while higher-denomination coins, including some $20 pieces, carried as passenger gold would have been more visible to the treasure salvors and the "eye" of the *Nemo*. Thus, it is likely that small denominations are under-represented among the coins recovered.

Listings are for items retained by CADG. Those retained by insurers are marked "ins." This list does not include coins that have not been conserved or attributed. Some adjustments were made to the list later.

Federal gold coins

$1 gold

1854 (1)

Quarter eagles

1834	1851 (11)
1843-O	1852 (2)
1845	1853 (3)
1846	1854
1846-O	1855
1847-O	1856-S (8, ins. 1)
1850 (2)	1857-S

$3 gold

1856-S (3)

Half eagles

1834 (5)	1848 (3)
1835	1848-C
1836	1849
1838 (2)	1849-C (ins. 1)
1840 (3)	1850-D (ins. 1)
1840-C	1851 (2)
1842-D	1852 (4)
1843 (4)	1852-C
1844-D	1852-D
1844-O (2)	1854 (2)
1845-D	1854-O (ins. 1)
1846 (2)	1855 (3)
1847 (8)	1855-C

Andrew Bowers and the "Eureka" bar, the largest of the ingots, at the Ship of Gold exhibit.

The History Channel interviewing me.

1855-S (11, ins. 1)　　1856-S (30, ins. 2)
1856　　　　　　　　　1857-S (12, ins. 7)

Eagles

1841	1851-O (2)
1843 (2)	1852 (2)
1843-O (2)	1852-O (2)
1844-O (2)	1853
1845-O (3)	1853-O
1846-O (3)	1854
1847 (7)	1854-O (2)
1847-O (6)	1854-S (13)
1848	1855 (2)
1848-O (2)	1855-S (6)
1849 (6)	1856-S (27, ins. 1)
1850 (2)	1857-S (9, ins. 3)

Double eagles

1850 (29)
1850-O
1851 (33)
1851-O (8)
1852 (32)
1852-O (4)
1853 (27, ins. 1)
1853-O (2)
1854 (19, ins. 1)
1854-S (25)
1855 (7)
1855-S (336, ins. 2)
1856 (6)
1856-S (1,138, ins. 15)
1857 (2)
1857-S (5,305, ins. 97)

Private and territorial gold coins

Moffat & Co.

1850 $5
1849 TEN DOL. (10)
1849 TEN D. (15)
1852 TEN D. Close Date (4)
1852 TEN D. Wide Date (8)

Dubosq & Co.

1850 $10 (1)

Baldwin & Co.

1851 $10 (1, ins. 1)

Augustus Humbert

1852/1 $10. 884 THOUS. (12)
1852 $10. 884 THOUS. (67)
1851 $50. Lettered edge. 880 THOUS. (3)
1851 $50. Reeded edge. 880 THOUS. (4)
1851 $50. Reeded edge. 887 THOUS.
　(1, ins. 1)

U.S. Assay Office of Gold

1852 $10. TEN DOLS. 884 THOUS.
　(90, ins. 2)
1853 $10. TEN D. 884 THOUS. (2, ins. 1)
1853 $10. TEN D. 900 THOUS. (8, ins. 1)
1852 $50. Reeded edge. 887 THOUS. (5)
1852 $50. Reeded edge. 900 THOUS. (1)

Wass, Molitor & Co.

1852 $10. TEN D. Small Head (9)
1852 $10. TEN D. Large Head (60)
1852 $10. TEN D. Small Close Date
　(2, ins. 2)
1855 $10. TEN D. (20, ins. 4)
1855 $50 (1)

Kellogg & Co.

1854 $20 (4)
1855 $20 (5)

Miscellaneous gold

1856 25¢ tokens (4)
1825 Hannover 10 thalers
1831 France. 20 francs
1851 Great Britain. Sovereign (1)

Gold ingots

Blake & Co., Sacramento: 34
Harris, Marchand & Co., Sacramento: 36
Harris, Marchand & Co., Marysville: 1
Henry Hentsch, San Francisco: 33
Justh & Hunter, Marysville (9,000 series): 28
Justh & Hunter, San Francisco (4,000 series): 59
Kellogg & Humbert, San Francisco: 342

Record-setting ingots
(from information marked on the ingots)

Lowest weight: 4.95 ounces • Serial number: 5190 • Blake & Co • Fineness: 795 • Value (1857): $81.34 [Same as lowest-stamped value ingot; a double record setter]

Highest weight: 933.94 ounces • Serial number: 1003 • Kellogg & Humbert • Fineness: 903 • Value (1857): $17,433.57 [Same as highest-stamped value ingot; a double record setter] • Dubbed the "Eureka!" bar

Lowest fineness: 580 • Serial number: 5222 • Blake & Co. • Troy ounces: 21.46 • Value (1857): $257.29

Highest fineness: 973 • Serial number: 3068 • Henry Hentsch • Troy ounces: 12.52 • Value (1857): $251.82

Lowest value (1857): $81.34 • Serial number: 5190 • Blake & Co. • Troy ounces: 4.95 • Fineness: 795 [Same as lowest-weight ingot; a double record setter]

Highest value (1857): $17,433.57 • Serial number: 1003 • Kellogg & Humbert • Troy ounces: 933.94 • Fineness: 903 [Same as highest-weight ingot; a double record setter] • Dubbed the "Eureka!" bar

The Second Expedition

By 2013, Tommy Thompson had disappeared and investors still had not received any money from the project. There was also a list of creditors who had not been paid. Recovery Limited Partnership (RLP), formed in 1985 to finance the SS *Central America* project, was rudderless. The Common Pleas Court of Franklin County, Ohio, appointed Ira Owen Kane, a prominent attorney and businessman, as the official receiver for Recovery Limited Partnership (RLP) and Columbus Exploration LLC, with James Henson also on the team.

Under the direction of the court to maximize the assets for the benefit of the investors and creditors, Kane began plans to revisit the SS *Central America* to resume recovery operations. The United States District Court of the Eastern District of Virginia confirmed RLP as the salvor in possession of the SS *Central America* in 2014.

Kane contracted with Odyssey Marine Exploration (see below) to return to the *Central America* and continue recovery operations that had started more than 25 years earlier. "We circulated a request for proposals to nine of the leading organizations in the deep-ocean exploration and recovery industry and established a rigorous proposal evaluation process," said Kane. "We found Odyssey's combination of experience, equipment, and personnel are unmatched in their industry."[401]

Under the arrangement Odyssey would conduct and underwrite the archaeological excavation, valuable cargo recovery, and shipboard conservation on behalf of RLP. In return, Odyssey was to receive 80% of the proceeds until a negotiated operations fee was reached. After that Odyssey was to receive 45%.

Odyssey Marine Exploration

Odyssey Marine Exploration, Inc., was founded in 1994 as Remarc International by John Morris and Greg Stemm to develop deep-ocean shipwreck projects. In the late 1990s the company began engaging in the exploration and recovery of intrinsically valuable shipwreck cargoes using remotely operated vehicles (ROVs), side-scan sonar, and other sophisticated devices. From the beginning, Odyssey was focused on conducting archaeologically sensitive excavations and sharing the finds with the public through books, television programming, Web sites, and exhibits. In January 2008, Greg Stemm was appointed CEO upon Morris's retirement. Listed on NASDAQ, the company attracted many investors who hoped to share in found treasures. Although the company made major discoveries and recoveries,

The *Odyssey Explorer* ship used in the 2014 recovery.

Some of the many gold nuggets recovered in the summer of 2014.

Archaeological curator Ellen Gerth speaks to guests of the Waterloo Region Museum in Kitchener, Ontario, Canada, during the grand opening of Odyssey's Shipwreck! Pirates & Treasure exhibit.

these were mainly of foreign ships carrying coins and artifacts. A remarkable success in the field of American numismatics was achieved with Odyssey's find of the SS *Republic*, lost at sea in October 1865 (the subject of chapter 16).

Its headquarters in Tampa, Florida, includes a world-class conservation facility housing more than 15,000 shipwreck artifacts. A traveling exhibit featuring over 500 recovered artifacts attracted more than two million visitors by autumn 2014. Ellen Gerth is the in-house curator who helped develop the exhibit and conducts research on numerous historical artifacts, and who we have consulted with on a number of projects. On October 1, 2014, Mark Gordon was named CEO of the company and Greg Stemm became chairman.

Success!

Exploration began at the wreck site on April 15, 2014. The mother ship was the *Odyssey Explorer*, a 251-foot dynamically positioned ship that furnished a stable platform. Accommodations on board included facilities for 42 crew members, scientists, technicians, and others, an archaeological laboratory, and facilities for conducting operations 24/7 for up to two months without returning to harbor. The 8-ton, 400-hp ROV, called *ZEUS*, performed the underwater work while being controlled and monitored from the *Odyssey Explorer* above. This same device had recovered items from the SS *Republic*. Craig T. Mullen served as director of operations for RLP and Bob Evans as the chief scientist and historian for RLP, both reporting to Ira Kane.

The first two-hour reconnaissance dive on April 15 yielded five gold ingots and two double eagles plus a handful of artifacts, a favorable prospect which confirmed the site had not been revisited and salvaged since 1991.

By May 13, 16 dives had been completed, and many items had been recovered from the more accessible spots. Included were 14 more ingots and over 800 gold coins, mostly double eagles, as well as nearly 9,000 silver dimes and 1,000 other silver coins. Extensive mapping and photography were also accomplished.[402]

ZEUS being lifted from the Atlantic Ocean.

Headquarters of Odyssey Marine Exploration, Inc., in Tampa, Florida.

In mid-May 2014 the *Odyssey Explorer* returned to Charleston, but it was back on the site on May 18, after a day's voyage from that port. During the next reporting period, ending on June 15, more than 900 coins and 25 ingots were found. The largest bar was by Henry Hentsch and was stamped with a weight of 319.22 ounces. The smallest bears the Kellogg & Humbert imprint and weighs 13.78 ounces. In addition many pieces of jewelry and miscellaneous artifacts continued to be brought to the surface.[403]

Recoveries continued during the third reporting period, June 16 to July 15, punctuated by a few days dodging Hurricane Arthur and a routine port call to offload finds and restock provisions. Sixteen dives were conducted, mostly focusing on the area from the stern to the aft end of the engine room. A large amount of coal had to be removed to another site on the sea floor. Two ingots, 4 eagles, 139 double eagles, 84 foreign silver coins, and a quantity of raw gold flakes and nuggets were found.[404]

The fourth reporting period from July 16 to August 15, 2014, included a return to Charleston on August 13 for a crew change and to refresh supplies. During this time there were 14 dives, the longest lasting more than 83 hours. Time spent included investigation of the southern debris field slightly away from the ship. Found were 6 copper coins and gold coins including 40 25-cent pieces, 36 50-cent pieces, 177 $1, 204 $2.50, 33 $3, 188 $5, 41 $10, 264 $20, and 51 foreign coins, plus more than 900 silver coins ranging from one trime to 36 half dollars. Nearly 700 of these silver coins were additional dimes.[405]

The fifth and final reporting period for the year covered August 16 to September 15, 2014. Hurricane Cristobal forced the ship to head farther out to sea for a few days. Fifteen dives were accomplished, the longest being 129 hours, or more than five days. This time around, fewer gold coins were found, including only 3 $1, 4 $2.50, 5 $5, 1 $10, and 22 $20. As had been the case all along, most of the double eagles were of the 1857-S variety.[406]

A large Kellogg & Humbert gold ingot, serial 503, from the 2014 finds.

Coin and Ingot Recoveries

RLP's chief scientist and historian, Bob Evans, was aboard the *Odyssey Explorer* for the entire 2014 expedition season. He had also served as chief scientist on the 1988–1991 expeditions to the *Central America* and later as curator for the treasure recovered from those early expeditions. Evans described the 2014 expedition in a July 2014 press release:

Suction attachment to the robotic arm on *ZEUS* recovering a double eagle on the sea floor.

The variety and quality of the coins being recovered is just astonishing. Of course there are spectacular $20 double eagles like we found back in the 1980s and 1990s, but the wide variety of other denominations makes this year's recoveries very different from the earlier finds. Among the silver coins I have seen what I believe are several of the finest known examples so far. The coins date from 1823 to 1857 and represent a wonderful diversity of denominations and mints, a time capsule of virtually all the coins that were used in 1857.[407]

The 2014 operations recovered more than 15,500 gold and silver coins, 45 gold bars, and hundreds of other gold nuggets, gold dust, jewelry, and other artifacts from the shipwreck site. Significant sections of the ship's structure and associated cultural-heritage artifacts and coins were located some distance from the main shipwreck, requiring excavation over a large area.

An extensive amount of knowledge has also been gained about the formation of the site. In addition to multibeam sonar surveys and photo-

mosaics, a 161,000 square-meter high-definition video survey was completed as well as a 4.5-kilometer by 10-kilometer survey utilizing Odyssey's Teledyne Reson dual-head SeaBat 7125 acoustic multibeam system. Ira Owen Kane, the court-appointed receiver, reviewed the extensive surveys, data, and other information gathered in 2014 with Odyssey to determine whether to re-commence recovery operations in 2015.

Details of the 2014 Recovery

The coin data presented by Odyssey Marine Exploration and given below is a preliminary inventory of American items based on shipboard observations. Minor adjustments to the inventory may occur as conservation of the coins and coin groups is completed.

Federal coins

Cents

1845
1851 (2)
1853

Half dimes

1852

Dimes

1838
Group of 9,669 not studied as of press time

Quarters

1805	1838	1843
1807	1839	1844-O
1833	1842-O (2)	1845 (2)

1850-O	1854-O (5)	1856 (8)
1853 (13)	1855 (18)	1856-O (7)
1853-O (2)	1855-S (13)	1856-S (3)
1854 (16)	1855	1857-S (4)

Group of 545 not evaluated as of press time

Half dollars

1810	1850-O	1855-O (5)
1824	1853 (3)	1855-S (4)
1830	1853-O (3)	1856
1832	1854 (4)	1856-O (8)
1846-O	1854-O (13)	1856-S (10)

Group of 324 not evaluated as of press time

$1 gold

1849 (17)	1852 (35)	1855-O (2)
1849-O (5)	1852-O (3)	1855-S (3)
1850 (10)	1853 (73)	1856 (8)
1851 (74)	1854[408] (22)	1856-S (40)
1851-C	1854-S (4)	1857-S (4)
1851-O (6)	1855 (13)	

Quarter eagles

1834 Classic Head (3)		
1835	1846	1851-O (4)
1836 (8)	1846-D (2)	1852 (60)
1838 (2)	1846-O (2)	1852-O (4)
1839-D	1847-C (2)	1853 (38)
1840	1847-D (2)	1854 (11)
1842-D	1847-O (4)	1854-O (9)
1842-O	1848-C	1855
1843 (5)	1849	1856 (4)
1843-C	1850 (15)	1856-O
1843-D (3)	1850-D	1856-S (66)
1843-O (9)	1850-O (4)	1857
1844-C	1851 (52)	1857-S (48)
1845 (4)	1851-D	

$3 gold

1855-S (10)
1856-S (36)
1857-S (15)

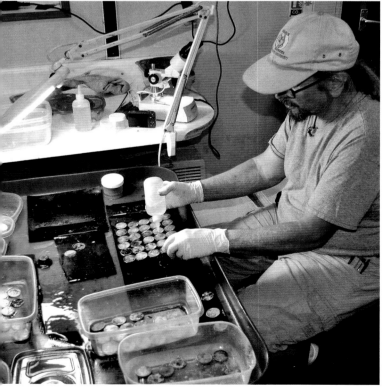

Chief scientist Bob Evans examines and documents gold coins while aboard the *Odyssey Explorer*.

A group of gold ingots discovered at the stern of the SS *Central America*.

ZEUS lifts a recovery basket with gold ingots for transport to the *Odyssey Explorer*.

One face of a Kellogg & Humbert ingot, serial 713, 13.78 troy ounces, value fineness 88, value stamped in 1857 $251.52.

Half eagles

1834 Classic Head (13)

1835 (2)	1845 (11)	1851-O (4)
1836 (8)	1845-D (2)	1852 (9)
1837 (2)	1845-O	1852-C (3)
1838 (7)	1846 (7)	1852-D (3)
1839	1846-O (3)	1853 (8)
1840 (2)	1847 (19)	1853-C
1841	1847-C	1853-D (5)
1841-C	1848 (7)	1854 (2)
1841-D	1848-C (2)	1854-O
1842 (2)	1848-D (3)	1855 (3)
1842-C	1849 (3)	1855-C
1843 (12)	1849-C	1855-O
1843-C (4)	1849-D	1855-S (30)
1843-D (2)	1850 (4)	1856 (2)
1843-O (4)	1850-D	1856-O
1844 (5)	1851 (7)	1856-S (52)
1844-D	1851-C	1857-S (52)
1844-O (3)	1851-D	

Eagles

1840	1848	1854
1841	1849 (10)	1854-S (13)
1842 (2)	1850 (2)	1855 (2)
1843-O (2)	1851 (2)	1855-S (2)
1844-O	1851-O (4)	1856-S (7)
1846-O (2)	1852 (2)	1857-S (4)
1847 (4)	1852-O	
1847-O (3)	1853 (2)	

Double eagles

1850 (14)	1852-O	1855-S (86)
1850-O (2)	1853 (14)	1856-S (304)
1851 (10)	1854 (12)	1857
1851-O (2)	1854-S[409]	1857-S (1,153)
1852 (22)	1855 (4)	

Private and territorial gold coins

Augustus Humbert, U.S. Assay Office of Gold

$10 1852 (3)
$10 1853
$20 1853 (20)

Kellogg & Co.

$20 1854 (24)
$20 1855 (23)

Moffat & Co.

$5 1849 (11)
$5 1850 (2)
$10 1849 (2)
$20 1853 (4)

Wass, Molitor & Co.

$5 1852 (2)
$10 1852 (3)
$10 1855
$20 1855 (2)

Miscellaneous gold

Dozens of small-denomination California gold coins
Many silver and gold foreign coins

Summary

Copper coins including some indiscernible: 14
Silver coins including foreign issues: 12,389
Gold coins including foreign issues: 3,133

Gold ingots

Harris, Marchand & Co.

Serial number: 6536 • Fineness: 731 (lowest in 2015 group) • Troy ounces: 14.70 • Value (1857): $222.13
Serial number: 6538 • Fineness: 682 • Troy ounces: 14.52 • Value (1857): $204.70
Serial number: 6542 • Fineness: 893 • Troy ounces: 25.18 • Value (1857): $470.03

Henry Hentsch

Serial number: 3127 • Fineness: 920 • Troy ounces: 58.56 • Value (1857): $1,113.69
Serial number: 3128 • Fineness: 815 • Troy ounces: 88.15 • Value (1857): $1,485.10
Serial number: 3225 • Fineness: 873 • Troy ounces: 119.45 • Value (1857): $2,155.65
Serial number: 3243 • Fineness: 892 • Troy ounces: 319.22 (highest in 2015 group) • Value (1857): $5,886.19 (highest in 2015 group)
Serial number: 3246 • Fineness: 938 • Troy ounces: 24.17 • Value (1857): $468.66

Justh & Hunter

Serial number: 4209 • Fineness: 820 • Troy ounces: 36.61 • Value (1857): $620.57
Serial number: 4274 • Fineness: 868 • Troy ounces: 142.70 • Value (1857): $2,560.49
Serial number: 4279 • Fineness: 924 • Troy ounces: 113.55 • Value (1857): $2,168.89
Serial number: 4307 • Fineness: 889 • Troy ounces: 51.78 • Value (1857): $951.57
Serial number: 4322 • Fineness: 839 • Troy ounces: 30.83 • Value (1857): $534.70
Serial number: 4338 • Fineness: 741 • Troy ounces: 7.54 (lowest in 2015 group) • Value (1857): $115.49 (lowest in 2015 group)
Serial number: 9483 • Fineness: 890 • Troy ounces: 313.54 • Value (1857): $5,774.54

Kellogg & Humbert

Serial number: 490 • Fineness: 857 • Troy ounces: 106.85 • Value (1857): $1,888.39

Serial number: 491 • Fineness: 871 • Troy ounces: 48.70 • Value (1857): $876.85

Serial number: 503 • Fineness: 889 • Troy ounces: 89.33 • Value (1857): $1,641.64

Serial number: 544 • Fineness: 875 • Troy ounces: 27.33 • Value (1857): $494.34

Serial number: 613 • Fineness: 850 • Troy ounces: 17.20 • Value (1857): $302.22

Serial number: 641 • Fineness: 874 • Troy ounces: 157.04 • Value (1857): $2,837.27

Serial number: 646 • Fineness: 870 • Troy ounces: 138.83 • Value (1857): $2,496.67

Serial number: 656 • Fineness: 892 • Troy ounces: 24.58 • Value (1857): $453.23

Serial number: 663 • Fineness: 882 • Troy ounces: 298.81 • Value (1857): $5,448.08

Serial number: 684 • Fineness: 882 • Troy ounces: 197.19 • Value (1857): $3,595.28

Serial number: 707 • Fineness: 967 (highest in 2015 group) • Troy ounces: 20.07 • Value (1857): $401.19

Serial number: 708 • Fineness: 882 • Troy ounces: 32.15 • Value (1857): $586.17

Serial number: 713 • Fineness: 883 • Troy ounces: 13.78 • Value (1857): $251.52

Serial number: 760 • Fineness: 900 • Troy ounces: 75.90 • Value (1857): $1,412.08

Serial number: 761 • Fineness: 901 • Troy ounces: 61.41 • Value (1857): $1,143.77

Serial number: 763 • Fineness: 890 • Troy ounces: 39.67 • Value (1857): $729.84

Serial number: 764 • Fineness: 889 • Troy ounces: 102.36 • Value (1857): $1,881.10

Serial number: 777 • Fineness: 872 • Troy ounces: 27.87 • Value (1857): $502.37

Serial number: 832 • Fineness: 873 • Troy ounces: 25.19 • Value (1857): $454.59

Serial number: 833 • Fineness: 843 • Troy ounces: 13.59 • Value (1857): $236.82

Serial number: 848 • Fineness: 895 • Troy ounces: 174.82 • Value (1857): $3,234.39

Serial number: 863 • Fineness: 891 • Troy ounces: 96.50 • Value (1857): $1,777.39

Serial number: 889 • Fineness: 843 • Troy ounces: 92.80 • Value (1857): $1.617.16

Serial number: 911 • Fineness: 875 • Troy ounces: 42.44 • Value (1857): $767.65

Serial number: 912 • Fineness: 899 • Troy ounces: 20.43 • Value (1857): $379.67

Serial number: 1008 • Fineness: 892 • Troy ounces: 41.62 • Value (1857): $767.44

Serial number: 1009 • Fineness: 884 • Troy ounces: 26.64 • Value (1857): $486.81

Serial number: 1010 • Fineness: 881 • Troy ounces: 167.53 • Value (1857): $3,051.03

Serial number: 1014 • Fineness: 879 • Troy ounces: 92.83 • Value (1857): $1,686.76

Serial number: 1018 • Fineness: 870 • Troy ounces: 113.74 • Value (1857): $2,045.55

chapter 15

The Fate of the SS *Brother Jonathan*

A gem Mint State 1865-S double eagle
from the SS *Brother Jonathan*.

The *Brother Jonathan* was one of dozens of vessels engaging in the Pacific Coast trade.[410] Launched at the shipyard of Perrine, Patterson & Stack, Williamsburg, New York, on November 2, 1850, the 1,181-ton ship was made of locust, white oak, live oak, and cedar and cost about $190,000.[411] Her measurements were 220 feet, 11 inches long by 36 feet wide with a draft of 13 feet, 10 inches. Power was provided by a vertical steam engine made by the Morgan Iron Works. Accommodations, including 24 staterooms, were provided for about 365 passengers. The staterooms offered extra amenities for those who wished to pay a higher fare, but most voyagers were content with simple berths; the original owner, Edward Mills, offered discount rates and attracted a poorer class of passengers.

The vessel started operations early in 1851 on the New York-to-Panama route, carrying cargo and gold seekers. During this year, she was involved in two separate disputes when travelers who had bought through-trip tickets from New York to San Francisco were brought to the Panamanian port of Chagres (later called Aspinwall, today's Colón) by the *Brother Jonathan*

but could not complete their connections on the western leg due to wrecks in the Pacific. The first incident on the Pacific side was precipitated when the steamer *Union*, with 236 passengers and $270,000 in gold, was wrecked early in the morning of July 5, 1851, when her helmsman, who with the rest of the crew was drunk from their Fourth of July celebration, fell asleep. The second problem was similar and occurred when the steamer *Monumental City* failed to arrive on schedule to complete the Pacific leg. In both instances, the relatively penurious passengers had bought cheap tickets through Mills' agency in New York City and became stranded when the higher-priced Pacific Mail Steamship Co. would not honor their tickets unless they paid a large surcharge.

Regardless of these issues, the ship seems to have had a good reputation. In an article, "Brother Jonathan: Pioneer Steamship of the Pacific Coast," Alfred L. Lomax described the ship early in its career:

People liked the *Brother Jonathan*. According to one who had booked return passage, the ship presented so impressive an appearance

when it was fully illuminated at night with its glittering, reflecting ornaments that it vied with the drawing-room of an imperial palace. Oilcloth of a bright and variegated pattern covered the floor. Crimson cushioned settees and chairs provided comfortable reading and writing facilities. The cuisine must have been excellent as meat was served regularly from freshly killed cattle, swine, sheep, and poultry which the vessel carried and kept on ice. . . .

Vanderbilt as Owner

This Atlantic schedule—apparently including very attractive settings for those aboard—continued until March 1852, when Commodore Cornelius Vanderbilt acquired the *Brother Jonathan* from Mills. The new owner was known for his filthy ships, spartan accommodations, emphasis on profits, and disregard for passengers' interest or safety. In one particularly memorable eight-month period in the 1850s, three of his steamers were wrecked.

Today, Vanderbilt's earlier poor reputation has been whitewashed. Unless one digs deeply into his biography, past his early involvement in steamships and also railroads, he emerges as a benefactor to the United States and more. His descendants became prominent in society, had multiple yachts, and were leading figures in Rhode Island. Regardless, many complaints about Vanderbilt's poor service have reached print at various points. Historian John Haskell Kemble commented:

> Vanderbilt's ships maintained a reputation which was hardly enviable. They were described in the press of both coasts as "floating pig sties," not half manned and badly provisioned, and their owner was characterized as the "Nero of the sea."[412]

Eric Heyl, another historian of renown, echoed the sentiments:

Some exceedingly bitter denunciations of Vanderbilt and the filthy conditions of his steamers, the poor and often spoiled food, and the ignorance and insolence of his captains and crews were published in the San Francisco daily newspapers. It was alleged that some of the Vanderbilt captains had never had any high-seas experience, but had been ferry-boat captains before being put in charge of the Pacific steamers.[413]

Upon acquiring the *Brother Jonathan*, Vanderbilt reconfigured the ship with three masts, a 400-horsepower steam engine, and additional accommodations (for a new capacity of 750 passengers). He also put the vessel on the San Francisco-to-San Juan del Sud (port at Nicaragua) route. The commodore hoped that crossing at Nicaragua, farther north than Panama, would offer a faster route to the gold fields, but he was mistaken; although the distance was shorter, the land segment was much larger, and the venture never was a success.

After operating the SS *Brother Jonathan* for slightly more than half a year, Vanderbilt transferred its title and those of his other ships to his Accessory Transit Company, operators of the Nicaragua Steamship Company. Under this flag, Vanderbilt maintained control of it for the next several years.[414] Among the ship's activities during this stretch was assisting in 1854 with the passage back to San Francisco of the ill-fated *Yankee Blade* passengers, whose story is recounted in chapter 13, "Gold Rush Treasure: SS *Yankee Blade*" (see page 223).

The vessel operated under Commodore Vanderbilt's ownership through 1856, when the government of Nicaragua revoked the charter of the Accessory Transit Company.[415] Then, in 1857, the ship was sold to John T. Wright of the Merchants Accommodation Line, who changed her name to the *Commodore*, a rather curious turn of events inasmuch as Vanderbilt's company had just stopped operating her.

North from San Francisco

The newly rechristened *Commodore* ran from San Francisco to Seattle and also called on Vancouver and Portland. British Columbia gold fever (see below) was rampant, and the *Commodore* and her sister ship, the *Pacific*, profited immensely from the related cargoes.

In 1861, the ship changed hands again, becoming the property of the California Steam Navigation Company. She underwent repairs at North's Shipyard in San Francisco to strengthen her superstructure, and the old dining room was eliminated in favor of a new one measuring 120 feet long on the upper deck. Additionally, one deck was eliminated, reducing the number from three to two. In December 1861, sporting its old name of *Brother Jonathan*, the ship was advertised as being ready:

> The new [*sic*] and splendid steamship *Brother Jonathan* built expressly for this route and with unequaled accommodations for passengers and freight, Samuel J. DeWolf, commander, will leave Pacific Street Wharf for the above ports [Portland and Victoria] on Thursday, December 19, 1861. . . .

California Steam Navigation Company poster.

Laden with Cargo and Lost

Lost: July 30, 1865 • **Location:** Near Crescent City, California •
Found: 1996 • **Treasure:** Gold coins

The ship's most eventful and last voyage commenced on July 28, 1865.[416] Burdened with freight far beyond her 900-ton capacity and riding low in the water, the *Brother Jonathan* left San Francisco headed north toward its intended destination of Vancouver Island. Captain Samuel J. DeWolf had strongly protested the overloading, but was told that if he complained further, there were many other ship captains who would like to have his job at the helm.

The passengers numbered nearly 180, a fraction of the capacity of close to 700. Among them were Mrs. J.C. Keenan, a popular proprietor of a San Francisco brothel, and seven girls in her employ, all heading north to seek new customers

and opportunities.[417] General George Wright, traveling with his wife, was on the way to assume his new post at Fort Vancouver under the Department of Columbia.

Victor Smith, who had recently survived the wreck of the *Golden Rule* on Roncador Reef, Ecuador, was also aboard, as was Anson C. Henry, governor of the Washington Territory. Fifty-four crew members manned the vessel. The cargo included two camels and a pair of horses, the latter the personal steeds of General Wright.

No sooner had she gone through the Golden Gate marking the exit from San Francisco Bay than the ship ran into a fierce gale. High winds continued as she passed Crescent City on the coast of Northern California on July 30, and shortly after 1:45 p.m. that day, she is said to have run onto rocks hidden beneath the surface off St. George's Point.[418] The collision ripped a great hole in front of the engine room, causing the foremast to topple across the deck. Three cannon shots were fired, alerting citizens on the nearby shore, which soon became crowded with spectators.

In a scene which has been variously described as ranging from calm to confused, six small boats (four Franklin Patent Metallic Lifeboats and two surf boats) were put into the water. Five were immediately swamped. Only one—a surf boat commanded by James Patterson (the third mate) and carrying three children, five women, and 10 crewmen—was able to reach shore, and those aboard turned out to be the only survivors from the 232 people comprising the crew and passengers.[419]

The quartermaster, who was one of the survivors, later told his tale:

> I took the helm at twelve o'clock. A northwest gale was blowing and we were four miles above Point St. George. The sea was running mountain-high and the ship was not making headway. The captain thought it best to turn back to Crescent City and wait until the storm had ceased. He ordered the helm hard to port. I obeyed and it steadied her. I kept on due east. This was about 12:45. When we made Seal Rock the captain said "Southeast by south." It was clear where we were, but foggy and smoky inshore.
>
> We ran until 1:50 when she struck with great force, knocking the passengers down and starting the deck planks. The captain stopped and backed her, but we could not move the vessel an inch. She rolled about five minutes, then gave a tremendous thump and part of the keel came alongside. By that time the wind and sea had slewed her around until her head came out of the sea and worked off a little. Then the foremast went through the bottom until the yard rested on the deck. Captain DeWolf

ordered everyone to look to his own safety and said that he would do the best for all.[420]

About 45 minutes after impact, the *Brother Jonathan* was at the bottom of the sea. At the time, the disaster represented the greatest loss of life of any shipwreck on the Pacific Coast of the United States. For days afterward, bodies—some wearing ineffective life jackets—floated ashore up and down the coast.[421] Many were buried in the Brother Jonathan Cemetery, a part of the Masonic cemetery which itself had been established in Crescent City about 10 years before the wreck.[422]

Readers of newspaper accounts found it curious and a sad reflection on human nature that 10 male *crew* members survived, but not a single adult male *passenger* was saved. Captain DeWolf's wife was among the women who lived. Later, she stated that the ship did not strike a rock of any kind, but, instead, had a hole torn in her bottom when a huge, heavy cast-iron ore crusher broke loose in the hold.[423]

It is believed that the ship's cargo was valued at $300,000 to $500,000, including machinery for a woolen mill; mining apparatus for the Owyhee district in eastern Oregon and Idaho; 346 barrels of whiskey; and $200,000 in payroll for U.S. troops at Fort Vancouver, Washington. One account stated that the payroll was in federal "greenback" notes, part of a shipment totaling $250,000 in such currency.[424]

It is also thought that the Wells Fargo agent on board, Joseph Lord, had with him about $250,000, and that close to $100,000—or even far more, depending upon the account—in jewelry and cash was in the safe of the purser, John S. Benton. William Logan, Indian agent for Uncle Sam, was on the voyage, and was said to be carrying with him $105,000 in gold in compensation payments—possibly, this was part of the purser's holdings.

In time, accounts of the coins and cash aboard the ill-fated ship achieved large proportions.

Salvage Attempts

As is the rule with sunken treasures, little factual information has reached print concerning early salvage of the *Brother Jonathan*. We do know that one of the first efforts was that of the steam tug *Mary Ann*, which left San Francisco on August 20, 1865, and sought the site without success.

Many parts and artifacts from the ship washed ashore during the weeks after the disaster. The ship's wheel was recovered, and for many years it was displayed over the bar in Scovill's tavern in Crescent City. A sailmaker and old-timer of that city named Captain Gee investigated the lost ship in 1890, but apparently achieved little success.[425]

In 1894, some fanfare was given to an adventurer—styling himself as the "Champion Deep Sea Diver"—who said he found the *Brother Jonathan* resting in good condition on the sea bed, walked her deck, and planned to raise her and put her back into service. Again, nothing tangible materialized. The Lund-Freese-Francisco explorers of 1916 seem not to have been chronicled in detail in any standard reference, nor were other efforts of the early 1900s, including one purported to have occurred in the 1930s.

Mention has been made of Frank L. Mooreman, a West Coast capitalist, who in 1927 was a partner with the U.S. government in exploration of the wreck. Uncle Sam was interested in Civil War military pay records which might be found, thus helping clear certain pension claims, while Moore was interested in the gold. Apparently, dissension arose among those involved. What gold or other treasure was recovered was not documented.[426]

Deep Sea Research

In 1991, Donald G. Knight and Harvey Harrington—both formerly of another exploration company, Sea-Epics Research—came together with experienced diver James Wadsley and founded Deep Sea Research (DSR) to recover coins from the SS *Brother Jonathan*. Others joined the firm later in 1991 and in 1992, including Sherman Harris and David L. Flohr. Using side-scan sonar and other technology, the group conducted searches for the wreck over the next two years.

Finally, on October 1, 1993, the ship was located and confirmed. Surveying began, and through 1994, salvage plans were made. In the meantime, the State of California objected to the planned recovery and went to court, but the legal representative for DSR, Fletcher C. Alford of the San Francisco law firm of Gordon & Rees, won this and several other legal actions on behalf of the company.

In the summer of 1996, some artifacts were recovered and were mostly given to the Del Norte Historical Society Museum. The Society was asked to make up a "want list" of other items that it would like and which had been seen or were likely to be on the wreck. Efforts were conducted with the M/V *Cavalier* serving as the mother ship, the *Xanadu* as the dive ship, and the one-man mini-sub *Snooper* and the two-man *Delta* assisting.

The "eureka!" moment happed on August 20, when Harrington saw a large quantity of gold coins on the surface of the wreck. Excitement prevailed. Subsequent dives brought hundreds of coins to the surface; these specimens were handled with care and transported by Brink's to a San Francisco-area bank vault, where they were conserved by Robert Johnson, a well-known numismatist. By the last day of the 1996 search, 875 coins were found, mostly $20 double eagles.

A year later, over a period of 15 days of saturation diving by an experienced team working from the M/V *American Salvor* and with assistance from the *Snooper*, 332 coins (again mostly double eagles) were found. During this season, my son Andrew and I spent a day aboard the *American Salvor* and watched the proceedings.

Later, much additional site exploration, mapping, and recovery of historical artifacts was conducted, with the found pieces going to the Del Norte County Museum. By the end of the search, $3,300,000 had been expended by DSR; in the last few years of the operations, the officers had received no salaries or compensation. Meanwhile, the State of California persisted in its effort to halt exploration and to otherwise cause difficulties. This was resolved in 1998 when the state agreed to cease its legal actions against DSR in return for a one-sixth share in the rare coins recovered.

The Treasure

The following listing of denominations, dates, mintmarks (as applicable), and grades represents a registry of rare coins recovered in 1996 and 1997 by DSR from the wreck of the *Brother Jonathan*, the last recovery operation taking place in August 1997.

The coins were divided into two categories. Those held by DSR were graded by PCGS and Bowers and Merena Galleries. Those awarded to the State of California were only graded as "circulated" or "Uncirculated." Note that one additional piece—a $5 gold coin encrusted in coral—was given to the Del Norte County Museum.

"Gradeflation" later took place, with the result that many coins in PCGS holders with the *Brother Jonathan* imprint are now graded higher in holders with no pedigree—a situation common to coins from certain other treasure wrecks.

Federal gold coins

Half eagles

1834, F-15
1835, F-15
1836, VF-20
1837, F-12
1838, VF-30
1839-D, VF-25
1840, F-12 (2)
1842-O, F-15
1843-O, G-4
1844, EF-40
1845, net EF-45
1845, F-15, VF-20, VF-25, VF-35
1845-O, VF-30
1846, VF-30
1847, F-15, net VF-35, VF-35
1848, net EF-40
1848-C, VF-35
1851, VG-10, VF-35
1852, VF-20, EF-40, net EF-45
1852-D, VF-35
1856, C-15, VF-15
1856-S, VF-30
1857-S, F-12

1858-S, VF-35
1859-S, EF-45
1860-S, VF-35, EF-40
1861, AU-50
1861-S, EF-40
1862-S, EF-40
1863-S, EF-45, AU-50
1865-S, net MS-60, MS-64

Eagles

1847, F-15
1861-S, EF-40
1865-S, MS-64

Double eagles

1850, VF-35
1852, VF-30, EF-40
1853, 3 Over 2, EF-45
1855-S, VF-35, EF-40
1856-S, AU-50, MS-62
1857, EF-45
1857-S, net EF-40, EF-40, EF-45, AU-50 (2), AU-53
1858-S, VF-25, VF-35, EF-40 (2), EF-45, AU-50
1859-S, net VF-20, VF-35 (3), EF-40 (3), net EF-45, EF-45 (4), AU-50 (2), AU-53
1860-S, VF-30, net VF-35, VF-35 (2), EF-40 (2), EF-45 (6), AU-50 (4), net AU-53, AU-55
1861, EF-45, net AU-50, AU-50, AU-53
1861-S, net EF-40 (4), EF-40 (4), net EF-45, EF-45 (13), AU-50 (11), AU-53 (6), AU-55 (5)
1862, AU-53
1862-S, EF-40 (5), EF-45 (20), AU-50 (14), AU-53 (17), AU-55, net MS-60, AU-58
1863-S, EF-40, EF-45 (10), net AU 50 (3), AU-50 (18), AU-53 (24), net AU-55, AU-55 (37), net AU-58, AU-58 (15), MS-60, MS-61 (3), MS-63 (2)

1864-S, EF-40, EF-45 (4), net AU-50 (2), AU-50 (8), AU-53 (5), AU-55 (27), net AU-58 (2), AU-58 (32), MS-60 (7), MS-61 (10), net MS-62, MS-62 (8), MS-63 (2)

1865, AU-55

1865-S, net AU-50 (2), net AU-55 (5), AU-55, net AU-58, AU-58 (22), net MS-60 (8), MS-60 (12), net MS-61, MS-61 (32), net MS-62 (5), MS-62 (111), MS-63 (190), MS-64 (142), MS-65 (14), MS-66 (2)

State of California (not graded, "circulated" unless otherwise noted)

$5 gold

1836	1846 D	1855-S
1838	1847-C	1857-S
1842-D	1851	1860-S
1843	1852	1861
1844-O	1853-D	1863

$10 gold

1849
1856-S

$20 gold

1852	1861
1855-S	1861-S (5)
1856-S (2)	1862-S (19)
1857-S (3)	1863-S (25, 2 Unc.)
1858-S (5)	1864-S (40, 9 Unc.)
1859-S (6)	1865
1860-S (7)	1865-S (61, 58 Unc.)

In 1999, DSR consigned most of the coins recovered from the *Brother Jonathan* to Bowers and Merena Galleries of Wolfeboro, New Hampshire. The sale was widely publicized, including with a special display at the Treasures of Mandalay Bay Museum in the Mandalay Bay Resort & Casino in Las Vegas.

The event, held in Los Angeles on May 29, created a lot of attention and resulted in strong prices. There were 842 lots, of which 793 were double eagles. In connection with the event, I wrote a book—*The Treasure Ship S.S. Brother Jonathan*—which garnered favorable reviews.

This event was a catalyst for the creation of a numismatic subculture: enthusiasts who desire to obtain one or more coins documented as coming from each of several major shipwrecks. This movement went into even higher gear soon afterward when large quantities of double eagles from the SS *Central America* (see chapter 14, "Gold Rush Treasure: SS *Central America*," page 231) became available.

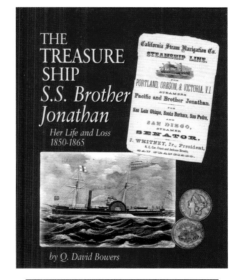

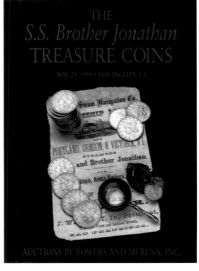

The *Brother Jonathan* book and auction catalog.

chapter 16

The SS *Republic* Treasure

From the days of Spanish galleons laden with gold and silver returning from Central and South America, the late summer and early autumn seasons have been known to be fraught with danger for sea-going vessels. Storms, sometimes referred to as cyclones and other times as fierce gales, could not be foretold of in years past and are still unpredictable in modern times.

The typical tropical depression or hurricane, as we refer to them now, rises in the Gulf of Mexico or the Caribbean Sea, tracks northward along the Atlantic Seaboard of the United States, and finally peters out in the North Atlantic—that is, right along some of the most historically important shipping routes. This chapter is yet another tragic yet numismatically important story of a craft that fell victim to such a storm in those waters.

To set the stage: on November 10, 1865, the *Daily Spy*, Worcester, Massachusetts, carried this account (forwarded from New York). The event had occurred several weeks earlier; in these days, news traveled slowly, telegraph lines were often down, and it was not until later that the story could be pieced together:

The steamer *Republic*, running on Cromwell's New Orleans line between that city and New York, was wrecked off the coast of Georgia . . . in a heavy gale of wind, proving a total loss. When the ship was on the point of going down, four boats and a raft put off from her.[427] Capt. Hawthorne [a passenger who had captained another vessel], who commanded one of the boats, states that he was assured by sailors that the persons placed on the raft were nearly if not all firemen and deckhands. When the Republic went down there were only two persons on board, one an elderly sea captain, and the other a German sailor. Had these two

The SS *Republic*.

had presence of mind enough to make an effort they would doubtless have been saved.

A report was current at Hilton Head when Capt. Hawthorne left, that another boat had arrived at Charleston, and also another one at Savannah. Capt. Hawthorne picked up seven persons from portions of the wreck after the steamer went down. It is generally believed that Lieut. Case of Boston was among those who took refuge in the second mate's boat. The lieutenant was indefatigable in his exertions to rescue his fellow passengers. Capt. Hawthorne was peculiarly fortunate in saving himself and family, but he lost everything else except the clothes he wore.

The *Savannah Herald* of the 31st ult., reports the arrival of the barkentine *Horace*

Beals with a boat from the *Republic*, picked up on the 26th, 20 miles east of Hunting Island, containing the following persons: S.E. Young, chief officer of the Republic. Passengers—Col. Wm. Nichols, Major R.S. Nichols, John H. Harloe, 1st Lieut. Lewis V. Casiare, Capt. George W. McNear, Chas. H. McNear, Horace D. Ellsworth, Ferdinand Muller, John C. Potter, George Long, James Cavana, fireman, and John Mancy, coal passer. They were in the life boat fifty hours without food or water. A demijohn of water placed aboard was broken by accident. They lost all their clothing and valuables, and were nearly naked.

Lost in a Hurricane

Lost: October 1865 • **Location:** Off the coast of Georgia • **Found**: 2003 • **Treasure:** Silver and gold coins

By the time she was lost at sea, the SS *Republic* had been in service for 12 years.[428] Built in Baltimore by John A. Robb, she was launched as the SS *Tennessee* on August 31, 1853. The two-deck ship was 210 feet long, 33 feet and 11 inches at the beam, and displaced 1,149 tons. Fitted with a vertical beam engine whose massive single piston was steam-powered by a pair of double-return-flue boilers and drove two 28-foot-diameter iron side wheels, the vessel could accommodate 100 passengers and about 5,000 barrels of cargo or the equivalent.

In 1854, the *Tennessee* was in service between Baltimore and Charleston, but the route proved to be unprofitable. She was put up for auction on March 22, 1855, but no buyer was found. Afterward, the ship went to England on a speculative voyage seeking profitable cargo, and then to Le Havre, France, from where goods were to be carried back across the Atlantic. During her return journey, she encountered a hurricane and was damaged, but by September the ship was berthed in New York, for sale and awaiting a buyer.

In late 1855, S. de Agreda Jove & Co. bought the ship, and in late January 1856 she became the first steamship to commence scheduled service between New York and South America. Then, in October 1856, she was sold to Charles Morgan and placed in service to and from New York and, separately, New Orleans to Nicaragua. The Nicaragua route was considered by some, especially Commodore Cornelius Vanderbilt, to be an alternative to the Panama crossing as a route to and from the California gold fields.

Interestingly, the ship carried American soldier of fortune William Walker and his mercenary troops to Nicaragua, where he sought to gain control of the country. In 1857, his army was defeated, and he was executed; the *Tennessee* then carried the straggling remnants of Walker's troops back to New York, arriving September 18, 1857. By that time, the Nicaragua route had been discontinued—the Panama Railroad had opened in 1855 and made the Atlantic-Pacific crossing easier, and domestic uncertainty in Nicaragua kept many travelers away—and so Morgan put the ship in scheduled service between New Orleans and Vera Cruz, Mexico, a profitable venture.

At the outbreak of the Civil War in April 1861, the *Tennessee* was taken over by the Confederacy and placed into service as a blockade runner. When New Orleans was retaken by Union forces on April 25, 1862, she was at the docks, loaded with a large cargo of cotton destined for Havana. She was subsequently commandeered, the U.S. flag hoisted over her, and became Admiral David Farragut's flagship for some of his operations on the Mississippi River.

Still in the Union's employ in September 1864, the Navy renamed her USS *Mobile*. The next month, she was caught in a gale near the mouth of the Rio Grande River and sustained severe damage to her hull. From there, the ship was put up for auction, sold to merchant Russell Sturgis for $25,000, repaired, and christened the SS *Republic*.

On May 13, 1865, she started on the New York–to–New Orleans route under charter to William H. Robeson's steamship line. By the time of her July 19, 1865, voyage, the charter had been assigned to the H.B. Cromwell & Co. steamship line servicing the same route—which would turn out to be the last the ship would travel.

The Fatal Voyage

The *Republic*'s last voyage began on October 18, 1865. She left New York, bound for New Orleans, with a reported $400,000 in gold coins.

Such a quantity was significant, as this was a very uncertain financial era; gold and silver coins of all denominations were being hoarded by the public, as they had been for several years. Federal bills in circulation, such as Legal Tender and National Bank notes, traded at a sharp discount to gold and silver. Specie brokers, exchange houses, and banks were well stocked with gold and silver coins and did a lively trade dealing in them. Traders and others expecting to do business in New Orleans necessarily bought such coins to take with them.

But back to the trip: on October 22, the *Republic* passed Cape Hatteras, well-known as a graveyard for passing ships. The following morning,

she was off the coast of Georgia when an east-northeasterly gale blew in. By evening, the storm had become a raging hurricane. The scenario was all too familiar to ship captains of the era, and in the vast majority of instances the challenge was to maintain forward speed and control until the storm was over.

On October 24, matters worsened, and the ship's paddlewheels stalled and couldn't carry the engine past dead center. Without power, the *Republic* was adrift and at the mercy of the elements. Steam was raised on the donkey boiler to run the pumps, but the next morning at nine o'clock, that boiler failed and water began to pour into the hold. With little time left to spare, the crew began preparing the four lifeboats. They also built a makeshift raft from the ship's spars and boards.

By 1:30 p.m. on October 25, the water was above the engine room floor, and all hands were called to help launch the safety vessels. By 4:00 p.m., after two days of valiant struggle to keep the vessel afloat, the *Republic* went down. Most of the passengers and crew were stowed safely on the four boats and the makeshift raft. The remaining survivors then jumped into the sea; swimming for their lives, some found safety aboard debris and passing craft, but two are believed to have drowned while swimming through the ship's floating debris.

Days later, all of the survivors aboard the four lifeboats were rescued by passing ships. Of the passengers who fled on the hastily constructed raft, only two remained when it was finally spotted seven days later by a U.S. Navy steamship near Cape Hatteras Light. Among newspaper accounts, the October 30 edition of the Charleston *Daily Herald* reported, "Her cargo was valuable, and in addition she had on board some $400,000 in treasure, which went down with the ship."

Ship Found!

In July 2003, Odyssey Marine Exploration Inc. found the wreck of the *Republic* off the coast of Georgia in about 1,700 feet of water.[429] Strewn on the sea floor was an array of gold coins, along with bottles and other artifacts.

The 8-ton, 400-hp robotic *ZEUS* prepares for a dive to the SS *Republic*.

A crab climbs aboard a recovery container filled with gold coins.

Recovery with the ROV *ZEUS* began in November 2003, and by early December more than 750 eagles and double eagles (but no other gold denominations) had been brought to the surface. More than 900 Liberty Seated half dollars had been found as well. The coins—estimated to be just a small part of the treasure—were sent to Numismatic Conservation Services (NCS) to be cared for and conserved.

Operations continued over the next months. A news release issued by Odyssey, January 27, 2004, included this update: "To date, more than 17,000 coins, with a total face value of $54,500 (approximately 14,230 silver and 2,950 gold coins) and over 750 other artifacts have been recovered."

The breakdown of the findings reflected what would have been a typical shipment at the time. Double eagles, the largest gold coins of the era, were the easiest denomination to use in large-scale commerce, as less effort was needed to count them. Half dollars would have been chosen for a similar reason, being the largest silver coins in circulation; silver dollars, which cost $1.04 each to produce, were minted as bullion coins, sold at an according price, and were mainly used in the maritime trade with China.

In bulk, such gold and silver coins were usually stored in one of two ways. For transactions within cities, and also for many shipments sent by sea, they were often put up in sturdy canvas bags. Wooden kegs furnished an alternative, and these were included aboard the *Republic*. While such kegs were more expensive, they had the advantage that large quantities of coins could be easily handled at the destination—as kegs can be rolled along the ground—and, unlike wooden crates, no special handling equipment was needed.

Moreover, a sealed wooden keg offered better security than a canvas bag. By that time there were many accounts of precious coins on shipboard being switched or pilfered, while to do that with a keg would have been more difficult and would have left obvious traces.

Note that many of the gold coins in the wreck of the *Republic* were found covered with a concretion, or thin film of grime. Careful attention by

NCS served to restore the pieces to their October 1865 appearance. As gold is the most inert and impervious of coinage metals, no harm had been done to them; if anything, the surface coating in many cases served to protect the original finish, including the frosty mint luster on some of the pieces. Many other gold coins were in pristine condition when they were found on the seabed.

Note also that most of the silver half dollars were etched by salt water and had surfaces showing porosity, sometimes so delicate that high magnification was needed to see this feature. Such were called "shipwreck effect" coins on certain holders. A limited number of other half dollars were found to be pristine when reviewed. The Numismatic Guaranty Corporation (NGC) certified any silver and gold coins that had no etching.

Silver Coins from the SS *Republic*

As detailed, the recovery of SS *Republic* coins commenced with vigor in late 2003 and continued through early 2004. At one check partway through 2004, about 31,000 silver coins and 3,425 gold pieces had been brought up from the depths, amounting in face value to slightly less than 18%

of the estimated coins lost. By late 2004, the count had crossed the 50,000 mark, mostly augmented by a cascade of silver half dollars.

Indeed, the silver coins found were nearly entirely in the form of half dollars. Among the half dollars, the lion's share consisted of Liberty Seated pieces, though coins dating back to 1832 of the earlier Capped Bust design were represented. Of note among the Liberty Seated examples was an "ordinary" 1861-O half dollar in exceptional Mint State condition shown to me by Greg Stemm; upon closer examination, the coin showed a tiny die crack at Miss Liberty's nose. Here, certainly, was an 1861-O half dollar that could be positively attributed to the Confederacy and minted after control was taken from the U.S. government. The same die had been used to strike four C.S.A. pattern half dollars.

Later, many of the *Republic* half dollars were viewed by Randall E. Wiley and attributed to 17 different die varieties, including early coins minted under federal auspices, later coins struck by the Louisiana state government, and the final mintage by the Confederate States of America.

A large cluster of half dollars probably originally representing the contents of a wooden barrel.

An 1861-O Liberty Seated half dollar. This obverse die has a tiny hairline crack from the bridge of the nose to the border, the same die used under Confederate auspices to make four 1861 Confederate States of America pattern half dollars.

The Confederate States-related 1861-O half dollars with the tiny die crack were especially important and were and sold at a premium because of this feature. Those attributed to Louisiana were also sold at an advance.

Beyond those thrilling rarities, the treasure find also included seven examples of the first Liberty Seated half dollar struck in San Francisco, the 1855-S—considered to be a key variety in any grade—and 174 later issues from that mint. Additionally, there were thousands of New Orleans issues and many Philadelphia coins.

Eagles from the SS *Republic*

In terms of value, although the silver half dollars were extremely important and valuable, the gold treasure found in the wreck of the SS *Republic*—primarily of double eagles and a lesser number of eagles, but no smaller gold denominations—was of incredible worth. Virtually all coins proved to be in excellent condition following their conservation, and many were identified as rarities or among the finest quality of their variety, or both.

Eagles ($10 gold coins) were found of all dates from 1838 onward, that year being the first of the Liberty Head design. Note that the distribution by date and mintmark of the recovered pieces roughly corresponds to distribution numbers. For example: by the time of the wreck in 1865, the largest quantity made of any date and mint of $10 gold coin was the 1847 (of which 862,258 were struck), and coins of this variety were the most numerous recovered from the SS *Republic*, with 221 conserved by NCS and graded by NGC by September 2004. Likewise, just one 1841-O

eagle—a rarity of which just 2,500 were made—was found.

The roster of other remarkably rare issues for which fewer than five coins were recovered includes:

1838 (4)	1858-O (4)	1862-S
1842 Small Date (4)	1858-S (4)	1863
	1859-O (2)	1863-S (3)
1852-O (3)	1860-O (4)	1864 (2)
1857-O (3)	1860-S (4)	1865
1858	1861-S (2)	
1865-S, 865 Over Inverted 186		

Certain of these combine great rarity with remarkable condition. One of the most storied rarities in the eagle series is the 1858, of which just 2,521 were struck, and the *Republic* coin was certified as AU-58, one of the finest known, with most of its original mint frost still remaining. The solitary 1865-S is of the curious variety with regular date over *inverted* date. The date was first punched into the die upside down, and then corrected.

Double Eagles from the SS *Republic*

Similar to the situation for the eagles, the double eagles found in the *Republic* wreck were dominated by the varieties with larger mintages. Every

A carpet of double eagles and other gold coins on the ocean floor.

A rare 1865-S eagle with the regular date punched over an inverted 1865, a die error. One was found in the treasure.

An 1854-O double eagle, the most valuable coin retrieved from the wreck of the *Republic*.

The only 1861-S Paquet Reverse double eagle found.

date and mintmark from the first year of issue (1850) to 1865—except for the 1856-O—was represented. The highlight of the find was an 1854-O rarity graded at a high About Uncirculated level. All of the coins were studied carefully, noting in some instances such varieties as 1854 Large Date and the scarcer Small Date (both listed in *A Giude Book of United States Coins*) and thus bringing them to the attention of collectors.

Large and small mintmark varieties of the 1855-S, 1860-S, and 1865-S were sorted out, too. Of the 1855-S coins, some had a large S mintmark, while others had a small S letter, the last being more numerous. Among those of 1860-S, 68 were found to have a small S mintmark, with just one having a large S Mintmark. With the 1865-S double eagles, slightly more than 200 had a small S, and fewer than three dozen had a large S. Then again, as few double eagle specialists seek different sizes of mintmarks, scarcer varieties often sell for little or no premium.

Finally, one of rare 1861-S "Paquet Reverse" pieces was also found in the treasure. Only 19,250 examples of this coin were struck before the director of the San Francisco Mint discontinued the special reverse die, which was made by engraver Anthony C. Paquet and is marked by tall, heavy letters. For reference, there were 97 examples of the 1861-S with the regular reverse style among the *Republic* coins.

Coin Treasures

If silver coins are included, the *Republic* yielded more coins than any other American shipwreck of the era. John Albanese, a long-time professional who had also advised concerning the SS *Central America*, was enlisted to bring the initial treasure to market. From 2004 to the present, this has been accomplished by dividing the pieces into categories of rarity, grade, and demand.

Marketing was done mainly through dealers in rare coins and distributors of collectibles. The higher-grade and more valuable coins were reserved for specific offers into the rare-coin market to dedicated buyers who added them to their collections. Odyssey's packaging included colorful brochures, DVDs, handsome cases, and other accoutrements that added to the pieces' desirability.

Most of the silver coins were offered at a premium from what comparable coins would have brought on the regular numismatic market. In contrast, nearly all of the rare double eagles and other pieces went directly to the numismatic com-

Visitors view gold coins from the SS *Republic*—part of a large traveling exhibit created by Odyssey Marine Exploration.

munity as coin enthusiasts sought specific dates, mintmarks, varieties, and grades.

Federal silver coins

Quarter dollars: 2
Half dollars: 47,263

Federal gold coins

Eagles

1838 (4)	1851-O (99)
1839 (9)	1852 (59)
1840 (11)	1852-O (3)
1841 (20)	1853, 3 Over 2 (6)
1841-O	1853 (59)
1842 (17)	1853-O (13)
1842-O (17)	1854 (22)
1843 (20)	1854-O (17)
1843-O (35)	1854-S (41)
1844-O (32)	1855 (44)
1845 (2)	1855-O (7)
1845-O (19)	1856 (22)
1846 (6)	1856-O (5)
1846-O, 6 Over 5 (13)	1856-S (27)
1846-O	1857 (9)
1847 (221)	1857-O (3)
1847-O (123)	1857-S (11)
1848 (39)	1858
1848-O (9)	1858-O (4)
1849 (167)	1858-S (4)
1849-O (8)	1859 (9)
1850 (72)	1859-O (2)
1850-O (16)	1860 (9)
1851 (33)	1860-O (4)
	1860-S (4)

1861 (60)	1863
1861-S (2)	1863-S (3)
1862 (9)	1864 (2)
1862-S	1865
1865-S	

Double eagles

1850 (55)	1858-O (8)
1850-O (10)	1858-S (68)
1851 (53)	1859 (3)
1851-O (15)	1859-O (2)
1852 (104)	1859-S (67)
1852-O (20)	1860 (96)
"1853/2"[430] (9)	1860-O
1853 (58)	1860-S (70)
1853-O (7)	1861 (459)
1854 (42)	1861-O
1854-O	1861-S (Paquet rev.)
1854-S (9)	1861-S (97)
1855 (18)	1862 (9)
1855-O (3)	1862-S (127)
1855-S (57)	1863 (35)
1856 (17)	1863-S (180)
1856-S (65)	1864 (42)
1857 (26)	1864-S (168)
1857-O (4)	1865 (320)
1857-S (86)	1865-S (253)
1858 (9)	

Artifacts from the Sea Bottom

If there had been no *coins* in the *Republic* wreck, it may not have been salvaged. Deep-ocean archaeological excavations cost millions of dollars to properly conduct, and to recoup funding for such operations, typically millions of dollars in value needs to be found in the form of coins or ingots. Still, we would be remiss to not at least mention the many important artifacts recovered in these operations.

As had been the case with the Columbus-America Discovery Group dives on the SS *Central America* from 1988 to 1991, the salvors of the *Republic* found a wealth of non-numismatic items, including countless relics in glass, metal, ceramic, and other materials that withstood the undersea environment for nearly 140 years. These discoveries are now being shared with the public through archaeological papers published in a series of volumes titled *Oceans Odyssey*, as well as exhibits and an online virtual museum (OdysseysVirtualMuseum.com).

A group of recovered Drake's Plantation Bitters bottles.

A Drake's Plantation Bitters bottle being carefully removed from the wreck.

Interestingly, bottles found on the *Republic* included patent medicines such as the popular Drake's Plantation Bitters, pickle bottles, condiment bottles, ink bottles, and more. Many of these remain in Odyssey's permanent collection and are on display in the company's traveling shipwreck exhibit as well as in other museums, while still others recovered in multiple quantities have found an eager reception by collectors. The hobby of bottle collecting, while not comparable in revenue to coins, is very dynamic.

Tintype of a young man with a bottle of Drake's Plantation Bitters.

chapter 17

Hoards of Commemorative Coins

The first U.S. commemorative coins offered to the public were the 1892 Columbian half dollars issued for the World's Columbian Exposition, held in Chicago a year late in 1893.[431] From that time until 1954, many different designs and varieties of silver half dollars were produced. Today, collectors seek 48 different basic motifs for a type set, or, more expansively, a complete set of 142 types, dates, and mintmarks.

In addition, there were two other silver commemoratives (the 1893 Isabella quarter dollar and the 1900 Lafayette silver dollar), as well as 14 gold commemoratives—10 varieties of gold dollars, 2 designs of the quarter eagle denomination, and 2 kinds of $50 pieces. These and the aforementioned half dollars represent what numismatists know as the "classic" era of commemorative coins; note that hoards of commemoratives of the "modern" era (1982 to date) are not discussed here.

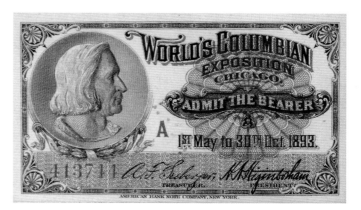

Silver Commemoratives

Unsold or saved: Various times before 1960 •
Found: Various times • **Treasure:** Commemorative coins

In general, silver commemoratives of the 1892–1954 era were produced to be sold at a premium for fairs and expositions (such as the 1893 Columbian, 1915 Panama-Pacific, and 1926 Sesquicentennial, among others); anniversaries of towns, counties, and states (such as 1927 Vermont Sesquicentennial, 1934 Maryland Tercentenary, 1936 York County Tercentenary, etc.); recognition of historical figures (1922 Grant Centennial, 1934–1938 Boone Bicentennial, 1946–1951 Booker T. Washington, etc.); or recognition of historical events (1920–1921 Pilgrim Tercentenary, 1924 Huguenot-Walloon Tercentenary, 1926–1939 Oregon Trail Memorial, etc.).

Many issues, including some of the preceding, were produced by private individuals or profit-oriented groups to exploit the collectors' market, and many of these did not commemorate a *nationally* meaningful anniversary or occasion. Perhaps most egregious in this regard is the 1936 Cincinnati half dollar, which was planned, ordered from the Treasury Department, and entirely sold by Thomas G. Melish, a businessman with close connections to Congress. These coins were made strictly for his private profit and bore reference to the 50th anniversary of that Cincinnati as "a Musical Center of America"—never mind that a diligent search of Cincinnati newspapers reveals nothing special at all happening 50 years earlier in 1886!

In a distribution situation for a classic commemorative, quantities of coins would be ordered from the Philadelphia (usually), Denver, and/or San Francisco mints and shipped to the issuing entities for face value plus die charges and transportation. These coins would then placed on sale at a premium, the actual prices solely determined by the issuer; no federal agencies had any say in the matter. Unsold coins were usually returned to the Treasury Department and melted, although in a few instances remainders were placed into circulation for face value.

In some instances—discussed below—groups and quantities were retained by the original distributor, sold in bulk to coin dealers, or otherwise retained in hoards after the main distribution had been completed. Note that if the following study had been compiled in 1950, many more hoards would be included, but today virtually all hoards have been dispersed. This has been due in part to owners desiring to have them certified by third-party services, which became popular with the advent of PCGS in 1986 and NGC in 1987. The concept of having valuable coins in bank-wrapped rolls is archaic today, though there are scattered exceptions, most notably a group of 500 1946-dated Iowa Centennial half dollars held by that state and intended for distribution in the year 2046.

Silver commemorative coins of the classic 1892–1954 era are listed in the approximate chronological order of production and distribution.

1892–1893 World's Columbian Exposition half dollars: Vast quantities of these were placed into circulation for face value, and examples did not command a significant premium on the collectors' market until decades later. I know of no original (non-numismatic) hoards of Mint State coins.

1893 World's Columbian Exposition Isabella quarter dollars: No hoards reported.

1900 Lafayette silver dollars: Relatively few of these were sold to coin collectors, and not much

excitement appeared in print concerning them. By a year or two later, examples were available on the market for less than the $2 issue price. Reporting in *The Numismatist*, January 1903, on a meeting of the Providence (Rhode Island) Curio & Numismatic Association, George C. Arnold noted: "Another member stated that early in November when he went to New York, he had purchased four Lafayette dollars for $1.10 each and these you remember were issued at $2 each, the total issue being only 50,000."

Arnold went on to relate: "Some 1,800 were left in the hands of the committee, 10,000 being returned from France" (where the statue depicted on the reverse of the coin was erected; these coins were among those intended to be sold at the 1900 Paris International Exhibition). It is also known that Chicago numismatist Virgil M. Brand acquired a cloth bag filled with 1,000 pieces.[432] This was sold after 1926 when his estate was dispersed.

Over time, approximately 36,000 Lafayette dollars were distributed. In line with the lack of interest, it is believed that some of the pieces were released into circulation at face value, and it is a certainty that many who acquired them at a $2 premium subsequently tired of the novelty and simply spent the pieces, for today it is not unusual to see examples in grades such as Extremely Fine and About Uncirculated.

The unsold remainder, amounting to 14,000 coins, went to the Treasury Building in Washington, D.C., where, unknown to collectors, the pieces were stored in cloth bags of 1,000 each in the same vault used to store large bundles of currency (including $5,000 and $10,000 notes).[433] In 1945, the Treasury Department converted the pieces to silver bullion, not realizing that the coins could have been sold at 10 times face value or more. Aubrey and Adeline Bebee, dealers who specialized in commemoratives, learned of the cache from government records, but, upon contacting the Treasury Department, found that their inquiry did not come in time to save the coins' destruction.

1915-S Panama-Pacific Exposition half dollars: No hoards reported.

1918 Illinois Centennial half dollars: A Springfield, Illinois, bank retained about 30,000 pieces until the "Bank Holiday" of March 1933, after which most went to dealers for a slight premium over face value. A small number may have also been released into circulation.

Large quantities of Illinois Centennial commemorative halves remained on the market until early 1936, at which time the numismatic demand for commemoratives of all kinds was such that the surplus was readily absorbed by the market.

1920 Maine Centennial half dollars: Just 50,000 Maine Centennial half dollars were struck (half of the original authorization) plus 28 pieces for the Assay Commission. Offered at $1 each, sales of the coins were fairly brisk, and 30,000 or more were sold soon after receipt. The others were kept by the office of the state treasurer and were parceled out through much of the year 1921, although quantities remained on hand for years afterward. Most if not all were distributed by the end of the 1930s.

1920–1921 Pilgrim Tercentenary half dollars: A large hoard of thousands of 1920 Pilgrim Tercentenary half dollars, all in original Mint cloth shipping bags, was sold by Paramount International Coin Corporation circa 1967–1968.[434] The market was not particularly strong at the time, and most of the coins went for about $8 each. Today they are widely dispersed and are valued much higher.

1921 Missouri Centennial half dollars: No hoards reported.

1921 Alabama Centennial half dollars: No hoards reported.

1922 Grant Memorial half dollars: No significant hoards have been reported, although there were scattered quantities in the market through at least the mid-1920s.

1923-S Monroe Doctrine Centennial half dollars: While it is certain that thousands of pieces were sold at the premium of $1 each, by and large the sales effort was a failure, and soon thereafter "nearly all went into circulation at face value,"[435] a situation which certainly did not please those who had paid $1 apiece.

1924 Huguenot-Walloon Tercentenary half dollars: No hoards reported.

1925 Lexington-Concord Sesquicentennial half dollars: No hoards reported.

1925 Stone Mountain Memorial half dollars: A number of hoards and groups were set aside at the time of issue, and occasionally these come on the market. At one time, financier Bernard Baruch was said to have owned more than 100,000 pieces. A number of Baruch's coins were sold circa 1956–1958 for $3.25 each for the benefit of the United Daughters of the Confederacy through the Citizens & Southern National Bank of Atlanta.[436] Others have been marketed since that time as well.

1925-S California Diamond Jubilee half dollars: In 1991, dealer Dwight Manley reported that he had been advised that a Southern California man owned a small hoard of about 400 pieces which had remained intact since the year of mintage.[437]

1925 Fort Vancouver Centennial half dollars: In 1982, a hoard of several hundred pieces surfaced. My firm purchased 257 of these and was told that this was a substantial majority of those found. One account had it that they had been the property of a historical society and museum, while another stated that they were owned by a local citizen who inadvertently turned them into a bank for face value!

1926 Sesquicentennial of American Independence half dollars: No hoards reported.

1926–1939 Oregon Trail half dollars: Wayte Raymond, who had distributed many of these coins at the time of their mintage, had on hand for years thereafter a tremendous supply of 1933-D, 1934-D, and other Oregon commemoratives.

1927 Vermont Sesquicentennial half dollars: No hoards reported.

1928 Hawaiian Sesquicentennial half dollars: One hoard traces its origin to a gesture of appreciation made by the president of the Bank of Hawaii to his employees. He put one of the commemorative coins on display and invited staff members to buy other such pieces wholesale for about $1 or $1.50 (recollections differ). However, when the displayed coin was swiped, the bank president became angry and locked up the remaining pieces—137 in all—and they remained untouched in a vault for more than a half century thereafter.

In 1985, the Bank of Hawaii brought the hoard back into daylight and consigned them to auction. On January 23, 1986, Bowers & Merena Galleries auctioned the coins to a new generation of numismatists.

1934 Maryland Tercentenary half dollars: No hoards reported.

1934–1938 Texas Centennial half dollars: Most were distributed or melted. B. Max Mehl bought

at least 1,000 by 1936,[438] but these were probably all sold. In later years, Amon G. Carter Jr. had hundreds of sets, and those too have been sold into the marketplace.

1934–1938 Daniel Boone Bicentennial half dollars: In the 1930s, Howard E. MacIntosh, owner of Tatham Stamp & Coin Company, purchased many hundreds—if not thousands—of Boone coins and sets of various issues. At the time of MacIntosh's death years later in 1958, many hundreds of pieces remained. These were later sold by New Netherlands Coin Co. Concerning these, John J. Ford Jr. recalled: "Among the hoard of commemoratives I remember the 1935 Boone sets with 'Small 1934,' which they only made 2,000 sets of, and MacIntosh had 180 to 200 sets."[439]

Maurice Rosen recalled that when he worked at First Coinvestors in the early 1970s, the firm purchased "two superb Mint State roll sets each of the 1937 P-D-S and 1938 P-D-S Boones; these were acquired from John J. Ford Jr. I believe during 1972–1973. There were other deals including a few rolls each of Clevelands, Elgins, Long Islands, and Roanokes."[440]

1935 Connecticut Tercentenary half dollars: No hoards reported.

1935–1939 Arkansas Centennial half dollars: No hoards reported.

1936 Arkansas Centennial-Robinson half dollars: In *The Numismatist* in February 1939, Stack's of New York City—the original distributor of the issue—placed an advertisement offering for sale to the highest bidder 500 unsold Arkansas

Centennial–Robinson half dollars (and also 500 sets of 1935 Texas Centennial half dollars). Bids were to be received on or before February 15, 1939.

That offering of Robinson pieces represented only a small portion of the unsold inventory, however. Eventually, a good portion of the remainder of coins—said to have amounted to 8,000 pieces—was wholesaled to Abe Kosoff, who maintained a coin business also located in New York. Even more large lots were sold to other dealers in the next few years; Arthur Kagin bought 4,000 coins late 1945 or early 1946.[441]

Large quantities of unsold Robinson half dollars were still in dealers' hands as late as the 1950s. I recall buying bulk groups of them from the Hollenbeck-Kagin Coin Company and Toivo Johnson. In 1991, an original mint bag of 1,000 coins was reported to exist in Arkansas.

1935 Hudson, New York, Sesquicentennial half dollars: No hoards reported.

1935–1936 California Pacific International Exposition half dollars: Although thousands of these coins were sold at the California-Pacific International Exposition and to the distributor's mail-order clients in the 1930s, quantities remained for years afterward. Anthony Swiatek and Walter H. Breen, writing in 1980, related that a large hoard of 31,050 pieces of the 1935-S issue—a staggering quantity amounting to a significant percentage of the net coinage after melting—was retained by an official associated with the Exposition and was not dispersed until after 1966.

In the market of the 1970s and 1980s, quantities of this particular coin changed hands from time to time. Dwight Manley advised me that beginning in the early 1980s, a Southern California individual whose grandfather had been associated with the Exposition dispersed more than 5,000 1935-S San Diego half dollars from a holding estimated at 10,000. The individual also sold his complete holding of 5,000 to 6,000 1936-D pieces. The grandfather had apparently originally obtained the pieces for face value.[442]

1935 Old Spanish Trail half dollars: These were distributed by promoter L.W. Hoffecker of El Paso, Texas, who issued many pronouncements about how fair he was being in the sale of the pieces, how they were soon sold out, etc.[443] However, much of what Hoffecker said and wrote was false. In a letter to Abe Kosoff, Numismatic Gallery, Beverly Hills, California, February 10, 1953, Hoffecker revealed—probably unintentionally—that not only had the coins not sold out in the 1930s, but that he still had a quantity of Old Spanish Trail half dollars on hand: "Received your letter of the 9th and say we have a very limited number of the Old Spanish Trail coins, and many collectors seem to like to buy from the designer of the coin, and we have no trouble selling 2 or 3 coins at $15 each every week." This was equal to a quantity of 100 to 150 coins sold per year.

Even many years later—February 1987, to be exact—coins clearly still remained, as when pieces from L.W. Hoffecker's estate were sold by Superior Galleries, the following commentary appeared on page 372 of the catalog: "The following group of sixty-three Old Spanish Trail half dollars . . . comes from the estate of L.W. Hoffecker. . . . "

Additionally, when the estate of Rev. Edward M. Catich—a Catholic priest who taught (but did not have his own parish) and was a coin dealer on the side—was appraised by Dean Oakes in the late 1970s, 400 Uncirculated 1935 Old Spanish Trail half dollars were found. The coins were subsequently sold for a million dollars at the height of the 1979–1980 coin investment boom. During that period, many commemoratives were pitched to investors who knew nothing about coins, but were attracted by their low mintages and reasonable prices; after such investors disappeared, the market crashed.[444]

1936 Providence, Rhode Island, Tercentenary half dollars: Well-known dealer Horace M. Grant was at the center of the distribution of this issue, which was fraught with phony news releases, made-up stories of the pieces being sold out within *six hours* of being put on sale, etc. Obviously, there was no real shortage, as in later years at least two large groups of hundreds or more sets (each with three coins, one each of the Philadelphia, Denver, and San Francisco varieties) came to light.

Another large quantity surfaced after the death of Howard E. MacIntosh in 1958. John J. Ford Jr. handled many of his coins and later commented that "MacIntosh had immense quantities of commemorative half dollars, which he had bought from the issuing commissions. How he did it, I don't know, but he had the coins. I do know that he was very thick with Horace Grant in Providence, Rhode Island, and that MacIntosh had a hell of a lot of Rhode Island halves."[445]

The Amon G. Carter Jr. estate (of Fort Worth, Texas), dispersed by John N. Rowe III in the 1980s, also contained hundreds of Rhode Island coins, these which had been held since the 1930s.

1936 Cleveland Centennial / Great Lakes Exposition half dollars: Enough 1936-dated Cleveland Centennial half dollars were minted that anyone desiring an example could have as many as he or she wanted at the time of issuance. For years thereafter, thousands of pieces remained unsold. Many of these went to dealers Abe Kosoff and Sol Kaplan, both close friends of distributor Thomas G. Melish (who also distributed the Cincinnati half dollars). In an effort to stimulate interest in Cleveland half dollars and to increase the value of those already in his possession, Kaplan ran numerous advertisements seeking to buy additional pieces.

As late as the 1950s it was not unusual for rolls (20 coins per roll) to be offered at coin conventions.

1936 Wisconsin Territorial Centennial half dollars: Remainder coins were still being sold by the state of Wisconsin in the 1950s.

1936 Cincinnati Music Center half dollars: No hoards reported.

1936 Long Island Tercentenary half dollars: In 1953 or 1954, John J. Ford Jr. bought 1,000 to 1,500 of this issue from the cash teller at the Williamsburg Savings Bank in Brooklyn. These had been stored in two or three original 500-coin cloth bags since 1936.[446]

1936 York County, Maine, Tercentenary half dollars: These coins were distributed by numismatist and American Numismatic Association member Walter P. Nichols, who endeavored to secure a wide market for them and to be honest in his news releases. After the initial burst of enthusiasm, about 6,000 remained unsold and continued to be distributed through the 1950s, well after Nichols' death on August 8, 1941.

Arlie Slabaugh related that the ANA sold pieces in the 1950s for $15.50 per group of 10, at which time the remainder was quickly liquidated. When my firm auctioned coins from the Nichols estate in 1984, a few York County Tercentenary half dollars were included, so technically it can be said that complete distribution was not concluded until that time.

1936 Bridgeport, Connecticut, Centennial half dollars: It was announced in *The Numismatist* in February 1938 that the unsold Bridgeport Centennial half dollars had been acquired by the Community Chest and Council of Bridgeport, which was going to offer them for sale. A quantity estimated to be on the order of several thousand pieces still remained unsold, and was eventually wholesaled for a small premium above face value through dealers.

Years later, Toivo Johnson acquired a large quantity, perhaps up to 2,000 pieces or so. I bought rolls of these pieces from Johnson in the 1950s and recall that substantial quantities were available to anyone desiring to purchase them. The remaining Johnson coins were later sold to Joe Flynn Jr. of Kansas City and First Coinvestors of New York. Maurice Rosen reported that when he worked at First Coinvestors circa 1972, "We dispersed 1,400 specimens of the Bridgeport half dollar. The coins were acquired from Toivo Johnson. Our cost was $25 each. These were 'original rolls,' assuming they were packaged that way in 1936, and based on today's grading would probably be at least MS-64."[447]

1936 Lynchburg, Virginia, Sesquicentennial half dollars: No hoards reported.

1936 Elgin, Illinois, Centennial half dollars: The distributor, L.W. Hoffecker, kept about 250 coins, which he parceled out over a long period of time.

1936 Albany, New York, Charter half dollars: In October 1936, the full authorized coinage of 25,000 pieces, plus 13 extra examples for the Assay Commission, was effected at the Philadelphia Mint. The Albany Dongan Charter Coin Committee offered them for sale at $2 each.

By this time, interest in commemoratives had dwindled sharply, and despite a lot of advertising puffery and hyperbole on the part of the issuing committee, quantities amounting to thousands of pieces remained unsold. Thus, the committee continued offering Albany half dollars for six more years. At one time, Abe Kosoff was given the opportunity to purchase the entire remaining stock for just $50 above face value for the lot, but he could find no one to sell to and so declined the offer.

In 1943, some 7,342 unsold and unwanted coins were sent to the Philadelphia Mint and melted. However, quantities still remained on hand.

Les Zeller advised me that circa 1954, it became known that the State Bank of Albany had between 1,600 and 2,400 undistributed pieces in its vaults and was willing to sell them for the issue price of $2 each. Jacob Cheris, Charles French, Dr. Kenneth Sartoris, and other local dealers and collectors quickly purchased the entire supply.

1936-S San Francisco–Oakland Bay Bridge half dollars: In the 1960s, it was not unusual to see small quantities of these offered on the collectors' market.

1936 Columbia, South Carolina, Sesquicentennial half dollars: No hoards reported.

1936 Delaware Tercentenary half dollars: No hoards reported.

1936 Battle of Gettysburg Anniversary half dollars: No hoards reported.

1936 Norfolk, Virginia Bicentennial half dollars: Although many unsold pieces were returned to the Mint and melted, at least several thousand were wholesaled to dealers. Bulk quantities remained in numismatic circles for years afterward.

1937 Roanoke Island, North Carolina, 350th Anniversary half dollars: No hoards reported.

1937 Battle of Antietam Anniversary half dollars: No hoards reported.

1938 New Rochelle, New York, 250th Anniversary half dollars: No hoards reported.

1946 Iowa Centennial half dollars: In November 1946, 100,057 coins were struck and shipped to the Iowa Centennial Committee in Des Moines in the same state. They sold well. Held back to be sold

50 years later in 1996 were 500 coins, and another 500 are held by the state to be sold in 2046.

1946–1951 Booker T. Washington Memorial half dollars: From 1946 to 1951, several million of these commemoratives were struck. Quantity per variety ranged widely, from a high of 1,000,546 Philadelphia Mint coins dated 1946 to only 6,004 each for the 1949 and 1950 P-D-S sets. While many coins were sold to numismatists and some went to the general public, it is believed that most were melted.

In the 1960s, rare-coin dealer Stephen J. Ruddel, of Arlington, Virginia, obtained thousands of hitherto undistributed sets and made a strong effort to popularize and distribute them to a new generation of numismatists, and undoubtedly many were sold this way.

1951–1954 Carver/Washington half dollars: In addition to the metal available from melting down earlier-dated Booker T. Washington half dollars, an unused authorization remained for earlier pieces of that issue that had not been struck, and this was applied to the new Carver/Washington issues as well, giving a maximum authorization of 3,415,631 pieces. Coins were produced in P-D-S sets of three, plus additional strikings of several issues—1952 Philadelphia, 1953-S, and 1954-S—intended for wide distribution (including through banks).

The effort was a failure, and many pieces were dumped at or close to face value. In the meantime, the collectors' market absorbed several thousand or more P-D-S sets, but most sets remained unsold. Eventually, 1,091,198 Carver-Washington coins were returned for melting.

John J. Ford Jr. recalled: "In the early 1950s we did business with the Chase Bank. Around 1955 they had large quantities of Booker T. Washington and Washington-Carver half dollars of certain dates and mints. These were available at face value, but nobody wanted them. With some effort I was able to market these. You couldn't sell the P-D-S sets, but there was a limited market for rolls and quantities of particular issues, like the large-mintage 1950-S, 1951, 1952, 1953-S, and 1954-S. We would get these in large quantities for the face value of fifty cents apiece, and then I would pay some guy a $10 or $15 tip for bringing them over to my office."[448]

Gold Commemoratives

Put away: Before 1930 • **Found:** Various times • **Treasure:** Gold coins

The first U.S. commemorative gold coins offered in quantity as souvenirs and sold at a premium were the 1903-dated Louisiana Purchase Exposition gold dollars in two styles: one bearing the portrait of Thomas Jefferson and the other of William McKinley.[449]

In the case of most gold classic commemoratives, the high face value of gold coins mitigated against dealers or collectors saving pieces in large numbers. Nearly all unsold pieces were returned to the Treasury Department and melted, with a few exceptions as noted below.[450] Coins are listed in chronological order of production and distribution.

1903 Louisiana Purchase Exposition, Jefferson, gold $1: No hoards reported.

1903 Louisiana Purchase Exposition, McKinley, gold $1: No hoards reported.

1904–1905 Lewis and Clark Exposition gold $1: No hoards reported.

1915-S Panama-Pacific Exposition gold $1: A total coinage of 25,034 Panama-Pacific International Exposition gold dollars were struck, with the extra 34 being reserved for assay. Distribution was through agent Farran Zerbe. Sales of the pieces at the Exposition were satisfactory, more or less; it is believed that thousands were sold.

When sales efforts terminated in the autumn of 1916, though, 10,000 remaining coins were shipped to the Treasury for melting. On the other hand, Zerbe did retain an ample quantity of additional unsold pieces at that time as well, and the net number of Panama-Pacific commemorative gold dollars eventually distributed totaled 15,000.

Examples of the 1915-S Panama-Pacific gold dollar remained plentiful on the numismatic market for decades thereafter, with B. Max Mehl in particular having a sizable holding. Some of Mehl's coins were later sold in the 1950s to Sol Kaplan, a Cincinnati dealer, through the efforts of Abe Kosoff, who obtained them from Mehl.

1915-S Panama-Pacific Exposition gold quarter eagle: No hoards reported.

1915-S Panama-Pacific Exposition gold $50, octagonal shape: No hoards reported.

1915-S Panama-Pacific Exposition gold $50, round shape: No hoards reported.

1916–1917 McKinley Memorial gold $1: In August and October 1916, a total of 20,026 McKinley commemorative gold dollars were struck at the Philadelphia Mint. In February 1917, a further 10,014 McKinley gold dollars of the same design, but dated 1917, were struck at the same facility.

Of the 30,000 or so pieces, about 20,000—most bearing the date 1916—were sold, and about 10,000 were returned to the Mint for melting. Half or more of the melted coins are believed to have been dated 1917, thus constituting much of the mintage of the latter date; apparently, the public bought very few 1917 coins at the time of their initial offering.

It is believed that Fort Worth, Texas, dealer B. Max Mehl bought about 7,000 of the 1916 coins and 3,000 or so of the 1917. Mehl then sold them to his mail-order clients for many years thereafter. A few other dealers may have purchased lesser quantities from the unsold remainder.

1922 Grant Memorial gold $1: These were made at the Philadelphia Mint in March 1922 in two varieties: 5,000 with a small incuse star in the right field, and 5,016 without this feature. Few details are known about the sales of the pieces, except that B. Max Mehl eventually came into possession of thousands of coins, paying little more than face value for them. Most were wholesaled to dealers, who parceled them out for a long period of time thereafter.

1926 Sesquicentennial of American Independence gold quarter eagle: In a Parke-Bernet sale of June 9, 1976, Lots 49 through 72 featured 71 examples of the 1926 Sesquicentennial of American Independence gold quarter eagle, including a bank-wrapped roll containing 46 pieces that had been found in a safe deposit box.[451]

chapter 18

The Great Treasury Hoard of Silver Dollars

The greatest of all U.S. coin hoards traces its roots to the Bland-Allison Act of February 28, 1878. At the time, silver prices were depressed on the international market, and hard times were being felt in Nevada, Colorado, and other domestic areas of production. So pressed, Western mining interests influenced congressmen to have Uncle Sam support the silver market in a classic case of a political boondoggle.

While I am against boondoggles as much as anyone (outside of elected office in Washington) is, if there have to be such things, then this certainly was a good one!

The aforementioned act was subsequently passed, and beginning in 1878, the Treasury Department was forced to buy tens of millions of ounces of silver each year and coin it into dollar coins. As such, the Philadelphia, Carson City, and San Francisco mints immediately began to turn out silver dollars in unprecedented quantities, and those facilities were joined in this activity by the New Orleans Mint in 1879. However, the pieces produced were neither wanted nor needed for commerce, and so most were put up in cloth bags of 1,000 coins and stored in vaults in the Treasury Building (Washington, D.C.), Federal Reserve offices, the various mints, and even post offices.

The mints would continue their breakneck silver dollar production pace through 1904, as legislative acts followed to add to the supply of silver when the Bland-Allison authorizations ran out. For example: after the Treasury Department began redeeming silver trade dollars in quantity in 1887, the coins were melted down and the silver was used to make Morgan dollars. The Sherman Silver Purchase Act of 1890 also added to the bullion supply, as did other scattered legislation including into the 1900s.

The government, meanwhile, began to run out of storage space. In one heroic instance, Uncle Sam built a vault—looking quite like a Greek temple—in the open courtyard of the Philadelphia Mint and stuffed it with incoming silver scheduled to be made into dollars.

Redeeming trade dollars at the New York Sub-Treasury.

Finally, in 1918 the Pittman Act mandated the melting of many of the long-stored dollars, and 270,232,722 were converted to bullion. The metal was used to coin other denominations and also to ship in international settlements. In 1921, however, there was a hurry-up call for more silver dollars as they were needed as backing for Silver Certificates, and millions more Morgan-design dollars were minted and put into storage.

Then, in December of 1921, the new Peace design was ready; coinage of these commenced,

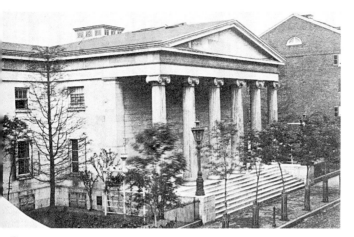

The second Philadelphia Mint coined Morgan dollars from 1878 to 1904 and again in 1921.

The San Francisco Mint coined Morgan dollars from 1878 to 1904 and again in 1921 and Peace dollars intermittently from 1922 to 1935.

The third Philadelphia Mint coined Morgan dollars from 1901 to 1904 and again in 1921 and Peace dollars from 1921 intermittently to 1935.

The New Orleans Mint coined Morgan dollars from 1879 to 1904.

The Carson City Mint coined Morgan dollars from 1878 to 1885 and from 1889 to 1893.

The Denver Mint coined Morgan dollars in 1921 and Peace dollars intermittently from 1922 to 1934.

to be continued intermittently through 1935, and again most went into storage.

Releases from Treasury Holdings

Some Morgan and Peace dollars did see the light of day not terribly long after their minting. Over a period of years in the 1920s and '30s, the Treasury Department would release bags of earlier-dated silver dollars, especially during the Christmas season, when there was a call for the pieces as gifts.

Occasionally, a bag of previously "rare" varieties would be released—such as several different Carson City dollar dates in the 1880s that were released in the 1930s—much to the delight of numismatists. Interestingly, in the early 1920s, the 1889-S Morgan dollar was considered to be a prime rarity (indeed, perhaps the rarest mintmarked issue in the series), but bags were released soon afterward, and it became easily available.

In time, numismatic passion for these pieces came to rest in a gray area. By 1962, the Morgan dollar market was a side branch of numismatics—hardly in the limelight, but not in the shadows either. There was a ready market for these, including in roll (20 coins) and bag quantities. However, they were not mainstream. Most numismatists sought Indian Head and Lincoln cents, Buffalo nickels, Mercury dimes, commemoratives, and other series of the 1800s and 1900s.

In the prime reference on values, the *Guide Book of United States Coins*, the great rarity among silver dollars by 1962 was the 1903-O, which cataloged $1,500 in Uncirculated grade, or more than any other variety. But even if you had $1,500 to spend in 1962, such coins were not to be found; it was believed that only a few Uncirculated pieces existed. When B. Max Mehl issued his Dunham Collection catalog in 1941, he put a frame around the description of the 1903-O rarity—most dealers had never even seen one.

Iron and steel vault set up in the courtyard of the Philadelphia Mint to store silver.

The rarity of this dollar had been recognized for a long time. In July 1925, *The Numismatist* included this letter from Howard R. Newcomb:

> There seems to be something peculiar about the standard silver dollar of 1903 issued from the New Orleans Mint. Although the government records a coinage of 4,450,000 pieces, I have failed to locate, in the last half dozen years, any specimens either in the hands of dealers or collectors, save one in my own collection and one in a prominent collection in Washington, D.C. They seem to be equally scarce even in circulation.

November 1962

Fireworks! In November 1962, from deep in a vault in the Philadelphia Mint that had been sealed in 1929 when a shipment of New Orleans Mint dollars had arrived for storage, a few 1,000-coin bags filled to the brim with sparkling, brilliant 1903-O dollars came forth! And those were followed by even more!

Accompanying these bags were some of two other highly prized rarities, as well: dollars of 1898-O and 1904-O. The "silver rush" was on, a stampede ensued, and within the next two years—until March 1964—the Treasury vaults were emptied of hundreds of millions of silver dollars. Large quantities were also paid out from storage in banks across the country, and in the process, the numismatic hobby underwent vast changes.

Bags of Uncirculated pieces of many dates were found, and there were groups of other issues, isolating only a dozen or so dates and mintmarks that were not found in rolls or larger quantities. In addition, some bags of circulated Liberty Seated silver dollars of mixed dates 1840–1873 were found, as were 1,000 or more heavily bagmarked Mint State 1859-O and 1860-O pieces.

Bags of silver dollars in a vault. In vaults that were not sealed, such bags were audited at intervals. They were tossed around, and no care was given to prevent damage.

More releases came, too, after the Treasury Department took stock of what rare coins were on hand (specifically, in the Treasury Building) later in 1964. Many bags of Carson City dollars were identified, and beginning in 1972 the Gen-

eral Services Administration (GSA) sold these to mail bids. The effort was mainly concentrated in the years up to 1974, but some sales occurred after that time.

Thus was laid the foundation of what today is the most popular of all early coin specialties—Morgan silver dollars. Books have been written about Morgan dollars, dealers have treated them as a prime focus, and even entire conventions have been built around them. Today, the vast majority of Mint State silver dollars of the 1800s that change hands are Morgans; they have captured the excitement and imagination of countless collectors.

To a lesser extent, Peace silver dollars have been in the limelight as well. Overall, an entire subculture of silver dollar collectors, dealers, and writers have become prominent.[452]

Numismatic Knowledge

A few notes on relative rarities before we dive into a breakdown of the issues. Firstly, it is to be remembered that although reading about the Treasury holdings is fascinating, many of the 1,000-coin bags referred to were simply "spent" in an era in which numismatic interest was just a fraction of what it became after 1962. This is particularly true of Peace silver dollars, which attracted very few buyers. Thus, a coin that existed in bag quantities in the 1940s can be quite elusive on the market today.

Also, consider that in the 1970s there was a speculative boom in the market for silver bullion, which multiplied in value to hit $52.35 per ounce on January 21, 1980. The increase—largely precipitated by the Hunt brothers of Texas attempting to corner the silver market—resulted in the melting of countless millions of Morgan and Peace dollars in worn grades, millions more of common varieties in Mint State, and even many other Mint State silver coin issues (notably rolls of Washington quarters from the 1940s onward and Franklin half dollars of the 1948–1963 era, as well as privately produced Franklin Mint medals).

I began gathering data on Treasury releases in the era they happened on a large scale starting in

November 1962. At that time, facts were scarce and rumors and opinions were plentiful. No one knew what would happen next. If bags of 1903-O dollars became common, would bags of 1893-S dollars appear as well? This placed a chill and uncertainty in the marketplace that lasted until early 1964. By that time nearly all silver dollars from the Treasury Department and from banks were in the marketplace, and order was made out of chaos.

After the 1960s, I continued my studies and interviews with dealers, bankers, and others involved in the Treasury release. Extensive details can be found in my two-volume set, *Silver Dollars and Trade Dollars of the United States: A Complete Encyclopedia*, 1993.

Regarding Rarity Today

Unlike the situation of a generation ago, research on the part of many "experts" regarding the rarity of coins is mostly limited to looking at the population reports of PCGS and NGC. Not to be an iconoclast, but much such research is beyond ridiculous for mainstream examples of popularly collected U.S. coins. Skeptical? Here is a prime example of reality:

In 1884, 1,136,000 Morgan dollars were struck at the Carson City Mint. Most of these went into storage at the time. In 1964, the Treasury Department found that 962,638 coins, amounting to 84.7% of the original mintage, were still in the Treasury Building in Washington. These were then turned over to the General Services Administration, which publicized them extensively and, starting in 1972, began offering them in mail bid sales. Eventually all sold, and at nice premiums.

As all of these were sold in the late 1900s to collectors and others who paid a premium and now are worth into three figures, one can logically assume that the vast majority have been certified. Right?

Wrong, far wrong. As of October 8, 2014, PCGS and NGC combined have only certified an 1884-CC silver dollar 153,354 times. I put it this way because this number does not necessarily represent different coins, as there have undoubtedly been many resubmissions.

The bottom line is this: a maximum of 16% of the coins sold at a premium have been certified. The point is to think for yourself in matters involving true rarity. Market levels and demand, and even certified grades, change countless times due to resubmission. Be a smart buyer!

LaVere Redfield

LaVere Redfield—whose name will name may be unfamiliar to many readers, but in the late 1900s it was often mentioned in the hobby—was a character worthy of a novel. He built a fortune in securities, and then moved to Reno, Nevada, where he became involved in real estate. He liked cash and "hard money" and would sometimes attend real estate auctions with grocery bags filled with paper money. At one time, he was jailed for false reporting to the IRS. Much more could be written about him, but for now we focus on his hoard, which came to light after his death in 1974.

In 1976, coins from his estate were auctioned as a single lot with Bowers and Ruddy Galleries (in a consortium with Joel Rettew and David Hall) bidding up to $7,200,000, after which A-Mark bid $7,300,000 and won. The group included 407,000 Morgan and Peace silver dollars, of which 351,259 were Uncirculated. These were later wholesaled into the marketplace, with all of the Carson City coins going to Paramount International Coin Co., of which David W. Akers was president. So as not to disturb the price structure, buyers were pledged to secrecy, but in time much information leaked out.

The quality of the Redfield coins ranged from ordinary upward, but there weren't many gems. Many of the Uncirculated coins were damaged by running them through a mechanical coin counter. Still, the Redfield coins were promoted with great intensity, and for years afterward mention was made of them in catalogs and elsewhere. As such, various mentions will be made in the following section of particularly large holdings of certain issues within the Redfield hoard.

Shining Light on Silver Dollars

Stored: 1800s onward • **Found:** Various times, notably 1962–1964 • **Treasure:** Bags of silver dollars

Here is a summary of Liberty Seated silver dollars (1840–1873), Morgan silver dollars (1878–1921), and Peace silver dollars (1921–1935) together with information about Treasury (mainly) and other hoards of each.[453]

Liberty Seated Silver Dollars

1840–1873 Liberty Seated silver dollars: Somewhat more than 10,000 circulated Liberty Seated dollars came to light during the Treasury release of 1962–1964, these being found late in 1962 and early 1963 in Federal Reserve banks in the Midwest. I had the pleasure of buying bags of unsorted pieces at the time. As they were taken out of bags, I arranged them in piles like poker chips.

Among early Liberty Seated dollars of the Without Motto type (1840–1865), the most plentiful date was 1847. Among dollars of the 1866–1873 years (the With Motto type), the most often seen was 1871. The typical coin graded Very Fine or Extremely Fine and had light gray toning. I recall no Mint State coins at all, nor any extremely worn ones. There were no great rarities such as an 1851 or 1852, but there were a number of scarcer dates such as 1844, 1848, and 1870-CC.

1859-O (circulation strike mintage 360,000): Somewhat more than 1,000 1859-O Liberty Seated dollars were found during the early days of the 1962–1964 Treasury release of silver dollars. Virtually all were heavily bagmarked or abraded.

1860-O (circulation strike mintage 515,000): Up to several thousand coins of this date and mintmark came to light during the 1962–1964 Treasury release of silver dollars. Nearly all were very heavily bagmarked.

Morgan Silver Dollars

1878, 8 Tail Feathers, Morgan silver dollars (circulation strike mintage estimated as 699,300+):[454] Morgan dollars with eight tail feathers were released in quantity in 1878 and in the immediately following years, and never were rare. In 1953, a number of bags came on the market, probably from storage at the Philadelphia Mint. From that point through the early 1960s, additional bags were released. Many came out in Las Vegas in the early 1960s; Philadelphia dealer Harry J. Forman bought several bags at that time.

1878, 7 Over 8 Tail Feathers, a.k.a. Doubled Tail Feathers (circulation strike mintage estimated as 544,000+): As far as I know, 1878, 7 Over 8 Tail Feathers, dollars were primarily issued mixed with the new 7 Tail Feathers dollars and, to a lesser extent, with the older 8 Tail Feathers pieces. As this variety was neither widely known nor widely collected until the 1960s (although scattered listings appeared in the 1950s), there is no numismatic documentation of Treasury releases.

When bags of 1878, 7 Tail Feathers, dollars were issued in the early 1960s, some of these contained 7 Over 8 Tail Feathers coins. In April 1964,

Florida dealer Charles Slade suggested that, based upon his knowledge of coins recently released by the Treasury, the 1878, 7 Over 8 Tail Feathers, was four to five times scarcer than the 1878, 8 Tail Feathers.

1878, 7 Tail Feathers (circulation strike mintage of the variety with parallel top arrow feather, a.k.a. Second Reverse, flat breast to eagle, is estimated as 7,200,000. Variety with slanting top arrow feather, a.k.a. Third Reverse, convex breast to eagle, is estimated as 2,000,000): The 7 Tail Feathers coins were not divided into Second and Third Reverse types until relatively recent times. Thus, in numismatic literature there is no record of when one reverse or the other was released in quantity. It is known that the 7 Tail Feathers dollars in general were distributed by the Treasury Department over a long period of time from the year of striking onward, and it has always been considered common.

A group of bags of this variety came out of the Treasury in 1953, and for a while they were especially plentiful in dealers' hands. Additional quantities of bags were paid out during the 1962–1964 Treasury release, especially during 1963, but no account was kept of them. In comparison to certain other issues, the quantities that came out in the early 1960s were small. Today, in the era of certification, these are usually found as singles.

1878-CC (circulation strike mintage 2,212,000): In the late 1930s, when quantities of Carson City coins were paid out by the Cash Room in the Treasury Building in Washington, D.C., very few 1878-CC dollars were among them. The scarcity of Mint State 1878-CC dollars in the marketplace continued until late 1946 or early 1947, when several bags came out of Washington, and a few others may have been paid out from storage at the San Francisco Mint (in addition to the Treasury Building in Washington, the San Francisco Mint became a storage depot for CC dollars after the Carson City Mint ceased operations).

Then, in 1950, large numbers of 1878-CC Morgan dollars came out of Treasury vaults, and the coins fell in value as they became one of the most plentiful varieties. Many more were paid out by the Treasury through the rest of the early '50s, and bags were handled by dealers on both coasts. Quite a few ended up in the hands of casino owners in Nevada.

By 1954, the 1878-CC was probably the most common Uncirculated dollar variety from the Carson City Mint in dealers' hands. Around that time, though, Treasury dispersals of the variety trickled down to a virtual halt. Perhaps additional bags were deeper in the vaults and thus inaccessible. Whatever the reason, when quantities of other CC dollars started coming out in large numbers in 1955, the 1878-CC was not well represented among them. However, there were some scattered exceptions, such as the 1958 release of 1878-CC bags in Montana.

Probably, well more than 100,000 coins were paid out by the Treasury from the early 1950s through the middle of that decade. I recall that in 1956, it was easy enough to buy a bag, and that around this time, Harry J. Forman bought three bags in Las Vegas.

Years later, during the Treasury release of 1962–1964, 60,993 1878-CC dollars were held back to be dispersed by the General Services Administration beginning in 1972. Note that this figure and other GSA hoard figures given in this text for Morgan silver dollars 1878-CC through 1893-CC do not include 84,165 cull coins and mixed circulated pieces, as well as 311 Carson City pieces of various dates which the GSA did not consider to be salable.[455]

All told, probably about 150,000 to 250,000 1878-CC dollars in Mint State were released in the 1950s, in the early 1960s, and in the GSA hoard.

1878-S (circulation strike mintage 9,774,000): It is believed that as of June 30, 1913, the majority of the original mintage of 1878-S (probably five to six million coins out of a total of 9,774,000), as well as nearly all of the original mintages of 1879-S, 1880-S, 1881-S, and 1882-S, were stored at the San Francisco Mint, to be paid out over a period of decades thereafter.

Especially large quantities were released in the early 1950s—so many that 1878-S coins were one of the most often seen Mint State Morgan dollars for years afterward. Many bags were also distributed later in the 1950s, as well as during the 1962—1964 dispersal. In *The Forecaster*, September 15, 1971, John Kamin gave his opinion that about 7% of the original mintage of 1878-S was released circa 1962–1964, a figure equal to about 600,000 coins.

Of the released coins, I know Harry J. Forman bought 10 bags from Phil Carlino; they probably came to Las Vegas by truck directly from the San Francisco Mint or the San Francisco Federal Reserve Bank. LaVere Redfield held many, too; this date was said to represent the fourth-largest single holding of Morgan silver dollars in his hoard.[456] One estimate placed the Redfield quantity at 5,000 coins and noted that the coins were in lower Mint State grade ranges.

By 1982, Wayne Miller considered the 1878-S to be the *least* available of the 1878–1882 San Francisco Mint Morgan dollar issues in Mint State. However, this was not the case earlier, and he recalled a January 1964 advertisement to buy all Uncirculated silver dollars with the exceptions of the following, which at the time were considered to be the *most* common: 1878-S Morgan, 1921 Morgan, 1922 Peace, and 1923 Peace.

1879 (circulation strike mintage 14,806,000):

As is the case with most other Philadelphia Mint coins in Mint State, the availability of this issue in early years is difficult to ascertain, as most collectors preferred Proofs, while Uncirculated coins—rare or not—were generally ignored.[457] Also, in the early 1900s, more numismatists collected encased postage stamps and Hard Times tokens than did mintmarked Morgan dollars. Regardless, in bank holdings it is evident that the 1879 Philadelphia Mint issue has been common virtually from the year of mintage.

Bags of this issue came on the market from storage at the Philadelphia Mint and possibly from Federal Reserve vaults in the late 1940s.

By 1950 and 1951, Mint State examples were commonly available. The 1879 dollars remained plentiful throughout the decade of the '50s, and the pieces were a common sight in Middle Atlantic-state banks. But as before, little numismatic attention was paid to them.

These and certain other Philadelphia Mint dollars were very annoying to those who enjoyed sorting through bags in bank vaults. Thankfully, by the time the 1962–1964 Treasury dispersal took place, most examples of such common dates were gone.

1879-CC (circulation strike mintage 756,000):

Years after the closing of the Carson City Mint, quantities of 1879-CC dollars were shipped in two directions for storage: westward to vaults in the San Francisco Mint, and eastward to Washington, D.C. Then, in 1942 and 1943, several bags of 1879-CC dollars were paid out at face value in San Francisco. Additionally, the Cash Room in the Treasury Building in Washington distributed at least several thousand Uncirculated 1879-CC dollars in the early- and mid-1950s, but by 1955 and 1956, the largesse stopped.

Sometime around this period, Harry J. Forman bought 500 coins from a bag of 1,000 pieces owned by J. Grove Loser, of Steelton, Pennsylvania, who, like Philadelphia dealer Charlie Dochkus, had a special "in" at the Cash Room.[458] Also, according to California dealer John Skubis, the Treasury unintentionally sold another bag to someone in "Montana or in Seattle," with the coins coming from storage in the San Francisco Mint. Meanwhile, the Treasury kept back slightly more than 4,000 coins, which may have been deep in a vault in the 1950s and thus not known to the numismatically wise people in the Cash Room.

As part of the GSA sales, 4,123 1879-CC dollars were sold. Of these, about 600 are thought to have been the Large CC Over Small CC (popularly, the "Capped CC"), variety. On that topic, the Redfield hoard (first marketed in 1976) was said by some to have had 400 to 500 pieces of the Large CC Over Small CC, nearly all of which were in lower grades and heavily bagmarked. However, in connection with the present book,

David W. Akers, the manager of Paramount at one time and the buyer from A-Mark of *all* the 1879-CC dollars in the Redfield hoard, stated, "The total was less than 100 pieces."[459]

This illustrates the difficulty of getting accurate information. I often find it necessary to interview several different people on a given subject.

1879-O (circulation strike mintage 2,887,000): I have no specific record of early Treasury releases, but quantities of this issue must have filtered onto the market over a long period of time. By the late 1940s and early 1950s, 1879-O Morgan dollars were considered to be on the scarce side and were not among issues *recently* released in mint-sealed bags. This changed in 1957, when an estimated 5 to 10 bags came out and went into the hands of dealers.

In the September 1957 issue of *The Numismatist*, Harry J. Forman advertised that he had 1879-O dollars in quantity. In March 1958, Dan's (Dan Morafka) was retailing 20-coin rolls at $37 each, which was equivalent to $1.85 per coin. Then, multiple bags of 1,000 Uncirculated coins came to light in late autumn 1962, and these with other New Orleans dollars were among the first of the Treasury releases that led to the depletion of the government supply of dollars.

Releases of 1879-O dollars continued well into the summer of 1963. However, the total quantity eventually released did not even remotely compare to such plentiful issues as 1883-O, 1884-O, 1885-O, 1898-O, 1903-O, and 1904-O. For some reason, the 1879-O issues did not get into the numismatic mainstream of bulk investment and dealer sales; perhaps most went to banks in remote areas. In time, the 1879-O once again became scarce in quantity lots. I do know that around 1975, Harry J. Forman bought a bag of 1879-O dollars from the estate of Paul Dinerman of Philadelphia,[460] and that this bag had come from the 1962–1964 Treasury release.

Note that many sealed bags of 1879-O, 1880-O, 1881-O, and 1882-O, dollars were found to have lightly circulated coins that were returned to the New Orleans Mint and put in storage. Wayne

Miller commented: "For reasons which have never been explained, these dollars were then gathered up after they had been lightly circulated, brought back to the Mint, and resealed into Mint bags. Mint sealed bags of these dates often contain over 90% lightly circulated pieces, including a few dollars from the Philadelphia, San Francisco, and Carson City mints, which happened to be circulating in the New Orleans area at the time of recall."[461]

1879-S (circulation strike mintage 9,110,000): The common belief is that most of the original coinage of 1879-S was held at the San Francisco Mint as of June 30, 1913 and was to be dispersed over a period of decades thereafter. Vast quantities of the issue were released from that source in the 1900s, particularly in 1942 (when many dozens, possibly hundreds, of bags were distributed) and the 1950s. Additionally, the Treasury Department released many additional bags in the 1962–1964 era. In *The Forecaster*, September 15, 1971, John Kamin ventured the suggestion that about 10% of the original mintage of 1879-S was released circa 1962–1964, a figure equal to about a million pieces.

Year in and year out, over a long period of time, the 1879-S has been readily available in quantity. Nearly all of these bags contained coins of the Third Reverse type, some Redfield hoard coins being a notable (and rare) exception.

1880 (circulation strike mintage 12,600,000): Bags of 1880 dollars probably came on the market over a long period of time, but there was little or no numismatic interest in them until well into the 1900s. I have been able to find no documentation of mass releases prior to the 1940s, but I do know that early in that decade, bags came on the market from storage in Philadelphia Mint vaults.

Dollars of this date remained plentiful throughout the 1950s, with a particularly large release occurring in 1955.

1880-CC (circulation strike mintage 591,000; net 495,000 after melting at the time of issue): Several bags of Uncirculated 1880-CC dollars were paid out from the Cash Room in the Treasury Building, Washington, D.C., in 1938. Apparently, the Cash Room payouts of this variety trickled to an end sometime in the late 1930s or early 1940s, and after that time the 1880-CC once again became scarce on the market.

Years later, history repeated itself: what occurred in 1938 happened again in 1955. Out of the vault in the Treasury Building in Washington, D.C. came many mint-sealed bags of the 1880-CC issue, and these went into the hands of dealers with the right connections. Steve Ruddel stated that, for starters, about 50 bags (50,000 coins, a popular release quantity for certain CC dollars) were paid out from the Treasury Building in that year.[462]

About 1957, Harry J. Forman bought several bags from Charles J. Dochkus, who had obtained them from the Cash Room. J. Grove Loser was properly fixed with Washington friends, and quite a few bags reached the market through his coin dealership. Quantities of the issue remained plentiful until 1959 and 1960, after which the supply dried up.

Circa 1962–1964, when the Treasury began releasing dollars in quantity, many more 1880-CC dollars came to light, and some additional bags were paid out. Then, in March 1964, the government took stock of the Treasury Building drain and called a halt, deciding to hold back 131,529 1880-CC coins.

These were sold by the GSA beginning in 1972. The GSA sale coins included examples of the 1880-CC, 80 Over 79, variety (a.k.a. Second Reverse coins); in total, these probably represented about 20% of the 1880-CC dollars released.

1880-O (circulation strike mintage 5,305,000):
Little record exists of releases or dealer offerings of quantities of 1880-O dollars. Circa 1946, a few bags were released, and for several years thereafter single coins were more plentiful in dealers' stocks than they had been earlier in the decade. Around 1956 and 1957, additional quantities came out from Treasury holdings, but again, the supply diminished, and 1880-O dollars became scarce in quantity in the early 1960s. The Treasury release

of New Orleans dollars beginning in late autumn 1962 and continuing at least through July 1963 also saw at least a few bags released, but I have located no specific documentation as to quantities, and they again must have been small.

As for later sales, a bag or more of 1880-O dollars came on the market in 1974, according to Wayne Miller in *The Morgan and Peace Dollar Textbook*. Then, in 1977, the Superior Stamp & Coin Company handled the R.D. Donovan hoard of silver dollars, which is said to have contained a bag or more of this issue.

The 1880-O is one of those Morgan dollar issues which does not immediately come to mind when scarce varieties are reviewed, but there aren't many mentioned in old-time releases.

1880-S (circulation strike mintage 8,900,000):
Most hold that, as of the end of June 1913, nearly all of the mintage of the 1880-S was in storage at the San Francisco Mint, from whence distribution was to occur for some years thereafter. As such, dollars of this date were available in quantities at face value from that location through the mid-1950s. In addition, numerous 1,000-coin bags were released by the Treasury from 1962 to 1964; in *The Forecaster*, September 15, 1971, John Kamin estimated that during that period, about 20% of the mintage (or 1,600,000 coins) was released.

The Redfield hoard contained dozens of bags of this issue, grading mostly MS-61 to MS-64 and just a few higher, according to John Highfill; indeed, the 1880-S is said to have represented the second-largest single holding of Morgan dollars in the Redfield property. Bag quantities of 1880-S dollars were also in the Continental-Illinois Bank hoard.[463]

On August 21, 1967, when trading in 1,000-coin bags of silver dollars commenced on the New York Mercantile Exchange, a bag of 1880-S dollars was displayed to watching commodities traders and brokers by coin dealer Charles Ross. The 1880-S dollars were said to be representative of a common date, such as those that would be traded.

In today's era of certified coins and wide distribution, it may be hard for modern readers to realize that in 1967 any well-funded person who wanted to put a few thousand *bags* of silver dollars in a vault would have had no trouble finding them!

1881 (circulation strike mintage 9,163,000): In the early 1950s, the 1881 Philadelphia Mint Morgan dollar was very common in Uncirculated grades in Eastern banks and elsewhere, indicating that many must have been released before that time. In addition, large quantities were dispersed in the late 1950s and early 1960s; in particular, quite a few bags came out in 1955, and after that time they were plentiful in dealers' hands for a while.

1881-CC (circulation strike mintage 296,000): At the time of mintage, probably fewer than 50,000 1881-CC dollars were released. As the years went on, the issue was recognized as scarce, although occasionally a few Uncirculated coins would come to light. For example, in 1938 and 1939, the Cash Room in the Treasury Building in Washington, D.C. parceled out a few Uncirculated coins, but this was not enough to seriously affect the market.

Later, in 1954, the Cash Room paid out several bags of 1881-CC dollars. Steve Ruddel stated that about 50 bags (50,000 coins) were released from the Treasury Building in 1955, and that this was just the beginning of a new wave of releases.[464] In the meantime, the San Francisco Mint shipped bags of 1881-CC dollars to Nevada casinos, where they were recognized as being desirable; many were resold to dealers, but it was also popular for casino operators in the downtown area of Las Vegas to squirrel away at face value "interesting" bags of Morgan dollars as part of their cash reserves. These were called a "stash."[465]

Despite these releases, the 1881-CC was relatively scarce once again by the early 1960s. However, the Treasury Building in Washington still had more, and the additional 147,485 Uncirculated pieces that remained in March 1964 were sold through the General Services Administration beginning in 1972.

1881-O (circulation strike mintage 5,708,000): Throughout the 1950s, a small but steady stream of Uncirculated 1881-O dollars trickled into the market. Then, beginning in late autumn 1962, many additional bags of the issue were released by the Treasury Department, and this dispersal continued through at least the summer of 1963.

Up to that point, 1881-O dollars had been somewhat scarce (although hardly rare) in Mint State preservation. Some mint-sealed bags of *slightly circulated* 1881-O dollars were also released.

1881-S (circulation strike mintage 12,760,000): The San Francisco Mint stored most of the original mintage of 1881-S as of June 30, 1913, the coins to be distributed over the decades that followed. In 1938, many bags were released, and during the 1950s, additional large quantities were paid out from storage in the minting facility.

Still, enough remained in government hands that many more millions of 1881-S dollars were released by the Treasury Department in the early 1960s, especially in 1963. In *The Forecaster*, September 15, 1971, John Kamin gave his opinion that about 50% of the original mintage of 1881-S was released circa 1962–1964, a figure equivalent to more than 6,000,000 coins.

Post-distribution, many thousands of 1881-S dollars were squirreled away by LaVere Redfield, whose estate is said to have had more 1881-S dollars than coins of any other date. Large quantities also went into the vaults of the Continental-Illinois Bank, where they were discovered by Chicago dealer Ed Milas. He was in the right place at the right time when the financial institution ran into trouble and had to liquidate its 1,500,000 silver dollars, many of which were of the 1881-S issue.

In later years, still more bags came to light. According to John J. Ford Jr., Harry J. Forman brought to him 126 bags (126,000 coins) of this date. Many were prooflike and deeply mirrored gems. Ford, in an interview on May 12, 1992, recalled that he handled 140 bags totally of 1881-S dollars.

Today the 1881-S dollar stands as the single most available Morgan silver dollar in gem Mint State preservation. Thus, it is an excellent "introductory coin" for anyone with a beginning interest in the series. However, the buyer is apt to be spoiled by the 1881-S, for the typical coin is very well struck and extremely attractive, not at all representative of many other issues in the series—for example, most New Orleans Mint coins are lightly struck.

1882 (circulation strike mintage 11,100,000): Mint State coins of this issue have been common for many years, even before the Treasury release of 1962–1964. Many of this date were stored at the Philadelphia Mint and also by the Federal Reserve System.

1882-CC (circulation strike mintage 1,133,000): For some time after striking, the Cash Room in the Treasury Building in Washington had a huge quantity of 1882-CC dollars. These were released sparingly over a period of time.

A sort of roller coaster followed. In 1938 and 1939, larger quantities became available at face value, but during the 1940s few 1882-CC dollars were released by the Treasury, and the price in the numismatic market crept up. Then, in 1955 bags came out from two storage areas: the San Francisco Mint and the Treasury Building in Washington. Steve Ruddel stated that about 50 bags (50,000 coins) were released from the Treasury Building in 1955, and that many more came out later.[466]

Later, the 1962–1964 Treasury releases apparently included some bags of 1882-CC, but probably not many, as when the government shut the floodgates of dollar distribution after those releases, 605,029 Uncirculated 1882-CC dollars—more than half the original mintage—remained on hand! These were subsequently sold through a series of auctions staged by the General Services Administration.

Today, Morgan dollars of 1882-CC, 1883-CC, and 1884-CC are the most often seen in GSA-sealed black plastic holders.

1882-O (circulation strike mintage 6,090,000): During the 1950s, every now and then a mint-sealed bag of 1882-O dollars would come on the market through some lucky finder who picked it up at a bank. Although this date was not in the common category at the time, it was not rare either.

Then, beginning in late autumn 1962, the floodgates opened, and hundreds of thousands of 1882-O dollars poured out into the market. When the dust settled early in 1963, a few months later, the 1882-O was solidly entrenched as one of the most common issues in the series. Distribution of 1882-O continued throughout most of 1963, until at least the autumn. Some mint-sealed bags of *slightly circulated* 1882-O dollars were also released.

1882-O, O Over S (circulation strike mintage is unknown; probably hundreds of thousands): These overmintmark coins were released as a small part of Treasury dispersals of 1882-O. No specific hoards reported.

1882-S (circulation strike mintage 9,250,000): The majority of the original coinage of 1882-S, supposedly to be paid out over a few decades, was in storage at the San Francisco Mint as of the end of June 1913. Later, some of these were transferred to the Treasury Building in Washington, D.C. However, enough coins dribbled onto the market over a period of years that 1882-S was never considered to be a rarity in Mint State.

Case in point: during the 1926 convention of the American Numismatic Association in Washington, D.C., numerous attendees were delighted to obtain at face value Uncirculated 1882-S dollars which were being paid out at the Cash Room of the Treasury Building in the same city. Also, for many years thereafter—through at least the early 1950s—1882-S dollars were available at face value from the San Francisco Mint.

Then, probably well more than a million were released by the Treasury Department in the 1962–1964 release, especially in 1963. In *The Forecaster*, September 15, 1971, John Kamin suggested that about 10% of the original mintage of 1882-S (about a million coins) was released in this period.

Post-release, dollars of the 1882-S issue were among the most abundant varieties in the Redfield and Continental-Illinois Bank hoards.

1883 (circulation strike mintage 12,290,000): The 1883 Morgan dollar was one of the most common dates seen in bag quantities in the early 1950s. Millions were released in the early 1960s as well. The Continental-Illinois Bank hoard held many, too: 12,000 to 15,000, to be more precise, including many high grade examples.

1883-CC (circulation strike mintage 1,204,000): A vast reserve of 1883-CC dollars was stored in the Treasury Building in Washington, D.C. From this source, examples trickled out over a period of years, with a significant release occurring in 1938 and 1939. Additionally, many bags were given out at face value in the 1950s, when dealers such as Charles J. Dochkus sought to buy them, but demand was such that the market could only absorb limited quantities.

Steve Ruddel stated that about 50 bags (50,000 coins) were released from the Treasury Building in 1955, and that at least that many were released of all other CC Mint Morgan dollars except 1879-CC, 1889-CC, and 1893-CC.[467] However,

by the late 1950s, the Treasury stopped paying them out. The subsequent silver dollar releases of the early 1960s included very few 1883-CC dollars.

As it turns out, a quantity amounting to 755,518 coins, or more than 62% of the original mintage, was held back. These were marketed by the General Services Administration beginning in 1972.

1883-O (circulation strike mintage 8,725,000): The 1883-O, minted in large quantities, was never rare in Mint State on the numismatic market. This date was released in bags of 1,000 coins as long ago as 1938 from the Treasury Building in Washington, D.C. That facility had also earlier paid out small quantities of this date; dealer John Zug was among those who obtained these for face value in the early 1930s.

Bags were distributed at later intervals as well, including a major release in 1952, followed by occasional bags until about 1957. Then, many more bags were released from a sealed vault in the Philadelphia Mint beginning in late autumn 1962, and this continued well into 1963. Some of the latter found their way to the Continental-Illinois Bank and were sold on the coin market about 15 years later.

As a result of these many large releases, today the 1883-O is very common in Mint State. The 1883-O, 1884-O, and 1885-O constituted the bulk of approximately 10 million coins released from the previously noted vault in the Philadelphia Mint. My estimate is that the breakdown of these three dates is about as follows: 1883-O: 1,500,000 to 2,500,000 coins; 1884-O: 2,500,000 to 4,000,000 coins; and 1885-O: 2,000,000 to 3,500,000 coins. Of course, these coins are in addition to hoard coins released from other vaults earlier.

While many 1883-O dollars were saved by the public, investors, and collectors, this date was common enough that other coins of the issue—possibly amounting to millions of pieces in total—went into circulation. Many of these were melted in the late 1970s and early 1980s during the sharp increase in silver bullion prices; during that period, common-date silver dollars found a more ready market to be melted down for bullion than they did as collectors' items on the numismatic market. Indeed, when silver hit $52.35 per ounce on January 21, 1980—in large part due to the Hunt brothers in Texas attempting to corner the market—melting could turn a tidy profit.

1883-S (circulation strike mintage 6,250,000): The 1883-S dollar in Mint State is one of the more curious Morgan dollars from a rarity and price history viewpoint. In the early 1900s, it was considered to be a common San Francisco issue. Single coins, rolls, and bags dribbled out from storage in the San Francisco Mint for many years.

In 1950, a few bags were released; John Skubis was known to have at least one bag of 1883-S in that decade, possibly more. Over time, such bags were broken up, and virtually every dealer in Morgan dollars had a good supply, often roll quantities, during that decade.

By the mid-1960s, most quantities of 1883-S dollars in dealers' stocks had been distributed, but singles abounded on the market. One by one, though, these singles found homes, and during the 1970s many collectors came to view the 1883-S as rare. Meanwhile, silver dollar hoarder LaVere Redfield had a full bag of 1,000 coins plus two additional specimens;[468] these coins were retailed by Paramount after the Redfield coins were auctioned in 1976. Today, most of the Redfield coins would grade in the MS-60 to MS-63 range.

Today, the 1883-S is considered to be among the more elusive San Francisco issues of the early years. Without doubt, and having no close challengers, the 1883-S is far rarer in Mint State than any other San Francisco Mint Morgan dollar from 1878 to 1883.

1884 (circulation strike mintage 14,070,000): Morgan dollars dated 1884 have been common for decades. The Treasury releases each year in the 1940s and 1950s, particularly at Christmas time when the holiday demand called for silver dollars for use as gifts, often contained bags of this and other Philadelphia Mint dates from 1878 through 1887. A particularly large release occurred in December 1954.

Later, the Treasury release of 1962–1964 saw additional quantities of the 1884 (and many other) Philadelphia Mint issue brought out from storage in government vaults. However, the number of bags of 1884 dollars released was small in comparison to certain New Orleans and San Francisco issues. Apparently, most 1884 dollars were distributed in the 1950s, and by the mid-1960s they were somewhat scarce in a comparative sense.

Sometime in the 1960s, 12 to 15 bags of 1884 dollars were added to the reserves of the Continental-Illinois Bank; these came to light about 15 years later.

1884-CC (circulation strike mintage 1,136,000): The 1884-CC Morgan dollar is one of the most remarkable coins in the annals of silver dollar history. In 1938, bags of this date were released, and the Cash Room in the Treasury Department paid out a steady stream of 1,000-coin bags during the 1950s. Dealer Steve Ruddel stated that about 50 bags (50,000 coins) were distributed from the Treasury Building in 1955.[469]

This being said, these earlier dispersals must not have amounted to much, nor could many 1884-CC coins have been included in the Treasury release of 1962–1964. This is because, out of the original production amounted to 1,136,000 pieces, 962,638 coins—amounting to 84.7% of the original mintage—were still in the hands of the Treasury Department after March 1964, when a halt was called to the great release that began in late autumn 1962.

Many of these remaining coins were sold by the General Services Administration through that organization's sales starting in 1972. Those coins would have gone primarily into the hands of numismatists and collectors, meaning most would continue to be preserved in their Uncirculated state. Today, the total number of Uncirculated 1884-CC dollars in existence is not known with precision, but it is undoubtedly more than a million; no wonder that *circulated* coins are rare!

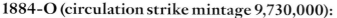

1884-O (circulation strike mintage 9,730,000): Mint-sealed bags of 1884-O Morgan dollars were released from storage in the Treasury Building in Washington, D.C. in 1933, 1934, 1938, and again in the 1950s. But these dispersals were insignificant compared to the veritable deluge of 1884-O dollars that spewed forth from storage in the Philadelphia Mint beginning in late autumn 1962. Some from the that distribution later showed up in the memorable hoard owned by the Continental-Illinois Bank.

The bulk of the approximately 10 million coins released from that vault in the Philadelphia Mint were of 1883-O, 1884-O, and 1885-O dates. While many went into the hands of investors, hoarders, and collectors, others—possibly amounting to millions of pieces in total—went into circulation and then became targets for melting in the late 1970s during the run-up in silver bullion prices.

1884-S (circulation strike mintage 3,200,000): In 1926, many coins of this issue were released to banks from storage at the San Francisco Mint. Additionally, limited numbers of this issue dribbled out from storage in the Treasury Building in Washington, D.C. as early as the early 1930s, and that continued through at least the very early 1950s. But if any full bags were paid out during this span, I have not learned of the situation.

Eventually, later in the 1950s, a few bags came out from storage at the Treasury. In 1957 and 1958, and possibly for a year or two later, additional quantities were paid out by this source. I have found no records of mint-sealed bags of 1884-S dollars changing hands on the numismatic market since, but as late as 1964, rolls of 20 Uncirculated coins were being advertised. By that time, Treasury holdings had long since been exhausted.

1885 (circulation strike mintage 17,785,000): Large quantities of Philadelphia Mint 1885 Morgan dollars were released by the Treasury Department from the 1930s through the 1950s, particularly in 1954, followed by many more

bags in the early 1960s. Single coins are very common today.

1885-CC (circulation strike mintage 228,000): Uncirculated 1885-CC dollars were considered to be very rare until the 1930s, when John Zug (of Bowie, Maryland) and a few others obtained small quantities from the Cash Room in the Treasury Building in Washington. Additionally, in 1941 and 1942, several bags were released, after which the supply seemed to dry up.

Then, in 1955, multiple bags came out of hiding in the Treasury Building, and 1885-CC dollars became common on the market. In 1958, even more bags were released in Montana; these were probably from storage at the San Francisco Mint or one of the Federal Reserve facilities. From that point, modest quantities of Uncirculated 1885-CC were turned loose during the Treasury dispersals of 1962–1964.

At the end of the Treasury release, 148,285 were held back for later sale by the General Services Administration. These were offered by the General Services Administration beginning in 1972. All but 31,569 sold, and those went in the final 1980 sale.

Note that earlier conventional wisdom had it that the Redfield hoard may have contained as many as 1,000 coins of this issue, but in connection with the present book, David W. Akers, former manager of Paramount (the firm that bought certain hoard coins from A-Mark), stated that there were far fewer than that.[470]

1885-O (circulation strike mintage 9,185,000): Following the closing of the New Orleans Mint in 1909, quantities of 1885-O dollars were shipped to the Treasury Building in Washington, D.C. and the Philadelphia Mint for long-term storage. Pieces of this issue began to be paid out from the Washington vault by the early 1930s, and they were released multiple-bag quantities in 1938, 1953, 1954, and 1957.

Then, in late autumn 1962 and continuing into early 1963, vast quantities (probably amounting to millions of coins) were released from storage at the Philadelphia Mint. Many of those ended up in the in the Continental-Illinois Bank hoard, while many others went into circulation and were subsequently melted in the late 1970s during the run-up in silver bullion prices; this fate befell many Treasury hoard dollars that were not considered to be rare at the time.

1885-S (circulation strike mintage 1,497,000): Quantities of 1885-S dollars were stored at the San Francisco Mint during the early part of the 1900s, but few people knew it. However, soon after World War II, the facility paid out a lot of early Morgan dollars, 1885-S pieces among them. From that point, awareness of the availability of dollars at the San Francisco Mint spread, and West Coast dealers tapped this source from time to time. By 1955, the 1885-S was sufficiently common in numismatic circles that bags had little premium value, and thus the supply of 1885-S dollars was steady for the next two or three years.

During the Treasury release of 1962–1964 (especially in 1963), more bags of 1885-S dollars were paid out, but I have no specific record of them. Steve Ruddel noted that 1885-S was among the hoard coins coming out in the early 1960s, but did not mention the quantities involved.[471] I suspect that most later quantity offerings of quantities of these coins—which seem to have been rolls rather than bags—were mainly left over from San Francisco Mint payouts of the mid-1950s.

In the years that followed the Treasury release, the 1885-S remained plentiful, but it was scarce in relation to some of the Morgan dollar varieties that had flooded the market in the early 1960s due to said dispersal. Writing in *The Morgan and Peace Dollar Textbook* in 1982, Wayne Miller stated this: "The 1885-S is still available in large quantities." However, he only told of two groups of 15 rolls each, or 600 coins—hardly a "large quantity" in comparison to such issues as 1879-S, 1880-S, 1881-S, etc., which commonly traded in bags.

Miller also gave details of a 1978 hoard of 35 to 40 rolls (700 to 800 coins), virtually all of which were of mediocre quality. "Not one coin could be called a gem."

1886 (circulation strike mintage 19,963,000): Quantities of 1886 dollars were released by the Treasury over a long period of years, with a large number coming out in 1951, 1952, and, especially, December 1954. During that period, though, anyone finding a $1,000 bag of 1886 dollars would "throw it back" to the bank, like a fisherman tossing back an undersized trout; bags of these and most other early Philadelphia Mint Morgan dollars were not wanted, even for face value. If a buyer could be found—and I remember the situation well—a good wholesale price would be only a slight amount over face value.

In the release of 1962–1964, the Treasury set free still more bags, some of which ended up in the coffers of the Continental-Illinois Bank. However, due to the melting of many millions of silver dollars in the bullion run-up of the late 1970s, Mint State coins are less plentiful today than hoard releases might indicate.

1886-O (circulation strike mintage 10,710,000): Among Morgan dollars, the 1886-O is somewhat of an anomaly. The mintage figure of 10,710,000 circulation strikes is overwhelming and even puts in the shade such common coins as the 1883-O, 1884-O, and 1885-O. By all rights, like these other coins, a million or more 1886-O dollars should have come to light in the great Treasury release of 1962–1964, and today a beautiful MS-65 1886-O should be in every collection. But this is not the case, and what *did* happen isn't known, at least not with certainty.

At or near the beginning of the 1900s, probably a few million coins of this issue—say 2,000,000 to 4,000,000—were placed into circulation and saw commercial use. Probably millions of other coins—perhaps as many as 6,000,000 to 8,000,000 pieces—went to the melting pot under the terms of the 1918 Pittman Act. Whatever happened, apparently no more than a few bags dribbled onto the market in the 1940s and 1950s.

In the Treasury release of 1962–1964, probably a few bags came out, but I have obtained no specific record of them. Harry J. Forman recalled that he never had an intact bag of 1886-O dollars, but he did find several hundred "minimum Uncirculated" coins in a bag containing various dates.

1886-S (circulation strike mintage 750,000): Apparently, very few pieces of this issue were released into circulation near the time of striking. It is believed that hundreds of thousands were melted under the 1918 Pittman Act provisions, although it is not possible to verify this today. Whatever the case, some additional coins were released into circulation in the mid-1920s from storage at the San Francisco Mint.

Beginning about 1942, and lasting until the late 1950s, bags were available at face value, but there were few takers. John Skubis, for one, recalls turning such offerings back for face value. Interestingly, there was a decent market for singles and a slight market for rolls, but apparently those who would have wanted bags—such as Nevada casino operators—could get them at face value without going through a coin dealer.

Note that in addition to the coins paid out by the San Francisco Mint, scattered bags were released by banks in the West (including some in Montana in 1956), and the 1962–1964 Treasury release included some 1886-S dollars (but probably not many).

In a commentary for this book, David W. Akers stated that there were 10 to 12 bags (10,000 to 12,000 coins) in the Redfield estate with "quite a few gem MS-64 and MS-65 coins."[472] Most Redfield coins were placed in red plastic holders and were optimistically graded to be mostly sold to investors; this was in an era before third-party certification.

1887, 7 Over 6 (circulation strike mintage unknown; part of 1887 mintage): No specific hoards have been recorded of the 1887, 7 Over 6, variety, except as a part of Treasury releases of dollars dated 1887 (a common date).

1887 (circulation strike mintage 20,290,000): The 1887 dollar was plentiful years ago, and additional Treasury releases from coins stored at the Philadelphia Mint took place in 1938, the 1940s, the 1950s (particularly in December 1954),

and the early 1960s. And even then, one lot of 100 bags existed as late as 1978.

The Continental-Illinois Bank hoard, which was estimated to contain as many as 1,000 original bags of brilliant Uncirculated dollars plus an estimated 500 bags of circulated coins (1,500,000 coins in total), included quantities of Mint State 1887 Morgans. The 1887 may have been, as Wayne Miller has written, the most plentiful Morgan dollar in terms of 1,000-coin bags still in existence by the early 1980s.

1887-O, 7 Over 6 (circulation strike mintage unknown; part of 1887-O): A group of 400 of these pieces was sold at the 1977 ANA convention and, possibly, was part of the 1962–1964 Treasury distribution of 1887-O dollars. This variety was not tracked in the earlier days, as it was not well known until the late 1900s.

1887-O (circulation strike mintage 11,550,000): On the coin market, the 1887-O Morgan dollar seems to have always been available in Mint State, as releases of mint-sealed bags are known to have occurred in 1938, 1953, 1957, and probably occurred in a few other years as well. Additionally, many pieces of the issue turned up in the 1962 emptying of the hoard of 10 million New Orleans coins from a sealed vault in Philadelphia (though it was not one of the more plentiful dates, comparatively). Still more bags from other Treasury holdings were released by the government as late as March 1964.

Reminiscing in *The Comprehensive U.S. Silver Dollar Encyclopedia*, Dean Tavenner said that he obtained one bag of prooflike 1887-O dollars with bagmarks in April 1964, just at the time his bank in Deer Lodge, Montana, was running out of silver dollars at face value. He also noted that Extremely Fine and About Uncirculated 1887-O dollars, as well as New Orleans dollars of certain other dates, were released in quantity in mint-sewn bags.

1887-S (circulation strike mintage 1,771,000): Apparently, many 1887-S dollars were put into circulation in the late 1800s, after which undistributed quantities remained in storage at the San Francisco Mint. I have located no record of any quantity of these dollars being released during the early 1900s, but beginning in late 1941 or early 1942, mint-sealed bags of 1,000 coins each were paid out at face value.

From that point until the early 1950s, bags continued to be available at face value from the Mint. However, in the mid-1950s, quantities began to be scarce, and releases slowed dramatically. An occasional bag or two must have come to light, for roll quantities remained plentiful until the end of the decade. But after the late 1950s the supply of 1887-S in quantity seems to have dried up almost entirely, and there is no record of the issue being included in the massive Treasury releases of 1962–1964 (although it is possible some may have been).

LaVere Redfield obtained an estimated 5 to 10 bags of this date, probably from Nevada casinos or from California dealers who had acquired them in the 1950s. Upon dispersal of the Redfield estate, these coins were found to be of "high quality" (per Wayne Miller's comment in his *Morgan and Peace Dollar Textbook*).

1888 (circulation strike mintage 19,183,000): As is the case with a number of other Philadelphia Mint issues, the 1888 was not considered to be a common coin in Mint State until the 1950s. Apparently, quantities were released into circulation at or near the time of mintage, and these quickly became worn. After that, many went into storage, while probably millions of others were undoubtedly melted under the 1918 Pittman Act.

Then, in the mid-1950s, 1888 dollars were released in quantity, probably by the millions. Few were saved by collectors, investors, or dealers, and most eventually ended up in mixed bags of Morgan dollars. The quantities were so vast that even though most bags were broken up, individual coins remained very common.

Finally, even more 1888 dollars were paid out during the great Treasury release of 1962–1964. In fact, bags of 1888 dollars were still being shipped by the Federal Reserve in March 1964,

the last month that silver dollars were available in quantity at face value from the government.

1888-O (circulation strike mintage 12,150,000): Like many of its sister New Orleans issues, the 1888-O dollars dribbled out of government storage and into the coin market in small quantities in 1946 and during the 1950s, especially from about 1955 to 1958. Some of these came from the Treasury Building in Washington, D.C., where they had been stored since the New Orleans Mint ceased operations.

Then, in 1962–1964, many more 1888-O dollars were released from a long-stored cache in a sealed vault at the Philadelphia Mint. This additional quantity may have amounted to more than 100,000 coins; some suggested that it might be many hundreds of thousands, if not a million or more.

As an example of the quantities of 1888-O dollars on the market for a decade after the Treasury release, Wayne Miller told of buying nine original mint sealed bags of 1888-O dollars in 1971 and examining 16 additional bags in the same six-week period, amounting to a total of 25,000 coins.

Then again, John V. Kamin wrote the following concerning quantities of 1888-O dollars:

"I disagree with Wayne Miller on how many bags of these came out. I was searching for quantity lots of 1888-O all during the 1960s, and only encountered a couple of bags. I don't know of any that came out after early 1964. 1888-O was always considered a premium date of silver dollars, as evidenced by the 1963 *Guide Book*, where it is listed at $6.50 in BU condition, while most other 'common date' silver dollars are listed at much lower prices, including some scarcer dates. I will be most pleased if 1888-O is considered a common date by Wayne Miller, and other dealers, for many more years, giving my friends a chance to buy up any bags that come on the market. I think 1888-O is at least 300 times scarcer than bags of 1883-O, 1884-O, 1885-O, and similar 'common date' bags!"[473]

Comments such as the preceding indicate that opinions about hoard quantities sometimes differ widely. As it is, I consider myself fortunate that I was present and participated in the silver dollar releases from the mid-1950s onward and later interviewed some of the largest "players" in the market.

1888-S (circulation strike mintage 657,000): The market and hoard history of the 1888-S bears a close resemblance to that of its cousin coin, the 1887-S. Like the 1887-S, the 1888-S was considered to be quite scarce in Mint State on the numismatic market until bags were released from storage in the San Francisco Mint in 1942. From that point until the mid-1950s, quantities could be obtained for face value from that source.

In 1956, more bags were released in Montana, but dealer and collector interest was limited and investor interest was nil. Most that were paid out went to Nevada casinos or to banks, where they were put into circulation and quickly descended the grading ladder to About Uncirculated or lower levels.

After the mid-1950s, the supply seems to have quickly dried up. The massive Treasury releases of 1962–1964 added few if any quantities to the supply of Mint State coins in numismatic and investment circles, although this is contrary to the conventional wisdom that many bags came out at that time.

The Redfield hoard (distributed in 1976) is said to have had 5 to 10 bags, including thousands of proof-like coins. Today, singles are easy enough to find.

1889 (circulation strike mintage 21,726,000): The story of the 1889 dollar echoes that of the 1888 piece and certain other Philadelphia Mint Morgan dollar issues of the 1880s. Many were placed into circulation in or near the time of mintage, after which quantities were relegated to storage, and it is likely that millions were then melted under the 1918 Pittman Act.

Occasional mint-sealed bags were paid out from those stored over a period of years—not enough that Mint State coins became common, but a sufficient quantity that 1889-dated dollars

never became expensive either. A few bags were released in the postwar market of the late 1940s.

Beginning about December 1954, large numbers of bags containing millions of coins were dispersed through banks, mainly in the East. Collectors, dealers, and what few investors there were looked at the gargantuan mintage figure and ignored the coins. Additional quantities continued to be paid out for a long time, including during the 1962–1964 Treasury releases; doubtless, many of these went to bullion melting pots in the heady silver bullion market of the late 1970s.

1889-CC (circulation strike mintage 350,000): When Carson City silver dollars were being paid out from the Cash Room in the Treasury Department in Washington, many thousands of all issues 1878–1893 were distributed—*except* for 1889-CC. Apparently, only a few single coins and rolls were given out, some of them as early as 1933 and 1934. By the 1950s, possibly only a few hundred coins remained on hand at the Cash Room. I have found no record of bags being distributed from Washington during that decade or any time later, and only *one* solitary coin was left in the Treasury when the government decided to hold back CC dollars after payouts were halted in March 1964!

It is probably the case that more 1889-CC dollars were stored at the San Francisco Mint and/or in Federal Reserve stocks in the West than at the Treasury Building. In 1925 and 1926, quantities of 1889-CC pieces were paid out at face value from storage at the San Francisco Mint. Bags that came to light in the 1950s are all from the San Francisco Mint vaults, as far as I know. Additionally, a bag of 1,000 pieces was released in Montana in the 1950s, and that was followed by another in the early 1960s. Apparently, the first bag contained many heavily marked coins of a quality that today would be called AU-55 or 58.

Harry Warner of Mill Valley, California, told Walter H. Breen that he once owned a bag of 1,000 coins of this issue. Ben Stack told Harry J. Forman that he bought two bags by advertising in 1954 in the *Las Vegas Sun*, and another was acquired in this way or by buying it separately.[474] One of these bags went to Irving Davidoff, owner of the Klondyke Coin Exchange in New York City; another was dispersed by the roll; the third was still owned by Ben Stack as of February 1976, for he offered it to me at that time. At the time the value was about $50 per coin, or $50,000 for a bag. Considering that is around the *Guide Book* price for a decent Mint State coin now, I should have bought it!

Today, individual 1889-CC dollars are very elusive in proportion to the demand for them, but likely a thousand or more are still in hiding. The issue is recognized as a prime rarity, and individual Mint State coins are few and far between on the open market.

1889-O (circulation strike mintage 11,875,000): Bags of 1889-O dollars were released over a period of time in later years, beginning at least as early as 1938 and continuing in small numbers to the mid-1950s. These pieces, coming from vaults in the Treasury Building in Washington, D.C., attracted little attention. The 1962–1964 Treasury release of specimens stored in a sealed vault in the Philadelphia Mint included 1889-O dollars, but it was not one of the more plentiful dates.

Harry J. Forman had at least one Treasury bag in 1962. Reminiscing in *The Comprehensive Silver Dollar Encyclopedia*, Dean Tavenner said that he obtained one bag of 1888-O dollars in April 1964, just as his bank in Deer Lodge, Montana, was running out of silver dollars to pass out at face value.

John Highfill reported having bags of this date and finding that 80% to 90% of the coins were flatly struck. Maurice Rosen's experience was similar; he told of handling bags of this issue, mostly consisting of MS-60 to MS-62 pieces and all of them lightly struck.

A bag of 1,000 pieces came on the market from Pennsylvania in 1979. John Love once had a bag of 1889-O dollars, mostly prooflike, in the same decade.

1889-S (circulation strike mintage 700,000): Until at least the early 1920s, the 1889-S was considered to be the rarest of all Morgan dollars, outranking such issues as the 1889-CC, 1892-S, 1893-S, and the Proof-only 1895. Most old-time collections lacked an example in any grade. This was largely because, at the time of minting, nearly all 1889-S dollars went into storage, mostly at the San Francisco Mint.

Finally, a few bags broke on the market in 1937, and many in the early 1940s, after which the 1889-S became common. Even during the early 1950s, quantities were available for face value at the San Francisco Mint. The sum of these releases is not known, but I imagine that somewhere on the order of 50,000 to 100,000 coins went into the hands of dealers, investors, collectors, casino owners, and others who saved them.

Today the 1889-S occupies a middle ground in the Morgan dollar series. With its relatively low mintage, it is one of the scarcer San Francisco Morgan dollars in Mint State, but it is hardly rare. The Redfield hoard (1976) is said to have contained several thousand Mint State coins, most of which were heavily bagmarked.

1890 (circulation strike mintage 16,802,000): Uncirculated 1890 dollars were available on the numismatic market virtually from the time of striking. Quantities were available in 1941 and 1942, the mid-1950s, and after that time, continuing through the great Treasury release of 1962–1964—and they were ignored by just about everyone. When it came to stashing away a few rolls or bags for investment, most hoarders seemed to prefer coins with mintmarks.

The bag quantities released by the Treasury in the 1950s and 1960s mostly consisted of coins in lower Mint State grades. Wayne Miller reported that many of these were coated with a dark, greasy substance that did not hurt the coins, but which had to be carefully removed with a solvent. This "vault grime" was common on bank-stored bags of circulated dollars and, in Europe, on quantities of double eagles hidden away in vaults. Acetone, which must be used with care, is sometimes used as the solvent for cleaning.

1890-CC (circulation strike mintage 2,309,041): After the Carson City Mint closed down its coinage facilities, quantities of undistributed dollars, including 1890-CC pieces, remained there. Later, many bags were shipped to the San Francisco Mint and to the Treasury Building in Washington, D.C., for storage.

In 1942 and 1943, the San Francisco Mint paid out many of these bags of 1890-CC dollars at face value. Probably two or three bags went to dealers and collectors at the time, and the rest went into circulation in the West, particularly in Nevada. Meanwhile, the Treasury was releasing bags as early as the early 1930s, and hundreds of these coins were snapped up by dealers and collectors. In 1941 and 1942, the Treasury released additional bags, after which the payouts slowed for the rest of the decade.

Then, in the early and mid-1950s, many more bags of Uncirculated 1890-CC dollars were released by the Treasury at face value to dealers with connections; a familiar story by now. Steve Ruddel, who was one of the most active dealers in Morgan dollars in quantity, stated that about 50 bags (50,000 coins) were released from the Treasury Building in 1955, and this was only the beginning of such dispersals.[475] Around the same time, more bags of these pieces were given out from storage in the San Francisco Mint—so in effect, there was a distribution on both coasts.

By 1956 and 1957, 1890-CC coins they were becoming scarce (though Harry J. Forman handled at least 10 bags during this time). The Treasury stock dwindling, an order was given in the late 1950s to stop paying them out. Thus, it is unlikely that many 1890-CC coins were involved during the 1962–1964 Treasury release of dollars. In 1964, when the Treasury took stock of its remaining holdings, only 3,949 1890-CC dollars

remained. These were sold in the 1970s by the General Services Administration. Outside of government distribution, the Redfield hoard is said to have contained about two bags, including many mirrorlike coins.

1890-O (circulation strike mintage 10,701,000): Probably at least 500,000 of these, if not far more, were held by the Treasury (and stored in Philadelphia) until the 1960s, and released during the 1962–1964 era. Earlier, 1890-O dollars had been paid out over a long period of decades, including an especially large release occurring in 1953 and 1954.

1890-S (circulation strike mintage 8,230,373): Quantities of 1890-S dollars were placed into circulation at or near the time of mintage. Many others were stored in the San Francisco Mint, and several million or more other examples probably were melted under the terms of the 1918 Pittman Act.

From among those coins stored, occasional bags were released over a long period of years. As a result, the 1890-S is one of the San Francisco Mint issues that has never been rare in Mint State—quite a contrast to its 1889-S sibling. Then, in the 1940s and 1950s, still more bags of the pieces were paid out.

The Redfield hoard (distributed 1976) was said to have contained 26 bags,[476] mostly MS-60 to 62 in grade, probably obtained from storage at the San Francisco Mint.

1891 (circulation strike mintage 8,693,556): The Federal Reserve released many bags of these in 1954 and 1955 and again in the late 1950s and very early 1960s (before the massive releases of 1962–1964). There were so many distributed that Harry J. Forman reported that virtually every bank in Philadelphia was loaded with them, and they were by far the most common dollar date available.

This being said, the 1891 dollar was not represented in quantity among the dollars dispersed in the Treasury distribution of 1962–1964. In a reversal of circumstances, the supply had been absorbed by the public and investors by the mid-1960s, and the 1891 was no longer considered to be among the more common dates.

1891-CC (circulation strike mintage 1,618,000): In the early 1900s, large quantities of Carson City dollars of the 1891 date were shipped to the San Francisco Mint for storage. Many bags from this group were paid out at face value in 1925, 1926, and the early 1940s (particularly in 1942). In fact, so many were released in the 1940s that silver dollar dealer specialists such as Norman Shultz stopped buying them, and by late 1942, the 1891-CC dollar was by far the commonest Carson City issue in collectors' and dealers' hands in Mint State.

The coins continued to be paid out at face value to dealers and others, and also shipped as part of Nevada casino coins, in the 1950s. Adding to the glut, bags of 1891-CC dollars were also released from the Cash Room in the Treasury Building—another recipient of stored coins at the closing of the Carson City Mint—in the 1950s. The quantities are not known, but dozens of bags were involved. Steve Ruddel stated that about 50 bags (50,000 coins) were released from the Treasury Building in 1955 alone. [477]

Around this time, Harry J. Forman bought at least 10 bags from John Skubis and Arnold Rosing; these originally came from San Francisco Mint storage. Dean Tavenner recalled that one bag was also released in Deer Lodge, Montana, circa 1958–1959, but by that time, no more were being released from Treasury stocks. As far as I know, few if any came out in the 1962–1964 Treasury release.

Still, there were some 1891-CC pieces on hand at the Treasury Building in Washington at the end of the great release, and these 5,687 leftover coins were sold by the GSA in the 1970s, with an additional 19 pieces later sold in the "mixed lot" offering.

Note also that the Redfield estate was estimated to have contained three to five bags of Mint State coins, most of which were heavily bagmarked. These probably came out of the San Francisco Mint, to Nevada casinos in the 1950s.

1891-O (circulation strike mintage 7,954,529): The 1891-O has received little publicity over the years. Part of this is because the typical coin is poorly struck (the illustrated example is above average and was hand-picked for quality) and aesthetically unappealing. Mint State coins have always been available on the market at low prices, probably indicating that occasional bags were released over a long span of time. A significant dispersal occurred circa 1946–1947, after which roll quantities were held by various dealer specialists. The supply then tightened.

Around 1955 and 1956, some bags were paid out of the Cash Room in the Treasury Department in Washington, and for a time the 1891-O was plentiful, but not common. The supply seems to have dried up after that, to the point at which Uncirculated specimens were scarce by October 1962. It was then, however, that many more New Orleans Mint coins were released in quantity from storage at the Philadelphia Mint.

Harry J. Forman, for one, subsequently handled many bags of 1891-O dollars in the early 1960s. Still, the issue was not common in the sense that 1883-O, 1884-O, and 1885-O dollars were. From the viewpoint of numismatic legislative history, the 1891-O dollar occupies a special niche in the annals of the denomination (for reasons that the reader may want to investigate).

1891-S (circulation strike mintage 5,296,000): Quantities of Uncirculated 1891-S dollars were stored at the San Francisco Mint after striking, and remained there for many years. From time to time, bags were released—not many, but enough to keep the market price in the "common date" category. Then, in 1941 and 1942, a major payout occurred. From that time through the next 10 years, 1891-S dollars were plentiful, especially in West Coast bank vaults and in the stocks of dealers there.

The supply seems to have diminished during the early 1950s, and by later in the decade bag quantities were no longer seen and roll holdings were sparse. It's been said that the 1962–1964 Treasury dispersals included a few 1891-S dollars, but I have no record of any significant quantity that came out. Probably, most had been paid out before that time.

The Redfield estate is said to have contained about 5,000 pieces, which Wayne Miller described as being well struck and lustrous but "with plentiful abrasions."

1892 (circulation strike mintage 1,036,000): Large quantities of Mint State 1892 dollars were released by the Treasury in the late 1950s and early 1960s, before which time they were rare. They quickly became very common from that point. Harry J. Forman reported that Uncirculated 1892 dollars were second only to 1891 dollars from the standpoint of availability through Philadelphia banks at the time, annoying to those searching for issues worth a premium.

However, by the time the Treasury began emptying its vaults in earnest, circa 1962–1964, most 1892 dollars had already been paid out. It has been suggested that the Redfield hoard had a partial bag of coins, and these mostly graded MS-60 to MS-62.

1892-CC (circulation strike mintage 1,352,000): When the Carson City Mint closed down, quantities of 1892-CC dollars were shipped for storage to the San Francisco Mint and, to a lesser extent, to the Treasury Building in Washington, D.C. From the San Francisco Mint, quantities were paid out over a period of years, including in 1925 and 1926 but particularly in the late 1940s and early 1950s. Meanwhile, some bags—but probably not many—were dispersed from the Cash Room in the Treasury Department in Washington up through 1953.

Then came a quantity dispersal: Steve Ruddel stated that about 50 bags (50,000 coins) of 1892-CC

dollars were released from the Treasury Building in 1955 alone. It seems that a vault was inspected and equal quantities of several dates were paid out.[478]

Later, few if any 1892-CCs were part of the Treasury release of 1962–1964. Then, when the government took stock of the situation in March 1964 and stopped paying out Morgan and Peace dollars of any and all dates, just a single Uncirculated 1892-CC dollar remained! The news of the non-availability of the 1892-CC in the surviving Treasury cache caused a run-up in prices in the 1960s and 1970s.

The Redfield estate contained 1,700 Uncirculated specimens, all of which were acquired by Paramount International Coin Corporation in 1976.[479] Wayne Miller in his *Morgan and Peace Dollar Textbook*, 1982, reported that as of that time, "large quantities of this date still exist in BU condition." Today they are found as singles or in small groups.

1892-O (circulation strike mintage 2,744,000): The 1892-O dollar has always been available in Mint State on the coin market. Generous quantities were released at and immediately following the time of mintage. A few bags were also released in the 1950s from storage in the Treasury Building in Washington, D.C. However, the great deluge of this issue came in late autumn 1962, during the unsealing of a vault in the Philadelphia Mint that held about 10 million Uncirculated New Orleans dollars.

After that time, Harry J. Forman handled at least 20 bags and reported that the issue was very common in bag quantities. The Redfield estate (1976) is said to have had two to four bags, with the coins heavily damaged by a counting machine used during the pre-auction appraisal.

In 1977, a bag from another source was dispersed; it was said to have contained numerous gems. Then, in the 1980s, Bowers and Merena Galleries handled a bag of 1892-O dollars from a Pennsylvania estate. Most coins in that group were in the range of about MS-62 to MS-63.

1892-S (circulation strike mintage 1,200,000): San Francisco Mint dispersals from storage in the

1940s and 1950s apparently yielded no bags of this date, nor were any among the untold millions of Morgan dollars paid out by the Treasury during the 1962–1964 emptying of government vaults.

However, it is known that at least one bag of 1892-S dollars was paid out by the San Francisco Mint decades earlier in 1925 and 1926. Few of those coins reached numismatic circles, as there was little collecting interest in Morgan dollar mintmarks at the time. Perhaps, some of the About Uncirculated coins now known came from that release.

1893 (circulation strike mintage 378,000): Many bags of 1893 dollars were released by the Treasury in the mid-1950s and very early 1960s. John Jay Ford Jr. handled at least one bag in 1952, dribbling out the contents for years, and John Love reported handling one bag circa 1959. However, few bags were in the 1962–1964 Treasury release.

At least one bag was sold by LaVere Redfield prior to his death, and multiple bags were bought by Superior Stamp & Coin Co. from Redfield's widow prior to the sale at auction of the Redfield silver dollars in January 1976, by which time the holding had been reduced to two to four bags.

1893-CC (circulation strike mintage 677,000): Mint bags of 1893-CC dollars came on the market at face value as early as 1920 through the Cash Room in the Treasury in Washington and, to a greater extent, from storage at the San Francisco Mint. However, the quantity was small in comparison to certain other Carson City dates, particularly those of the early and mid-1880s.

The supply seems to have been exhausted by the late 1950s, and there are no records of any quantities being paid out after that time. How-

ever, the 1893-CC was sufficiently plentiful during the 1950s that Harry J. Forman handled at least 10 bags (10,000 coins), and other quantities were bought and sold by other dollar specialists. We also know that a bag of 1,000 was released through a bank in Great Falls, Montana, in 1955.

Just one solitary coin turned up in the General Services Administration's holdings, which were made up of coins held back in March 1964 after the Treasury release. The Redfield estate contained a single bag of 1,000 coins, most of which were damaged when they were run through a mechanical counting machine.[480] Note that most 1893-CC dollars are very extensively bagmarked (they share "honors" with 1895-S in this regard).

1893-O (circulation strike mintage 300,000): A few bags of 1893-O dollars were paid out at face value from the Cash Room of the Treasury Building from about 1948 to 1955. These may have been released a few coins at a time, rather than in intact 1,000-coin bags, but regardless furnished the source for dealers' stocks.

Around 1958 or 1959, it was realized that even rolls of this issue were scarce. After that, I have no record of bags of 1893-O being included in the 1962–1964 Treasury releases.

1893-S (circulation strike mintage 100,000): I have located no record of any 1,000-coin bags of this issue being released in the 1900s. However, 20 examples of 1893-S are said to have been found mixed in with a bag of Uncirculated 1894-S dollars that came to light in Great Falls, Montana, in the early 1950s (reported by Wayne Miller). These were sold into the market over a period of years, and all were gone by the mid-1970s.

Harry Warner told Walter H. Breen that he knew of a mint bag of 1,000 1893-S dollars, but this has not been seen, and I have been able to find nothing to confirm it. In the early 1970s, dealer Aaron Stollman told Maurice Rosen that he had handled a brilliant Uncirculated roll of 1893-S.[481] Regardless, the 1893-S is a landmark rarity in Mint State today.

1894 (circulation strike mintage 110,000):
Several 1,000-coin bags of Uncirculated 1894 dollars were released in the 1950s and early 1960s. Additionally, a bag from Great Falls, Montana, was sold by John B. Love around 1961, and a bag containing a mixture of Uncirculated 1893 and 1894 dollars was located in San Francisco in the early 1960s. As far as I know, though, this date was not represented in significant quantities in the Treasury release of 1962–1964.

1894-O (circulation strike mintage 1,723,000):
A few bags of Uncirculated 1894-O dollars came on the market in the East during the early 1950s. Then, when many New Orleans Mint dollars came out from storage in a sealed vault at the Philadelphia Mint during the dispersal of 1962–1964, other 1894-O coins (but probably not more than a few thousand coins) came to light.

Around that time, Steve Ruddel told Wayne Miller that he declined to buy a bag of Uncirculated 1894-O dollars (and also a bag of 1896-O dollars) for $3 per coin because "at that time no one knew what was going to be available next." Harry J. Forman at one point handled one bag of this date, and Wayne Miller wrote that in the 1970s, groups of 20 to 100 coins (one to five rolls) were common.

1894-S (circulation strike mintage 1,260,000):
Bags of 1894-S dollars were distributed in San Francisco in the 1950s; John Skubis was among the buyers and paid face value for a bag. Several bags were also released in Deer Lodge, Montana, in the early 1950s; one of these bags contained 20 1893-S dollars mixed in with 980 1894-S pieces.

Apparently, most quantities of 1894-S dollars were released well in advance of the Treasury dispersal of 1962–1964, and this is one date that did not get a "play" during the fast and furious trading times of the early 1960s. Years later, in 1982, Wayne Miller wrote that many hoards containing up to 100 coins had appeared on the market in recent years. Today, pieces from this issue are often offered as single coins.

1895 (circulation strike mintage 12,000, probably an erroneous listing): It is not known for sure if any circulation strikes of this issue were made. Mint records indicate 12,000, but these may have represented coins dated 1894.

I have never seen a Mint State 1895, and perhaps none exist. No hoards are rumored or known, although the search for such has been the Holy Grail of Morgan dollar specialists for decades. Proofs of 1895 were minted to the extent of 880 pieces, and these represent the only *known* supply of the date.

1895-O (circulation strike mintage 450,000):
Around the 1950s, some Mint State coins of this issue were released from storage in the Treasury Building in Washington, D.C. Facts are scarce, but the total was probably between a few dozen and a couple hundred.

In my many interviews with dealers, investors, and others concerning hoards, no one ever mentioned the 1895-O; Harry J. Forman, who has handled as many New Orleans Mint dollars as anyone, never heard of a quantity of true Mint State 1895-O dollars. Apparently, no 1895-O dollars were represented in the Treasury release of 1962–1964, either. Still, it was not considered to be anything special until more recent years—the true rarity of high-level Mint State 1895-O dollars was not appreciated until the 1990s!

1895-S (circulation strike mintage 400,000):
Examples of 1895-S filtered out of the San Francisco Mint over a long period of years in the normal course of business. We know specifically that a few bags of 1895-S dollars were released in

1942, and from then through the very early 1950s more bags were paid out. Then, the distribution stopped, and by 1955, 1895-S dollars were considered to be rare. John Skubis recalled that K.O. Cunningham, of Nevada, offered a bag for sale at this time, but John did not buy it for he was fearful that a lot more would be released at face value.

Indeed, some additional coins were released, but most went to casinos or the public rather than to dealers. The Redfield estate had a mint bag of 1,000 coins,[482] nearly all of which coins were bag-marked, and many of which were said to have been damaged by a coin counting machine. Mint State 1895-S dollars are known for their extensive bagmarks, a characteristic also common among 1893-CC dollars.

1896 (circulation strike mintage 9,976,000):
Vast quantities of Uncirculated 1896 dollars were released in the mid-1950s and early 1960s, making this one of the most plentiful of all Philadelphia Mint dollars and one of the most frequently seen Morgan dollars dated in the 1890s. John B. Love handled 16 or 17 bags from the Redfield estate, selling many of these to John Kamin of *The Forecaster* newsletter. However, the Redfield coins were just a drop in the ocean in relation to the total number of Uncirculated coins in existence.

1896-O (circulation strike mintage 4,900,000):
In 1953, New York dealer Philip Maul broke up one or possibly two bags of this issue. A few more bags came out in 1956, but little attention seems to have been paid to this date. It was considered neither rare nor common and striking was not of the best, and for these reasons 1896-O dollars were not especially sought.

In the early 1960s, some additional bags came out, probably from storage in the Philadelphia Mint. John B. Love recalled buying a bag of coins in Billings, Montana, and noted that the coins were weakly struck and that there was not a prooflike coin in the lot. Steve Ruddel, dealer in quantities of dollars in the early 1960s, told of turning down a bag at a low price, as he did not

know if this was just the tip of the iceberg; for all he (or anyone else) knew, hundreds of bags might have been forthcoming (as in the case with 1898-O and other issues).

A few other bags of 1896-O dollars did turn up in the early 1960s, but the number could not have been large. Harry J. Forman, an astute observer of the Morgan dollar scene, stated that he had neither heard of nor handled a bag of this issue. Today, survivors in Mint State are nearly all in lower ranges such as MS-60 and MS-61.

1896-S (circulation strike mintage 5,000,000):
Bags of 1896-S Uncirculated dollars were paid out from the San Francisco Mint during the very early 1950s, when scant attention was paid to them as they had little value at the time. A few years later, John Skubis and Arnold Rosing jointly bought a bag which turned up at a bank in Oakland, California. Perhaps another bag or two came out as well during that era.

The issue seems to have been plentiful enough as singles in the 1950s and 1960s, but rare in quantity, although it should be noted that Harry J. Forman advertised a 20-coin roll in May 1965. At least several hundred coins found their way to the holdings of Reno investor LaVere Redfield and were later included in his estate. Reportedly, most of the Redfield coins would grade from MS-60 to 63 if evaluated today. Finally, Wayne Miller reported that roll quantities of 1896-S dollars appeared on the market in the early 1970s, but by the early 1980s they were largely dispersed.

1897 (circulation strike mintage 2,822,000):
Once considered rare, Morgan dollars of 1897 were later released in large quantities, and by the 1950s mint bags were common in Eastern banks. By that time, they had no premium value, so no attention was paid to them. The Treasury release of 1962–1964 brought forth still more bags, probably by the hundreds or more, and even more were released in Montana early in 1963 and in California and Nevada shortly thereafter.

Later, in the mid-1970s, an estimated 16 to 18 bags were discovered in the Redfield estate and were sold through John B. Love, reportedly many to John Kamin, publisher of *The Forecaster* newsletter. In 1982, Wayne Miller wrote: "This date is a favorite of promoters because it is readily available and has a deceptively low mintage."

A lot of water has gone under the numismatic bridge since 1982, and what was common then is less so now; at least, what was concentrated in just a few places then is apt to be widely dispersed now. I recall that in the 1950s I could have bought a truckload of Mint State 1897 Morgan dollars (or any one of several other dates) for face value. Now, even a single bag of this common date would be worthy of notice if it came on the market. Still, in terms of single coins, they are second only to the common 1896 in terms of availability among dollars of the 1890s.

1897-O (circulation strike mintage 4,004,000):
In the late 1940s and again in the early 1950s, a few bags of 1897-O dollars came on the market in the East in the greater area comprising New Jersey, eastern Pennsylvania, and southern New York. These were from storage in the Treasury Building in Washington, D.C. It has been said that a few bags of 1897-O dollars—coming from storage in a sealed vault at the Philadelphia Mint—were also part of the Treasury release of 1962–1964, but I have found no specific record of them.

Harry J. Forman, who never handled a bag of 1897-O dollars, reported that New York dealer Joel Coen is said to have had 10 rolls (200 coins) that might have come from that 1962–1964 distribution. Regardless, there was little investor interest at the time of any of these releases, and the 1897-O issue is not one to have attracted much attention, for the typical piece is lightly struck and unattractive.

1897-S (circulation strike mintage 5,825,000):
The 1897-S was released in bag quantities from the San Francisco Mint in the mid-1920s, 1950s, and early 1960s. It was not worth a significant premium at any of those times, nor was it ever considered to be a scarce date.

As such, many from the distributions of the 1950s and 1960s went to the gaming tables in Reno and Las Vegas, and quantities persisted on

the coin market for much of the 1970s. LaVere Redfield reportedly had as many as 20 bags.

1898 (circulation strike mintage 5,884,000):
The 1898 was released in large quantities by the Treasury Department through the Federal Reserve, and by the mid-1950s Mint State coins were very common in Eastern banks. Before that time, however, Uncirculated coins were scarce or even rare.

Additional large quantities were released in the late 1950s and early 1960s. By the mid-1970s, most such quantities had been widely dispersed, with the result that the Redfield estate holding—estimated to have been about 16 to 18 bags—was a novelty at the time. Most of these Redfield coins went to John Kamin, publisher of *The Forecaster* newsletter.

1898-O (circulation strike mintage 4,440,000):
If you had been a collector of Uncirculated Morgan dollars in September 1962, high on your want list alongside the 1903-O and 1904-O would have been the 1898-O. These three were the most formidable rarities among Mint State New Orleans dollars, and even the most in-depth dealer's stock was not likely to have an example of any one of the three!

The 1962 *Guide Book* listed the value of the 1898-O at $300, or double the price of the revered 1889-CC. None were to be had in quantity, and even singles were elusive; although a few bags had come out of storage in the Treasury Building in Washington, D.C. in the 1940s and early 1950s, the coins had largely slipped into circulation, except for a few hundred pieces of these that went into dealers' stocks.

But then, in November 1962, the long-sealed vault at the Philadelphia Mint containing many New Orleans Mint dollars was opened, and these became very common. Within a few months, bags of 1,000 were available in the $1,200 range! Just how many bags of 1898-O dollars were released is uncertain, but it was at least many hundreds, if not a thousand or more—the latter quantity amounting to 1,000,000 or more coins.

It was not long after this that the public became fascinated with Morgan silver dollars, and collectors who had ignored the series earlier became interested. Thus, the number of available Morgan dollars multiplied many times over, but the number of collectors interested also multiplied. The rest is history.

1898-S (circulation strike mintage 4,102,000): The Treasury Department released numerous bags of 1898-S dollars in the mid-1920s and again in the 1940s and 1950s, primarily from storage in the San Francisco Mint. The coins had little value as collectors' items in the 1920s, however, and they were even less popular in the 1940s and early 1950s. Thus, they were widely dispersed, including to visitors of Nevada casinos.

By the time of the 1962–1964 Treasury dispersal, most 1898-S dollars were gone. The Redfield estate auctioned in 1976 contained "several thousand prooflike Uncirculated coins, some of which were very nice."[483]

1899 (circulation strike mintage 330,000): From the early 1950s through the very early 1960s, numerous bags came to light. Probably, somewhere between 50,000 and 100,000 Mint State coins were released at the time. Harry J. Forman reported handling about 10 bags, mostly obtained from Las Vegas (an unusual source for Philadelphia dollars), and he later bought additional quantities. Unfortunately, his success in the marketplace prompted certain small-minded competitors to spread the word that these were overpriced and would soon fall in value!

The Treasury dispersal of 1962–1964 saw more 1899 dollars brought out into the open from long-term storage. Bags were also released in

Montana early in 1963 and in California and Nevada shortly thereafter. Today, 1899 dollars are usually seen one coin at a time.

1899-O (circulation strike mintage 12,290,000): Beginning in 1947 and 1948 and continuing through the early 1950s, several bags of 1899-O dollars were released in the East from storage in the Treasury Building in Washington, D.C., and were distributed among banks. Prior to this time, the 1899-O had been a rarity in Mint State, although few collectors or dealers realized this. A few dealers took advantage of these early releases and stocked up on a bag or two or a few rolls.

Eventually, in October 1962, large quantities of bags of this issue became available. Indeed, 1899-O coins were among the first silver dollars in quantity to see the light of day.

1899-S (circulation strike mintage 2,562,000): A steady stream of Uncirculated 1899-S dollars—singly, in groups, and by the bag—was paid out by the San Francisco Mint from 1942 through the mid-1950s. As such, only a few bags were left by the time of the Treasury release of 1962–1964.

Conventional wisdom had it that the Redfield hoard had a bag of high quality coins (per Wayne Miller) or less than a full bag of coins in MS-60 to 63 (per John Highfill). A contribution to the present book from David W. Akers clarifies the situation: "Redfield had several thousand coins, some of which were very nice, as Wayne Miller says."[484]

1900 (circulation strike mintage 8,830,000): Bags of 1,000 dollars of these pieces were released on the East Coast in the 1950s, and the issue came to be recognized as a common date. By the time of the massive Treasury release of 1962–1964, most had been paid out.

1900-O (circulation strike mintage 12,590,000): After the New Orleans Mint was closed, many bags of 1900-O dollars were shipped to the Treasury Building in Washington, D.C. Some were then shipped in 1929 to the Philadelphia Mint for storage, while others dribbled out from the Treasury Building holding from the early 1930s through at least the early 1950s.

Unlike the 1898-O, 1903-O, and 1904-O—all of which were deemed to be great rarities in Uncirculated grade—the 1889-O, 1890-O, 1894-O, 1896-O, 1897-O, 1899-O, 1900-O, and 1901-O were on the market in bag and roll quantities in the early part of the 1950s decade. For example, Philip Maul, a Hudson, New York dealer, advertised rolls of these particular issues in *The Numismatist* in September 1953.

Later, in the late autumn 1962 dispersal of New Orleans dollars from long-term storage at the Philadelphia Mint, the aforementioned bags of 1900-O coins shipped to that location were brought to the forefront. Hundreds of thousands were released. Quantities must have been broken up after that, though; Wayne Miller wrote in 1982 that in rolls, 1900-O was believed to be scarcer than 1898-O, 1899-O, 1902-O, and 1904-O, and ran a close contest with 1901-O. Today, there are plenty of singles to go around.

1900-O, O Over CC (circulation strike mintage unknown; a small part of 1900-O): Bags of 1900-O dollars had the overmintmark O Over CC coins mixed in. In the mid-1980s, Bowers and Merena Galleries handled a quantity of unsearched Mint State 1900-O dollars from a Montana holding, and about a third to a quarter were 1900-O, O Over CC. However, I believe that this was an unusual situation, and that the total population of 1900-O, O Over CC, dollars is only a tiny fraction of that of 1900-O.

In 1992, Dwight Manley obtained and began the dispersal of a full original bag of 1900-O, O Over CC, dollars from a Chicago source. The distribution of grades (PCGS certification) was as follows: 1 coin in MS-67, 10 in MS-66, 150 in MS-65, 260 in MS-64, 340 in MS-63, and 239 from MS-60 through 62 (not certified).[485]

1900-S (circulation strike mintage 3,540,000): Vast quantities of 1900-S dollars were stored at the San Francisco Mint. These were paid out over a period of years in the late 1930s, 1940s, and 1950s. Many went to Nevada casinos in the

latter decade. Then, in the 1962–1964 period, many additional bags were released in the Treasury dispersal. By the time that government stocks were exhausted, 1900-S was a plentiful coin in the hands of investors, dealers, and the public.

1901 (circulation strike mintage 6,962,000): As far as is known, this date was not represented in any Treasury releases of the 1940s, 1950s, or early 1960s. Today, Mint State coins are scarce and anything truly MS-63 or finer is a great rarity.

On the other hand, well-worn pieces are extremely common. It seems that nearly all were released into circulation in an era in which very few collectors were interested in Morgan dollars, and those who were interested chose to buy Proofs.

1901-O (circulation strike mintage 13,320,000): The beginning of the story is familiar: after the New Orleans Mint ceased business, quantities of silver dollars were shipped to Washington, D.C. and Philadelphia for storage. From vaults in the Treasury Building in Washington, D.C., Uncirculated 1901-O dollars dribbled out onto the market from the early 1930s onward.

Then, in 1953, a major release occurred, and this was followed by distributions through the mid-1950s. Obtaining coins indirectly from the Treasury, Philip Maul advertised rolls in *The Numismatist* in September 1953. In the September 1957 issue of *The Numismatist*, Harry J. Forman also advertised that he had Uncirculated specimens of 1901-O available in quantity. In general, anyone who stocked Uncirculated dollars was apt to have a supply of this date.

All this being said, any quantities released in the 1950s paled in significance to the amount dispersed in late autumn 1962, when a long-sealed vault in the Philadelphia Mint was opened. Countless thousands of sparkling, new 1901-O dollars were released.

1901-S (circulation strike mintage 2,284,000): 1901-S dollars were paid out by the San Francisco Mint over a long period of years, beginning at least by 1925. In addition, bags of this issue were stored in the Treasury Building in Washington, D.C. and were released from time to time starting in the 1930s. Quantities remained in dealers' hands as recently as the 1950s.

In later years, though, the 1901-S became harder to find. Quantities released in the Treasury dispersal of 1962–1964 were probably small. Interestingly, John B. Love noted in *The Comprehensive U.S. Silver Dollar Encyclopedia* that two bags of these were found in Idaho in the early 1960s and were bought by Bill Holdman in Great Falls, Montana.

1902 (circulation strike mintage 7,994,000): Like a number of other Philadelphia Mint Morgan dollars, the 1902 in Mint State was elusive before the 1930s. Circa 1947–1948, the Treasury paid out bags of 1902 dollars, but still they remained somewhat scarce. Then, in the early 1950s, additional quantities were paid out, and in the closing years of the decade, many bags came to light.

Today, probably well over 100,000 Mint State coins exist, but these are usually seen just a few coins at a time or as singles.

1902-O (circulation strike mintage 8,636,000): Although 1902-O dollars seeped out over a period of years from storage in the Treasury Building in Washington, D.C., especially in the late 1950s and very early 1960s (before autumn 1962), the date was not considered common until a vast torrent of hundreds of thousands emerged from a sealed vault in the Philadelphia Mint in late autumn 1962 and the ensuing months. Earlier, the 1902-O had been considered to be a rarity in Mint State, and for a period of years it was priced higher than, for example, the 1884-S.

1902-S (circulation strike mintage 1,530,000): Large quantities of 1902-S dollars were paid out from storage at the San Francisco Mint over a long period of years, with substantial releases occurring in the late 1920s, 1940s, and early 1950s, plus at other intervals. David W. Akers stated that in the Redfield estate there were "several thousand pieces, but not many of high quality."[486]

1903 (circulation strike mintage 4,652,000): Mint State specimens of 1903 dollars remained elusive until 1955, when many bags were paid out in the East. Later, in the 1960s, a dealer in Salinas, California made a specialty of 1903 Philadelphia Mint Morgan dollars and at one time accumulated a cache amounting to more than 50 bags (50,000 coins).[487] The Redfield estate, meanwhile, is said to have had less than a bag of coins, grading MS-60 to 63.

1903-O (circulation strike mintage 4,450,000): In terms of historical significance relative to Treasury hoards and its impact on the numismatic hobby, 1903-O is *the* Morgan dollar of all time. In fact, in all of American numismatics, there is probably no other single coin that led the way for sweeping changes as did the 1903-O.

As noted in the introduction to the present chapter, the 1903-O was a formidable rarity until November 1962. How many were involved in the release at that time is not known, and guesses have ranged from 60,000 or so to more than 1,000,000. Wayne Miller's estimate is 60,000 to 100,000. Probably, the truth lies somewhere between 60,000 and several hundred thousand; I suggest 200,000 to 350,000.

Regardless, after the news broke of the coins' release, I was offered a few bags for $17,000 each in late 1962 or early 1963 by a Detroit source. I declined, as I was fearful that about four million more coins would be coming out of the Treasury, but I was wrong on the four million, and time would have vindicated a purchase at $17,000 per bag.

Today the 1903-O is an affordable reminder of one of the most sensational events in American numismatic history. As these pieces are rare in worn grades—indicating the issue did not go into circulation—but the present population is not comparable to the total original striking, it is probable that most of the 4,450,000 coins minted were melted under the Pittman Act of 1918.

1903-S (circulation strike mintage 1,241,000): Quantities of 1903-S dollars were stored at the San Francisco Mint and paid out in small numbers through November 1953. At that time, several bags were released, and that was followed by other dispersals during the next several years. Dealer John Skubis was among those who procured a bag in this era.

By the late 1950s, apparently most coins of this issue were gone from government storage, and the issue was not represented to any extent in the 1962–1964 Treasury release.

1904 (circulation strike mintage 2,788,000): Quantities of 1904 dollars dribbled onto the market in 1941 and 1942, in the 1950s, and again in the early 1960s, but there were apparently no *major* releases at any specific time. Thus, quantity offerings by dealers were few and far between. A very mediocre bag of 1904 dollars entered the market early in 1979; Wayne Miller examined nearly 300 pieces from the lot, but found no gems.

1904-O (circulation strike mintage 3,720,000): In late autumn 1962, vast quantities of 1904-O dollars—well more than 1,000,000 coins—were released from long-term storage at the Philadelphia Mint. Additional bags of 1904-O dollars were released from storage in the Treasury Building in Washington, D.C., from which location some coins had dribbled out in small numbers since the 1930s.

Prior to these releases, the 1904-O in Mint State had been considered one of the prime rarities in the Morgan series along with 1898-O and, especially, 1903-O. Today, however, there are more 1904-O Mint State dollars in existence than there are of any other New Orleans dollar after 1885-O.

1904-S (circulation strike mintage 2,304,000): Although the San Francisco Mint served as a storage depot for its own coins, many bags of Uncirculated 1904-S dollars were shipped to the Treasury Building in Washington, D.C. From time to time in the 1930s and 1940s, an occasional bag would be paid out from there, and in 1941 and 1942, there was a particularly large release that augmented dealers' stocks for a long time.

Case in point: a perusal of advertisements of the 1950s will reveal that most dealers had a supply of Mint State 1904-S dollars. One or more bags of 1904-S dollars also came out through Los Angeles banks in the early 1950s; Bebee's, having recently moved from Chicago to Omaha, bought some from this hoard.

The issue was not plentiful for everyone, though; John Skubis, who was one of the most active dealers in bulk San Francisco Mint dollars in the 1950s, recalled that the 1904-S was one of only three dates of S-mintmark coins that he did *not* handle by the bagful. Supplies dried up after a while, too—I have found no accounts of any being in the 1962–1964 Treasury release, none were in the Redfield estate, and today it is one of the rarer issues.

1921 (circulation strike mintage 44,690,000): Many bags of this issue were released over time. Eventually, examples became so common that dealers' buying prices for Uncirculated bags and rolls of Morgan dollars often said "except 1921." Although there is no way of knowing, it is likely that most 1921 dollars of the three mints were melted during the silver craze of the late 1970s.

In Nevada casinos in the very early 1960s, this and the Denver version of the same year were the most seen dollar varieties on roulette and other gaming tables. Note that all 1921 Morgan dollars—Philadelphia, Denver, and San Francisco—are from dies in shallow relief and tend to show friction and bagmarks even after slight jostling in mint bags.

1921-D (circulation strike mintage 20,345,000): Vast quantities of Mint State 1921-D dollars were released in the 1950s and early 1960s. The issue was considered common, and most dealers did not desire to buy them. Most were probably melted in the 1970s, and today far fewer single Mint State 1921-D dollars exist than do those of 1921 from Philadelphia and San Francisco.

1921-S (circulation strike mintage 21,695,000): Dollars of this date and mint were scarce during the 1920s, for relatively few were released. This changed when quantities were paid out from storage at the San Francisco Mint at intervals from the 1930s through the 1950s, but the issue was little esteemed in those times (not even casino operators and other silver dollar hoarders liked the 1921 Morgan from any of the three mints or wanted to save them) and thus few original mint-sealed bags were saved. Most were probably melted in the 1970s.

Peace Silver Dollars

1921 Peace silver dollars (circulation strike mintage 1,006,473): I have never heard of even one original 1,000-coin mint bag of this issue coming on the market, and when I asked Philadelphia dealer Harry J. Forman, he knew of no original bags either. In fact, during extensive research I never came across a quantity offering of any kind—I've never even seen an original Uncirculated *roll* of 20 coins!

This makes the 1921 Peace dollar unique among coins of this design, for all other Peace dollar varieties 1922–1935 were available at one time or another in multiple-roll and bag quantities several years or more after they were minted.[488] Dealer Maurice Rosen reported that, around 1979 or 1980, he bought a roll of Uncirculated pieces from Don Apte, and that: "If my recollection is accurate, they would make today's MS-64

and 65 grades. All were frosty white with above average surface characteristics for the issue."[489] Of course, a roll of 20 pieces is hardly a hoard.

1922 (circulation strike mintage 51,737,000): Mint-sealed bags of 1,000 Mint State 1922 Peace dollars seem to have been released over a stretch of several years, with the result that this date has never been rare. In fact, it became an annoyance for Eastern dealers searching for rare dates when they found shipments to their banks from the Federal Reserve consisted of $1,000 bags of this date.

Particularly large quantities were released through banks in 1949 and 1950, but there was little call for them by numismatists. Bags were still readily available in 1953 and 1954—but they largely remained in bank vaults, unwanted—and were still being distributed by the Treasury as late as March 1964. In later years, bags traded frequently; in 1982, Wayne Miller wrote that in one recent year he and his partner sold 40 bags (40,000 coins).

1922-D (circulation strike mintage 15,063,000): Bags of 1922-D dollars were available on the market in the 1940s and very early 1950s. No one paid much attention to this date, though, and most languished in bank vaults or were paid out for circulation in the West or use in gambling casinos. Bags of 1,000 Uncirculated coins were still readily available in 1953 and 1954.

Many years later, in the late 1980s and early 1990s, a hoard of 50 bags (50,000 coins) began to be marketed. Dwight Manley examined them and found that the average bag of 1,000 coins contained Mint State examples approximately as follows: 5 coins in MS-66; 70 in MS-65; 200 in MS-64; 225 in MS-63; and 500 in MS-60 to MS-62.[490]

1922-S (circulation strike mintage 17,475,000): In 1941, 1922-S—as well as 1926-S—dollars were released in quantity through the San Francisco Mint, where they had been stored for many years. Several bags or more came on the market, but the demand for Peace dollars was not very great.

Probably no more than two or three thousand went into numismatic channels at the time, although more could have been obtained from the Mint had dealers desired them. Quite a few went to Reno, which had an active casino industry (the growth of Las Vegas was yet to come).

Later, in the spring and summer of 1942, many more bags of 1922-S, 1923-S, 1925-S, 1926-S, and 1927-S dollars were paid out by the San Francisco Mint. These mostly went to banks and into general circulation in some areas of the West, where they became worn. No one ever thought they would become scarce. Indeed, quantities continued to come on the market through 1956, though by that time the end was drawing near and the mint would soon be out of them.

Bags of 1922-S dollars were in the Redfield hoard, and, according to John Highfill, represented the largest single holding of any Peace dollar issue in this famous group. A number of Redfield bags, mostly containing weakly struck MS-60 to MS-63 coins, were marketed through Paramount International Coin Corporation after the 1976 dispersal of the hoard.

1923 (circulation strike mintage 30,800,000):

Bags of 1923 Peace dollars descended upon the channels of commerce in the mid-1940s, remained common in bank holdings through the early 1960s, and were paid out by the Treasury until the early months of 1964. After that, these bags were frequently in the hands of investors (in particular) and dealers.

In all grades from well-worn to high-grade Mint State, the 1923 may account for 5% to 10% of the silver dollars in existence today, as suggested by Wayne Miller in his 1982 text.

1923-D (circulation strike mintage 6,811,000):

In an article in the July 1925 edition of *The Numismatist*, collector E.S. Thresher stated that in June 1919 he embarked on a search to find each and every date of coin variety believed to be available in circulation. In the Peace dollar series, still a relatively new specialty when he wrote his letter, he had located every issue from 1921 through 1925 except for 1923-D, 1925-D, and 1925-S, the last two not having been released yet.

From this, it is apparent that the 1923-D was rare in its own time, and may not have been released in as late as early 1925. This scarcity was alleviated somewhat when many bags of the issue were later paid out by the Treasury Department from the late 1930s through at least the 1950s, after which time the government stock of mint-sealed bags of this issue was largely depleted.

1923-S (circulation strike mintage 19,020,000):

1923-S dollars were readily available throughout the 1930s, and in the spring and summer of 1942, the San Francisco Mint paid out many bags. In 1949 and 1950, more bags of 1923-S dollars came on the market and were obtainable through banks in the San Francisco and Oakland area, and in 1953 and 1954, many others went to casinos in Las Vegas and Reno while a few went to silver dollar hoarders.

Quantities continued to be dispersed in 1955 and 1956, and it is said that still more came to light during the Treasury release of 1962–1964. This may be where LaVere Redfield obtained his; his estate is said to have had quite a few bags. Those coins graded MS-60 to 63 and were weakly struck, noted John Highfill in his *Comprehensive U.S. Silver Dollar Encyclopedia*.

1924 (circulation strike mintage 11,811,000):

Many 1,000-coin mint-sealed bags of this date came out in 1949 and 1950, these on top of a number that were released before that time. A few years later, in 1953 and 1954, there were large quantities in Eastern banks. However, there was little dealer interest in buying them, even for face value, and these stocks remained in bank vaults through the rest of the decade.

John Kamin found even more in later years: "I had often been of the opinion that 1924 and 1925 Philadelphia Mint dollars were about equal in rarity, that is substantially more common than the scarcer dates such as 1927-S, 1928, and 1934-S, but about 100 times scarcer than the super-common 1922 and 1923 Peace dollars and

1921 Morgan dollars. But then, around 1969, I bumped into a hoard containing nearly 100 bags of 1924 Peace dollars, with no other dates in the group, from the Tennessee area."[491]

1924-S (circulation strike mintage 1,728,000): Unlike the 1922-S, 1923-S, and 1926-S, of which many bags came on the market from the San Francisco Mint in the 1940s and 1950s, quantities of 1924-S seem to have been paid out only occasionally. However, this particular issue was and is notorious for being extensively bagmarked, a situation which facilitated their being ignored by numismatists.[492]

A few 1,000-coin bags were released in the late 1950s and were quickly absorbed at prices of about double face value, a high premium at the time. The Redfield estate is said to have had a few hundred individual Uncirculated coins, but no bags.

1925 (circulation strike mintage 10,198,000): In 1940, the 1925 Peace dollar was considered to be the rarest Philadelphia Mint issue in Mint State, but by 1945 it had dropped slightly in rank to second-rarest (after the 1923). In numerous offerings early in the 1940s, it was priced higher than the valuable 1934-S, but by late 1940s, enough had been released from Treasury vaults that the 1925 Peace dollar was demoted to the status of a plentiful issue.

Still, catalog values remained high until hundreds of bags were released in 1954 and 1955, after which the date became very common. I remember selling a large quantity obtained for face value at a Pennsylvania bank to Charles E. Green, of Chicago, who traded under his wife's name of R. Green.

1925-S (circulation strike mintage 1,610,000): In 1938 and again in the spring and summer of 1942, many bags of 1925-S Peace dollars were paid out by the San Francisco Mint. The issue became common in dealers' stocks. However, the numismatic market for Peace dollars was limited, and it would continue to be so for many years;[493] I imagine that following the 1942 release no more than two or three thousand Uncirculated

pieces were sold to collectors during the ensuing 12-month period.

In 1949 and 1950, many more bags of 1925-S dollars came out through San Francisco, Oakland, and other California banks, but there was little interest in them at the time. Some additional bags were paid out in the late 1950s; this last quantity was not large, but at least 10 to 20 bags went into the hands of dealers. Those may have included the five bags that were later owned by LaVere Redfield of Reno.

1926 (circulation strike mintage 1,939,000): In a November 1941 advertisement in *The Numismatist*, the Hollenbeck Stamp & Coin Stores referred to the 1926 Peace dollar as the scarcest coin in the series. The honor for the scarcest issue changed from time to time, as hoards were dispersed, and thus this coin was dethroned.

In 1944, bags of the issue were released. Several authorities—John Highfill, Walter H. Breen, and Wayne Miller among them—reported that most of these were extensively bagmarked. Then, in 1953 and 1954, a large number of additional bags came out through Eastern banks. They were generally ignored, as at this point it was felt that 1926 dollars would be forever common. Those bags were soon dispersed, though, and as the decade wore on, not many others came to light (although a few are said to have emerged from 1962 to 1964).

1926-D (circulation strike mintage 2,348,700): While large releases of S-Mint bags of Peace dollars were well documented, and while similar releases of Philadelphia coins were also publicized, relatively little was said about Denver issues. Accordingly, I did not find a single verified instance of a bag of 1926-D dollars being released before 1950 during the course of research from the 1950s onward—and yet many must have been. It is my guess that most slipped quietly into the channels of commerce before that time.

It is known that a bag or two came out in the Midwest around 1953 or 1954 and were quickly absorbed. It has been suggested that a few bags came out in the Treasury release of 1962–1964.

Years later, in 1982, Wayne Miller wrote that rolls were plentiful.

1926-S (circulation strike mintage 6,980,000):
In 1941, quantities of 1926-S dollars were released through the San Francisco Mint, where they had been stored for 15 years. Several bags came on the market, but the demand for Peace dollars was not very great. Although plenty could have been obtained from the Mint had dealers desired them, probably no more than two or three thousand coins went into numismatic channels at the time, and even this estimate may be overly generous. Quite a few went to casinos in Reno, Nevada.

More bags came out later, in the spring and summer of 1942. Quantities remained unsold in dealers' stocks, and for a long time the 1926-S was considered to be very common. Still more bags were released in 1949 and 1950, mainly through banks in the San Francisco and Oakland area; later in the 1950s, particularly from 1953 through 1956; and even as late as during the 1962–1964 Treasury dispersal.

And yet despite these myriad releases, most 1926-S dollars floating on the market had found homes by the early 1970s, and the issue was not often seen in quantity. In 1982, Wayne Miller wrote that the issue was rarer than 1926-D; that is, until the Redfield coins came on the market.

That hoard, dispersed in 1976, contained several or more bags, probably obtained from Nevada casinos in the late 1950s and early 1960s. John Highfill has written that the 1926-S was the third-most plentiful Redfield hoard Peace dollar issue, but that many were damaged by the mechanical counting machine used by the firm hired to inventory the group. All of these Redfield 1926-S dollars went to numismatists and investors.

1927 (circulation strike mintage 848,000):
The low-mintage 1927 is a coin that has slipped through the cracks so far as news of bag releases is concerned. Little about this date appeared in print years ago. Today, the 1927 Philadelphia issue ranks as one of the scarcer Peace dollar issues in higher levels of Mint State, although it has never been in the numismatic limelight.

1927-D (circulation strike mintage 1,268,900):
In the late 1930s, the 1927-D dollar was considered to be one of the scarcer varieties in the Peace dollar series. In late 1939, several bags broke in the Midwest, but soon this supply dwindled, and once again the 1927-D gained the status of being an elusive issue. However, in keeping with most other dates, it was not necessarily expensive.

Later, in the Treasury releases of 1962–1964 came and went, few if any quantities of 1927-D Peace dollars were released. By 1982, Wayne Miller noted that scarcely any rolls—never mind bags—had appeared on the market during his career, and that Mint State 1927-Ds were rarities.

That changed on June 23, 1992, when Sotheby's auctioned two and a half original bags of 1927-D dollars (a hoard amounting to 2,500 coins) in groups which added up to about $400,000 when the auctioneer cried "Sold!" for the final lot. Two thousand coins were in two original Denver Mint cloth bags bearing serial numbers 5758 and 5799, while the remaining 500 coins were in a Bank of Denver bag.

These 2,500 coins were a 25th anniversary present from a man to his wife, "a nice touch," commented David E. Tripp, who cataloged the pieces.[494] Dwight Manley examined the group at Sotheby's prior to the sale and estimated the grades to be as follows: 50 coins in MS-65; 300 in MS-64; 550 in MS-63; 700 in MS-61 and MS-62; and 900 in MS-60.[495]

1927-S (circulation strike mintage 866,000):
On the coin market in 1935 and 1936, a 1927-S dollar in Uncirculated grade was just another common issue. However, most became scattered fairly quickly, and for a time in 1938 they were scarce in numismatic hands. Around that time, a few bags were released from the San Francisco Mint, but these too became widely distributed.

In the summer of 1942, more bags came out, and the price slipped, but just slightly; probably not more than a couple thousand additional specimens emerged from storage at that time. For a while after this, the 1927-S Peace dollar remained basically scarce on the numismatic market, as hundreds of thousands were in storage at the San

Francisco Mint but would remain so for a bit longer. Whenever the occasional group of bags came on the market in this interim period, the price would fall, as the low-mintage 1927-S dollars were scarce in Uncirculated preservation, but specialists in Peace dollars were even scarcer.

Then, in 1949 and 1950, many bags of 1927-S dollars came on the market through the San Francisco Mint, which paid them out to banks in the area. In 1953 and 1954, another group of bags came out in the San Francisco area, and this time dealers took the opportunity to stock up on what they could use, but not too many, for it was realized that the vault at the San Francisco Mint could be tapped if any more were needed.

There was yet another turn in the road, though, as before anyone was truly aware of it, the supply had become dispersed into circulation over the California border to the casinos in Nevada and elsewhere. Thus, by 1960, 1927-S dollars were considered to be somewhat scarce once more.

Several or more bags are said to have been in the Redfield estate. Wayne Miller said that the Redfield coins were of generally high quality, while John Highfill took a different stance and stated that many were in lower grades such as MS-60 to 63 and were damaged by the mechanical counting machine used in the appraisal process. Apparently, many coins were somewhat prooflike on the obverse, due to minute striae from die polishing.

1928 (circulation strike mintage 360,649): In terms of quantities of this issue, I have never seen, nor have I a firm record of an original mint-sealed bag of 1928 pieces being preserved. Rolls, meanwhile, came on the market occasionally through about the 1970s.

Single 1928 coins were a different story. In the 1950s, high-grade examples were common in unsorted lots I examined in banks in Pennsylvania—so much so that I did not bother to keep more than a few. MS-63 was a typical grade in retrospect, probably equal to MS-64 or finer today.

Note that dollars of this date have a distinctive beveled rim, making them easily detectable in a bag, even if the date is hidden under another coin.

1928-S (circulation strike mintage 1,632,000): Many bags of 1928-S dollars came on the market in the late 1930s and early 1940s. More bags were released in 1949 and 1950, when the San Francisco Mint distributed them through banks in its area and by direct shipment to Nevada casinos. There was little numismatic interest in them, however, as Peace dollars were not a popular series, and the market was in a slump, too.[496]

John Highfill wrote that possibly four to six bags of this issue were in the Redfield hoard when it was dispersed in 1976, and that most of the coins had deep scratches from a mechanical counting machine employed while the coins were being inventoried. Most were also extensively bagmarked; from all of the comments about his coins in John Highfill's book, it seems that Redfield was the antithesis of a connoisseur.

1934 (circulation strike mintage 954,057): Bags of 1934 dollars were paid out through Eastern banks from the 1930s onward. Little documentation of 1,000-coin bags exists, and I do not know if any original mint-sealed bags survived. Interestingly, this is one issue which for many years seemed to be "common" and "ordinary" per conventional wisdom, but anyone checking closely would find that few if any quantities were to be had.

1934-D (circulation strike mintage 1,569,500): I am not aware of any bag quantities reported during my many interviews years ago. Individual Mint State coins were and are available easily enough, though.

1934-S (circulation strike mintage 1,011,000): Probably many thousands of 1934-S dollars were released from the mid-1930s through the mid-1940s. I estimate that perhaps an additional bag or two or three (1,000 to 3,000 coins) saw distribution from the San Francisco Mint in the late 1940s through the mid-1950s. Around that time, a San Francisco dealer told me that he personally saw more than one million coins of the issue still stored at the local mint, which made a good story and impressed me at the time; however, the same dealer was interviewed by me later and did not remember having seen such a hoard, and so his account is just an entertaining numismatic tale.

Anyway: by the early 1960s, Uncirculated specimens of the 1934-S had been largely absent from dealers' stocks for nearly 15 years. Often in that era, listings of Mint State Peace dollars would commence with 1921 and end with 1935-S, and give prices for each issue, except for 1934-S which would be marked "Wanted." Notable is that while the 1934-S was not realized for its rarity until the 1950s, prices had risen beginning in the late 1940s.

A hoard of several hundred pieces turned up in San Francisco not too much later in the 1960s (per Wayne Miller and others) and was distributed over a long period of time. At the January 1978 Florida United Numismatists Convention, a group of 35 pieces was broken up; by that time, such a holding was considered unusual.

1935 (circulation strike mintage 1,576,000): I never encountered a mint-sealed bag of these, though rolls sometimes come on the market. David W. Akers recalled buying a group of 200 superb gem coins from RARCOA in the late 1970s.[497]

1935-S (circulation strike mintage 1,964,000): Many bags of 1935-S dollars were released by the San Francisco Mint to banks in its immediate area in 1949 and 1950. Most of these coins showed only light traces of handling and were what would be called gems a generation later. Unfortunately, there was relatively little numismatic interest in them, and while Norman Shultz and several other dealers of the time bought a total of a bag or two, most were ignored and eventually slipped into circulation. I recall being offered a bag of them around 1955 and declining to buy at $1,200; I couldn't figure out what to do with more than a few dozen pieces (what a mistake!).

Later, Wayne Miller wrote that a hoard of this date came on the market in San Francisco in the 1960s and was dispersed over a period of time. The Redfield estate had a number of bags, but most of the coins were poorly struck.

U.S. Gold Coins Found in Foreign Countries

Collecting U.S. gold coins by date and mintmark varieties has not always been popular; the specialty was largely ignored in earlier years. Case in point: writing in 1893 in his *Treatise on Mint Marks*, Augustus G. Heaton stated that he knew of *no one* in the numismatic community that collected mintmark issues of half eagles, eagles, and double eagles. Later, when Edgar H. Adams published his *Official Premium List of U.S. and Territorial Gold Coins* in 1909, not much interest in large denominations was shown, either.

Virgil Brand, millionaire Chicago brewer who began collecting in the 1880s and by the time of his death in 1926 owned more than 300,000 coins, was different in that he had many large-denomination gold coins by mintmark varieties. However, as the numismatic market for them was nil, his heirs—brothers Armin and Horace—simply turned most of them in at banks for face value.

It was not until the 1940s that there was a great flurry of interest in collecting gold. As the focus of this chapter—U.S. gold coins that were repatriated after World War II—would have been of far less excitement without passionate collectors, it is worth examining said flurry before detailing the pieces that came back to our shores.

The 1930s

The government began calling in gold coins in 1933 but provided an exception for numismatic coins. As such, many collectors started paying closer attention to them. Baltimore collector Louis E. Eliasberg commenced his interest in 1935 and began acquiring as many different dates and mintmarks as he could find. Floyd Starr, a Philadelphia collector since the 1920s, did the same thing, as did others.

Meanwhile, the public turned in countless millions of dollars in gold coins to banks for face value. Dealer Thomas L. Elder of Philadelphia published buying lists that he circulated to bank tellers, pointing out that all gold dollars, quarter eagles, and $3 gold coins had numismatic value, and some of low mintages or with C or D mintmarks had extra value. Pioneer and territorial gold coins were on the list as well. Many treasures were thus saved from melting.

Thomas L. Elder.

Still, surrendered gold piled up in Treasury facilities, especially at the Philadelphia Mint, and in 1937, the order was given to melt them all. By that time, though, there was enough collector interest, including in high denominations, and attuned Mint and Treasury Department workers picked out coins of interest, substituting common coins of the same denominations. The government came out even, and numismatists had the chance to buy many rarities.

Some issues—such as the 1932 double eagle—were of legendary rarity before 1937, as few had been released. As holders of these coins sold them to dealers, they became widely available. Abe Kosoff, whose Numismatic Gallery office was in New York City, recalled paying out large amounts of cash to sellers of 1932 double eagles who came by train from Philadelphia. He also bought multiple examples of the even rarer 1933, including four that he sold to California collector R.E. Naftzger Jr.

Some gold coins that were not popular at all at the time they were made, the 1908 to 1929 Indian Head quarter eagles and half eagles being prime examples, now found buyers. The market for commemorative coins, which had reached a speculative peak in prices in 1936, had crashed, too, and thus some of those who had specialized in commemoratives had more time for gold coins.

The Watershed Green Collection Sale

In the 1940s, the auction catalogs of several firms—notably B. Max Mehl, Numismatic Gallery (Abe Kosoff and Abner Kreisberg), and Stack's—showcased several collections that featured large-denomination gold coins by dates and mints. This further fueled interest in gold, as did the search for rare specimens by Louis E. Eliasberg Sr., Jacob Shapiro (a.k.a. Jake Bell), and several other collectors.

Especially in the limelight in the numismatic market of the 1940s were rare varieties of Saint-Gaudens double eagles such as the 1924-D and S, 1925-D and S, 1926-D and S, 1927-D and S, and all issues after 1928. Most prized of all was the 1926-D double eagle, which was viewed as one of

the greatest of all U.S. rarities. Second on the "most wanted" list was the 1924-S, and some considered it to be number one. Curiously, the 1927-D, considered today to be the rarest issue of the 1920s, received very little attention back then.

In April 1949, Mehl offered the Dr. Charles W. Green Collection—billed as including the only complete set of date and mintmark varieties (through 1932) of double eagles ever sold—for sale to mail bids. The *pièce de résistance* was this:

> Lot 916: 1926-D Uncirculated with mint lustre. Only in the recent few years has the real rarity of this coin been recognized. In 1944 this coin was catalogued for only $100. In 1946 it was catalogued for $200, and now it is catalogued at $1,000. The rarity of this coin may well be surmised from the fact that none of the great collections of double eagles offered on the market in the last few years had a specimen of it, such great collections as the Bell, "The World's Greatest," and others. This is the first specimen ever to be offered at auction.

As was true of many Mehl offerings, there was more to the story. Perhaps Mehl forgot about the listing of a 1926-D in the 1946 offering by the Numismatic Gallery of the F.C.C. Boyd cabinet (billed as "The World's Finest Collection"), despite the fact that it was illustrated and occupied a full page!

Regardless, the Green coin created a sensation, realizing two and one-half times its estimate. Collectors and dealers went wild, and from that point great interest was focused on later-date mint-marked double eagles. That 1926-D and the 1924-S in the same sale were the catalyst of the

Abe Kosoff.

Abner Kreisberg.

great rush that developed in collecting Saint-Gaudens double eagles by date and mint.

Indeed, in the Numismatic Gallery catalog of the sale of the Adolphe Menjou Collection in 1950, Abe Kosoff stated that the 1924-S was "the rarest of all double eagles; perhaps there are less than five extant." This would have put it on about par with the famous 1913 Liberty Head nickel and the 1885 trade dollar, of which just five were (and still are) known of each.

Dynamic New Era of Collecting

Such well-publicized and successful sales, coupled with the rise in collector interest, made the return of gold coins from Europe all the more noteworthy. It was in 1955 that the dam broke, and the "Bank of France" yielded dozens upon dozens of previously rare varieties after Paul Wittlin—a California professional working with Dayton, Ohio, dealer James F. Kelly—provided lists of desired dates and mints to bankers there. From various banks in Paris, long-stored gold coins were examined, and over a period of time the 1926-D descended from being the *crème de la crème* coin of the double eagle series to being simply "scarce" or "rare." Within a few years, probably 100 to 200 came to light from French banks and other locations. Ditto for the 1924-S, 1926-S, and certain other issues.[498]

This would only be the beginning, though, as the finds set off a treasure hunt in other overseas banks. Switzerland proved to be a particularly rich source, as millions of U.S. gold coins—primarily of the half eagle, eagle, and double eagle denominations—were stored there. Such coins had been received in various transactions, but particularly as exchange payments during the general era 1880–1932, after which the pieces had remained there. These foreign banks had never been the slightest bit interested in holding U.S. paper money, and when President Franklin D. Roosevelt called in gold coins in 1933 and 1934, they held on to their gold reserves more tightly than ever.

Of course, that policy changed when numismatists came offering high premiums for the coins.

Indeed, by the late 1950s, several Swiss banks—primarily based in Zürich—had established numismatic departments specifically to sell the pieces. Typically, purchases of gold coins were conducted by a bank officer taking a prospective buyer to a private room and discussing the customer's wants.

I visited several of these banks in the early 1960s. I recall that at one prominent bank in Zürich, I asked what the price would be for a large quantity of unsorted Saint-Gaudens double eagles in Uncirculated grade. The banker told me that he could quote a figure then and there for 100,000 pieces, but if I wanted more than that he would have to excuse himself for a moment and check with others. I could not afford any such number, despite their current market price of about $40 each (the coins had a melt-down value of about $35, and during the 1950s the bulk price on the numismatic market had been as low as $36 or $37). In the end, it turned out the banker was aware of rare dates and owned a copy of the *Guide Book of United States Coins*, and he separately sold me a few dozen scarce issues for higher premiums.

While I suspect many similarly sized deals occurred, there were bigger movers and shakers involved, too. For example: in New York City, the Lentex Corporation—primarily a dealer in platinum—imported vast quantities of U.S. double eagles from Europe. Those of numismatic significance were bought and marketed by New Netherlands Coin Company (who had first peek at each shipment) and others.

Additionally, erstwhile jeweler-turned-numismatist James F. Kelly was active in the importation of gold coins during this period, working from a pine-paneled office in the basement of his home in Englewood, Ohio. He always had a large selection of the highly prized Carson City double eagles; usually, when an ordinary Liberty Head $20 sold for $40 to $50, a "CC" issue would sell for $60 to $80. Kelly's typical pieces were in grades of Very Fine and Extremely Fine, punctuated by an occasional About Uncirculated and an even more occasional Uncirculated coin. I found these to be scarce in French and Swiss holdings, so Kelly found them somewhere else; when asked, he stated that his source was a supplier in Argentina or, on other occasions, Venezuela. It was really none of my business—good for him if he found them in both countries.

A final note on the coins that came forth during this era before we move along. While double eagles, eagles, and half eagles were far more common, quite a few $2.50 quarter eagle coins came to light in Europe along the way as well, among which were Uncirculated specimens of the Liberty Head design dates from the 1880s to 1907 (with most being in the early 1900s). Some of the latter were beautiful, frosty gems. Also, European banks occasionally furnished gold dollars and $3 pieces—typically worn issues—but I am not aware of any cache of a particular date, not even one with dates in the 1880s (the range in which most high-level Mint State pieces in existence today are dated).

More Investors Arrive

Gold-buying activity in the United States snowballed from this point, and before long there was a great nationwide interest in squirreling away gold coins, especially double eagles, as a hedge against inflation and as security in the event that the American monetary system collapsed. Eventually, this became the "hard money" or "tangible asset" sector of the investment community.

I recall that one of our numismatic customers in Los Angeles started Monex in the 1970s and went on to offer financing for bulk coins and bullion, over time doing *hundreds of millions* of dollars in business. Other big players beginning around that time included A-Mark, MTB (Manfred, Tordella & Brookes), Mocatta Metals, and the Republic Bank (New York). While these firms sold many coins to collectors, most went to investors who knew little or nothing about coins. I personally had many customers who had no numismatic inclinations but felt a comfort in having a modest quantity of gold.

Of course, such public interest in hoarding gold coins had a longer standing in Europe, what with the unfortunate experiences of two world wars and untold political and economic turmoil, and by the 1960s bullion exchanges or sales counters were familiar sights in many banks and currency exchanges across the continent. Such smaller displays were in the nature of boutiques—not staffed by anyone with numismatic knowledge—and offered examples of popular gold coins from England, France, and Germany mainly, but also restrikes from the Austrian Mint and usually some U.S. and Mexican gold coins (particularly the large 50-pesos denomination, typically bearing the date 1947).

It was my experience in the 1960s and 1970s that such boutiques, if they had anything rare in the U.S. series, usually had counterfeits. This was particularly true of $1 and $3 gold pieces, for which fakes abounded for many different dates. These phony coins were occasionally seen in the stocks of numismatically knowledgeable Swiss banks as well. I recall helpfully pointing out a rather obvious counterfeit $3 on display in Zürich and receiving a reply to this effect: "Well, I guess you won't want to buy this one." The coin remained on display.

Also, on a trip through Greece in 1978, I saw that many banks had U.S. gold coins for sale—not many coins, but a counter exhibit—and nearly all were fakes. At that time, several U.S. citizens lived full-time in Europe and acted as suppliers and pickers for stateside firms.

An Overview of Foreign Hoards

Exported: 1933 and earlier • **Discovered by numismatists:** 1950s • **Treasure:** Gold coins

To prevent price drops and to avoid scaring buyers, very little information was ever given in print as to what specific gold coins were imported from Europe, especially if there were a cache or quantity of a given date. However, after a time the existence of such coins is revealed by their plenitude on the market and their increased listings in the population reports issued by commercial grading services such as ANACS (prominent then), the Numismatic Guaranty Corporation of America, and the Professional Coin Grading Service.

In the years since the initial wave, importation of U.S. gold coins from overseas sources has remained a part of the trade, but spectacular finds occur much less frequently today. As a general rule of thumb, overseas hoards from the 1950s onward have included these items:

Gold Dollars

Relatively few *authentic* gold dollars have turned up overseas.[499] Most of the genuine examples seen are in circulated grades and dated in the 1850s. Counterfeits abound, but are rarely imported by numismatists, as buyers on this side of the Atlantic are too knowledgeable. Significant quantities of these forgeries are brought in by tourists, however, and today just about any gold specialist sees them with some frequency.

Quarter Eagles

Quarter eagles are fairly scarce as a denomination in foreign hoards, but thousands have been imported. Those dated from 1834 to about 1880 are nearly always in circulated grades. Most early

pieces are of the Liberty Head style, but some Classic Heads are mixed among them. Occasionally a Charlotte or Dahlonega coin will be found. In general, availability is in proportion to original mintages, except that earlier dates are scarcer than later ones; this is true of all pre-1880 denominations, and there is seemingly a straight-line diminution in this regard.

Quarter eagles from about 1880 to 1907—the later part of the Liberty Head era—are typically Mint State, especially if dated in the 1900s, and some examples are frosty gems. Indian Head quarter eagles from 1908 to 1929 are a mixed bag and are typically Extremely Fine or About Uncirculated, although some Mint State coins have been found. The reason for their typically lower grades is the design; the flat field, normally the area in lowest relief on a coin, is on these pieces the highest part (except for mintmarked issues, for which the raised mintmark is higher yet). Thus, even with a minimal amount of contact, such pieces show abrasions.

$3 Gold Coins

The situation for $3 gold coins parallels that of gold dollars. Lots of fakes are on the overseas market, where they appeal to bargain-seekers. Reality hits when the coins are brought back home to the United States and shown to a reputable rare coin dealer or grading service. Notwithstanding this comment, a few authentic $3 coins have turned up over the years.

I recall an amusing incident in the 1960s: a fairly steady customer who specialized in gold coins went to Europe and returned with about a dozen different dates of $3 coins dated from 1854 into the 1880s. Giving him a magnifying glass, I pointed out that all had been struck from the same die, as evident from tiny characteristics. He became quite angry with me, and I never saw him again.

Half Eagles

Classic Head half eagles from 1834 to 1838 are scarce but available in the annals of overseas hoards; these are typically Very Fine or Extremely Fine. Liberty Head issues of the 1839–1880 years nearly always have evidence of circulation (the branch mint coins especially), whereas pieces of that design dated 1880 to 1908 are a mixture of Very Fine, Extremely Fine, and Mint State grades.

Indian Head half eagles from 1908 to 1929 are virtually all of the 1908–1916 years, and are typically in Very Fine, Extremely Fine, or About Uncirculated grades. In general, gem examples of half eagles of any design are elusive in foreign bank hoards and in many instances very rare, there being a few exceptions among issues of the 1900s.

Eagles

Liberty Head eagles of 1838 to 1907 are plentiful, especially those dated toward the end of the

range. Those dated before about 1880 are nearly always circulated and in grades of Very Fine, Extremely Fine, or About Uncirculated, while those from about 1880 to 1907 are mixed and include many Extremely Fine and About Uncirculated coins. Any Mint State pieces dated before 1900 are usually heavily bagmarked, although highly lustrous.

Among issues of the early 1900s, gems can be found of certain dates, and prodigious quantities of 1901-S coins have turned up. However, most of these have been sold into the general investment (not numismatic) market, thus there is hardly a glut. If anything, this means that a gem coin of a common issue is available for a reasonable price, making it easy to get a nice one for a type set.

As for pieces of the Indian design (dated 1907–1933), many coins have turned up, including numerous choice examples dated 1926 and 1932. Earlier issues range from Very Fine to Mint State; if the latter, usually towards the low end of that grade. A peculiarity of the Indian design is that the cheek of Miss Liberty is apt to acquire many contact marks and friction while the fields remain frosty. As such, grading practices were apt to vary widely in the late 1900s, and one person's About Uncirculated could be another's Mint State; in 1996, Greg Roberts, who has handled as many eagles in quantity as has anyone, commented that the typical Mint State eagle of this design is apt to be closer to MS-60 in grade than to MS-65.[500] Thankfully, third-party certification has eliminated much of the uncertainty today.

A representative find of Indian Head eagles was mentioned in this 1996 catalog description by David W. Akers:

> 1911-S Indian $10, PCGS Mint State-65: A gorgeous, original coin with full mint frost, excellent lustre, and superb color, a modulated medium orange and greenish gold. Almost no marks of any kind occurring since striking, but there is a die imperfection in the lower left obverse field that is nearly always seen on this date, and often on the 1913 S. Undoubtedly one of the finest examples from a mini-hoard

(less than 100 pieces) that came out of Europe in the late 1970s. Prior to the appearance of this group, the 1911 S was all but unknown in Mint State, much less in gem condition.[501]

Double Eagles

While they were in production, double eagles were the workhorse denomination in the U.S. gold series, as it was easier account for a single piece valued at $20 than two eagles, four half eagles, or eight quarter eagles. Of course, the same principle holds true outside the United States, and so the double eagle also became the denomination of choice for international trade when vast quantities were shipped overseas.

Today, Liberty Head double eagles dated from 1850 through about 1880 that have come back from international sources are typically Very Fine, Extremely Fine, or About Uncirculated. For certain issues of the 1860s and 1870s, Mint State pieces exist, but they are nearly always very heavily bagmarked—even cut or scratched—typically looking as if they have been "through the mill."

Liberty Head dates of the 1880s and 1890s exist in the same grades, although Mint State pieces are more numerous, typically grading MS-60 to about MS-63. Often a variety can be common in MS-63 grade but a great rarity if MS-65. Also note that it is my opinion that there seems to have been a "grade inflation," or loosening of interpretations among graders, and what is called MS-60 today might have been called an About Uncirculated coin a decade or so ago.

Among Liberty Head double eagles of the early 1900s, several issues are scarce due to their low mintages. In contrast, the 1901-S, 1904, and 1904-S coins are common as gems, have mostly been sold outside of the numismatic market, and furnish the opportunity for relatively inexpensive "type" coins.

Finally, Saint-Gaudens double eagles from 1907 to 1932 are typically Mint State at the levels of MS-60 to MS-63, although the Philadelphia Mint dates of the mid-1920s average higher and are often seen MS-63 to MS-65. What's rare and what's not can be determined by checking grading service population reports and popular price guides; the market tends to adjust itself nicely and correctly over a period of time.

Seventh Street

36-10

X

35 N. 7

1   1 Office Bldg Brick
0   2 Coinage Bldg   "
       3 Smelting House

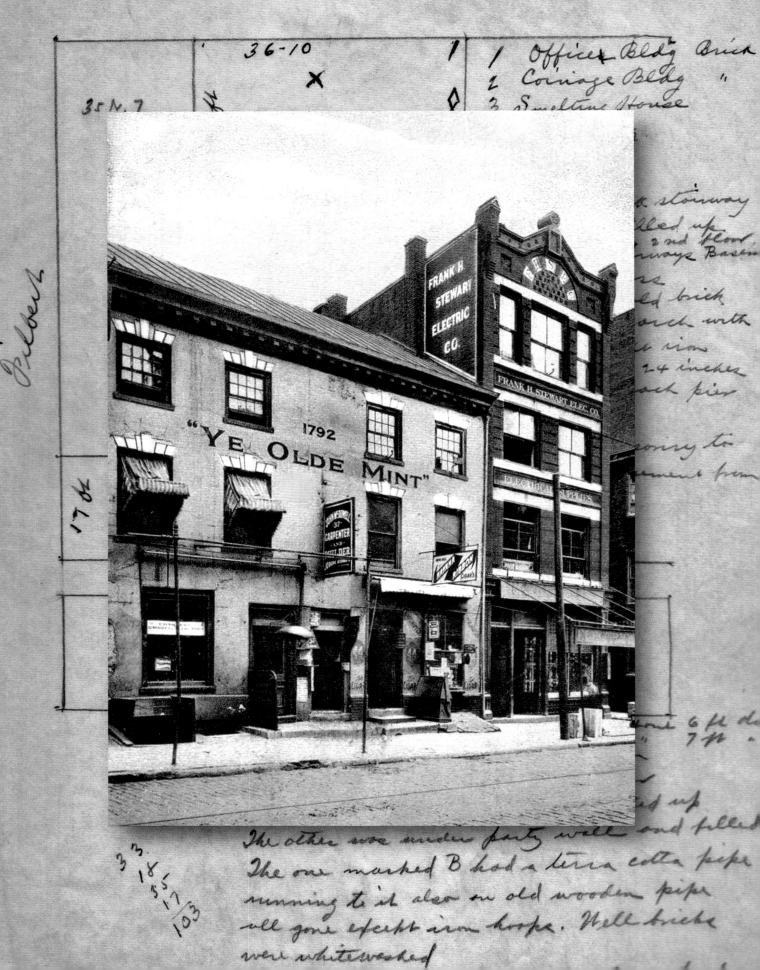

a stairway
led up
2nd floor
ways Basen
s
ld brick
ch with
irom
24 inches
ach piers

soury to
ement from

one 6 ft d
" 7 ft

ed up
The other was under party wall and filled
The one marked B had a terra cotta pipe
running to it also an old wooden pipe
all gone except iron hoops. Well bricks
were whitewashed

3 3.
18 '
5 5
17
103

Secrets of the Philadelphia Mint

The Philadelphia Mint, which since 1792 has operated in four subsequent locations within that city, has yielded many numismatic treasures over the years. As many of these delicacies have been wrapped in red tape and bureaucracy, and the complete truth will never be known concerning their origin. However, based upon numismatic observation, Mint correspondence, and knowledge of the characters involved, some strong theories have been brought forward.

Already, various hoards of silver dollars in certain mints have been discussed. Here, we explore a few tales with unique relation to the nation's primary coining facility.

Dies Found in the First Mint

Deaccessioned: 1800s • **Acquired by numismatists:** 1800s • **Treasure:** Coinage dies

Today numismatists are familiar with several different varieties of "restrikes" of coins of the 1800s made up from old dies, often mismatched (with obverses mated to incorrect reverses). Quite probably some of them had their genesis from the caches of dies described below.

Portrait of Joseph J. Mickley from the obverse of an 1867 medal by W.H. Key.

The following appeared in the January 1879 issue of the *American Journal of Numismatics*:

Editorial

The statement that the dies, hubs, &c. of U.S. coins, advertised for sale with the Mickley Collection, were seized by the United States authorities, has given rise to a great deal of comment. We have received from a gentleman in Philadelphia the following account of the affair:

"A few days previous to the sale, the United States authorities claimed the above, viz.: Some 20 obverse and reverse dies of the U.S. coinage, mostly in a damaged and corroded condition, the same having been condemned by the Mint authorities above 'half a century ago,' and as tradition says was the custom in those days, 'sold for old iron.' Since then we have grown more *artful*, and it has been deemed politic under existing laws, that the whole multitude of dated dies should be annually destroyed in the presence of three designated officers of the Mint.

"In the above described lots in the catalog, there was not a complete *pair* of obverse and reverse dies. Even the obverse die of the half-cent of 1811 was muled with the reverse die of a different year. We cannot conceive by what authority the government, after making sale of its 'refuse material,' could seize upon the same property without tendering some compensation. There is scarcely a numismatist in the United States, but who is aware of the existence and whereabouts of similar dies, and who is also aware of the many "re-strikes"—*known to be such*—being made from the dies, say of the 1804 cent, the 1811 half-cent, and of the 1823 cent, outside of the Mint.

"Philadelphia, December, 1878.
"R. Coulton Davis."[502]

From what we have seen in the public prints in reference to this matter, we infer that the government authorities were somewhat hasty in their action, and claimed the property without first satisfying themselves as to the ownership. No one would for a moment suspect Mr. Mickley of any wrongdoing in the matter. The affair was settled, we believe, by a payment to the family of the estimated value of the dies, which were then presented to the Mint, and subsequently destroyed.

Charles Warner Remembers

This related article is from *The Numismatist*, December 1910 and sheds much light on the matter. Charles K. Warner was a diecutter and token maker.

A store card issued by Charles K. Warner.

Coin Dies Abandoned in the Old U.S. Mint

Reminiscences of Charles K. Warner

Various publications in recent months regarding the first United States Mint and the many discussions of the use and misuse of coin dies in early Mint days have been subjects of extraordinary interest to Charles K. Warner, the veteran medallist of Philadelphia.

In comparison with the recent destruction of all coinage dies excepting those in actual use, and the now prescribed rigid regulations as to the care and destruction of dies,[503] the following communication to *The Numismatist* from Mr. Warner makes interesting reading at this time:

"I have at times in the past promised to write you something regarding my boyhood days around the old Mint building, which still stands on the east side of Seventh street and which was pictured and featured in the January and February *Numismatist* of this year.

"My father, the late John S. Warner, who from 1823 to 1868 was the oldest established medallist in the United States, was well acquainted with a certain William Sellers who for many years conducted the business of a silversmith in the old Mint building. He occupied the entire first floor and a greater part of the basement.

"In the latter part of 1857 Mr. Sellers gave to my father a large number of old coin dies which were a part of a great lot of both obverse and reverse dies for all the silver and copper denominations that Sellers found in the old building when he first occupied it years before. It was stated at that time that these were found among general rubbish when the basement was cleaned. Most of the dies were considerably rusted, chipped on the edges, or cracked across the face. My father having no use for the old dies gave them to a particular friend of his, the then Chief Coiner of the Mint, which was then located in Chestnut street near Broad.

"As a lad I frequently visited the old Mint building on errands to Mr. Sellers for my father. I often played about the building with a son of Sellers, who was about my age. I well remember the old vault. I could have easily explored the vault, and no doubt could have found many things which, if preserved, would be of great interest today, but lad that I was I had no interest in such things."

It is seen that the Mint sold no old dies at all, contrary to the Davis letter, but they were found among trash by John S. Warner and given to an unnamed Mint official.

The Philadelphia Mint as it appeared in 1854, by that time in private hands and the home to several businesses.

Lots of Stories

Other stories, theories, and reminiscences about old dies from the first Mint abound, often differing widely from each other. Walter H. Breen related that certain dies had been sold as scrap metal as early as 1833:

The 1823 [large cent] was long believed scarce enough in upper grades that when Joseph J. Mickley found the broken original obverse die among batches of scrap metal sold by the Mint (1833), he and his friends eventually decided to make restrikes, using an 1813 reverse from a similar source. These dies suffered still more extensive breaks, but continued to be used at intervals for decades, at least until a later owner defaced them. . . . [504]

Never mind that the Mint in 1833 sold no old dies to Mickley or anyone else.

The 1804 "restrike" cent is not a restrike at all. The obverse is from an 1803 die altered to read 1804. The reverse is from a die used in 1820.

Further from Breen:

1804 restrike [cent]. Copper. Struck about 1858 by parties unknown (Mickley? Dickeson?) from rusted dies retrieved from scrap metal sold by the Mint in 1833. Obverse altered from 1803 Sheldon-261, reverse of 1820. Both dies hand-strengthened. [505]

This story should also be taken with a grain of salt, as neither Joseph J. Mickley nor Montroville W. Dickeson can be connected with restriking coins from Mint dies in 1858 or at any other time.

Still more from Breen, this ascribed to an 1816 Mint disposal of dies:

The 1811 [half cent] restrike was struck outside the Mint about 1859 from genuine dies (the regular 1811 Close Date obverse with the 1802 reverse), which the teen-aged Joseph J. Mickley had retrieved in 1816 among rusted and broken dies sold by Mint personnel as scrap metal.

For many years the coin dealer Capt. John W. Haseltine used to claim that only six were struck; the correct number seems to be 12, of which 11 are traced. [506]

Yet another dubious account: There is no evidence that Mickley, born in 1799, was anything beyond a teenaged boy beginning his interest in coins around 1816.

Regardless, a final tale, this from the January 1907 issue of *Coins, Paper Money, Etc., For Sale,* issued by Lancaster, Pennsylvania, dealer Charles Steigerwalt. Today the so-called "restrikes" are eminently collectible as such, but Steigerwalt was no fan of them:

> A certain kind of 1804 and 1823 cents have appeared in sale catalogs for years as "Mint Restrikes." The recent catalogers may be excused on the plea of ignorance, but when these rank counterfeits are sold by those who have being doing so for years, it is time collectors knew their true character.
>
> While at a recent sale, the lacking information regarding the 1823 was given by an aged collector, who told how, years ago, he had found the dies in New York, probably sold with old iron from the Mint, brought them to Philadelphia, had a collar made, which was lacking, and the coins struck by a man named Miller on 7th Street, that city.[507]
>
> Later, the dies came into possession of a then leading dealer there and, when his store was sold out in 1885[508], the writer finding them among a lot of old dies purchased, they were at once destroyed so effectually that no more will ever come from that source. These coins never saw the Mint, and are counterfeits pure and simple.
>
> It was supposed the 1804 came from the same source as the 1823, but the originator of those disclaimed any knowledge of the 1804. An effort was made in a recent sale catalog to throw an air of mystery around this 1804.

That is simply ridiculous. The obverse has been identified as an 1803, but as that date was too common, a crude 4 was cut over the 3 and a reverse of the same period after the fraction was omitted, probably of about 1816 or later, was used in striking these abominations. By whom struck is unknown, but it was at a period long after, when the dies were rusty, and certainly not in the Mint.

Like the Breen stories, there is a problem with Steigerwalt's account—specifically that he "at once destroyed" the dies for the 1823 restrike. In actuality, cent specialist Doug Smith offered them for sale to me in the 1950s (I declined as I did not know what their legality was), and the dies still exist today.

Other Dies, Other Times

There are even more instances of dies from various Mint disposals reaching the private sector. In the 1800s, many superannuated dies were used to create "restrikes," including those mentioned above, often in different metals from the originals or with mismatched obverses and reverses.

The list of such productions is a long one; many pieces are described in detail in Andrew W. Pollock's *United States Pattern Coins and Related Issues* and earlier texts on the pattern series and in an appendix in *United States Pattern Coins* by Dr. J. Hewitt Judd. Examples range from a white metal piece struck using an 1806 half dollar obverse die and a postal embossed stamp die for the reverse (probably made in the 1800s) to impressions made in 1962 from the rusted reverse

The 1823 "restrike" cent.
These were made at intervals over the years.

Obverse striking in copper from an
1822 half dollar die discarded in the early 1900s.

die of an 1814 dime with legend incorrectly spaced so as to read STATESOFAMERICA. These latter pieces were made to the extent of 536 examples in Edinburgh, Scotland, to the order of Robert Bashlow, and were typically combined with a modern obverse die lettered GOD PRESERVE PHILADELPHIA AND THE LORDS PROPRIETERS.[509]

In the American Numismatic Society's collection today are such productions as an 1818 cent Newcomb-9, 1805 25¢ Browning-2, 1806 50¢ Overton-102, 1806 O-123/4, and an 1803 $10

(not a die variety known to exist in original gold striking form).[510]

A couple more tidbits: toward the end of the 1900s, a number of obverse and reverse dies for Carson City silver and gold coins—some defaced and others not—were found buried near the mint building. They had been discarded, and it was thought this was a good way to dispose of them.

And also in the late 1900s, the U.S. Mint sold certain commemorative coin dies that were very lightly canceled with two line cuts across the face.

Two Tons of Three-Cent Pieces

Circulated: 1850s–1862 • **Found:** 1882

As certain denominations and coinage formats became obsolete, pieces of those denominations were called in by the Treasury Department. Many accounts of such redemptions were printed over the years, including this one in the October 1882 *American Journal of Numismatics*, reprinted from the *Boston Herald*:

> The United States Mint in Philadelphia has lately received over two tons of three-cent silver coins, which by act of Congress have been abolished from the national coin-

age. This is said to be, however, only about one-fifth of the quantity of these small coins which are to be brought from the various Sub-Treasuries in the country, there having already been redeemed more than ten tons.

The three-cent pieces now in the Mint would fill three large wagons. They are to be recoined into dimes, as the three-cent nickel pieces are to take the place of the old silver three-cent coins. The Treasury Department is redeeming the small coins as fast as possible, and in a few years they will entirely disappear, and only the nickels will be in circulation. The coins have lost a very considerable percent of their intrinsic value by usage, in some cases amounting to as much as 25%. In fact, they were rapidly wearing out. This is one reason why they were abolished and the harder and more convenient nickel substituted.

Finds at the 1792 Mint Site

Lost: 1792–1832 • **Found:** 1907–1911

In the early 1900s, Philadelphia electrical contractor Frank H. Stewart purchased the original Mint buildings, which had been used for coinage from 1792 until a new Mint structure was occupied in 1832. Between the time of that move and Stewart's purchase, the old premises had housed a variety of private businesses, including that of John S. Warner, who found many old dies (see account in "Dies Found in the First Mint," page 335).

In 1907, Stewart began to clear the area to make way for new construction by razing one of the smaller buildings. Then, in 1911, he attempted to have the City of Philadelphia and other groups preserve the main buildings (two connected structures), suggesting that they be relocated to Fairmount Park. Viewing the prospect as an exceedingly expensive undertaking, no interest was forthcoming from any officials or civic organizations.

Accordingly, in the same year the front or main buildings were razed. During the process, Stewart acquired several numismatic artifacts which were exhibited Congress Hall at 6th and Chestnut streets in the same city.

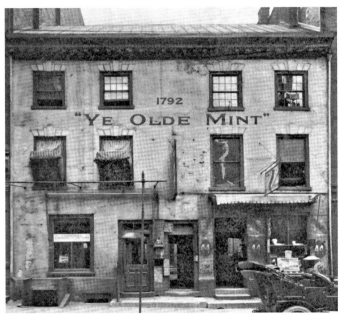

The Mint when Stewart owned it.

Front of the Coinage Building as it appeared in 1911. By this time, most of the Mint buildings were in sorry condition.

Rear of the Coinage Building as it appeared in 1911.

Some of the many items found when Stewart razed the building in 1911. Planchet for a silver center cent and a piece of copper from which a half cent planchet was cut.

Later, in 1924, Stewart wrote a fine book about the Mint, its history, and his experiences while demolishing it. He related that the following coins and related items had been found (partial listing):

> Draped Bust half cent, circa 1800–1808, date not readable (some of these pieces were probably loose change lost by employees and visitors, not undistributed coins)
>
> 1825 half cent, corroded
>
> Two blank planchets for 1792 silver-center cents; this find was learned of by J.C. Mitchelson, numismatist of Tariffville, Connecticut, who came to Philadelphia in an effort to persuade Stewart to part with them[511]
>
> 1816 copper cent
>
> 1826 copper cent, corroded
>
> 1832 copper cent. Worn, perhaps VF-30 grade
>
> 1834 copper cent. Worn, perhaps VF-20 grade
>
> 1795 half dime, pattern struck in copper, "damaged"
>
> Half dollar planchet, no further description
>
> Half dollar coinage die showing the "eagle side." Sent to the Secret Service in Washington; later disposition not known
>
> Early silver dollar, date not stated, edge lettered ONE HUNDRED FOR A DOLLAR
>
> 1804 $5, pattern struck in copper
>
> Various blank planchets and planchet cutter scrap (such scrap was known as scissel, a term not generally used today)[512]

From Within the Mint

Minted: 1800s • **Disclosed:** 1909

To relate the story of many rare patterns that came from the Philadelphia Mint in the early 1900s, we begin with John W. Haseltine. Born in 1838, the longtime Philadelphia resident became interested in coin collecting by the 1860s, worked with dealer Ebenezer Mason in 1869, and eventually started his own business. He had very close connections to certain individuals at the Mint—probably in the Medal Department—who produced patterns, restrikes, and Proofs.

Thus, it was Haseltine who acted as the funnel to distribute Proof "restrikes" of 1801, 1802, and 1803 silver dollars and Class III 1804 dollars in the early 1870s. By the early 1900s, he was considered an old-timer in the trade and was nicknamed "The Numismatic Refrigerator" for his "rarities on ice," a stock from which he withdrew morsels for sale from time to time. He frequently surprised numismatists with Proofs, patterns, and other rarities—some of which were not previously known to exist, such as the silver Proof trade dollars of 1884 (10 minted) and 1885 (5 minted), which he made known to the collecting community in 1907 and 1908. These glittering gems were said to have come from the estate of his father-in-law, William Idler (1808–1901), who was engaged in the coin trade in the early 1850s and also had close connections to the Mint.

At the 1908 American Numismatic Association convention in Philadelphia, Haseltine regaled listeners with tales, somewhat embellished, of the olden days in the coin trade. By this time, he was associated in business with Stephen K. Nagy, and the two had an established customer in William H. Woodin (1868–1934), a manufacturer of railroad and other heavy equipment who at one time served as the chairman of the American Car & Foundry Company.

Sometime during the year of said convention, Haseltine acquired either from his own stock or from the current holdings at the Mint two coins, the existence of which were not known earlier: one each of two different varieties of 1877 "half union" $50 coins struck in gold.

Woodin—one of the first U.S. numismatists to take a serious interest in collecting gold coins of lower denominations by date and mintmark, and at one time the owner of the unique 1870-S $3 gold piece—was offered these pieces and purchased them forthwith. The price paid by Woodin was $10,000 each, far and away a record for any U.S. coin up to that time, and a feature story about these treasures was published in *The Numismatist*.

One of two varieties of the 1877 pattern gold half union or $50 piece, each unique and a showpiece in the National Numismatic Collection. In 1909, these caused a major controversy. This variety is known as Judd-1548 as described in *United States Pattern Coins*.

At this, an unexpected furor arose; it was said by some that the $50 gold patterns never should have left the Mint, and also that they might have done so *recently*. Normally, bygones were bygones and there was no commotion at all about rarities that had slipped away from the Mint to enrich certain employees within the halls of that venerable coinage institution—but in this case, Haseltine and Nagy re-acquired the pieces from Woodin to quiet the matter.

The coins were then presented to the Mint Cabinet, where they were duly put on display. In exchange, the Mint searched its vaults and came up with several *crates* of old pattern coins, some of which dated back to the Gobrecht era,[513] to be given to Woodin. He subsequently partnered with the era's pre-eminent numismatic scholar, Edgar H. Adams, and the two used the coins for the basis of a book on the patterns: *United States Pattern, Trial and Experimental Pieces*, published by the American Numismatic Society in 1913.

Following the Patterns to Present Day

No inventory of the 1909 Mint hoard of patterns was ever published, but from later evidence it was deduced that even a partial list would have included thousands of pieces, many previously unlisted. Emphasis seems to have been on coins dated in the 1870s and early 1880s. All of a sudden, dozens or more specimens of certain beautiful designs by engravers James B. Longacre, William Barber, and George T. Morgan were revealed. Quite possibly the most recently dated coins in the cache were several hundred duplicates of the cent and five-cent shield-design patterns dated 1896.

1839 pattern half dollar by Christian Gobrecht featuring a Large Letters reverse die introduced slightly later. J-97.

Pattern bronze cent by James B. Longacre adapting a Flying Eagle design created by Christian Gobrecht in 1838. This pattern is slightly smaller than a standard copper cent of the era. J-178.

Most of the coins remained in Woodin's possession for many years. Toward the end of his life, he would serve as President Franklin D. Roosevelt's first secretary of the Treasury, holding the office from March 5, 1933, to December 31 of the same year. He resigned in poor health, having been ill for most of his term to that point. In the meantime, Henry Morgenthau Jr. had served as acting secretary for much of the time. Under Woodin's watch (with Morgenthau as surrogate), there were vast changes in Treasury procedures involving gold coins and bullion. In 1933 the United States coinage included $20 gold coins that would later become quite prized and also somewhat controversial.[514]

Woodin passed away on May 4, 1934. His pattern coins came on the market privately during the 1930s and 1940s, with a few stragglers in the 1950s, and by now are widely dispersed in many different collections. Years ago, I bought several hundred of these coins from Woodin's friend Robert K. Botsford; these pieces were long-forgotten leftovers came from the estate of the deceased, who had maintained a residence in nearby Berwick, Pennsylvania.

As for the $50 gold union patterns, they are today in the National Numismatic Collection at the Smithsonian Institution, Washington, D.C.

1870 Pattern Standard Silver half dollar by Longacre. Rather than being patterns made to test a design or concept, several hundred varieties were made in copper, aluminum (as here), and silver, and with plain or reeded edge. Collectors could not order them openly at the time, but could buy them from favored dealers who had connections with Mint officials. J-1357.

1877 pattern half dollar in silver by George T. Morgan. Patterns of this year were made in dozens of die combinations in copper and silver and could be quietly purchased from favored dealers or those closely tied to Mint officials. J-1512.

1879 $4 gold coin or "Stella" struck in aluminum. These were made under a veil of secrecy and were not known to numismatists until some were found in the crates of patterns traded to William H. Woodin in 1909. This hoard had many other unknown varieties of patterns, restrikes, and other numismatic delicacies. J-1640.

chapter 21

Notable Single-Coin Finds

While a "hoard" probably should include several coins, there are many single-coin finds that are worth mentioning, at least in passing. Several interesting ones are delineated in this chapter.

The possibilities are virtually endless, as just about every coin that is worn and rare was at some time found by someone. Thus, this is but a sampler.

"A Queer Piece of Money"

Hidden or lost: 1600s • **Found:** 1893 • **Treasure:** Willow Tree shilling

This account appeared in H.E. Morey's *Numismatic Quarterly and Catalogue*, January 1894:

> While digging a cellar on the Deacon Faulkner estate in Malden [Massachusetts], an Irishman found a queer piece of money. A gentleman passing by offered the Irishman a quarter for it. Pat accepted at once, pleased at getting something he could spend, while the gentleman added a fine Willow Tree shilling to his collection.

Note that there is a possibility this might have been a joke rather than a legitimate report, as it was common at the time to poke fun at the innocent nature of Irishmen, and "Pat" was sometimes used as a generic name in this regard. Also, as an aside, the town of more numismatic news out of Malden was published in this same edition of the journal, and this time the find was definitely not all it was cracked up to be:

> A portion of the famous buried treasure of the late Captain Kidd [*very* late!] was found in Malden recently, or rather that is what a workman thought while digging on Hawthorne Street when he struck a two-quart pail filled with shining metal coins. He was an employee of Lyman B. Jordan and was digging a post-hole when he struck a metallic substance.
>
> Investigation proved the find to be a pail containing coins of the denominations of dollars, halves, and quarters. They were new and were dated 1860 and 1863. The man's dream of wealth was shattered, however, after he had them tested, for they proved counterfeit. How or when they were buried there is a mystery.

In an Irish Farmhouse

Lost: 1700s or 1800s • **Found:** 1904 • **Treasure:** 1787 Clinton copper and other coins

Sometime before early 1905, presumably in the warmer months of the preceding year, an American numismatist made a tour of Ireland.[515] Stopping at a rural farmhouse, the collector engaged its owner in conversation. Finally, the topic turned to old coins, and "the farmer said he had a few stowed away somewhere that he had no use for."

After duly rummaging around, the farmer brought forth a small box that appeared to be filled with old Roman coins of low value, perhaps from centuries earlier when Romans occupied Britain. Glancing quickly over the lot, the visitor saw nothing of value, offered a couple of dollars, consummated a transaction, and put the coins in his trunk. Later, after returning to the United States, the collector opened the box:

> Upon examining the coins he was surprised to find a beautiful specimen of a New York cent of the date of 1787, one of the rarest of the

colonial coins. This coin is known as the Clinton cent, having been issued when George Clinton was governor of New York, and bearing his portrait. The coin was worth up in the hundreds of dollars, but just how much no one knows, for there are only four of them known.

The 1787 Clinton copper is indeed a major rarity, and today it is believed that only 10 to 12 are known. Whether the Irish find was one of these, or was a copy (such as made by James Bolen) that was "laundered" through this tale, is not known. If genuine, today it would merit a full page in an auction catalog.

A Find in France

Exported: 1800s • **Found:** Circa 1904 • **Treasure:** $50 gold "slug"

A remarkable "find" was made in Europe by a "millionaire collector from one of the New England states," who visited the head of one of the larger French financial institutions. This account appeared in a 1905 newspaper story:

> The banker said that in one of their branch banks was a $50 gold piece which he could have at face value, and welcome.
>
> Of course, the collector could not eat or sleep until he had located the coveted coin. It was found to be just as represented, in splendid condition. The new owner now says that $500 would not buy it. And there are hundreds of other chances awaiting the lucky man in the thousand and one old shops in European cities.[516]

One can but speculate if the aforementioned $50 piece was one that had been part of a $200,000 shipment of octagonal $50 coins—some 4,000 pieces—from New York City to Liverpool on the steamer *Asia*, cited in a newspaper account on January 13, 1853.[517]

Going, Going, Gone!

Misplaced: Early 1900s • **Found:** 1905 • **Treasure:** 1794 dollar

The *Worcester Evening Post*, April 26, 1905, recounted this tale:

> New York, April 26.—Karl Fraenkle sold an old safe for $29 on Saturday. The man who bought the safe and carted it away made one of the greatest bargains on record. For inside the safe was $20,000 worth of stock of the Central Brewing Company, much valuable jewelry bequeathed to Mr. Fraenkle by his wife, and a collection of old coins—one a United States silver dollar of 1794, worth several hundred dollars.
>
> The forgetful Mr. Fraenkle also forgot to give the combination of the safe to the man who bought it. But from the moment the safe left his possession until yesterday, Fraenkle rushed frantically around the city yelling figuratively, "New safes for old." Then, by good luck, he found the safe and still locked in it were his stock jewels, coins.
>
> Karl Fraenkle, who is wealthy, has kept for many years an old-fashioned saloon at No. 331 Bowery, next to the Dry Dock Savings Bank. His failing health determined him to retire from business. He sold his saloon fixtures at auction Saturday.
>
> On Friday he cleaned out the old safe all but one drawer. In it lay the $20,000 worth of stock of the brewing company of which Fraenkle is the director, his dead wife's jewels, and the coins.
>
> "I leave them here until tomorrow," said Fraenkle, and he closed the safe's doors.
>
> Saturday came and the auctioneer and the buyers. Bidding was not lively on the safe.
>
> "Going at 29!" cried the auctioneer—going, going—gone!

"One of Three Known"

Hidden or lost: 1600s • **Found:** 1910 • **Treasure:** Pine Tree shilling

This find appeared in newspapers on October 24, 1910:

Coin Made in 1652
Found in Field

Cassius D. Phelps, a South Williamstown merchant, while plowing in a field, found one of the rarest of American coins, a Massachusetts Pine Tree shilling, for which he has refused $300. It is one of the first coins which was minted in the Massachusetts Bay Colony and is dated 1652, thirty-two years after the landing of the Pilgrims at Plymouth.

There are only two others like it in existence, and neither is as good a specimen as this one. One is owned by a Boston collector and cost him $212, and the other is owned in Albany, and no price will be placed upon it.[518]

As is true of many, indeed most accounts of coin finds in the popular press, the preceding yields virtually nothing in the way of numismatic information. At the time an ordinary Massachusetts 1652 Pine Tree shilling would have been worth just a few dollars.

An 1804 Dollar in a Pot of Coins

Hidden: 1800s • **Found:** December 26, 1913 • **Treasure:** 1804 dollar (or was it?)

The 1804 silver dollar, of which only 15 are known, has been dubbed the "King of U.S. Coins." Its story is fascinating, and it begins with a contradiction: Although these rare pieces are dated 1804, no dollars bearing this date were struck in this year.

In actuality, the first 1804 dollars were not struck until 1834, when they were made at the Mint as presentation pieces. Years later—starting in 1859—additional pieces were struck using a different reverse die. Today, there are 6 of the first striking known and 9 of the second.

This information was not known to numismatists until later in the 1900s, though, allowing the rarity of these pieces to spawn all sorts of wondrous tales. Today's reader can well imagine the excitement that this news article, datelined December 27, 1913, New Haven, Connecticut, caused among collectors at the time:

Numismatists flocked to this city today in an effort to get possession of the 1804 silver dollar which was found in a pot of coins and old documents unearthed at the excavation for the Yale hockey rink in this city yesterday.

Col. J.P. Hart of Philadelphia, representing a wealthy collector of that city, was early on the ground with an offer of $2,000 for the coin and obtained permission to take it to New York to further its authenticity. Other offers, one of $1,200 for the coin, have already been received.

On January 8, 1914, a further account emanated from New Haven:

The 1804 silver dollar found several weeks ago at the excavating for the Arena-Centerfreeze Company's hockey rink is still undisposed of, and the numismatists have not completed their examination of it. It has been pronounced genuine, but there is some question as to whether it was issued in 1804, or is one of the few struck off the die in 1858.

The coin was found by William Sullivan, an assistant foreman of the work of excavation.

Under the Connecticut law the property found belongs to the Arena-Centerfreeze Company. What happened to this "1804 silver dollar" is not known. More likely, it was adjudged spurious. In any event, the ardor for its possession seems to have subsided by two weeks after its discovery.

Tangential Tales

Though not all are strictly finds, nor confirmed examples of an 1804 silver dollar, a few other stories involving the "King of Coins" can be told before leaving the subject.

Édouard Frossard, a leading dealer in the late 1800s.

One tale[519] informs us of a special visitor to the Mint (shades of Sir Rowland Winn; see "An Englishman Visits America" in chapter 2, page 53). Édouard Frossard in his house organ, *Numisma*, May 1884, told of a "perfectly struck, brilliant, nearly Proof, almost high relief, sharp, strong dollar of 1804" in an oval morocco presentation case, with this inscribed in gold lettering on the outside cover:

Presented to Frank S. Houghton, Esq're, on the occasion of his visit at the National Mint in Philadelphia July 4th 1804, his fortieth birthday, Elias Boudinot, Director.

Other accounts relate to 1804 dollars lost at sea (near China, Central America, or Africa) or seized by pirates. One such comes from Dr. Ivan C. Michels, in his 1880 book, *The Current Gold and Silver Coins of All Nations*:

1804 Dollar—similar to the dollar of 1803. This dollar has become exceedingly scarce, and the last sale of a fine specimen was made at $1,000. Of this dollar, according to returns of the United States Mint records, 19,570 pieces were struck, and, with the exception of a few, were all exported to Africa. . . .

In 1804, an expedition was started from the United States against Tripoli, headed by Captain Eaton and Hamet Carmanly, exile and elder brother of the Bashaw of Tripoli. Their march lay across a thousand miles of desert; yet it was accomplished, with indescribable fatigue and suffering, in 50 days. To pay the expenses of this little army of mounted Arabs and 70 American seamen, these 1804 dollars were shipped to the coast of Africa, and only very few of them, if any, were brought back by the returned victors. . . .

One 1804 dollar was even swiped by a tramp, as in this caper. It must have been a slow day for news on July 22, 1895, when *The New York Daily Tribune* informed its readers of two men named Schultz and a great rarity:

Judge Fitzgerald, sitting Sessions, the other day had before him a man named Charles Schultz, who was arraigned for theft. The complainant was one Felix Schultz, who said he had recently been appealed to for assistance by a stranger, who gave his name as Charles Schultz. It was evident from his appearance that he was in hard luck. Felix Schultz was moved by the sad story told by Charles to take him into his house, where food and a night's lodging were generously provided.

The next morning Charles had gone and so had Felix's new trousers, his grandfather's gold watch and chain and some money and coins that were in the pockets. The police were promptly informed of the case, and Charles was arrested and arraigned before Judge Fitzgerald. T.F. Gibbons, a lawyer, of No. 105 West Tenth Street, appeared for Felix Schultz. During the examination it was discovered that Charles had Felix's trousers on, and he admitted that he had pawned the jewelry.

As Judge Fitzgerald was about to sentence Charles to Sing Sing, Felix importuned him to mitigate the sentence if Charles would tell what he had done with a pocket-piece, a silver dollar of the coinage of 1804, that he prized from the fact it had been in his family for three generations.

Judge Fitzgerald asked the prisoner what he had done with the coin. The prisoner said he had tried to pass it in a saloon, but the proprietor refused to take it because it was so old. He then, on the advice of the bartender, took the coin to a dealer in old coins in Broadway, who offered him $75 for it. He concluded to try other dealers in coins. He named the Scott Stamp and Coin Company (Ltd.), in East Twenty-Third Street, who, he asserted, purchased it for $90.

"We have begun a suit against the Scott Company, of East Twenty-Third Street, for the recovery of this coin," said Mr. Gibbons, "and the case is to be tried before Judge Roesh on the 30th inst. The Scott Company has made a general denial of ever having purchased the coin."

Of the 1804 dollars, all but 12 that were issued were returned to the Mint owing to an omission in stamping them. Of the 12 outstanding, 11 have been accounted for and this coin which is in dispute is supposed to be the missing one.

Mr. Gibbons said he had demanded $5,000 from the Scott Company. He also said that an uptown dealer cataloged the coin as being worth from $600 to $2,400.[520]

As a parting commentary on rare 1804 dollars, it is perhaps significant, certainly interesting, to reprint this news clipping dated Bunkie, Louisiana, March 4, 1930:

The proverbial end-of-the-rainbow story came true yesterday for Forest Normand, Avoyelles Parish farmer, when he plowed up a pot of silver coins on his farm near here. While plowing, he noticed a few coins turned up, and upon closer investigation, unearthed an old iron pot, rusty with age, containing more than 3,000 pieces of Spanish silver, coins from 1763 to 1805. Included in the find was an American silver dollar bearing the date 1804 with the likeness of George Washington.[521]

Presumably, this is the ultimate U.S. rarity, an 1804 silver dollar showing the "father of our country" rather than Miss Liberty!

A Long-Lost Proof Set

Lost or saved: 1800s • Found: 1940s • Treasure: 1842 Proof set

In the 1930s and 1940s, Oscar G. Schilke used to advertise in newspapers to buy coins. In addition, he had an arrangement with certain banks in Connecticut and New York whereby he would visit their lobbies and conduct free coin appraisals for bank clients. Over a period of time, he acquired many interesting things.

One of his prize finds was brought to him by a Connecticut lady who found a group of copper and silver coins in a small case stored under some other things in a bedroom chest of drawers. Oscar could hardly believe his eyes as he contemplated a glittering U.S. Proof coin set of the year 1842, containing one each of the half cent, large cent, half dime, dime, quarter dollar, half dollar, and silver dollar.

While such a set is exceedingly rare and of immense value, this particular 1842 group contained a special rarity: the Liberty Seated quarter dollar was of the variety with Small Date numerals. In that year, all quarter dollars made at the Philadelphia Mint for circulation in commerce had the date in larger numerals. A few presentation Proof sets—probably not more than a dozen or two—contained quarters from a special Small Date die. This was one of them.

Today, fewer than 10 1842 Small Date quarters are known, and the Schilke Collection specimen, which later appeared in the Century Collection Sale (1965), may be the finest of these.

A Little Princess Comes Out of Hiding

Lost: 1800s • **Found:** Circa 1960 • **Treasure:** 1841 quarter eagle

In the early 1960s, a lady who lived near Hamilton, New York—a quiet little town best known as the home of Colgate University—found an old gold coin among her family heirlooms. Taking it to Empire Coin Company, she was delighted to find that it was no ordinary gold coin, but was one of the very rarest dates in the quarter eagle series, the 1841.

Known as "The Little Princess," an appellation given to it years earlier by Abe Kosoff, this particular Philadelphia Mint variety was struck to the extent of perhaps fewer than a couple dozen. By 1960, fewer than 10 were known to exist.

Jim Ruddy and I checked the woman's coin carefully and then showed it to several other numismatists including John Jay Pittman (of Rochester, New York) and John N. Rowe III (of Dallas, Texas). All agreed that it was, indeed, a genuine 1841 "Little Princess," and this new discovery was added to the short roster of the pieces known. Soon thereafter, it was sold to a gold coin specialist.

If You Find Just One Large Cent . . .

Hidden or lost: Late 1700s or early 1800s •
Found: 1974 or earlier • **Treasure:** 1793 Chain large cent rarity

If you find just one old large cent, if it is a 1793, you've hit the jackpot![522] There were three major designs of cents this year—the Chain, the Wreath, and the Liberty Cap types—and while an example of any of these can be very valuable, this story relates to the earliest design, the Chain style.

So-called due to the continuous chain of 15 (one for each state) links on the reverse, these cents are found with several die varieties, the most famous of which is that with the name of our country abbreviated as AMERI.[523] The engraver probably believed that the full word AMERICA would not fit comfortably on this particular die—though he was able to include it on later dies.

On with the story: one day in June 1974, a woman walked into the New York City office of the Sotheby Parke Bernet auction house. She showed coin expert David E. Tripp a leather pouch which held some poorly preserved English copper pieces of the late 1700s—pieces of no numismatic account or monetary importance. But there was one more coin: a gorgeous 1793 United States cent, a Chain AMERI!

Tripp accepted the coin for a forthcoming auction sale. Seeking to share his excitement, he took it to the Park Avenue office of Lester Merkin, who carefully treated it with a badger's hair brush and, with the agreement of David Tripp, assigned the quite conservative (in the opinion of certain later viewers) grade of EF-45, with traces of mint luster, to it.[524] The coin crossed the auction block and fetched $13,000, the buyer being Maryland professional numismatist Julian Leidman.[525]

The story of a "penny selling for $13,000" hit the news wire services, but there was a little problem: the date was transposed, and articles were published about Sotheby's selling a *1973* cent, a coin worth just face value, for $13,000! "As a result, I was deluged with letters and calls to the extent that I dreaded coming to the office," Tripp later recalled.

Such is the life of a rare coin dealer!

If You Find Just One Double Eagle . . .

Hidden or lost: Late 1800s • **Found:** 1977 • **Treasure:** 1870-CC double eagle

Variation on a theme: if you find just one old double eagle, if it is an 1870-CC, you've hit the jackpot![526]

One day at his desk at Sotheby Parke Bernet in spring 1977, David E. Tripp received a coin in the mail from Nevada. Upon inspection, it proved to be somewhat worn and not particularly attractive, but no matter: it was the most highly prized of all double eagles made at the short-lived Carson City Mint, an 1870-CC!

In Tripp's words:

> I called the man to discuss his good luck, but he was too poor to own a telephone. I wrote him and suggested he call me collect. When I told him what he had, he was astonished.
>
> It is probably the lowest-grade piece among the few known 1870-CC double eagles, but when it sold it fetched $10,000!

A Hitherto Unknown Half Dime

Saved or hidden: Circa 1870s • **Found:** Circa 1977 • **Treasure:** Unique 1870-S half dime

One of the most significant numismatic discoveries of the late 1900s took place in the late 1970s, when RARCOA dazzled the hobby by announcing that an 1870-S half dime had come to light.[527] The coin had previously been purchased over the counter at a suburban Chicago coin shop as a common-date coin, and only later was the S mintmark on the reverse noticed! The coin was then sold to RARCOA.

The remarkable new discovery was exhibited at several conventions. I had the privilege of examining it closely. Indeed, not only was the coin not known, but the very fact that it was ever made was not known either. The coin had not been listed in the *Guide Book*, *The Standard Catalogue of United States Coins*, or any other references, nor had it been mentioned in any official Mint Reports.

Shortly after the announcement of the discovery, John Abbott, a well-known Michigan coin dealer, began seeking to buy the piece. What was it worth? The thought went through the mind of Ed Milas, the owner of RARCOA. It was decided that when Bowers and Ruddy Galleries auctioned the Garrett Collection 1804 silver dollar as a part of a series of sales being conducted for The Johns

Hopkins University, the asking price of that rarity *plus $25,000* would be a reasonable figure for the unique 1870-S.

On the evening of March 26, 1980, in a fantastic "fight" among enthusiastic bidders on the auction floor, the 1804 silver dollar broke all past records and soared to $400,000—thus setting the auction sale record for any U.S. silver coin! Abbott subsequently acquired the 1870-S half dime, though it is not confirmed if he paid $425,000 (as prescribed by the previously mentioned agreement) or another amount.

The coinage of certain 1870-S denominations has been partially an enigma; for example, the silver dollar of that date and mintmark is a great rarity—about a dozen are known—but there are no mintage reports in government records. It is thought that one other 1870-S half dime may have been struck, this one placed in the cornerstone of the second facility of the San Francisco Mint. Similarly, it is believed that of the 1870-S $3 gold piece, two examples were struck—one of which is confirmed today and the other presumably in the cornerstone. It seems the San Francisco Mint kept sloppy or incomplete records at the time.

Found on a Deserted Beach

Lost: In the 1800s • **Found:** 1983 • **Treasure:** Rare Schultz & Co. $5 gold coin

On the afternoon of Christmas Day in 1982, James Owens, operator of a roofing company in Sand City, California, was prospecting with his metal detector on a deserted beach near Monterey. A strong storm had passed through recently, churning up the sand and perhaps revealing things long forgotten. He was in the right place at the right time; responding to a "beep," he poked in the sand and found a $5 gold piece struck by Schultz & Co. in San Francisco in 1851!

Not Struck for Long

Before we visit the fate of the found coin, a bit of background information on the manufacturer is in order.

Schultz & Co., comprised of Judge G.W. Schultz and William Thompson Garratt, was one of a number of private coiners who operated in San Francisco in the early days of the Gold Rush. As early as 1850, Garratt conducted a brass foundry on Clay Street, San Francisco, behind Baldwin & Company's coining establishment; there, Garratt produced many of the dies used for private coinage by other firms in the city.

His partnership with Schultz, however, operated for just a short time and was dissolved in April 1851 through circumstances brought about by unfavorable publicity. Samples of the firm's coinage were examined by assayer Augustus Humbert—the United States Treasury-appointed assayer of gold, who worked under a Treasury contract in the offices of private coiner Moffat & Company—and were found to average just $4.87 in intrinsic value each.

Such an amount might seem reasonable today, but it was considered at the time to be too lightweight. The prevailing philosophy was that private coiners earned their compensation by charging a refining and minting fee, and the resultant coins should have a melt-down value extremely close to their face value. Those firms whose values were less were thought to be doubly profiting.

As it turns out, three Schultz & Co. $5 pieces assayed at the Philadelphia Mint in 1851 showed an average intrinsic value of $4.94. However, by the time this news reached California, the Schultz half eagles were already widely discredited, as were those of other coiners except for Moffat.

In later years Garratt furnished a description of his early activities:

> We made a great many dies for private coining. Albert Küner, who is still in business here, would do the engraving and I the turning—that is, the machine work on the dies, for which at the time we would get $100 per day per man on that special job. After that, Schultz took a notion to go into coining for Burgoyne & Co. and Argenti & Co., who were bankers here at the time. They would buy the dust and we would do the coining.[528] We ran for a while, and then Schultz and I separated, he taking the coining establishment and I the foundry, he keeping the room over the foundry for his business. He continued only a short time before the Legislature passed a law prohibiting private coining.
>
> We took gold at $16 an ounce, and put it through the refining process, and then would add 10% copper. That of course would take a very little copper, just enough to make the coin hard enough to wear. I think the Legislature prohibited it altogether; I am not exactly clear on that point. Moffat was allowed to go ahead. We continued in the same place after Schultz had quit. We had moved from Clay Street down to Leidesdorff, near Sacramento [Street]. While we were there we separated. He continued coining until he was shut off by the Legislature; it might have been two months.[529] From that he went up into the mountains and I continued with the business. Judge Schultz was connected with the Gold Mountain Quartz Mining Co.

Pioneer Gold's Allure

With such a short window of striking, the rarity of piece that Owens found is obvious; indeed, fewer than a dozen examples are confirmed to exist. The coin, illustrated here, was consigned to the Pacific Coast Auction Galleries and sold in June 1987 for $49,500 to a Santa Barbara dealer. That same dealer said he was prepared to pay an additional $25,000 if that had been necessary.[530]

From that point, the coin was off the market for a generation. Then, it reappeared—graded

MS-62 by NGC and thought to be the finest known—in Heritage Auctions' sale in April 2014, where it crossed the block at $340,750.

No "Small Potatoes" Here!

Hidden or lost: 1600s or later • **Found:** February 1990 • **Treasure:** NE silver sixpence

Still another variation on a theme: If you find just one old American colonial coin, if it is a New England (Massachusetts) silver sixpence minted in 1652, you've hit the jackpot![531] While some Massachusetts silver varieties are a bit rarer, the NE sixpence is certainly in the front row and commands a lot of attention!

The discovery at hand occurred on a cold February night in 1991, in East Hampton, New York. Lillian P. Rade and her coin-collecting husband Ron were looking for coins in a potato field when Lillian's metal detector gave off a delightful buzz, indicating that something was in the offing. Using an ice pick to probe the frozen earth, a small hole was dug and a little silver disc was found. Mrs. Rade's initial reaction was not one of great excitement: "When I first saw it, I thought the coin was junk." Hardly any markings could be seen, except for "NE" on one side and "VI" on the other.

That evening, the Rades looked through Ron's numismatic library to see if anything matched the little silver piece they had unearthed. Aha! It seemed to be a rare New England shilling! After that, the couple took it to New York dealer Stack's, who advised them to send it to the American Numismatic Association Authentication Bureau in Colorado Springs. After due inspection, J.P. Martin of the ANA staff, working with consultants including Michael Hodder, pronounced it to be absolutely genuine and thanked the Rades "on behalf of coin collectors everywhere for bringing this numismatic rarity to light."

Subsequently, the coin was given to Sotheby's for auction and crossed the block in November 1991. In its catalog description, David E. Tripp drew upon the notes of Michael Hodder and suggested that it was one of just eight specimens of the NE silver sixpence known to exist. When the dust settled in the sale room, the Rades were $32,000 richer, less a modest commission to the auction house—no "small potatoes" this!

chapter 22

Undiscovered Treasures on Land

There are many stories of railroad and stagecoach holdups, bank robberies, and other stolen or lost coins, but most leave the reader in suspense. Was the loot ever recovered? Probably yes in many instances and no in many others.

This chapter includes some stories of coin hoards, holdup booty, and other potential treasures believed to be largely lost, perhaps awaiting discovery and the writing of new stories.

The following listings are from many sources. Some pirate treasures are included here for general interest.[532]

Stories of stagecoach robberies are plentiful, but few provide details of the treasure stolen.

Lost Treasures State by State

Alabama Treasures Waiting to be Found

The Nuñez family treasure is said to be buried near an old river ferry site at Seminole in Baldwin County.

Along the Alabama seacoast, pirate treasures may be buried, including some caches by Jean Lafitte at Bayou Batre and elsewhere.

On the shore of Bay Minette in Baldwin County, some Spanish-American gold may have been cached. Nearby and not far from Fort Morgan, pirates may have buried some treasure.

C.E. Sharps, a wealthy mill owner in Alabama, liked to keep his money in gold coins. He also liked to keep it hidden, according to one account. In June 1899, he drowned, taking the secret of his "huge cache of gold" to the grave.[533]

The steamer *White Horse* on the Yukon River.

Alaska Treasures Waiting to be Found

There are scattered reports of missing gold in the Yukon. In this region, gold was moved by coach and, more often, by boat on the Yukon River.

A safe deposit box in Juneau is said to contain a number of rare $10 national currency notes from that city, put away long ago by a mine owner in the district.

Arizona Treasures Waiting to be Found

Bars of gold remain hidden in the San Francisco Mountains in Coconino County. If stamped with the markings of territorial assayers, they would have significant numismatic value.

Train robbers' loot secreted near Bisbee Junction has never been found.

Treasure from a holdup at Canyon Station remains undiscovered. Will C. Barnes commented: "A large natural cave on Posta Quemada Canyon, eight miles off the Tucson-Douglas highway and 19 miles east of Tucson. On south slope of Wrong Mountain in the Rincon Range. Owned by the state. First discovered by a man named Rolls, 1879. A Southern Pacific Railroad train was robbed in 1884, and the robbers trailed to this cave. One man was found dead. The others escaped. On Christmas, 1902, some Tucson people found some old Wells-Fargo sacks which proved to be part of the 1884 holdup upon identification in San Francisco."[534]

Hashknife Charley's missing 38 gold bars, near Sononita, Santa Cruz County, may have assayers' stamps on them, but no one will know until they are found.

A safe and its contents proved to be missing after a flash flood in Fools Gulch northeast of Wickenburg. Possibly, the treasure remains underground in some dry stream bed today.

Treasure taken by pirates from the steamer *Gila* lies somewhere near Crescent Spring, Mohave County.

A thousand pounds of silver dollars taken in a train robbery in the Dos Cabezas Mountains near Willcox remains unaccounted for. At 56 pounds per $1,000 face value, this would amount to close to 20,000 coins.

On November 5, 1871, a stagecoach containing an Army payroll of $100,000 was held up nine miles west of Wickenburg. It is still missing.[535]

In addition to coin accounts, stories abound of lost silver (mostly) and gold mines in Arizona. The legend of the Lost Dutchman Mine at Superstition Mountain is a staple item in folklore of the state.

Arkansas Treasures Waiting to be Found

The fortune of a mill owner is said to have been buried near Huntsville, Madison County, and partially recovered at a later date.

John Murrel, notorious bandit, buried treasures on Stuart Island near Lake Village in Chicot County. Murrel made many depredations in the Mississippi River watershed area and is said to have had "HT," for "Horse Thief," branded on a thumb as part of his conviction for that crime. Loot from his various robberies is said to have been buried in different places in Arkansas, Mississippi, Louisiana, and elsewhere. Murrel also engaged in nefarious activities along the Natchez Trace.

Many Spanish-American gold coins brought overland from Texas and Mexico are said to have been hidden here and there around the state. Not much to go on with information as vague as this!

On or near the land once owned by John Avants along the Cosatot River is a vast fortune transported overland from Mexico in several wagons.

California Treasures Waiting to be Found

Approximately $200,000 in gold coins may be hidden near Scotty's Castle in Death Valley, today a tourist attraction. Scotty is mentioned in many stories published over the years; he may have had lots of money or he may have had none, depending upon what you read, but he was certainly a fascinating character.

The fortune of a French saddle maker is concealed on the Rancho Santa Teresa near San Jose.

In the Trinity Mountains near Cecilville in Siskiyou County, $80,000 in stolen money was hidden by "Rattlesnake Dick."

Scene on the Mokelumne River in the Gold Rush days.

Loot from the Bentz Company robbery hidden near Biggs in Colusa County has never come to light.

Treasure from the holdup of the Bodie stagecoach north of Bodie in Mono County—as well as a strongbox taken from the same stagecoach at Freeman Junction, about 60 miles east of Bakersfield—remain lost.

Famous bandit Joaquin Murietta hid some loot in Arroyo Cantoova and Hornitos, among many other places. It remains undiscovered.

At Mokelumne Hill along Route 49 in the Mother Lode country, a cache of $50 gold coins is said to be in an old foundation wall.

Hijackers' loot of $30,000 was once stashed at Camp Oak Grove, San Gabriel Mountains, Los Angeles County, and may still be there.

A bandit's underground hiding place near Avila, San Luis Obispo County, is said to have been the depository for much loot.

In Los Angeles, a pirate treasure is said to have been buried where Elysian Park is now. If so, this might be a tough one to spirit away without notice, for the Los Angeles Police Department has a training site there. Best to go at night on Sunday or a holiday.

Treasure taken from a Death Valley wagon train that was burned is, perhaps, somewhere in that vast desert area.

Treasure from the Fallbrook stagecoach on the Butterfield line between Temecula and Pala in San Diego County is still missing.

Gold bars from the Freemont (or Frémont) Mine near Amador City are said to have been hidden in the area.

Gold coins were lost in Horse Canyon near Tehachapi.

Treasure belonging to an innkeeper near the old Warner Ranch at Aguana in San Diego County awaits discovery.

Coins hidden in the hills near Isabella, Kern County, have never been found.

A "fortune in gold coins" hidden in Cucamonga in 1862 remains missing.[536]

Dr. John Marsh's cache of $40,000 in gold coins—said to be at Marsh Creek, east side of Mount Diablo, near Brentwood, Contra Costa County—would be worth many multiples of its face value if it were found today.

Lieutenant Jonas Wilson's poker winnings—no description at hand—are said to be hidden somewhere in Hoaglin Valley at the foot of Haman Ridge, Trinity County.

Coins lost near Ventucopa, Santa Barbara County, are still missing.

Gold "slugs" and coins, the treasure of the Mariposa tax collector, remain lost on Deadman's Creek near Agua Fria, Mariposa County.

Loot from a Needles bank robbery, near Oro Grande, San Bernardino County, is supposedly still missing.

The SS *Mollie Stevens*, laden with gold bullion, was lost on Owens Lake in the Owens Valley in May 1882, according to one account.[537] Another account has it that she served well on the lake from about 1874 until she caught fire and was destroyed in a beaching process; she was apparently meant to be beached alongside the *Bessie Brady* so that parts from her, including the steam engine, could be used on the latter vessel.[538]

Gold "slugs" hidden at the old Forty Mile House near Shingle Springs near El Dorado County have never come to light.

A lost cache of "octagonal gold coins" in the Panamint Mountains remains unaccounted for. Interestingly, the name of those mountains is from a good wish expressed to gold miners: "I hope you pan a mint."

The "Rifle Barrel payroll" hidden near French Gulch, Shasta County, has remained missing for generations.

Treasure taken by the Ruggles brothers from the Redding stagecoach and buried near Middle Creek about six miles from Redding, Shasta County, is nowhere to be found. The brothers were hanged after the robbery.

Assets of a saloonkeeper hidden at the junction of Greenhorn Gulch and Freeman Gulch, Kern County, await the lucky finder.

"Treasure of the San Francisco Mint" at Shelter Cove near Point Delgado, Humboldt County, no doubt would prove interesting if found.

Loot from the Sonora stagecoach was hidden near Snelling, Merced County.

A tub filled with gold coins was hidden at Yankee Hill near Sonora, Tuolumne County.

Somewhere in the North Beach area of San Francisco is hidden $1 million in gold stolen from the Bank of California by Henry Meiggs.[539]

In addition, just about all of the old Spanish missions along the coast have treasure tales connected with them. Stories of lost mines in the Sierras and Mother Lode country also abound.

Colorado Treasures Waiting to be Found

Bandits' stolen treasure of $100,000 was hidden east of Clifford in Lincoln County.

Much treasure is apparently buried at the site of Bent's Fort on the old Santa Fe Trail.

"Treasure of the Denver Mint," apparently including silver dimes, was concealed in a chasm on the Gunnison River between Crawford and Montrose. The tale of "The Treasure of the Lost Dimes of Denver" might be related: four wagons, each carrying three or four kegs of newly minted dimes, fell off a precipice in the Black Canyon and disappeared.

Some of these coins may have been found in the 1940s, when a treasure hunter showed another treasure hunter, Jim Wilson, an old camera case filled with "time tarnished dimes. Wilson and he located a site among some rocks and found more dimes. They marked the spot, intending to return. When they did they could not find the marker."[540]

At Robbers' Roost near Fort Collins, a lot of stagecoach holdup loot is hidden.

Treasure of the paymaster of Fort Garland was stashed on Trinchera Creek, Costilla County.

Two barrels of coins belonging to Henry Sefton were lost at the Gomez Ranch, Sangre de Cristo Mountains, Huerfano County.

Some of Jesse James's treasure is said to have been cached in Half Moon Gulch, southwest of Leadville. Of course, accounts of his hidden loot abound and are ascribed to many different Western states.

Approximately $100,000 in gold hidden by outlaws near Manitou Springs—at the foot of Pikes Peak—has never been found.

The "Bloody Espinosas," obviously an unsavory group, buried treasure near the present-day town of Cascade in Ute Pass in the late 1860s.

A chest filled with gold was hidden on Ralston Creek Road between Central City and Denver.

Coins hidden by the Reynolds gang near Hand Cart Gulch, Park County, have never turned up.

Train robbery loot hidden near Grand Valley, Garfield County, remains undiscovered.

Near Monument, between Colorado Springs and Denver, the Butch Cassidy gang is said to have stashed $100,000 from bank robberies.

Treasure from a wagon train hidden near La Junta, Otero County, has never been found.

Connecticut Treasures Waiting to be Found

Tuxis Island off Milford is said to have yielded "a great quantity of 18th century coins" for a group of campers in 1903. Perhaps more remain.[541]

The beach at Penfield Reef near Fairfield may be worthwhile, as in 1888 George Hawley found a cache of gold and silver coins all dated 1795.[542] If, perchance, these were U.S. coins, this has to be one of the most interesting finds around. Too bad we don't have more details.

Delaware Treasures Waiting to be Found

The Atlantic coastal areas of Delaware have yielded many coins over the years, numerous examples of which have washed up on the shore. The salvage of the *DeBraak* and accounts of the *Faithful Steward* are numerous and can be found on the internet and elsewhere. Many other ships have been wrecked off Delaware and in her inlets and bays, and doubtless there is treasure waiting to be found. Most such coins are probably Spanish-American or British.

District of Columbia Treasures Waiting to be Found

A private residence once occupied by the commandant of the United States Marine Corps is said to have $25,000 hidden within.

Who knows what may be cached in the Treasury Building on Pennsylvania Avenue. We have one story of a cache there (see chapter 10, "Treasure

The Treasury Building in Washington, D.C.

in the Treasury Building," page 159), but what other old coins or currency might be lurking? What we need is a numismatic detective with a license to snoop, and for said detective to spend a week or two looking around!

Also, do cases of Washington Seasons medals still survive somewhere in the War Department (the facilities of which are now occupied by the State Department)? Many were never distributed.

Florida Treasures Waiting to be Found

Stories of Florida treasures are dominated by accounts of buried pirate treasure and sunken Spanish galleons, both of which antedate indigenous American coinage. Note, though, nearly all finds to this point have been associated with the latter and not the former. Of course, loot is still loot, and the treasure-hunting community is particularly active along the Florida coast, with numerous shops offering scuba equipment, electronic treasure detectors, guidebooks, and other useful items.

In his *History Under the Sea*, 1965, Mendel Peterson gave advice concerning potentially profitable sites for undersea treasure exploration, noting: "The reefs of the Florida Keys and coast of Florida north to Cape Kennedy [Cape Canaveral], which is one of the richest spots." Further: "Almost any bar lying near harbor approaches on the Atlantic coast will yield sites. On the eastern side of the Florida Passage to the Bahamas formed a dangerous barrier for ships, and these reefs and keys are littered with sites."

Fowler's Bluff on the Gulf Coast may be a productive site for the seeker of pirate treasure.

At the headwaters of Carter's Mill Creek in the northern part of the state, Indians may have cached a fortune in gold coins received from the British as payment for their depredations on settlers.

At Amelia Island there may be much buried pirate treasure.

F.L. Coffman reported that "an old treasure hunter, Bill Sneed," found $625,000 in gold bullion and coins at the mouth of the Suwanee River, a part of a treasure of gold coins valued at $5,000,000. I knew Bill Sneed, who in the 1950s operated the Wilmary Motel in Lakeland, Florida, and recall that he enjoyed regaling his acquaintances with tall tales, but had relatively few rare coins as evidence to verify his finds.

José Gaspar, better known as Gasparilla the pirate, is said to have buried many treasures along the Gulf Coast.

An excursion boat in Silver Springs, Florida in 1894. It was popular for tourists to toss coins overboard and see them resting on the bottom through crystal clear water.

Near Fort Walton on Choctawhatchee Bay on the Gulf Coast, pirate Billy Bowlegs may have cached many gold and silver coins.

Members of the notorious Ashley gang were killed in 1924. Their loot is missing and may be near Canal Point on Lake Okeechobee and/or at an inlet near Peck's Lake on the Intracoastal Waterway.[543]

On the bottom beneath the sparkling waters of Silver Springs, near Ocala, are coins tossed by tourists from the 1800s onward. Beware of alligators if you go.

Georgia Treasures
Waiting to be Found

A certain Mr. Duncan—a prosperous businessman who lived in Griffin, Georgia—did not trust banks, but kept coins and bills stored here and there around the house. His wife feared for his and her safety, as his wealth was well known, and someone might break in. At her insistence, he consolidated all of this money, rumored to amount to at least $100,000, and said he would take it to a bank. However, he had second thoughts and buried it in a peach orchard instead.

Some months later, Duncan was disabled by a heart attack. While bedridden, he attempted to gesture as to where the trove was hidden, but he could not make himself understood. He died shortly thereafter, taking the secret of the location with him.[544]

The old Lions House on Third Street in Columbus is supposed to contain hidden treasure.

At Blackbeard's Island, the treasure of its namesake is said to have been buried. More of his chests (or whatever he used for storage) may be on Ossabaw Island.

Various citizens of the state buried coins and other treasures to prevent capture by William

Tecumseh Sherman during his famous (or infamous) march through the countryside, during which his troops pillaged and burned everything in sight.[545]

SHERMAN'S CAMPAIGN, 1864.

The route that Sherman took on his campaign through the South in 1865, Raleigh to Savannah to Atlanta.

Near LaGrange, a wealthy plantation owner named Lipscomb accumulated about $100,000 in silver and gold coins and buried the treasure in two places near his house just before the Civil War. He enlisted the aid of a faithful servant whenever he dug up the ground to make a "deposit" or simply to review what he had stored.

One day he wanted to visit his coins, but his servant was not around, and Lipscomb could not locate the sites. Forewarned, he later recorded directions to the spots, but after Lipscomb died, his widow was not able to locate the directions. Today the treasure is still missing.[546]

At Milledgeville, Baldwin County, a treasure of remarkable proportions is said to be hidden under a house.

In Savannah, the pirate treasure of John Flint may be concealed in or near a house he once occupied on Broad Street.

Many gold and silver coins that were once holdings of the Confederate States of America Treasury may be hidden on the south bank of the Savannah River (or near Washington, Georgia; or Abbeville, Georgia; or near Richmond, Virginia; or in the false bottom of a horse-drawn coach; or divvied up among trusted officers, who each did their own hiding; or in a railroad car, etc.). Narratives relate that military payrolls from both sides were hidden during the war on various occasions when their security became endangered.

Idaho Treasures Waiting to be Found

Multiple stagecoach booty possibilities: A cache from one holdup was hidden on the south side of the Boise River near Boise, another stash may still be secreted near Camas Creek in Jefferson County, and yet another near Grimes Creek in Boise County awaits discovery.

Robbers hid $75,000 in loot near the Shoshone Ice Caves in Lincoln County.

North of Boise, a strongbox with $50,000 in stagecoach loot is hidden.

A robber's treasure secreted near Lewiston, if discovered, will be found by accident, as the territory described covers a very large area (a common theme for many "clues" to such caches).

Treasure, possibly from a Wells Fargo stagecoach holdup, may still be at Mud Lake, southwest of Idaho Falls.

In McCammon, Bannock County, about $100,000 taken from an 1865 stagecoach heist is hidden. The bandits were chased by a posse and killed.

Money taken from a pack train by robbers between White Bird and Dixie, Idaho County has never been accounted for.

Bandits stole $118,000 and buried it in the area of Humphrey in Clark County, where it may still be today.

Loot of the Henry Plummer gang, hidden in Beaver Canyon near Spencer, Clark County, remains unlocated.

A large number of Gold Certificates owned by Virgil Brumbach are lost in Soldier's Canyon, east of Saint Maries, Shoshone County.

Illinois Treasures Waiting to be Found

In the late 1860s, on the 1200 block of North State Street in Chicago, Felix and Ellen Conway spent their married years. The two were not on friendly terms with each other, however, and Felix, upon being diagnosed with an incurable illness, dug deeply in his backyard and buried $250,000 in gold coins without telling his wife. He did tell his doctor of the cache, though, and suggested that once both husband and wife had passed to her reward, said doctor could recover it.

As it turns out, the doctor himself became ill and neared death, at which time he told his son of the fortune in store. However, the doctor's son died as well, all while Ellen Conway continued to live until at the age of 92 she passed away. She never found the treasure, and today, the exact location of the gold coins is not known, but they are presumed to still be there.[547]

Near old John Hill's Fort at Carlyle, Clinton County, a buried fortune remains for the lucky finder.

Cave-In-Rock in Hardin County was long used as a hideaway by many robbers and other unsavory characters, including the Harpes Gang and the notorious Wilson, and it is said much loot remains secreted there. Robert M. Coates has written:

"From Red Bank [on the Ohio River] on down to the town of Smithland, the river traversed its most dangerous section. Shoals abounded, sand bars lay just below the ripple of the surface, and islands split the channel. . . . Landsmen most of the travelers were, as they came poling down in their barges. . . . A whole hierarchy of piracy had arisen to prey on them. The first of these was a man named Wilson. . . . He took his stand at a cave in the bluff along shore, a cave with deep chambers and hidden recesses. He posted a sign on the river bank: 'Wilson's Liquor Vault & House for Entertainment.' The cave was known as the Cave Inn, later twisted to Cave-In-Rock. It had a long chapter in the history of river piracy. Boat-wreckers waited along the bank. Watching a boat pass, they would offer to pilot it through the channel. If the unskilled steersman chose to run the rapids unaided, it was more than likely he would run aground. If he hired a pilot, the chance of his grounding became a certainty. Once beached, the boat and its occupants fell easily before the attack of Wilson's gang."[548]

Indiana Treasures Waiting to be Found

In or near Rockford, Jackson County, $98,000 taken in a train robbery is buried.

On May 22, 1868, the Reno gang (Clinton, Frank, John, Simon, and William) held up the J.M. & I. Railroad train at Marshfield, Indiana, about 20 miles south of Seymour, and escaped with $90,000 cash described as being in "new notes." After another escapade or two, the brothers were tossed into jail in New Albany in December of the same year. Then, on December 11 a group of do-gooders went to New Albany, entered the jail, seized the prisoners, and hanged them. Meanwhile, what happened to the stolen currency was not stated.[549]

An 1824 half dollar counterstamped to commemorate Lafayette's visit to the United States.

In the mid-1820s, during the Marquis de Lafayette's return visit to the United States, one of Lafayette's carriage drivers stashed $8,000 in gold in the ground in Connelton, Perry County.

Iowa Treasures Waiting to be Found

Near Redfield in Dallas County, a gang of outlaws buried their ill-gotten coins.

A long time ago, outlaws gathered in Bellevue, Jackson County, and buried treasure in the area.

At Kelly's Bluff in Dubuque, a well-to-do miner buried his personal fortune. Some of it was later discovered, but more remains to be found.

Horse thieves buried their treasure near Sabula, Jackson County.

Kansas Treasures Waiting to be Found

Treasure of an Army paymaster was lost near Lawrence, Douglas County.

Wells Fargo treasure was hidden west of Dodge City, Ford County.

Bandit loot hidden at Point of Rocks, northwest of Elkhart, Morton County, remains concealed.

Near Point of Rocks, wagon trains headed for California were plundered by outlaws who buried their loot in the area. Note that this may be another version of the preceding story simply described differently by a different source.

Treasure from a wagon train of forty-niners headed to California was hidden southwest of Offerle, Edwards County. Curious that treasure would be taken *to* California—sort of like taking coals to Newcastle or owls to Athens, it would seem.

Yet another wagon train treasure is said to have been concealed near old Fort Dodge.

A wagon train from Mexico with a vast fortune aboard was attacked by Indians. Some travelers survived with their money and buried it in the area.

A group of forty-niners returning from California with $50,000 in a buckskin bag buried their treasure near Offerle, Edwards County, before being killed by Indians.

On November 1, 1969, Jack Hazelwood—a 32-year-old Wichita coin dealer who was also well known on the national scene—disappeared. Left behind were his wife of 14 years, four children, and many puzzled friends and business acquaintances. Gone with him was a number of coins of considerable value.

An entrepreneur *par excellence*, or at least seemingly so, he owned the Wichita Coin & Stamp Co. and HZD Enterprises (said to be the largest wholesale coin dealer in America) and had connections to more than 20 other businesses, some in other states. He also represented Bankers Investment Co. of Hutchinson, Kansas, and made loans against coins deposited with him as collateral in two vaults in the Southwestern National Bank in Wichita, amounting to about $1 million, it was said.

Before his disappearance, he had ordered sets of coins on approval from various dealers, stating he wanted to show them to a client. Jerry Cohen and Abner Kreisberg sent a year-by-year set of

Mint State Liberty Walking half dollars (1916–1947) and other coins on an invoice in the tens of thousands of dollars. Hazelwood took the shipment, told his wife he was driving to Tulsa on a coin deal and was not seen again.

After his disappearance, a crime scene—or was it?—was found in his coin store. Although there were no signs of forced entry, safes and display cases had been emptied, blood was on the floor, and bullet holes were in a wall. Hazelwood's car, suitcase, torn shirt, and tie, as well as a piece of rope, and two bullet casings were found.

It was later discovered that Hazelwood was at least $400,000 in debt, that there were many fake contracts, and most if not all of his apparent success was a sham. To this day there are no answers.[550]

Kentucky Treasures Waiting to be Found

Just before the Civil War, William Pettit hid treasure at Alleghany Hall, south of Lexington.

Indians are said to have buried an immense treasure including many coins (some of which have been found now and then) in the Winchester area.

In Hueysville, Thayer County, a well-to-do landowner buried a large quantity of gold coins around the beginning of the 1900s.

Contents of a chest of silver and gold coins stolen from a bank in Nicholasville, Kentucky, may lie on the bottom of King's Mill Pond. A few coins were recovered by a fishing guide in 1910.[551]

Louisiana Treasures Waiting to be Found

Stories of the treasure buried in Louisiana and other Gulf of Mexico places by pirate Jean Lafitte have filled several books. Lafitte—who is alternately viewed as a hero or a scoundrel, and who was of help to the government during the War of 1812—plundered many ships and quite possibly buried strongboxes and chests filled with many

U.S. coins, although probably most are Mexican or from other Spanish-American mints.

Within Louisiana, especially good possibilities for the location of Lafitte's gold and silver include such places as near Shell Beach Drive in Lake Charles; Opelousas in St. Landry Parish; an island in Lake Borge (such island has eluded mapmakers); the banks of the Mississippi River upstream from New Orleans; Caillou Island; the LeBleu plantation site in Calcasieu Parish; Pecan Island near Westwego in Jefferson Parish; Kelso's Island; Isle Dernier; and Jefferson Island near Lafayette.

clients and in time became wealthy—so much so that she built a fine home, Maison Blanche, on Lake Pontchartrain near New Orleans. When she died in 1881, her fortune (estimated at $2 million) could not be located.

Honey Island in St. Tammany Parish may be one of many places in the Mississippi River area where John Murrel hid his loot (see also information under "Arkansas Treasures Waiting to be Found," page 357). Outlaw James Copeland may have also cached coins on this island (as well as along many other coastal areas).

The Parlange Plantation treasure, near New Roads, Pointe Coupee Parish, is part of a cache originally comprising nearly a half million dollars' ($300,000 appears in several accounts, $500,000 in another) worth of silver and gold coins. Stored in three metal strongboxes or chests, it was buried early in the Civil War. The owner, Madame Virginie Parlange, feared that Union soldiers would ravage the plantation, which had been built by Marquis Vincent de Ternant in 1750.

The Yankee troops arrived in due course but were friendly to the owner after she greeted them in a warm fashion and even invited them to dinner. After the war, her son followed his mother's instructions and unearthed two of the chests, but the third could not be found. It was presumed that the two slaves who had helped bury the chests—both of whom had since decamped to Texas—had

Union troops roamed throughout the South, often pillaging and looting. Many citizens buried coins as a precaution.

Marsh Island may be where coins salvaged at an early date from Spanish wrecks off Padre Island (Texas) were brought for safekeeping.[552]

Marie Laveau, the beautiful "Voodoo Queen," offered fortune telling and consultation to various

unearthed the coins and had reburied them elsewhere. Although several attempts were made to locate the treasure, the coins remain missing to this very day.[553]

The Gabriel Fuselier plantation in St. Landry Parish is believed to be the site for coins buried during the Civil War era.

In Magnolia Cemetery in East Baton Rouge Parish, there may be something buried besides bodies (that being gold and silver coins). One might imagine that digging there would be discouraged, however.

An entire "shipload of gold" may be at the bottom of the Amite River close to the site of where Galvez Town used to be, near present-day Oak Grove in West Carroll Parish.[554]

The site of the old French settlement Fort Iberville, in Plaquemines Parish, is said by some to be where $160,000 in gold treasure is buried.[555]

Various plantations on inland waterways are said to be rich possibilities for very impressive treasures. Of the more than 1,000 large plantations that operated along the Mississippi River and elsewhere in the state, only a few hundred remained active after the Civil War.

In Natchitoches Parish at an old landing on the Red River, hidden treasure worth several thousand dollars has been found over the years, and it is said that this is just the beginning.

In Hulls Lake at Selma, Grant Parish, the loot from a bank robbery was hidden, never to be found.

On the banks of the Red River near Acme, many gold coins are said to have been buried circa 1861.

In a bayou near the Chretien Plantation a large quantity of coins is said to have been hidden prior to the Civil War. Some of this treasure may have been from pirates who had some sort of an arrangement with the owner of the estate.

Maine Treasures Waiting to be Found

The coast of Maine is said to have been an especially popular place for such pirates as Captain Kidd, Captain Bellamy, and their ilk to bury treasure. All of Bellamy's gold and silver may have been hidden near the coastal town of Machias—but, on the other hand, it may have been buried elsewhere (such is the nature of pirate treasure accounts, and if enough of them are read, the reader comes back full circle to the starting place).

After all, there are more islands off the coast than can be counted, and many of these have been suggested as burial sites for the ill-gotten gains of buccaneers and privateers, too. The trio of Deer Isle, Vinalhaven and North Haven (constituting the main part of the Fox Islands group); Fort Popham (built in 1861 as a deterrent should the Confederacy invade the Pine Tree State); Reef Ram Island; Mount Desert Island (a vast acreage now a national park and the location of Ship Bottom Bay); Monhegan Island; Elm Island; Bailey Island; and Money Cave (sounds particularly interesting!) on Isle du Haut are among the isles reflected in treasure lore.

Captain Kidd and his pirate crew burying treasure.

The possibilities are seemingly endless; such is the nature of pirate treasure accounts, and if enough of them are read, the reader comes back full circle to the starting place. Note that if and when any such treasure is found, most probably it will consist primarily of Spanish-American coins, although there is the possibility that some Massachusetts silver could be included. Pirates aside, the coastal areas of Maine have yielded their share of Massachusetts Pine Tree shillings and related pieces over the years (see various accounts in chapter 1). Note that because Maine's population has grown relatively slowly in the past 150 years, it is more likely that old sites there have not been overwhelmed by new construction, developments, etc. Thus, certain areas may yield treasures.

Also, the water itself may hold considerable wealth; the "stern rockbound coast" (as one poet put it) of New England, and of Maine in particular, spelled disaster to many coastwise ships that became lost in fog or darkness. Many of their hulks remain today at the bottom of the sea, some with coins scattered in the sand nearby.

At Cedar Ledges east of Ram Island in Casco Bay, three kettles of gold coins were found on Thanksgiving Day, 1852, and more may still be there.[556]

On Richmond Island, offshore from Cape Elizabeth, a vast treasure of Spanish-American and other gold and silver coins was found in 1855. Many of the pieces were given to the Maine Historical Society.

Maryland Treasures Waiting to be Found

A French immigrant is said to have buried $100,000 in coins near Catonsville.

At or near the old Croissant Mansion in California—a census-designated place in St. Mary's County, not the state—a treasure is said to be hidden.

Near Salisbury, about $30,000 in treasure had already been found by the early 1950s, and legend has it that more awaits lucky searchers.

Maryland coastal areas are said to conceal some of Captain Kidd's treasure, some of which may be inland near the old Mansion House in northwest Baltimore.[557]

Maryland has a rich colonial history, and without doubt many town and commercial sites conceal coins awaiting seekers using electronic detectors.

Chesapeake Bay has had its share of ship losses, but any coins remaining on the sea bottom are probably the personal property of passengers rather than lost treasure cargo.

Massachusetts Treasures Waiting to be Found

In Salisbury, Essex County, $175,000 in buried treasure has never been found.

Nantucket, Martha's Vineyard, Marblehead, Snake Island, Plum Island (near Newburyport), Cape Cod and other coastal regions are said to have been popular places for secreting pirate gold and silver. Captain Kidd's name is often associated with such accounts.

As an aside, anyone wanting to read exciting tales of pirates operating off the coast of Massachusetts need but acquire several of the books written by the late Edward Rowe Snow, who for many years was the prime American chronicler of sea lore. Snow related that it was common practice for pirates to be tried (loose interpretation of this judicial term) in Boston and their corpses put in shackles and chains and taken to islands in Boston harbor to be strung up from a gibbet in full view of passing ships as a warning of what happens to buccaneers when they are caught.

Among those so displayed was Jack Quelch, who often operated out of Marblehead; his corpse was put in chains and strung up at Nix's Mate, a small island in Boston harbor, where it rotted away, although some remains could be viewed for several years thereafter.[558]

The banks of the Parker River near Byfield may be worthwhile sites to hunt for treasure, including over $200,000 worth of gold and silver in a chest.[559]

At Dalton in Berkshire County, loot stolen by Hessian mercenary soldiers during the American Revolution is said to be buried.

Near old Tenney Castle at Methuen, Essex County, two eccentric brothers are said to have hidden a fortune.

At Deer Island near Winthrop, 1,200 Mexican 8 reales were dug up in 1906, and who knows how many more there might be. The beaches at Ipswich and Salisbury are said to frequently yield 8-real Mexican silver coins dated circa 1715. Short Beach and Grover's Cliff as well as nearby Nahant and Revere were used as cache sites for pirate silver and gold.[560]

What treasures might be buried along the Massachusetts coastline?

Early in 1932, William Hesslein of New Haven, Connecticut—the self-styled "best known dealer in the United States"—disappeared, along with his coins and other items. Active from the late 1800s until he went missing, he seems to have had a fine trade, selling to such clients as J.M. Clapp and relocating to the busy center of Boston in 1913.

Hesslein was a frequent advertiser in *The Numismatist*. In the March 1905 issue, he advertised that he had for sale to the highest bidders the finest known New England shilling; the finest known small planchet Pine Tree shilling; a Fine Carolina Elephant token; a Very Good Higley copper of the three-hammer variety; a Fine New York Excelsior cent; a Proof 1836 gold "ring dollar;" an 1848 quarter eagle with the CAL. counterstamp; the finest known 1803, Small 3, half dollar; a white metal example of the Low-1 Hard Times token, one of the finest known 1799 cents, and other pieces.

Later, in the May 1929 issue of the same publication, he advertised:

> Facts and not braggadocio. Have been established over 30 years. I was the first advertiser in many of the scientific and mechanical magazines in this country. In that time I have spent thousands of dollars keeping myself before the public, spending in the aggregate considerably more than any dealer in the world. I claim to be the best-known dealer in the United States. In the last sale there were distributed over 1,500 public auction sale catalogues, and no dead wood, either, all live collectors. My sales are public auction sales conducted under the supervision of a licensed auctioneer and all are welcome to attend. Can this be done at the so-called mail order auction sales? My next sale will be the last of the season and will be a specially good one. There still is time if you wish to place any material in this very important sale.

A few years later, he was gone without a trace. Then, long after Hesslein's vanishing, in the May 1941 edition of *Hobbies* magazine, Thomas L.

Elder recalled: "One day we mysteriously missed Hesslein. He had mysteriously disappeared, probably a suicide, maybe by drowning. His wife and son came into my office some months after and with sober faces said they never could trace Mr. Hesslein and never knew what became of him." What happened to his coins is still a mystery.

Michigan Treasures Waiting to be Found

A fortune belonging to François Fontenay is said to be buried on Presque Isle near Detroit.

Many treasures are said to be aboard sunken ships off the shores of Michigan. Over the years, many thousands of ships have gone down in Lake Michigan and the other Great Lakes. Though most carried commodities such as ore, grain, lumber, and coal, some number of coins was undoubtedly on board each one.

Minnesota Treasures Waiting to be Found

In a stand of trees at Henderson, Sibley County, a treasure is buried.

In the woods near Wadena, a group of bandits buried their loot and were killed shortly thereafter by a posse.

Mississippi Treasures Waiting to be Found

Near the old Gore mansion in Calhoun City, valuable treasure was hidden in the earth.

Bandit James Copeland is said to have hidden gold coins in coastal areas in Mississippi in the 1840s and 1850s.

Pirate Patrick Scott is said to have buried some treasure in the early 1800s near Ocean Springs, Jackson County.

A treasure of gold coins may have been buried at Beaux Bridge in St. Martin's Parish by the slaves of Narcisse Thibodeaux in the early 1800s.

The Pirate's House near Bay St. Louis is said to offer multiple possibilities, including the finding of underground tunnels facilitating the clandestine transfer of gold and silver from shore to the house.

The treasure of a merchant named Gaines is said to have been hidden in Greene County, and although quite a bit of it was recovered in the late 1800s, much remains undiscovered.

Just before the Civil War, the Pickett family buried its fortune near the edge of Vicksburg.

Robbers are said to have buried two kegs of gold near Greenwood in 1865.

At Mathiston in Choctaw County, many buried gold coins are waiting to be found.

Joe Hare, a bandit who once operated around Fayette, Jefferson County, may have buried his treasure in the area.

Patrick Scott, one of the lesser-known pirates in folklore, is said to have picked Ocean Springs, Jackson City, to cache his coins.

At Pass Christian in Harrison County, a Captain Dane is supposed to have buried $200,000 beneath an old oak tree. The tree may not still be there, but the treasure near it has never been discovered. The money, in Spanish-American gold coins, belonged to a woman passenger of the *Nightingale*, who in the aftermath of a love triangle, was locked in a cabin when the ship sank. Great material for a novel, it would seem!

The Copeland gang looted the Bay St. Louis area in the early 1800s and buried their treasure in Catahoula Swamp.

Missouri Treasures Waiting to be Found

Near Waynesville in Pulaski County, a wealthy forty-niner is said to have buried $60,000 in the hills.

In the river near St. Louis, there are said to be several coin-laden steamship wrecks.

Montana Treasures Waiting to be Found

Much of the loot of the Henry Plummer gang (which was also active in Idaho) was hidden near Sun River, Cascade County, and several other areas—possibly including Virginia City and ghost towns including Bannack, Deer Lodge, and Haugan.[561]

The Horsethief Cache near Billings is said to be where cattle rustlers hid treasure (presumably coins, not cows or horses).

Robbers' Roost at Sheridan, Madison County, is where thieves secreted their plunder.

At Drummond in Granite County, a Chinese miner is said to have buried five pounds of gold in a can under a tree.

Treasure taken from General Custer's troops after his "last stand" in Big Horn County is said to have been hidden in the area (although one can only with great difficulty imagine Army troops having much treasure). Separately, a few scattered coins such as Shield nickels have been found on the site in recent generations and, called "half dimes," were shown in an issue of *National Geographic Magazine* in the 1990s.

Virginia City was the site of extensive gold discoveries in the 1860s. It is said that much treasure is still hidden in the region.

Nebraska Treasures Waiting to be Found

Jesse James is said to have hidden loot here and there in Nebraska, such as at Devil's Nest near Crafton, Knox County.

Believed to be hidden near Sargent, Custer County is $40,000 stolen from a bank in Kearney.

Gold miners returning from California were robbed near Lexington, Dawson County, and their treasure is buried in the area.

Robbers' Cave near Macy, Thurston County, may contain much treasure.

Nevada Treasures Waiting to be Found

The unrecovered booty of highwaymen stashed in Nevada includes but is not limited to: stagecoach robbery loot hidden near Columbus, Esmeralda County; Wells Fargo treasure from the Empire Stage, near Carson City; coins from a 1916 stagecoach robbery hidden north of the ghost town of Jarbridge, Elko county; tens of thousands of dollars in takings known as the stagecoach treasure of Williams Station on Harrison Creek near Hill Beacher Road, Elko County; and another stagecoach treasure hidden near Genoa, Douglas County.

The payroll intended for workers at the Candaleria Mines was stolen and said to be hidden near Mina, Mineral County.

Lost gold from the Mormon caravan, between Cave Valley and Ash Meadows near Carp, Lincoln County, has never been located.

Money left behind in the winter of 1846–1847 by the ill-fated Donner expedition in the High Sierras (see chapter 2, "The Ill-Fated Donner Party," page 39) may still be hidden somewhere, perhaps in the region of Shafter, Elko County.

A miser's fortune was hidden near the old Pogue Station southeast of Eureka, White Pine County.

A bank robber's treasure was hidden near Six Mile Canyon near the road from Carson City to the ghost town of Ramsey.

Note that, as is the case with many Western states, Nevada also has many treasure stories concerning lost silver or gold *mines* (as opposed to coins or other forms of treasure).

New Hampshire Treasures Waiting to be Found

Near Colebrook in Coos County, far in the northern regions of the state and quite distant from the sea, some of Captain Kidd's treasure is said to have been buried, and "old coins have been found." If so, there is a remote possibility that such a cache could have or still does include Massachusetts silver coins. However, it is difficult to imagine that Captain Kidd would have spent a week or more journeying to this remote inland location after he anchored his ship on the New Hampshire coast.

A treasure buried in the 1940s in Dublin, New Hampshire, has never been found.

Governor John Wentworth is said by some to have buried $25,000 in coins and silverware near Portsmouth, presumably before fleeing to the north during the parlous times of the Revolutionary War. It is known that Wentworth was a man of considerable wealth.

The Isles of Shoals off the coast of New Hampshire and just about every landing along the state's short (about 17 miles) seacoast have been long regarded as prime sources for hunting pirate treasure, although little has actually been found there. Said to be a particularly rich possibility in this offshore group is Smuttynose Island, and apparently pirate Jack Quelch thought this was a great location to bury silver and gold.

Ned Low and William Fly were two other pirates who liked the area too. Cotton Mather, the Massachusetts diarist and prominent justice, recorded that Fly's career was especially bloodthirsty, but lasted only 35 days before he was tried and hanged in Boston, where Fly helped the hangman tie the knot for his neck.

Note that Appledore Island, not far away, is also said to be laden with treasure just waiting to be found, and ditto for Star Island. And Londoner Island, later called Lunging Island, is where Blackbeard is said to have buried treasure—specifically, on the side of the island facing the Star Island Hotel across the water.

The lower reaches of the Piscataqua River, which empties into the Atlantic at Portsmouth, are said to be where Samuel Bellamy cached some supplies and possibly coins.

Panoramic view of the Isles of Shoals.

New Jersey Treasures Waiting to be Found

With all of its shoreline, New Jersey was an enticing place to bury treasure for pirates, and some did stash their plunder there. As such, it is not unusual for old coins to wash up on beaches after storms, high tides, or (especially) a combination of both of these events. Asbury Park, Stone Harbor, Beach Haven, and other coastal sites have been mentioned in this regard, and additional pirate gold is said to be secreted at several places including Perth Amboy and Cape May.

Near Colt's Neck and near Farmingdale, both in Monmouth County, robbers who terrorized the pine barrens are said to have buried their loot.

Near Caldwell, a German naval officer is said to have secreted a treasure before he was killed.

New Mexico Treasures Waiting to be Found

Money from the Cooney stagecoach, hidden near Cooney, Grant County, has never been found.

Stagecoach treasure hidden in Doubtful Canyon near Steins Peak, Hidalgo County is unlocated.

Lost treasure of Fort Bayard, Grant County, remains unfound.

At Devoy's Peak near Mount Dora, much outlaw loot is hidden.

Missing cash from a train robbery to the tune of $100,000 is believed hidden near the Lava Beds southeast of Grants, Valencia County.

A Texas outlaw's stash may still be concealed at Pump Canyon, San Juan County.

A number of gold ingots, weighing in total between 17 and 20 tons, is believed by some to be hidden near Shiprock, San Juan County. It is believed by others to be imaginary, but it makes an interesting story nonetheless.

Gold bars have been missing for many decades at Tres Piedras in the San Juan Mountains, Taos County.

About 25 miles east of Springer, Colfax County, there may be hidden some $40,000 in gold coins from a wagon train.

New York Treasures Waiting to be Found

At the old Jeffery Amherst Fort site at Crown Point, Essex County, treasure may have been buried.

In the Montezuma Swamp near Seneca Falls, the Loomis gang is said to have buried much loot.

At Grand Island in Lake Erie, not far from Niagara Falls, a fortune is said to have been hidden by an early resident.

A ship holding a vast fortune was lost many years ago near Hell's Gate in the East River, and although the area is not large, the hulk of the vessel in question has never been found.

The notorious Captain Kidd is said to have buried much treasure in coastal areas, especially at Gardiners Island. Most probably, if such still exists, it includes few American coins.

There are numerous accounts of lost chests, sunken ships, etc., near Manhattan in the East River, Hudson River, and New York harbor areas. Long Island, with its extensive sandy beaches, is said to also offer many possibilities.

The missing coins stolen from Waldo C. Newcomer, president of the National Exchange Bank of Baltimore and a consummate coin collector, would probably be worth in the millions if they could be found. The story goes back to the summer of 1913, when Newcomer was vacationing with his family at Rye Beach, New Hampshire (which was a popular resort then and still is now). Meanwhile, his many numismatic rarities, rarely shown to anyone, were stored at his home in a special cabinet—this measuring five feet high, sporting 15 drawers, fitted with locks, and protected by a recently installed burglar alarm system.

Newcomer returned home on September 15 and busied himself with catching up on things since his June 20 departure. Two days later, he looked at his coin cabinet and saw that drawers were unlocked and trays were in disarray. After taking inventory, he determined that about 1,200 coins had disappeared, including hundreds of silver coins and about 150 gold pieces.

Detectives were put on the trail. A break came when a man with a heavy case came to the Columbus Avenue Branch of the Corn Exchange Safe Deposit Vaults in New York City. The superintendent of the facility, Stanley R. Walker, was surprised to be offered a $50 gold coin in payment. He accepted it and, possibly because it seemed strange, kept it, no doubt substituting other funds for the box rental. He made note of the man's name and address, Frederick Holtz, 242 West 42nd Street in the city.

Not long afterward, Walker made a trip to Philadelphia for some reason and registered at the Ritz-Carlton Hotel. He paid for his stay with the same $50 gold piece that he had received for the safe deposit box; apparently, it had lost its novelty for him. The hotel cashier who received the payment noticed the coin's unusual character, though, and thinking that it might be valuable showed it to two of the hotel's bellboys, August Kungle and Nicholas Turner.

The pair offered to find out, and they made their way to dealer S. Hudson Chapman, where they offered to sell it for $75. Chapman recognized the coin as a very rare 1855 Kellogg & Co. coin minted in San Francisco and concluded it was the one recently reported as stolen from Newcomer. Chapman subsequently had the young men arrested, but their story to the authorities as to how they acquired the coin was investigated and was found to be truthful.

Stanley R. Walker was arrested next as he was suspected of being the culprit, but Walker told his story, and Frederick Holtz was identified as the thief. He was eventually tracked down, perhaps when he came to visit his safe deposit box, and the suspect was put in jail.

As it turns out, Holtz's real name was found to be Otto Henry Houst. His supposed address was false as well—a theatre. It was also learned that he was an electrician and had worked with the Holmes Burglar Alarm Telephone Company in Baltimore in installing a system in Newcomer's home—no wonder an alarm never sounded!

Of Newcomer's gold coins, all but one—an 1829 Small Date half eagle—was recovered. Houst said at first that the rest of the coins, including the silver pieces, were too heavy, and that he threw them in the North River. He later changed his story to say he buried the coins in two chamois bags near a marked tree in Kingston, New York; then, he changed his story again and said that he had bought a farm in the town of Rosendale, eight miles north of Kingston, and had buried the coins there in a place known as

Waldo C. Newcomer.

$5 note signed by Newcomer as president.

"The Cottages" about 300 feet from his house and near a Catholic cemetery.

Detectives searched the area and found a few silver coins, but not the two bags. Meanwhile, Houst was still in jail. He said he had great remorse, pleaded poverty, and told of his distressed childhood. Perhaps Newcomer did not press charges. It is not known if he went free after the search or if he served additional time, but he was eventually released.

Later, Houst, his wife and their six children moved to near Kingston, New York, where he continued to work as an electrician—including installing alarm systems—and became a minister in a local church. He was viewed as an upstanding citizen, and when he died on January 17, 1949, more than 100 members of the Kingston Masonic Lodge were among the many people who attended his funeral.

Meanwhile, Newcomer rebuilt and added to his collection. Unfortunately, he ran into financial difficulty during the Depression and had to consign his collection to B. Max Mehl in 1932. He died of heart failure on July 29, 1934, never seeing his silver coins—which included a rare 1878-S half dollar and a Proof 1895 dollar—again. They remain missing to this day; perhaps a treasure to be found.[562]

North Carolina Treasures Waiting to be Found

A stranger is said to have buried a bag filled with gold near the old Brummels Inn at High Point.

In the early 1900s, some old Spanish-American coins—including some dated 1788—were found on the James Robert Thomas property in Waynesville. More may still be there.

On the bottom of the Pamlico River, an old brick vault is said to have been found by fishermen, within which were several kettles and more than 200 Spanish-American gold coins. For reasons hard to figure out, the fisher folk are said to have reburied the treasure on a nearby shore, where it was lost track of, as flooding changed the profile of the river bank.

Near Chimney Rock, Round Top Mountain—which forms one side of Hickory Nut Gap—a pot of gold is said to have been buried by a group of six Englishmen in colonial days. A copy of a map indicating the site is in the Library of Congress. Several explorations have been made, but no success has been reported.[563]

Plum Point in Beaufort County was a burial spot for pirate booty, and to prove the contention, it is said that some has already been recovered there.

Near Wrightsville Beach, there is a place aptly named Money Island. Could its moniker allude to unfound riches?

The Great Dismal Swamp may be where Frenchmen fleeing a British warship hid gold during the early days of colonization.

North Dakota Treasures Waiting to be Found

Along the Missouri River near Bismarck, forty-niners laden with gold from California are said to have buried treasure worth $90,000 to prevent its capture by Indians.

At Rolla in Rolette County, bank robbers hid loot in the foothills of Turtle Mountain.

The paymaster for Hudson's Bay Company buried $40,000 in the area of Lignite, Burke County, just before an attack by robbers.

Ohio Treasures Waiting to be Found

The Bridge family pot of gold was buried near Eaton, Preble County, in the early 1800s and has never been recovered.

At Rockford, Mercer County, some loot of bank robbers has been found, but more is believed to be in the area.

Oklahoma Treasures Waiting to be Found

Gold belonging to a cattleman of Atoka is believed to be lost.

Half a bushel of silver coins hidden by bandits on Holsum Valley road, Le Flore County, has never been found.

At Roman Nose State Park, near Watonga, Blaine County, the loot of several old-time outlaw gangs is said to be buried.

Robber's Cave State Park, near Wilburton, Latimer County, offers obvious possibilities.

An outlaw's treasure on Boggy Creek—near Boswell, Choctaw County—awaits a lucky searcher.

Treasure formerly the property of California emigrants is supposedly hidden on Fish Creek near the old Edwards Post south of Holdenville, Hughes County.

Loot that Charles "Pretty Boy" Floyd hid near Sallisaw, Sequoyah County, may still be there.

Treasure from Captain Golden's wagon train was hidden at Big Caney Creek, south of Artillery Mound, near Boulanger, Osage County.

Loot of the Dalton gang was hidden in various locations around the state, including in caves at Sand Springs.

Dick Estes's outlaw gold treasure on Panther Creek, about 10 miles north of Cache, Comanche County, has not been found.

The lost gold of Fort Arbuckle, on or near the old Fort Sill Military Reservation, is still missing.

Glass jars containing $58,000 or more in coins were secreted near Sulphur Canyon Bridge, which is not far from Clayton in Pushmataha County.

Robber Henry Starr's ill-gotten gains may be cached near Rose and Pryor, Mayes County.

Treasure in the ghost town of Ingalls, east of Stillwater, Payne County, awaits the discoverer.

The Dillon gang is said to have buried treasure in and around Mannford, Creek County.

Joe Vann's treasure may be found on the site of his old mansion in Webbers Falls, Muskogee County.

Kenton in Cimarron County was once a center for banditry, and stolen treasure is still hidden in the area.

Near Rattan at Seven Devil Mountain, $50,000 in gold coins—this being from the loot of a bank robbery—is said to be hidden. The bandit gave directions to where the coins were cached before he was hanged, but later attempts to locate the coins proved futile.[564]

The safe taken from the Kosoma train at Buck Creek, near Antlers, Pushmataha County, has been missing for a long time.

Silver dollars were lost near Summerfield, Le Flore County.

An Army paymaster's cache may be hidden at Twin Mounds, near Jennings, Pawnee County. Similarly, an Army payroll was hidden at Cache, Comanche County, to prevent capture by Indians.

Loot buried by bank robber Al Spencer may be hidden in the Osage Hills west of the Verdigris River in northeastern Oklahoma.[565]

Note that there are many stories of Jesse James's loot being hidden in the state.

Oregon Treasures Waiting to be Found

A buried fortune may or may not be on the Baker Ranch on Birch Creek, south of Pilot Rock, Umatilla County.

At Mount Hood, in the area of Government Camp, Clackamas County, stolen treasure was buried.

Pirate treasure is said to be buried near Cascade Head, Lincoln County.

In Baker City, some of the two-ounce gold "buttons" made during the gold rush there in 1907 may be in safe deposit boxes or elsewhere. Only three or four are known today from an original production of many dozens.

Many ships in the coastwise trade have been wrecked off the coast of Oregon, and it is said that some contained money from passengers' purses and from safes. Factual accounts of coins are scarce, though.

At Horse Thief Meadows near Parkdale, Hood River County, $25,000 from a stagecoach robbery is believed to be hidden.

Pennsylvania Treasures Waiting to be Found

Many Indian peace medals were given out by early settlers. Many pieces, now oxidized or corroded, have been excavated, but more probably remain.

At a place called Asylum on the upper reaches of the Susquehanna River, escapees from the French Revolution (and some displaced Frenchmen from the West Indies as well) are said to have concealed their wealth during the mid-1790s.

Near Aristes, Pennsylvania, at 1:41 in the afternoon of June 17, 1948, a four-engine United Airlines DC-6 crashed and broke into pieces, killing all aboard. The tragedy occurred when carbon dioxide sprayed into the cargo hold to quench a supposed fire (there was none), crept into the cockpit, and incapacitated the crew. It was said that $250,000 aboard in small bills was never found.

The Doane Gang of Tories stashed $100,000 in loot near Wernersville, Bucks County.

Money gathered by settlers at the communal settlement of Ephrata Cloisters is said to be concealed somewhere in that area.

Rhode Island Treasures Waiting to be Found

There are lots of pirate treasure stories associated with the beaches and inlets of this seacoast state. Specifically, Pirates' Cave on the southern reaches of Conanicut Island in Narragansett Bay may or may not be aptly designated.

Conanicut Island as shown on an 1866 map.

South Carolina Treasures Waiting to be Found

Most treasure stories relating to this state concern pirate loot, such as treasure hidden at the appropriately named Pirate House on Church

Street, Charleston; the site of old Fort Randall; Tilghman's Point on Little River; and Murrell's Inlet in Georgetown County.

Hampton Plantation, located northeast of Charleston, is where Edgar Allan Poe is said to have written his "Gold Bug" story in the 1840s, obviously an excellent omen for a place said by later generations to conceal treasures. A cache of 198 gold coins hidden during the Civil War was found there, though no numismatic description of the pieces has been encountered. Could there be more waiting to be found?

As an aside, George Washington is said to have slept at this plantation, and Archibald Rutledge (1883–1973) once owned the place.

South Dakota Treasures Waiting to be Found

Money may still be hidden on the site of a burned ranch near Redfern, Pennington County.

Loot from the holdup of the "Old Ironsides" Canyon Springs stagecoach is believed to be hidden near the junction of Prairie and Rapid creeks near Rapid City.

Buried treasure of the Gordon Stockade at French Creek, Lawrence County, remains lost.

Fruit jars filled with cash, the Mexican Ed Sanchez treasure, is hidden on Dirty Woman Creek near the old town of Grinston, Custer County.

Loot amounting to $140,000 was taken in a stagecoach holdup in 1878, hidden along a creek near Fairburn, Custer County, and never found. The treasure was being sent from a mining camp to a bank. The bandits were chased by a posse and killed.[566]

Near Hat Creek, in Rumford, Fall River County, a strongbox taken in an 1877 stagecoach robbery remains missing. This may be the same as $30,000 in gold coins in a treasure chest reported taken in a train robbery.[567]

A steamboat was lost near Riverside Park, Pierre, in the 1860s, with much gold aboard.

At the bottom of Long Lake, near Lake City, Marshall County, a "flour sack full of gold" is said to be hidden.

Miners laden with gold returning from the Virginia City, Montana, area in the 1860s buried their treasure near Deadwood before being killed by Indians.

Tennessee Treasures Waiting to be Found

The Touhy gang from Chicago stashed $60,000 near Newport.

Wartburg in Morgan County is where much gold brought back from California in the 1850s remains buried.

The parts of the Natchez Trace that wound through the forested areas of the state are said to offer many possibilities for robbers' loot, including some from notorious Samuel Mason and his son.

John Murrel, a bandit in early times mentioned in other accounts (see information under "Arkansas Treasures Waiting to be Found," page 357, and "Louisiana Treasures Waiting to be Found," page 365), is said to have cached up to $1,000,000 worth of treasure near Denmark, Madison County.

During the Civil War, much treasure was buried near Dover, Stewart County.

Texas Treasures Waiting to be Found

Gold bars were lost in Paisano Pass in Brewster County, near the Brewster-Presidio county line.

The gold and other treasure of Emperor Maximilian may be buried at Castle Gap, about 15 miles east of Horsehead Crossing, where a 15-wagon caravan carrying said riches was ambushed circa 1866 by ex-Confederate soldiers and other opportunists. Does this treasure exist? If so, does it include gold coins?[568]

Notorious Texas outlaw Sam Bass and his sidekick, Joel Collins, went to Big Springs, Nebraska, and held up the Union Pacific Railroad, escaping with a payroll of 3,000 freshly minted 1877 double eagles in a trunk. Although $25,000 worth of coins and jewelry (this would have been 1,250 double eagles if the jewelry had been minimal) was recovered, Collins and Bass died without revealing where the rest of the loot was. It is said that Bass had hidden his part in Cove Hollow—about 30 miles from Denton, Texas—where it may still be today.[569]

In spring 1894, four men held up the First National Bank in Bowie, Texas, and rode away with 500 double eagles ($10,000) and $18,000 in currency (among which might have been some $10 and $20 notes of the robbed bank, which issued its own bills). Before crossing the flooded Red River, the men decided to bury the heavy coins so as not to impede their crossing—though it seems highly unlikely that at the rate of 125 coins per man, with each coin weighing about one ounce, they would really have been a problem.

Anyway, the men were later captured and hanged, but not before one of the desperadoes confided to a lawman named Palmore that the gold was buried beneath a large tree, supposedly in a stand of cottonwoods near where the Red River meets the Little Wichita River.[570]

A cache of coins hidden by robbers near or on Biloxi Creek, not far from Lufkin, Angelina County, has never been discovered.

In Illinois, a gang of desperadoes held up a train, escaped with $350,000 in loot, and for some reason took it near San Antonio to hide it. They apparently hid it well, as it has never been found.

Treasure taken from the Butterfield Stage was hidden at Castle Gap, near King Mountain, Upton County.

A lost cache of double eagles in Palo Duro Canyon, Armstrong County, will certainly yield surprises if found.

A Missouri wagon train treasure, possibly amounting to as much as $30 million worth, was hidden near Willow Springs, northeast of Monahans, Winkler County.

Forty-niners who were headed back east laden with gold from California chose to bury their treasure in Buffalo Gap, Taylor County, when ambushed by Indians.

The missing Musgraves treasure of gold coins is said to be near Cotulla, La Salle County.[571]

Stagecoach robbery loot was hidden in Rattlesnake Cave—a.k.a. Skeleton Cave, for one of the bandits' remains are supposed to still be there—near old Fort Concho, west of San Angelo, Tom Green County.

The missing $100,000 on the old Riddles Ranch near Fort Worth has never turned up.

The Sanderson train robbery loot, near Sue Peak, Brewster County, remains missing.

More loot from another train holdup is believed to be hidden at the southwest edge of Stanton, Martin County.

Stories abound of pirate Jean Lafitte's treasures hidden at various places along the Gulf of Mexico coast and of gold and other treasures brought to Texas from Mexico only to meet various fates. Similarly, Mexican troops involved in various battles (the Alamo, for example) are said to have hidden coins in various places.

In a story reminiscent of those of Jack Hazelwood and William Hesslein (see information under "Kansas Treasures Waiting to be Found" and "Massachusetts Treasures Waiting to be Found," respectively), a coin dealer's dubious actions resulted in another lost accumulation, this somewhere in Texas. The dealer in question here is one Robert Henry Burnie—known as R.H. Burnie—who rose to some prominence with the 1955 publication of a 96-page work, *Small California and Territorial Gold Coins: Quarter Dollars, Half Dollars, Dollars*. This was well received, and within a short time it became the standard reference in the series.

Burnie, who did much of his business by mail order, relocated in 1956 from Pascagoula, Mississippi, to Texarkana, Texas. There, he devised a coin auction listing many rare items. Response was excellent, and in keeping with his terms of sale, successful bidders mailed him tens of thousands of dollars in payment, perhaps more. At about the same time, he requested rare coins from dealers to show to an important new client, and many coins and sets were sent to him.

From there, things went squirrely. In what was only the tip of the iceberg, *The Numismatist* reported this in May 1957: "R.H. Burnie, 40, of Pascagoula, Mississippi, and Texarkana, Texas, who conducted a fraudulent coin auction last year and fled to Mexico to avoid prosecution, was sentenced to five three-year prison terms by Federal Judge Joe Sheehy in Tyler, Texas, March 15. Burnie had pleaded guilty to swindling coin collectors of $35,000. Sentences are to run concurrently."

Today, his inventory and coins sent to him on approval remain missing.

Utah Treasures Waiting to be Found

An Army payroll treasure remains missing near Castle Dale, Emery County.

Train robbers' loot hidden near Bear River City, about four miles north of Corinne, Box Elder County, has never been found. Ditto for the take from the Corinne stagecoach robbery, also believed to be concealed near Corinne.

Caleb Rhodes, of Mountain Home, Duchesne County, had much wealth from an unknown source. Some of this, or perhaps a secret gold mine, awaits discovery.

Members of the Donner Party, on the way to California, are said to have hidden valuable coins near Silver Island Mountain, near Wendover, Tooele County, in autumn 1846 (see also chapter 2, "The Ill-Fated Donner Party," page 39, and information in this chapter under "Nevada Treasures Waiting to be Found," page 371).

The Castlegate payroll treasure near Hanksville, Wayne County, has been missing for a long time.

Robbers' loot from the Emery bank holdup was hidden at Hondo Arch near Emery.

The Mountain Meadow Massacre treasure is said to be hidden about 30 miles south of Cedar City, Iron County. This dreadful encounter has been written about by Mark Twain and others, and it seems unlikely that any treasure was actually left behind by the perpetrators of this sad event, a very dark chapter in the history of Utah.

Mormon gold coins are said to be stored in a vault in Salt Lake City.

The "Wild Bunch treasure," about $28,000, was secreted at a cabin near Brown's Hole, San Juan County.

Vermont Treasures Waiting to be Found

One does not usually associate Spanish explorers and expeditions with the Green Mountain State, but in 1952 Tom Penfield told of two treasures buried by Spaniards in Vermont, one of gold on the slopes of Ludlow Mountain.

Virginia Treasures Waiting to be Found

On a hill near McGaheysville, Rockingham County, a treasure was buried, according to local accounts.

In Fauquier County, William Kirk amassed a large fortune by the late 1700s and is said to have hidden it on the grounds of his estate, thus accounting for various scattered discoveries of coins in later years. However, the bulk of the treasure remains unlocated.

Major General George Cornwallis, whose surrender effectively ended the Revolutionary War, is said to have cached his own coins, as well as those captured during his earlier forays, to prevent their seizure by the U.S. troops. These coins and other precious items may still be found in or around Yorktown, if you are lucky enough to look in the right place.

On or near Chincoteague Island, on a wooded knoll overlooking the water, ten strongboxes filled with treasure may have been buried by pirate Charles Wilson.

In Prince William County, Confederate raider John S. Mosby captured a troop of Union forces who had in their possession many coins, jewels, and other items pilfered from Virginia homes. Mosby hid these items in the area, and they still may be there.

In 1794, the family of Baron François Pierre de Tubeuf, who lived in Washington County, was killed by outlaws. The criminals may have hidden the baron's money nearby, for when they were captured there were no coins in their possession.[572]

Near Richmond, $10,000,000 or more in gold coins—part of the much-discussed "Treasure of the Confederacy," a loan from England—is said to be buried. This can be discounted as fiction, however, according to most modern scholars of the subject.

The tale is probably derived from an account in the *New York Times*, October 31, 1947, "British Loan to Confederacy Thought Buried in Virginia." It was related that Virginia Governor William M. Tuck had recently received a letter from F.L. Weathers, of Greenville, South Carolina, who related that his grandfather, a Confederate soldier, had helped bury $10 million to $11 million in gold, a loan from the British government, in an iron box.

"I know the exact location in Virginia where the money is buried," Mr. Weathers wrote. "Some time ago I talked with a resident of that area, who said that the place I have mentioned has remained undisturbed since the close of the Civil War." Governor Tuck told reporters that, in view of the state's annual budget, he would be grateful if such a treasure could be found. Apparently, Weathers declined the governor's invitation to come to Virginia and act upon his information.

On an old plantation near Front Royal, somewhere along where a tree-lined drive was once located in front of the mansion's portico, a pot of silver coins may have been buried in 1861.

Roanoke was home to numerous wealthy families before the Civil War. Many treasures of these people were hidden in and around the city, where they may remain to the present day.

In Saltville, Abraham Smith and his sons are said to have buried $46,000 worth of silver and gold coins under a roadbed during the Civil War to prevent them from falling into the hands of Union soldiers.

Thomas Jefferson Beale may or may not have deposited hundreds of thousands of dollars' worth of gold and silver coins and gold nuggets somewhere in the state in the early 1800s. A more precise location is supposedly described in a cipher message.

In Page County, Edwin Powell is believed to have buried a large quantity of silver coins in the early 1700s. The site may be under a rock into which the design of a horseshoe is carved.

Then again, Powell is believed to have been a counterfeiter, so there is no guarantee that, if found, the treasure will consist of genuine Spanish-American silver coins, other coins circulating in the area at the time, or fakes.[573]

One of the more fanciful tales holds that Charles II of England, who was on the throne from 1660 to 1685, was fearful of being deposed, and in an early-day version of what many dictators and their kin would do to national treasuries years later, he sent some trusted aides with a large holding of coins to be secreted abroad—in this case, in the colony of Virginia. Note that if it exists, part of this treasure may even include some ancient Roman coins.[574]

The coastal areas of the state are rich hunting grounds for anyone equipped with an electronic metal detector, and many old coins have been found, usually one at a time.

Washington Treasures Waiting to be Found

Captain Johnson's cache of gold may still be at the old Johnson home site in Ilwaco, Pacific County.

On Vashon Island in Puget Sound, a logger buried gold in 1877, and it remains unlocated.

The treasure of Captain James Scarborough is believed to be hidden at Fort Columbia.

Sarah Smith Collard of Seattle traveled widely and is said to have hidden money in out-of-the-

way places on her journeys, including $500,000 in an old clock and several $1,000 bills in another location. In the 1950s, the administrator of her estate was seeking clues as to where some of the money was; how successful he was in finding information or the treasure is unknown.[575]

Robbers' Roost is the site of buried loot. Note that several different places in the Western United States bear the name "Robbers' Roost;" this one is near Fruitland.

In 1863, $20,000 in gold coins was hidden in the base of a bluff on the stage road from Walla Walla, Washington, about a day's ride on horseback on the way to Lewiston, Idaho.[576]

West Virginia Treasures Waiting to be Found

What is now the State of West Virginia was before October 20, 1863, part of the State of Virginia; the present-day locations of the towns are filed under the West Virginia heading.

Dennis Adams buried his wealth in Kermit in the early 1900s. It has never been found.

Near Chapmanville, a payroll in coins destined for Union troops may be buried on the west bank of the Buyandotte River, while an even larger payroll may be secreted in Upshur County, near or in Rock Cave.

In 1758, a group of Shawnee Indians attacked a settlement in a remote area, captured those who lived there, and took their coins and other possessions away. These have never been found and may have been buried on the slopes of South Fork Mountain.

The outlaw sons of John Jennings may have buried loot in and around Wetzel County.

In Jefferson County, Rezin Davis Shepherd may have buried coins on his land in the 1850s and early 1860s.

Near the Buckhannon River in Randolph County, two separate hoards of coins may be hidden.

Around 1820, Colonel Joseph Van Swearingen, a Revolutionary War veteran, is said to have buried much of his fortune about a half mile north of Shepherdstown in Jefferson County.

In 1917, a draft evader is said to have buried $150,000 in the vicinity of Marlowe, Berkeley County.

Wisconsin Treasures Waiting to be Found

Near Antigo, a bunch of bank robbers hid their loot, but were never able to come back to get it.

The Dillinger gang hid $250,000 in currency in the woods near Mercer in 1934.

Notorioius bank robber John Dillinger.

Outlaws considered Bogus Bluff, near Gotham, Richland County, to be a good hiding place for coins. Many may still remain there today.

On Stockton Island (one of the Apostle Islands near Bayfield), treasure is supposed to have been hidden by British soldiers.

Wyoming Treasures Waiting to be Found

Bandits' loot hidden near old Fort Laramie has never been found.

The Jack Slade gang hid treasure in Slade Canyon, near Sunrise, Platte County.

Stagecoach holdup loot amounting to $37,000 was hidden in 1878 near Newcastle, Weston County, and remains missing.

The coins of an Army paymaster were buried at Smoot, Lincoln County, to avoid capture by Indians.

"Teton" Jackson buried his loot at Cache Creek near Jackson Hole. This is may be the same treasure detailed in a report of $150,000 in stolen gold hidden in the area.

In the vicinity of Baggs, Carbon County, outlaw treasure is hidden.

Gold coins were found in 1916 at Rock River, Albany County, but they are believed to be just a small part of a treasure that is still unlocated.

Train holdup booty secreted near Rock Springs, Sweetwater County, remains untraced.

Stagecoach treasure near Newcastle, Weston County, has been lost for decades.

chapter 23

Unrecovered Sunken Treasures

A ship is the most living of inanimate things.
—Oliver Wendell Holmes

The possibilities for coin treasures lost underwater and still waiting to be found are nigh-endless. We start with the number of shipwrecks worldwide in the past several centuries, which has amounted to hundreds of thousands, if smaller vessels are included; one estimate places the total at close to a million.[577]

Narrowing the scope to those sunken treasures related to the United States, we have a few more concrete figures, but the quantity soon becomes just about as unwieldy and nebulous. For example, Edward Rowe Snow—New England's best-known chronicler of things nautical and interesting—published a list of 1,119 wrecks of larger ships, mostly of the 1800s and early 1900s, that had wrecked off the coast of just the *southern part* of New England.[578] There are also more than 7,000 documented larger sunken ships known in the Great Lakes.[579] A listing of wrecks on the Mississippi and tributary river system would reach into the thousands as well; countless additional ships are at the bottom of the Atlantic Ocean off Cape Hatteras, North Carolina; and individual disasters, such as the port fires in Sacramento and St. Louis, sometimes claim a couple dozen or more ships at a time.

Looking specifically for vessels with U.S. coins, the most likely candidates are those that not only are said to have contained specie, but also operated after about 1820—especially on ocean voyages that *originated* in the United States or on inland waters. Specie cargoes before about 1820 are likely to have contained Mexican-American or other non-U.S. coins; these, of course, are still of importance to the numismatist, but are not the focus of this book.

Speaking of specie, there is a common snag encountered when attempting to determine whether or not a ship had any on board—coins carried as ship cargoes were rarely identified as such. As noted in chapter 7 as part of the description of the Economite Hoard (see page 125), tens of thousands of dollars' worth of gold coins shipped to the Harmonists by canal boat from Philadelphia were listed as *machinery* on the manifest. And earlier, in the 1700s, it was popular to designate coins as *hardware* when shipping them from one place to another by stage or ship. Thus, from historical records we will not always gain numismatically informative descriptions of what was aboard the thousands of ships that were wrecked in or near American waters.

This being said, it is worth noting that in the absence of proof of specie on board, what a given ship carried as its main cargo can give some indication as to the likelihood of coins being found in a sunken vessel. For instance, passenger vessels are likely in most instances to have had money aboard as travelers' belongings, and some few ships had treasure or other coins aboard as commercial cargo. However, most ships were used to transmit merchandise or commodities, and it is highly unlikely that a wrecked freighter with a cargo of lumber or fertilizer will ever yield anything significant in the way of rare coins. Indeed, most veteran explorers of underwater wrecks have never found much in the way of numismatically valuable specimens, despite inspecting dozens of wrecks over a long period of years.

And in the end, it is a fact of life that in the majority of instances when a wreck carrying coins is located, the huge expenses—properly registering with state officials, quieting potential claims, and paying for professional divers and equipment—overwhelm any chance of profit, even if the recovery is significant. Clive Cussler,

who has salvaged several dozen wrecks and who has written extensively on the subject, commented in 1996 that except for the *Nuestra Señora de la Atocha* and SS *Central America* recoveries, very few undersea efforts have ever yielded a profit to their discoverers.[580] And now that all the facts are in, including information not known until the late 1990s, the *Central America* recovery by the first expedition was a loss to the investors, as chronicled in detail in chapter 14.

Value Estimates and Reality

In virtually all printed accounts of marine treasures, estimates of the value of coins aboard are apt to be wild guesses supported by little in the way of facts, let alone information of a useful numismatic nature. It is also usually not stated how such estimates were derived; some are based upon contemporary statements of how much gold or other cargo was lost, and in such instances, today's coin values would be considerably higher.

Then again, even given information as to the face value of coins lost in a wreck a century or more ago, anyone wishing to evaluate the potential treasure today can do no better than make estimates. If a numismatist is involved in such estimates, the figure may have some semblance to reality. Otherwise, the sky's the limit for wild guesses. Donald Shomette, marine author and historian, was quoted by the *Los Angeles Times* as saying, "The real profit for treasure hunters comes from raising money from investors."

The varying condition of the lost treasure also complicates value estimates. Copper coins corrode in sea water, and silver coins do not fare well either, while gold coins are sometimes quite resistant to such effects. Water in lakes and rivers is kinder to coins, but still a large amount of oxidation will take place on copper and silver coins over a period of time. It's interesting to note that if silver coins are immersed in salt water in contact with iron (ship's nails, boiler supports, etc.), the electrolytic action of the salt water will oxidize the iron first and preserve the silver virtually unharmed; unfortunately, this fortuitous juxtaposition of iron and silver has occurred with only a few coins on only a few wrecks.

Unsalvaged Wrecks with Coins Aboard

All these caveats—the chances of a wreck not containing coins, the slim probability for profit, and the inaccuracy of value estimates—aside, hope springs eternal. The thrill of finding something special remains a powerful attraction, and there is something incredibly romantic about a *treasure coin*.

Perhaps deep sea treasure hunting is like winning the *America's Cup*—money will be the reward, but it will not be nearly enough to cover expenses. Maybe some future chronicler will tell of the finding of rare silver and gold coins of the 1820s in sandy dunes of Long Island—the lost treasure of the *Vineyard*—or possibly someone will reveal details of gold coins recovered in Long Island Sound from the wreck of the *Lexington* tragedy.

Meanwhile, here are some potential sources for interesting coins as gleaned from several thousand treasure and nautical accounts. For general interest, as in the preceding chapter, information for certain wrecks having other than United States coins is given.

1679, September. *Griffon.* In the water off Hessel, Mackinac County, the ship may include gold coins intended for use to purchase furs. This ship—under the control of Robert Cavelier, Sieur de LaSalle—departed from what is today Green Bay, Wisconsin, on September 18, 1679, and was never heard from again, thus creating one of the most tantalizing mysteries in Great Lakes nautical lore.[581] Any coins aboard would of necessity be foreign, perhaps including French provincial intended for Canada, although it is not impossible that some New England silver coins could have been among them as well.

In the summer of 2013, researchers claimed to have found the wreckage of the *Griffon*, but this claim has not been confirmed as of October 2014.

1799. *Defense.* This privateer is said to have sunk off the coast of Stonington, Connecticut, with $500,000 in captured booty, of which some might have been U.S. coins. Any of those that could be recovered today, if in reasonably good condition, would have immense value.

Early 1800s. Unknown name. A schooner with a cargo of gold bullion is said to have been wrecked off the point of Little Bay de Noc, near Escanaba in Lake Michigan.[582] Possibly this is the same as an unidentified vessel that sank off Poverty Island, Big Bay de Noc, Delta County, Michigan, mentioned in another source.[583]

1820, January 17. *Midas.* This ship was lost off Boston, Massachusetts, incoming from Santo Domingo. A large quantity of specie was supposedly aboard, and if so, this ship certainly had an appropriate name, hearkening to the mythical king who could turn anything to gold with his touch! Whether the specie was in the form of U.S. coins is not known, and while it seems somewhat unlikely, you never can tell.

1823, February 8. *Tennessee.* A steamer of 416 tons built in Cincinnati in 1819, the ship departed New Orleans with 300 or more festive passengers aboard, who had pulled away from the shore in a party mood, shouting and waving.[584] Soon it was nightfall, the sky and river were dark, and at a bend above Natchez the steamer snagged.

One passenger grabbed a skiff, rowed slightly away from the stricken steamer, and implored a passenger aboard to throw him his saddlebags which were filled with money; this effort in lieu of his working to save others. The engineer of the ship was given the opportunity to board a small yawl and go to safety, but he elected to remain aboard in an effort to run the *Tennessee* onto a sandbar so the passengers could be saved. Unfortunately, the ship went down in the swirling current, taking with it the noble engineer, who was in the steam-engine room, and about 30 others.

1827, January 15. *Panthea*. This vessel was lost on the east side of Holyhead harbor, England, inbound from New York City. Cargo was said to have included specie, some of which was salvaged soon after the disaster. As for the rest of the specie, one cannot help but wonder if it might have included U.S. gold coins. If so, here is an immense treasure even if only a few coins are found—all U.S. gold coins minted prior to 1827 are exceedingly valuable today.

1837, May 9. *Ben Sherrod*. This 393-ton steamer, built in 1836 on the Ohio River at New Albany, Indiana, departed the levee at New Orleans at about ten o'clock on Sunday morning, May 6, 1837, under the command of a Captain Castleman. The vessel was what was known as a "Tennessee cotton boat," and on this trip had a cargo of 1,500 to 2,000 bales of cotton piled up and filling nearly all of the lower outside decks. There was also a large quantity of gold and silver coins consigned to banks in Tennessee, much "passenger gold," several rigs of horses and carriages and other commercial goods—not to mention many families and other excursionists aboard for the joyful occasion of a scenic cruise.

The trip was going well, all were having a good time, and time passed quickly. On the evening of May 8, the boat was engaged in an exciting race with the steamboat *Prairie*, on her way to St. Louis. As the rival drew close to the *Ben Sherrod*, it was necessary for the latter to stop at Fort Adams, during which time the *Prairie* passed her. Great vexation was manifested by some of the passengers that the *Prairie* should get to Natchez first.

Regardless, the captain retired to his berth and left the deck in the charge of an officer. A barrel of whiskey was opened, and some of the

crew indulged heavily. Later, after the steamer left Fort Adams—full speed ahead and without regard to safety—the wood piled up near the furnaces caught fire several times, and was only partially extinguished due to the inebriated state of the crew.

By one o'clock in the morning of May 9, the fire was out of control. The ship spun around a couple of times, then hit a sandbar. The excursionists woke from their dreams to find a fiery hell—some tried to get away in boats, but their craft capsized. Others jumped into the water.

Two other steamers came into view, the *Columbus* and the *Statesman*, and saved many. Still, the death toll amounted to somewhere between 72 and 200 persons (estimates vary), among whom were Captain Castleman's father and one of the captain's children.[585]

1837, June. *Aurora*. This schooner, sailing under the U.S. flag, was on the way from Havana to New York City when she sunk in the Atlantic close to shore off North Carolina. The weather was moderate, and with some effort Captain Richard Sheridan and his crew were able to struggle ashore, unharmed. Lost on board was a shipment of gold coins consigned in Havana to Don Francis Stoughton, the Spanish consul in New York City.

Captain Sheridan was later arrested and charged with fraud. Authorities stated that he, in cahoots with two of his crew members, had staged the wreck. The cargo, including 264 doubloons valued at $4,000 (for once, the computation seems to be about right; doubloons were worth about $16 each), was secretly taken from the ship at the time she went down and, later on shore, converted into U.S. coins. Sheridan was ordered to pay restitution amounting to $4,919, including costs, and was clapped into jail.[586]

As an aside, there are so many coastal shipwrecks off North Carolina like this one that it is said an observer from the air can see dozens of dark hulks littering the sea bottom within a mile of the shore on a calm, sunny day.

1841, March 11 (departure date). *President*. This 1,863-ton ship, which belonged to the

British & American Steam Navigation Company, was lost with 136 aboard in mid-ocean on the way from New York City to Liverpool, the latter being the leading British port at the time. Specie said to have been worth $30,000—belonging to stage actor and comedian Tyrone Power, ancestor of the film actor of the same name—was aboard.

A message from Power, "President sinking fast," was found in a bottle many weeks later. This is the only message known from the missing ship. Her captain, Richard Roberts, had expressed the sentiment that the vessel was jinxed and had presciently called her "the coffin ship" before departure. Following the loss of the *President*, the British & American Steam Navigation Company went into bankruptcy.

1841, February 22. *Creole*. This steamer of 192 tons was built in Pittsburgh in 1839. It burned on the Mississippi River at Torras, Louisiana, on the way from New Orleans to Natchez, with the loss of 34 lives, $100,000 in coins, and many bales of cotton.[587]

1841, August 9. *Erie*. Built in Erie, Pennsylvania, in 1837, this ship was a steamer of 497 tons and was first berthed at Presque Isle. She burned in Lake Erie off Silver Creek, New York, 30 to 35 miles from Buffalo, on a voyage from that port to Chicago. The loss of an estimated 242 lives marks this as one of the most tragic nautical disasters ever associated with the Great Lakes.

Gold and silver coins said to have been worth about $200,000 were salvaged in 1856 (another account says $2,000 in 1854) when the wreck was raised, but there may be more specie on the lake bottom. Also, when the derelict hull was being towed, it sank in 11 fathoms of water about four miles from shore, possibly containing some treasure.

One estimate published in 1957 suggested that the original treasure was worth $100,000 and that some still remained unsalvaged at the time. Later, in 1960, a group of divers found in the hull an estimated $1,200 worth of English sovereigns, kroner, and rubles.[588]

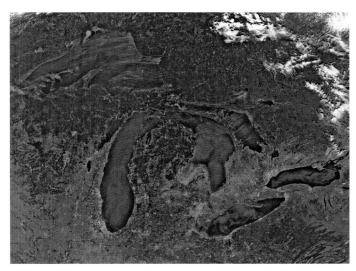

Not all tales of sunken treasure pertain to the high seas; the Great Lakes have claimed their fair share of ships.

1843, July 1. *Columbia*. This British ship of the Cunard Line, 1,138 tons, was one of four vessels (the others being the *Acadia*, *Britannia*, and *Caledonia*) on hand when the line was started by Samuel Cunard in 1840. She was wrecked—thankfully, without loss of life—in strong currents and heavy fog in the Bay of Fundy, off Devil's Limb Rock, about a mile from the coast of Cape Sable Island, Nova Scotia, Canada. The ship had departed from Boston and was on the way to Nova Scotia. A considerable value in specie was said to have been aboard; much was salvaged along with luggage and cargo shortly after the disaster, but some may remain in the derelict hull.

1846, June 11. *Lexington*. This ship sunk in Lake Erie off Point Mouille, near Ashtabula, Ohio, with $300,000 in gold aboard.[589]

1850. *Anthony Wayne*. Sunk in Lake Erie near Buffalo, New York, with $60,000 in gold aboard.[590]

1850, March 4. *Orline St. John*. This steamer of 349 tons, built in Louisville in 1847, was wrecked in the Alabama River at Bridgeport, about four miles south of Montgomery, Alabama. Forty-one lives were lost. A Colonel Rodman was aboard and is said to have been in charge of about $250,000 worth of gold. Salvage efforts took place shortly thereafter, and it is not known what might have been recovered or missed.[591]

1851, June. *Salle Fearn.* En route from New Orleans to Liverpool, this vessel caught fire and was lost in the middle of the Atlantic Ocean. The cargo of cotton and about $120,000 worth of gold was partially salvaged soon thereafter. One might surmise that many New Orleans Mint gold coins could have been aboard.

1852, August 19–20. *Atlantic.* This 1,155-ton sidewheel steamer, measuring 267 feet in length and featuring luxurious first-class accommodations, was built in Newport, Michigan, in 1849. In 1852, she collided with the grain freighter *Ogdensburg* in Lake Erie about six miles east of Long Point Island, Ontario, on the well-traveled route from Buffalo to Detroit.[592] The wreck, with about $30,000 face value in registered gold aboard, took an estimated 130 to 350 lives. Many of the passengers were Norwegian immigrants huddled in steerage.

Gold, silver, and various artifacts were recovered in the 1990s by the Mar Dive Corporation, Los Angeles. Published estimates of the modern-day value were as high as $200,000,000, but reality was far less. The matter of ownership went to court, and a man named Fletcher, who had found the wreck on September 1, 1984, was awarded title. However, additional claimants had emerged as well, as others had visited the wreck on various times from the 1800s onward.

Still, the whole matter was moot, as the ship had sunk in Canadian waters and the treasure was awarded to the Province of Ontario (never mind that both ships were from the United States). It is presumed that some treasure remains and is yet to be recovered.

1854, September 27. *Arctic.* Launched on January 28, 1850, this large and well-appointed

steamship was built by William H. Brown for the New York & Liverpool U.S. Mail Steamship Company, familiarly known as the Collins Line. On September 27, 1854, in heavy seas about 50 miles off of Cape Race, she was rammed by the *Vesta*, a small French steamer. Those aboard the *Arctic* did not think they had cause to worry, though, and even launched a lifeboat to assist the other ship.

As it turns out, there was cause to worry, despite assurances of the captain and crew that there was no problem. Not long after impact, it was learned that the *Arctic* was taking on water and was in serious danger. Nonchalance changed to tragedy as lifeboats became swamped in the high waves, and 322 people lost their lives. Meanwhile, the *Vesta* limped into port in Newfoundland under its own power.

As for the numismatically relevant content of this tale, the *Arctic* may not have had a cargo of treasure aboard, but at least one American coin of great numismatic significance was lost. In his *American Numismatical Manual*, Dr. Montroville W. Dickeson discusses a prime rarity, the 1733 Rosa Americana pattern penny, noting he knew of the existence of only four, now only three, specimens: "The fourth was purchased in England for the sum of £7, or $35, for Charles Bushnell, Esq., of New York City, unfortunately placed on board the steamer *Arctic*, to be transmitted to him, on her last and fatal voyage, and its pigmy proportions are now added to the vast accumulations that lie imbedded in the sands of the Atlantic Ocean."

1854, September 30. *Eliza Thornton*. Lost at Pedro Branco off the coast of China, this U.S. brig was on the way from San Francisco to Hong Kong and is said to have carried quite a bit of gold (although silver seems more likely, as the Chinese preferred this metal). Some passengers laden with coins jumped into the water to save themselves and their treasure, but lost both.

1856, October 29. *Superior*. This 567-ton steamer was built in Perrysburg, Ohio, in 1845. She is said to have had a goodly amount of specie

aboard when she was stranded off Grand Island on the way from Niagara, New York, to Lake Michigan. Thirty-four lives were lost.

1858, May 7. *Ostervald*. Wrecked in the Caribbean Sea about 50 miles off the coast of present-day Belize, this ship was on the way from New Orleans to Liverpool with $45,000 or so worth of specie aboard. Much was salvaged shortly after the disaster, but some may remain.

1858, October 15. *Water Witch*. Lost off St. Thomas Island in the Virgin Islands on the way from St. Thomas to Maracaibo, this vessel had specie aboard, but whether this included U.S. coins is not known. Put this in the "maybe so, maybe so, but probably no" category.

1859, November 14. *Heidelberg*. Lost off the coast of Florida on the way from New Orleans to LeHavre, France, the ship contained specie, some of which was recovered not long after the vessel went down. Note that ships departing with specie from New Orleans in the 1850s are prime candidates for having had New Orleans Mint coins aboard.

1860, November 10. *Dakatah*. This ship sunk in Lake Erie, near Long Point, Ontario, with $60,000 in gold aboard.[593]

1862, November. *Black Hawk*. This brig, laden with cargo including stained glass and specie, was lost in Lake Michigan about four miles north of Frankfort, Michigan. The stained glass would have little value today, as the state of the art in that field progressed rapidly after 1862, but the coins—total value at the time unknown—might just include some interesting U.S. pieces.

1863, August. *Georges Sand*. This ship, named after the pseudonym used by a famous female writer,[594] was on her way from San Francisco to Hong Kong when she was wrecked on a reef off Dongsha Qundao, China. Rumors of a great value in gold coins aboard circulated, some estimates crossing the $1 million mark, but the actual worth was probably considerably less than that. The coins were probably mostly silver, as Chinese merchants and bankers strongly preferred that metal.

1865, November. *Westmoreland*. This vessel sunk in Lake Michigan, north of North Manitou Island, with $100,000 in gold aboard.[595]

1868, September 15. *Parkersburg*. This ship, with much specie aboard, was lost in the Bay of Fonseca, Honduras, while on the way from Panama. Much was salvaged shortly thereafter, but some treasure may remain.

1870, February 22. *Golden City*. This steamer of 3,374 tons, built by William H. Webb, New York City, was launched on June 24, 1863. On the night of February 21, 1870, on the run from San Francisco to Panama, she encountered heavy fog. After 6:00 the next morning, the ship—still in zero-visibility conditions—ran with great force on a sandbar about 10 miles north of Point Lazaro (a.k.a. Cape San Lazaro) at Magdalena Bay, or about 225 miles north of the tip of Baja California.

From here, accounts differ. One states that the *Golden City*'s 400 or so passengers and the crew went ashore and remained there until February 25, when the *Colorado* was seen on her way north, but that the ship was not able to take the stranded people aboard at that point on the coast. That account continues by saying the castaways then had to walk to a landing point about 25 miles away—a trek on which they encountered much difficulty and some became lost—but that everyone eventually reached safety, and at least some of the treasure was recovered.[596]

A different account, meanwhile, says the *Golden City* burned and $300,000 in treasure was lost.[597]

1871, February 9. *Crescent City*. This 2,039-ton vessel owned by the Liverpool & Mississippi Steamship Company was on the way from New Orleans to Liverpool when she was wrecked near Galley Head, Ireland. Her cargo was said to have included 40 boxes of gold and/or silver coins

valued at more than $100,000, of which some 20 boxes were salvaged shortly after the wreck.

1871, February 12. *Republic*. Traveling from Port-au-Prince, Haiti, to Cape Lookout, North Carolina, this ship was said to have had a large amount of specie aboard when she was wrecked 60 miles offshore from her destination.

1871. *Yangtze*. On the way from New York City to Fuzhou, China, this elegant clipper ship was wrecked at the Paracel Islands. Her cargo is said to have included specie, presumably intended for the purchase of tea.

1871, October 17. *R.G. Coburn*. This ship sunk in Lake Huron off Harbor Beach with $105,000 in gold aboard.[598]

1872, August 24. *America*. This 4,560-ton sidewheel steamer owned by the Pacific Mail Line was en route from California to Yokohama, Japan, and was burned in the destination harbor, perhaps due to an incendiary (though this was never proved). On board were several hundred Chinese, primarily returning from California. Most passengers were taken off safely, but 60 to 70 perished. The latter are said to have been lost because they refused to leave the burning ship without taking with them their heavy wooden boxes filled with coins. The ship was afire for all of the following day and was a hazard to navigation, despite attempts of the Italian corvette *Vettor Pisani* to sink her with howitzer fire.

Gold and Mexican coins variously said to be worth from about $400,000[599] to $1,600,000 were aboard, although it seems that there was probably a lot of "passenger silver" that was not accounted for, among which were likely San Francisco Mint half dollars. At least some of these coins were said to have been stored in an iron-lined compartment with wooden braces extending through the corners, and the heat from the fire was so intense that much liquid metal ran through the brace holes. About $300,000 worth of metal was salvaged,[600] But whether any coins escaped being melted is not known.

1872, December 5. *Sacramento.* This steamer of 2,682 tons was built by William H. Webb in New York in 1864. On the night of December 5, 1872, she was running about 10 miles off the shore of Port Antonio, Baja California, and hit an uncharted reef. The *Montana* took off many of her passengers on December 11, but the captain and 20 crewmen stayed aboard to guard the cargo.

In the end, there was no loss of life, but gold valued at up to $2,000,000 may have been aboard and gone down with the boat.[601]

1873, September 21. *City of Detroit.* A steamer of 682 tons built in Marine City, Michigan, in 1866, one account says she was lost in Lake Erie two miles north of Port Barcelona, New York, with $100,000 in gold aboard.[602] Another account, however, mentions the ship as being sunk in Saginaw Bay near the treasure-laden schooner *Fay.*[603]

1874, December 17–18. *Japan.* This 4,351-ton U.S. sidewheel steamer, under the flag of the Pacific Mail Steamship Co., was on the way from San Francisco to Hong Kong when she caught fire and burned in the South China Sea. Her cargo is said to have included $365,000 in specie and additional gold, of which more than $180,000 was recovered by 1878 but some is still unaccounted for.

1877, February 6. *Bavaria.* This British steamer of 2,300 tons sailed under the flag of the Dominion Line. She caught fire and burned in the Atlantic Ocean while traveling from New Orleans to Liverpool. Specie valued at about $260,000 was aboard; part of this was said to be stolen by the crew at the time of the wreck, possibly as the conclusion to a dastardly plot hatched beforehand, a scenario that happened now and then.

1893, October 11. *Dean Richmond.* Owned by the Western Transportation Company, this 1,257-ton steamer was built in Cleveland, Ohio, in 1864. She was wrecked about a mile off Van Buren Point in Lake Erie, near Dunkirk, New York, en route from Toledo to Buffalo. The cargo included gold valued at $141,000 and additional treasure in the form of silver coins.[604] Not far away on the lake bottom is said to be the *City of Detroit.*[605]

1897, March 8. *Ville de St. Nazaire.* Under Captain Jaqueneau, this 2,640-ton French ship operated by the Compagnie Générale Transatlantique departed New York City with 9 passengers, 74 crew members, and cargo said to have included gold and headed toward the West Indies. On the first day out, she sprung a leak, but upon due consideration the breach was not deemed sufficiently serious to warrant returning to port.

On the next day the leak worsened, and on the following day the ship ran into an unexpected hurricane in that treacherous area known as the "Graveyard of the Atlantic" off Cape Hatteras, North Carolina. As her compartments filled with sea water, the captain ordered the ship to be abandoned, and all took to the lifeboats. While many were later rescued, 34 died from exposure.

1898, November 27. *Portland.* Operated by the Portland Steam Packet Company, this 2,284-ton wooden sidewheel paddle-steamer under Captain H.H. Blanchard left the India Wharf at Boston bound for Portland, Maine, on the evening of November 26, 1898. Her cargo, valued at several hundred thousand dollars or more, is said to have included jewelry and specie.

The weather was uncertain, and for a time Captain Blanchard considered postponing the voyage. In the end, though, he decided to adhere to the scheduled 7:00 p.m. departure.

At sea, the weather proved to be much rougher than anticipated, and heavy waves from an especially fierce gale damaged the *Portland*'s superstructure. At the same time, there was much destruction along coast; it was truly a forbidding night to be out in the open sea.

Around nine o'clock the next morning, Captain O.S. Fisher of the Cape Cod Life Saving Station saw a large paddlewheel steamer of unknown name, but possibly the *Portland*, offshore, and heard four blasts from the ship's siren. The weather closed in, visibility decreased to near zero, and the ship was not seen again.

By midnight, November 27–28, cabin furniture, personal effects, and many bodies had washed ashore on Cape Cod, giving mute testimony that a disaster had occurred at sea. Not a single soul lived to tell what happened, and no messages or other clues were ever found. It was supposed, however, that the ship broke up around nine o'clock on the evening of November 27 about 10 to 15 miles north of the cape.[606]

1901, February 22. *City of Rio de Janeiro*. This U.S. passenger steamship had left Yokohama, Japan, on February 2, 1901, and crossed the Pacific without incident. By the wee hours of February 22, she was within San Francisco Bay,[607] but she ran into pea-soup fog about 2,000 feet off Fort Point. Visibility was absolutely zero. So near, yet so far. What to do?

Captain William Ward had been warned of the dangers of proceeding, even slowly, in such conditions, but in his eagerness to reach port he disregarded such advice. This proved to be a fatal

mistake, as just past 4:30 a.m., the ship struck rocks. With a hole below her waterline, she continued under steam for nearly 20 minutes, but then sunk.

Down to the bottom of San Francisco Bay plunged a fortune in coins and cash, of which more than $2 million is said to have been recovered but some may still remain. The death toll included Captain Ward and between 103 and 128 others (estimates vary). Only 81 people survived.

1901, August 15. *Islander*. This ship went down in Stevens Passage between the Admiralty and Douglas Islands in the southern reaches of the Alaska's Pacific coast with a reported $3,000,000 in gold and $400,000 in currency aboard. Forty people lost their lives.[608]

1909, January 24. HMS *Republic*. This 585-foot, 15,378-ton White Star ocean liner was on her way from New York City to stops in the Mediterranean Sea, including Genoa and Alexandria, when she crashed into the 5,018-ton steamer *Florida*. Many of the passengers were taken aboard the latter vessel, and meanwhile the *Republic*'s radio distress signals were heard by the White Star liner *Baltic* and by the *Furnessia*, which came to the scene and took passengers from the *Florida*.

The U.S. revenue tugboat *Gresham* shortly took the damaged *Republic* under tow, but eventually she was lost in 45 fathoms—ostensibly shallow enough for recovery, but in a region of strong and changing currents. With her was lost an estimated $3,000,000 worth of large-denomination U.S. gold coins, according to some later accounts, although facts are elusive. The final death toll included two first-class passengers aboard the *Republic* and four crew members of the *Florida*.

The exploration of sunken ships sometimes yields numismatic wonders—and in other instances, such as that of the HMS *Republic*, salvagers come back with other kinds of artifacts.

Although this wreck is well known and numerous salvage attempts have been made, including by Martin Bayerle, no success in finding gold coins has been reported.[609] In the summer of 1987, more than $1 million was spent on a recovery effort that yielded champagne bottles, cut glass, tableware, and other artifacts, thought to be from the first-class pantry, but no gold.[610] One can imagine that if the cargo included a mixed assortment of eagles and double eagles—these being the two highest denominations in use at the time—perhaps 20,000 coins or so would have been involved.

Into the 2000s, Bayerle was still seeking gold. Theories concerning the rich cargo included a "politically sensitive and secret" $3 million shipment of recently minted U.S. gold eagles, including $2 million in gold coins purchased on January 12, 1909, from the National City Bank in New York and destined for Russia toward payment of a loan. No shipping manifests confirming such gold have ever been located, though.[611]

1909, December 8. *Clarion*. Built in 1881, this 1,712-ton ship was operated by the Erie & Western Transport Company of Canada. She caught fire and was lost off Point Pelee, Lake Erie, Ontario. Her cargo included specie.

1911. *R.J. Cochrane*. Sunk off Angel Island in San Francisco Bay, this ship had a cargo of $96,000 in gold.[612]

1911, May 12. *Merida*. This passenger ship, on a run from Havana to New York City, was rammed by the *Admiral Farragut* and sunk in the Atlantic Ocean off the Virginia Capes. She was said to have been carrying much treasure from Mexico, but several visits to the site by diving crews have yielded nothing in this regard.

1917, February 25. *Laconia*. This Cunard Line steamer of 18,099 tons, Captain Irvine at the helm, was torpedoed by a German submarine about 160 miles west-northwest of Fastnet, Ireland, while on the way from the United States to England. The hit occurred just after 9:00 p.m. on the ship's starboard side, near the engine room. Damage was done, but the attack was not fatal.

However, 20 minutes later another torpedo slammed into the engine room on the same side, spelling the ship's doom. She sank in the darkness at about 10:20 p.m. Of the 292 people aboard, 12 were killed.

She was said to have had 132 boxes of specie aboard, amounting to over a million ounces of silver. The ship was located by salvors shortly thereafter, but no report was given of any recovery of the coins.

1917, March 21. *Healdton*. This 4,489-ton U.S. tanker was torpedoed by a German submarine in the North Sea off the Netherlands. Some rumors had it that $3 million in gold was aboard.

1918, June 25. *Atlantian*. On her way from Galveston, Texas, to Liverpool, England, she was lost about 110 miles west-northwest of Eagle Island, Ireland. Her cargo is believed to have included gold and silver.

1931, September 11. *Columbia*. This steamship sunk off of Port Tasco, Mexico, with about $800,000 in coins aboard. Shortly thereafter, the Merritt, Chapman & Scott Salvage Corporation retrieved about $705,000 worth, and Lieutenant Harry E. Rieseberg, a California treasure hunter of renown, found more about two decades later, but the rest may still be there.[613]

chapter 24

Treasure Hunting Electronic Style

From the 1970s to the present time, seeking coins with electronic metal detectors—or "coinshooting"—has been a great hobby for thousands. These "detectorists," as they are called, are a passionate bunch, and many belong to clubs and subscribe to magazines.[614] They hunt on beaches, vacant downtown lots, city parks, and other places where people gathered years ago; they search in old cellars and foundations; and they explore ghost towns.

The typical experienced coin hunter operating in the Western United States is likely to have found a few silver dollars and perhaps one or two gold coins, plus an array of old-time loose change. In the Eastern United States, coins are more apt to be bronze or smaller silver denominations, but anything can and has happened. In general, there have been countless numismatically valuable coins found by electronic means from the late 1900s to date, and devices bearing such names as Fisher, Garrett, and White (there are others as well) can mean many happy hours for the treasure hunter.

It is worth mentioning here that while most coinshooting is casual in practice, precautions must be taken before serious searches for significant treasures on private property (say, gold said to be hidden on a plantation). To avoid legal problems, some type of a written agreement from the land owner granting permission to explore is necessary, though often overlooked. Such a document should give a general description of what is sought (old coins, artifacts, or whatever), the time limits for the search, and the "consideration" (reward) for the land owner—either expressed as a flat fee or a percentage arrangement. Various brochures issued by the manufacturers of metal-detecting devices often give suggestions.

Finally, note that coinshooting on National Historic Sites is nearly always forbidden, and obtaining permission to look for hidden things in city parks, school grounds, and other publicly owned places often involves a lot of red tape. For this reason, many treasure seekers do it on an informal (read: *illegal*) basis—not from desire to break the law, but from frustration. Of course, this is not to suggest that "thou shall go and do likewise"—simply an observation.

A Gallery of Finds by Detectorists

From thousands of stories reviewed, the following items have been selected to give a cross section of significant numismatic finds of older coins.

Found in an Old Springhouse: The time is in the early 1990s, and the place is "somewhere" in the United States.[615] The printed account of this particular find gave no geographical information at all—likely because this would result in claimants materializing from all directions—but some leafless trees in an included photo suggest it took place in an area which has both deciduous trees and a winter season (eliminating, for example, the Mojave Desert and the state of Florida).

Our detectorist is Roy Zeper, who had memories from his childhood of exploring a large estate, perhaps on a square mile or more of land with a grand mansion. Years later, he drove by the same place to see that most of the landscape had been developed for housing. On a corner, however, was a damp area with an old springhouse in decrepitude; years earlier, it had been used to store milk, meat, and other things in cool surroundings.

Equipped with a Fisher 1265-X metal detector, Zeper and his wife asked permission to prowl around. The device picked up a strong signal near the base of one of the interior stone walls. Zeper used a hand trowel to loosen a likely rock, then pulled it free to reveal a muddy Mason jar filled with coins. Inspection soon revealed Indian Head cents, bronze two-cent pieces, nickels, dimes, quarters, half dollars, and many silver dollars! The oldest coin was a half dollar of 1812 in perhaps Extremely Fine grade.

Gold Coins from a Demolition Site: Detectorists had been exploring a city demolition site, location not specified, where a double eagle had been found recently. Luck was with them, and another double eagle was found in short order, followed by four more all stuck together, followed by even more—the total reached 14 by the day's end.

Three more double eagles were found the next day, another was located a few days later, and an 1899 eagle was recovered as well. A coin dealer subsequently advised that all but one coin from the site was Mint State. A photograph accompanying the printed account revealed that the double eagles were dated from 1877 to 1906, suggesting that the coins had been secreted on or after 1906.

A Bordello in the Desert: Somewhere in the vast Mojave Desert, there was once a house of prostitution.[616] By the 1970s, it was sufficiently

defunct—the madam and her ladies of the night had long since departed—and only its old foundation remained. Russ Dieffenbaucher, a treasure hunter from Bakersfield, California, poked around the place with his electronic metal detector and found five half eagles, an eagle, and 40 silver dollars in an old Mason jar, perhaps remaining from the receipts of decades earlier.

The half eagles were dated 1881-S, 1892-S, 1901-S, and two of 1909-D, while the eagle was a 1902-S. Dieffenbaucher had long experience in hunting for coins, and in other places he turned up 60 or 70 Indian Head cents over a period of years, assorted gold coins, and other pieces. His oldest find was described as an 1819 copper cent so worn that he had to soak it in catsup until the date "was finally raised" so it could be seen.

The "Goat Doctor" Find: Not far from the bordello foundation (see the preceding entry), in a canyon in the foothills of the Sierra Mountains, the aptly named "Jimmy Sierra"—actually the nickname of James Normandi, one of the Western United States' best-known treasure hunters—made a major find one day in October 1980. Equipped with a White's 6000/D Series 2 metal detector (a brand which he distributes) and accompanied by Ed Milota, Ray Bolduc, and Don Arthur, the explorer found a "large Wells Fargo bag containing over 2,000 silver dollars."

This was only the half of it, though, as in the same place a year later Sierra dug up a rusted strongbox stuffed with $2,500 in Silver Certificates and more silver dollars and half dollars.[617] The silver face value alone amounted to more than $15,000, ranking this as one of the greatest buried treasures ever found in the United States!

The site was an old orchard that formerly belonged to a so-called "goat doctor," otherwise described in the account as a faith healer and self-taught chiropractor, perhaps specializing in using extracts from goat glands to cure various afflictions of his patients. Whatever he did, customers were willing to pay in silver, and plenty of it—over a period of many years from about 1920 to 1950, his customers handed over a wide variety of coins that would prove to be treasures. One cannot help but wonder why the "goat doctor" never recovered his earnings.

Good Times on Dollar Creek in Utah: Dan Davis and his sons were enjoying the day by a creek in Utah. It was the dry season, and although there was enough water for fishing, the level was far below normal.[618] One of the boys was idly tossing rocks into the water, and one hit a black rock . . . no! It was actually a little pile of blackened coins!

Upon close inspection, 136 silver dollars and 87 other coins were found, including one struck in gold! Dan shared the good news with his friend Boyd M. Jolley, who gave the place the nickname "Dollar Creek" after he went there with his Daytona-brand detector and found 21 more coins, including five silver dollars (one a low-mintage 1885-CC).

Coin Hunting in Westchester County, New York: North of Manhattan, in the residential area within Westchester County, John V. Dimaio sought treasure with his electronic detector for 15 years.[619] His biggest find came from an area with a 20-foot perimeter, where coins must have been scattered or hidden in the 1880s or later. An inventory listed half eagles of 1881 and 1881-S; eagles of 1848-O, 1880, and two dated 1882; an 1822 Spanish gold coin; an 1874 German

gold coin; and U.S. half dollars of 1818 (8 Over 7 variety), 1842-O, 1859, 1871, two of 1876-CC, and three of 1877. In addition, he found an 1877 Liberty Seated quarter and an 1853 English shilling. Quite a varied group!

Coins Plus a Rattlesnake: Randy Grantham of Las Vegas, Nevada, and his friend Scott Hardow were new to treasure hunting in the 1980s. For a while, they sniffed around with their electronic detectors in parks and schoolyards, finding some old pocket change. Seeking bigger things, they headed into the Crescent Peak area. Before long, they came upon the littered landscape of what seemed to be an old mining site, long since abandoned.

Amid old bottles, rusted scraps of metal and the like, Randy got a promising signal, dug about six inches into the dry soil, and found a silver dollar. This was just the beginning, and in short order the remains of a broken glass jar were found to contain two half eagles, two eagles, and three double eagles, the latest dated 1906. Additionally, plenty more silver dollars, dated from 1878 onward, were found—159 in all.

Also found on the same trip was a rattlesnake, but little was said about that critter. There are some things that treasure hunters do not want to find!

Quantity, Perhaps with Quality: During one month, Dick and Nancy Waters found the incredible total of 2,490 coins with their Fisher 1210-X and 1260-X metal detectors! A photograph indicates that this was a varied lot, but no numismatic information was given.

Note that an account such as this can be replicated many times—just about anyone with an electronic detector and a well-populated beach can report some degree of success—perhaps not 2,490 pieces!

Two for Two: David Crasep, of Carmel Valley, California, found two gold coins on two consecutive days by using a Fisher CZ-6 electronic detector. His treasures were an 1847-D half eagle and an 1829 Peruvian two escudos.

Slave Hire Badges: In the early 1800s in Charleston, South Carolina, owners of slaves had to register them with local authorities and pay a yearly tax or fee. Each slave was then given a copper badge to wear, upon which was stamped his main occupation (such as PORTER, FISHER, CARPENTER, etc.). These are sometimes called "slave hire badges."

From time to time, these have attracted attention in numismatic circles, as when Michael Hodder cataloged two important groups of them for Stack's, and when Rich Hartzog offered many pieces for sale. Using a Fisher detector, Rudy Wyatt of Charleston has found more than 30. Extensive information can be found in Russell Rulau's *Standard Catalog of U.S. Tokens 1700–1900.*

A Lake Tahoe Find: Old coins are often found in jars, as with one discovery by a detectorist in the late 1900s on the shore of Lake Tahoe at an old home site. Upon inspection, a dozen coins—quarter eagles and half eagles, all dated before 1900—were found.

Pine Tree Threepence Found in New Hampshire: Tom Brown, of Hudson, New Hampshire, was searching with his Garrett Master Hunter CX detector in a farm field near the Merrimack River when he found an example of one of the earliest American series—a Pine Tree threepence.

"When I uncovered it about three inches down in the sandy soil, I didn't know exactly what I had at first," he explains. "I didn't know I had a coin. When I got home and carefully washed off the dirt, I saw the date 1652 and knew it was an important find." The New Englander said he felt

the coin, which gets its name from the crude outline of a pine tree it carries, was worth about $5,000. "It's a coin collection in itself," he says. "I look at it every day."

As it turns out, Brown is an experienced and savvy coinshooter. With the new Garrett detector, he has discovered large cents, two-cent pieces, Indian Head cents, a Civil War token, and an 1818 Spanish-American real (a coin that was used throughout the United States in the 1800s). He has concentrated his searches in old towns, which gives him numerous opportunities in New England.

Also, before he turns on his detector, Mr. Brown heads for the local library for a bit of detective work. He searches records for old meeting sites, such as churches. "If it's all pavement, you're out of luck," he said. When Brown finds an open field, he heads "for the oldest tree and begins searching there." Some of his best finds have come under old trees, he says.

Coin Hunting in Southern New Jersey: Starting in October 1986, Wayne H. Selby jumped into the hobby of electronic treasure hunting. Seventy-one sites in and around Burlington County, New Jersey, yielded considerably more than 1,000 coins, as well as numerous other artifacts. His finds included many Spanish-American coins; large copper cents including a 1793 Chain cent and 22 Liberty Cap cents, among those a 1793 and an 1804; early federal silver coins including 1803 and 1805 half dimes and a 1799 silver dollar; and coppers of the 1780s including a Georgius Triumpho piece, 5 of the Nova Constellatio design, 3 of Vermont, 43 of New Jersey, 11 of Connecticut, 5 of Virginia, 2 of Fugio type, and 2 of Machin's Mills.[620]

Glass Jar Yields Treasure in Illinois: James E. Brewer of Illinois, a Garrett detector in hand, was exploring the sites of long-demolished schools that he found in a 1938 plat book of Livingston County. At one such location, he "began scanning near the old foundation and found many items, such as square glass ink wells, green copper conduit pipes and lightning arresters. But no coins!"

Then, his luck changed. "Scanning at the corner, I received a very strong reading. The cursor indicated a dollar-size object, but after digging nine to 10 inches, I recovered a fruit jar full of someone's unfortunate loss. Now, a quart jar is quite a find to me, and my heart almost stopped when I dug it up."

Brewer found its contents included 70 Indian Head cents, the oldest dated 1866 and worth $250 in Uncirculated condition; six silver half dollars, the oldest an 1875 Liberty Seated; 37 silver dimes, the oldest dated 1853; 2 half dimes; 9 silver quarters; and 1 Morgan dollar dated 1921. Quite a find for one day!

Found Near the First U.S. Mint Site: In 2006 in Philadelphia, coinshooter Matt Mille found with his metal detector a partial 1798 dollar die trial near the site of the first Mint on North Seventh Street. The site today is occupied by the William J. Green Federal Center.[621]

Finds in Southern New England: Jim Bailey, a Rhode Island detectorist and numismatist, has found many American and foreign coins in recent years. His two most interesting finds are a 1652 Oak Tree shilling, Noe-14 variety, and a 1786 New Jersey copper, Maris 17-J. He also found a Washington inaugural button in September 2014.

Beaches, fields, forests, urban areas—all are potential treasure troves for coinshooters.

chapter 25

Paper Money Hoards

Paper money hoards are scarcer than those containing coins, most probably because the archetype hoarder liked "hard money," especially if made of gold or silver. However, over the years a number of important caches of paper notes have been found, some of which are delineated here.[622]

The King City Bank Hoard

Put away: Early 1900s • **Disclosed:** 1949 • **Treasure:** Federal currency

If you own a high-grade $5 Series of 1882 Brown Back or $5 1902 Date Back note from First National Bank of King City, Missouri, you owe a debt of gratitude to a reclusive hoarder named Mary Hammer for preserving it for you.[623] Unfortunately, she paid the ultimate price for her contribution to your collection—her story is among the most tragic in American numismatics.

Hammer, age 82, lived alone under meager circumstances on her 400-acre farm nine miles north of King City, Missouri (about 25 miles north of St. Joseph). She was crippled by rheumatism, walked with difficulty, and paid her bills in cash from funds hidden years earlier in containers kept in her kitchen and bedroom. She was last seen alive on January 18, 1949, immediately prior to a six-inch snowfall, which began that day and was followed by several days of sub-zero weather.

The story of her demise began when, according to later court testimony, Elsie Emrich (about 40 years of age) and neighbor Fredie McQuinn were talking with Elsie's son Harold at the B. & C. Café in a nearby town on the afternoon before the snowfall. Harold mentioned that there was a lot of scrap iron on the Hammer farm and that it would be great if someone could go there with him to get it. Elsie added that Mary also had a lot of money.

Fredie and Harold subsequently broke into Mary's home and threatened her; Mary, pleading for her safety, directed them to three one-gallon containers of money from under her bed. There were federal bills, First National Bank of King City notes, gold coins, silver dollars, and some loose change. Harold then struck Mary three times with her crutch, probably killing her; if not, the sub-zero temperature did. Her frozen body was found on January 22.

On January 24, Harold and two friends, Tommy Beal and Columbus McCrary, went back to the farm and ransacked the house, finding more money. They split up about $4,000 in cash. The three men then went on a drinking spree in St. Joseph and started to spend the money. Two bartenders refused to take unfamiliar-looking notes, but a third one did.

As time passed, though, suspicions were aroused when old bills (including Gold Certificates) continued to be spent. Arrests were made after a lot of detective work, and Harold Emrich and Fredie McQuinn received 15-year sentences, Elsie Emrich got 7 years, and several others got lighter sentences.

Paper-money expert Peter Huntoon gave this summary of the paper money in 2014, based on his research:

> We know that a good percentage of the notes were Series of 1882 Brown Backs and Series of 1902 Date Backs from the First National Bank of King City. Those notes have been turning up in the numismatic market for decades. Thanks to this hoard, these earlier notes from the bank are hugely over represented for a

bank of its size. The bank was liquidated in 1924 when it had a circulation of $100,000.

The 71 King City notes reported in the census maintained by the National Currency Foundation—not all from the hoard—reveal that the hoard contained consecutive runs of Uncirculated notes directly from the King City bank, because notes from tightly knit runs of serial numbers survive. Most notable are 1882 Brown Back $5s with Treasury serials close together. It is obvious that her hoard included cut sheets of Brown Backs and possibly 1902 Date Backs. The high grade King City notes date from 1907 to 1914, so the hoard was amassed at least during that period.

The King City notes comprised just a fraction of the whole. There were plenty of circulated notes in the hoard, both national and non-national. Those now in collections bear no hint as to their provenance from the hoard. The hoard contained at least 600 to 750 notes using the $6,000 low-end estimate for it size. If you contemplate the $12,000 figure also mentioned in the court records, there is a lot of room to dream about many more notes, most of which were simply cashed in. It was in the 1950s, and such notes had no numismatic value.

First National Bank of Davenport Hoard

Put away: 1860s and later • **Disclosed:** 1950s–1994 • **Treasure:** Currency and coins

The Davenport Bank Hoard began to be dispersed in the 1950s, but there were enough items remaining on hand in 1994 that about $600,000 worth of rare numismatic items was sold to two buyers. Dean Oakes, who seems to have had an inside track on quite a few caches and treasures in the Midwest, appraised the remaining coins and bills in 1990 and assisted with the 1994 sale.[624]

Accumulation and First Dispersals

The story goes back more than a century, to when the First National Bank of Davenport, Iowa, was organized on June 22, 1863, with Charter No. 15. It was the very first National Bank in America to open its doors, though not by intention: authorities in Washington, D.C., had instructed banks under the new charter system to start business on a given Monday, but someone misunderstood the directions. Apparently the notice arrived on Saturday, and the bank threw open its doors right away, beating everyone else by 48 hours!

The First National Bank of Davenport, Iowa as it appeared in the early 1900s.

The bank issued national currency with its own imprint. Many thousands of dollars' worth of these notes, from the early First Charter bills of the 1860s, continuing through later issues, was stored as "vault cash" by the bank. Denominations ranged from $1 to $100.[625]

The hoard that thus accumulated was generally unknown in numismatic circles until 1957, when Dean Oakes was shown an Original Series "Lazy Two" $2 note of the bank by Phil Sorensen, of Mechanicsville, Iowa, who said that the bank in Davenport still had a lot of these and other early notes and that, in fact, he had seen "a little pile" of Lazy Two notes a few years earlier.

In the same decade, numismatists Ted Hammer and Loyd B. Gettys, both of Iowa, had access to the bank hoard, and on behalf of the institution offered many notes for sale, among which was an example of the $100 "Watermelon" Coin Note of 1890, one of the great classics in U.S. currency.

After the 1950s, however, the remaining items in the bank were more or less forgotten.

The $100 "Watermelon" Coin Note of 1890.

"Rediscovery"

About 1980, Oakes—remembering his conversation with Phil Sorenson of years earlier—decided to check on the hoard. Seeking to establish a connection with the Davenport institution, Oakes and his business partner at the time, John Hickman, went to their local bank in Iowa City to see if anyone could help.

At the time, the Davenport Bank & Trust Company—successor to the First National Bank of Davenport—was under the presidency of V.O. Figgie, who had held the post since 1942 (and would continue to do so until 1992; he died in 1995). Oakes learned that Figgie was a very conservative man who usually would not give information to outsiders. However, an officer in Iowa City knew someone in the Trust Department in the Davenport bank, and the door was opened.

A day later, Hickman and Oakes made arrangements to visit Davenport. Opening the vault was like seeing the inside of Fort Knox, Oakes later recalled. Among the treasures were $2 red-seal notes from 1928 to 1953 with a face value of $18,000; an original bag of $20 face value of 1883 Without CENTS Liberty Head nickels, some 400 coins in all, that had been put in the vault in 1883; $100 face value in 1946 Iowa silver commemorative half dollars; 50 $500 bills; 50 $1,000 bills with consecutive serial numbers; one $5,000 bill; a type set of Original Series notes (Gettys and Hammer had disposed of the main cache of these in the 1950s, it was learned); a group of red-seal $100 notes on the First National Bank of Davenport; about $300 to $400 worth of gold coins that had been turned in to the bank during the 1930s and 1940s and kept there; about 15 $1,000 bags of silver dollars (common issues such as 1882-O, 1887, and 1921 Morgan); 30 bags of common silver coins put away in the early 1960s; and rolls of 1948 Franklin half dollars.

Additional items among the paper money holdings included 10 bundles with bank straps on them dated 1868 and 1871, these together amounting to 1,000 notes of the $5 Legal Tender notes of 1862, 1863, and 1869 and representing 10% of the $50,000 the old First National Bank was required to keep on hand to satisfy the requirements of its charter. The notes were well used, but yielded a few examples of the Friedberg-61, a variety considered to be rare.[626] Also well-represented were Silver Certificates of 1880 and 1891 through the $100 value and Legal Tender notes of all series through the $100 and $500 Series of 1880.

In 1990, the Davenport Bank & Trust Company sold out to the Norwest Bank chain, and this is when Oakes appraised the holding. The aforementioned 1994 sale that he assisted with involved two buyers—one for the coins and the other for the paper money.

Oops! Into the Trash!

Put away: 1864 • **Found:** Circa 1962 • **Treasure:** Confederate $5 and $10 notes

Circa 1962, a banker walked into the premises of Spink & Son, Ltd., rare coin dealers on King Street, St. James, London. With him were several bundles of Confederate States of America $5 and $10 notes issued in 1864 and shipped to England at that time, possibly in payment for goods.[627] The notes had been found sealed in an old vault. Apparently, there were tens of thousands of each denomination.

As it happened, Douglas G. Liddell, manager of Spink's numismatic department, was not in his office that day, and it fell to a newly hired young man to wait upon the banker. "Confederate notes are worthless, and we are not interested in buying them," the employee stated. Still, the banker left a couple packs of these "worthless" notes behind, with his business card, in the hope that Spink's might want some at another time.

A month or two later, I was in London and met the employee in question while poking around the various cabinets at Spink's. He paused for a moment, then remembered that he had a few hundred of those Confederate notes that the banker had left behind during his recent visit. I recognized them as being of numismatic worth, and wanted to buy them, which I did for sixpence each, and then asked if there were more. The seller looked up the telephone number of the banker, made a call, and learned that the entire rest of the hoard—again, tens of thousands of notes—had been pitched in the trash a few days earlier!

The Oat Bin Hoard

Hidden: 1800s • **Found:** By 1966 • **Treasure:** Rare currency

In the annals of hoards of scarce, rare, and interesting U.S. paper money, the so-called Oat Bin Hoard ranks as one of the more significant finds.[628] The story begins in 1966 with Dr. Howard Carter of Leawood, Kansas.

Carter owned a bank in Kingswood, Missouri, and through its connections put out inquiries seeking old currency. From time to time, he was rewarded by success, but never so much as when he learned of an estate found in the southern part of Missouri that had a wondrous quantity of paper money. He thus purchased the fabulous Oat Bin Hoard, a cache of paper money comprising more than $28,000 face value that had been "brought to the Midwest from Virginia shortly after the Civil War. They were later found in an oat bin that had not been emptied for many years."[629]

The hoard—which had over the years been supplemented with more notes, probably acquired in the Midwest after the initial migration— featured such treasures as a $1,000 Legal Tender note of the early 1860s. A premium of some type was paid above face value, and the estate representatives and Carter were both satisfied.

Subsequently, the new owner took the notes to the American Numismatic Association Convention (held that year in Bal Harbour, Florida) seeking to sell them to collectors. But despite his having printed a list that included a Dakota Territory note, only a few had been sold after several days had passed at the show.

Then, Dean Oakes in partnership with his fellow Iowan, Don Jensen, went to Dr. Carter's hotel room and viewed a sampling of the notes. A week later, the pair went to Leawood, Kansas, and bought the entire deal. Oakes and Jensen went as partners in the National Bank notes in the group, and Oakes on his own bought the "type" currency. The Nationals were mostly from Booneville, Missouri, and several Kansas towns including St. Marys, Wamego, and Topeka.

Thievery

Oakes and Jensen held on to at least a portion of the notes for a couple of years, as in 1968, they brought a display of 50 of the choicest Oat Bin Hoard notes—mostly Original Series Charter National Bank issues—to the Professional Numismatists Guild show in Chicago. It was there that they were stolen!

Oakes and Jensen acted quickly, running advertisements in coin publications seeking information, and with the assistance of Chicago dealer Dennis Forgue compiled a listing of the missing notes and serial numbers. In due course, two notes—a rare Texas Original Series $20 and a rare Selma, Alabama, $100 note—turned up in the hands of a small-town dealer in Wisconsin, not far from the Illinois border. The new "owner" of the pieces offered them for sale, so Jensen notified the Federal Bureau of Investigation and, together with an agent, arranged a "buy."

Soon, Don and his "cousin," supposedly tagging along because he wanted to buy an old car in the same town, met with the holder of the notes and inspected them. They suggested that the $2,000 asking price was too high and countered with $1,800 in the form of several cashiers' checks, and this offer was accepted. Then, minutes later, FBI agents grabbed the seller of the stolen notes as he went out the back door to his car and confiscated the checks!

The two notes were also confiscated, for evidence, but were later returned by the FBI to the rightful owners.

What About the Rest?

Fast forward to spring 1979, 11 years after the theft: 48 notes were still missing. As luck would have it, the two men who happened to hold them at the time walked into RARCOA, the Chicago dealership where numismatist Dennis Forgue was employed. Forgue was quite familiar with the missing items, having helped make up a list of

them earlier, so he feigned interest in acquiring the notes, set up an appointment three days later to "buy" them.

At the scheduled hour, the men reappeared and were greeted by the police. The men had various alibis and excuses, but could not prove they held title to the notes, so they were confiscated and returned to Oakes and Jensen. Unfortunately, the statute of limitations on the theft was 10 years, so no prosecution could be made. Regardless, Forgue deservedly received the PNG's Sol Kaplan Award for his work in the recovery.

The notes were subsequently offered in an auction by Hickman & Oakes (John Hickman and Dean Oakes) on November 24, 1979, and were widely dispersed.

The Ella Overby Hoard

Put away: Early 1900s • **Found:** 1960s • **Treasure:** Rare currency

This remarkable holding of old-time bills had been the property of one Ella Overby, resident of the small village of Starbuck, Minnesota. Sometime around 1910, her husband—who worked for the railroad—passed away at an early age, and for many years afterward she received a pension from the railroad line. Each month when her check would arrive, she would take it to the local

bank, cash it into bills, and put the currency in an envelope.

She lived very frugally (for meat, she bought wieners one at a time at the local market) and thus did not have to draw upon the money that continued to accumulate in the envelopes. Her spartan style of life continued until she died in the early 1960s, when the executor of her estate advertised that the hoard of notes would be sold as a single lot.

Numismatist Mort Melamed of Minneapolis learned of it in this manner and in due course was the high bidder among several dealers who inspected the holding. His personal interest was National Bank notes from Minnesota, which were represented in the hoard by an amazing quantity of 130 or more from the hitherto "rare" town of Starbuck. The firm of Hickman & Waters bought the other National Bank notes, while Dean Oakes bought the "type" notes, among which were about 75 of the Chief Onepapa $5 Silver Certificates in high grades (including some with consecutive numbers); a couple of hundred large-size $1 notes with Washington's portrait; and many others, the entire estate comprising about $130,000 face value. Note that many small-size notes of 1929 and later, Federal Reserve notes, and other items with little or no numismatic value from the hoard were cashed in for face value.[630]

The Society of Free Quakers Hoard

Put away: Circa 1786 • **Disclosed:** Over a period of years from 1957 onward • **Treasure:** Currency issued in the 1700s

This hoard consisted of 27 bills of credit issued by four jurisdictions: Pennsylvania (7 notes), New Jersey (13), Delaware (2), and Maryland (5).[631] Dates on the bills range from 1770 to 1786, with more than half dated 1785 or 1786. It was kept together by the treasurer of the Free Quakers, and eventually wrapped and sealed with the hand-written notation "£27.10.0." on the front of the wrapper. As that is the total face value of the items in the hoard today (after converting the Maryland bills denominated in dollars into their value in pounds, shillings and pence at the rate of 7 shillings and 6 pence per dollar), we know that this hoard has remained intact since it was set aside.

The bills presumably became worthless while in the treasurer's hands and thus could not be spent. As such, the hoard—along with the Society's minutes, accounts, reports, correspondence, birth registers, burial records, library list, and other records—was donated intact to the American Philosophical Society in Philadelphia. Fortunately, the notes were retained over time despite not having value, and it now provides today's students with a first-hand view of what a Philadel-phia religious institution would have had in the back of its cash box during the period of depreciation of our paper currency. A complete tally of the bills in the hoard has been made, by issuing authority, date, denomination, serial number, and in some cases, signers.

The hall of the American Philosophical Society, which now serves as the museum of the organization.

A Jar Stuffed With Money

Hidden or lost: By the early 1930s • **Found:** May 31, 1971 • **Treasure:** Gold Certificates

On May 31, 1971, R.W. Kirkland, of Carrollton, Texas, was operating a backhoe as part of a storm sewer construction project. Assisting were C.D. Doolittle and L.C. Stanciel. As a bucket load of earth was dumped, a jar tumbled out. Upon inspection, it was found to contain a staggering $47,400 face value in Gold Certificates! Such certificates were issued during the late 1800s and early 1900s by the U.S. Treasury Department and were payable in gold coins upon demand.

Obviously a man of very high personal standards, the first thing Kirkland did upon the discovery was to call the local sheriff's office, after which the sheriff himself appeared and took possession of the treasure trove. Of course, word of the find spread, and "claims were filed immediately" by five people including present and past owners of the land. In the end, though, District Court Judge Spencer Carver of Dallas ruled on December 29, 1971, that the finders were keepers, with the largest share going to Kirkland. Virtue, indeed, had its reward.[632]

Estherville, Iowa, Rarities

Hidden or lost: Early 1900s • **Found:** 1970s • **Treasure:** Rare currency

In the 1970s, the small town of Estherville, Iowa, and a related hoard became well known to numismatists through an interesting course of events.[633] The man who set these events in motion was Bill Higgins, founder of the Higgins Museum of paper money in Okoboji, Iowa, who sought to own and display one or more notes from each of the banks in the state that had issued currency with their own imprint.[634] The trouble was that he and other currency collectors were having no luck finding the issues of the First National Bank of Estherville—one of two banks in the small town, each of which had issued National Bank notes—thus, broader channels had to used, and a tiny place in the hinterlands of Iowa was brought to the fore of many minds.

Part of the difficulty in locating the notes spurred from the fact that the bank in question (organized on January 23, 1892, with a capital of $50,000) had issued notes of only two denominations, $50 and $100. Not only were there no known examples of either, but the general rarity of such high-value bills—typically, if a bank issued notes, they were of the $5, $10, or $20 denominations—further complicated matters.

As such, it would take some effort to track down an example. Being of an innovative turn of mind, John Hickman, curator of the Higgins Museum, came up with the idea of broadcasting on a nearby radio station in Spencer, Iowa, that a reward of $50 would be given to any listener who might provide information leading to the purchase of one of these Estherville bills. Not long after, a farmer who had been plowing his field all morning came into his house for lunch, heard of the reward, and asked his daughter to telephone the Higgins Museum to say she knew of *one* such note.

Hickman, a well-known currency collector and dealer himself, was asked to go to Estherville and check the note. There, he met the old farmer, Fred Clayton, and his daughter. He was then cautiously shown a $50 Series of 1882 National Bank note from Estherville, and, after first paying the $50 reward, was allowed to purchase the note itself for an additional amount.

A $5 Chief Onepapa note like those found in the farmer's cache.

Clayton then asked Hickman if he would buy more than one note, and, if so, would additional $50 rewards be paid for others. In due course, Hickman parted with two more rewards and purchased another $50 note and a $100 note! At that time, the farmer asked:

Do you buy other old money? We have other large-size old bills. My wife used to sell eggs and kept the money at home. When the banks closed in the 1930s we lived off her egg money. We still have a small box full of this kind of cash. I took them to the bank, but they told me that they will only accept the small notes now, and that the large ones are not worth anything.

The old farmer was delighted to learn from Hickman that these notes indeed had value, even more than the denominations printed on them. After Clayton died, his family found the cache, which amounted to about $2,000 to $3,000 face value. Among the pieces in the hoard were Gold Certificates, three beautiful $20 "Technicolor"

notes, 20 to 25 of the $5 Chief Onepapa notes, and some cut sheets. Each of the National Bank notes had been folded twice, yielding three vertical creases apiece.

The notes from the farmer's estate, some gold coins, and other miscellaneous items were made up into four or five lots and offered for sealed bids by the estate executor. Don Mark bought the group and sold the "type" notes, including the $5 Onepapa bills, to Dean Oakes. He kept for himself the National Bank notes, among which were about 30 bills of the $10 and $20 denominations from Terril, Iowa.

The Wood River Currency Hoard

Hidden or lost: Early 1900s • **Found:** 1974 • **Treasure:** Rare currency

The Wood River Hoard came to light under circumstances that were never revealed. Dean Oakes and John Hickman later purchased the group from a Nebraska dealer, Marvin Luke, and concluded that it had been hidden in the early part of the 1900s.[635]

The notes appeared to have been tightly rolled up and stored in dry circumstances—not buried in the earth—perhaps in one or more cans, as some showed slight evidence of rust stains or, in some instances, larger areas of discoloration. The notes were on the Wood River National Bank in Nebraska and were of the 1902–1908 Date Back series.

Inspection and counting of the 236 notes acquired by Oakes revealed that for every $20 bill in the hoard, there were three of the $10 denomination. This and serial number evidence suggested that they had been printed in the usual format of the time, in sheets of four notes, $10-$10-$10-$20, then cut apart and stored.

The notes were later marketed to collectors including by listing the notes in Hickman & Oakes' 60th Price List, 1974, the last issued by that firm.

The Secret of a Picture Frame

Hidden or lost: By the early 1900s • **Found:** By 1994 • **Treasure:** Rare currency

One can never tell what might be hidden behind an old picture or print mounted years ago in a frame.[636] This tale, involving Iowa numismatist Don Jensen, proves as much.

On a memorable occasion, the significance of which was not realized until later, an Omaha dealer in antiques attended an auction and bought a framed picture, apparently of no particular importance. Probably, it sold for practically nothing and seemed to be a bargain. No doubt, someone could use the frame for a modern piece of art or old family photograph, and there was always a ready market for such things, providing they were cheap.

Upon going home and taking the unwanted image from its wooden frame, the new owner was delighted to find 130 pieces of paper money. The notes were subsequently sold to a fellow in Iowa, who in turn told Jensen about them. One particularly important example was a rare $10 Series of 1882 Brown Back from Keokuk, Iowa. Another was a $20 Series of 1902 Red Seal note from the rare location of Juneau, Alaska, this being the only such note known from that state!

Other notes in the stash were from such locations as Smith Centre, Kansas; Pawnee, Oklahoma; Pender, Nebraska; Stockton, Kansas; and Mounds, Oklahoma, to give just a short list. This picture-frame hoard was large in scope and excellent in numismatic content, certainly a winning combination.

The War Department Find

Hidden or lost: After the Civil War • **Found:** By 1998 • **Treasure:** Confederate notes

After the Civil War ended, the federal government took the position that Confederate States of America paper notes were its property. Large quantities of the bills, worthless commercially, were confiscated in Richmond, the capital of the Confederacy. They were later shipped to the War Department in Washington, where they were stored out of sight for many years. Within this stash, the rarity of certain varieties was recognized at an early time, and one or more unidentified people with numismatic knowledge removed

any "Montgomery Notes" and other key pieces—specifically what these were is not known today.

Eventually, a different hoard of Confederate notes—this held by the Treasury Department and amounting to $60 million face value—"was destroyed to relieve the congested condition of the Treasury vaults. The currency comprised the 'sinews of war' in the Confederate Treasury at Richmond, and was seized by the federal troops when the Southern capital was captured."[637]

The War Department's remaining notes meanwhile continued to escape in such fate, though, and that entity's cache of more than 600,000 bills was eventually sent on "temporary loan" to the National Archives. Then, in February 1988 the bills were moved to their present location—the National Numismatic Collection in the Smithsonian Institution.

In their new home, curator Dr. Richard G. Doty and his staff sorted them by Criswell catalog numbers and placed them on edge in rectangular cardboard boxes. Although there were no rarities remaining, many interesting sub-varieties such as inverted backs, minor printing errors, and mismatched plate letters were found.

I have seen the cache on several visits to the Smithsonian; the typical bill is signed, issued, and is in Very Fine or so grade. The large remainder consists of low-denomination bills, 70,000 notes from 1861, and others of later years through 1864. Nearly 1,000 CSA bonds are there as well.

The George Hoard

Put away: Circa 1781 • **Disclosed:** 2001 • **Treasure:** New Jersey and other bills of credit

The approximately 55 bills in this hoard had been stashed in the ceiling of an old Freehold Township, New Jersey, farm house in about 1781. An ancestor of the owner at the time of discovery apparently did the hiding, though the owner did not know this until the hoard came to light in dramatic fashion;[638] a portion of the ceiling of the house gave way during a night storm, bringing the bills down with it.

After this shocking revelation, the owner took the bills to a friend who operated a coin shop in Freehold. Through the friend, the bills were sold to collectors over time; unfortunately, only 35 of them remained at the time the balance of the hoard was photocopied and cataloged. All but three of those were New Jersey bills, issued over a 25-year period from 1757 to 1781. One New York bill and two pieces of Continental currency were also in the hoard.

A detailed list of the 35 bills by date, denomination, signers, and serial numbers was published in the *Colonial Newsletter* in 2002.

A £6 bill of the June 14, 1763, issue of the colony of New Jersey, from the George Hoard.

Bills in an Old Barn ────────────

Hidden or lost: Early 1900s • **Found:** 2008 • **Treasure:** U.S. paper money

On a rainy day in early April 2005, four men were set to do a roofing job on a house one of them had rented in Methuen, Massachusetts. Fearing that predicted rain would make the work risky, they decided to do lawn work instead. One of them was digging up a small tree when his shovel hit a rotten wooden box containing metal cans filled with paper money dated from about 1899 to 1929.

The men transferred the currency to a milk can and took it to the Village Coin Shop, located about 10 minutes away across the state border in Plaistow, New Hampshire. Owner Domenic Mangano, who had no information about the source of the hoard other than what he was told by the men, agreed to help them identify, sort and catalog what they had.

After the owners publicized the find, excitement prevailed, and Mangano went with the men to New York City to appear on NBC's *Today Show*, *Fox News*, CNN, and ABC's *Good Morning America* to share information about their fabulous find. Still more media attention followed, and on April 26, a *Boston Globe* story by David Abel noted that the hoard was reported to contain more than 900 $1 bills, 200 $2 bills, and 300 $20 bills. Legal Tender notes, National Bank notes, Gold Certificates, and Silver Certificates were also in the find, and one report estimated the value to be between $50,000 and $125,000.

The treasure continued to have wide interest. Loving the publicity they were receiving, the four men separately told of their good fortune to various reporters and others, but with widely varying details. Suspicions were aroused, the four were arrested. Although stories varied, it seems likely that on another job on a farm near Newbury, Massachusetts, the men found the paper money under the roof of a barn and made off with it, not telling the owner. Charges against the finders were eventually dismissed, though, and what eventually happened to the notes was not reported.[639]

The Cornell Hoard of Colonial Bills ──────

Hidden or lost: Mid-1700s • **Revealed:** 2010 • **Treasure:** North Carolina colonial bills

In 2010, the Colonial Williamsburg Foundation, of which Erik Goldstein is the curator of mechanical arts and numismatics, revealed its acquisition by anonymous donation of more than 6,600 bills issued by the province of South Carolina in colonial days.[640] In the autumn of that year, some of the bills were included in a new exhibit, "Dollars, Farthings & Fables: Money & Medals from the Colonial Williamsburg Collection," in the DeWitt Wallace Decorative Arts Museum.

The bills were of various denominations, were issued from 1748 to 1775, and in 1775 had a value of about £7,176 sterling. The accumulation was dubbed the "Cornell Hoard" after the man who formed it, Samuel Cornell.

The Hoard's Long Road Home

As a young man, Cornell moved from New York to New Bern, North Carolina. There, he engaged in the mercantile trade—and possibly currency speculation, too, as suggested in a news release from Colonial Williamsburg—and gained substantial wealth. He was involved in finance, as well, including providing a loan of £8,000 for the governor's mansion in New Bern, in appreciation for which he was appointed to His Majesty's Council for North Carolina.

In 1775, as the Revolutionary War began, Cornell and some other colonial governors (including Governor John Wentworth of New Hampshire, who went to Nova Scotia and became governor there) fled to safety. Cornell sailed to London, but two years later he sailed to New York City, then occupied by British troops, seemingly taking his cache of North Carolina bills with him. Then, after he died in 1781, his will left most of his wealth to his five daughters.

The bills seem to have remained in the family until 1913, when they were offered, along with Cornell papers and documents, to the New York Public Library, which published the letters. In the 1970s, the New York Public Library sold the hoard to a dealer, who split it apart, about half of the bills going to the individual that eventually donated them to the Colonial Williamsburg Foundation.

Other Hoards Here and There

One unresolved story involves more than 1,000 pieces of old currency in $500 and $1,000 U.S. bills that came on the market in the early 1990s. Additionally, I saw an equal or larger hoard in 2005 at the ANA's World's Fair of Money convention. This hoard of circulated bills had been brought from Russia, I was told.

While we're at it, what happened to the seven $10,000 bills that Amon Carter Jr. sometimes carried in his suit coat pocket as conversation pieces? And that reminds me of the $1 million in $10,000 bills once on display at Binion's Horseshoe Club in Las Vegas . . . these were a great attraction until their combination of face and numismatic value—$10,000 notes were bringing $40,000 to $60,000 or more at the time—convinced the proprietors to sell them. The bills were quickly absorbed by collectors through Lyn Knight and other dealers.

My sons Wynn and Lee and myself at
Binion's Horseshoe Club in 1973 with $1 million in $10,000 bills.
Elsewhere in the lobby was a punning sign that read:
"If you want credit here, go to Helen Waite."

chapter 26

Hoaxes, Fantasies, and Questioned Finds

P.T. Barnum said that people love to be "humbugged" (fooled). History is strewn with phenomena, objects, and situations that were hailed as marvelous, but were later found to be fakes: the Piltdown Man, the Mormon "salamander letter," the Hitler diaries, telescope sightings of life on the Moon and canals on Mars, the long-lost *Vortigern and Rowena* play by Shakespeare, and countless others.

And aren't the Loch Ness Monster, the Shroud of Turin, the yeti, and flying saucers still in the news today, with believers and disbelievers each having opinions? At least most people agree the earth is round, not flat.

Numismatics has its share of such stuff. This category includes restrikes or fantasies made later than the dates they bear and other items that have been questioned by numismatists, as well as "finds" that relate to the American series and have been attributed to old-time hoards or discoveries but were more likely assembled in later times. In addition, various "theories" and "facts" that were presented to account for the rarity of certain issues are recited, some of which are quite amusing to read today.

Mention also should be made here of the process of "laundering" coins, these being fakes, copies, fantasies, and other items that appear on the numismatic market backed by sometimes impressive "pedigrees." Innovation and imagination know no bounds when it comes to bringing questionable coins to market; according to what some would have their victims believe, these "rarities" have been found by metal detectors, have descended in the families of former Mint engravers or employees, or have been located in old safe deposit boxes, barns, pirate chests, or woodpiles.

Some particularly enterprising owners of spurious items have consigned them to auctions overseas, so the coins can be "discovered" by American collectors who believe they have a chance to secure bargains that few other stateside numismatists know about. And in another instance (not given in this book), a would-be salvor of undersea wrecks sprinkled some modern fake Spanish-American coins on the sea bottom, "discovered" them, and sold them to eager buyers.

Finally, a couple of handy rules for numismatists: A phony coin accompanied by an elegant pedigree or story is still a phony coin. Also, when exciting treasure stories are found to be false, there is rarely any follow-up by the media to inform the public of the deception. Regardless, the accounts forthwith and others like them have a great measure of entertainment value.

The Boscawen Hoard

In 1854, a Mr. Getchell advised numismatist Dr. Ammi Brown that he had some *1650*-dated Massachusetts silver Pine Tree shillings, as well as some with the normal 1652 date that he had obtained from an old man in Boscawen, New Hampshire. Unsurprisingly, the 1650-dated pieces were later adjudged counterfeit.[641]

The Chelsea Hoard

A reporter for the *Boston Journal* wrote of this experience in Chelsea, Massachusetts, for the issue of June 16, 1856:

> We had the pleasure of seeing today some of the Pine Tree money of Massachusetts, which was dug up some time since at Chelsea. There were a shilling, sixpence, threepence, and twopence, dated 1652, in almost as good preservation as if they had been coined one year [ago] only, every letter and figure upon them being perfectly clear and distinct; they probably have been entombed for more than one hundred and fifty years. The bottle in which they were found, and several of the coins, were purchased by a gentleman to be presented to the British Museum.

This notice caught the eye of reader "Nummus," who hastened to pen a commentary for the *Boston Transcript*, August 16, 1856, noting in part:

> It is remarkable to observe how many different means unprincipled people resort to replenish their empty purses. Too proud to work for an honest livelihood, and too indolent to engage in some legitimate pursuit, their wits are constantly at work devising new ways to fatten themselves upon the industry of others. . . .
>
> A few weeks since a paragraph appeared in several of our papers, stating that a large number of pine tree coins had been recently dug up in this vicinity. No sooner had this announcement been made than complete sets of this coinage poured into our city. NE shillings and sixpence, before so rare, together with some other pieces never before seen, were to be found exposed for sale in this city. . . . It has, however, turned out that all of these pieces are counterfeit, and made by a man in New York City, who represents them to be originals. . . .

The perpetrator was one Thomas Wyatt, who lived on Mercer Street in New York City circa 1840–1860. He had apparently struck or had made to his order a dozen "sets" of Massachusetts silver coins, each containing one each of the NE shilling and sixpence; an Oak Tree shilling and twopence; a Pine tree sixpence, threepence, and hitherto unknown one pence; and a Good Samaritan shilling.[642]

A knowledgeable numismatist, Wyatt wrote *Memoirs of the Generals, Commodores, and Other Commanders Who Distinguished Themselves in the American Army and Navy During the Wars of the Revolution and 1812* (Philadelphia, 1847) and *A Description of the National Medals of America, Presented to the Officers of the Wars of the Revolution and 1812* (New York, 1854) and once assisted Prof. Daniel E. Groux[643] in the making of reproductions of rare U.S. medals. His interests were varied and also included natural history, religion, military history, conchology, and other fields; why he turned to forgery in this instance is unknown.

The Great Fugio Copper Find

This is the story of one of the most famous numismatic hoaxes.[644] Though no treasure or hoard ever existed, the tale nonetheless has attracted much attention over the years.

It begins with several accounts from the 1800s, which relate that 14-year-old C. Wyllys Betts visited a site in New Haven, Connecticut, where certain 1787 Fugio copper coins had been minted under federal government contract years earlier.[645] There he supposedly located several original dies from which "New Haven restrikes" were later made in copper, brass, silver, and gold; these

So-called 1787 Fugio copper restrike,
Newman 104-FF, Whitman-17560.

Horatio N. Rust as depicted on a Numismatic Gallery token
issued by Augustus B. Sage in 1859, dies by George H. Lovett.

"restrike" coins differed from all originals inasmuch as the linked rings on the reverse were much thinner.

These pieces and the story behind them were generally accepted for some time; during the 1900s, the restrikes were a stock item for many dealers, and an account similar to that just given concerning the fortuitous find of C. Wyllys Betts found its way into various modern references, including *A Guide Book of United States Coins*. The real origin of the coins seems to have been a bit different, though.

A Likelier Scenario

The more probable—though still somewhat dubious—story of the New Haven restrikes starts with Horatio N. Rust (1828–1906), a prominent collector who was most active from the 1850s through at least the 1880s. Rust related that circa 1860, while residing in New York City, he resolved to learn more about the Fugio coppers minted in 1787. Realizing that specimens had been struck in New Haven, he decided to spend a day there, investigate the situation, and "if possible find the dies."

On that trip, he vainly searched in old newspaper files for information, but he also spent the evening with a coin collector who, as it turned out, was a fountainhead of information. The 1787 Fugio copper coins had been struck, Rust's host said, by the firm of Broome & Platt, hardware jobbers. Some of the equipment still existed, he added, and was in the hands of a hardware dealer on Chapel Street. An impromptu visit was arranged.

As luck would have it, on the desk of the hardware store cashier were two original Fugio dies being used as paperweights! Also, Rust learned during the visit that there had been a third die, but that it had been loaned to a man in Bridgeport and never returned.

Note that Rust later changed his recollections to finding two *pair* of dies during his visit and learning about one missing die;

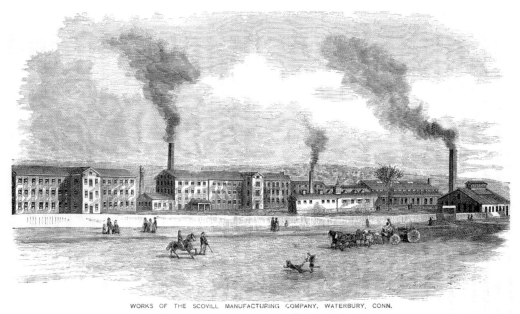

WORKS OF THE SCOVILL MANUFACTURING COMPANY, WATERBURY, CONN.

The Scovill Manufacturing Co., Waterbury, Connecticut.

regardless, we know he bought some dies on the spot and, in his words:

> [I] took them to Waterbury, Conn., and struck several hundred for cabinet specimens. I had one struck in gold and several in silver and for many years used them as exchanges in collecting coins. I printed an account of finding the dies on a slip, which I gave with each restrike, that all might know what they were. After coming to California I sold the dies to a coin collector in Philadelphia. Recently I noted in an eastern paper that a Ring cent in gold had been found. Probably it is the one I struck in 1860.

Henry Chapman's catalog of the George Parsons Collection, June 1914, reprinted the text of Rust's paper slip:

> First United States Cent, known as the Ring or Franklin Cent. July 6, 1787, the United States government ordered the minting of its first coin. Messrs. Groome [sic] & Platt, New Haven, Conn., did some part of the coinage. About the year 1860 the undersigned found (and still retains) the original dies among their effects in New Haven. The dies were taken to Waterbury, Conn., and a few coins struck for cabinet specimens, the enclosed being one of the restrikes.
>
> Horatio N. Rust
>
> Chicago, 1875.

More Research

Though it has more truth to it than the Betts story, Rust's scenario is flawed in that certain workmanship of the dies is of a technology not in use in 1787. It seems likely that new "1787 Fugio" hubs were made by the Scovill Manufacturing Company in Waterbury, and from these hubs several new dies were made. These included not only the dies for the "New Haven restrikes," but also for several varieties of rare "Fugio patterns" which were listed by Sylvester S. Crosby in *Early Coins of America*.

Note that the same basic idea—that these may have been "possibly a manufacture of new dies" and not original—was long ago suggested by W.C. Prime in his 1860-copyrighted book, *Coins, Medals and Seals*.

As for the extent of the restrikes, the following appeared in the *American Journal of Numismatics*, January 1873, and gives some mintage figures:

Mind Your Business; Ring, or Franklin Cent

> The first owners of the dies of this cent, as far as we can learn, were Broom [sic] & Platt, hardware dealers, of New Haven, Conn. There were three sets of dies; our informant, Mr. H.N. Rust, tells us that he found a single die at Bridgeport, Conn., in 1858; afterwards he obtained the remaining five parts of the dies in the store formerly occupied by Broom & Platt, in New Haven.[646]
>
> Mr. Rust sold three of the dies to a dealer in New York City, but who did not succeed in obtaining good impressions from them. Mr. R. had some three or four hundred pieces struck at Waterbury, Conn., in a metal composed of copper and nickel, also a few in silver, and one only in gold.

Today, probably several hundred of the copper and brass pieces (most of which look somewhat alike) exist, a few dozen silver coins, and several in gold.

To Find Treasure, Go to Africa

Dr. Ivan C. Michels's 1880 (and other editions) book, *The Current Gold and Silver Coins of All Nations*, included helpful information about the history and rarity of many U.S. issues, but it also included some fanciful tales to explain the rarity of certain issues. In these two instances, the reader might well come to the conclusion that a trip to Africa would yield a numismatic bounty.

The first example involves the mysterious 1801 half eagle, of which none are known to exist today and considerable dispute has been advanced among collectors. We know that the U.S. Mint report for 1801 returns a coinage of 26,006 pieces; that one-time Mint director James Ross Snowden attested to that fact; and that the *Annual Report of Director of U.S. Mint*, 1879, states that at the value of 1801 half eagles struck amounted to $130,030.00 (which adds up perfectly).

Per contra, William S. Appleton, of Boston, ignored the half eagle of 1801 in his summary of U.S. coins; there was never a specimen to be found in the Mint Cabinet (now National Numismatic Collection); and Dr. M.W. Dickeson, in his *American Numismatical Manual*, 1859, says:

> 26,006 pieces were coined, as per report of the U.S. Mint, and yet every piece has escaped the eagle eyes of numismatologists: Not a single piece having been seen by them. . . . There is a mystery connected with it wholly inexplicable to us.

Dr. Ivan C. Michels gave the answer:

> For the seeming total disappearance of this coin, a theory—and only a theory can be advanced, namely: On the 10th of June

1801, the Bashaw of Tripoli, a petty prince of the Barbary States, in the north of Africa, declared war against the United States. Ships of Algiers, Tunis, Tripoli, and Morocco captured American vessels; and, not satisfied with ordinary piratical plundering, they reduced the crew and passengers of the captured vessels to a condition of servitude. Captain Bainbridge was dispatched to cruise in the Mediterranean in order to protect American commerce. Before leaving the U.S. shores it is surmised that the purser of his vessel was provided with half eagles of that year's coinage; if so, it is but probable that only a few coins ever reached our shores again.

Michels also points the reader to Africa for the rare 1799 cent, which today is among the most valuable early large cents and the nebulous mintage of which is lumped in with that of 1798:

> This cent, owing to a heavy export of the same by a New England merchant in 1799, to the coast of Africa, has become very scarce, and when in fine condition sells at a heavy premium.

Dr. Michels asserted that a considerable quantity of 1799-dated large cents were exported to Africa.

The Kroll Hoard of California Gold

Herman Kroll, a jeweler with premises at 37 John Street, New York City, apparently produced large quantities of Liberty Head "California gold coins," mainly of the 25¢ and 50¢ denominations, in both octagonal and round shapes. Although these are believed to have been made sometime between the 1880s and the early 1900s, they bear earlier dates in the 1850s and 1860s.[647]

Many of these coins were sold to pioneer gold specialist A.C. Nygren, and nearly a thousand appeared in Henry Chapman's sale of the Nygren Collection, held April 29, 1924. Additionally, certain of Kroll's dies survived to a later date and were used to strike additional pieces sometime after the early 1960s.

Opinion as to the original intent of the Kroll pieces has been divided. Specialist and author Kenneth Lee considered them to be controversial and inauthentic and did not integrate them into his book on California gold. On the other hand, Walter H. Breen and Ronald Gillio featured and illustrated them in their 1983 work, *California Pioneer Fractional Gold*, relating much of the preceding and assigning them and others to Period Three (1883 onward) issues.

Nagy Productions

The revelations of Stephen K. Nagy, a well-known Philadelphia dealer and one-time business associate of J.W. Haseltine, were the subjects of many articles in the first decade of the 1900s. Together, Nagy and Haseltine introduced the previously unknown 1884 and 1885 trade dollars to the numismatic community in 1907, stating that 5 and 10 had been struck of each, respectively; and in 1909, their sale of the two unique varieties of 1877 gold $50 half union patterns created a furor.

On his own, Nagy apparently produced (or had produced for him) certain fantasy pieces at the beginning of the 1900s. Examples include Templeton Reid "trial pieces" of gold coins, including the $XXV denomination, struck on U.S. large cents (typically of the Draped Bust type).[648] These were "laundered," presumably by Nagy, through various dealers with no mention being made of their non-contemporary origin. Nagy was also responsible for Massachusetts and California Company $5 coins in various metals, which were made from new dies emulating originals produced decades earlier. Today, such fantasies are highly collectible in their own right.

Further Information Down the Road

I had the opportunity to interview Stephen K. Nagy in the 1950s when I started compiling the recollections of old timers. He told me he knew of the existence of several hundred Proof restrike dollars of the dates 1801–1803, for he had helped sell them to a Colorado collector; that he had sold many restrikes of the 1836–1839 silver dollar patterns and had put a "secret mark," the nature of which was not disclosed, on every piece which went through his hands; and that he had information on the 1884 and 1885 trade dollars which would be disclosed someday. That "someday" never arrived.

He also related that he had obtained a 1926-S $10 gold eagle from the Philadelphia Mint in 1926, and this was shown on one of his inventories. Although dies for such were made at that mint, no such coins are known today.

Nagy died in Philadelphia in 1959 at the age of 72. In later years, Nagy's nephew Earl Moore furnished even more information about his uncle.

My uncle was married but childless because of his wife's health. He treated me as a son and I spent many weekends at his shop and accompanied him on trips to New York and elsewhere. But he was close mouthed but big of heart. Back in those days, dealers were not generally friendly with each other. I can't tell you much about Merkin, although I did meet him several times. I enclosed some photo-copies of documents I inherited and donated some to the Smithsonian or sold over a period of years. Perhaps they may be of research value or useful for samples of signatures at the Mint.[649]

The Hauser Gold Coin Find

On August 23, 1923, Lee Hauser—a 23-year-old laborer on a road project near Hagerstown, Maryland—located a double eagle.[650] This was the prelude to a major find: a tin container the size of a large cigar box, stuffed with gold coins, was soon unearthed! Apparently, Hauser's co-workers gathered around, and his employer, George W. Ingram, also gazing upon the scene, generously stated that the coins belonged to the finder.

The matter was not so simply settled, though. The Department of Justice soon sent four agents to investigate the theory that the coins could have been part of a cache hidden by Grover Cleveland Bergdoll, who was described as a World War draft evader and German sympathizer. Bergdoll, who with his brother Erwin was said to have operated from a hotel in Hagerstown, was suspected to have received five valises filled with money in exchange for certain illegal information.

As it turns out, Bergdoll had actually taken the money to Germany. Meanwhile, excitement prevailed as news of Hauser's gold treasure spread, but the finder soon began to deny having located any such cache of gold coins, and his sister Esther told the press that the entire story was a hoax. No more questions or publicity was wanted by the finder.

Whether the whole matter was a hoax or not remains the subject of conjecture today. In any event, Uncle Sam's agents went away coinless.

1940s–1960s: Numismatic Fantasies and Daydreams

Someone with a barely passing grasp ("a little knowledge is a dangerous thing") of history and a good measure of imagination is believed to have inspired the creation in the 1950s of a group of large cents, half dollars, and other coins counterstamped with modern-style letters with variations on the Wells Fargo name including WELLS FARGO / U.S. / R.W.P.O / EXPRESS (probably intended to represent "Railway Post Office") and the even more improbable WELLS FARGO / BONDED / LEWIS & CLARKE.

The large cents were said to have been used in Nevada as chits or receipts by Wells Fargo on its Pony Express stagecoaches. The problems with this story are many, including the facts that large cents were never used in the Western United States; the Pony Express (which employed single riders, not stagecoaches) was not established until 1860, by which time large cents were obsolete; the correct spelling is Lewis and Clark (and their expedition took place in the first decade of the 1800s, decades before Wells, Fargo & Co. was formed by Henry Wells and William Fargo in 1852); etc.

Related in concept are coins with large, modern-style letters counterstamped with LOUISIANA / 4 BITS and TEXAS / 4 BITS.[651] Also related, groups of coins of the early 1800s crudely counterstamped UNION MINE / 5 Dol. / OREG. / TERR came on the market circa 1958 and again circa 1970. "They should fool no one except the most uninitiated," token specialist Alan V. Weinberg advised token expert Russell Rulau.[652]

The Secret of an Old Mill

This tale had its genesis when a knowledgeable old-time collector of U.S. large cents conspired with a young coin dealer and decided to use a high-grade 1793 Chain cent from the former's collection to play a joke on a coin shop owner they both knew. They enlisted two friends to carry it out.[653] The pair presented this story, much of which—if not all—was false:

In the early 1950s, a young married couple (actually the friends) owned a property in rural Connecticut. An old grist mill from the 1790s was on the land; its water wheel had long ceased turning, and the snows and rains of many seasons had penetrated the loose wooden siding. Derelict probably since the last century, the structure seemed to be on the verge of collapse.

Regardless, the husband and wife decided to explore it. Who knows, perhaps something interesting could be found—some old newspapers, record books, or other artifacts from the long-ago time when the mill was important in local agricultural commerce. Hours were spent poking about in nooks and crannies until darkness gathered. They continued their search early the next day, encouraged by finding an old almanac, an Indian Head penny, and a few old books.

Eventually, something truly worthwhile did come up! A cavity was found behind a loose board in a storeroom, and after other boards were quickly pried away, a metal-banded wooden keg filled to the brim with old pennies was revealed. Picking one up, the husband noted that it had a woman's head on one side and the date 1793. On the back side was a chain design and some lettering.

He then reached in for a generous handful, then a double handful. All of the pennies looked

the same and all were made in 1793. There seemed to be thousands of them. Could these have any value to a collector?

Determined to find out, the couple took one of the copper pennies with them the next time they visited New York City. Showing it to a coin shop owner and telling of the thousands more left at home, they were told, in effect, "Yes, these old coins could have value—not a great amount, but enough to make it worthwhile for you to bring in the whole batch for my offer. Right now, could I buy the sample you brought with you?"

"What would you offer?"

"How much do you want for it?"

"You are the expert. You tell us. That is why we brought it here."

"How about ten dollars?"

"Wow! That sounds great! We never thought it would be worth that much! However, we don't want to sell it right now, but we will be back soon, now that we know they are so valuable and you want to buy them."

In the end, a nice story, but without a word of truth.

Scrooge McDuck

For comic relief, mention should probably be made of Walt Disney's cartoon character, Scrooge McDuck, uncle to ducklings Huey, Dewey, and Louie. McDuck loved money, and he had three *cubic acres* of the stuff, in which he enjoyed cavorting, diving, etc. In one cartoon, he took a fancy to 1916 Standing Liberty quarter dollars and tried to hoard every one in existence, which he almost did.

Luckily for collectors, a miserly duck does not own all 1916 Standing Liberty quarters.

The Rare 1841-O Half Eagle

In the 1950s, the *Guide Book of United States Coins* listed the 1841-O half eagle with the notation that just 50 were struck. No one had ever seen one, and an inspection of the inventory of the Colonel E.H.R. Green Collection of half eagles revealed that he did not own one, despite owning many other rarities. None could be found in old auction catalogs.

I discussed this with John J. Pittman, a leading collector of the day, who said, "I think I have one somewhere." John was fond of hinting at rarities he owned—and he had a great many. However, some years later he could not remember telling me that he had an 1841-O; a forgotten joke, it seems.

Treasure Lost, Found (?), and Lost Again

This is the story of a treasure that at one time created a mini-Klondike rush on a Missouri farm, but of which the details have since become obscured.[654] While apparently someone who recognized New Orleans Mint coins was on hand at the time, his or her identity has become lost, and the treasure itself is almost a total fabrication—but not quite.

The hoarder was Wilson Tilley, a well-to-do Missouri farmer engaged in the horse and mule trade who, like many in the border states, sided with the Confederacy during the Civil War. Sentiment for the South ran high in the area, and a Confederate flag was put up on the county courthouse lawn. Waynesville historian Theodore Wolff commented that local citizens were urged to take the banner down, but did not do so until Union General John C. Frémont moved

in close to the town and sent cavalry to enforce his presence.

Tilley had accumulated a private reserve of gold and silver coins, and with the onset of the conflict in 1861, he buried them on his property, as having obvious wealth could have been dangerous at the time. Although no accounting was kept, it is believed that the face value amounted to about $2,400, a sizable amount in that era.

He would not live to dig up his funds, though, as on September 10, 1861, Tilley was murdered and his home was burned to the ground. His children fled into the woods to escape danger. His wife Elizabeth was away on a visit to nearby Waynesville; she returned to bury her husband on the property. Eventually, a new house was built on the site.

Details of the Violence

Local history has it that horsemen forgotten by Frémont had remained in the area to live off the land. Known as "bushwhackers," these renegade ex-soldiers pillaged and murdered at will, and if someone was believed to have wealth, they became a target for plunder or worse. Historian Wolff has written that in Waynesville on the same day of Tilley's death, just such a party of bushwhackers hanged a Mr. Burchard, who refused to say where his own money was hidden. Also, the home of Lottie Christenson, an abutter to the Tilley farm, was looted and burned that day.

As for the specifics of Tilley's demise, legends prove plentiful, but facts are elusive. Some said he was killed for being a Confederate sympathizer, others that he was murdered for his wealth. One account has it that he was shot and then hoisted up into a tree; another has him hanged, and his body dropped on a road to serve as a warning to others with a rebel leaning. Still another story avers that he was shot and castrated.

Regardless, we know that in a shooting match between Union troops and insurgents occurring about a year later, a wounded man named Oscar Blount was taken prisoner, labeled a bushwhacker, and confessed to being a party in the Waynesville rampage that resulted in Tilley's murder.

A later generation of Tilleys would believe that while Elizabeth may have dug up several hundred dollars' worth of these coins to finance the rebuilding of her home, the larger part remained hidden. Perhaps even she did not know where it was.

A Fleeting Find

A century after the Civil War, on December 5, 1962, a crew was bulldozing land in a farm field to build new barracks buildings for Fort Leonard Wood, south of Waynesville. Contractor James Mace was at the controls when his blade caught on two homemade maple boxes, each about the size of a cigar box and somewhat deteriorated. Contemporary accounts had it that one box burst open and spilled its contents, revealing a vast array of old silver coins!

Mace and his co-workers converged on the broken boxes and grabbed what they could. Word

spread, as such tales have a way of doing, and by nightfall a swarm of treasure hunters with metal detectors turned the site into a free-for-all. Hundreds of additional silver coins were found, mostly of the half dollar denomination, apparently these from the first box.

The second box, meanwhile, was found to be chock full of half dimes and quarter dollars, most or all from the New Orleans Mint; the pieces were reported to be of the Liberty Seated design and bear dates from 1840 to 1861. The next day, many soldiers from Fort Leonard Wood descended upon the area and with detectors and shovels found a few more coins plus some nails and other items, including relics from Tilley's burned-out homestead.

At this point, though, the contents of the hoard—and thus, the evidence that it existed—seem to disappear into the ether. Neither local historians nor regional numismatists seem to know where the pieces went, even though there must have been many thousands of specimens. Some have thus suggested that the treasure itself is a legend.

More than two decades later, in 1984, Kim Combs—curator of the small museum at Fort Leonard Wood—learned of the tale, and he sought to wrap facts around the fuzzy story. Information about farmer Tilley and his murder could not be found, and although a Springfield (Missouri) minister recalled that the second, intact box was confiscated in its entirety by the authorities at Fort Leonard Wood in 1962, no evidence could be found to substantiate this. The same Springfield man reported that each box had $1,000 face value in silver. If so, each box would have had to have been larger than the "cigar box" size earlier described as the coins would have weighed about 56 pounds. Most probably, at least some coins were found that day in 1962—perhaps even quite a few. If the face value was indeed $2,000 and was composed of quarters, half dollars, and other, smaller silver coins, this would indicate that somewhat more than 5,000 pieces were found.

But where did they all go? And can anyone identify even a single piece directly attributable to this remarkable find? Perhaps the coins exist here and there in collections, whose owners have no clue as to their tragic pedigree—or is the entire matter fiction?

Questionable and Fake Western Gold Bars

In the West, during the Gold Rush era and in later years, many assayers and mining companies produced gold bars, also called ingots. Although some pieces issued by official California state assayer Frederick D. Kohler and by Moffat & Co. circulated as money, the vast majority of these ingots were used for transporting precious metal to distant locations, where it could be stored or shipped—for example, the hundreds of bars found in the wreck of the SS *Central America* were intended for this purpose. Also, while some of these bars got into public hands and were buried or otherwise stored and forgotten under various circumstances, most bars were melted soon after they were made due to their high intrinsic value.

Regardless, there was for years not much numismatic interest in collecting these, in large part because of their unavailability (due to the aforementioned melting and shipping) and, to a lesser extent, lack of information concerning them. Alden Scott Boyer, who served as the president of the American Numismatic Association in the early 1930s, had a collection of ingots by 1950, but no inventory has been found of them, nor is anything known about their dispersal. B. Max Mehl also had a collection of ingots, likewise undocumented.

Eventually, though, there was at least one notable push to acquire these bars and find out more. Beginning in the 1950s, John J. Ford Jr. mounted an intensive advertising campaign to locate such pieces in the Western mining states, often enlisting his friend Paul Franklin to act as an intermediary and do the footwork. Brochures were printed, advertisements were run, notices were inserted in mailings, spreads were printed in the catalogs of Ford's New Netherlands Coin Company, and other efforts were undertaken.

Over a period of time, this unprecedented publicity created a great deal of interest and resulted in dozens of gold bars coming to light, most of them of hitherto unknown varieties. But then, in the 1960s, some numismatists questioned the authenticity of certain of the ingots, and this erupted into a major controversy by the end of the decade, complete with name-calling, debates, and various scholars taking sides.

Modern Investigation

In 2013, Karl V. Moulton published a comprehensive study—*John J. Ford, Jr. and the "Franklin Hoard"*—on the topic of Ford's findings. Correspondence from the Ford estate revealed that he had indeed engaged in falsehoods, telling one person one thing about an ingot and another person something entirely different.

Also, careful examination of the unquestionably authentic ingots from the SS *Central America*—the nature of which was not known until that treasure was made public in 1999—revealed the techniques of leading San Francisco assayers and the information they stamped on them, and with this knowledge it was realized that many of the ingots featured and sold by Ford ranged from highly questionable to downright fake. These included many that were not known to numismatists except through Ford.

The bars in question seem to have been made by the numismatic equivalent of reverse engineering. Names of assayers were found in directories published in the 1850s, 1860s, and 1870, and modern ingots were made with their imprints. At the time, these could not be compared with any others, as they had not been known to numismatists earlier.

Moulton further documented that a lot of Ford's stories were contrived, including the origin of certain U.S. Assay Office of Gold pieces now known to be fake. Still, I hasten to say that 99.99% of the coins, tokens, medals, and paper money sold by Ford over the years are unquestionably genuine. It is only the Franklin-Ford ingots, the "Republic of Texas" fraudulent counterstamps, and some fake Gold Rush era coins as well that tarnish his memory.

1950s to Date: Numismatic Rarities are Found

In the 1950s and 1960s, copies of many thousands of U.S. rarities were cast in base metals and were at one time sold by a company (not a regular coin dealer) in Yonkers, New York, for $2 each, with price lists being sent to dealers. These included copies of the 1783 Nova Constellatio 1000 units, or one mark, piece (note that the copy was cast from another copy, that one made in the 1800s, and not from the original); 1776 Continental "dollars;" 1776 New Hampshire pattern coppers; and others.

In addition, large numbers of imitation 1855 Blake & Company $20 pioneer gold coins, made in base metal washed with a gold-colored substance, were sold, possibly by another distributor.

Also common was a forgery purporting to be a $20 gold ingot issued by Parsons & Co. in Colorado, as well as gold-colored base metal copies of the 1787 Brasher doubloon.

All of these things contributed to giving legitimate coin dealers countless headaches, as phones jangled with people thinking they had found a fortune but not wanting to be told that what they had was a worthless fake. Later, the Hobby Protection Act required that copies be marked as such, but enough earlier copies remain that these pieces will deceive for centuries to come, and even if a copy were to be marked COPY, a determined person can remove or fill in the lettering.

Republic of Texas Gold Coins

These pieces are authentic Spanish-American gold coins of the 1830s, but with modern fantasy counterstamps. On the obverse, a star surrounded by a wreath has the outer legend REPUBLIC OF TEXAS. On the reverse, a liberty cap (such as found on Mexican coins of the early 1800s) is surrounded with the legend HOUSTON TREAS. DEPT. 16 D. 8 E. 21 C.

In his book, *American and Canadian Countermarked Coins*, p. 147, Dr. Gregory Brunk illus-

trated a specimen and commented: "These pieces were discovered in the early 1960s, and they appear to be struck from coin dies. Their origin is uncertain. Some think they are recent fantasies."

Walter H. Breen related to me that in the 1950s that he was enlisted by John J. Ford Jr. to help create the designs for these based upon historical records—more reverse engineering. Subsequently, the New Netherlands Coin Co., which was conducted by Ford and Charles M. Wormser, advertised in *The Numismatist* and elsewhere to buy South American gold doubloons. New dies for the counterstamps were made in Milan, Italy, and impressions were struck on authentic doubloons and at least one trial striking in lead or white metal.

Breen said that F.C.C. Boyd had conceived the whole idea as a prank, possibly to see what a well-known Eastern dealer would say when he was shown a handful. The story would be told that these were surprises among some doubloons purchased as a result of the New Netherlands advertising. However, the pieces seem to have been suppressed.

Mormon Gold Coin "Patterns"

In the early 1960s, a large group of Mormon "pattern" coins surfaced and were represented as being from an old Ohio hoard, where the coins had been for many decades. All were one-sided (uniface), and some had wire shanks attached to their backs. The designs were those used on the Salt Lake City coinage of the Mormons, circa 1849–1860.

Opinion as to the authenticity of these was mixed at the time, with some numismatists calling them modern counterfeits and others considering them to be rare patterns. Years later, in his 1981 book *Private Gold Coins and Patterns of the United States*, Donald H. Kagin described them thus: "All restrikes probably made during the 50-year anniversary in 1898."

Bordello Tokens and Other Fantasies

Token makers in the past half century have on occasion let their numismatic imaginations run wild. In one instance dating to the 1960s, collectors of tokens were delighted to find that a bordello in a Colorado mining camp in the Rockies west of Denver had issued tokens redeemable by its patrons during the 1800s. Certainly, tokens from a madam in a red light district were more interesting to own than those issued by dry-goods merchants or livery stables.

Then, it developed that not just one, but several Rocky Mountain bordellos issued brass tokens. Many additional pieces came on the market, obviously from an old hoard. Then more appeared, and then still more. Before long, such tokens—often lightly etched, worn, or weathered—became common in Colorado souvenir shops. In the end, it was revealed that all had been made in recent times by a Chicago manufacturer of tokens.

A couple more examples of such fantasies cropped up in more recent times. In an article in *Numismatic News*, July 9, 1996, token specialist

David E. Schenkman described two tokens. One was marked DRINK COCA-COLA, GOOD ONLY AT 1904 WORLD'S FAIR, FREE, and the other had the inscription U.S. DEPT. OF INDIAN AFFAIRS / VALUE $10 / HAY, GRAIN, FARM GOODS. Schenkman commented:

> Fantasies such as this have plagued the antique, collectibles, numismatic markets for more than 20 years, and during that time many people have paid good money for worthless pieces of metal.

In the *Token and Medal Society Journal*, August 1996, Schenkman described still more:

> Copper octagonal token marked FORT WAGNER / SOUTH CAROLINE / 1863, etc.

> Brass token marked EMPIRE CITY MINE / 1876 / EMPIRE, COLO. Reverse inscribed COLORADO GOLD / 5 / DOLLARS.

Brass token marked THE TOPIC SALOON / 1890 / LEADVILLE / COLO.

Typically, "research" for such a token-making project involves reverse engineering, starting with checking old newspapers, directories, and other old sources for the names and specialties of merchants, tradesmen, and others. Then, a sketch or design is made of a token of the type that *might have been* issued by such an establishment, the wording on the token matching known genuine tokens produced by other firms of the same era or locality. Finally, the services of a die shop or token-making enterprise are enlisted, with privacy requested, and fantasies are created.

Missing 1916 Standing Liberty Quarters

In the Pennsylvania Dutch area of Pennsylvania in the 1950s, an enthusiastic numismatist was fond of displaying *one* of his treasures: a gem Uncirculated 1916 Standing Liberty quarter, a classic rare issue worthy of the admiration of just about anyone. Over a period of time, this single coin generated several stories of its being taken from an original bank-wrapped roll of 40 coins still in existence and, better yet, from one of four original rolls. When asked about the veracity of such rumors, the numismatist simply gave a knowing wink.

The man died, and his children became embroiled in a big squabble with each other when only a single rare 1916 quarter could be found, as they just "knew" that their dad had owned dozens more, but none of the siblings could identify which of the others had pilfered them and wasn't telling. In actuality, probably there was only a single coin to begin with.

Misuses of Mint Medals

The Philadelphia Mint maintains on sale many back-dated medals, some of which were first made in the early 1800s. Some pieces are from original dies, others are from modern copy dies, but none bear any notation such as "copy" or "restrike," federal law and the Hobby Protection Act notwithstanding (although it can be argued that a modern "restrike" from copy dies may not be a copy if there were no originals from the same dies).

Indeed, the practice and the pieces are described in detail in *Medals of the United States Mint Issued for Public Sale, Department of the Treasury*, a work published by the Government Printing Office in 1972; the foreword noted in part: "All of the medals listed in this catalog are offered for purchase by the public. Order forms appear in the appendix."

Although the Treasury Department and Bureau of the Mint had no intention to deceive, many of these restruck and copy medals were later offered by others as originals. In a typical scenario, someone with a silver-plated copper restrike (or, infrequently, a silver restrike) of an Indian Peace medal of the 1800s—an original of which would be worth thousands of dollars—will give it the appearance of having been used by an Indian years ago by tumbling it in a machine to give it the appearance of wear and drilling a hole at the top for suspension.

Hundreds of these have been so altered, and typically sold at "bargain" prices at gun shows and antiques shows. A sales pitch goes something like this: "I bought this medal, don't know what it is worth, but as I didn't pay much for it, you can have it for only $300." The seller does not represent that it was a fake and later can claim that he sold it "as-is."

Every so often, a small group or "hoard" of such restrikes comes on the market, usually accompanied by a tale of the pieces having been found by a metal detector in territory once occupied by Indians, or something along this line. All professional numismatists who specialize in tokens and medals have heard many such stories of the elation—and then woe—of people who

have bought these "bargains." In the 1960s, I personally had the painful experience of telling Paul Eakins (operator of a tourist attraction in Sikeston, Missouri, and not a numismatist but a fan of Americana) that his collection of Indian peace medals were all modern.

Indian Head and Lincoln Cent Rarities

In the mid-1970s, a man of the San Francisco Bay area visited Los Angeles dealers and brought with him hundreds of 1877 and 1909-S Indian Head cents, 1909-S V.D.B. Lincoln cents, and other rare issues, most of which were lustrous brown Uncirculated with somewhat pinkish edges. The pieces were said to have been put away years earlier.

An alert professional became suspicious of the coins and called in the Secret Service. After ques-

tioning, the owner confessed to making them; however, he was of an innovative turn of mind and claimed that he did nothing wrong, as he had acquired very worn specimens of these varieties and by a casting process had simply "augmented" them by adding more metal. The final disposition of the case is not known.

$1,000 for a Worthless Dime

Thomas K. DeLorey recalled this:

While I was working at ANACS, we had a middle aged man come in one day with a rare 1894-S dime he had just purchased on a vacation to the Philippines. The coin might be worth many tens of thousands of dollars, and he wanted us to authenticate it. Unfortunately, it was a Philadelphia Mint coin with an added S, very professionally done. It seems that the man, a collector, had been in the habit of inquiring in small towns if anybody had any old coins, and in one town a storekeeper said he knew an old man who had a rarity. He closed his shop and drove the collector on a circuitous route up in the hills, and introduced him to the old man, who said that during the war he had rescued an American pilot and hidden him from the Japanese, and in gratitude the pilot had given him this very valuable rarity. Now that he was old, he wished to sell the

coin. Eventually they settled upon a price of $1,000, which the American paid quickly, concealing his excitement at obtaining such a bargain.

Upon returning to the U.S. the collector rushed to Colorado Springs, where I examined the coin and gave him the bad news. He was angry he had been duped (and, I guess, because he was not going to make the huge profit he was anticipating!) and was prepared to fly back to the Philippines to try to get his money back when I convinced him he had been had by professional con men and his money was gone. Since then I have heard a similar story from a dealer, involving another 1894-S. These con men, or others, may be spreading the rumors about rare coins to lure in other suckers. Of course, there is not much an American can do after the fact if he is cheated in a foreign country and buys 'bargain' coins for cash.[655]

Stories such as this abound and often involve eager collectors shelling out cash while on trips a long way from home to buy "rarities" at below-wholesale prices. The sellers, meanwhile, want the matter kept secret from relatives (or business partners, etc.) or don't want Uncle Sam (or the French customs agents, or the British tax authorities, etc.) to know about it; reasons are many and diverse. Then, days, weeks, and thousands of miles later, the coins are offered to rare coin dealers or are submitted for authentication or grading, and are found to be worthless fakes.

"Mystery Tokens" Found on Long Island

The September 6, 1994, issue of *Numismatic News* included an article by Christopher Batio, "Mystery 'Tokens' Dug Up on Long Island Shore," which told of what was viewed by some as a fabulous find near Fort Salonga, New York. Working with a metal detector, a treasure hunter . . .

> . . . dug up more than 100 roughly round chunks of what looked like copper and pewter . . . that look like tokens that would have been meant to circulate during the Revolutionary War. . . . More than 10 different types [were found]. All but one is dated between 1774 and 1779, yet none of them corresponds with any known tokens of the colonial or Revolutionary period. This fact makes them immediately suspect to numismatists. What are they then? Fantasy issues produced sometime after the Revolution? Someone's experiments, as old as the Revolutionary period? Unfinished buttons?

The truth of these pieces would come out soon enough. On October 24, 1994, Russell Rulau, well-known token expert and author, corresponded with Rufus B. Langhams, a local (Huntington, New York) historian who had been called upon to research the pieces. In fact, Langhams had written a monograph on them, *Long Island Revolutionary Coins, Patterns & Tokens 1774–1779*, which was offered for sale by the town of Huntington.

Of course, he'd done so before Rulau let him know that there was no historical backing to support these having been made in the 1770s:

> The items are, on their face, too good to be true and thus suspect. They could have been made a century ago for some personal whim; a number of Americans overcome by nostalgia made their own coin-like items in the 1850–1880 period and these are pretty well documented, but new ones may turn up. . . .[656]

The pieces were said to have been found on the shore of Long Island Sound. Inscriptions on the pieces included UNITE OR DIE, UNITY, CONTINENTAL CENT OR PENCE, ONE CENT, PASS AS ONE PENCE, and PLATT'S TAVERN / HUNTINGTON. It should be noted that a correct rendering of the denomination of one penny would be PENNY, for "pence" is the plural term. Further, the first American coin denominated ONE CENT was the Massachusetts cent of 1787. The decimal system of coinage, with cents, was not used in America until long after the period of 1774 to 1779; Continental Currency notes of the 1770s are denominated in Spanish milled dollars (divisions of which were reales, not cents).

The Philippines Hoard

An American stationed or living in the Philippines wrote many detailed letters to rare coin dealers describing a vast treasure of U.S. coins buried in the Philippines circa 1940 to prevent capture by the Japanese. The story grew in the telling, and after a while the hoard was said to have included an 1804 silver dollar, Proof trade dollars of 1884 and 1885, and a bag of 1933 eagles!

Although the prospect seemed to be quite exciting at first to those contacted, no coins are known to have materialized, and as more and more classic rarities were added to the list, skepticism grew until further letters on the subject went directly to the wastebasket.

A Hoard of 1911-D Half Eagles

In 1996, Michael Fahey, authenticator for the ANACS grading service at ANA Headquarters in Colorado Springs, reported that he had recently inspected a hoard of counterfeit 1911-D half eagles. Fahey stated at the time, "This counterfeit has been in our photomicrograph files since the 1970s and was most likely first introduced in the 1960s. When I first started working as an authenticator for ANACS in the early 1980s, this counterfeit turned up at coin shows and then dried up, but now it appears to be back."[657]

The Chapman Pedigrees

When a coin can be pedigreed to a well-known numismatist, its value and desirability are often enhanced. When it comes to such pedigrees, the name of Philadelphia dealer Henry Chapman (1859–1935) ranks especially high, for he and his brother S. Hudson Chapman (1857–1931) handled many really outstanding coins and collections in their time.

In an attempt to capitalize on this trend, an "enterprising" Californian in the 1980s acquired some old, unused Henry Chapman coin envelopes and used them to store recently acquired inventory items from various sources, thus giving his stock the appearance of a long-forgotten holding.

In short order, however, the deception was discovered, and the "Henry Chapman pedigree" idea came to a quick end.

In a similar tale, another inventive numismatist did the same thing in the 1960s with B. Max Mehl (1884–1957) envelopes.

Henry Chapman.

Breen's Undocumented Finds

Walter Breen's Complete Encyclopedia of U.S. and Colonial Coins was published in 1988 and became a very valuable reference for many areas of coinage, as it was more comprehensive than anything published earlier. In the years since the work's publication, many researchers have endeavored to learn about certain hoards he mentioned—some of 1871 and 1872 Liberty Seated silver dollars being examples—but have been unable to do so.

Although not all the details are known, it seems likely that most hoards reported by Breen are factual, especially when cross-referenced to earlier sources, but that some are pure fiction. Other examples are represented by imaginary or mis-stated hoards of certain double eagles, to which comments by David W. Akers have been added:

1908-S: The report of a bag of 1,000 found in Central America has not yet been verified.

(David W. Akers: Not true; no such bag was found. It never will be verified.).

1910-S: A bag of 1,000 was discovered about 1983 in Central America. (Akers: There were many more than just 1,000 pieces.)

1913-S: The report of a bag of 1,000 found in Central America has not yet been verified. (Akers: Not true; no such bag was found.)

1922-S: At least 7,000 Uncs. turned up in summer 1983. (Akers: Only a few hundred coins were found, some of which were of high quality.)

1926-S: The report of a bag of 1,000 Uncs. from Central America remains unconfirmed. (Akers: No such bag was found.)[658]

The Wells Fargo Coin Hoard

A few decades hence, a story made the rounds that a vast hoard of mint-sealed bags of gold and silver coins put away years ago by Wells Fargo & Co. had been discovered in a Chicago (or, according to another account, San Francisco) bank vault, and a Southern California (or Chicago, or New Hampshire) dealer had an agreement to buy it. Bags of rare 1927-D double eagles and 1919-S Liberty Walking half dollars were just two of many treasures in this vault, it was said, and the aggregate was said to total many tens of millions of dollars in numismatic value. However, after a year or two, rumors subsided, and so far as is known, no newly found 1927-D double eagles or other rarities in quantity have come on the market.

Then, in 1996, I saw an inventory said to have been made of the hoard, which differed in its composition from some of the accounts heard earlier (for example, the inventory showed just a single 1927-D double eagle, but it did include 4,000 1919-S half dollars). This delineation occupied many pages and, at the very least, would have required a lot of effort to create. The list began with early half cents and ended with late-date double eagles.

Among single coin rarities were gold Proofs more or less continuous from the 1850s onward; an 1884 Proof trade dollar (highly unusual, as numismatists believe that all 10 pieces stated to have been struck are presently accounted for); Carson City coins by date sequence, including an Extremely Fine 1870-CC double eagle and a choice Uncirculated 1871-CC dime; an 1873-S half dollar *without* arrows (no others known to exist); and many other delicacies. The composition was that of a very large and impressive numismatic collection, plus unbelievable quantities of certain rare (as well as common-date) coins.

The numerous great rarities would have to indicate that such an accumulation was formed by one or more persons who were prescient enough in the late 1800s continuing well into the 1900s to acquire many fine items; financially capable of storing huge quantities face-value wise of double eagles and other items for many decades; and alive through the 1930s to keep adding to the collection. And, this string of events would have had to have been accomplished without a peep about this activity appearing in any numismatic catalogs or magazines over a period of nearly a century.

Pardon me if I am skeptical, but I am not the only one. In reviewing this list, professional numismatist Thomas K. DeLorey mused that it was unusual that the Ark of the Covenant and the Holy Grail were not also included in the hoard![659]

A Bag of 1889-CC Dollars and More

The story sounded good enough: In a bank vault in Southern California, a man—now quite old—put away many numismatic treasures years ago, among which was an original 1,000-coin bag of now-rare 1889-CC Morgan silver dollars. Desirous of selling these and other rarities, the man had his attorney contact various rare-coin dealers from California to New England. Eager to get the inside track on this cache, the dealers kept their own counsel.

After a while during which no 1889-CC dollars or other coins materialized, though, they began comparing notes after and became suspicious. One had even given the attorney $5,000 worth of

Canadian "maple leaf" one-ounce gold coins toward purchases, and others made cash deposits, but the attorney had disappeared.[660]

No 1889-CC Morgan dollars came from this supposed cache.

Forty-Niner's Treasure Found in Death Valley

The Associated Press broke the story:

It was like something right out of the movie *Raiders of the Lost Ark*. An archaeologist's search of a desert cave yielded a wooden chest filled with gold and silver coins, apparently hidden 149 years ago during an ill-fated Gold Rush expedition across the harsh California desert.

Among the treasures were journals documenting the wagon train trek Forty Niner William Robinson, who was among some 100 men, women, and children seeking the gold-laden foothills of the Sierra Nevada but ending up in the merciless Death Valley.

"I was just blown away," archaeologist Jerry Freeman said Monday. "Nothing pre-

pared me for this." Freeman, a semi-retired substitute teacher with a degree in archaeology from Long Beach City College, said he has always been fascinated with the pioneers who left Salt Lake City in an ill-conceived attempt to skirt the south end of the Sierra Nevada and ended up crossing Death Valley in November 1849. "I consider them some of the most intrepid pioneers in U.S. history," said Freeman, 56, of Pearblossom. Eventually, the pioneers ended up near what is now Valencia in northern Los Angeles County, 300 miles southwest of their original destination.

Freeman organized a five-person archaeological team, including his two adult daughters, to follow the pioneers' route in December. He made his discovery in November during a reconnaissance hike. The chest was propped up on boulders and a board but remained hidden in mint condition, seemingly unscathed by time. A hymnal tucked inside the trunk contained a hauntingly poignant letter written by Robinson: "My Dear Edwin, Note, now we should have gone around. . . . If I'm not home by February, then I probably will not make it out. . . ." Robinson died 26 days later on Jan. 28, 1850.

Freeman stated that on November 28, 1988, he hiked to Pinto Peak and found a boning knife and oxen shoe, which prompted him to investigate a nearby ridge. The chest was unearthed from the deeper of two caves. The team found a manifest of the trunk's contents dated Jan. 2, 1850, along with nearly 80 pieces of currency, including $5 and $10 gold pieces and a number of silver dollars. None of the money appears to have dates after 1849, Freeman said. He estimated the total worth at $500,000. . . .

This find attracted the attention of the numismatic community. Russell Kaye submitted this to *Coin World*, and the story was published on March 13, 2000, under the title of "'Treasure' find disappointing: Evidence points to more recent origin for 'Death Valley Hoard'" (excerpted):

Blair Davenport, curator of the museum at Furnace Creek in Death Valley, on March 6, 1999, allowed me to examine the 80 coins found in the trunk. The group comprises 34 copper coins, mostly large cents, 39 silver coins, and seven gold coins. The silver includes five Spanish colonial 8 reals, all with Oriental chopmarks. The seven gold coins are all United States federal issues with denominations ranging from gold dollars to $10 eagles. The overall appearance of these coins is not what would be expected of a hoard stashed away during the middle of last century, but more typical of what might be found on the bourse floor of a coin show.

The copper portion contained three half cents including an 1837 Feuchtwanger token. The 31 remaining large cents contained a fairly good mix of dates from 1797 to 1849, with 20 different dates represented. Several characteristics of this group immediately appeared to be inconsistent with a hoard left during the mid-19th century.

First, none of the coins were in particularly high grade. All showed varying degrees of wear, with many of the latest dates in low grades. Second, the patina and surface condition of the copper coins varied greatly. Some specimens, such as the 1848 and 1826 cents, showed considerable corrosion, apparently from direct burial in the ground, while others displayed smooth surfaces with even wear, like the 1831 and 1838 cents. Nearly all showed some damage including holes, digs, scratches, or corrosion.

The 39 silver coins, again, did not have the look of coins left in a chest for 150 years. None were in relatively high grade, even among the pieces dated in the late 1840s. An 1848 Seated Liberty half dime grades only Good and an 1848-O Seated Liberty half dollar is only in Fair condition due to excessive wear. It is hard to imagine how these coins could have received so much wear in the short period of time between when they were minted and January 1850, when they are alleged to have been left.

As with the copper, there also was no uniformity in appearance among the silver coins. Many of the coins had been cleaned at some point with some slight retoning and others with traces of old heavy toning in the devices that had been stripped away at some point. A 150-year-old hoard that has been stored under the same conditions should exhibit some similarity in toning. This was not the case with this group. . . .

The seven gold coins in the group included two gold dollars, a $2.50 quarter eagle, two $5 half eagles, and two $10 eagles. The quarter eagles and half eagles were all dated 1834 or 1836, grading in the VG to Very Fine range.

The eagles were dated 1845 and 1847, and both were cleaned, grading VF, at best. Again, this is an unlikely degree of wear for coins only in circulation for a couple of years.

However, the real damning evidence was found in the gold dollars. First, it is unlikely that there would be any gold dollars in the group, as production of these coins didn't start until May 1849. The first shipments probably went to banks in the large Eastern cities. It seems unlikely that many (if any) of these new coins found their way to the frontier, west of the Mississippi and to Salt Lake City before the fall of 1849 when William Robinson and about 1,000 others left for the California gold fields.

What is even more unusual is that one of the gold dollars had obviously been used in jewelry as evidenced by large black marks where the coin had been soldered, and extensive scratching around the date. These scratches made the date difficult to read, and the park officials had identified the coin as having "no date." Careful examination with a 10-power loupe clearly identified the coin as an 1853. The lower loop of the 5 and much of the 3 in the date still remain visible. This is obviously conclusive evidence that these coins were not left in what is now Death Valley National Park during 1850.

This wasn't the only evidence that conclusively indicated a later date for the trunk's placement. A piece of porcelain found in the trunk is marked "Made in Germany." Many numismatists familiar with European history are aware that there was no "Germany" until 1873, when various German states were united to form Germany. In addition, there were problems with other items in the trunk, including the fact that some had residue from adhesives not in use until the 1900s, possibly from price or identification labels.

As it turns out, the "Death Valley Hoard" was not likely left behind by 19th-century pioneers trekking through that unforgiving desert.

About the Author and Foreword Writers

Q. David Bowers entered the rare-coin business in 1953, when he was a teenager. He is chairman emeritus of Stack's Bowers Galleries and is numismatic director of Whitman Publishing. He served as president of the American Numismatic Association (1983–1985) and president of the Professional Numismatists Guild (1977–1979); he is a recipient of the highest honor bestowed by the ANA (the Farran Zerbe Award); he was the first ANA member to be named Numismatist of the Year (1995); and he has been inducted into the Numismatic Hall of Fame maintained by the ANA.

Bowers is the author of more than 50 books, including many on U.S. federal coins; hundreds of auction and other catalogs; and several thousand articles, including columns in *Coin World* (now the longest-running by any author in numismatic history), *The Numismatist*, and other publications. His books have earned more "Book of the Year Award" honors bestowed by the Numismatic Literary Guild than have those of any other author.

He has been important in the sale of many of the most valuable coin collections ever sold at auction—the Ambassador and Mrs. R. Henry Norweb Collection ($24 million), the Garrett Collection for The Johns Hopkins University ($25 million), the Harry W. Bass, Jr. Collection ($45 million), the Eliasberg Collection ($55+ million), the John J. Ford, Jr. Collection (nearly $60 million), and others. When the all-time-high auction record for a rare coin was achieved, for a gem 1794 dollar sold in 2013, Bowers cataloged it and his firm sold it. Regarding treasures, he has been involved in the publicity and distribution of quite a few, including the SS *New York*, SS *Central America*, and the SS *Brother Jonathan*, and he worked with curator Ellen Gerth of Odyssey Marine Exploration regarding the SS *Republic*.

Bowers is a trustee of the New Hampshire Historical Society and a fellow of the American Antiquarian Society, the American Numismatic Society, and the Massachusetts Historical Society. In Wolfeboro, New Hampshire, he serves on the board of selectmen and is the town historian. He has been a consultant for the Smithsonian Institution, the Treasury Department, and the U.S. Mint, and is research editor of the *Guide Book of United States Coins* (the hobby's best-selling "Red Book").

Kenneth Bressett has actively promoted the study and hobby of numismatics since the 1940s. His published works on the subject cover a wide range of topics and extend from short articles to standard reference books on such diverse areas as ancient coins, paper money, English, and U.S. coins. He has served for many years as the editor of *A Guide Book of United States Coins*, popularly known as the "Red Book"—at more than 23 million copies, one of the best-selling nonfiction titles of all time.

Throughout his career he has worked as an author, editor, and publisher of books and products for coin collectors. He has also taught the subject to hundreds of students through courses at Colorado College and other places. From 1983 to 1988, he served the American Numismatic Association as Director of Coin Authentication and Educational Programs. Subsequently he served on the ANA Board of Governors, and as Vice President and President.

Bressett was appointed to the U.S. Assay Commission in 1966 by President Lyndon Johnson and in 1996 was made a member of the Citizens Commemorative Coin Advisory Committee. As a former consultant to the United States Mint, he was instrumental in originating the 50 State Quarters® Program, and in selecting many of the coins' reverse designs. He has received numerous awards in recognition of his service and dedication to numismatics, including election to the National Numismatic Hall of Fame, the American Numismatic Association Medal of Merit, the Ferran Zerbe award, and the Numismatic Literary Guild's Clemy Award.

Bob Evans is a geologist by academic background. His professional experience includes projects and employment involving a broad range of scientific, historical, and curatorial pursuits and studies. He is best known for his work with discovering the long-lost SS *Central America*—the subject of his foreword to this book and also chapter 14. It is a story, an adventure, a treasure with no equal in American history. As the project's chief scientist and historian, Evans became the curator of the treasure, and developed techniques to safely remove the decades of mineral and rust deposits obscuring the surfaces of the coins and bars.

His research articles published in *The Numismatist* have earned him two of the American Numismatic Association's top honors: the Heath Literary Award and the Wayte and Olga Raymond Literary Award. His "Ship of Gold" Numismatic Theatre program at the ANA convention in 2000 drew an unprecedented 400 attendees, a record that still stands. Other programs and seminars have drawn wide audiences.

In 2014 a resolution of various complicated legal issues enabled a return expedition to the site of the SS *Central America* shipwreck after an absence of 23 years, for which Evans resumed his role as chief scientist and historian (and on-site numismatist). The expedition, using the latest technology, yielded new discoveries, additional treasure, artifacts, scientific findings, and insights, and continuing analysis of the recovered treasure and the enormous data set generated by this expedition will yield further information. Evans has traveled widely as the curator of the treasure, and he has appeared on many television programs from the 1980s to modern times.

Evans resides with his wife Jane on a small farm in the hills of eastern Ohio. He works as a scientific and curatorial consultant, and he continues to enjoy traveling and teaching about the SS *Central America* and other shipwreck treasures.

Credits and Acknowledgements

Information-gathering for this book began in the 1950s and has continued to the present, with the assistance of many contributors over the years. Much information compiled here would have otherwise been lost to history. The following people and organizations, listed alphabetically, have been notably helpful, some decades ago, others in recent times.

John W. Adams provided an illustration. The late **David W. Akers** discussed hoards with which he was familiar and made several valuable suggestions. **John Albanese** assisted with research on the SS *Central America*. **Jeff Ambio** helped in the search for images. **Gene** and **Audra Andries** sent a clipping from the *St. Louis Globe-Democrat* about a 1960 find. **Roy D. Ash** corresponded concerning hoards of Liberty Seated silver coins, including the New Orleans find. **Leonard Augsburger** furnished extensive information about the Baltimore hoard of gold coins found in the 1930s.

Jim Bailey shared information about his detectorist finds. **Laura L. Barton** of Odyssey Marine Exploration provided information, including inventories and illustrations of the 2014 exploration of the SS *Central America*. The late **Harry W. Bass Jr.** assisted with historical information. **Wendy Beattie**, of Littleton Coin Co., helped with hoard information. **Anne Bentley**, curator of art, Massachusetts Historical Society, helped in several ways. **Ray Bolduc** provided information on gold coins found in California. **Mark Borckardt** helped in several ways. **Barbara Brandt** sent several newspaper clippings on the Sun Valley hoard. **Karen Bridges** photographed many coins and supplied images. **Roger Boye** provided a list of undiscovered treasures and a map showing various locations. **Kenneth E. Bressett**, senior editor of *A Guide Book of United States Coins*, wrote a foreword and suggested several areas for inquiry. **Roger W. Burdette** gave permission to use information from his three *Renaissance of American Coinage* books, including a Treasury hoard of gold coins featured in *Renaissance of American Coinage 1909–1915*, 2007. He also contributed Merkers Kaiseroda Mine Treasure for chapter 10. **Milt Butterworth Jr.** supplied images relating to the SS *Central America*.

Robert Ellis Cahill provided information on pirate treasures and sent a copy of one of his books on the subject. **Winthrop Carner** assisted with an inquiry. **Frank Campbell**, librarian of the American Numismatic Society in the 1990s, furnished copies of auction listings from the 1800s and Economite hoard data. **Robert J. Chandler**, former curator of Wells Fargo & Co. Historical Services in San Francisco, helped with much research relative to Gold Rush coins and treasures. **Lynn Chen**, librarian of the American Numismatic Association in the 1990s, provided several catalogs and books for study. The author worked with **Christie's**, New York City, in 2000 and created for them the first auction catalog with SS *Central America* gold. The late **W. Murray Clark** shared recollections of Vermont hoarder Alexander Miller. The image of the 1820 large cent, Newcomb-13, appearing on page 110 is from the **Classics Collection**. The illustration entitled "Gold Mining in California" appearing on page 151 is by **Currier & Ives**.

John W. Dannreuther discussed several hoards and helped in other ways. **Joe Darnell** submitted a clipping about a find in Valmy, Wisconsin. **Hal Dawson**, of Garrett Metal Detectors and editor of *Searcher*, provided a file of clippings. The officers and directors of **Deep Sea Research, Inc.** (David L. Flohr, Harvey Harrington, Sherman Harris, and James Wadsley) collaborated in chronicling the SS *Brother Jonathan*. **Beth Deisher**, editor of *Coin World* from 1985 to 2012, helped with research and furnished many articles. **Thomas K. DeLorey** provided a citation relative to the Aaron White hoard, related an experience concerning a remarkable hoard of double eagles and another regarding an 1894-S dime, and after reading the manuscript made several valuable suggestions, amplifications, and corrections. **Lou Dieke**

provided information on a gold coin cache. **R.L. Dixon Sr.** sent a 1901-dated clipping from the *Brunswick* (Maine) *Telegraph*, relating to a find. The late **Richard Doty**, senior curator of the National Numismatic Collection at the Smithsonian Institution, helped in many ways.

John F. Eaves sent a clipping about the cornerstone of the Lutheran Home near Allentown, Pennsylvania. **Robin Edgerly** assisted with graphics, reproduction of photographs, and etchings. **Bruce Ellis** sent a clipping. **Bob Evans** shared information about the finding of the wreck of the SS *Central America*, wrote a foreword, and helped in many other ways.

C. John Ferreri provided an illustration. The late **John J. Ford Jr.** reviewed certain information in the author's files in the 1990s and helped in several ways. **Carl Francis**, late of Harvard University, provided information. **Roberta French** transcribed several accounts and helped with searching for citations in old magazines and books. The illustration of a country store in the 1800s appearing on page 119 is by **A.B. Frost**. The late **George Fuld** assisted with research, sent copies of several citations, and helped with several clarifications. **Kathy Fuller-Seeley** reviewed parts of the manuscript and made suggestions.

Jeff Garrett provided several leads for investigation of hoards, notably the gold find in Jackson, Tennessee. The **Gentlemen of Fortune** group (Craig DeRouen, Gary and Renée Hebert, and Avery Munson) discovered the wreck of the SS *New York* and provided information concerning it. **Ellen Gerth**, Odyssey Marine Exploration, Inc., provided extensive information about the SS *Republic*, the SS *Central America*, and other Odyssey Marine Exploration finds. **Ronald J. Gillio** gave details of the Wells Fargo hoard of 1908 double eagles and helped in other ways. **David Gladfelter** provided two essays on finds of colonial paper money. The engraving of the SS *Winfield Scott* appearing on page 216 is from the edition of Gleason's Pictorial Drawing Room Companion dated May 31, 1851. **Ira Goldberg** and **Larry Goldberg** assisted with research on the SS *Central America*, provided images of cents—including the image of the 1816 large cent, Newcomb-2, from the R.E. Naftzger Jr. Collection and appearing on page 110—and helped in other ways. **James C. Gray** shared ideas on sea-salvaged gold coins. **Philip D. Greco** furnished information about the cornerstone of the Boston branch of the Bank of the United States and a cache found on Cape Cod.

David Hall furnished information. **James L. Halperin** furnished information about a hoard of 1821 cents. **Thomas J. Hammond** contributed an account of the Alexandria find of Kellogg gold $20 pieces. **David Harper**, editor of *Numismatic News*, helped locate information concerning a hoard. The print entitled "The Panic in Wall Street" appearing on page 68 is from the edition of *Harper's Weekly* dated October 10, 1857. The illustration of trade dollar redemption at the New York Sub-Treasury appearing on page 291 is from the edition of *Harper's Weekly* dated June 4, 1887. The illustration of silver dollars in a vault appearing on page 294 is from the edition of *Harper's Weekly* dated July 15, 1893. The photo of crates of gold being loaded onto a steamship appearing on page 166 is from the edition of *Harper's Weekly* dated April 1, 1899. The lithograph of the Old Sugar House and Middle Dutch Church appearing on page 156 is by **George Hayward** and originally appeared in *Valentine's Manual*. **Heritage Auctions** (HA.com) provided access to images from their Permanent Auction Archives. **Michael Hodder** created several entries (including accounts of the HMS *Feversham*), furnished numerous citations, and provided certain annotations. **Fred Holabird** provided the photo of Tom Sebring (dated July 30, 2005) appearing on page 220. A coin from the **Dan Holmes** collection is illustrated. **Wayne Homren**, editor of *The E-Sylum*, sent several newspaper clippings about varied subjects including the SS *Central America*, the supposed find of an 1804 silver dollar, and others.

Scott M. Hopkins added to information about the Umpqua River hoard. **Mark Hotz** furnished an item associated with the Panama Railroad, commented about the counterstamped quarter dollars of 1815 and 1825, and shared an experience concerning a visit to a numismatically important site on Eden Street, Baltimore. **William M. House** provided a specimen of an Aaron White medal. **Peter Huntoon** furnished images of three notes from famous hoards and supplied all of the information for the King City, Missouri, hoard described in chapter 25. **Bennie Hutchins** provided information about the Prairie Town, Illinois, hoard.

The map of California appearing on page 181 was created by **I.T. Hinton, Simpkin and Marshall**.

Don Jensen provided information about a currency hoard. **R.W. Julian** made valuable suggestions.

The late **Arthur M. Kagin** shared recollections of various commemorative hoards and other caches he handled. **Donald H. Kagin** granted permission to use material from his book, *Private Gold Coins and Patterns of the United States*, and furnished information on the Saddle Ridge Hoard. **Christine Karstedt** facilitated certain of the author's research and inquiries. **Richard Kelly** provided information about the Waldo C. Newcomer theft of 1913. **David Klinger** furnished an image. **Normand E. Klare**, author of *The Final Voyage of the Central America 1857*, assisted with research. The late **Abner Kreisberg** answered an inquiry about gold dollars of the 1879–1881 years.

James Lamb, rare-coin expert at Christie's, furnished an illustration. **Robert H. Lande** provided much information concerning the SS *Winfield Scott*. **David W. Lange** shared his research and comments concerning the Cogswell time capsule. **Karen M. Lee**, former associate curator of the National Numismatic Collection at the Smithsonian Institution, helped in several ways. **Robert D. Leonard Jr.** supplied an inventory of items found in the sea-floor wreckage of the SS *Winfield Scott* and much supporting material, including correspondence with various numismatists. **David Lindvall** made several important suggestions. The photo of a portion of the Miller Hoard appearing on page 75 is courtesy **Littleton Coin Co. John Lupia** provided original citations and helped in other ways.

Dwight N. Manley sponsored research relating to the California Gold Rush, sponsored the "Ship of Gold" exhibit of SS *Central America* finds and artifacts, and helped in other ways in the late 1990s and early 2000s. The map of Boston appearing on page 6 is courtesy the **Massachusetts Historical Society. John McCloskey**, Liberty Seated Collectors Club, sent information on several hoards for which he had records. **Patrick McMahon**, of the Museum of Fine Arts, Boston, provided an inventory of a Massachusetts State House time capsule opened and resealed in 2015. The image of the 1819 large cent, Newcomb-9, appearing on page 110 is from the **Medio Collection. Jennifer Meers** helped with treasure ship and other information. **Wayne Miller** was interviewed and provided information about two hoards, one that came to light in Montana and the other in California. **Rosalie Minnerly** helped with research, the gathering of information, and coordination. **Evelyn R. Mishkin** did copyediting and provided suggestions. **Karl Moulton** acquainted the author with the Charles White Collection (containing a hoard) and provided a catalog of it; likewise, the Judge J.P. Putnam hoard information came from him; he also provided a comprehensive historical file as well as his own thoughts and ideas concerning the hoard of 1815 and 1825, 5 Over 3, quarter dollars with E and L counterstamps. **Rich Mulcahy** furnished a suggestion. **Tom Mulvaney** provided photographs via Jeff Garrett. Colonel **William Bain Murray** discussed coins retrieved from the wreck of the *Arabia*. **Don Munro** furnished copies of several hundred newspaper accounts relating to treasures and hoards.

The late **R.E. Naftzger Jr.** assisted with certain information

on gold coins, and photographs from his collection via Ira and Larry Goldberg were used. The Proof 1881 gold dollar appearing on page 98 and the railroad station vignette appearing on page 110 (which is from a $2 note of the Cuba Bank of Cuba, New York) are courtesy the **National Numismatic Collection** of the Smithsonian Institution. **Eric P. Newman** supplied an 1863 advertisement for quantities of copper-nickel cents and provided a recollection of the dispersal of the Stepney Depot hoard, from which he obtained a key 1776 Machin's Mills copper. **James "Jimmy Sierra" Normandi** provided information about several finds in which he was involved during the course of treasure hunting with an electronic detector.

Dean Oakes was interviewed and provided information on several coin and currency hoards including the "Oat Bin" hoard, the Davenport Bank hoard, and the Ella Overby hoard. **Florence Ogg**, Suffolk County (New York) Vanderbilt Museum, sent several clippings relating to the *Lexington*. The photo of field hands in Economy Village appearing on page 126 is courtesy **Old Economy Village. Nancy Oliver** provided information about the Waldo C. Newcomer theft of 1913. **Joel J. Orosz** contributed comments suggestions and reviewed the manuscript. The illustration of the Donner camp appearing on page 41 is from the edition of *Overland Monthly* dated January 1917. **Dan Owens** provided newspaper accounts of shipwrecks from the 1800s, located modern descriptions and citations about wrecks, and helped in other valuable ways.

John Pack provided images. The photo of the Harmonist Church, circa 1880, appearing on page 124 is courtesy **Pennsylvania Historical and Museum Commission** and **Pennsylvania State Archives** (Group 354, photograph 35, "Church," Old Economy Village Archives, State Library of Pennsylvania). **Andrew W. Pollock III** suggested avenues for research and found information regarding the Lord St. Oswald Collection sold in 1964. **Donald Prybyzerski** sent several clippings and accounts concerning the 1840 *Lexington* disaster.

Kenneth W. Rendell loaned items, including documents, prints, and letter sheets from his extensive private archives, and helped in other ways. The image of the Mint State 1821 large cent appearing on page 117 is courtesy the **Richard Jewell Collection. Steve Roach**, former editor and now editor-at-large of *Coin World*, furnished many articles. **Greg Roberts** discussed hoards of gold coins. **Kaye Robinson** furnished images of the Saddle Ridge Hoard. **Jay Roe** provided information about gold coins salvaged from the SS *Winfield Scott*. The 1787 New Jersey copper appearing on page 22 is courtesy the **Roger Siboni Collection. Bob Ross** provided details of coins found in Glasgow, Kentucky. The late **Russ Rulau** helped with information concerning the Aaron White hoard and corresponded about various tokens. The late **Margo Russell**, editor of *Coin World* from 1961 to 1985, furnished many clippings relating to coin hoards.

Harry E. Salyards reviewed the manuscript and made valuable suggestions. **Thomas H. Sebring** discussed various shipwreck hoards and made several suggestions. **Daniel Frank Sedwick** provided certain information. **Ernie Segundo** sent articles and other information about an 1851 Schultz & Co. $5. **Neil Shafer** provided recollections of a cache of coins that may have belonged to nineteenth-century numismatist R. Coulton Davis. **Raymond Shepherd**, curator of Old Economy Village, provided much hitherto unknown information about the settlement there, the coin hoard, the Museum of Curiosities, and other aspects of what seems to have been a veritable financial center in western Pennsylvania in the mid-1800s. The images of the 1817 large cent, Newcomb-14, and 1818 large cent, Newcomb-10, appearing on page 110 are from the **Sherman Collection. Robert W. Shippee** made valuable suggestions. **Pete Smith** discussed the Aaron White and Economite hoards, provided information concerning

A.M. Smith's remarkable holdings and life, and supplied an image. **Paul T. Stimmler** sent a newspaper clipping. Stack's Bowers Galleries furnished images and helped in many other ways. **David Sundman**, Littleton Coin Co., sent several old-time newspaper clippings about coin hoards and helped in other ways.

Eric Tate of Odyssey Marine Exploration provided information regarding coins recovered from the SS *Republic*. **Gerald Tebben**, feature writer for the *Columbus Dispatch*, provided newspaper articles and other information over a long period of time. **Anthony Terranova** made several suggestions concerning colonial and early American coins. **Tommy Thompson** shared information about the finding of the wreck of the SS *Central America*. **David E. Tripp** corresponded concerning a gold hoard, a cache of 1927-D Peace dollars, and other treasure matters; he and his wife **Susan** have helped in many research matters over the years, beginning with our association in the sale of the Garrett Collection of U.S. coins for The Johns Hopkins University (1979–1981) and continuing with our sale of the Virgil M. Brand Collection (1983–1984). **Dennis Tucker** furnished the photograph of Daisy and Hyacinth on page 61.

The photo of the Merkers Salt Mine appearing on page 174 is courtesy the **U.S. Army Signal Corps**.

Bob Vail suggested several citations from old auction catalogs. **Carolyn Van Praag**, Fisher Research Laboratory, sent information concerning finds made by the firm's electronic metal detectors. **Mark Van Winkle** provided information on numismatic hoards. **Doug Veal** furnished an extensive file of clippings from treasure-hunting magazines. The map of Anacapa Island appearing on page 219 originally appeared with the article "Small Change: California Small Denomination Gold and the Wreck of the Winfield Scott," which appeared in the *Ventura Historical Society Quarterly*, Volume 47, No. 4, 2003. The illustration on page 5 (a selection of coins relating to early America) is a page from the *Visitor's Guide to the U.S. Mint*, by A.M. Smith. **Kenneth V. Voss** furnished a 1984 clipping about a Civil War treasure.

Alan V. Weinberg provided illustrations and a newspaper article relating to the SS *Central America* and helped in several other valuable ways, providing style and copyediting suggestions.

Fred Weinberg suggested an avenue for further exploration. **Stephanie Westover**, Littleton Coin Co., provided images. **Randall E. Wiley** suggested sources for Liberty Seated hoard information and answered an inquiry. **Ray Williams** provided information on electronic treasure finds published in the *C4 Newsletter*. **Richard E. Winslow III** located several historical accounts relating to treasures lost at sea. The research of **Douglas Winter** regarding gold coins was a valuable resource. **Mark B. Wolf** sent a file of clippings and citations. **William M. Wright Jr.** sent a story about a hoard of Indian Head cents.

Keith Zaner discussed 1815 and 1825 quarter dollars with E and L counterstamps.

Institutions and other entities whose libraries and research facilities were utilized by the author include: the American Antiquarian Society (Worcester, MA); American Numismatic Association (Colorado Springs, CO); American Numismatic Society (New York City, NY); Bancroft Library (Berkeley, CA); California State University at Long Beach; California State University at Sacramento; Circus World Museum (Baraboo, WI); Del Norte County Historical Society and the Del Norte County Museum (Crescent City, CA); Doheny Library, University of Southern California (Los Angeles, CA); Harvard University (Cambridge, MA); Huntington Beach Central Library (CA); Huntington Library (San Marino, CA); Idaho State Historical Society; Library of Congress (Washington, D.C.); Mariners Museum (Newport News, VA); Massachusetts Historical Society (Boston, MA); Museum of Fine Arts (Boston, MA); New York Public Library (New York, NY); Oakland Museum of California; Odyssey Marine Exploration (Tampa, FL); Peabody Essex Museum (Salem, MA); Port Angeles Library and Historical Society (Port Angeles, WA); Steamship Historical Society of America (Baltimore, MD); National Archives (D.C. and VA); New Hampshire Historical Society (Concord, NH); San Francisco Maritime Museum; San Francisco Maritime National Historical Park; J. Porter Shaw Library (San Francisco); Smithsonian Institution Museum of American History; University of California at Los Angeles; and Western Heritage Museum (Omaha, NE).

Endnotes

1. Readers who are not numismatically knowledgeable may wish to consult *A Guide Book of U.S. Coins*, Kenneth E. Bressett, editor, an inexpensive reference guide (contains prices, is published annually, also contains a list of sources for information). In addition, many of the books mentioned in the endnotes are available through coin dealers and numismatic booksellers and furnish worthwhile reading.

2. There were 20 shillings to the British pound. Years later in the 1790s, when U.S. dollars became a reality, a British pound was worth about $4.85, although exchange rates varied over a period of time.

3. See Sylvester S. Crosby, *Early Coins of America*, for original legislation and selected contemporary commentaries.

4. Quoted in the *American Journal of Numismatics*, 1890, p. 31; also *AJN*, 1881, p. 46. Another early citation was in the *Salem Gazette*, July 11/18, 1737. Sydney P. Noe, *Pine Tree Coinage of Massachusetts*, 1952, p. 17, wrote that this find "bears all the marks of gross exaggeration," but does not elaborate upon his opinion.

5. Sydney P. Noe, "A Coin Hoard in Maine," *The Numismatist*, February 1943; other sources.

6. Submitted by Don Munro.

7. *Pine Tree Coinage of Massachusetts*, 1952, p. 16; he did not state the basis for his assigning of this date, considerably later that the last date found on coins. This reference book is also the source for "Noe numbers" assigned to various dies and combinations.

8. Sources: Sydney P. Noe, *Massachusetts Pine Tree Coinage*, 1952, p. 14 (Noe's information was from *The Historical Magazine*, October 1863); Walter H. Breen, "Survey of American Coin Hoards," *The Numismatist*, January 1952; and W. Elliot Woodward auction catalogs, including John F. McCoy et al., June 21, 1864, and the Levick, Emery, Illsley, Abbey sale of October 1864 (Woodward had been a resident of Roxbury, Massachusetts since 1848).

9. Following the potato famine of 1846 and relief shipments from America in 1847, vast numbers of Irish citizens immigrated to the United States to start new lives in the land of opportunity and plenty. By the 1870s, they constituted a significant percentage of laborers in the Atlantic seaboard states and certain other locations. In the 1860s, there were more Irishmen working in the Comstock Lode in Nevada than were men of any other single nationality or native-born Americans (see Eliot Lord, *Comstock Mining and Miners*, 1883, appendices).

10. Sources: *American Journal of Numismatics*, 1877, p. 92; *AJN*, 1878, p. 105 (signed "C.H.B.," probably Charles H. Betts); and Sydney P. Noe, *Pine Tree Coinage of Massachusetts*, 1952, p. 16. Walter H. Breen, "Survey of American Coin Hoards," *The Numismatist*, January 1952, commented that the Haines Willow Tree shilling, Noe 11 (dies 30C), later appeared in the C.T. Whitman sale, 1893, Lot 103; later in the Jenks Collection sale, 1921; Mabel B. Garvan; Yale University.

11. Essentially the same comment appeared in Charles Steigerwalt's *Coin Journal*, September 1880: "A few Pine and Oak Tree Shillings were recently found in a small cove in Boothbay Harbor, Me. The finder hoping to secure more keeps secret the exact place of discovery." Steigerwalt, of Lancaster, Pennsylvania, was best known for his fixed price lists and catalogs.

12. Bangs & Co. was a general auction room at which venue various art and collectible objects, as well as wholesale merchandise, were offered for bids. Catalogs were prepared by private firms or individuals, including Woodward, who paid a fee to Bangs for the use of their facilities.

13. Source: Sydney P. Noe, *Pine Tree Coinage of Massachusetts*, 1952, p. 18. Numismatically, such a corroded coin would have relatively little value unless it was a rare die variety. However, the pedigree, if carried along with such a coin as it changed hands over the years, would add value to collectors with an interest in history.

14. The circulation of private one-cent tokens would reach a peak in 1837 and 1838, when millions of such pieces flooded commercial channels at a time when silver and gold coins were not being paid out by banks and were hoarded by the public; these are known as Hard Times tokens by numismatists today. During the Civil War, especially in the year 1863, countless millions of cent-size bronze (mostly) tokens again filled a need when specie payments had been suspended by the Treasury Department and banks.

15. Dickeson's book appeared in 1860 and 1865 printings as well, then slightly retitled as *American Numismatic Manual*. This folio-sized volume was an authoritative reference in the hobby at that time. Even today, it remains impressive, despite much information having been proved incorrect or having been superseded.

16. John Jacob Eckfeldt (1733–1818), patriarch of a long line of Eckfeldts who would become associated with American coinage, especially the Philadelphia Mint.

17. A different person from the Dudley who was employed at the Rahway (New Jersey) mint (some citations state he later cut dies for certain varieties of New Jersey copper coinage, but he seems to have been a laborer who worked in other jobs there, was not paid his due, and later sued to collect back wages).

18. This identifies A. Dubois as the die engraver. Presumably, Eckfeldt and Swanwick supplied blank, unhardened dies.

19. It would be interesting to learn the earlier use(s) of this particular coining press. Coins dated prior to 1783 and made in the United States are very few in number (but include, as an example, the 1776 Continental Currency "dollar").

20. *Coin World*, January 9, 1980, p. 1; Walter H. Breen, *Encyclopedia*, 1988, pp. 113, 116.

21. In the 1860s, the term "Proof" was not well defined and was often used in various texts, auction catalogs, etc., to refer to Mint State coins that had what today would be called a "prooflike" surface; these coins, of course, were in addition to what we know as regular Proofs specifically minted as such.

22. This is Prime's reference to Horatio N. Rust's Fugio die discovery caper.

23. Walter H. Breen, *Encyclopedia*, 1988, p. 147; and other sources.

24. *Ibid*. p. 143. Kempson was a prolific coiner of Conder tokens.

25. Sources include Eric P. Newman, *Coinage for Colonial Virginia*, 1956; and Walter H. Breen, "Survey of American Coin Hoards," *The Numismatist*, January 1952.

26. Among these being the Robert Gilmor Jr. collection assembled during the early 1800s; the Waldo C. Newcomer collection of the early 1900s and dispersed by B. Max Mehl in the early 1930s; the John Work Garrett collection (built upon the

foundation established by T. Harrison Garrett); and the Louis E. Eliasberg collection. For many years, Frank G. Duffield, editor of *The Numismatist*, maintained his offices and created that publication there.

27. The latter from Walter H. Breen, *Encyclopedia*, 1988, p. 31. No source was given.

28. Recollection of the author, who bought many of these pieces; Jonah Shapiro, who operated the Syracuse Stamp & Coin Co., was also an active buyer.

29. Die variety information is from John M. Kleeberg.

30. *The Numismatist*, March 1924, p. 243, quoting an unidentified press clipping. The 1780 piece was not of American origin, as no indigenous copper issues bear that date.

31. Text and research for this account are by Michael Hodder; also see his article, "When Morristown Made Coins," *The Numismatist*, August 1993, pp. 1099–1102, 1159–1162.

32. As quoted in Sylvester S. Crosby, *Early Coins of America*, 1875, p. 282. Crosby also cited early information about several other New Jersey mint locations. The mentioned book, *The Hole at the North Pole*, treated the "theory of concentric spheres," which proposed that another civilization existed beneath the surface of the earth as we know it, and could be accessed via an opening in the Arctic.

33. National brand cardboard coin albums with celluloid slides were made in Shippensburg, Pennsylvania, by M.L. Beistle and marketed by Wayte Raymond of New York City.

34. Attributions of Connecticut copper coins are to Henry Miller's numbers, as published in *State Coinage of New England*, American Numismatic Society, 1919. Hillyer C. Ryder's attributions for Vermont and Massachusetts coppers are included in the same book.

35. Walter H. Breen, "Survey of American Coin Hoards," *The Numismatist*, January 1952. Here edited.

36. Norman Stack related to Michael Hodder that a client of Stack's, Edward Hessberg, happened to visit the firm when Norman was examining some of the Connecticut coppers, and said, "I'll take the lot." The coins Breen examined were those owned by Hessberg. (Michael Hodder, commentary, July 1, 1996)

37. Letter, August 7, 1996, after reviewing a draft of this account.

38. Voyageur: Traveling (often by canoe) fur-gathering agent, woodsman, and trader who visited various remote sites. A voyageur is depicted as part of a standard reverse design on many Canadian silver dollars from the 1930s onward.

39. "The American Fur Trade," *Merchants' Magazine and Commercial Review*, New York, 1840, Vol. III, pp. 199, 200.

40. Letter, January 25, 2015.

41. Via a listing in *Rare Coin Review* No. 31, 1978, p. 11.

42. Fort Vancouver formed the subject for a U.S. commemorative half dollar in 1925.

43. Michael Hodder contribution to text. Anthony Terranova, in a letter dated October 15, 1996, stated that he had personally seen the group.

44. Walter H. Breen, *Encyclopedia*, 1988, p. 129.

45. Much more information can be found in Q. David Bowers's *The Whitman Encyclopedia of Colonial and Early American Coins*, Whitman Publishing LLC, 2007.

46. Paul Gilkes, "Counter Box Yields Colonial Hoard," *Coin World*, September 30, 2002; John Andrew, "Hoard of 19 Baltimore Sixpence Tops Morton & Eden's Nov. 13–14 Auction," *Coin World*, January 13, 2003.

47. Submitted by Don Munro.

48. *Portsmouth* (NH) *Oracle*, August 15, 1818.

49. *Boston Commercial Gazette*, September 10, 1818.

50. *Essex Register*, Salem, Massachusetts, October 21, 1818.

51. A specimen (Valentine-2) appeared in W. Elliot Woodward's John F. McCoy Collection sale, May 1864, Lot 609. In later years, Woodward suggested that the hoard may have been sold by Ms. Rea in the 1860s or 1870s, but the latter decade seems improbable given the sale of one in 1864 (how easy it is to forget!). See Walter H. Breen, "A Survey of United States Coin Hoards," *The Numismatist*, January 1952, but information there differs greatly from what the same writer had to say in his *Encyclopedia*, 1988, p. 276 ("about 100"; there the date of the find is given as 1880, and it is called the Wadsworth-Rea hoard; in his 1952 work, the "Wadsworth" find is used to describe 1794 half dimes).

Wadsworth-Rea nomenclature is also used in a commentary in Breen's half cent *Encyclopedia*, 1983, p. 38. Valentine attributions are to Daniel W. Valentine, *The United States Half Dimes*, American Numismatic Society, 1931.

52. As quoted in the *American Journal of Numismatics*, October 1880, p. 43.

53. Citation from Bob Vail. Also see Walter H. Breen, "Survey of American Coin Hoards," *The Numismatist*, January 1952; and Walter H. Breen, *Encyclopedia*, 1988, p. 276.

54. Putnam-Woodward connection courtesy of Karl Moulton, letter, September 10, 1996, with enclosures.

55. This sale was originally scheduled to be held in September or October, 1862, but was delayed. The sale date of November 11–14, 1862, was pasted as a correction on the front page of the catalog. The auction venue was the sale room of Messrs. Bangs, Merwin & Co., Irving Buildings, 594 and 596 Broadway.

56. Coins were first struck in Carson City in 1870 and first reviewed by the Assay Commission in 1871. In 1863 (the year for which coins were being reviewed by the Assay Commission in 1864), there were two active mints, Philadelphia and San Francisco.

57. Certain information is from Francis Pessolano-Filos, *The Assay Medals, the Assay Commissions, 1841–1977*, pp. 155, 159, 162, and 168.

58. Those stored at the Mint were melted by spring 1857, per an account of Director James Ross Snowden in *A Description of Ancient and Modern Coins in the Cabinet of the Mint of the United States*, 1860.

59. Citation suggested by Bob Vail. Copy of Woodward's sale catalog furnished by Karl Moulton.

60. Apparently Woodward had forgotten his immediately preceding comment, "Another lot so fine probably does not exist." Moreover, it took some modern-day digging in reference books to determine that Putnam was on the Assay Commission for the first time in 1864 and that he neither served in 1855 nor obtained his cents as a commission member at that time, as the Woodward catalog seems to imply.

61. It is not clear whether all the coins in this and the following lot were Uncirculated, or whether some were in the grade of Very Fine.

62. Adapted from several sources, especially and extensively H.H. Bancroft, *The History of California*, Vol. V, Chapter XX; the numismatic portion and inventory are from Philip W. Whiteley, "Coin Find Reveals Pioneer Money Usages," *The Numismatist*, August 1963.

63. Bancroft, p. 526, notes that he located the names of about 200 male immigrants and supposed that there may have been another hundred, plus families, for the trans-Sierra route circa 1845–1848; this number is lower than the many thousands noted in some overviews of the subject. Many others took alternate routes. After the discovery of gold, in-migration became almost continuous and numbers reached into the many thousands.

64. This happened to numerous travelers on other routes as well. It was not unusual for westward emigrants to burn their abandoned wagons, so as not to help "competitors" who might otherwise have an easier trip to California, but there is no record of the Donner Party doing this.

65. The Oregon Trail, most of which was to the north of the several routes followed by overland emigrants to California, was used by several thousand travelers during the 1842 to 1845 period. Its dangers were better recognized than were those of the southern paths to the Pacific Coast.

66. Keseberg had come to the United States from Germany two years earlier. His wife Philipine and their two children, Louis Jr. and Ada, were also traveling with the Donner Party. Keseberg later went to trial. Bancroft, pp. 541–543, discussed the alleged murder in detail, giving his view that Keseberg was not guilty.

67. Probably actually Spanish-American coins, perhaps from the Mexico City Mint.

68. Boyd's obituary appeared in *The Numismatist*, October 1958, p. 1180. Boyd died on September 7, 1958, at the age of 71. He had been an executive of the Union News Company (a subsidiary of the American News Co.). Further, "One of America's prominent numismatists, Boyd was Life Member No. 5 of the American Numismatic Association and a fellow and benefactor of the American Numismatic Society. . . . In 1937 and 1938 he was an appraiser of the Col. Green Collection."

69. Conversation with the author, June 27, 1996.

70. Walter H. Breen, "Survey of American Coin Hoards," *The Numismatist*, January 1952, modified by his comments in the same journal, October 1952, p. 1010 (pointing out inaccuracies in the Chapman account, this new information having been gained by Breen from old-time numismatist John F. Jones, who had known and visited Collins); Walter H. Breen, *Encyclopedia*, 1988, p. 169.

71. It seems unlikely that the group was comprised entirely of rarities; such is the nature of popular accounts in newspapers. From an account, "Europe Hunting Place for Coins," in the *Boston Sunday Herald*, April 30, 1905, furnished by David M. Sundman.

72. Walter H. Breen, *Encyclopedia*, 1988, pp. 165, 166, Henry Chapman and the 200 estimate. Alternatively, Breen's half cent *Encyclopedia*, 1983, p. 276, places the number as "many hundreds"; there as Chapman brothers.

73. Walter H. Breen, half cent *Encyclopedia*, 1983, p. 338.

74. Walter H. Breen, *Encyclopedia*, 1988, p. 171; also personal recollection of author concerning the availability of the coins in the 1950s.

75. *Ibid*. p. 211. Roger W. Burdette comment (correspondence, November 17, 2014): "This is utter nonsense. There was no standard keg size for cents or half-cents. Banks did not keep minor/copper coins in reserves – only gold, silver and certain government securities were permitted post-Civil War." As noted elsewhere, many of Breen's facts have been discredited—but a number of them are given in this text so that readers will be aware they were reviewed.

76. *Ibid*. pp. 165, 166. Walter H. Breen, half cent *Encyclopedia*, 1983, p. 201, gives the find date as "sometime between 1935 and 1937" and notes that estimated quantities have ranged from 30 to 100 pieces; further, "there was an earlier (before 1910?) hoard of darker specimens, variously graded as About Uncirculated or brown Uncirculated; this must have included hundreds of pieces." Some mentions of hoards in the Breen half cent *Encyclopedia* (for example, the 1796 With Pole, p. 162; the 1804 B-7 Spiked Chin, p. 245; 1804 B-11, p. 252, etc.) are highly inferential; Breen suggests that just because multiple Mint State specimens exist today, "there may have been a small hoard"

(see p. 245). The present book omits such unconfirmed hoards.

77. Foster is little remembered today by numismatic historians, but in his time he was one of the most admired people in the profession. His integrity was of the highest order, and he had a warm personality. His advertisements and listings were sometimes titled "Suitcase Specials," reflective of his carrying part of his inventory to conventions in a small traveling bag.

78. Jasper Robertson, M.D., of Hoosick Falls, New York (located only a few miles from Troy, on the road to Bennington, Vermont), is one of many numismatists of the era of the 1930s to the 1950s who assembled a fine cabinet of coins, but whose activities were never chronicled in print. In the 1950s, Jim Ruddy and I—then trading as the Empire Coin Co., Johnson City, New York—acquired via Dave Nethaway the Robertson collection of copper, nickel, and silver coins. As I recall, most of the coins from 1880s onward were gems, as were many earlier pieces. Years later, the Robertson gold coins were sold at auction by Mid-American Rare Coin Galleries (Jeff Garrett and Ron Guth).

79. Charles French, conversation with author.

80. The viewing of these coins was probably circa 1955–1957.

81. Walter H. Breen kept extensive notes on U.S. coins for many years, only to have many of them stolen or misplaced in the 1970s when he was working in New York City. Thus, some of his thoughts were lost forever, others were recalled quite accurately, and still others were incorrectly remembered by the time he wrote his 1988 *Encyclopedia*. Most probably, at an earlier time he had more information concerning these 1841-O coins.

82. Letter, August 1996, here slightly edited; additional information sent on September 4, 1996, this including copies of certain p.s of the book, *Barren County Heritage*, 1980.

83. Bill Ashworth, "Rockbridge Treasure Valued Above $1,000," *Richmond Times Dispatch*, March 9, 1959 (main source). Also, Emmett W. Tardy, "A Buried Treasure Unearthed," *Numismatic Scrapbook Magazine*, April 1959; "Treasure Unearthed," *The Numismatist*, May 1959 (both as cited by John Kleeberg).

84. Recollection of John J. Ford Jr., conversation, June 24, 1996; also the

New Netherlands Coin Co. auction catalogs as cited.

85. Many if not most of the 1831-dated coins had small, mostly triangular marks on the lower third of the obverse, particularly on the bust, perhaps artifacts of some type of coin-ejecting device used at the Mint. Since that time, the author has kept an eye out for other 1831 halves with these marks and has seen them on many other Mint State examples.

86. Walter H. Breen, *Encyclopedia*, 1988, p. 280.

87. Personal recollections of the author; interviews at the time; comments furnished by James F. Ruddy. Both James F. Ruddy and the author were in London at the time, and we both viewed the lots; as noted, Jim Ruddy attended the sale, which was held at Christie's auction rooms, close by Spink & Son, Ltd.

88. Walter H. Breen, *Encyclopedia*, 1988, p. 423, among other listings. Robert P. Hilt II, *Die Varieties of Early United States Coins*, 1980, stated that certain of the coins were "presentation pieces," and similar comments have reached print elsewhere, never mind that documentation is non-existent.

89. During lot viewing the coins were appreciated for their high quality (mostly About Uncirculated and Uncirculated) by the intending American buyers, but the writer recalls no one saying at the time that they looked like presentation or "special" coins. The prevailing sentiment in 1964 was that someone who was not a numismatist brought some pocket change to England from America in 1795, and the coins had been kept together since that time. The assortment of coins was random, with some duplication and with obvious gaps—hardly what a numismatist would have sought or requested if given *carte blanche* as a guest at the Mint. Walter H. Breen was not present at lot viewing or the sale itself.

90. *Journal of the American Bibliomania Society*, the leading organization of numismatic book collectors.

91. Jack Collins had nearly completed a manuscript on the 1794 silver dollar—giving provenances of all known specimens—and had sought to learn more about the origin of the two Lord St. Oswald specimens.

92. Information from an American Auction Association sale (Q. David

Bowers and James F. Ruddy), February 7, 1974, lots 10–16.

93. Adapted from David W. Lange's article, "Henry D. Cogswell and His Curious Time Capsule," *Calcoin News*, Summer 1984, courtesy of the writer.

94. Adapted from Carrie Dolan, "Found: $150,000 Silver Coin Cache," *Oakland* (Michigan) *Press*, reprinted in *Treasure Magazine*, October 1979; copy furnished by Doug Veal.

95. $1,000 face value in silver coins weighs about 56 pounds.

96. Sources include *Coin World*, November 24, 1982, account by New Orleans dealer James H. Cohen, "New Orleans Hoard Yields O-Mint Treasures"; this is the source of the specifically quoted commentaries. Also Walter H. Breen, *Encyclopedia*, 1988, p. 346; interview with Les Zeller, a New York dealer who made these a specialty and purchased many; personal recollection of the author.

97. Chris Pilliod reported in *Gobrecht Journal*, March 1992, pp. 44, 45, that of the 21 specimens of 1841-O he studied, 11 were of the doubled obverse variety.

98. Published by Larry Briggs Rare Coins, 1991. Various die combinations of the era are discussed, and several comments are made concerning those found in the New Orleans hoard. The variety of which more than 200 are known is Briggs's 2-C.

99. Roy D. Ash, letter, August 26, 1996; notes edited and adapted to reflect material not already given.

100. Information from David E. Tripp, cataloger of the sale.

101. Attributions to the die variety description in Al C. Overton's book, *Early Half Dollar Die Varieties 1794–1836*, 1990 edition (edited by Donald Parsley).

102. Adapted from an article, "Woman Discovers Some Buried Booty," by Jesse Garza, *Milwaukee Journal-Sentinel*, August 11, 1996; submitted to the author by Gerald Murack and, separately, by Joe Darnell.

103. Information from Richard Snow, July 8, 2014.

104. *Coinage for Colonial Virginia*, 1956, pp. 33, 34. Inventory is from Newman, comments following each coin are by the present writer with certain adaptations from Newman.

105. From an Associated Press story, January 7, 2015.

106. Information from Patrick McMahon, Museum of Fine Arts, Boston. A nod to Anne Bentley, curator, Massachusetts Historical Society, as well. Modern images are from the Museum of Fine Arts.

107. Ohio Life's main business was banking, and its bills of exchange were accepted in virtually all parts of the United States.

108. Margaret G. Myers, *The New York Money Market*, Vol. I., 1931, p. 142. This work also gives many details about the worsening conditions of banks during the year and the high ratio of paper money and credit in relation to coin reserves. Myers' detailed account of the Panic of 1857 does not mention any effect from losses of gold coins en route from California.

109. The Chemical Bank was severely criticized by its competitors for not suspending. Shortly afterward, Chemical Bank's privileges at the New York Clearing House were revoked!

110. The financial difficulties of 1857 are mentioned in the chapter devoted to the SS *Central America* and its treasure. An excellent account of the crisis is found in R.M. Devens, *Our First Century*, pp. 644–652.

111. Sus = sow; pendens = suspended or pendant.

112. Di oboli = two oboli, a small Greek copper coin; deux sous = two sous, a small French copper coin; toll ens = rooting. Perhaps White intended to convey the sentiment that paper dollars were worth two cents each in terms of coins.

113. Woodward's comment in his May 1884 J.N.T. Levick Collection catalog. Levick was arguably the leading U.S. collector of tokens in his era. Today, the White tokens are still considered somewhat scarce. All seen by the writer have been with mirrored Proof surfaces.

114. *Standard Catalog of United States Tokens 1700–1900*, pp. 271, 272. Russell Rulau suggests these tokens "were apparently struck by the Thomas Kettle firm in Birmingham, England," but this does not seem likely to the present writer.

115. This medal was described and illustrated by George and Melvin Fuld in *The Numismatist*, June 1959.

116. Benjamin P. Wright, "American Store or Business Cards," serialized in *The Numismatist*, 1898–1901; this token is Wright's no. 1230. John F. Jones, "The Aaron White Hoard of

Coins," *The Numismatist*, February 1938 (Jones interviewed Frossard, who told him of the hoard contents and of 5,000 copper cents sold for 2¢ apiece). Walter H. Breen, "A Survey of American Coin Hoards," *The Numismatist*, October 1952. White's tokens are described in the Hibler-Kappen text, So-Called Dollars, as HK-829, 830, and 831. A satirical medal related in concept is Betts-115 (C. Wyllys Betts, *American Colonial History Illustrated by Contemporary Medals*, 1894), of 1720, with a legend that translates to "credit is as dead as a rat," and showing (per Betts) "a man lying dead on rocky ground grasping a winged caduceus in his right hand, and in his left a packet, inscribed ['letters of exchange'], his cocked hat has fallen near him."

117. *Evening Star*, Washington, D.C., March 2, 1910.

118. Adapted from an interview with Wayne Miller conducted by the author in Denver, Colorado, August 16, 1996; reviewed and edited by Wayne Miller, letter, September 26, 1996.

119. *Ibid.*

120. Information from David M. Sundman, letters, September 7 and 13, 1996; Christie's catalog of the Miller automobiles, September 1996; article in the *Union Leader* (Manchester, NH), September 6, 1996, "His Mystery Was Vintage Cars, Collection of Vermont Man Estimated at $1.24 M," by Anne Wallace Allen. Other sources are subsequently cited.

121. Conversation with the author, October 11, 1996. The Clark family members have been fine personal friends for many years.

122. David Hewett, "Three-Day Auction Disperses First Part of Miller Estate," *Maine Antique Digest*, October 1996. The sale was held on behalf of a court-appointed asset management team, the Stratvest Group.

123. "Miller Auto Trove Exceeds Wildest Expectations; Brings $2.18 Million," *Maine Antique Digest*, October 1996. Certain information also from John R. White, "A Car Auction of Legend," *Boston Globe*, September 14, 1996.

124. The reverse of this Vermont token is similar to certain others listed by Russ Rulau in his *Standard Catalog of United States Tokens*, pieces described as having been issued by the Brooks News Company, Jamestown, New York. In a conversation with David M. Sundman, September 17, 1996, Russell Rulau commented that the Drury token is the only variety known to him that has the word "Miss" as part of the name of its issuer.

125. Information from David M. Sundman, letters, September 18 and 20, 1996; certain information also from the Williamstown Historical Society; subsequent footnote information from the Rulau *Standard Catalog of United States Tokens 1700–1900*. Also R.G. Dun's *Mercantile Agency Credit Report*, July 1909.

126. R.G. Dun's *Mercantile Agency Credit Report*, July 1909.

127. For an expanded and extensively illustrated account of the Miller hoard, see Q. David Bowers, *Coins and Collectors: Golden Anniversary Edition*, 2014.

128. Citation suggested by Bob Vail.

129. Much information is from by Karl Moulton, who acquainted the author with White and furnished copies of the two auction catalogs quoted.

130. This may have been the 1820, 20 Over 19 overdate—one does not know in retrospect—but, on the other hand, it probably was not. Harlan P. Smith was an accomplished numismatist and was familiar with the 1820, 20 Over 19, not a rare variety, and also knew well the Type Table published by John W. Haseltine in 1881, which listed known varieties. This "1820 over '18" captured his attention and quite possibly represented a variety that awaits rediscovery by a new generation of specialists. Here is a "treasure" possibility for the alert half dollar specialist.

131. As cataloger H.P. Smith stated that the variety is "seldom found," this would imply that he had seen at least a few others. Relevant to the Charles White Collection coin, Thomas K. DeLorey, letter, September 26, 1996, commented: "This is most likely Wiley-Bugert #101 as listed for the 1840-O, struck from a leftover reverse die of the Capped Bust type of 1838–1839 on which the mint marks were on the obverse. See their article in the Coinage of the Americas Conference proceedings for 1987. Apparently, credit for the original publication of this should now be given to Harlan P. Smith."

132. This may have been a hub created by Charles Cushing Wright in New York City to create dies shipped to San Francisco for the 1851 (*sic*) $50 coinage of August Humbert, United States assayer of gold.

133. This would have been a U.S. Mint hub die, era unknown, except that in 1838 and 1839 certain pattern half dollars (but no known eagles) were made with a Liberty head and stars. In 1838, the coinage of eagles, suspended since 1804, was resumed now utilizing a Liberty head by Christian Gobrecht.

134. This could have been any one of various Franklin busts or even a Civil War token obverse die later (circa 1900–1910) believed to have used by Stephen K. Nagy to create impressions by flattening the obverses of copper cents dated in the 1840s and 1850s. This latter piece is listed as No. 14990 in Gregory Brunk's *American and Canadian Countermarked Coins* and also illustrated with a full-p. photograph on p. 202 of that book.

135. For detailed information, see Bowers, *Virgil Brand, the Man and His Era: Profile of a Numismatist*, 1983.

136. Pete Smith, *American Numismatic Biographies*, 1992, p. 189.

137. A January 26, 1937, financial report on MacIntosh (copy furnished by David M. Sundman) noted that he was 26 years old at the time, married, and began dealing in stamps in 1927, later adding "numismatology." His mother, Caroline H. MacIntosh, was a partner. Further, "The business occupies a 20 by 35 ft. space in a frame building located on a corner in a thickly populated residential district of the middle class. Management rests with the owners, and 6 to 10 are employed." MacIntosh's obituary appeared in *The Numismatist*, October 1958, p. 1180, and noted in part: "MacIntosh, 47, took his own life by firing a 32-caliber bullet through his head in the basement of his home. . . . Recently he had worked about two hours daily following illness and an operation. He conducted a real estate business and a coin company."

138. Information from Pete Smith, letter, September 8, 1996; also Pete Smith, *American Numismatic Biographies*, p. 217. *The Numismatist*, June 1935, p. 398, Bolender sale announcement.

139. Recollection of John J. Ford Jr., conversation, June 27, 1996. For more information about Morgan's special, but confidential, services to favored numismatists see the 1921 Proof Morgan and 1922 Peace dollars offered in the Norweb Collection catalog, November 1988.

140. Pete Smith, *American Numismatic Biographies*, 1992, p. 105. F.C.C. Boyd was an appraiser of the coin part of the estate and evaluated the Green holdings in 1937 and 1938.

141. Walter H. Breen, *Encyclopedia*, 1988, p. 299.

142. *Ibid.*, p. 337: "When Col. Green inherited his mother's millions, he became a collector of (among other things) railroad cars, pornographic films; and among his immense numismatic holdings was a hoard of over 200 Uncirculated 1796 quarter dollars, of which at least 100 were more or less prooflike—their fields more mirrorlike than on the others. Abe Kosoff and André DeCoppet dispersed many of these to date and type collectors during the 1940s." It is believed that Kosoff acquired the Green coins through Philadelphia dealer James G. Macallister; accounts vary. Separately, John J. Ford Jr., conversation, June 27, 1996, stated that in the 1940s he had inspected the quarters when they were part of the Green estate, but that Macallister had bought them.

143. Walter H. Breen, *Encyclopedia*, 1988, spread the word about Gies. On p. 323, he related concerning Barber dimes that he "obtained rolls of all of them"; on p. 358, he credited Gies with having rolls of all Barber quarter dollars; on p. 410, he said the same thing about Barber halves. William Pukall and Wayte Raymond were also credited with having most or all Barber coins in roll form, also a highly unlikely scenario.

144. Ford, conversation with the author, June 27, 1996.

145. Walter H. Breen, *Encyclopedia*, 1988, p. 173; related information is in Breen's half cent *Encyclopedia*, p. 450. John J. Ford Jr., conversation, June 27, 1996. Seller Collection, March 1980, lots 3056–3059, there stated to have been from Thomas L. Elder, and illustrated on the cover of the sale catalog. Additional 1854 half cents of somewhat lesser quality, but from the Ford holdings, appeared in the Bowers and Ruddy sale of the Park Forest Collection and other consignments, October 1980, lots 2061–2064.

146. Walter H. Breen, *Encyclopedia*, 1988, p. 228; citation from Dr. George Fuld's comment in Kagin's Van Cleave Collection sale, 1986, under Lot 5012. The writer has found no other mention of this remarkable group.

147. Roger W. Burdette, correspondence, November 17, 2014.

148. Personal experience of the author with William Pukall.

149. Conversation with the author.

150. Letter, July 7, 1996.

151. Ted Hammer, "Hoard Defies Searchers," *Coin World*, November 30, 1977, and "Unclaimed Hoard Scheduled to Wichita Auction Block," December 7, 1977.

152. "Large Hoard of Pan-Pacs Overhangs Market."

153. Simsbury has its own numismatic connection as a source of copper for the Higley threepence coinage of 1737–1739.

154. Information is from Joseph C. Mitchelson's obituary in *The Numismatist*, October 1911, and personal visits to the Connecticut State Library in the 1980s and 1990s with curators Kathleen Plourde, David White, and Dean Nelson. David Corrigan of the Library also assisted.

155. His first offering of 1942, 2 Over 1, dimes appeared in the February 1945 issue.

156. David M. Sundman, conversation, July 11, 1996, and letter, July 22, 1996. Certain of these coins were offered in the Littleton Showcase, July and August 1996, p. 1. James Reardon, Littleton's chief buyer, acted in the transaction. The quantities of coins given as "highlights" do not necessarily reflect the quantities or proportions of the coins found by Mr. Moscow, as many pieces had been sold by Mr. Shaw over the years. An article on Morris Moscow, "Cache-ing in on T.A.," by Gersh Kuntzman, appeared in the *New York Post*, August 14, 1996.

157. David M. Sundman, letter, October 18, 1996.

158. This coin was offered in the Stack's Bowers Galleries ANA Sale, August 4, 2014, lot 3123.

159. In the 1800s, New Hampshire decreed that all transactions, to be legal, had to be expressed in the British system of pounds, shillings, and pence. In 1950, an alert state legislator noted that this law was still in effect! It was promptly changed.

160. *The Numismatist*, August 1917, p. 329.

161. Sources include Walter H. Breen, "A Survey of American Coin Hoards," *The Numismatist*, January 1952; Walter H. Breen, *Encyclopedia*, 1988,

p. 189; Dr. William H. Sheldon, Dorothy I. Paschal, and Walter H. Breen, *Penny Whimsy*, 1958, pp. 189, 190. Breen (1952) lists these further sources: Walter H. Breen, *Copper Coinage Figures Revised*, in the May–June 1951 *Coin Collector's Journal*; George H. Clapp and Howard R. Newcomb, *United States Cents of the Years 1795, 1796, 1797 and 1800*, p. 17; Adam Eckfeldt, "Cent Book," 1796–1803, bound manuscript volume in R.G. 104, Treasury Section, National Archives, Washington, D.C.; same source, treasurer's receipts for copper coins; Joseph N.T. Levick, "Reminiscences of Coin Collecting," *American Journal of Numismatics*, December 1868 (the reference there to "Mr. C." is to Edward D. Cogan); Dr. W.H. Sheldon and Homer K. Downing, *Early American Cents*, 1949, pp. 11, 173–175, 183, 190–192; various W. Elliot Woodward auction catalogs, including lots 620–622 of October 1864 (Levick, Emery, Illsley, Abbey), Lot 316 of December 1866 (Jencks and Paine), Lot 972 of January 23, 1882 ("Elmira"), Lot 673 and the photographic plate in front of the catalog of January 8, 1884 (Ely), and Lot 15 of January 21, 1889 (Stetson). Note that with regard to these catalog citations, Breen said: "The accounts in the 'Elmira' and Stetson catalogs vary slightly, but the substitution of Nichols for Goodhue in the last-named was probably a slip of memory; W.E.W. was then very old, nearly blind, and generally declining. All of his late catalogs were put out with help from younger dealers, and many show rambling reminiscences not seen before 1879 except in rare tantalizing fragments."

162. However, in most modern references and citations, the 1816 is included; *e.g.*, John D. Wright, *The Cent Book*, 1992, p. 4, concerning 1816 Newcomb-2: "Possibly a few thousand Mint State examples survive from the Randall Hoard circa 1867."

163. The 1830s represent the first decade of growing popularity of the railroad. This is only relevant if, indeed, a railroad platform was involved. Atlanta, settled in 1833, was founded in 1837 at the end of the Western & Atlantic Railroad and at first was named Terminus. There were, however, many other Georgia cities and towns antedating the railroad that could have received a keg of copper cents in the 1820s, shortly after their manufacture. Further, it is likely that

no railroad platform was involved (see later endnote).

164. Walter H. Breen, "Survey of American Coin Hoards," *The Numismatist*, January 1952.

165. Thus negating the "railroad platform" theory mentioned by others later, unless the hoard was beneath a railroad platform and also buried in the earth.

166. At the time, one-cent pieces were legal tender only to the amount of 10¢. Although they normally circulated at par and probably could have been spent at par in the 1860s, from time to time—including for a period in the 1840s and 1850s— cents were in oversupply in certain commercial channels (such as in New York City from 1841 through 1853) and traded at a discount from face value.

167. Significant contemporary mention that they were in just one keg, and it was small. The hoard "grew" as later stories of it reached print.

168. Rarity information is from Walter H. Breen, *United States Minor Coinages 1793–1916*, p. 11.

169. Walter H. Breen, *Encyclopedia*, 1988, p. 202.

170. Walter H. Breen, *Encyclopedia*, 1988, p. 211, 212. Dickeson suggests that the "milling of the edges"—the rim on the coins—is not sufficiently raised to protect the surfaces from contact marks and undue wear.

171. Citation furnished by Bob Vail.

172. *The Traveller's Guide Throughout the Middle and Northern States*, G.M. Davison, Saratoga Springs, New York, 1834, p. 69.

173. Citation suggested by Bob Vail.

174. Certain information is from Bowers, *The Strange Career of Dr. Wilkins: A Numismatic Inquiry*, 1987, pp. 11, 12, with the quotation about Gould being from *Collector's Blue Book*, May 1914.

175. Citation suggested by Bob Vail. Certain information about Morey is from *American Numismatic Biographies*, Pete Smith, 1992. It is likely that the profits earned by Morey, Mehl, and other issuers of premium catalogs were primarily from the sale of the catalogs, not by profits from rare coins bought from catalog buyers.

176. Adapted from an account by Howland Wood, "Buried Coins," *American Journal of Numismatics*, October 1910, pp. 156, 157. This is how numismatic "facts" are created; Howland Wood had no

way of knowing whether these were unconsciously deposited, that they "rolled out one by one," etc.

177. The actual motto is MIND YOUR BUSINESS (with no "OWN"); the inscription, "Fugio," meaning "I fly"—a reference to the rapid passage of time—appears on the obverse of the coin, not the edge, but it is near the rim. Congress awarded a contract for their coinage in 1787.

178. Published in the *Boston Herald*, January 10, 1914. Citation provided by David M. Sundman, Littleton Coin Co.

179. Recollection of Oscar G. Schilke to the author.

180. John D. Wright, *The Cent Book*, 1992, pp. 81, 82. James L. Halperin, letter, July 1, 1996. New England Rare Coin Auctions, October 1981 Long Beach Sale, lots 58–64.

181. July 2, 1996, "Large Cent Hoard Discovered."

182. September 17, 1996, "Large Cent Hoard Departs from Expected Pattern."

183. Neil Carothers, *Fractional Money*, 1930, p. 187.

184. Citation furnished by Eric P. Newman.

185. History repeats itself, and an article in *Coin World*, July 22, 1964, told of a sagging (but, apparently, not collapsed) floor. "Braden Coin Hoard Set for Sale" related that $60,000 in coins had been located in the lodgings of the late Clarence Braden, of Jefferson, Texas, who was described as a frugal professor. The coins, of which perhaps $3,000 worth was numismatically valuable, were "found in shoe boxes and cigar boxes under Braden's bed and in a closet; weight of the coins caused the apartment's floor to sag."

186. Catalogue copy furnished by Frank Campbell, American Numismatic Society, New York City. Citation suggested by Bob Vail.

187. Recollection of the author.

188. "Turns in Cent Hoard," *Coin World*, January 31, 1979, p. 60.

189. Information from Shepherd per conversation, October 10, 1996, and material subsequently sent including *A Guide to Old Economy*, by Daniel B. Reibel; "Old Economy Village," a brochure issued by the Pennsylvania Historical and Museum Association; "Harmonie Herald," by The Harmonie Associates, Ambridge, Pennsylvania; and copies of historical

records, museum accession records, financial and coin-deposit data, and other information. Excerpts from three books by Karl J.R. Arndt, who for 60 years (1934–1994) was the primary person with access to the Harmony Society files, were also sent: *George Rapp's Harmony Society 1785–1847* (Rutherford: Fairleigh Dickinson University Press, 1965); *George Rapp's Successors and Material Heirs 1847–1917* (Rutherford, 1971); and *George Rapp's Years of Glory: Economy on the Ohio 1834–1847* (New York: Peter Lang, 1987). Certain information concerning the Rappites in Indiana is from John E. Faris, *The Romance of Forgotten Towns*, 1924, which discusses the formation of the movement and quotes accounts by Robert Dale Owen, son of Robert Owen, purchaser of the Indiana tract from the Rappites.

190. The Millerites, active in the 1830s and 1840s, placed the arrival of the millennium at the forefront of their beliefs, but unlike the Rappites, the Millerites are remembered by historians as not being very industrious and, in fact, often relaxed or lazy while they awaited the return of Christ. The Rappites (Harmonists) are said to have been as close to the Lutheran doctrine as any branch of Protestantism, but they had their own set of practices. The practice of celibacy was taken from the teachings of St. Paul, who believed that celibacy was better than the state of being married.

191. Faris, p. 166. One non-believer suggested that these footprints had been hewn from a rock quarried near St. Louis.

192. Flower visited Harmony in 1819 and is remembered as the Englishman who founded Albion, Illinois. It was he who went to England to visit Robert Owen to try to interest him in buying the Harmony village. See Faris, pp. 165, 166, 168. Albion is the Latin designation for England.

193. Furnished by Raymond Shepherd, curator, October 11, 1996.

194. Baker managed the Society's store. Later, he became head of the Society, in turn to be followed by Jacob Henrici. Baker (1793–1868) exhibited great ability in shepherding the Harmonists' assets.

195. *George Rapp's Successors and Material Heirs*, 1971, pp. 66–68.

196. Raymond Shepherd, curator, conversation of October 10, 1996.

197. Sources include Walter H. Breen, "Survey of American Coin Hoards," *The Numismatist*, January 1952; *Coin Collector's Journal*, March 1881; and Sydney P. Noe, *Coin Hoards*, American Numismatic Society, 1921 (primarily derived from the CCJ account of 1881). A modern commentary is found in "Another Visit to Economy, Pennsylvania," John Kovach, *John Reich Journal*, July 1993.

198. Morgan may have buried his own treasure seized in other raids against the Yankees, per W.C. Jameson, "General John H. Morgan's Buried Treasure," *Buried Treasures of the Ozarks and Appalachians*, pp. 293–297.

199. Here presented in edited form. It is obvious that most of these numbers are approximate.

200. Daniel B. Reibel, *A Guide to Old Economy*, p. 9.

201. Inventory from Raymond Shepherd, letter, October 11, 1996.

202. Sources include Karl Moulton, letters, August 22 and 31, 1996, enclosing historical citations and extensive numismatic commentary, part of his research for a long-term book project on the large-size quarter dollars of 1796–1828; Kenneth E. Bressett, conversation, August 19, 1996; Walter H. Breen, *Encyclopedia*, 1988, pp. 340–342; correspondence with Mark Hotz; several conversations, July 1996, with Keith Zaner of *Coin World*, who was preparing an article on the topic (which appeared in the issue of August 26, 1996, "Theories Galore"); and the author's long-time interest in the subject. Gregory Brunk, *American and Canadian Countermarked Coins*, mentions these on p. 65 and among other observations quotes Frank G. Duffield's commentary on them (*The Numismatist*, 1919, Duffield nos. 1345 and 1346).

203. Ard W. Browning, whose book *Early Quarter Dollars of the United States, 1796–1838* was published by Wayte Raymond in 1925, is himself the center of a numismatic mystery. The obviously talented Mr. Browning apparently published no earlier or later works on coins, but arose in full bloom in 1925 to present the collecting community with a first-class reference book on this rather specialized series.

204. 1825 B-3 is also mentioned in the literature including the Breen update of Browning's 1925 work, but has not been verified by any observed

photographs or inspections of coins as of 1996 (see Karl Moulton, letter, August 31, 1996).

205. At the time, Haseltine's store was at 1225 Chestnut Street, Philadelphia, and Randall was at 1905 Chestnut Street, a separation of seven blocks (punctuated by the U.S. Mint at Chestnut and 13th). In *Numisma*, January 1880, Edouard Frossard noted: "Messrs. Haseltine and Randall of Philadelphia are now engaged in a descriptive list of the United States Silver Dollars, Half Dollars, and Quarters, a work for which their long experience and thorough knowledge of the subject eminently qualifies them. Mr. Haseltine informs us that the work will describe minutely all the known varieties." In March 1880, Frossard noted that Haseltine commented the work was "progressing favorably, and that orders for copies are coming in from every quarter." The "Catalogue of John W. Haseltine's TYPE TABLE . . ." bears on the cover the notation, "catalog by John W. Haseltine" with no mention of Randall, who seems to have been plagiarized, as he was the main author.

206. A virtually identical "obnoxious" description was used for Lot 958 in the same cataloger's sale of October 25–27, 1886.

207. Another counterstamp on these quarters, the letter R, was occasionally mentioned years ago, but it seems to have been recalled incorrectly, as no pieces have been located by modern scholars. Sometimes it was said that R meant regular or regulation weight.

208. Also see Heritage's 1996 ANA Convention Sale, Lot 7059, which mentions a theory by Karl Moulton that the E and L could have been reference marks relating to star and date placement and alignment. Concerning counterstamping rare coins for numismatic identification, very few collectors if any would want to do this today; the procedure is hardly recommended.

209. Mark Hotz, "Mint Counterstamped Large Size Bust Quarters 1815 & 1825," December 1987; Bill Subjack, "E & L Counterstamps— Another Theory," December 1987; Mark Hotz, "Those Darned Counterstamped Bust Quarters—The Saga Continues," October 1990. Also see commentary by Bowers under Lot 1121 in the Harold A. Blauvelt Collection Sale, February 1977.

210. As related by Davis to Pete Smith, August 1996; Smith, letter, September 8, 1996.

211. From an account in *A Complete History of the Marquis de Lafayette*, "by an officer in the late Army," Hartford, 1847, pp. 497, 498. The Bunker Hill Monument was not completed until 1842.

212. Letter, September 10, 1996.

213. Kenneth E. Bressett, conversation, August 19, 1996, commented that he had never seen a well-worn one in many years of making notes about the counterstamps. Most pieces offered in the auctions in the 1881–1883 era studied by Karl Moulton were Uncirculated. (It could also be argued that well-worn pieces were of insufficient value in the 1800s to merit auction descriptions.)

214. Thomas Parker, *History of Farmington, Maine*, second edition, 1875, p. 168.

215. Sources include newspaper accounts and John M. Kleeberg, *Numismatic Finds of the Americas*, pp. 217, 218.

216. Paul Gilkes, "Dealer Marketing Hoard Coins," *Coin World*, May 2, 2005; other accounts.

217. Sources include: William Weir, *Sixty Years in Canada*, 1903; Weir was the secretary of the Tariff Reform Association of 1858 and the government agent for the exportation of U.S. silver coins in 1870. Also Neil Carothers, *Fractional Money*, 1930, pp. 217, 218, 259, 260. A related commentary appears in the *American Journal of Numismatics*, March 1870, p. 87, under "A 'New Dominion' Coinage."

218. *Fractional Money*, p. 218.

219. Weir, p. 138.

220. Weir, p. 151 and subsequent p.s.

221. Quoted commentary from the *American Journal of Numismatics*, March 1870, p. 87. The "old lady with the broomstick" was a whimsical description of the Liberty Seated half dollar, the "broomstick" being the liberty cap and pole.

222. Weir, p. 159. At the time, London was the world's premier market and price arbiter for gold and silver.

223. *Fractional Money*, pp. 259–260, here slightly edited.

224. Walter H. Breen, *Encyclopedia*, 1988, p. 401.

225. Sources include *American Journal of Numismatics*, April 1875, pp. 90, 91; April 1876, p. 87; January 1876, p. 66.

226. To a lesser extent, Proof Morgan dollars were not popular, and many were not spent. In the 1870s and 1880s, dollars had great purchasing power and thus were not retained casually. Numismatists who collected American silver coins usually retained just the smaller denominations and were interested only in Proofs. Mintmarked issues were ignored, as were large-denomination Proofs.

227. An article by David Helfer, "1855-S Half Dollars in the China Trade," *Gobrecht Journal*, July 1993, included this comment and is one of the very few numismatic citations seen on the subject: "It is my opinion that in all probability a substantial number of these pieces were shipped to China to purchase goods in the China trade. In the Far East these coins would have been viewed as merely bullion and traded to the Chinese by American ship captains." Four examples of counterstamped 1855-S half dollars were illustrated.

228. Walter H. Breen, *Encyclopedia*, 1988, p. 401.

229. There was a shift in preference, and in later years—including in the present era—gold is very much appreciated by the Chinese, in addition to the traditional silver.

230. Recollection of the author.

231. Louis Helfenstein Collection auction held August 1964. The sale catalog, with a "scenic" color cover featuring partially opened cabinet drawers laden with large cents, created a sensation in the numismatic community at the time and gave a great boost to his auction business. Merkin, a long-time private collector, was also a professional clarinetist. From the late 1950s to the 1970s, he conducted 32 auction sales. George F. Kolbe auctioned his library in 1984, and after his 1992 death, Stack's auctioned his coins.

232. Conversation with the author, June 27, 1996.

233. H.A. Wise, *Captain Brand of the Centipede, a Pirate of Eminence in the West Indies*, 1864, p. 138.

234. George Eliot was the pen name of British writer Mary Ann Evans. *Silas Marner: The Weaver of Raveloe*, published in 1861, is perhaps the consummate piece of fiction relating to the hoarding of gold coins.

235. When it comes to finding gold treasures, "silence is golden," as the saying goes. Indeed, discretion may be just as valuable as the discovery

of the gold coins themselves in terms of legal fees saved, etc. (not a recommendation, but merely an observation).

236. Thomas Hood, "Miss Kilmansegg," c. 1841–1843.

237. Adapted from "An Old Newfoundland Savings Hoard," R.J. Graham, *Canadian Numismatic Journal*, July–August 1986, reprinted from the *Transactions of the Canadian Numismatic Research Society*, Summer 1986.

238. Joseph Hooper, "Hooper's Restrikes: A California Find," *The Numismatist*, October 1906, cited by John Kleeberg.

239. Citation furnished by David M. Sundman, Littleton Coin Co.

240. To the author it seems unlikely that British prisoners of war held by Americans would have retained valuable coins. There is probably another explanation as to the origin of this hoard. The founding date on the Sage token differs from that in the narrative. It seems to have been built as a refinery by the Livingston family in 1754.

241. Sources used by Thomas J. Hammond: Q. David Bowers, *The History of United States Coinage*, 1979; Vi Bruning, personal interview, August 8, 1994; "Find of $1,160 in Kellogg & Co. Double Eagles," *The Numismatist*, January 1915, p. 27; "Found Sack of Old Gold," *Hebron Journal*, November 20, 1914, p. 1; *History of the State of Nebraska*, 2 volumes, Chicago: Western Historical, 1882; Donald H. Kagin, *Private Gold Coins and Patterns of the United States, Pricing Supplement*, 1982; Ane McBride, personal interview, August 8, 1994; *Nebraska History Magazine*, April–June 1933, p. 136; Wayte Raymond, *Private Gold Coins Struck in the United States, 1830–1861*, 1931; Russell H. Renz, *Private Gold Coinage of the United States*, 1938; Jackie Williamson, personal interview, August 8, 1994; R.S. Yeoman (Kenneth E. Bressett, editor), *A Guide Book of United States Coins*, 47th edition, 1993. Photographs were supplied by Thomas J. Hammond.

242. *History*, p. 1450.

243. This philosophy would come to the fore in the 1896 presidential election campaign pitting William Jennings Bryan (with his famous "Cross of Gold" speech showcasing the farmer) against William McKinley.

244. Quoted from *History*, p. 1443. This was written in an era in which the Indians were generally viewed as being savages, while white settlers were seen as virtually blameless.

245. *The Numismatist*, p. 27.

246. Walter H. Breen, *Encyclopedia*, 1988, p. 651, not stating a source: "Many Uncirculated survivors dated 1854 came from the Thayer County hoard."

247. Information concerning this hoard, including the notes, is from Roger W. Burdette, *Renaissance of American Coinage 1909–1917*, Seneca Mill Press, 2007.

248. U.S. Mint, NARA-CP, op. cit., entry 229, box 297. Letter dated February 12, 1912, to Ashbrook from MacVeagh.

249. U.S. Mint, NARA-CP, op. cit., entry 229, box 297. Memorandum dated January 29, 1912, to MacVeagh from Andrew (here lightly edited).

250. U.S. Mint, NARA-CP, op. cit., entry 229, box 297. Letter dated September 3, 1912, to Roberts from Norris. The receipt from Chapman was dated July 18, suggesting that either there was a delay in transferring the coins to him, or Comparette had neglected to obtain a receipt as required by Roberts.

251. There were two major types of half eagles minted in 1834. The rarer pieces are those with the Capped Head to Left obverse design and the motto E PLURIBUS UNUM on the reverse, which were minted prior to the summer of the year. Pieces minted in August and later, bearing the so-called Classic Head portrait by Chief Engraver William Kneass, lack the motto. These were made in much larger numbers and most probably represent what the two boys found.

252. From a 1926 account in the *New York Times* quoted by B.A. Tompkins, *Treasure*, p. 163.

253. The account appeared in many places, including in the *New York Times*, June 1, 1926; also quoted in *The Numismatist*, July 1926, p. 397, "Finds $200,000 in Gold Coin Buried by Father." The editor of *The Numismatist* could not resist adding: "If any of those $20 gold pieces minted in 1850 'and before' ever reach the auction room, we predict a small-size riot among collectors for front seats at the sale."

254. A few pattern $20 pieces were made at the Philadelphia Mint in 1849. The Mormons in Salt Lake City also

made a small number of $20 coins that year, but these never circulated in Kentucky or Tennessee.

255. Adapted from a report in *The Numismatist*, October 1927, p. 626, "Philadelphians Find Gold Coins Among Debris." The editor of *The Numismatist* gently remarked that the 1843 double eagle story "may easily have been a typographical error." Such inaccuracies in the popular press were common, as in an unrelated account in *The New York Times* which told readers about U.S. gold dollars minted in 1847 (numismatists know that the first such gold dollars were dated 1849).

256. Adapted from a press account in *The Numismatist*, February 1929, p. 68, "Workmen Dug Up Coins and Jewelry."

257. Undated article from the *Oconomowoc Enterprise* quoted in *The Numismatist*, July 1931, p. 527, "Gold Coins Dug Up in Wisconsin."

258. Again, this is precisely why only a small percentage of hoards have ever been reported over the years.

259. Adapted from *The Numismatist*, September 1931, p. 642, "Many Gold Coins Unearthed at Buffalo, Illinois."

260. Adapted from *The Numismatist*, September 1932, p. 583, "Rush for Buried Coins at Saratoga Springs, N.Y." At one time, this town had many different bottlers and sellers of mineral water.

261. On October 24, 2014, Leonard Augsburger reviewed this section and made extensive changes based upon his research and his book, *Treasure in the Cellar*, 2008.

262. *The Numismatist*, October 1934, p. 677, "A Large Quantity of Gold U.S. Coins Unearthed." Actually, Baltimore was allied with the Union, and federal troops were not an uncommon sight.

263. *The Numismatist*, April 1935, p. 237, "Baltimore Hoard of Gold Coins to Be Sold at Auction."

264. Yale Merrill's son became a rare-coin dealer many years later; Mark Hotz, who became a dealer in his own right, was once in his employ. Hotz visited 132 South Eden Street in Baltimore in the 1990s to see what remained on the site, but found that the gold-bearing house was long gone and that the entire block was occupied by two commercial warehouses (see Mark Hotz, letter, September 16, 1996).

265. From an unattributed press clipping reprinted in *The Numismatist*, July 1935, p. 420, "Possibly Some Rarities Here." Never mind that the Civil War did not begin until 1861, and the latest coin was dated 1854.

266. *The Numismatist*, March 1937, p. 199, "A $20 Gold Coin with Pattern Reverse." Walter H. Breen, "A Survey of American Coin Hoards," *The Numismatist*, January 1952.

267. *The Numismatist*, April 1938, p. 333, "Hoard of Gold Coins Found in Bloomsburg, Pa."

268. Adapted from a report by Judge L.B. Handley, who administered the estates of Mr. and Mrs. Cooper, as published in *The Numismatist*, June 1943.

269. "Gold Coins Valued at $1,830 Ploughed Up on A.L. Bain Farm Twelve Miles South of Kerens," *Corsicana* (Texas) *Daily Sun*, April 16, 1947, as cited by John Kleeberg.

270. F.L. Coffman, pp. 139–149. The same writer said that he and Dr. Body subsequently found $18,000 in gold coins hidden in the wall of a house, but no details were given.

271. Adapted from Roger W. Burdette, "U.S. Mint & Nazi Gold, Merkers *Kaiseroda* Salt Mine Treasure," *Journal of Numismatic Research*, Summer 2013, Issue 3, pp. 53–61.

272. NARA-CP, Record Group 260, Records Relating to Shipments of Gold and Silver, compiled 1945–1947; Records Relating to Shipments of Gold and Silver; "Netherlands."

273. Ziemke, Earl F., *The U.S. Army in the Occupation of Germany 1944–1946*, Center of Military History, United States Army, Washington, D.C., 1990, pp. 228–231. The term "salt mine" refers to potassium, sodium, magnesium and other chemical salts, not just ordinary table salt.

274. Greg Bradsher, "Nazi Gold: The Merkers Mine Treasure," *Prologue: Quarterly of the National Archives and Records Administration*, Spring 1999, p. 12.

275. Letter, October 12, 1996.

276. Letter, June 25, 1996.

277. Walter H. Breen, *Encyclopedia*, 1988, pp. 480, 481, gives Charles E. Green (Chicago dealer) and Horace L.P. Brand (of Chicago, a brother to super-collector Virgil Brand and co-heir of the fabulous Brand estate following Virgil's death in 1926). If Brand was the source, further information can be found in the

extensive Brand archives in the library of the American Numismatic Society, New York.

278. Adapted from an Associated Press dispatch, "Map Leads to Buried $100,000 Gold Coins," datelined Mount Prospect, Illinois, and published in the *St. Louis Globe-Democrat*, March 31, 1960; clipping furnished by Gene and Audra Andries.

279. Today it is estimated that fewer than 50 examples of the 1931-D exist.

280. "Arkansas Worker Finds Gold Hoard," *Coin World*, January 27, 1965, p. 41.

281. "Indians Locate Gold Coin Hoard," *Coin World*, July 19, 1967.

282. Recollection of the author.

283. Sold at auction by Bowers and Ruddy Galleries, June 20–22, 1977, lots 3422–3432.

284. Adapted from Mark Richards, "Found: $26,000 Coin Hoard," *Treasure Found Magazine*, Summer 1978; copy furnished by Doug Veal.

285. Information provided by Ray Bolduc, letter, August 1996; Lou Dieke furnished a photograph.

286. Information furnished by David E. Tripp, letter, August 1996; he appraised the coins and assisted in their sale.

287. Clearly Breen's assumption that the coins in the present inventory were from Virgil M. Brand is erroneous, considering that Brand died on June 20, 1926, while the hoard contained 14 double eagles dated 1927.

288. "Wisconsin Hoard Yields 19th Century U.S. Gold," *Coin World*, April 11, 1984, p. 57.

289. Adapted from Bob Grant, "Treasure Hunter Hits Gold Coin Bonanza," *Treasure Magazine*, November 1984; copy furnished by Doug Veal.

290. Sources include Associated Press accounts of the discovered treasure, mostly from October 1 to 7, 1985; letters from numismatists James C. Gray and John Dannreuther in 1996 and 1997; interviews with others who wished to remain anonymous; correspondence with John Lupia. Also, Thomas L. Aud, *Gold is the Key: Murder, Robbery, and the Gold Rush in Jackson, Tennessee*, BrayBee Publishing Co. LLC, 2012, gives additional information.

291. Correspondence, May 18, 2000.

292. *The Merchants' and Bankers' Almanac for 1855*; *Banker's Magazine*, August 1856, p. 84.

293. Ebenezer Finley McKnight (1806–1877).

294. Stated in a letter to his sister, Mrs. Jane Turner, in Lake County, Indiana; citation given by Thomas L. Aud.

295. *Augusta* (GA) *Chronicle*, June 20, 1859. Irwin; dozens of accounts from February 1859 into 1860 concerning the robbery and its aftermath.

296. Stated in a letter to his sister, Mrs. Jane Turner, in Lake County, Indiana; citation given by Thomas L. Aud.

297. *Augusta* (GA) *Chronicle*, February 8, 1859; *Evening Post*, New York City, February 11, 1859; related news accounts.

298. Letter, September 23, 1996.

299. Offered and sold in the catalog of the auctions by Bowers and Merena of the Kissel and Victoria Collections, September 1989, lots 556–606.

300. Letter, September 6, 1996.

301. Sources include several articles sent by Barbara Brandt from *The Wood River Journal*, published in Ketchum, Idaho; Paul Gilkes, "Judge Awards Gold Coin Hoard to Rolling Stone Publisher," *Coin World*, February 8, 1999; Tad Friend, "The Gold Diggers," *The New Yorker*, May 31, 1999.

302. Communication to the author, February 3, 2004, for inclusion in *A Guide Book of Double Eagle Gold Coins*, Whitman Publishing LLC, 2004.

303. The main sources of information, as well as each of the illustrations, were Don Kagin and his associate David McCarthy through e-mail correspondence, supplemented by coverage in *Coin World*, *Numismatic News*, and *COINage* magazine.

304. Paul Gilkes, "Early Sales of Saddle Ridge Coins Top $4.1M," *Coin World*, June 16, 2014.

305. Much of this text was written by Michael Hodder.

306. *The Intelligencer, No. XIX*, December 2, 1728, as given in Dean Swift's *Works* (quoted in *Historical Magazine*, February 1869, p. 117). Presumably, this referred to Spanish-American silver, but it could have pertained to Massachusetts silver coins just as easily. "Notes on Coins," by William Kelby, in the same issue of *Historical Magazine*, p. 115, notes that the 1652 Massachusetts silver coinage arose in part from the need to convert large amounts of captured Spanish silver brought to New England by buccaneers in 1651.

307. William M. Lytle, *Merchant Steam Vessels of the United States 1807–1868*. Passenger accounts and other information in S.A. Howland, *Steamboat Disasters and Railroad Accidents in the United States*, 1840, are the basis for several later stories of the wreck. A dramatization of the final hours of the Lexington appears as Part 1 in Clive Cussler, *The Sea Hunters: True Adventures with Famous Shipwrecks*, 1996, and relates the Longfellow anecdote.

308. Another bad news-good news "missing the boat" account appears under the discussion of the SS *Central America*, relative to a passenger who arrived at the dock in Havana after the ship had sailed.

309. Engraving drawn on stone by William K. Hewitt. Published by N. Currier, 2 Spruce Street, New York. Many copies were printed as extras to the *New York Sun*. Four different versions of the print are known to collectors today and are described in *Currier & Ives: A Catalogue Raisonné*, Gale Research Co., 1984, p. 35.

310. The following account is adapted and paraphrased from the original 1840 *Extra Sun* story as published by Currier; John H. Morrison's *History of American Steam Navigation*, 1903; and testimony given before the 26th Congress. Certain other information is from Jeannette Edwards Rattray, *Ship Ashore!*, 1956.

311. On coastwise ships, the pilot—who was familiar (or supposed to be) with shoals, reefs, and other hazards to navigation—directed the course of the ship, while the captain was in charge of the crew and passengers.

312. Alternatively, cold, but not as cold as usual for the season; accounts varied.

313. There were at least three other captains aboard as passengers: E.J. Kimball, B.D. Foster, and Ichabod D. Carver (who was soon to be married). Hilliard, age 24, provided a detailed account of his experience that was appended to the aforementioned Nathaniel Currier print.

314. Italics per the original account. Captain Terrill was counting on high tide to carry his ship over a sand bar, otherwise he would have had to wait until the next high tide, thus causing a delay and diminishing his profits.

315. Conversation, October 8, 1996; note, October 14, 1996.

316. Actually, the ship had caught fire on January 2, 1840; a small box ignited and was quickly extinguished.

317. It was Vanderbilt's practice to exact tribute from his competitors to induce him to stay away from a route or to keep rates high.

318. As quoted by Dr. Clarence A. Wood, *Long Island Forum*, 1950.

319. Charles Ellms, *The Tragedy of the Seas; or Sorrow on the Ocean, Lake, and River, from Shipwreck, Plague, Fire, and Famine*, copyright 1841, edition of 1846, imprint of Loomis & Peck, Philadelphia, p. 422, as part of a chapter, "The Burning of the Steamboat Lexington."

320. *The Atlas of Ship Wrecks & Treasure: The History, Location, and Treasures of Ships Lost at Sea*, by Nigel Pickford, 1994, called the Lexington an "American luxury liner" and stated that $800 in specie was recovered at the time of loss. The same writer stated that the ship was wrecked on November 19, 1846. The "luxury" term is in several modern accounts, but the author has not encountered it in any narratives from the 1800s.

321. *Long Island Newsday*, October 12, 1983; copy furnished to the author by Donald Prybyzerski. The group of treasure hunters had been founded by Clive Cussler. His 1996 book, *The Sea Hunters: True Adventures with Famous Shipwrecks*, gives a description of the Lexington and commented that it furnishes a potential site for modern-day divers, although conditions can be dangerous. Relics from the wreck are on display at the Vanderbilt Museum on Long Island.

322. Conversation, October 8, 1996; note, October 14, 1996.

323. *Niles' National Register*, August 1, 1840; James Sprunt, *Chronicles of the Cape Fear River 1660–1916*, second edition, p. 195; almanacs; news accounts.

324. Certain information is from Ben Marich and Roger Howard, published in 2000 by JW Fishers, manufacturers of electronic detection equipment, in Issue 8-1, submitted by Fishers.

325. Numismatists will recognize Allaire and his New Jersey village and company in connection with Hard Times tokens and paper money.

326. James P. Baughman, *Charles Morgan and the Development of Southern Transportation*, p. 45.

327. Walter H. Breen, *Encyclopedia*, 1988, p. 529. Similar information is found in Douglas Winter, *Charlotte Mint Gold Coins: 1838–1861*, 1987, pp. 113, 117.

328. John Haskell Kemble, *The Panama Route, 1848–1869*, p. 92.

329. Tony Jaggers, *A Shipwreck Guide to the Bahamas, Turks and Caicos, 1500 to 1990*, p. 18.

330. John Haskell Kemble, p. 238.

331. Letter, June 22, 1996.

332. One account says 235 feet in length, draft of 20 feet; often ship specifications in contemporary (as well as later) publications are approximate.

333. John Haskell Kemble, *The Panama Route, 1848–1869*, 1990 edition, p. 252.

334. Ernest A. Wiltsee, *Gold Rush Steamers of the Pacific*, p. 80; John Haskell Kemble, p. 252.

335. Ernest A. Wiltsee, p. 82.

336. John Haskell Kemble, p. 65.

337. Blunt, who had graduated from the Naval Academy at Annapolis in 1849, was sent as his first assignment to participate in the Government Geodetic Survey of the Coast of Oregon and California.

338. Livestock pens were used only on Pacific coastal steamers; on the Atlantic side, meat was packed in ice in New York City for trips in both directions, including the return from Panama. Meat was segregated by type, with beef in one group of barrels, chicken in another, pork in still another, etc.

339. Certain information adapted from an account, "Arrival of the *California*, Loss of the *Winfield Scott*, No Lives Lost, Safety of the Mails and Treasure," *Alta California*, December 7, 1853, p. 2. Purser Watkins of the stricken ship provided most of the details to the newspaper. The "Let her rip!" account appears in the Edward Bosqui narrative subsequently quoted and in other texts.

340. *Ibid.*

341. The *California* had departed from Panama on November 19, 1853, with 500 passengers and 254 mail bags, some of which had connected from New York on the SS *Illinois* and from New Orleans on the SS *United States*. On November 30, on the way to San Francisco, the *California* had passed "the boilers and other remains of steamer *Independence*, high and dry on the shore of [Santa] Margarita Island." The *Independence*, a 613-ton steamer owned by Cornelius Vanderbilt, was wrecked on March 16, 1852, and 122 lives were lost of 283 aboard.

342. The *Republic*, an 852-ton, 201-foot wooden sidewheel steamer, had been put in service in 1849 for the Baltimore Steam Packet Co. Like so many Eastern steamers, in 1851 she was sold to Western interests and entered the lucrative Pacific Coast run, mainly calling at ports along the California shore, her activity at the time of the *Winfield Scott* wreck. Later she plied the San Francisco-to-Portland and Victoria routes. In the 1860s, her engine was taken out and put in the *Del Norte*, and later the hull was scrapped or simply rotted away (accounts differ). The 337-ton *Southerner* was launched as the *Aurora* in 1846, then sold to the Navy in January 1847 and renamed the *Scorpion*. It was rebuilt after October 1848 and renamed the *Isthmus*, and in 1854 renamed the *Southerner*. At that time the steamer was employed on the San Francisco-to-San Diego run. After sailing from the port of Umpqua, Washington, in December 1854, she struck a sandbar at the mouth of the Columbia River, sprang a leak, and was lost; all passengers were saved, but the cargo went down with the ship (see Ernest A. Wiltsee, pp. 129, 131, 150, 151; and John Haskell Kemble, p. 232, there as the *Isthmus*).

343. Ernest A. Wiltsee, pp. 130–132, quoting accounts in the *Alta California*, December 7, 13, and 15, 1853. Ernest A. Wiltsee, p. 348, notes that the vessel hand-stamped its mail, this being marked "Steamer Winfield Scott." Captain Blunt was dismissed by the Pacific Mail Steamship Company, although he was never formally censured. He was not able to find employment as a captain elsewhere. He died in 1854, some said of a broken heart, despite a comment in the *Alta California*, December 7, 1853, "We do not think that his well-established reputation as a careful and skillful navigator will suffer from this unfortunate loss."

344. Information concerning the wreck exploration is adapted from: Glenn E. Miller, "Ghostly Gold," *Skin Diver*, March 1967; Dick Anderson, "There is Gold on the *Winfield Scott*," *Skin Diver*, September 1969, which also reprinted a news account from the *Panama Herald*, December 27, 1853; Anderson, "Yes, Virginia, There is a *Winfield Scott* Treasure," September 1972; Anderson, Argosy Treasure Hunting, 1977 Annual, "Gold from the Winfield Scott."

345. Jay Roe, letter, September 3, 1996, enclosing inventory of the Croft pieces, which Roe had obtained years earlier from Walter H. Breen.

346. Frontier & Diviercy (Pierre Frontier, Eugène Diviercy), 81 Bush Street, San Francisco.

347. Antoine Louis Nouizillet was located at 58 Kearny Street, San Francisco, circa 1852–1854 and was associated at times with M. Deriberpe and Isadore(?) Routhier.

348. Deriberpe, an engraver, maintained premises at 58 Kearny Street, San Francisco, in 1852 and 1853 and was associated at one time with Nouizillet.

349. Numismatic information is from Robert D. Leonard Jr., furnished to the author, August 1996; also furnished were copies of letters from Leonard to dealer Kenneth W. Lee, August 13, 1978, and Lee to Leonard, August 18, 1978, as well as magazine articles and research notes. Probably, many more coins were recovered over the years and not reported to anyone. Attributions are to Walter H. Breen and Ronald Gillio's *California Pioneer Fractional Gold*, 1983. "Small Change: California Small Denomination Gold and the Wreck of the Winfield Scott," *Ventura Historical Society Quarterly*, Volume 47, No. 4, 2003, a copy of which was supplied by Robert H. Lande, was another source; Jack Totheroh furnished most of the numismatic information for that study. The coins illustrated in this chapter are representative and not specifically attributed to the SS *Winfield Scott*.

350. Further sources include: Walter H. Breen and Ronald J. Gillio, *California Pioneer Fractional Gold*, 1983, pp. 5, 6, most of which information came from Robert D. Leonard; Frank Soulé, John H. Gihon, M.D., and James Nisbet, *The Annals of San Francisco*, 1855, p. 473. A modern description of the wreck site is found in Darren Douglas, *Guide to Shipwreck Diving, Southern California*, 1990, pp. 49–52. Sidewheel spokes and scattered parts of the ship can be seen. Visibility changes as sands cover and uncover the wreckage.

351. John Haskell Kemble, p. 68. Humbug was a popular term for deception or fraud. The ballad was published in the *Panama Weekly Herald*, October 17, 1853, this being shortly before the SS *Yankee Blade* entered service.

352. Ernest A. Wiltsee, p. 252. The *Yankee Blade* is discussed in Don B. Marshall, *California Shipwrecks*, 1978, pp. 34, 35. An illustration of the ill-fated ship, from the Bancroft Library, is reproduced on p. 41. A modern description of the wreck site is found in Darren Douglas, *Guide to Shipwreck Diving, Southern California*, 1990, pp. 24–27. Large sections of the steam engine cylinders can still be seen, as can parts of the paddlewheels, brass fittings, and other items.

353. Ernest A. Wiltsee, pp. 138, 139.

354. *Ibid.* Another account, this one the statement of Captain Bell, passenger on the rescue ship *Goliah*.

355. Further, the passenger lists that do exist are usually rife with misspellings and wrong information.

356. Sources include accounts in *Alta California*, October 10, 11, 16, 22, and December 1, 1854; also January 5, 7, 10, 14, 16, 18, 23, 26, and 27, and April 6, 1855. Also *New York Times*, November 10, 1854, and January 26, 1855. Copies furnished to the author by Dan Owens.

357. *Alta California*, December 10, 1854. Soon thereafter the *Sonora* was to be the venue for an on-board theft of treasure in which it was reported that six $20 gold coins had been hidden by the boatswain, "$300 to $400 was found sewn up in one of the beds," etc., this being a part of 96 boxes of treasure containing $15,000 to $25,000 each, and two bags, one with $15,000 and the other containing "a few thousands" (latter account in *Alta California*, January 5, 1855).

358. Erik Heyl, *Early American Steamers*, 1953, pp. 395, 463.

359. Per some reports; specie (minted silver and gold coins) was the normal form of shipment. For example, the *New York Times*, November 10, 1854, mentioned "the specie on board." However, "gold dust" is mentioned in several contemporary accounts, a common naïve synonym for coins and ingots.

360. *Three Years' Wanderings of a Connecticut Yankee in South America, Africa, Australia, and California*, 1860, p. 323.

361. Equivalent at the time to a month's wages for a typical laborer on the East Coast.

362. November 10, 1854. Accounts from several eyewitnesses were printed.

363. The *Alta California*, October 10, 1854, quoted an account stating that 850 passengers from the *Yankee Blade* were taken aboard to add to the 135 already on the *Goliah*. The 145-foot wooden sidewheel steamer was built in 1848 as a tug, but was later sent to California to do service on the Sacramento River, there bearing the name *Defender*. In 1854, she was rebuilt, refitted, renamed *Goliah*, and put into use as a coastwise steamer. Her name is incorrectly spelled as *Goliath* in some accounts, a logical error. Years later, she served as a tow boat in Puget Sound and was dismantled in 1899.

364. John Haskell Kemble, pp. 144 (account from *San Francisco Prices Current and Shipping List*, October 14, 1854) and 252; Oscar Lewis, *Sea Routes to the Gold Fields*, pp. 239, 240, 248–250 (among others); Ernest A. Wiltsee, pp. 144–147 (the quotation of a small part of Vought's extensive commentary is from this source; unlike most other observers, Vought did not criticize the captain—under whom he had served); Richard M. Benson, *Steamships and Motorships of the West Coast*, p. 80; William M. Lytle, p. 245. *Harper's New Monthly Magazine*, January 1855, p. 110 (there the number of deaths was given as "about 30"; John Haskell Kemble, p. 144, states "some 30 lives were lost"; other estimates were as low as 15).

365. *New York Times*, November 10, 1854. Another account in the same issue placed the number of passengers aboard at 812 plus a crew of 122, for a total of 934, of which "we are satisfied that not more than 50 perished."

366. Normand E. Klare, *The Final Voyage of the Central America 1857*, pp. 54, 55.

367. Reported in *Alta California*, October 16, 1854.

368. Ernest A. Wiltsee, p. 148.

369. *Alta California*, January 10, 1855.

370. F.L. Coffman (who called her a schooner and estimated her treasure to be worth from $4 million to $32 million), p. 260.

371. In the case of gold coins minted in California, and some others minted in other locations, silver existed as an "impurity" as part of the 10% copper alloy; silver, too, is readily attacked by salt water.

372. Perry had a strong numismatic interest; his holdings included Hard Times tokens, an original 1836 Gobrecht silver dollar, and various world coins.

373. Law, an important member of the firm earlier in the decade, had since departed, and it was desired several years earlier to rename the ship. However, there were regulations against this, and the renaming did not occur until 1857, after the law was changed. This was her second voyage under the SS *Central America* flag. Changing the name of a ship was bad luck, some said.

374. Erik Heyl, p. 171.

375. *New York Herald*, September 21, 1857; Judy Conrad, *Story of an American Tragedy*, 1988, p. 16.

376. *New York Herald*, September 27, 1857; Judy Conrad, p. 17.

377. *New York Times*, September 23, 1857; Judy Conrad, p. 18.

378. Herndon's leadership prevented the disgraceful panic of the crew that had taken place in 1854 on the doomed Collins Line *Arctic*, in which the crew prevented women and children from boarding lifeboats in order to save themselves.

379. Account in Frank Leslie's *Illustrated Newspaper*, October 3, 1857.

380. Normand E. Klare, p. 200.

381. Of the bark *Jane A. Falkenberg* out of San Francisco.

382. Interview with Jane Badger, *New York Times*, September 24, 1857; Judy Conrad, pp. 28, 41; Normand E. Klare, p. 199 (there, Badger's gold is valued at $17,000 to $20,000).

383. Normand E. Klare, p. 200.

384. This scenario seems highly dramatized. By September 1857, there were relatively few miners with enough cash reserves to return to the East and live lives of luxury. Other accounts do not support the stories of earning permanent wealth in the gold fields. However, the *Central America* did have its share of wealthy non-miners aboard and, perhaps, a few miners of similar means.

385. R.M. Devens, *Our First Century*, pp. 642, 643. $20,000 worth of gold dust is mentioned and may be the same anecdote as $17,500 to $20,000 in coin mentioned in other accounts; scarcely two retellings of the *Central America* disaster were alike in all details.

386. From review of the manuscript.

387. Normand E. Klare, p. 199. Another account, per Bob Evans correspondence, November 14, 2014, states that Birch had sent his $70,000 on another steamer, probably one that left San Francisco on August 5.

388. Normand E. Klare, p. 200. Perhaps reminiscent of the humorous

rejoinder relating to accumulated worldly treasures, "If I can't take it with me, I'm not going."

389. Normand E. Klare, p. 116, noted that Caldwell had mined the gold himself in California; this was equal in value to about 15 years' wages for a working man at the time. Account of William Chase, *Detroit Free Press*, September 23, 1857; Judy Conrad, p. 46. Caldwell was picked up by the Ellen.

390. *American Journal of Numismatics*, May 1867, p. 9. Most modern (1980s and 1990s) accounts of the *Central America* have overlooked this numismatist. However, he is mentioned (but not with a numismatic connection) by Normand E. Klare, pp. 213, 214, as being a "political and personal friend" of President James Buchanan. Although no account is given of Graham's experience aboard the ship, it is stated that on October 19, 1857, Graham petitioned President Buchanan to give an award to Captain Hiram Burt of the brig *Marine*, who assisted in the rescue of passengers.

391. Passenger lists were not complete, and accounts vary. The numbers quoted here are from Normand E. Klare, p. 247.

392. Also see the story of Aaron White in chapter 3, "Hoarders and Misers," p. 67.

393. Certain of Milt Butterworth's images have been used to illustrate the work of CADG.

394. William T. Gibbs, *Coin World*, September 27, 1989.

395. Beth Deisher, *Coin World*, September 14, 1992.

396. William T. Gibbs, *Coin World*, September 27, 1989.

397. McNall owned Numismatic Fine Arts, a 51% interest in the Superior Galleries coin dealership and auction business, and was the main stockholder of the Los Angeles Kings hockey team. Some years later, his business empire collapsed.

398. An impossible scenario, as the Panic of 1857 began on August 24, 1857, by which time the SS *Central America* had already departed.

399. Paul Gilkes, "Insurers want to sell S.S. *Central America* gold," *Coin World*, October 5, 1998.

400. This listing represents all coins examined and conserved by Bob Evans as of June 22, 2001.

401. "Odyssey Marine Exploration Selected for Recovery of S.S. *Central America* Gold," *Globe Newswire*, March 3, 2014.

402. Report #14-01 issued by Odyssey Marine Exploration, covering April 15, 2014, to May 13, 2014.

403. Report #14-02 issued by Odyssey Marine Exploration, covering May 14, 2014, to June 15, 2014.

404. Report #14-03 issued by Odyssey Marine Exploration, covering June 16, 2014, to July 15, 2014.

405. Report #14-04 issued by Odyssey Marine Exploration, covering July 16, 2014, to August 15, 2014.

406. Report #14-05 issued by Odyssey Marine Exploration, covering August 16, 2014, to September 15, 2014.

407. http://ir.odysseymarine.com/releasedetail.cfm?ReleaseID=860611.

408. Type not specified.

409. The fact that only one 1854-S is in the inventory may suggested that most of these were shipped to the East and thus became scarce in circulation in California.

410. Brother Jonathan was a popular term for America as part of the "family" of lands in the British empire, an early-day counterpart of Uncle Sam (England was sometimes known as John Bull). A clever Yankee in a play, *The Contrast*, written by Royall Tyler and produced in 1787 as America's first stage comedy, was named Brother Jonathan. In 1842, the *Brother Jonathan*, published in New York, became America's first illustrated weekly paper. The name was often used in cartoons and elsewhere to denote a shrewd or clever young boy or a U.S. citizen contemplating some new turn of politics or invention. A token made by George H. Lovett in 1858, 31 mm, shows John Bull and Brother Jonathan exchanging lightning bolts across the sea. At the left is HOW ARE YOU JONATHAN. At right, PURTY WELL OLD FELLER / HOW'S YOURSELF. This chapter corrects some earlier versions of the story, such as John J. Ford Jr. having gold ingots that were carried on the ship, now a tale believed to be false.

411. Concerning the weight of the ship, William M. Lytle states 1,359 tons. Erik Heyl, *Early* pp. 63, 64, gives an excellent account of the *Brother Jonathan*.

412. John Haskell Kemble, *The Panama Route, 1848–1869*, p. 96, for this

specific quotation attributed to the San Francisco *Alta California*, July 14, 1860; numerous other comments in the same vein are given elsewhere in the text.

413. Erik Heyl, p. 407, in an account of the negligent breakdown at sea of Vanderbilt's steamer *Samuel S. Lewis*.

414. Erik Heyl, p. 64.

415. Later, Vanderbilt increased his fortune and became a major force in the operations of the New York Central Railroad. His heirs spent money lavishly on personal pleasures, including luxurious yachts and The Breakers, renowned as the most lavish "cottage" at the seashore in Newport, Rhode Island.

416. An excellent account and a passenger list of the *Brother Jonathan* are found in Don B. Marshall, 1978, pp. 157–167. Harry Rieseberg and A.A. Mikalow, *Fell's Guide to Sunken Treasure Ships of the World*, 1965, pp. 138, 139, "The Deep-Fathomed Tomb of the *Brother Jonathan*," includes useful information.

417. Don B. Marshall, p. 159. In keeping with popular parlance, certain later accounts referred to the ladies as "soiled doves" and "fallen angels."

418. Also known as St. George Point. A crag known as Jonathan's Rock is said to have administered the fatal hull puncture.

419. William M. Lytle gives the deaths as 171. Don B. Marshall, p. 157, quotes a contemporary account stating that one lifeboat was successfully launched, two were swamped, and three remained on board. Later stories varied.

420. Citation furnished by John J. Ford Jr.

421. Life jackets of the era were of two main types: with hollow tin compartments which were subject to leaking if damaged, and cork-filled.

422. In 1955, the Del Norte County Historical Society registered the cemetery as a State Historical Landmark.

423. Don B. Marshall, p. 161. The same writer discounted Captain DeWolf's supposed last words, "Tell them if they hadn't overloaded me, this would not have happened!" It seems improbable that a cargo shift caused the wreck, in view of the quartermaster's testimony that the *Brother Jonathan* was, for a time after its impact, firmly stuck on a reef.

424. Dudley L. McClure, "$250,000 Face Value Now Worth Millions: Shipwreck Deposited Legal Tender Notes with Davy Jones, Recovery Still Possible?" *Numismatic News*, April 17, 1976. This writer suggested: "Probably because the *Brother Jonathan* losses in paper currency seemed to lack impact, the dollar totals consistently reached the public prints in terms of gold and silver coins." The same account mentioned "a few ingots which somehow were recovered, possibly having come ashore in trunks, boxes, crates, and other such flotsam from the wreck."

425. B.A. Tompkins, *Treasure*, pp. 164, 165.

426. *Ibid.*, pp. 164, 165.

427. Actually, two lifeboats, the captain's gig, and the ship's dinghy. The raft was hastily constructed aboard the ship as it was sinking. Information from Ellen Gerth.

428. Certain information from Ellen Gerth of Odyssey Marine, to author, January 2004.

429. Sources include discussion with Greg Stemm, January 8, 2004; "Another Atlantic Shipwreck Gives Up Treasure Coins," William T. Gibbs, *Coin World*, January 5, 2004; "NCS Conserves Treasure," *Numismatic News*, January 6, 2004; other media releases by Odyssey.

430. Repunched date, not a true overdate.

431. In conjunction with this chapter, a perusal of the commemorative listings in *A Guide Book of United States Coins*, or another standard source, will give information about mintages, designs, and reasons for issue. For expanded information and technical details, Bowers, *Commemorative Coins of the United States: A Complete Encyclopedia*, may be useful.

432. Information from David E. Tripp, letter, September 13, 1996.

433. However, circa 1903 at least 10 bags of Lafayette dollars were photographed in this vault, and the image was subsequently reproduced on several widely distributed postcards.

434. Recollection of Raymond N. Merena to author; Merena was general manager of Paramount when these coins were sold.

435. *Coinage of Commemorative 50-Cent Pieces*, p. 29; Government Printing Office, 1936.

436. The monograph, *The Selling of the Stone Mountain Half Dollar*, by William D. Hyder and R.W. Colbert, gives more information on this and numerous other aspects of the distribution.

437. Conversation with the author, January 8, 1991.

438. *Coinage of Commemorative 50-Cent Pieces*, Government Printing Office, 1936.

439. Recollection of John J. Ford Jr. to the author, February 20, 1991.

440. Letter, March 28, 1991.

441. Letter, August 24, 1996.

442. Telephone conversation with the author, January 8, 1991.

443. Details and specific references appear in Bowers, *Commemorative Coins of the United States: A Complete Encyclopedia*, pp. 301–311.

444. Dean Oakes, interview, August 12, 1996. Father Catich, who always wore a black cleric collar, was a familiar figure at coin conventions in the 1950s, often in the company of his friend and fellow Iowan Loyd Gettys.

445. Interview with the author, February 20, 1991.

446. Interview with the author, February 20, 1991.

447. Letter, March 28, 1991. Also, Anthony Swiatek, "Barnum Appears on Bridgeport Obverse," *Coin World*, May 29, 1991, p. 96.

448. Interview with the author, February 20, 1991.

449. The 1848 gold quarter eagle with CAL. counterstamped on the reverse was produced at the Philadelphia Mint using metal recently received from California and is truly the first American commemorative. However, these were not sold at a premium to the general public. The method of distribution is not known.

450. For complete information on the designers, issuing commissions, methods of distribution, prices over the years, and other aspects of silver and gold commemoratives, the writer's *Commemorative Coins of the United States: A Complete Encyclopedia*, 1991, gives much information for the specialist, as does *The Encyclopedia of United States Silver & Gold Commemorative Coins*, 1981, by Anthony Swiatek and Walter H. Breen. *The Commemorative Trail*, edited by Helen Carmody and published by the Society for U.S. Commemorative Coins, provides a continuing source for research findings, collecting ideas, and other topics of interest.

451. Information from the cataloger, David E. Tripp, letter, September 13, 1996.

452. In the writer's *Silver Dollars and Trade Dollars of the United States: A Complete Encyclopedia*, many pages are devoted to the Treasury hoards of silver dollars together with comments concerning the number released of each date and mintmark.

453. In my two-volume study, *Silver Dollars and Trade Dollars of the United States: A Complete Encyclopedia*, I discuss each of these Treasury releases in detail and give recollections of many of the people who were involved in the distributions and finds. Certain of the figures given here are adapted from that text.

454. All mintage figures for circulation strike 1878 dollars given in this text are estimates, despite their precise-appearing aspects.

455. Excellent details concerning the GSA sales are to be found in the Van Allen-Mallis book, *Comprehensive Catalog and Encyclopedia of Morgan & Peace Dollars*, third edition.

456. Information concerning the Redfield hoard of dollars is largely conjectural, as no specific figures were ever released. Sources for information in the present text include the writings of John Highfill, Wayne Miller, and Les Fox; expanded information is found in Bowers, *Silver Dollars and Trade Dollars of the United States: A Complete Encyclopedia*. Also see information in this chapter on the Redfield Hoard for expanded commentary.

457. Although Proofs were preferred over circulation strikes, the total number of numismatists seriously interested in collecting Proofs was very small. Many Proofs were spent.

458. Interview with Harry J. Forman, September 9, 1992.

459. Letter, July 7, 1996. Other citations by David W. Akers concerning silver dollars in this book supersede figures and estimates in earlier books, including Bowers, *Silver Dollars and Trade Dollars of the United States: A Complete Encyclopedia*.

460. Conversation with the author, August 11, 1992.

461. Wayne Miller, *The Morgan and Peace Dollar Textbook*, p. 85.

462. Advertisement in *The Numismatist*, January 1964.

463. As reported by Clark A. Samuelson and Leon E. Hendrickson in "The Continental-Illinois Bank Deal," part of John Highfill's *The Comprehensive U.S. Silver Dollar Encyclopedia*. These bank hoard coins were mostly from earlier Treasury bulk releases from the 1950s through and including the large dispersals of 1962–1964. Chicago dealer Edward Milas figured prominently in the dispersal of the Continental-Illinois coins.

464. Advertisement in *The Numismatist*, January 1964.

465. The writer recalls that Amon G. Carter Jr., of Fort Worth, Texas, was the numismatic advisor to two downtown casinos, both of which had quantities of Carson City dollars. I had the opportunity to go behind the scenes, including on catwalks over the gambling tables and in vaults were silver dollars were stored.

466. Advertisement in *The Numismatist*, January 1964.

467. *Ibid.*

468. David W. Akers, letter, July 7, 1996; this information is new to the silver dollar field and supersedes earlier estimates.

469. Advertisement in *The Numismatist*, January 1964.

470. Letter, July 7, 1996.

471. Advertisement in *The Numismatist*, January 1964.

472. Letter, July 7, 1996.

473. Letter, October 29, 1992.

474. Benjamin J. Stack (1925–1984) operated the Imperial Coin Company in Las Vegas at the time.

475. Advertisement in *The Numismatist*, January 1964.

476. David W. Akers, letter, July 7, 1996; this information is new to the silver dollar field and supersedes earlier estimates.

477. Advertisement in *The Numismatist*, January 1964.

478. *Ibid.*

479. David W. Akers, letter, July 7, 1996; this information was new to the silver dollar field at the time.

480. *Ibid.*; this information was new to the silver dollar field in 1996 and superseded earlier estimates.

481. Undated commentary from Maurice Rosen, received by the author, November 2, 1992.

482. David W. Akers, letter, July 7, 1996; this information was new to the silver dollar field and superseded earlier estimates.

483. *Ibid.*

484. Letter, July 7, 1996. David W. Akers was general manager of Paramount International Coin Corporation, who bought these coins from A-Mark, successful bidder for the Redfield estate dollars.

485. Dwight Manley, letter, October 28, 1992.

486. Letter, July 7, 1996.

487. Recollection of Steve Markoff; telephone conversation with the author, April 15, 1992.

488. A June 12, 1936, audit of Vault 5, Cage 10 in the Philadelphia Mint showed 154,800 1921 Peace dollars, 18,800 1928 dollars, 23,000 1934 dollars, and 2,500 1935 dollars. Information from Roger W. Burdette.

489. Letter, September 8, 1992.

490. Letter, July 6, 1992.

491. Letter, September 8, 1992.

492. As a rule of thumb, Philadelphia Mint Peace dollars of all dates are seen less extensively bagmarked than mintmarked varieties. This is a combination of their being handled less often in banks and in the Treasury Department, and their generally plentiful quantities, which permitted a lot of picking and choosing by numismatists. Branch mint dollars of 1922–1925 and those dated 1927-S and 1928-S are usually extensively bagmarked. Branch mint dollars of 1926, 1934, and 1935, as well as 1927-D, are much less so.

493. Although Morgan silver dollars (1878–1921) often appeared attractive after having been jostled about in mint bags for many years, this was not true of Peace dollars. Often a very small amount of handling resulted in the coins becoming unsightly with heavy marks, particularly on the obverse portrait and surrounding field. Add to that the planchet abrasions often seen (particularly on San Francisco and Denver coins of the early 1920s) on the higher parts of the eagle, and the result was an overall "scruffy" appearance. While hoards of Peace dollars released in the 1940s and 1950s are historically interesting to read about, probably most such coins went back into circulation (in the West) or became part of mixed-date bags and holdings (in the East). Although no records survive, of the many thousands of 1925-S dollars paid out in 1942, probably no more than a thousand or two ever reached numismatists who preserved them.

494. Letter, August 1996.

495. Letter, July 6, 1992.

496. The rare-coin market rose steadily from 1943 until 1948, after which it stumbled and fell. The years 1949 and 1950 were very slow. Revival began in 1951, and in 1952 the New Netherlands Coin Co. section of the ANA Convention sale may have furnished the spark of enthusiasm that signaled a strong growth in numismatic interest.

497. Letter, July 7, 1996.

498. "Rare Double Eagles Discovered in Europe," *Numismatic Scrapbook Magazine*, September 1955, p. 1354. "An enterprising dealer furnished the Bank of France with a list of rare dates. . . . That is why a 1926-S sold in the convention auction for less than $700 as compared to its former $2,000 price tag."

499. All illustrations are of genuine coins.

500. Conversation, September 26, 1996.

501. From the "Chicago '96" sale, a joint public auction by RARCOA (Ed Milas) and David W. Akers, p., 72, Lot 449.

502. Davis, a pharmacist, was a numismatic scholar. Pattern coins were among his specialties.

503. The Mint deviated from this policy numerous times in this era and in later years as well.

504. Walter H. Breen, *Encyclopedia*, 1988, p. 202.

505. *Ibid.*, p. 198.

506. *Ibid.*, p. 170.

507. Certainly this circa 1907 meeting with the finder of the dies could not have been with J.J. Mickley (born in 1799, died in 1878), who Breen incorrectly stated was the finder of the dies and the person responsible for first making restrikes from them. The Steigerwalt account implies that his 1907 interviewee was the sole person responsible. A fine biography of Steigerwalt is found in John W. Adams, *United States Numismatic Literature, Vol. I*, pp. 105, 106.

508. Perhaps E.L. Mason Jr., who moved from Philadelphia to Boston in early 1884.

509. See Walter H. Breen, *Encyclopedia*, 1988, p. 303, for further information including the seizure of these pieces by the Secret Service. The deliberate "PROPRIETERS" misspelling is in imitation of a 1694-dated copper coin bearing legends relating to the Carolinas. Bashlow, who lived near Washington Square, New York City,

was one of the more innovative rare-coin dealers and made restrikes of several other issues, most notably the 1861 Confederate States of America cent (from copy dies by August Frank of Philadelphia). Circa 1958–1960, Bashlow imported vast quantities of obsolete bronze British farthings, Conder tokens, and other British issues to America and sold them here. He died in the late 1970s in a hotel fire in Zaragoza, Spain.

510. As studied by Michael Hodder.

511. Today, Mitchelson's collection is preserved by the Connecticut State Library in Hartford.

512. Frank Stewart, *History of the First U.S. Mint*. Also see Leonard Augsburger and Joel Orosz, *The Secret History of the U.S. Mint*, 2011, pp. 111–114.

513. Sources include contemporary articles in *The Numismatist* and conversations between the author and Stephen K. Nagy, circa 1957; also information from Robert K. Botsford to the author in the 1950s. Botsford lived in Nescopeck, Pennsylvania, and was a close friend to Woodin, whose family home was in Berwick, Pennsylvania. Otherwise, Woodin mainly resided in New York City.

514. Of the 445,500 pieces struck of the 1933 double eagle, 100,000 were minted in March 1933, 200,000 in April, and 145,500 in May. On April 3, 1933, Franklin Roosevelt dictated that all gold coins be delivered to the secretary of the Treasury by May 1, 1933. Exactly why hundreds of thousands of pieces were subsequently minted in April and May that year only a student of government logic can answer. In any event, years after the fact the government took the position that all 1933 double eagles in the hands of collectors could not be legally held. Woodin, a very qualified numismatist and specialist in gold coins, had made no such declaration in 1933, nor did Morgenthau. In fact, 1933 double eagles were openly bought and sold for the next decade. It was not until 1944 that Uncle Sam went on a witch hunt for the pieces. Later the government had seized a 1933 double eagle that was said by some to have been in the King Farouk Collection and which had passed into the hands of a London dealer. Others said it was a coin owned by Jeff Browning and consigned for sale to Michael Brownlee, who offered it for sale to a number of dealers from whom I gained information.

515. From an account, "Europe Hunting Place for Coins," in the *Boston Sunday Herald*, April 30, 1905, furnished by David M. Sundman.

516. *Ibid.*

517. Mentioned by Edgar H. Adams, *Private Gold Coinage*, 1912, p. 51.

518. As quoted in the *American Journal of Numismatics*, 1910, p. 178.

519. Adapted from Eric P. Newman and Kenneth E. Bressett, *The Fantastic 1804 Dollar*, 1962, Chapter III, "Disappearance Stories."

520. Citation furnished by Wayne Homren.

521. Quoted by Lyle Saxon, *Lafitte the Pirate*, 1930, p. 296.

522. Information from David E. Tripp, letter, September 13, 1996, and Sotheby's catalog description.

523. Variety Sheldon-1 as described in William H. Sheldon's *Early American Cents* (1949) and *Penny Whimsy* (1958).

524. Many numismatists use camel's hair; Dr. William H. Sheldon, *Penny Whimsy*, 1958, p. 45, suggested goat's hair; Merkin preferred the hair of the badger (see David E. Tripp, letter, October 2, 1996). Brushing an old copper coin gently is a time-honored tradition employed by many advanced collectors.

525. Sotheby Parke Bernet sale of November 20, 1974, Lot 59.

526. Information from David E. Tripp, letter, September 13, 1996, and Sotheby Parke Bernet catalog description, sale of September 27, 1977, Lot 175: "Weakly struck on left side, obverse and reverse, dig through T of TRUST, otherwise Fine and exceptionally rare."

527. Certain information courtesy of Dennis Forgue and Thomas K. DeLorey, communication, October 11, 1996.

528. No coins are known today with either the Burgoyne or Argenti imprints.

529. This seems to be incorrect; no legislative action against Schultz is known.

530. Harvey Arden, "East of Eden: California's Mid-Coast," *National Geographic*, April 1984. Information supplied by Ernie Segundo.

531. Information from David E. Tripp, letter, September 13, 1996, and Sotheby's catalog description, sale of November 21, 1991, Lot 108. This coin was also featured in *The Numismatist*, September 1991, pp. 1385, 1386 (source of the Rade quotation).

532. More than 200 books, pamphlets, treasure guides, maps, pirate accounts, tourist guides, etc., including the following, were reviewed in the search for stories: Nina and William Anderson, *Southern Treasures*, 1987; Norman Carlisle and David Michelson, *The Complete Guide to Treasure Hunting*, 1973; Robert M. Coates, *The Outlaw Years: The History of the Land Pirates of the Natchez Trace*, 1930 (also gives many accounts of river pirates along the Ohio in particular); F.L. Coffman, *1001 Lost, Buried, or Sunken Treasures*, 1957 (a generous part of the 1,000 figure is a long list of sunken ships without details as to what they contained); W.C. Jameson, *Buried Treasures of the South*, 1992; Michael P. Henson, *A Guide to Treasure in Virginia and West Virginia*, 1982; Charles D. Miller, *Encyclopedia of Buried Treasure*, 1965; Thomas Penfield, several titles including *Wild Bill Hickok Guide to Lost Treasures*, Rand McNally, 1952, *Directory of Buried or Sunken Treasures and Lost Mines of the United States*, and *A Guide to Treasure in Arkansas, Louisiana, and Mississippi*; Thomas Probert, *Lost Mine and Buried Treasures of the West*, 1977; Harry E. Rieseberg, *Fell's Complete Guide to Buried Treasure on Land and Sea*, 1970; Robert Ellis Cahill, *New England's Pirates and Lost Treasures*, 1987.

533. W.C. Jameson, *Buried Treasures of the Ozarks and the Appalachians*, 1993.

534. *Arizona Place Names*, 1988 reprint, p. 105.

535. Brad Williams and Choral Pepper, *Lost Legends of the West*, 1970, and *Lost Treasures of the West*, 1975, reprinted as a single volume, pp. 36–50.

536. Brad Williams and Choral Pepper, *Lost Legends of the West*, 1970, and *Lost Treasures of the West*, 1975, reprinted as a single volume, pp. 132–136.

537. Thomas Probert, 1977.

538. Don B. Marshall, *California Shipwrecks*, 1978, p. 15.

539. Brad Williams and Choral Pepper, *Lost Legends of the West*, 1970, and *Lost Treasures of the West*, 1975, reprinted as a single volume, pp. 225–233.

540. Ed Rochette, "The Treasure of the Lost Dimes of Denver!" *Journal of the BCCS*, Summer 1990.

541. Robert Ellis Cahill, 1987, p. 58.

542. *Ibid.*

543. Charles Garrett, *Treasure Caches Can Be Found*, 2004, pp. 163–165.

544. W.C. Jameson, *Buried Treasures of the South*, 1992, pp. 48–51.

545. Sherman had intended to follow a career in finance, but he suffered greatly in the Panic of 1857 and its immediate antecedents. Thus, the Union eventually gained one of its foremost heroes.

546. W.C. Jameson, pp. 58–62.

547. F.L. Coffman, pp. 99–101.

548. Robert M. Coates, *The Outlaw Years: The History of the Land Pirates of the Natchez Trace*, account occupying many pages and most of two chapters; this book contains many dramatized accounts of the Natchez Trace (which went from eastern Tennessee, up through Kentucky, through the middle of Tennessee, the northwest corner of Alabama, continuing through Mississippi to the city of Natchez on the Mississippi River). Also, Otto A. Rothert, *The Outlaws of Cave-in-Rock*, 1924.

549. James Mitchell Guthrie (editor), *Indiana Sesquicentennial Commission*, 1966 anthology of newspaper articles, pp. 76–78. Sent by Mark B. Wolf.

550. Kansas Genealogical Trails on the Internet, quoting newspaper articles published years later in the *Wichita Eagle*, *Wichita Beacon*, and *Wichita Eagle-Beacon*, submitted by Lori DeWinkler.

551. W.C. Jameson, *Buried Treasures of the Ozarks and the Appalachians*, 1993.

552. Nina and William Anderson, p. 17.

553. W.C. Jameson, *Buried Treasures of the South*, 1992, pp. 87–89; other sources.

554. Thomas Penfield, *Wild Bill Hickok Guide to Lost Treasures*, 1952.

555. Nina and William Anderson, p. 19.

556. Robert Ellis Cahill, 1987, p. 58.

557. Thomas Penfield, 1952.

558. Robert Ellis Cahill, 1987, p. 45.

559. *Ibid.*, pp. 56, 57.

560. *Ibid.*, p. 53.

561. Charles Garrett, *Treasure Caches Can Be Found*, 2004, pp. 169, 170; other sources.

562. Condensed and adapted from "Where's Waldo's Coins," by Nancy Oliver and Richard Kelly, *The Numismatist*, November 2014, by permission.

563. Nina and William Anderson, p. 16.

564. F.L. Coffman, pp. 80, 81.

565. Charles Garrett, *Treasure Caches Can Be Found*, 2004, pp. 167–169.

566. F.L. Coffman, p. 179, and other sources.

567. *Ibid.*, p. 178.

568. F.L. Coffman, pp. 83, 84.

569. W.C. Jameson, *Buried Treasures of Texas*, 1991.

570. *Ibid.*

571. The name is reminiscent of the treasure hunt mentioned in the fictional Sherlock Holmes detective story by A. Conan Doyle, "The Musgrave Ritual."

572. Nina and William Anderson, p. 22.

573. *Ibid.*, p. 19.

574. *Ibid.*, pp. 20, 21.

575. F.L. Coffman, pp. 103, 104.

576. Williams and Choral Pepper, *Lost Legends of the West*, 1970, and *Lost Treasures of the West*, 1975, reprinted as a single volume, pp. 332–341.

577. F.L. Coffman, p. 4.

578. Yankee Publishing Co., 1943, pp. 348–354 (set in almost microscopic type!). List furnished to Snow by Miss E.E. Freeman, of Wellfleet, Massachusetts, who examined the records of the United States Engineers at Newport, Rhode Island.

579. F.L. Coffman, pp. 5 and 122, notes that federal records document 7,167 ships lost in the Great Lakes from 1679 through 1951, with more than $300,000,000 in cargo lost in each of lakes Erie, Huron, Michigan, and Superior. In the 20 years from 1878 to 1898, some 5,999 ships were wrecked or lost on the Great Lakes. Another guide places the number at more than 10,000.

580. In his 1996 book, *The Deep Sea Hunter*.

581. Robert F. Burgess, *Sinkings, Salvages, and Shipwrecks*, 1970, pp. 150–152, among other sources.

582. F.L. Coffman, p. 123.

583. Thomas Penfield, 1952.

584. Account adapted from Ellms, pp. 345, 346; William M. Lytle; and other sources.

585. Ellms, 1841, pp. 343–354 (includes passenger recollection); William M. Lytle, pp. 18 and 219; other sources.

586. David Stick, *Graveyard of the Atlantic*, 1951, pp. 22, 23.

587. William M. Lytle, pp. 42, 222; Nina and William Anderson, *Southern Treasures*, 1987, p. 142.

588. F.L. Coffman, p. 125; Robert F. Burgess, p. 152, stated that original records are "reputed" to have placed the treasure at $100,000, further noting that the passengers were mainly German and Norwegian immigrants. Probably, no accounting was ever made of the passengers' money. Robert F. Burgess also furnished information about the 1960 recovery.

589. F.L. Coffman, p. 127; also Thomas Penfield, 1952. William M. Lytle lists seven steamers named *Lexington*, but not this one.

590. F.L. Coffman, p. 127. William M. Lytle, pp. 10, 220, 235, gives conflicting information, listing the ship as 390 tons, made in Perrysburg, Ohio, in 1837, and wrecked at Vermilion, Ohio, on April 28, 1850, with a loss of 22 lives. Elsewhere, it is listed as 400 tons, built in Trenton, Michigan, 1849, and also lost at the same place and date. Such confusion is in part the result of multiple ships having this popular name. Also, there were various formulas for computing tonnage (the weight of water displaced) by using various measurements of length, breadth, and depth, and the same ship often appeared with different weights in different accounts.

591. Not to be confused with the *Orline St. John*, a bark built in 1848 and owned by William Bradstreet of Gardner, Massachusetts. That ship went down off Cape Hatteras on February 21, 1854, under circumstances that would prove very distressful to the survivors, who practiced cannibalism (see David Stick, *Graveyard of the Atlantic*, 1951, pp. 48, 49).

592. The 352-ton *Ogdensburg*, built in 1852, survived the Atlantic collision, but was star-crossed and met her end in another collision, with the schooner *Snow Bird*, on September 30, 1864.

593. F.L. Coffman, p. 126. Also spelled as Dakotah and Dacotah.

594. George (Georges in French) Sand was the penname of the French novelist and playwright Amandine Aurore Lucie Dupin, the Baroness Dudevant (1804–1876), remembered by the literati for her novels including *Lélia* (1833) and *Consuelo* (1842).

595. F.L. Coffman, p. 126; also Thomas Penfield, 1952.

596. Erik Heyl, pp. 185, 186.

597. F.L. Coffman, p. 263.

598. F.L. Coffman, p. 126. However, one must be very cautious of accounts of

specie lost in Eastern and Midwestern domestic commerce during the general period from 1862 to 1876, as gold and silver coins were not being paid out by the Treasury Department, and none were in general circulation. Such coins did circulate in the West at that time.

599. Charles Hocking, p. 28, drawing upon Lloyd's insurance information, suggests 400,000 Mexican silver dollars.

600. Per an account in the *New York Herald*, November 2, 1872.

601. Erik Heyl, p. 373; F.L. Coffman, p. 70 (source of $2 million figure).

602. F.L. Coffman, p. 126. William M. Lytle, pp. 33, 275, there as fate unknown.

603. Thomas Penfield, 1952 (who, separately, places the *City of Detroit* as being near the *Dean Richmond*).

604. F.L. Coffman, p. 126, gives the sinking date as August 19, 1893. William M. Lytle, pp. 46 (as 1,083 tons), 268 (different date of loss, given as burnt on October 29, 1871.

605. Thomas Penfield, 1952.

606. F.L. Coffman, p. 183, values the cargo at $3,000,000; on p. 247 of the same book, it is valued at $200,000.

607. Sources include Jim Gibbs, *Disaster Log of Ships: A Pictorial Account of Shipwrecks, California to Alaska*, 1971: pp. 12 and 40; Charles Hocking, p. 147. As the *City of Rio de Janeiro* was inbound to the United States from Japan, presumably relatively little of the specie aboard was in the form of United States coins.

608. Adrian L. Lonsdale and H.R. Kaplan, *A Guide to Sunken Ships*, 1964, p. 177.

609. Charles Hocking, *Dictionary of Disasters at Sea During the Age of Steam*, 1969, p. 586; Robert Ellis Cahill, *Finding New England's Shipwrecks and Treasures*, Chandler-Smith Publishing House, 1984, pp. 48, 49.

610. Some of these items were sold at auction by Guernsey's in Newport, Rhode Island on June 12, 1988.

611. Paul Gilkes, "Chasing the Treasure of the R.M.S. *Republic*," *Coin World*, August 2, 1999; Paul Gilkes, "1909 Shipwreck May Hold $1 Billion in Gold," *Coin World*, July 23, 2001; Laurel J. Sweet, "Searching for Billions," *Boston Herald*, July 7, 2005.

612. F.L. Coffman, p. 260.

613. F.L. Coffman, pp. 118–119. Merritt, Chapman & Scott also investigated the wreck of the *DeBraak* in 1932.

614. Illustrations in this chapter, unless stated otherwise, are representative and not coins specifically attached to the accounts. Accounts of finds by Garrett and Fisher electronic detectors were furnished by those two companies. Ray Williams provided information from the C4 Newsletter.

615. Adapted from Roy Zeper, "The Springhouse Cache," *Western & Eastern Treasures Magazine*, February 1992; copy furnished by Doug Veal.

616. Adapted from Dr. Richard M. Fales, "Ill-Gotten Gold Uncovered!" *Treasure Found Magazine*, Winter 1977; copy furnished by Doug Veal.

617. Unfortunately, the silver dollars were stolen from the finder in a burglary in February 1982 (James Normandi, letter, October 3, 1996, enclosing articles on the find as published in the spring of 1981 and March 1982, respectively, in *Treasure Found* and *Treasure Magazine*).

618. Adapted from Boyd M. Jolley, "Found: $1,000 Silver and Gold Coin Cache," *Treasure Found Magazine*, Summer 1978; copy furnished by Doug Veal.

619. Adapted from "Gold & Silver Coins Cache," *Western & Eastern Treasures Magazine*, March 1990; copy furnished by Doug Veal.

620. Wayne H. Shelby, "Survey of Colonial Coins Recovered in Southern New Jersey," *C4 Newsletter*, Winter 2003; "Survey of Colonial Coins Recovered in Southern New Jersey. Part II," *C4 Newsletter*, Summer 2005. Detailed inventory by sites.

621. Leonard Augsburger and Joel Orosz, *The Secret History of the First U.S. Mint*, pp. 241–243.

622. Images are of notes that are attributed to the hoards mentioned.

623. Adapted from a draft, "King City, Missouri, Blood Money," furnished by Peter Huntoon, October 28, 2014. Daryl Crotts provided certain research.

624. Adapted from an interview by the author with Dean Oakes in Denver, Colorado, August 12, 1996.

625. Details of the bank's evolution and mergers over the years and quantities of notes issued may be found in John Hickman and Dean Oakes, *Standard Catalogue of National Bank Notes*, p. 283.

626. Per Robert Friedberg, *United States Paper Money*, various editions from the 1950s onward.

627. Or for some other reason not presently known. Before many months had passed on the calendar in 1864, the financial reputation of the Confederacy hit rock bottom, and its paper was poorly regarded.

628. Adapted from an interview by the author with Dean Oakes in Denver, Colorado, August 12, 1996.

629. Information is also from "Storied 'Oat Bin' Nationals Go to Auction," *Bank Note Reporter*, November 1979, p. 1. Citation furnished by David Harper.

630. Adapted from an interview by the author with Dean Oakes in Denver, Colorado, August 12, 1996, plus other information sent by mail on October 8, 1996.

631. Research and text by David Gladfelter.

632. "Judge Awards Hoard of Gold Certificates to Workers," *Coin World*, January 12, 1972, p. 15.

633. Adapted from an interview by the author with Dean Oakes in Denver, Colorado, August 12, 1996; additional commentaries and notes submitted by Dean Oakes, October 8, 1996. Town name misspelled "Esterville" in some printed accounts.

634. In a newsletter dated September 1996, currency dealer Lyn F. Knight noted that the Higgins Museum in Okoboji, Iowa, is a "Mecca" for collectors of National Bank notes. In the collection there are more than 2,400 such notes from various cities and towns and about 20,000 photographic postcards. The holdings represent the combined work of the late Bill Higgins and his associate, the late John Hickman. A research library may be used by visiting scholars.

635. Adapted from an interview by the author with Dean Oakes in Denver, Colorado, August 12, 1996.

636. Adapted from an interview by the author with Don Jensen in Denver, Colorado, August 12, 1996. In addition, Jensen, letter, October 15, 1996.

637. Account in the *Louisville Courier-Journal* quoted in *The Numismatist*, July 1920.

638. Research and text by David Gladfelter.

639. Sources include articles by David Abel, *Boston Globe*, April 26, 2005; Caroline Louise Cole and David

Abel, *Boston Globe*, April 29 and April 30, 2005; Caroline Louise Cole and Kathleen Burge, *Boston Globe*, May 1, 2005; O'Ryan Johnson, *Boston Herald*, April 29 and May 2, 2005; Marie Szanizlo, *Boston Herald*, April 30, 2005; David C. Kranz, *Numismatic News*, May 17, 2005; and Eric von Klinger, *Coin World*, May 23. 2005.

640. Sources include *Coin World*, November 22, 2010, and news releases by Colonial Williamsburg.

641. See Sylvester S. Crosby, *Early Coins of America*, 1875, pp. 62–67; Sydney P. Noe, *Pine Tree Coinage of Massachusetts*, 1952, p. 42; Don Taxay, *Counterfeit, Mis-Struck and Unofficial U.S. Coins*, 1963, pp. 133–135. Two of these 1650 shillings later went into the Charles I. Bushnell Collection.

642. See Richard D. Kenney, *Struck Copies of Early American Coins*, 1952, pp. 1, 2; Sylvester S. Crosby, *Early Coins of America*, 1875, p. 74 (silver penny illustrated from a 1763 work by Martin Folkes, "Tables of English Silver and Gold Coins," which may have been Wyatt's inspiration; in 1856 there were no American numismatic references in print concerning the series); Sydney P. Noe, *New England and Willow Tree Coinages*, 1943, pp. 50–55; Noe, *Pine Tree Coinage of Massachusetts*, 1952, p. 47 and other citations; Don Taxay, *Counterfeit, Mis-Struck and Unofficial U.S. Coins*, 1963, pp. 137–139. Also Eric P. Newman, *The Secret of the Good Samaritan Shilling*, 1959, various pages; p. 43 includes biographical notes on Wyatt, and the Newman plates illustrate Wyatt and other copies/forgeries. Wyatt copies were first illustrated in the Clay Collection sale catalog, 1871.

643. Seemingly a remarkable person on the collecting scene, in the mid-1850s Groux announced that he would soon publish a three-volume set of books on American numismatics. Apparently, he ran out of steam, for after a flurry of activity including visiting collectors up and down the Atlantic Seaboard, nothing further happened.

644. Chapter 26 of the present work describes other fantasy hoards.

645. Life dates: 1845–1887. Betts was criticized for creating fantasy rarities with legends implying the coins were part of the American colonial series. In actuality, it seems there was no intent to deceive, just to amuse. His master work, *American Colonial History Illustrated by Contemporary Medals* was published posthumously in 1894 and today remains the standard reference on the subject.

646. This account, yet another version of the "1787 die find," states that Rust first found a single die in Bridgeport and later found five dies in New Haven!

647. Backdating small denomination California gold coins was not an unusual procedure, and numerous other coiners did it. Kroll's productions were late in the game and were considered more as tokens or souvenirs than as pieces made for use as small change.

648. Several different $10 and $25 pieces are described and illustrated by Donald Kagin, *Private Gold Coins and Patterns of the United States*, p. 378, it being his opinion that the dies were original as made for Reid in the 1830s, but not used until many decades later when Nagy had impressions struck.

649. Letter, September 12, 1999. Earl Moore was prominent in the field of historical autographs.

650. B.A. Tompkins, *Treasure*, p. 110, citing the August 25, 1923, issue of the *New York Times*, "Hauser Hoax," and other sources.

651. See *American and Canadian Countermarked Coins*, Dr. Gregory G. Brunk, p. 188 (Wells Fargo). Also p. 110 (Louisiana) and p. 174 (Texas) of that work. Also description of history of these pieces from a Western numismatist having some for sale (letter to author, 1980s).

652. Rulau described the UNION MINE pieces on pp. 245, 246 of *Standard Catalogue of United States Tokens, 1700–1900*, 1993. In addition, Alan V. Weinberg, note, October 16, 1996.

653. Recollection of the former "young coin dealer," John J. Ford Jr., to the author, circa 1958. This also appeared in the author's "The Joys of Collecting" column in *Coin World*, November 25, 1996. The caper was conducted by Ford and F.C.C. Boyd.

654. Adapted from "Civil War Treasure," by Leo Mullen, *St. Louis Post-Dispatch*, April 15, 1984; clipping furnished by Kenneth V. Voss.

655. Letter, September 29, 1996.

656. Copies of correspondence with Rufus B. Langhans furnished to the author by Russell Rulau.

657. *Coin World*, October 7, 1996, p. 32.

658. Letter, July 7, 1996.

659. Letter, September 29, 1996.

660. David Hall comment to author, August 29, 1996; Hall had not been involved, but related two accounts of other dealers who were. An Eastern dealer also had this experience.

Index